AF456094

DATABASE SEMANTICS

Semantic Issues in Multimedia Systems

IFIP - The International Federation for Information Processing

IFIP was founded in 1960 under the auspices of UNESCO, following the First World Computer Congress held in Paris the previous year. An umbrella organization for societies working in information processing, IFIP's aim is two-fold: to support information processing within its member countries and to encourage technology transfer to developing nations. As its mission statement clearly states,

IFIP's mission is to be the leading, truly international, apolitical organization which encourages and assists in the development, exploitation and application of information technology for the benefit of all people.

IFIP is a non-profitmaking organization, run almost solely by 2500 volunteers. It operates through a number of technical committees, which organize events and publications. IFIP's events range from an international congress to local seminars, but the most important are:

- The IFIP World Computer Congress, held every second year;
- open conferences;
- working conferences.

The flagship event is the IFIP World Computer Congress, at which both invited and contributed papers are presented. Contributed papers are rigorously refereed and the rejection rate is high.

As with the Congress, participation in the open conferences is open to all and papers may be invited or submitted. Again, submitted papers are stringently refereed.

The working conferences are structured differently. They are usually run by a working group and attendance is small and by invitation only. Their purpose is to create an atmosphere conducive to innovation and development. Refereeing is less rigorous and papers are subjected to extensive group discussion.

Publications arising from IFIP events vary. The papers presented at the IFIP World Computer Congress and at open conferences are published as conference proceedings, while the results of the working conferences are often published as collections of selected and edited papers.

Any national society whose primary activity is in information may apply to become a full member of IFIP, although full membership is restricted to one society per country. Full members are entitled to vote at the annual General Assembly, National societies preferring a less committed involvement may apply for associate or corresponding membership. Associate members enjoy the same benefits as full members, but without voting rights. Corresponding members are not represented in IFIP bodies. Affiliated membership is open to non-national societies, and individual and honorary membership schemes are also offered.

DATABASE SEMANTICS

Semantic Issues in Multimedia Systems

IFIP TC2/WG2.6 Eighth Working Conference on Database Semantics (DS-8)
Rotorua, New Zealand, January 4-8, 1999

edited by

Robert Meersman
Vrije Universiteit Brussel

Zahir Tari
Royal Melbourne Institute of Technology

Scott Stevens
Carnegie Mellon University

SPRINGER SCIENCE+BUSINESS MEDIA, LLC

Library of Congress Cataloging-in-Publication Data

A C.I.P. Catalogue record for this book is available
from the Library of Congress.

DOI 10.1007/978-0-387-35561-0

Printed on acid-free paper.
www.springer.com/mycopy

Contents

Preface

Multimedia Technology has been capturing popular imagination in recent times. For the general public, multimedia is often synonymous with the World Wide Web. At the time of this conference, microprocessors continue to follow Moore's law, doubling every 18 months and the capacity of fiber-optics is doubling every 12 months. But Internet traffic is doubling every 4 months. What is the effect of today's use of the Web on Internet traffic? A telling statistic relates to how much time, measured in clicks per site visited, people spend on Web sites. Studies show the mean number of clicks per site ranges between 8 and 10, the median is between 3 and 4, while the mode is 1!

Amongst other things, these statistics show that today's search engines provide many irrelevant items in their result sets. Users don't know a site is unrelated to their search until after they visit it. User satisfaction is reason enough to provide mechanisms to solve this problem. But as Internet use grows exponentially faster than Internet resources, solutions become imperative.

It is clear that such solutions will involve more than just technologies such as faster processors and higher bandwidth communications. The quality of the underlying databases and support process become key components. Modern advanced multimedia systems require a paradigm shift to allow the representation and manipulation of complex text, image, audio, and video information. An essential characteristic of this shift is clearly defined semantics for multimedia databases.

This the Eighth Data Semantics Working Conference (DS-8) focused on those issues that involve the semantics of the information represented, stored, and manipulated by multimedia systems. Topics and issues covered included: data modeling and query languages for media such as audio, video, and images; methodological aspects of multimedia database design, information retrieval, knowledge discovery, and data mining; and multimedia user interfaces.

This proceedings contains three keynote speeches and 20 papers. One of the expressed purposes of the conference was to provide an active forum for researchers and practitioners to present and exchange research results. This collection of papers offers the reader a glimpse of the excitement and enthusiasm of DS-8.

The organization of both the conference and this book is composed of seven sections: the keynote speeches and six thematic areas. The six broad areas are: Video Data Modeling and Use; Image Databases; Applications of Multimedia Systems; Multimedia Modeling in General; Multimedia Information Retrieval; and Semantics and Metadata.

The three keynote speeches were by Ramesh Jain from the University of San Diego, U.S.A. and PRAJA, Inc.; Hermann Maurer from the University of Technology, Graz, Austria; and Masao Sakauchi from the University of Tokyo, Japan. Professor Jain talked about Presence Technology (PT). Presence systems blend component technologies like computer vision, signal understanding, and multimedia information systems into a system that enables users to perceive, move around, and interact with remote live environments.

Professor Maurer asked questions like, "Can WWW be Successful when 10% of all links will be broken by the end of 1998?" and "Can the WWW evolve into a usable environment or must we start all over again?"

Professor Sakauchi, proposed a new framework for developing applications and services. The "Multimedia Mediation Mechanism" provides services for diverse multimedia environments such as streaming video and real-time environmental monitoring.

One of the most active research area today concerns computer mediated digital video. The section on Video Data Modeling and Use contains papers ranging from issues in quality of service to syntactical and semantical descriptions of video for archiving and intelligent retrieval of video.

Digital pictures are increasingly important. Large image databases such as those from earth observing satellites are obvious applications. But even in the home, the advent of inexpensive digital cameras and photo-realistic ink jet printers will cause personal photography to become digital. The section on Image Databases contains papers on content-based image retrieval and view mechanisms.

All of the underlying multimedia techniques are of little value without applications. The section on Applications of Multimedia Systems contains papers on systems highlighting user interface semantics and query mechanisms for image databases.

Regardless of the application, multimedia modeling is crucial. The sections on Multimedia Modeling in General and Semantics and Metadata contain discussions on semantic models and metadata for objects ranging from static objects such as documents to temporal objects such as video and audio.

Searching and finding information becomes more difficult when the database contains multimedia objects. The section on Multimedia Information Retrieval presents key ideas in the search and retrieval of distributed heterogeneous databases.

As is often the case, we had many more excellent submissions than the conference or its proceedings could accommodate. The papers contained here are an outstanding sample of the exciting work that is progressing worldwide in the area of semantic issues in multimedia systems.

We would like to thank all of the people that made this working conference such a success, especially the authors and our program committee. Without their essential input this conference would, of course, not have been possible.

ROBERT MEERSMAN, SCOTT STEVENS, ZAHIR TARI

Conference Chair:

Tharam Dillon — LaTrobe University, Australia

Program Co-Chairs:

Robert Meersman — Free University of Brussels, Belgium
Zahir Tari — RMIT, Australia
Scott Stevens — Carnegie Mellon University, USA

Tutorial Chair:

Omran Bukhres — Purdue University, USA

Organising Chair:

Justo Diaz — University of Auckland, New Zealand

Publicity Chair:

Arkady Zaslavsky — Monash University, Australia

Program Committee:

A. Abbadi (UC Santa Barbara)	R. Agrawal (IBM San Jose)
P. Apers (Univ. of Twente)	E. Bertino (Univ. of Milano)
T. Catarci (Univ. of Rome)	E. Chang (LaTrobe Univ.)
S. Christodoulakis (Univ. of Crete)	M. Christel (Carnegie Mellon Univ.)
A. Delis (Polytechnic Univ.)	S. Gibbs (GMD-VMSD)
F. Golshani (Arizona Univ.)	W. Grosky (Wayne St. Univ.)
T. Ichikawa (Hiroshima Univ.)	R. Jain (UCSD)
M. Kim (Konkuk Univ.)	R. King (Univ. of Colorado)
W. Klas (Univ. of Ulm)	P. Liu (Siemens Corporate Research)
J. McGovern (RMIT)	E. Neuhold (GMD-IPSI)
T. Ozsu (Univ. of Alberta)	M. Papazoglou (Tilburg Univ.)
E. Pissaloux (Univ. of Rouen)	C. Pu (Oregon Graduate Inst.)
R. Sacks-Davis (RMIT)	H. Samet (Univ. of Maryland)
T. Sellis (National Technical Univ.)	A. Sheth (Univ. of Georgia)
S. Spaccapietra (EPFL)	V.S. Subrahmanian (Univ. of Maryland)
M. Takizawa (Tokyo Denki Univ.)	A.M. Tjoa (Vienna Univ. of Technology)
M. Vazirgiannis (Athens Univ.)	G. Weikum (Univ. of Saarland)

Additional Referee:

W.G. Aref	C. Bertram
H. Blanken	K.S. Candan
C. Esperana	E.H. Cho
U. Cetintemel	M. Hirakawa
S. Hollfelder	O. Liecht
T.S. Lima	B. List
D. Merkl	K. Parasuraman
D. Revel	S. Sampath
G. Santucci	M. Sifer
A. Soffer	J. Thom
A. Yoshitaka	A. Zben
J. Walpole	D. Wu

1 SEMANTIC INTERACTIVITY IN PRESENCE SYSTEMS

Ramesh Jain

PRAJA inc. and
University of California, San Diego
jain@ece.ucsd.edu

Presence Technology (PT) is targeted to the needs of people who want to be part of a remote, live environment. Presence systems blend component technologies like computer vision, signal understanding, heterogeneous sensor fusion, live-media delivery, telepresence, databases, and multimedia information systems into a novel set of functionality that enables the user to perceive, move around, enquire about, and interact with the remote, live environment through her reception and control devices. PT creates the opportunity to perform different tasks: watch an event, tour and explore a location, meet and communicate with others, monitor the environment for a potential situation, perform a query on the perceived objects and events, and recreate past observations. Technically, the framework offers computer-mediated access to multi-sensory information in an environment, integrates the sensory information into a situation model of the environment, and delivers, at the user's request, the relevant part of the assimilated information through a multimodal interface.

This framework departs from all previous architectures for multimedia content delivery or retrieval systems in two important ways. First, it does not just acquire and passively route a sensor content to a user (although it can be made to do so) like video streamers or web cameras. It integrates all sensor inputs into a composite model of the live environment. This model, called the environment model (EM), acts like a short-term database, and maintains the spatiotemporal state of the complete environment, as observed from all sensors taken together. By virtue of this integration, the EM holds a situationally complete view of the observed space. The second point of departure is that in a Presence system, the user not only perceives sensory inputs, but also actively interacts with it. This interaction, whether effected by an explicit query for more contextual information about an observed object, a request to track an object in the environment, or a notification request when any observed object enters a user-designated region, transcends any query operations found in current state of the art multimedia information retrieval systems. Indeed, we contend that content-based interactivity on live, dynamic objects is the next generation of capabilities beyond the content-based query operations on stored, mono-stream media objects offered by today's systems. Hence we believe that the ability to perform an action on the remote environment by a client-side action is a significant aspect of the Presence Technology.

PT is an extension of the Multiple Perspective Interactive Video project at the Visual Computing Laboratory, University of California, San Diego. In this paper we will present results from PRAJA Presence system implemented to bring an early version of PT for different application. We will present a demo of this system to explain different technical components of the system.

2 TOWARDS THE CONSTRUCTION OF THE MULTIMEDIA MEDIATION MECHANISM

Masao Sakauchi

Institute of Industrial Science, University of Tokyo
7-22-1 Roppongi, Minato-ku, Tokyo 106-8558, Japan
sakauchi@sak.iis.u-tokyo.ac.jp

Abstract: Multimedia Information Environments based on video are now growing rapidly. Especially three types of environments, i.e. "Stream type Multimedia Environment" by digital TV broadcasting, "Real-world type Multimedia Environment" monitoring roads and towns, and "Network type Multimedia Environment" on the WWW are especially promising targets. In this paper, a new framework for developing applications and services from these three Multimedia Environments named by "the Multimedia Mediation Mechanism", is proposed and discussed. In the Stream type Multimedia Mediation System, basic functions including video stream description, data retrieval, data integration, event discovery and data creation are designed. New interactive video services, personal media services are developed on the network as application. In the Real-world type Multimedia Mediation System, basic functions including construction of mediation map, locating functions, object recognition and event discovery are designed. Several applications for ITS (Intelligent Transport System) etc. are also developed. In the Network type Multimedia Mediation System, various advanced search engines are developed.

2.1 INTRODUCTION

Rapid expansion of multimedia information space based on video or image data is being realized by means of various distribution tools. Three types of multimedia information spaces (or environments), i.e. "in the digital broadcasting stream", "in the real-world" and "on the Internet" are especially promising. On the other hand, from social and economic viewpoints, importance of information processing techniques which can create real value for human activity or life should be surely recognized.

Considering these two backgrounds, we are now developing a new multimedia database system, named the Multimedia Mediation Mechanism (or System) of application-oriented middleware for realization of functions, services demanded by human and society.

In this paper, the framework of the Multimedia Mediation System, the basic functions for realizing three types of concrete Multimedia Mediation Systems of Stream type Multimedia System, Real-world type Multimedia System and Network type Multimedia System will be discussed with several embodiment, mainly based on our research project (http://shinpro.sak.iis.u-tokyo.ac.jp/index-e.html).

2.2 THREE TYPES OF "MULTIMEDIA ENVIRONMENT" AND THE MULTIMEDIA MEDIATION SYSTEM

Fig. 2.1 shows the framework of the Multimedia Mediation System (MMS). The MMS consists of three types of individual mediation system, i.e. the Stream type MM System, the Real-world type MM System and the Network type MM System, corresponding to Stream type, Real-world type and Network type MM Environment, respectively.

⟨ Stream type MMS ⟩

Needless to say, one of the typical leaders of multimedia information (contents) providers is broadcasting. Commercial-based satellite digital broadcasting with over hundreds of channels have already started in USA, Japan, Europe and Asia. Another digital broadcasting in the form of CATV, ordinary surface wave TV, or Fibernet communication also have already been or will be planed soon. In such situations, where we'll be able to enjoy hundreds or thousands of broadcasting channels, much more user-oriented and intelligent access to the tremendous amount of "contents stream" will be required as shown in the top-left part of Fig. 2.1.

In this Stream type MMS, the mediator functions would be most important for user, which help them to pick up useful and required data from the stream and to make their own customized contents for new service and business.

⟨ Real-world type MMS ⟩

We Japanese, suffered severe earthquake damage at Kobe in January, 1995. This tragedy taught us the importance of realtime acquisition of our city information for disaster mitigation. Multimedia communication technology enables us to establish a new type of database which collects and analyzes realtime situations (video information) to tell us "What's going on in the city" on real-world. Let's call this type as "Real-world type MM Environment" as shown in the top-middle part of Fig. 2.1.

Though this type of systems generally have not been considered as multimedia system, they have promising possibility to realize new services and busi-

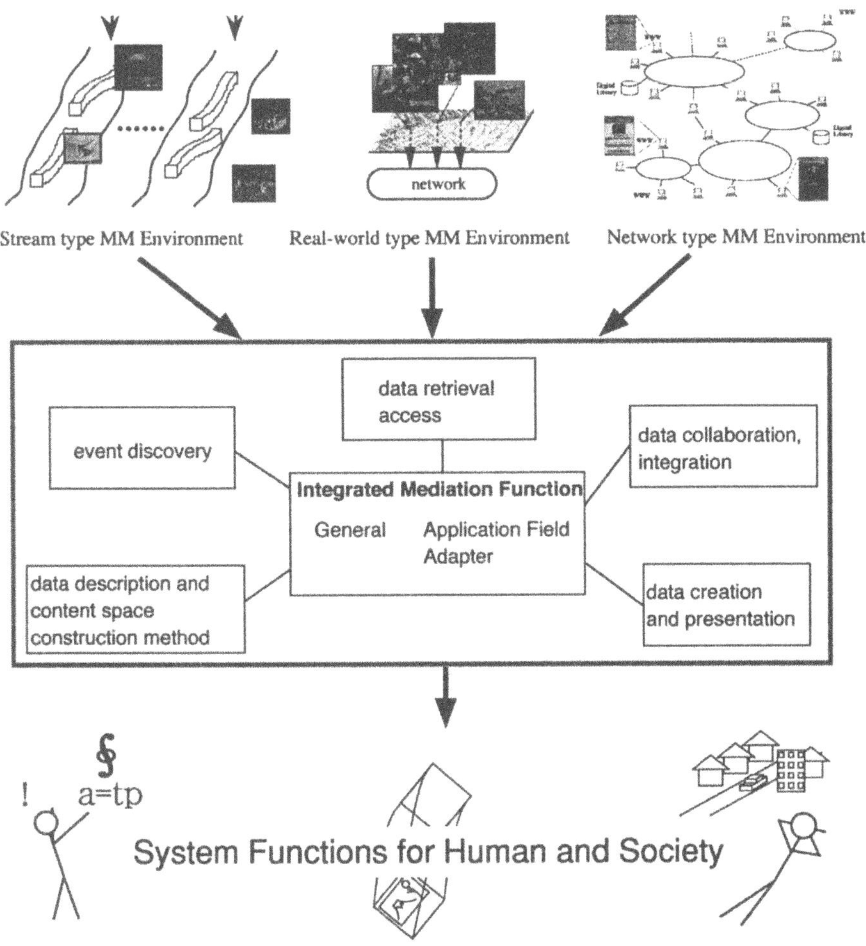

Figure 2.1: Framework of Multimedia Mediation System

ness with real time integration of real-world situations and existing another databases. Expecting fields in this category include disaster mitigation, intelligent transport systems (ITS), advanced environment management, advanced utilization of high resolution satellite images etc.

⟨ Network type MMS ⟩

The "Internet" data services including the WWW are now becoming more and more popular. Tremendous amount of services provide multimedia information even in the form of video and images. Hereafter, this means that most databases will be scattered where contents are generated and such situations will grow uncontrollably. Such dispersed databases should be called here the "Network type MM Environment" as one of our promising targets as shown in the top-right part of Fig. 2.1.

There are many "what to do" for this environment. We believe, however, mediator functions, which inform users what kinds of data exist in the network, or where is their useful or desired information, and help to collect and relate them to the user's applications, are the most important. Such "contexing" of the network multimedia data should be the main function in the database. Their typical and first-step trials are the "Yahoo" directory service or another search engines for text data. Various trials and functions, however, will be required for more general multimedia data in the network.

Basic functions in order to create various services and applications from these three environments are the core part of the MMS as shown in the lower part of Fig. 2.1. In the followings, more concrete discussion for each individual MM systems, will be given based on our research project.

2.3 STREAM TYPE MULTIMEDIA MEDIATION SYSTEM

More detailed basic mediation functions for the Stream type MMS are shown in Fig. 2.2. In this case, target multimedia data include video stream in digital broadcasting, video contents etc. New interactive video services and personal media services are examples of target applications.

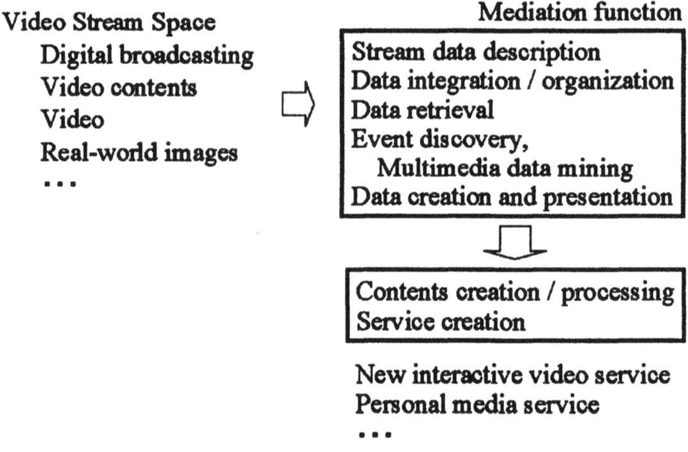

Figure 2.2: Stream type Multimedia Mediation System

Detailed mediation functions include stream data description, data integration / organization, data retrieval, event discovery / multimedia data mining, data creation and presentation for applications. Concrete examples in our project for Stream type MM functions are listed below.

Stream data description functions

- Interactive description [6]
  - Interactive object description on the network
- Automatic description [7][8][9][10]
  - Object description using synchronized video, audio and documents
  - Advanced video analysis using natural language processing
  - Face identification system using video and transcripts

Data retrieval, Presentation functions

- Live hypermedia system [11][12]
  - Automated picking up of video sequence by Scene Description Language
- Music stream data retrieval
  - Music retrieval using musical interval, melody and lyrics
- Data creation / Presentation [13][14]
  - Video editing based on script processing

Because we have no room to describe about those researches in detail, please access to references or (http://shinpro.sak.iis.u-tokyo.ac.jp/index-e.html). Only several examples are overviewed here.

Fig. 2.3 shows the framework adopted for description of video data, where description labels for both video frame (scene) and objects in the frame. Those descriptions are written by object-oriented video scene description language SVSDL. Various operations for management of these description have been developed by Java environment.

Fig. 2.4 illustrates an example of these basic operations. Contents of video description in this example are generated automatically, by our video understanding method using logical synchronization among video, sounds and document based on devised DP matching technique.

Fig. 2.5 shows an example of "edit operation" of video streams. A user can easily realize his/her own video authoring just by using much easier text processing (editing), because video streams have tight timing synchronization with scenario documents by SVSDL description.

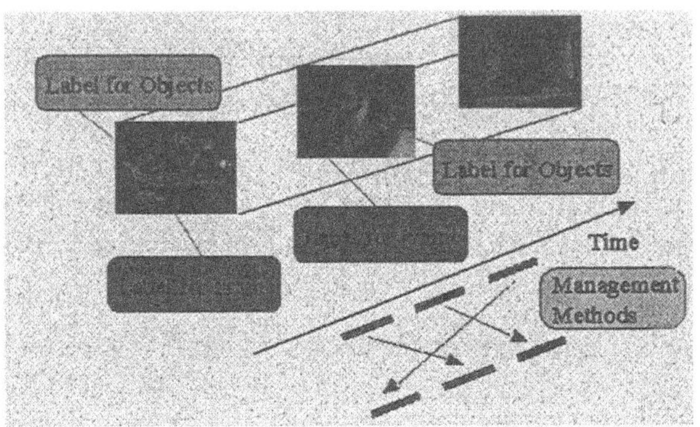

Figure 2.3: Framework of Video Data Description

Figure 2.4: Prototype System

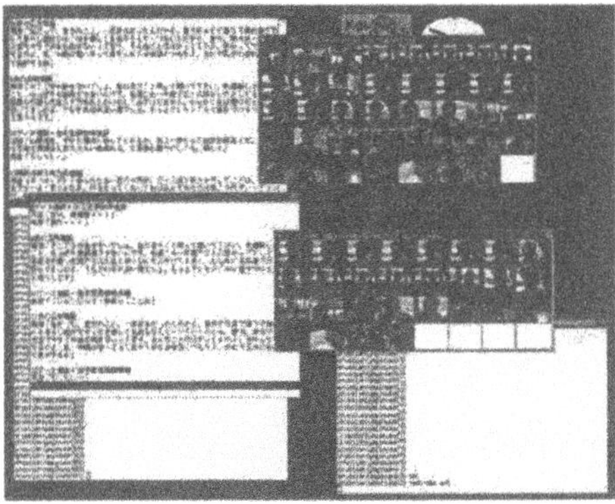

Figure 2.5: Editing by Script

2.4 REAL-WORLD TYPE MULTIMEDIA MEDIATION SYSTEM

Fig. 2.6 shows more detailed basic mediation function for the Real-world type MMS. In this case, the target multimedia data include various data from robot cameras, mobile units or network sites, reflecting realtime situations in the real-world, such as town scenes or traffic on the roads. Intelligent transport system (ITS), various applications for town life, social security system are examples of target applications.

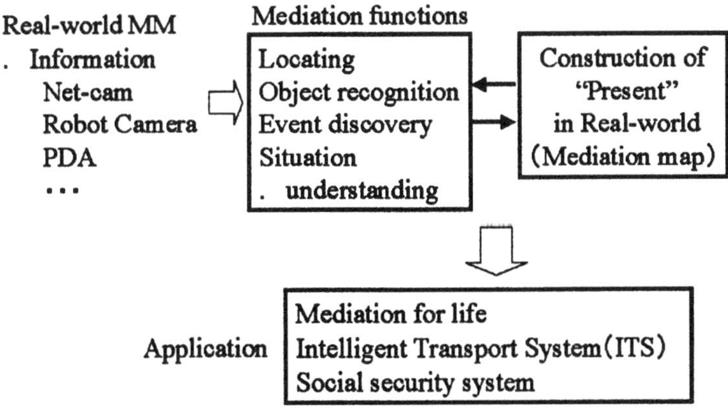

Figure 2.6: Real-world type Multimedia Mediation System

Detailed mediation functions include contraction of present situations in the real-world, locating function for objects in images or video, object recognition, event discovery from real world images or video stream. Concrete examples in our project for Real-world type MM functions are listed below.

- Object description, mediation map construction function [15]
  - Object description using digital city map and video for urban scene
- Object description function [16]
  - Extraction of 3D information from video of traffic
- Data creation, mediation map function [17]
  - Realization of AR by acquiring a radiance distribution
- Others
  - Mediation function for Real-world contents (Map, Net-cam, High resolution satellite image etc.)

Only two of those are overviewed below. Fig. 2.7 shows one method of object description (or recognition) of urban scenes in distant views. Considering urban scenes in distant views, the buildings which are very high or have special shapes are very prominent. We propose an approach for understanding urban scenes in distant views first by recognizing key buildings appearing as silhouette using a model-based object recognition scheme. A city map-database with 3D descriptions of the rooftops of the buildings is used to build a world model. The feature correspondences between the images and the model are established using a dynamic programming technique. Rough viewing parameters for location and orientation can be obtained from the sensors. Although these parameters are not precise, the information about which buildings appear as silhouettes can be obtained. Based on this information, a model consisting of building's rooftop line segments is constructed for recognition. The feature correspondences between the images and the model are established using a dynamic programming technique. The correspondence hypotheses are then verified to ensure that the correspondences are reliable and accurate. Incorrect feature correspondences caused by sensor uncertainty and image clutter are modified, based on a similarity evaluation method. Using this method, the buildings appearing as silhouette in distant views can be identified as shown in Fig. 2.7.

Fig. 2.8 shows another method of recognizing urban scenes in close-range views. In the case of close-range images, only part of a building's surface can be seen clearly instead of building's shape. Therefore, we prefer to use appearance matching rather than shape matching used in recognizing buildings in distant view. For the recognition of a single building, we use an eigen window method which is an effective appearance-based method. The space being modeled by the eigen windows is intensive patterns in the image. The reliability of the eigen window method is also discussed under the transformations

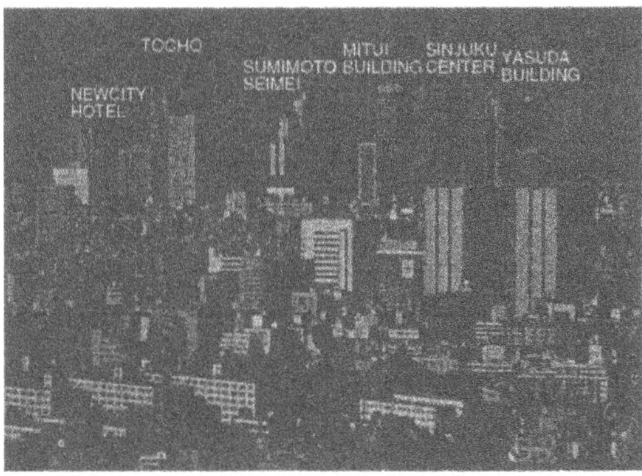

Figure 2.7: Recognizing Buildings in Distant View

of translation, rotation, scale, and viewing angle. When a number of buildings are present in an image, like scenes we see while walking along a road, we segment the image into building regions based on edge distributions. A building in a separated region can be recognized by the same method as recognizing a single building. However, considering that there are many buildings in an urban scene, the recognizing process will be time-consuming, and it is possible that some buildings might be in similar appearance. Fortunately, buildings with similar appearances are often on different streets. A digital map provides spatial relations of buildings, for example, along the Aoyama St. in Tokyo there is Honda building and beside Aoyama Twin Tower. We build a building image database having the same relations as in the map to support recognition. Images of these buildings are shown on the left of Fig. 2.8. We use the features of extracted building regions such as color to represent the context of a scene, and use this description to retrieve candidate roads from the building image database. The retrieval result is shown on the right of Fig. 2.8. We build eigen spaces for the buildings along each road. A building in a separated region can be recognized by being projected into eigen spaces of the candidate roads. Therefore the retrieval results can be verified.

2.5 NETWORK TYPE MULTIMEDIA MEDIATION SYSTEM

Fig. 2.9 shows more detailed basic mediation functions for the Network type MMS. In this case, mediation functions for realizing advanced search engine or mediation for solution include Event discovery (data mining),data retrieval, data collaboration or interface for mediation.

Concrete examples in our project for Network type MM functions are listed below.

- Data retrieval function [18][19]

Figure 2.8: Recognizing Buildings in Close Range View

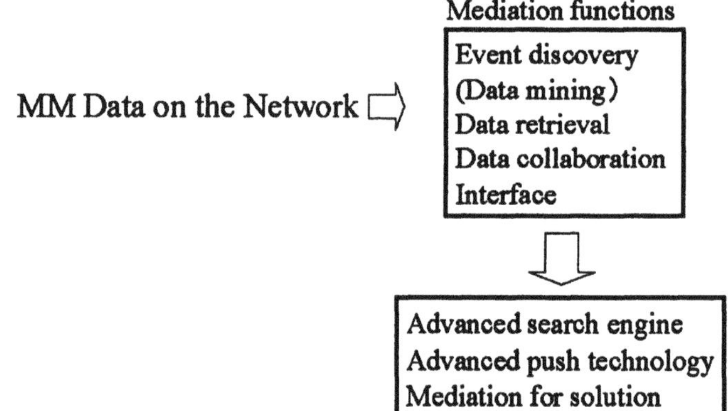

Figure 2.9: Network type Multimedia Mediation System

  - Advanced search engine

- Data Collaboration function [20]
  - Data organization using concept information system
  - Collaboration based on visualization of information mediation

- Others [21]
  - High speed data mining mechanism etc.

Fig. 2.10 shows operation of GIRLS (Global Image Retrieval and Linking System) as one of these examples. GIRLS for the image data in the WWW has been developed as the embodiment of such database systems. In GIRLS, a search robot named BOYS automatically gathers typical images and layout information and URL from the WWW to construct the database for retrieval and linking based on the image contents. The system provides users with open functions including retrieval of images or logo's in the WWW data space, linkage to the original homepages with images imagined by users, feedback to the retrieval performance. In the example for the GIRLS operation in Fig. 2.10, similarity retrieval results to the given layout homepage are shown.

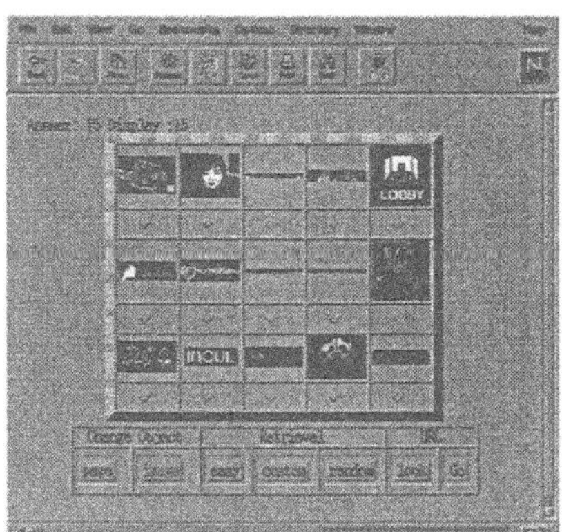
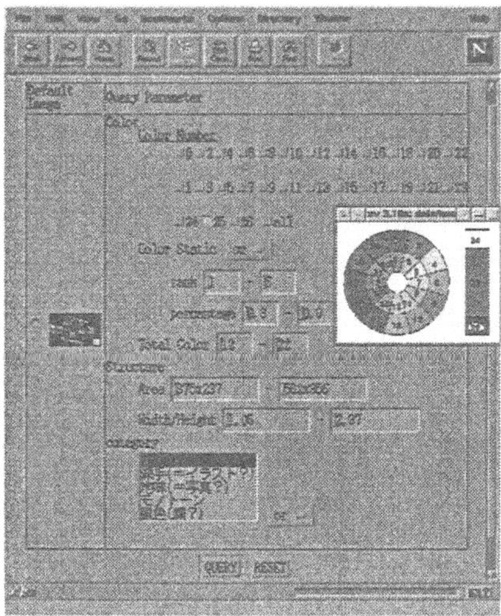

Figure 2.10: Image Search Engine GIRLS (Global Image Retrieval and Linking System)

2.6 CONCLUSIONS

In this paper, the Multimedia Mediation System has been proposed and discussed in order to provide various applications and services. Three types of individual systems include promising field of digital broadcasting applications, ITS applications and network search engines.

Our project is now growing toward realization of useful middleware for multimedia data spaces.

Acknowledgments

This work is supported as the Grant-in-Aid for Creative Basic Researh #09NP1401: "Research on Multimedia Mediation Mechanism for Realization of Human-oriented Information Environments" by the Ministry of Education, Science, Sports and Culture, Government of Japan.

References

[1] M.Sakauchi, "Video Information Media from the Viewpoint of Computer – Proposal of Multimedia Date Mediator," *The Journal of the Institute of Image Information and Television Engineers*, vol.51, no.1, 1997

[2] M.Sakauchi, T.Satou and Y.Yaginuma, "Multimedia database systems for the contents mediator," *The Transaction of the Institute of Electronics, Information and Communication Engineers*, vol.E79–D, no.6, pp.641–646, 1996

[3] Y.Yaginuma, T.Yatabe, T.Satou, J.Tatemura and M.Sakauchi, "Four Promising Multimedia Databases and Their Embodiments," *Multimedia Tools and Applications*, Kluwer Academic Publishers, 5, pp.65–77, 1997

[4] M.Sakauchi, "Image retrieval and image understanding," *IEEE Multi-media Computing Magazine*, vol.1, no.1, pp.79–81, 1994

[5] M.Sakauchi, Y.Ohsawa and T.Sagara, "Construction and application of multimedia geographical database," *Journal of Institute of Geographical Information Systems of Japan*, vol.3, no.2, pp.53–58, 1995

[6] T.Yatabe, T.Ohba and M.Sakauchi, "A Proposal of Structured Video Database Using Multiple Users' Description on the Network," *Technical Report of the Institute of Electronics, Information and Communication Engineers*, PRMU97–64, pp.63–68, 1997

[7] Y.Yaginuma and M.Sakauchi, "Construction of Intelligent TV Drama Database based on the Synchronization between Image, Sound and Script," *Proc. of Pacific Workshop on Distributed Multimedia Systems*, pp.125–132, 1996

[8] Y.Yaginuma and M.Sakauchi, "A proposal of the synchronization method between drama image, sound and scenario document using DP matching," *The Transaction of the Institute of Electronics, Information and Communication Engineers*, vol.J79–D–II, no.5, pp.747–755, 1996

[9] N.Izumi, Y.Yaginuma, H.Nakagawa and M.Sakauchi, "Construction of Existence/Action Map Based on the Script Analysis," *The Journal of The Institute of Electronics, Information and Communication Engineers D-II*, vol.J79-D-II, no.11, pp.1993–1996, 1996

[10] S.Satoh and T.Kanade, "Name-It: Association of face and name in video," *Proc. of Computer Vision and Pattern Recognition*, pp.368–373, 1997

[11] T.Satou and M.Sakauchi, "Data acquisition in live hyper media," *Proc. of IEEE International Conference on Multimedia Computing and Systems '95*, pp.175–181, 1995

[12] T.Satou and M.Sakauchi, "Video information acquisition on live hypermedia," *The Journal of The Institute of Electronics, Information and Communication Engineers*, vol.J79-D-II, no.4, pp.559–567, 1996

[13] Y.Yaginuma and M.Sakauchi, "Content-based Drama Editing based on Inter-media Synchronization," *Proc. of IEEE International Conference on Multimedia Computing and Systems '96*, pp.322–329, 1996

[14] Y.Yaginuma and M.Sakauchi, "A proposal of a video editing method using synchronized scenario document," *The Transaction of the Institute of Electronics, Information and Communication Engineers*, vol.J79-D-II, no.4, pp.547–558, 1996

[15] P.Liu, W.Wu, K.Ikeuchi and M.Sakauchi, "Recognition of Urban Scene Using Silhouette of Buildings and City Map Database," *Proc. of the 3rd Asian Conference on Computer Vision*, 1998

[16] C.X.Li, P.T.Wang, H.T.Zen and M.Sakauchi, "Creation of Plane-Spatiotemporal-Image Using a Selected Slit," *Proc.of IAPR Workshop on Machine Vision Applications '96*, 1996

[17] I.Sato, Y.Sato and K.Ikeuchi, "Seamless Integration of Computer Generated Objects into a Real Scene Based on a Real Illumination Distribution," *The Transaction of the Institute of Electronics, Information and Communication Engineers*, vol.J81-D-II, no.5, pp.861–871, 1998

[18] T.Yatabe, H.Takaha, T.Satoh and M.Sakauchi, "Open Image Search Engine System GIRLS using image infomation," *Proc. of Advanced Database Symposium*, pp.139–145, 1996

[19] S.Sugawara, K.Yamamoto and Y.Sakai, "A Study on Image Searching Method in Super Distributed Database," *Proc. of IEEE GLOBECOM '97*, vol.2, pp.736, 1997

[20] Y.Takama and M.Ishizuka, "Application of Fish Eye Vector Based on Concept Structure for Information Organization Supporting Tool," *Technical Report of Japan Society for Artificial Intelligence*, SIG-FAI-9702-17, pp.97–102, 1997

[21] T.Shintani and M.Kitsuregawa, "Parallel Mining Algorithms for Generalized Association Rules with Classification Hierarchy," *Proc. of ACM SIGMOD International Conference on Management of Data*, 1998

3 CAN WWW BE SUCCESSFUL?

Hermann Maurer

IICM, Graz University of Technology, Graz, Austria

hmaurer@iicm.edu

Abstract: Considering the fact that the number of WWW servers and users keeps exploding the title of this paper sounds strange, to say the least. However, while every organisation without their own proper URL starts to feel like an outcast, there are clouds over the future of the WWW.

After all, the number of "broken links" keeps rising every month, not just in absolute numbers but also percentage-wise. Estimates have it that by the year 2000 almost 10 % of all links will be broken, i.e. will (when clicked at) produce the infamous message "Error 404. Object not found". The situation is not restricted to the Internet, but applies as well to WWW based Intranet solutions. A well-known Fortune 100 company, when systematically checking their Intranet, found 4000 links that were not working. The overall situation is worse: search engines are unable to cope with the chaos on the web, returning too many hits, documents found are obsolete, secure payment procedures are still a rarity, and so is making money with what one offers on the WWW, etc.

Thus, it is no wonder that insiders are starting to ask the question: will WWW be able to evolve into a truly usable environment, or will it be necessary to "start all over again", with an entirely new "Web2", or whatever you might call it. After all, such things have happened before: the amateur film has not evolved to but has been replaced by video; musical records of once have been replaced by CD's; and Videotex, even the fairly wide-spread Minitel of France, was wiped out by WWW. Are we going to witness another revolution? Or is there a reasonable migration-path to what we surely need: a Web2?

Some of the main weaknesses of ordinary WWW will be discussed in this paper. It will also be argued that having WWW interfaces on top of traditional databases does not solve the problem. Rather, a more integrated approach of four competing paradigms is necessary to solve the problems we encounter today. Solutions of this type are starting to be used in a growing number of large Intranets, making it possible that they will "spill over" into the Internet. For the majority of users unnoticeable, this may well mean the replacement of the WWW as we now see it by more modern solutions, by a Web2.

3.1 INTRODUCTION

The World Wide Web (WWW) keeps exploding. The majority of persons concerned with the WWW believe, without much reflection, that the expansion witnessed will continue, and that the WWW will be the infrastructure of the often quoted information society of the future. There is little doubt that the information society will be based on a sophisticated network of service providers that can be reached (eventually) by most people at any point and at any time. However, it is our contention that it is not at all clear whether such a network of the future will evolve from WWW, or whether it will derive from new basic concepts. In this paper we will argue that such a "Web2" will have to have much functionality that is difficult to fit on top of current WWW architecture. Thus, the question arises whether there is an evolutionary path from current WWW to a Web2, or whether a Web2 will emerge that will make WWW as obsolete as Videotex was made by WWW, or as 8 mm (amateur) movies were made obsolete by videocameras. We will not answer this question in this paper, but we will show that the question is justified, and that the challenge to an evolutionary path from WWW to a Web2 is indeed formidable.

The paper is structured as follows. In the next section we will present some arguments why a Web2 is needed. In the following section, the main part of this paper, we will point out various serious shortcomings of the original WWW concept and add some comments on how they are currently being addressed. We will then briefly mention that some, but by far not all, shortcomings of the WWW concept have been taken care of by some developments the author of this paper was involved in. In the final section we return to the main point raised in this paper: can WWW evolve to a Web2, or do we need a new approach altogether?

3.2 WHY WWW WON'T KEEP EXPANDING IN ITS PRESENT FORM

It has been often said that the WWW is the "largest information repository the world has ever had - but also the most chaotic one". Both points are correct, yet the significance of the second one is often not taken serious enough. The WWW is not just chaotic, it is getting more and more so: the percentage of broken links has risen from 4 % in 1996 to over 6 % in 1998 and - as the hypertext pioneer Nielsen is being quoted - is likely to hit 10 % by 2000. The rise in working WWW servers that contain obsolete data is equally alarming: a recent sample shows that less than 20 % of all servers contain reliable and up-to-date information. Relevant information is ever harder to find: the enthusiasm with which search engines like Alta Vista have been welcomed is being replaced by the feeling that without human intervention too much useless information is found; the resulting new search engines that work with substantial teams of specialists to weed out and categorize information are trying to cure symptoms, but not the underlying disease; and this is true, independent of whether such human-assisted directories are still called search engines, or "meta-servers", or "Web portals". At the same time as "relevant" information is every harder to locate, more and more robots "harvesting" servers keep increasing the load on servers intolerably; also, large WWW sites are exponentially hard to administer. A plethora of tools developed to assist do indeed help to some extent, yet basically just cover up flaws in a system that was designed for curtain purposes but is now used for entirely different ones: It is important to understand that all that is going to be mentioned in terms of shortcomings of the WWW is not a criticism of the original WWW design: the team of Berners-Lee, Cailliau et al [1] at CERN developed WWW for a specific purpose: to make a growing archive of text-only physics reports available to the world. Little could they know that WWW would be (mis)used as a network with huge amounts of dynamically changing multimedia data, used in an increasingly interactive fashion. For their purposes. the original concepts of WWW were sufficient, and ingeniously simple. It is this very simplicity that created the WWW explosion, yet it is the same simplicity that is now turning into a handicap. Programming became popular because of simple-to-learn and simple-to-use programming languages like FORTRAN or BASIC. Yet nobody in his right mind would design large application programs using such languages today. It is the contention of this paper that a similar paradigm shift must and will happen with respect to WWW. FORTRAN is still alive as FORTRAN version X (whatever X is) and is useful for special-purpose applications; WWW version X may still be alive in 10 years and be used for some niche applications. But maybe the world of information will not be dominated by such better WWW but by entirely different Web2 systems.

Summarizing, the WWW has serious deficiencies for today's and tomorrow's applications, that prohibit both users and administrators to get the best out of a system of distributed services we have come to expect the WWW to be. We will analyze some of the major weaknesses of WWW in the next section. The future will show whether WWW can evolve to embrace all such features or whether new systems might supersede WWW at some stage.

3.3 SHORTCOMINGS OF WWW THAT WILL EVENTUALLY STIFFLE FURTHER GROWTH

In this section we discuss some of the problems inherent in WWW architecture. This is by no means a complete list, but it will prove the point this paper wants to make: some dramatic changes at the very basis of WWW will be necessary if WWW is to evolve to a useful Web2.

3.3.1 The communication protocol

The standard HTTP protocol used in WWW is a stateless, non-connection oriented protocol and offers no way to provide a "quality guarantee", i.e. a guaranteed bandwidth as required for many streaming multimedia applications, particular audio and video. The fact that the protocol is stateless makes it necessary to use crutches such as "cookies" and "session keys" to preserve information on what users have done before. Connection oriented protocols are much more efficient when substantial sessions are carried out with one server. And the fact that security issues are not addressed in HTTP has required the addition of e.g. SSL (secure socket layer) constructs, or new protocols such as HTTPS.

The weaknesses of HTTP are well-known to the community. And it has to be said there - and will not be repeated in all sections (although it applies to most) that the W3C (the WWW Consortium headed by Berners-Lee) [18] is trying very hard to push improvements. Unfortunately, the W3C is hampered by two major facts: (i) the main industry players often act independently of the W3C and (ii) the issue of backward compatibility is always looming. And this is exactly the hot issue addressed in this paper: is it possible to carry through the innovations necessary under such circumstances?

3.3.2 The document model

The basic document in a WWW server is an HTML-page. HTML is a simple logical mark-up language derived from SGML that allows users to specify titles, subtitles, the start of a new paragraph, etc, but leaves the actual representation on the computer screen to the viewer that interprets the HTML code. Under pressure from groups that wanted more control "on how things look on the screen" the simplicity and device independency of HTML was soon destroyed by introducing presentation mark-ups (allowing to define font size, colors, in-line images, etc.) and hence creating device (e.g. screen-resolution) dependence. Further, HTML today does not really exist anymore: there is one version by Microsoft, another by Netscape and despite the commandable efforts of the W3C mentioned earlier no real new HTML standard that is accepted by all major players is in sight. The problems with HTML are accerbated by the fact that all "meta-information" including link information is embedded in the document. We will return to the problem of why embedding information about information x into information x is undesirable, but we want to mention the general problem of meta-information at this point: storing a document without information about it(when it was created, who created it, what is the topic of the document,who owns it, etc.) is almost like putting photos in a photo-album without noting down when and where the photo was taken, what is seen on the photo, etc. In ordinary HTML a "meta-tag" does exist, but with no further structure behind it the use of it is very limited [6]. Yet meta-information is crucial for finding relevant documents, for defining the semantic structure of a document, etc.

As a result of the deficiencies mentioned, a powerful derivative of SGML, the so-called XML standard was introduced in 1996. It is much more powerful than HTML, allows logical and semantical mark-ups, allows presentation specific instructions using style sheets, allows the incorporation of meta-information and a somewhat more flexible link management than HTML [18].

It is to be seen whether XML will catch on on a large scale. Some say it is "too little, too late". The reason for this is that many organisations, dissatisfied with HTML, have started to use their WWW servers as repository for

PostScript, PDF, Winword, etc. files. I.e. the uniform presentation protocol of the original WWW has already made place to a mixture of many formats. And while this is evident in case of text-oriented material the situation concerning video and animation formats is still more chaotic. The idea to use JAVA applets (running on a "virtual machine" in "any environment") has made the situation concerning media-rich applications a bit simpler, yet does not present a solution on its own.

Worse, however, is the fact that important other issues have not even been seriously considered, yet: such issues include the definition of various types of access rights, provisions for versioning, for charging, for transclusions in the sense of Ted Nelson [3], for distributed editing, for document locking during transactions, etc.

3.3.3 The access model

WWW is based on the idea that information is accessed using links. We will discuss in section 3.4 why the link concept and related issues as available in today's WWW systems are not suitable for a Web2, but we want to make another important claim in this section.

The claim, in a nutshell is that information systems should not be built around a single data access paradigm, but should seamlessly combine the four major paradigms known in computer science. Those four paradigms are:

(i) Access by searching: In titles, keywords, fulltext with all kinds of extensions and combinations, as is e.g. done in search programs such as Verity and Fulcrum. Note that searches (including full-text searches) should also be supported in non-HTML files (e.g. in PDF and Winword files), i.e. any good search program needs "filters" for a large set of file formats.

(ii) Access by structure: Much of our thinking is in terms of categories, classifications, menues, directories (or whatever you want to call it). It is thus natural that the document space of a WWW server should allow (arbitrary many, possibly overlapping, possibly user-defined) hierarchical or DAG-like views. The advantages of such approach not only for locating information but also for link reduction, re-usability of modules and easing server administration have been discussed in detail before, e.g. in [4] and [5].

(iii) Access by attributes: This type of access, also called access by meta-data, is closely related to relational databases. Documents or document groups can have a set of attributes and those can be used in SQL-type (or simple versions thereof) queries to locate data.

(iv) Access by links: The classical WWW approach with all its advantages ("intuitive", "associative") and all its disadvantages ("the Web is a huge Spaghetti-bowl of links by now" according to R. Cailliau, one of the inventors of WWW; "the getting lost in hyperspace syndrome", etc.)

It is our contention that neither of the above approaches on its own is sufficient. Hence pure WWW systems relying on links only (iv) will not work well in some situations, nor will systems that are purely based on attributes (iii) like relational databases; nor are systems based only on search engines (i) or menues (ii) suitable for all situations. It should also be clear that a "serial combination" like a WWW (link-based) interface to a relational database will be sub-optimal in some cases, nor will any fixed combination of the four paradigms (i) - (iv) provide an ideal solution for all applications.

Rather, a seamless applications dependent mix of the four access strategies is what is needed, and with the exception of Hyperwave (see [4], [6], and [7]) no current WWW technology provides this feature that will be essential for any Web2.

3.3.4 The link model

Links in ordinary WWW servers are compared with goto-statements already in [8]. This leads to the obvious consequences that links should be replaced by structure as much as possible. The remaining links should be at least maintained automatically by the system, and should have a number of other desirable properties. In ordinary WWW links are uni-directional, have no attributes, and their anchors are embedded in the HTML page. It has been argued at length, particularly in [9], but also in [4] and [5] that links (as implemented already in Brown University's Intermedia system almost 10 years ago!) must be bi-directional, be treated as objects with their own attributes (so that e.g. some links are only visible to some people, or only for a certain time) and their anchors must not be embedded within the documents (so that e.g. adding a link can be done without write-access to the document where the link is added).

Indeed there are more general issues at stake: links (and other "tags" that are commonly seen as part of the document) should not only be separate from the document, but one document may well have different sets of such tags associated with it. Depending who and how one reaches a document completely different sets of links, but also different items in different forms might be displayed.

There is also another issue that has to be addressed rather sooner than later: at the moment, anyone can link to other pages. However, owners of pages may resent that links point to their pages (e.g. since they want users to first go through some title page with advertisements). Thus, future WWW systems have to provide means for blocking links to certain areas of the database!

3.3.5 Making WWW more interactive

Ordinary WWW is basically a "static", "read-only" affair. Mind you, using forms or JAVA certain kinds of interactions are possible. In general, however, WWW allows to retrieve some information but does not allow to work with it. Work with it means that users should be allowed to created notes and links on any document for themselves or a specific group of users, thus providing the possibility for individualisation, customization and cooperation.

Private and shared workspaces to re-arrange and transclude information should be provided, news-group like discussion facilities integrated, and bookmarks should be kept on servers rather than on clients to allow bookmark-sharing as a powerful tool of communication and cooperation.

Current ordinary WWW technology is a far cry away from such facilities, although serious attempts to integrate them can e.g. be seen in [10] and [11].

It is our contention that a Web2 will have to be orders of magnitude more interactive than current WWW. And simple "push-technology" now available on some WWW systems is not sufficient, although some variantes of it like the "query object" in Hyperwave [12] are first steps in the right direction.

3.3.6 Other issues

The above subsections have listed a few of the important issues unresolved in ordinary WWW, yet essential for a Web2. The list can be expanded arbitrarily. We just want to show the complexity of the issues by mentioning a more or less random selection of three other points.

- WWW does not allow distributed editing: it is the webmaster who controls what is inserted where, how it is accessed, what links go into a document and emanate form it. However, much more flexibility is needed: not only must it be possible to appoint subadministrators who can work in certain parts of the WWW database, but this process should be recursive, providing a full hierarchy of administrators, i.e. fully distributed editing. Moreover, adding links and views for personal or group use must be possible even without document editing privileges.

- Caching information in servers is crucial for performance and for decreasing network load. At the moment, however, caching poses serious problems: when accessing a document in a cache how can it be assured that no obsolete copy is shown; and if a document is cached from a server (even if no pricing is involved) caching distorts the hitrate of pages, the "holy grail" of WWW advertising. Consequently, many pages carry the information "don't cache me". First, such information might be ignored by some servers; second if it is not ignored the benefits of caching disappear. What is clearly needed is a more sophisticated caching protocol: the server A knows when a document X of A is cached in server B. If X is changed in A, B is notified of the change, and accessing X on B results in fetching a new copy from A; further, if X is accessed on B, a message to that extent is sent to A so that the hit-rate of X on A remains correct despite the caching; a similar mechanism can be used even if charges are attached to X.

- The whole area of subscriptions, payments, micro-payments, charging, etc. is still much in flux, yet is clearly as essential for e-commerce as truly secure transactions. For example, billing mechanisms on servers that are time-dependent (news get cheaper as they get older!) and a host of similar situations can be handled today, if at all, only by "tons of" CGI scripts, see [6], not "exactly" what is desirable!

3.4 WHAT CAN BE DONE ABOUT THE SHORTCOMINGS OF ORDINARY WWW?

Many but by far not all of the problem areas mentioned have been tackled in the meantime by a sheer endless list of add-ons, like CGI scripts, JAVA applets, JAVA scripts, Active-X components, etc. Some of the more fancy WWW applications resemble a shaky platform (ordinary WWW) onto which - using a less then perfect operating system (Windows) and a less than fully reliable "platform independent" programming language (JAVA) - fancy buildings of amazing complexity have been built. This cannot continue.

More solid approaches use standard databases (such as Oracle) as platform and provide the feeling of WWW through a WWW interface. This works perfectly for some well-structured applications but tends to fail in complex Web Based Information Systems [7], when Web Based Knowledge Management [6] is attempted, or even when just heterogeneous information with a dynamically changing structure is to be dealt with.

A more integrative approach is taken by Hyperwave [12] and hence warrants evaluation when considering the implementation of complex WWW-based applications. Looking at the issues raised Hyperwave is not much help concerning protocols (its own connection-oriented protocol cannot be used with standard clients, hence Hyperwave is also forced to work with HTTP); it does support a much more general document and access model, solves most of the problems of link management, goes a long way towards making WWW more interactive by allowing private and group views, annotations and links but scratches only the surface as far as distributed editing, caching or billing is concerned.

3.5 WILL WWW SURVIVE?

The shortcomings of current WWW as outlined make it clear that a Web2 will be necessary to handle the kind of interactive, communicative, information- and transaction-oriented system that is desparately needed.

Attempts by the W3C, and systems such as Hyperwave are trying to build an evolutionary path from current WWW to a Web2. However, the Web2 will differ from current WWW to an extent that it is not clear whether the evolutionary path that always has to take into account backward compatibility will not exact too high a price, and that a new Web2 that is not compatible with current WWW might not be the better solution.

One thing is clear: if anyone is building a complex application based on WWW with "tons of" customized CGI scripts those solutions will not carry over easily to a Web2. Hence one recommendation is fairly obvious: for small applications one can use simple WWW servers; for large applications one should use a standard database with WWW interface or an integrated solution such a Hyperwave. Solutions that are taylor-made by adding many customized CGI scripts to simple servers will be hard to maintain, and the roll-over to a Web2 will be difficult, to say the least.

The important fact to notice is: WWW will not survive as is, it will be replaced by a Web2, sooner rather than later. However, this will not be very noticeable for users. Rather, the brunt of the "conversion" will be on the shoulder of those running WWW services today and it is up to them to use tools that will make the migration to a Web2 easy.

References

[1] Berners-Lee, T., Cailliau, R., Groff, J.-F., Pollerman, B. (1992). World-Wide Web – The Information Universe, *Electronic Networking* 2,1 , 52-58.

[2] *W3C - The World Wide Web Consortium*, see http://www.w3.org

[3] Nelson, T.H. (1987). *Literary machines.* Edition 87.1, 702 South Michingan, South Bend, IN 46618, USA

[4] Maurer, H. (1997). What We Want from WWW as Distributed Multimedia System, *Proceedings of the VSMM'97*, Geneva, IEEE, 148-155.

[5] Maurer, H. (1998). Large WWW-Systems: New Phenomena, Problems and Solutions, *Proceedings of the 21st Annual Conference of the GfKl, 1997, Classification, Data Analysis, and Datahighways.* Balderjahn, Mathar, Schader (eds.), Springer, 270-276.

[6] Maurer, H. (1998). Web-Based Knowledge Management; Internet Watch, *Computer* (March 98), IEEE, 122-123.

[7] Maurer, H. (1998). Modern WIS, *Communications of the ACM 41,7*, 114-115.

[8] Van Dam, A. (1998). Hypertext'87, Keynote address; *Communications of the ACM 31, 7*, 887-895.

[9] Maurer, H. (ed.) (1996). *HyperWAve: The Next Generation Web Solution.* Addison-Wesley Longman, London.

[10] Dietinger, Th., Maurer, H. (1997). GENTLE – (GEneral Networked Training and Learning Environment), *Proceedings of ED-MEDIA & ED-TELECOM 98*, Freiburg, Germany, AACE, 274-280.

[11] Maurer, H. (1998). Using the WWW System Hyperwave as the Basis of a General Networked Teaching and Learning Environment, *CIT, vol. 6, 1* (special issue).

[12] *Hyperwave*, see http://www.hyperwave.com

4 RESOURCE PREDICTION AND ADMISSION CONTROL FOR INTERACTIVE VIDEO

Karl Aberer, Silvia Hollfelder

GMD – German National Research Center for Information Technology
IPSI (Integrated Publication and Information Systems Institute)
Dolivostr. 15, D-64293 Darmstadt, Germany *
{aberer|hollfeld}@darmstadt.gmd.de

Abstract: Highly interactive multimedia applications, like browsing in video databases, generate strongly varying loads on the media server during the presentation of media data. Existing admission control approaches for limiting the number of concurrent users and thus guaranteeing acceptable service quality are only suited for applications with uniform load characteristics like video-on-demand. We propose a session-oriented approach to admission control that is based on the stochastical model of Continuous Time Markov Chains, which allows to describe the different presentation states occurring in the interactive access to the multimedia database. The model is derived from semantic information on the forthcoming browsing session. In particular, it considers the relevance of the videos to the user. In this way a more precise prediction on resource usage can be given for achieving the two goals of Quality of Service (QoS) and good server utilization. The admission control mechanism is part of a multimedia database architecture for supporting efficient browsing in large video collections.

4.1 INTRODUCTION

Large digital collections of multimedia data, like Digital Libraries (DL), are getting increasingly important due to the widespread use of information networks like the World Wide Web. The amount of data available in digital multime-

*Partial funding by the ESPRIT joint project (Long Term Research No. 9141) **HERMES** (Foundations of High Performance Multimedia Information Management Systems).

dia collections is huge. Thus, a user needs to be supported to efficiently explore the digital collections by preselecting the data. Besides Digital Libraries, other applications also require this type of access, for example, previewing in pay-per-view systems or telelearning applications, where scholars from various disciplines study videos as primary source material [25].

In this article we focus on the problem of browsing multimedia data collections, in particular video collections. Browsing in video collections is particularly relevant, since content-based querying on video data is still not well supported. Browsing differs from other types of accesses to video databases, in particular video-on-demand applications. Only the relevant parts of the video are accessed and no complete videos need to be streamed to the user. By limiting data delivery to the relevant portions of videos the system throughput can be improved [3]. Frequent user interactions in browsing scenarios, like selection of videos, that are encoded in various formats, use of VCR-functions, and simultaneous presentation of videos, cause highly varying data consumption rates during a browsing session. In addition, the required Quality of Service (QoS) may vary for different requests [18].

Thus, the media storage components have to provide mechanisms which are able to deal with this characteristics of highly interactive multimedia applications. In order to achieve the required presentation quality, the clients compete for limited resources on the server. The basic strategies to deal with limited resources can be classified as optimistic or pessimistic ones.

With optimistic strategies all requests are served as well as possible (best effort). These strategies are typically used in client-pull architectures, where the client aperiodically requests small chunks of media data at the server during presentation [16]. The client-pull architecture is best suited for interactive applications with varying resource requirements. In case of user interactions, the client only has to change its data request behavior, for example, it will request larger blocks of a media or send more frequent requests. Bottlenecks are dealt with either by the server or clients with various strategies, e.g., by means of quality adaptation mechanisms at the client [8] or at the server [20, 21].

With pessimistic strategies full guarantees, based on worst-case resource requirements, or stochastical guarantees, are made at the server in advance. An admission control mechanism usually checks at the server if enough resources are available for the adequate delivery of data to a new media request. If there are enough resources available, the client is admitted and the resources are reserved until the end of the presentation. For interactive applications reservations based on stochastically specified resource parameters (i.e., mean rate with high rate deviation) waste server resources. Heuristic predictions on the future resource consumption of a client are more appropriate since the resource demands may vary extremely. This prediction can either be based on the past behavior of a client, or can be predicted by exploiting knowledge on the semantics of the request. Both approaches have their pros and cons. History based predicitions do not require high-level understanding of the semantics of the request and truly reflect the actual system usage. Thus, as long as the users behave in a uniform way, this approach appears to be appropriate. On the other hand, the implicit heuristic assumption that user behavior does not change may be inappropriate if opposite knowledge exists. Therefore, in situations in which knowledge on the forthcoming access behavior is available, it might be substantial to derive predictions from that, though, inevitably, many assumptions and heuristics might be involved in the prediction. We give a concrete example for illustration. If users request access to a multimedia database for unrestricted browsing, a uniform model of usage is appropriate and access can be granted if it can be derived from access statistics that sufficient resources are available. If users request access to a multimedia database to browse a pre-specified subset of data, e.g. given by the result of a retrieval request, this subset may bear certain characteristics which allow much more precise estimations of future resource usage. For example, only low quality videos have been selected, and thus resource consumption is substantially lower than in the general case where both low and high quality videos are accessed equally.

In a previous paper, we have introduced an admission control framework that exploited the client request history as an indicator for its future behavior [7]. This approach is fully application-independent and it does not exploit available knowledge on the application semantics for improved estimations of expected resource requirements. In this paper, we will make predictions for the resource demands of browsing sessions in multimedia databases based on the semantics of the request. We propose an admission control mechanism for browsing applications which models the user behavior in a browsing session. The model is based on information that is extracted from the set of browsing candidates selected by a preceding retrieval request. We assume that the starting point to a browsing session is given by a retrieval request. The result of the retrieval is a hit list with corresponding relevance values for each hit. From this information we derive a Continuous Time Markov Chain (CTMC) which stochastically models the presumable behavior of a user. From the CTMC we can derive a stochastic prediction of the future resource consumption of the client. This prediction is then used as an admission criterion. Thus, admission to the clients is granted in a session-oriented manner. The benefit of the session-oriented approach is that after an interaction an admitted client will get media data with low delay. Especially in browsing applications with frequent scene switches this is of high importance. We expect that our techniques are not only suitable for browsing applications but with some adaptations also applicable for other types of access to multimedia databases, in particular preorchestrated multimedia presentations.

The paper is structured as follows: We first introduce the browsing system architecture in Section 4.2. In Section 4.3, we model different types of browsing scenarios by using the CTMC model. In Section 4.4, we describe how resource predictions can be made on the basis of the CTMC models and how they are used as admission control criteria. We conclude the paper with related work, in Section 4.5, and remarks on the future research direction in Section 4.6.

4.2 SYSTEM ARCHITECTURE

In this chapter, we describe the architecture of a multimedia retrieval and browsing system that is under development at GMD-IPSI. It is designed to support highly interactive browsing applications [19]. The system supports (1) conceptual access to data, (2) continuous media presentation by means of client-side buffering mechanism, and (3) admission control for highly interactive applications.

Our browsing prototype is based on a client/server architecture. It consists of the following components: a Multimedia Database Management System (MM-DBMS) that is responsible for the storage and retrieval of meta data and media objects, a multimedia retrieval engine, an admission control module to restrict the access to the limited resouces on the server and to schedule data requests, a client-side buffering mechanism for media data, and a user interface for query formulation and result presentation. Figure 4.1 displays the relationships of the different components. These are described now, in more detail.

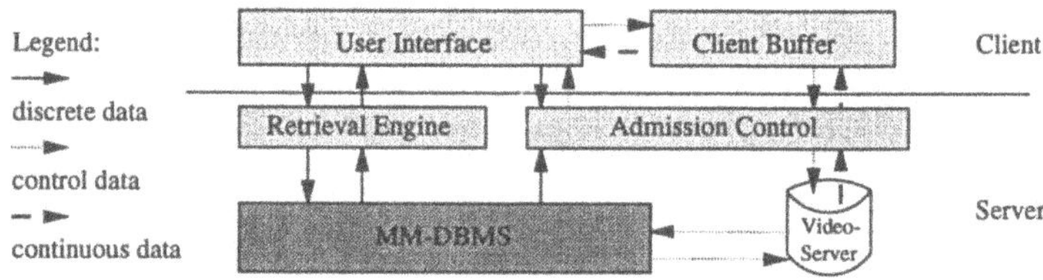

Figure 4.1: System architecture

4.2.1 *Multimedia Database Management System*

Our browsing prototype is implemented on the object-relational DBMS Informix Dynamic Server (IDS). The IDS enables the integration of so-called DataBlades which provide a flexible extension mechanism for new datatypes and their corresponding functions. We use the Video Foundation DataBlade [10] as basis for managing video data. The IDS DBMS stores the discrete data like text and images and the meta data for videos. The Video Foundation DataBlade enables to manage access to the external storage managers and devices. The external storage managers handle the storage of the various media streams. Thus, the media data and meta data of the media are stored separately.

4.2.2 *Retrieval Engine*

The Retrieval Engine provides content-based access by employing different multimedia retrieval techniques, like feature extraction, feature aggregation, and classification for videos on scene granularity. Content-based access to media data is supported by conceptual queries. For example, when a user is interested in indoor shots he specifies "artificial light" and "artefacts". The queries are mapped according to a rule base to requests expressed in constraints on feature values [19]. As a query result a hit list of stills, scenes, and videos is returned, together with relevance values - ranging between 0 and 1. The relevance values corresponding to a conceptual query are calculated by means of feature aggregation on video scene granularity. The basic image features, like edge analysis, grayscale, and entropy, are annotated in the IDS as meta data since feature extraction is a time consuming task. The features relate to single frames or scenes of a media. Rules define search criteria on the feature level which can be executed on the meta data [12]. Since meta data management is important to the browsing application, a MM-DBMS based implementation is best suited for providing the needed support for the retrieval engine [3].

4.2.3 Admission Control

The admission control module is located on top of the video server. It is responsible to manage the limited server resources such as disk bandwidth and buffer space. Thus, given the delay-sensitivity of multimedia presentations, there is a limited number of clients that can be admitted for the service. The admission control module has access to meta data stored in the IDS DBMS.

In our architecture, an admission control module for highly interactive browsing applications is provided that considers the varying data rate requirements. Its tasks are divided into: (1) the admission of new clients, when it is assumed that system resources are sufficient, (2) the scheduling and adaptation of the single data requests of the admitted clients.

4.2.4 Client Buffering

Since the Video Foundatation DataBlade does not support continuous presentation, we developed the Continuous Long Field DataBlade. It manages continuous data transport, client-side buffering, and client-side quality adaptation in distributed environments [9]. Additionally, we enhanced the client buffer strategy to support browsing applications by means of a content-based preloading and replacement strategy. It considers, in addition to the current presentation state, the relevance to a conceptual query result, too [5]. The goal is to keep the most important scenes, corresponding to the current presentation state and to a previous query, in the buffer.

4.2.5 User Interface

The user interface enables the specification of a conceptual query that is sent to the retrieval engine and the selection of result scenes for presentation. At the server, the access to hits requested in a retrieval session are subject to admission control. During presentation the user has the possibility to control the presentation through VCR-interactions and to jump interactively to other hits.

4.3 MODELING OF BROWSING APPLICATIONS

A major difficulty in estimating resource usage in interactive applications is the high variability of resource requirements. In this section, we will use a stochastical model, namely Continuous Time Markov Chains, to describe user interactions. It can be used to estimate future resource demands and, thus, to provide a more precise criterion for an admission control mechanism. The admission control mechanism itself will be discussed in the subsequent section 4.4. We will use multimedia browsing sessions as an application scenario for inspecting multimedia retrieval results.

4.3.1 Modeling of Multimedia Sessions as Continuous Time Markov Chains

The retrieval and browsing system described in Section 4.2 delivers a result list L that contains references to scenes of videos or whole videos together with their relevance values as the result of a retrieval query. Thus an element $l_i \in L, i = 1, \ldots, |L|$ is of the form $l_i =< scene_i, rv_i >$, where $scene_i$ is an identifier for a video scene and $rv_i \in [0, 1]$ is a relevance value. Additionally, it is possible to compute physical information on the video scene from the meta data in the multimedia database, in particular, its duration $d(scene_i) \in R^+$ and the datarate $rate(scene_i) \in R^+$.

This information is available when a browsing session is started. The browsing session itself can be viewed as a state transition system, where the user switches between states for presenting particular videos and idle states for selecting the next video to be presented. For resource control it is important to consider, in addition to those states, the temporal dimension, i.e., the holding time of a state. A well established model to describe such state transition systems stochastically are Continuous Time Markov Chains (CTMC) [22].

A state transition process is specified in a CTMC by a set of states I, by holding times $\frac{1}{v_i}, i \in I$, and by transition probabilities $p_{i,j}$, with $i, j \in I, i \neq j$ and $\sum_{j \neq i} p_{i,j} = 1$ for all $i \in I$. If the system jumps into state i, it stays in state i an exponentially distributed holding time with mean $\frac{1}{v_i}$ independently of how the system reached state i and how long it took to get there. If the system leaves state i, it jumps to state j with probability $p_{i,j}$ independently of the holding time of the state i. States are memory-less, which is called the Markovian property, i.e., the history how a state is reached is not relevant [22]. CTMCs are an extension of discrete time Markov chains, which do not model the holding times in the states.

Using CTMC for the modeling of a browsing session, the session states, i.e., the playback of a video scene or an idle time, are represented as corresponding states of a CTMC. The sojourn time or holding time in a state is the time until a user decides to change presentation process by an interaction. The transition probabilities denote the probability that a user switches from one session state to another one.

In our approach, we assume that the parameters determining a CTMC, i.e., the transition probabilities and the holding times of a state, are related to the relevance values rv_i of a hit $l_i \in L, i \in I$. When a user finds a large number of hits he will not inspect all of them since the total presentation duration is too long. Typically, a user selects those scenes that have a high relevance with respect to the query. Furthermore, the time a user will spend to view a hit is dependent on its duration. The structure of the CTMC used to model the browsing session and the detailed relationship between the relevance values and the CTMC parameters are the subject of the next subsections.

4.3.2 Modeling Browsing Behavior by CTMCs

Depending on the application, a user may pursue different goals in a browsing session. Some users may aim at getting an overview of all hits in the hit list (sneak preview), others may intend to extract detailed information from the hit list. This results in different browsing behaviors. In the following, we will discuss different possible browsing behaviors and model them by CTMCs. This discussion is not intended to exhaustively explore the issue of how browsing sessions are structured, but to illustrate how different assumptions on the nature of browsing sessions lead to structurally very different CTMC models. From this, we will eventually analyse the computational methods required for a resource prediction used for admission control.

In the following, we first make a simplifying assumption on result viewing. We neglect different VCR-presentation states, like fast forward, fast rewind, and slow motion. We consider only two principle states, namely the *idle states* in which the user selects the next scene and no resources are consumed, and the *playback states* where particular videos are viewed in standard playback mode. Only transitions back and forth between idle states and playback states are possible. Later we will indicate how to model different modes of presentation.

The structural differences in CTMC models for browsing result from accounting for the browsing history in different ways. Since the CTMC itself is memory-less any historical information needs to be encoded into additional states.

4.3.3 Memory-free Browsing

In the simplest case, the selection of the next step is fully independent of the previous browsing steps. For modelling this situation it is sufficient to use one single idle state is and playback states $1, \ldots, |L|$ for the presentation of the different videos in the hit list. The transition probability $p_{is,i}$ is a function of rv_i only. We choose the probabilities to be distributed in the same way as the relevance values, i.e., we use the *normalized relevance values* $\overline{rv}_i$ of a hit l_i, given by

$$\overline{rv}_i = \frac{rv_i}{\sum_{j=1}^{|L|} rv_j}, i = 1, \ldots, |L|$$

as transition probabilities. Then $p_{is,i} = \overline{rv}_i$ and $\sum_{i=1,\ldots,|L|} p_{is,i} = 1$, whereas always $p_{i,is} = 1$. An advanced model might use a weighting function in addition, e.g., to overproportionally increase the probability that videos of higher relevance are viewed.

For the holding times, we assume the following heuristic model: for short scenes, the mean of the exponentially distributed holding time is proportional to the length of the scene. There is a minimum presentation time d_{min} and the mean is limited by a maximal presentation duration $d_{min} + d_{max}$. In addition, we weight the mean by the relevance of the video, i.e. more relevant videos are viewed longer than less relevant ones. This heuristics is reflected in the following formula for the mean holding time:

$$1/v_i = d_{min} + d_{max} \frac{d(scene_i)}{d(scene_i) + d_{max}} rv_i, \; i = 1, \ldots, |L|$$

Example. To demonstrate the concepts, we use a running example in the following. A user query with 5 result scenes ($|L| = 5$) delivers the results shown in Table 4.1.

Table 4.1: Example of query result list.

	d	$rate$	rv
$scene_1$	$5sec$	$1.5Mb/s$	0.8
$scene_2$	$60sec$	$0.8Mb/s$	0.7
$scene_3$	$20sec$	$4.0Mb/s$	0.7
$scene_4$	$10sec$	$1.5Mb/s$	0.1
$scene_5$	$20sec$	$4.0Mb/s$	0.05

By setting $d_{max} = 30sec$ and $d_{min} = 3sec$ we get the following (rounded) values for the holding times: $\frac{1}{v_1} = 6.4, \frac{1}{v_2} = 17, \frac{1}{v_3} = 11.4, \frac{1}{v_4} = 3.75, \frac{1}{v_5} = 3.6$. For the idle state is, we assume a mean holding time $\frac{1}{v_{is}} = 5$ which means it takes an average of 5 seconds to select the next presentation.

The transition probabilites in the example are then: $p_{is,1} = 0.34, p_{is,2} = 0.3, p_{is,3} = 0.3, p_{is,4} = 0.04, p_{is,5} = 0.02$.

In Figure 4.2 the CTMC is given for the example. The numbers at the arrows represent the transition probabilities between the states.

4.3.4 *General history-dependent Browsing*

In the most general model for browsing the transition probabilities are fully dependent on the browsing history. In order to model this case we have to use a CTMC with the tree structure indicated in Figure 4.3. The root represents the start state, the nodes at the first level represent all hits selected first, the nodes at the second level all hits selected second, and so on. In this way,

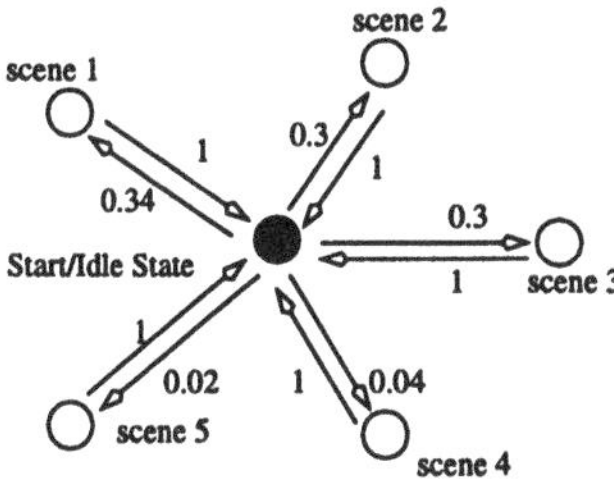

Figure 4.2: CTMC for memory-free browsing

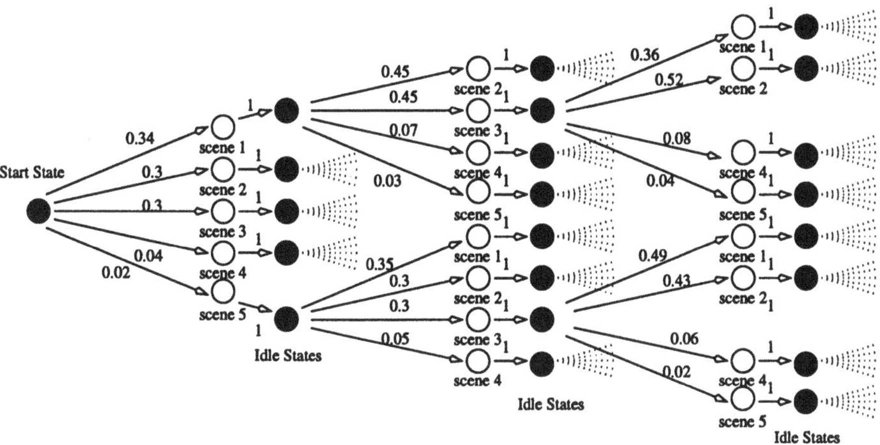

Figure 4.3: CTMC with tree structure for general history-dependent browsing

the CTMC represents all possible session histories. Each state represents a different viewing sequence of earlier videos and, since repetitions are possible, we end up with an infinite number of states. In contrast to the previous case, we have to distinguish a start state ss and different idle states is_h for each different presentation history h consisting of the sequence of videos that have been presented before.

We discuss now a simple model of how the transition probabilities can depend on the previous browsing history. A video that has just been viewed is not likely to be selected again. However, the longer a video has not been selected and the more other videos have been selected the more likely it becomes that the video will be selected again. Assume, that the browsing session is in the idle state

is_h belonging to a certain sequence of videos that have been selected before. Then for every scene $scene_i, i = 1, \ldots, |L|$ we modify the relevance values for videos that have previously been viewed as follows:

$$rv'_i = \overline{rv_i}\frac{2n}{n + |L|},$$

where n is the number of times $scene_i$ has not been viewed in the history h. From the modified relevance values, we compute the normalized relevance values $\overline{rv'_i}$ and use them as transition probabilities. Note, that for $n = 0$ we get $rv'_i = 0$ and for $n = |L|$ we get $rv'_i = rv_i$. The factor is monotonically increasing for $n > 0$.

Assume that in our running example $scene_1$ has just been viewed. Then the modified relevance values rv'_1 for $scene_1$ used to compute the transition probability for the consecutive steps are $0, 0.11, 0.19, 0.26, 0.30, 0.34$ assuming the video is not selected within those steps. Note that these values are not normalized yet. A fragment of the CTMC with normalized $\overline{rv'_i}$ values as transition probabilities, visualized as numbers at the arrows, is given in Figure 4.3. The dotted lines represent missing paths that are omitted due to the lack of space.

4.3.5 *Browsing without Repetition*

Up to now, we have assumed that the user is free to select any video for viewing an arbitrary number of times. We now investigate how further constraints on the selection of videos to be viewed impact the CTMC model for browsing.

The first additional constraint we consider is, that the user can view each video only once. Thus, we will obtain a finite CTMC as opposed to the previously discussed case of general, history-dependent browsing, where an infinite CTMC has become necessary. The general structure of the resulting CTMC is depicted in Figure 4.4. Since we assume that each video will be viewed only once, the number of subsequent states decreases in each level by the state that has been presented already and, thereby, the one-step transition probabilities increase for the remaining videos.

The transition probabilities are determined at each level from the normalized relevance values of the remaining videos. They are given for the case of our running example in Figure 4.4.

4.3.6 *Browsing in Relevance Order*

This is a very restricted form of browsing where the user can access the query result only in the order of their relevance values. Thus, the user basically only determines the holding times for each video that is viewed. In this case, we obtain a degenerated CTMC with a (nearly) linear structure, as displayed in Figure 4.5 for our running example. The state on the left side represents the start state, the relevance values rv of the hits viewed in the playback states decrease from left to right. States with the same relevance are modeled by alternative state sequences that are accessed with the same probability.

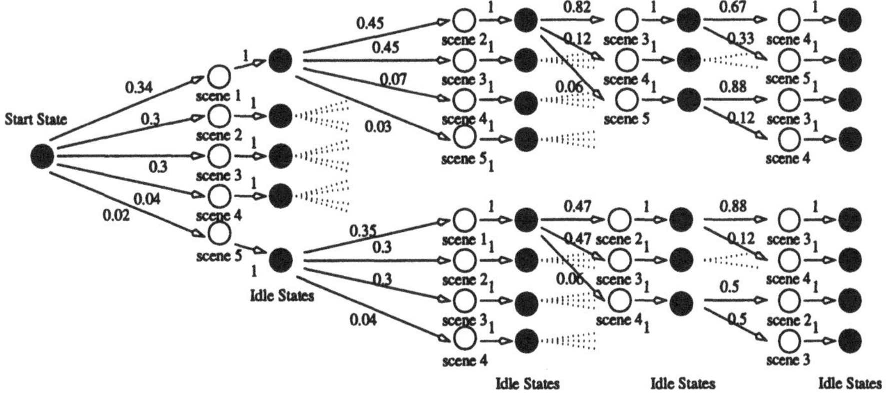

Figure 4.4: CTMC with tree structure for browsing without repetition

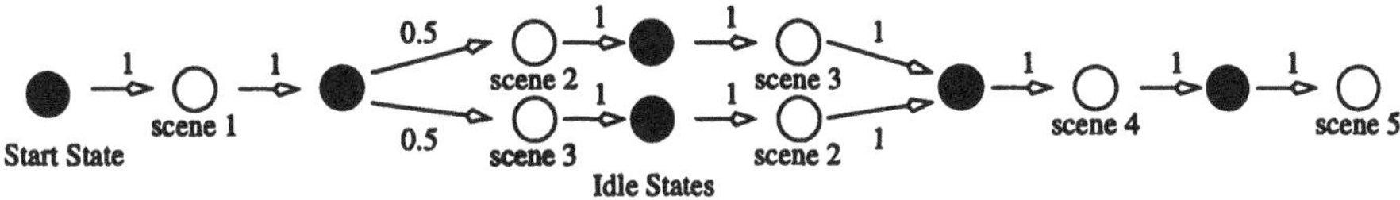

Figure 4.5: CTMC with sequential linear browsing

4.3.7 Representation of VCR-functionality

As indicated earlier, in the different CTMC models, we have used the simplifying assumption that the viewing of videos is represented by a single playback state in the CTMC. In practice, a user may use VCR-functionality. In the following we sketch how this can be accommodated within a CTMC model.

We assume now that, during the presentation of a video, a user may switch to a fast forward, fast rewind, or slow motion state. We determine that these interactions are only accessible from the playback state and extend thus a CTMC in the following way: for each video of the hit list, we introduce additional VCR-states for fast forward, fast rewind, and slow motion. We assume fixed transition probabilities from the playback state to the VCR-states. The transition probability from the VCR-state to its playback state is always 1. The holding times can be derived from the holding times of the playback state, for example, by decreasing it for fast forward and fast rewind and increasing it for slow motion.

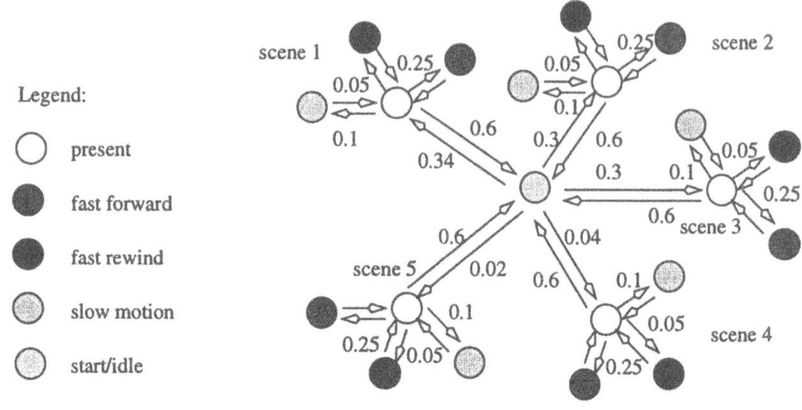

Figure 4.6: CTMC for memory-free browsing with VCR-functionality

We illustrate the extended CTMC for our running example in the case of memory-free browsing. As transition probabilities to the VCR-states, we have arbitrarily chosen $p_{present,ff} = 0.25, p_{present,fr} = 0.05, p_{present,sm} = 0.1$ in this example. Figure 4.6 displays the corresponding CTMC when VCR-functionality is supported. Since the transition probabilities from the VCR-states to the present state are all equal to 1 they are not displayed in the figure.

4.3.8 Possible Refinements of the Modeling Approach

Appearently, in the modelling, a number of assumptions have been made on parameters and functions that capture certain characteristics of browsing sessions. It is beyond the scope of this paper to devise methods of how concrete parameters can be analytically derived from evaluations of concrete behavior of users. This is an important direction for future work. Such an approach allows not only to come up with better-substantiated heuristics on the user behavior, but would also allow to determine the necessary parameters individually for different users or application scenarios. As a drawback, individualized user parameters require additional bookkeeping mechanisms.

Some of the models introduced were very complex. One can devise different ways of how the complexity could be reduced in order to obtain computationally more feasible models for browsing sessions, without giving up too much precision in the prediction. One obvious approach would be to aggregate states with similar characteristics, e.g., comparable resource consumption and holding time, and, thus, to substantially reduce the number of states in the model. Another possibility would be to allow for small errors and just omit less important scenes, i.e., those with low relevance.

In this paper, we have used a rather abstract view on how the occurence of a video within a query result is related to the probability that it will be accessed. Other parameters than the relevance value may influence the access probability to a video. In particular, the way in which the result list is presented at the user interface can play a substantial role. For example, for videos with the same or similar relevance value, the position in the result list can be of importance, or if the result hits are presented in a page oriented way, hits on the first page are more likely to be accessed than on later pages etc.. Thus the way, of how a multimedia presentation is generated from the hit list is certainly of relevance to the access behavior of the user. This discussion also shows that similar methods for modeling the user access to multimedia data may be employed for general preorchestrated multimedia presentations.

4.4 ADMISSION CONTROL USING RESOURCE PREDICTION

4.4.1 Analysis of CTMC Models

In the previous section, we have modeled browsing behavior with CTMCs under various assumptions of how browsing might be performed. The main purpose was to explore the question which structures occur in the CTMC models, how these structures are related to different assumptions on how browsing is performed, and how the resulting CTMCs are suited to compute a resource prediction.

The first important question in analyzing CTMCs is whether we have an open or a closed CTMC at hand. A CTMC is called closed if every state can be reached from every other state. This classification is important with regard to the applicable analysis methods. One distinguishes transient analysis and equilibrium analysis. Equilibrium analysis determines certain measures that are attached to a CTMC with regard to long term behavior. Transient analysis determines those measures over a given (short) finite time span. Equilibrium analysis is only applicable to closed CTMCs. With transient analysis we can also analyse CTMCs of infinite size, as they occured in the case of general history-dependent browsing.

For the computational complexity of the analysis, the size of the CTMC is of importance. Both, for the CTMC model for general history-dependent browsing and for browsing without repetition the size of the (relevant fragment of the) model grows exponentially in the number of hits, when a transient analysis is performed. For memory-less and sequential browsing the size of the CTMC is linear to the number of hits.

In this paper we will not be able to give a conclusive statement on which model and which type of analysis will prevail as the most relevant one. Rather, we will give the analysis for a selected case, namely memory-less browsing. As analysis method, we will use an equilibrium analysis. There are a number of reasons why this choice is reasonable and practical as well, in particular, considering the requirement that the resource predicition has to be performed efficiently.

From the computational viewpoint, encoding of histories into CTMCs leads to combinatorially explosive sizes of the resulting models and, thus, to prohibitively high costs in the analysis. In addition, equilibrium analysis is computationally simpler than transient analysis. A problem which further complicates transient analysis is the choice of the expected duration of the browsing session. This does not occur in equilibrium analysis.

When the impact of the history on the transition probabilities is small the equilibrium analysis is a good approximation of the transient analysis. This is also the case when only a few hits will be viewed in a browsing section, since then only a few transition probabilities change, too. In addition, there exists the possibility to redo the equilibrium analysis at a later stage with modified parameters and to accomodate changes that result from the previous history.

4.4.2 Resource Estimation for memory-less Browsing using Equilibrium Analysis

Since for each playback state the corresponding data rates are known, it is possible to stochastically determine an overall expected data rate for a single client session, based on its CTMC model for browsing. In the following, we will give the necessary steps to perform this calculation. Details on the mathematical background of this calculation can be found in [22].

A closed CTMC with bounded rates $v_i, i \in I$ has a unique equilibrium distribution $P_i, i \in I$, where the P_i can be interpreted as the probability that the CTMC is in state i. In order to compute this equilibrium distribution one first transforms it into a discrete Markov chain by introducing so called transition rates $q_{i,j}$ with

$$q_{i,j} = v_i p_{i,j}, \text{with } i,j \in I, j \neq i. \tag{4.1}$$

Based on the transition rates, the equilibrium distribution can be determined by solving the following system of linear equations, which has a unique solution.

$$v_i P_i = \sum_{k \neq i} q_{k,i} P_k, i \in I \tag{4.2}$$

$$\sum_{k \in I} P_k = 1. \tag{4.3}$$

For the concrete case of the CTMC for memory-less browsing we can compute the expected data rate as follows. Given holding times v_{is} and $v_i, i = 1, \ldots, |L|$ we get $v_i P_i = q_{is,i} P_{is}$ since the states i can only be reached from $state_{is}$ and thus

$$P_i = \frac{v_{is}}{v_i} p_{is,i} P_{is} \text{ for } i = 1, \ldots, |L| \tag{4.4}$$

using equation 4.1.

Substituting equation 4.3 for our concrete case with $\sum_{i \in |L|} P_i + P_{is} = 1$ and using equation 4.4 yields

$$P_{is} = \frac{1}{1 + \sum_{i=1,\ldots,|L|} \frac{v_{is}}{v_i} p_{is,i}} \tag{4.5}$$

from which the other values P_i can be immediately derived.

The expected value $E(i)$ of resources required by state i within the long-run analysis is determined then by

$$E(i) = P_i * res(i)$$

where $res(i)$ is the amount of resources consumed in state i.

The expected amount of resources required by a client c within a browsing session is then

$$E_c = \sum_{i \in I} E(i).$$

Since idle states do not consume resources, the expected resource demand is then computed for our concrete case as

$$E_c = \sum_{i=1,\ldots,|L|} P_i * rate(scene_i).$$

This derivation shows that for the CTMC for memory-less browsing we can derive the equilibrium distribution and, thus, the expected resource demand in linear time cost in the size of the result list.

For our running example, we obtain by means of using equation 4.4 and the v_i and p_i values from Section 4.3.3 the equilibrium probabilities

$$P_{is} = 0.31, P_1 = 0.14, P_2 = 0.32, P_3 = 0.21, P_4 = 0.01, P_5 = 0.005.$$

Note, though the first video has higher relevance the probability that the system is in the state of presenting the second or third video is higher. This is due to the fact that those videos have substantially longer holding times. The expected resource demand for this client session is then $E_c = 1.35 Mb/s$.

4.4.3 *Admission Control of Pending Clients*

The MM-DBMS limits the number of active clients that are allowed to simultaneously perform a browsing session for inspecting the hit list. Thus when a client issues a query, the results will only be presented if sufficient resources are available. For determining whether sufficient resources are available the prediction models introduced in the previous section are employed. A client that has been admitted will be served for the complete browsing session, with high probability in the required quality.

Let us assume the system has already admitted clients $c_1, \ldots, c_k$ and a new client c_p requests admission. Then the admission control mechanism computes the expected resource demand of the running clients $E_{c_j}, j = 1, \ldots, c_k$, and the expected resource demand E_{c_p} of the new client. Then the admission criterion is

$$E_{c_p} + \sum_{j=1,\ldots,c_k} E_{c_j} < \tau * s_{max},$$

where s_{max} is the amount of maximal available resources and $\tau \in [0,1]$ is a safety margin to allow small deviations from the expected resource usage. The quantity τ determines how close the average load values may approach the maximum server load, and thus how much tolerance is available to compensate for deviations between predicted and real server load. High values of τ represent a permissive admission policy, while low values of τ represent a cautious admission policy. For a large number of possible clients, such a criterion based on an estimation of the average resource usage appears to be appropriate, since deviations from the average values of single clients can be expected to compensate for statistical reasons. For a small number of clients, other admission criteria based, for example, on maximum expected resource usage or maximum expected deviation, can be considered in addition.

The actual resource usage of a client can be determined a posteriori by analyzing its requests to the system. This technique has been used in [7] to devise an alternative admission control mechanism, based on the lookback to past system behavior. It may occur that the predicted resource usage of a client and the actual resource usage systematically deviate from each other. In such a case, it is quite clear, that one can use the information on the actual behavior to systematically correct future predictions. A detailed discussion of this approach is, however, beyond the scope of this paper.

For the concrete realization of the admission control mechanism a number of further issues need to be resolved, like the definition of admission points, the treatment of rejected clients, the recomputation of predictions for admitted clients and the reaction to overload situations. Some solutions to that extent have been presented in [7], in particular, a complete specification of an admission control algorithm.

4.5 RELATED WORK

Most approaches to admission control consider the requests of *single* media streams. The resource requirements are prespecified by the media request in terms of constant rate or little rate deviations [16]. The available system resources are calculated by stochastic [13], [24] or deterministic approaches [23], [14]. Based on the knowledge about the already reserved and freely available resources, it is possible to reject requests in case of server overloads. Most concepts providing stochastical service guarantees assume stochastical retrieval time from storage system which we do not consider. For example, [24] exploit the variation in access times from disk. In the following, we focus on strategies that consider interactive applications.

A priori reservation. To guarantee a given QoS worst-case assumptions about the required data rate can be made. Obviously, in case of reservation of this high data rate server resources are wasted and the number of clients that can be served in parallel is decreased. Dey-Sircar et al. [4] give stochastical guarantees by means of reserving separate server bandwidth for VCR-interactions. The drawback of their work is that they assume interactions to occur rarely.

Re-admission at interaction points. A straightforward way to use standard admission control policies with interactive applications is to perform admission control for each single media object request that can occur as the result of an interaction as described in Gollapudi and Zhang [6]. One drawback of their approach is, in contrast to our session-oriented approach, that each client request is subject to the admission control. This means, for example, when the first scene of a video is admitted there is no guarantee for the immediately admission of the subsequent scenes of the same presentation. This may lead to unacceptable delay in presentation when too many clients send requests. Moreover, the admission of one continuous media stream of a multimedia presentation does not necessarily guarantee the timely admission of another continuous media stream that has to be synchronized with the already admitted streams.

Smooth the application data rates. Some approaches to admission control for interactive applications propose to "smooth" the data rate deviations to achieve a relatively constant workload. Shenoy and Vin [17] reduce the high data rate for fast forward and fast rewind of MPEG-videos by encoding the stream in base and enhanced layers. The encoding of the base layer is done by reducing the temporal and spatial resolution. For fast forward, only the base layer is used. Chen, Kandlur, and Yu [2] suggest segment skipping where a segment can be a set of Group of Pictures (GoP) of an MPEG-video. For fast forward or fast rewind, some segments are skipped. Chen, Krishnamurthy, Little, and Venkatesch [1] change the order of MPEG-frames to a priority sequence. For fast forward and fast rewind, only the most important frames (I- and P-Frames) are pushed to the client. The higher data rate is reduced by quality adaptation on the temporal dimension of other requests by a dynamic resource reservation. Reddy [15] reduces the latency of "urgent" requests, but neglects varying bandwidth requirements. The smoothing approach is, however, restricted to relativley simple interactive scenarios where interactions take place within the presentation of one single media stream.

Inspect the past system behavior. In earlier work, we presented a general admission control mechanism which is applicable for varying resource requirements of highly interactive applications [7]. It consists of (1) the admission of new clients when server resources are available and (2) the scheduling and adaptation of requests of admitted clients. For the admission of new clients, we inspect the past system behavior. For a large number of parallel sessions, the average client consumption is a good estimate for prediction. Data rate variations are accounted for by introducing a safety margin. Thus, an admitted client is supposed to obtain sufficient resources. If in spite of the admission control resource bottlenecks occur, strategies for rescheduling requests are used to achieve high QoS by means of load balancing. In the worst case quality adaptations are required to enable guaranteed continuous delivery.

Usage of application semantics. Zhao and Tripathi [26] propose a session-based reservation approach for multimedia applications with varying resource requirements. A multimedia session consists of the presentation of multiple multimedia objects that have to be synchronized in temporal order. The temporal order of the presentation is known at admission time. They propose an "advanced resource reservation" mechanism, i.e., to reserve resources for time intervals in the future. The goal of the approach is to determine a starting point for the presentation for which all required resources (i.e., network and end system) are available. The basic reservation model does not consider user interactions. They propose the following extensions for interactions: (1) the specification of a minimum upper bound which is not economically and (2) re-admission at interaction point as discussed earlier in this section.

The use of continuous-time Markov chains for modeling the access behavior in a multimedia database system to support the efficient vertical data migration between the tertiary and secondary storage has been devised in [11]. This shows that the application of the CTMCs to model resource usage in multimedia databases is not only limited to admission control but is applicable to other aspects of resource management as well.

4.6 CONCLUSION

In this paper, we presented a session-oriented admission control mechanism for highly interactive browsing applications by considering application semantics for the admission of new clients. It is based on the stochastical resource prediction of clients. We assume that the user behavior is related to the relevance values of a conceptual query and specify the user behavior as Continuous Time Markov Chains.

A Java based implementation of the admission algorithm within the IDS based system architecture described in Section 4.2 is under way. Future work will concentrate on the refinement and evaluation of the approach and on learning models for user profiles. An evaluation of the concept will strongly depend on the availability of sufficient real-world data against which the proposed models can be calibrated. From this data the statistical parameters of the Markov chain models can be learned to adapt the admission control framework to particular application scenarios. In combination with the retrospective approach to admission control by inspection of past system behavior, the goal is a self-adapting admission control framework for multimedia database access.

References

[1] Huang-Jen Chen, Anand Krishnamurthy, Thomas D. C. Little, and Dinesh Venkatesch. A scalable video-on-demand service for the provision of

VCR-like functions. In *Proc. 2nd Intl. Conf. on Multimedia Computing and Systems*, pages 65–72, May 1995.

[2] Ming-Syan Chen, Dilip D. Kandlur, and Philip S. Yu. Support for fully interactive playout in a disk-array-based video server. In *ACM Multimedia*, 1994.

[3] Stavros Christodoulakis and Peter Triantafillou. Research and development issues for large-scale multimedia information systems. *ACM Computing Surveys*, December 1995.

[4] Jayanta K. Dey-Sircar, James D. Salehi, James F. Kurose, and Don Towsley. Providing VCR capabilities in large-scale video servers. In *ACM Multimedia*, pages 25–32, 1994.

[5] André Everts, Silvia Hollfelder, and Ulrich Thiel. Browsing descriptors and content-based presentation support for videos. In *GI-Workshop Multimedia Systeme, in conjunction with Informatik'98, (GI-Jahrestagung Informatik zwischen Bild und Sprache)*, September 1998. To be published.

[6] Sreenivas Gollapudi and Aidong Zhang. Netmedia: A client-server distributed multimedia environment. In *Proc. of Third Intl. Workshop on Multimedia Database Management Systems*, pages 352–363, August 1996.

[7] Silvia Hollfelder and Karl Aberer. An admission control framework for applications with variable consumption rates in client-pull architectures. In *Proceedings of Multimedia Information Systems (MIS'98)*, Istanbul, September 1998. To be published, also appeared as GMD Technical Report, Sankt Augustin, Nr. 8, April 1998.

[8] Silvia Hollfelder, Achim Kraiss, and Thomas C. Rakow. A client-controlled adaptation framework for multimedia database systems. In *Proc. of European Workshop on Interactive Distributed Multimedia Systems and Telecommunication Services (IDMS'97)*, Darmstadt, Germany, Sept 1997.

[9] Silvia Hollfelder, Florian Schmidt, Matthias Hemmje, and Karl Aberer. Transparent integration of continuous media support into a multimedia DBMS. In *Proceedings of IADT '98*, Berlin, 1998. Enlarged version published as GMD Technical Report, Nr. 1104, Sankt Augustin, Germany, December. 1997.

[10] Informix. *Video Foundation DataBlade Module User's Guide, Version 1.1.* INFORMIX Press, June 1997. Version 1.1.

[11] Achim Kraiss and Gerhard Weikum. Vertical data migration in large near-line document archives based on markov-chain predictions. In *VLDB*, pages 246–255, 1997.

[12] Adrian Müller and André Everts. Interactive image retrieval by means of abductive inference. In *RIAO 97 Conference Proceedings – Computer-Assisted Information Searching on Internet*, pages 450–466, June 1997.

[13] Guido Nerjes, Peter Muth, and Gerhard Weikum. Stochastic performance guarantees for mixed workloads in a multimedia information system. In

Proc. of the IEEE International Workshop on Research Issues in Data Engineering (RIDE'97), Birmingham, UK, April 1997.

[14] Banu Özden, Rajeev Rastogi, Avi Silberschatz, and P. S. Narayanan. The Fellini multimedia storage server. In S. M. Chung, editor, *Multimedia Information Storage and Management*. Kluwer Academic Publishers, 1996.

[15] Narasimha Reddy. Improving latency in interactive video server. In *Proc. of SPIE Multimedia Computing and Networking Conference*, pages 108–112, February 1997.

[16] Siram S. Roa, Harrick M. Vin, and Asis Tarafdar. Comparative evaluation of server-push and client-pull architectures for multimedia servers. In *Proc. of Nossdav 96*, pages 45–48, 1996.

[17] Prashant J. Shenoy and Harrick M. Vin. Efficient support for scan operations in video servers. In *Proc. of the Third ACM Conference on Multimedia*, 1995.

[18] Ralf Steinmetz and Klara Nahrstedt. *Multimedia: Computing, Communications and Applications.* Prentice Hall Series in innovative technology. Prentice Hall, 1995.

[19] Ulrich Thiel, Silvia Hollfelder, and Andre Everts. Multimedia management and query processing issues in distributed digital libraries: A HERMES perspective. In Roland R. Wagner, editor, *Proc. of the 9th Int. Workshop on Database and Expert Systems DEXA'98*, pages 84–89, August 1998.

[20] Heiko Thimm and Wolfgang Klas. Delta-sets for optimized reactive adaptive playout management. In *Proc. 12th Int. Conf. On Data Engineering (ICDE)*, pages 584–592, 1996.

[21] Heiko Thimm, Wolfgang Klas, Crispin Cowan, Jonathan Walpole, and Calton Pu. Optimization of adaptive data-flows for competing multimedia presentational database sessions. In *IEEE International Conference on Multimedia Computing and Systems*, pages 584–592, June 1997.

[22] Henk C. Tijms. *Stochastic Models. An Algorithmic Approach.* Wiley series in probability and mathematical statistics. Wiley, 1994.

[23] Harrick M. Vin, Alok Goyal, and Pawan Goyal. Algorithms for designing large-scale multimedia servers. *Computer Communications*, March 1995.

[24] Harrick M. Vin, Pawan Goyal, Alok Goyal, and Anshuman Goyal. A statistical admission control algorithm for multimedia servers. In *Proc. of the ACM Multimedia*, pages 33–40, October 1994.

[25] M. M. Yeung, B.-L. Yeo, W. Wolf, and B. Liu. Video browsing using clustering and scene transitions on compressed sequences. In *IS &T SPIE Multimedia Computing and Networking*, 1995.

[26] Wei Zhao and Satish K. Tripathi. A resource reservation scheme for synchronized distributed multimedia sessions. *Multimedia Tools and Applications*, (7):133–146, July 1998.

5 DATA SEMANTICS FOR IMPROVING RETRIEVAL PERFORMANCE OF DIGITAL NEWS VIDEO SYSTEMS

G. Ahanger
T.D.C. Little

8 Saint Mary's Street
Multimedia Communications Laboratory
Department of Electrical and Computer Engineering
Boston University, Boston, Massachusetts 02215, USA
(617) 353-8042, (617) 353-6440 fax
{gulrukh,tdcl}@bu.edu

Abstract: We propose a novel four-step hybrid approach for retrieval and composition of video newscasts based on information contained in different metadata sets. In the first step, we use conventional retrieval techniques to isolate video segments from the data universe using segment metadata. In the second step, retrieved segments are clustered into potential news items using a dynamic technique sensitive to the information contained in the segments. In the third step, we apply a transitive search technique to increase the recall of the retrieval system. In the final step, we increase recall performance by identifying segments possessing creation-time relationships.

A quantitative analysis of the performance of the process on a newscast composition shows an increase in recall by 23% for the third step of the process and 48% for the fourth step, over the conventional keyword-based search technique used in the first step.

5.1 INTRODUCTION

A challenging problem in video-based applications is achieving rapid search and retrieval of content from a large corpus. Because of the computational cost of real-time image-based analysis for searching such large data sets we

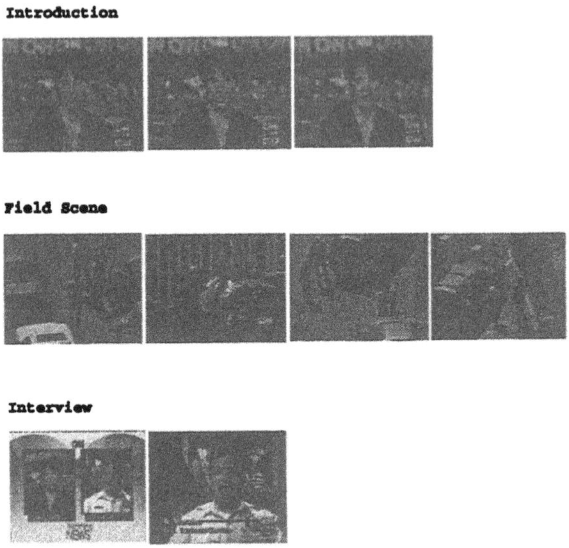

Figure 5.1: Scenes from an Example News Item

pursue techniques based on off-line or semi-automated classification, indexing, and cataloging. Therein lies the need for "bridge" techniques that have rich semantics for representing motion-image-based concepts and content, yet are supported by fast and efficient algorithms for real-time search and retrieval. At this intersection we have been investigating techniques for video concept representation and manipulation. In particular we have sought the goal of automatic composition of news stories, or newscasts based on an archive of digital video with supporting metadata.

To retrieve video clips we need to process video data so that they are in clip-queryable form. We need to extract information from video clips, represent the information in a manner that can be used to process queries, and provide a mechanism for formulating queries. Presentation of discrete clips matching a query is not engaging. After retrieval, composition of these clips towards a theme (e.g., a news topic) adds value to the presentation.

The general process in automatic composition of news (or any) digital video towards a theme is based on selecting desired video data within some domain (e.g., sports), filtering redundant data, clustering similar data in sub-themes, and composing the retrieved data into a logical and thematically-correct order [1]. All of these tasks are possible if we have sufficient information about the content of the video data. Therefore, information (metadata) acquisition and techniques to match, filter, and compose video data are critical to the performance of a video composition system. The quality of data retrieved depends on the type of metadata and the matching technique used.

Table 5.1: Example Transcripts of Several Segments

Introduction	*Field Scene*	*Interview*
A ONE-YEAR-OLD BABY BOY IS SAFE WITH HIS MOTHER THIS MORNING, THE DAY AFTER HIS OWN FATHER USED HIM AS A HOSTAGE. POLICE SAY IT WAS A DESPERATE ATTEMPT TO MAKE IT ACROSS THE MEXICAN BORDER TO AVOID ARREST. CNN'S ANNE MCDERMOTT HAS THE DRAMATIC STORY.	A MAN EMERGED FROM HIS CAR AT THE U.S. MEXICAN BORDER, CARRYING HIS LITTLE SON, AND A KNIFE. WITNESSES WITNESSES SAY HE HELD THE KNIFE TO HIS SON, LATER, TO HIMSELF. AND IT ALL PLAYED OUT LIVE TV. OFFICIALS AND POLICE FROM BOTH SIDES OF THE BORDER...	DARYN: JUST IN THE RIGHT PLACE AT RIGHT TIME ESPECIALLY FOR THIS LITTLE BABY. CAN YOU TELL US WHAT YOU WERE SAYING TO THE MAN POLICE IDENTIFIED AS EDDIE PRICE AND WHAT HE WAS SAYING ON BACK TO YOU? I JUST ASSURED HIM THAT THE BABY WOULD BE OKAY...

However, news audio and video (and associated closed-captioning) do not necessarily possess correlated concepts (Fig. 5.1). For example, it is common in broadcast news items that once an event is introduced, in subsequent segments the critical keywords are alluded to and not specifically mentioned (e.g., Table 5.1, the name Eddie Price is mentioned only in the third scene). Segments can share other keywords and can be related transitively. If a search is performed on a person's name, then all related segments are not necessarily retrieved. Similarly, related video segments can have different visuals. It is not prudent to rely on a single source of information about the segments in retrieval and composition (e.g., transcripts or content descriptions). The information tends to vary among the segments related to a news item. Therefore, we require new techniques to retrieve all the related segments or to improve the recall [16] of the video composition system.

In this paper, we propose a transitive video composition and retrieval approach that improves recall. That is, once a query is matched against unstructured metadata, the components retrieved are again used as queries to retrieve additional video segments with information belonging to the same news item. The recall can be further enhanced if the union of different metadata sets is used to retrieve all segments of a news item (Fig. 5.2). However, the union operation does not always guarantee full recall as a response to a query. This is because no segment belonging to a particular instance of a news item may be present among the segments acquired after the transitive search (data acquired from different sources or over a period of time containing data about the same news event).

This work is an outcome of our observations of generative semantics in the different forms of information associated with news video data. The information can be in the visuals or in the audio associated with the video. We also study the common bond among the segments belonging to a single news item. The composition should possess a smooth flow of information with no redundancy.

Annotated metadata are the information extracted from video data. In our previous work [3, 12] we have classified annotated metadata that are required for a newscast composition as content metadata and structural metadata. The

Table 5.2: Content Metadata

Entity	Tangible object that are part of a video stream. The entities can be further sub-classified, (e.g., persons, and vehicles).
Location	Place shown in video. (e.g., place, city, and country).
Event	Center or focus of a news item.
Category	Classification of news items.

Table 5.3: Structural Metadata

1. Headline	Synopsis of the news event.	
2. Introduction	Anchor introduces the story.	
3. Body	Describes the existing situation.	
	a. Speech	Formal presentation of views without any interaction from a reporter.
	b. Comment	Informal interview of people at the scene in the presence of wild sound.
	c. Wild Scene	Current scenes from the location.
	d. Interview	One or more people answering formal structured questions.
	e. Enactment	Accurate scenes of situations that are already past.
4. Enclose	Contains the current closing lines.	

content metadata organize unstructured information within video data (i.e., objects and interpretations within video data or across structural elements). Some of the information extracted from news video data is shown in Table 5.2. Information such as the objects present in visuals, the category of a news item, and the main concept (focus or center [7]) depicted by the new item are stored as metadata. The structural metadata organize linear video data for a news item into a hierarchy [2] of structural objects as shown in Table 5.3.

The development of the proposed hybrid video data retrieval technique is based the availability of segment metadata. We have explored the use of these data for the following reasons.

- By utilizing both annotated metadata and closed-caption metadata, precision of the composition system increases. For example, keywords of "Reno, Clinton, fund, raising," if matched against closed-caption metadata, can retrieve information about a place called "Reno" (Nevada). Therefore, annotated metadata can be used to specify that only a person called "Reno" (Janet Reno) should be matched. The results from

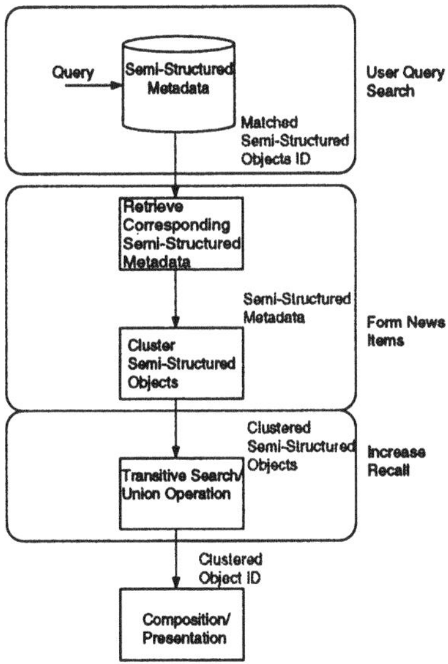

Figure 5.2: Process Diagram for Newscast Video Composition

annotated and closed-captioned searching can be intersected for better precision.

- Recall of a keyword-based search improves if more keywords associated with an event are used. Transcripts provide enriched but unstructured metadata, and can also be used to improve recall. Utilizing transcripts increase the number of keywords in a query; therefore, in some cases precision of the results will be compromised (irrelevant data are retrieved). The transitive search technique is based on this principle (Section 5.4).

- If the relationships among segments of a news event are stored, recall of a system can be increased. For example, if news about "Clinton" is retrieved, then related segment types can be retrieved even if the word "Clinton" is not in them.

As a result of the above observations, we propose a hybrid approach that is based on the union of metadata sets and keyword vector-based clustering as illustrated in Fig. 5.2. The precision of vector-based clustering improves by using multiple indexing schemes and multiple sets of metadata (annotated and unstructured). Unstructured data describe loosely organized data such as free-form text of the video transcripts.

The organization of the remainder of this paper is as follows: In Section 5.2 we describe existing techniques for video data retrieval. In Section 5.3 we discuss metadata required for query processing, classification of annotated metadata, and the proposed query processing technique. In Section 5.4 we present an analysis of the proposed approach. In Section 5.5 we present of our observations. Section 5.6 concludes the paper.

5.2 RELATED WORK IN VIDEO INFORMATION RETRIEVAL

A variety of approaches have been proposed for the retrieval of video data. They can be divided into annotation-metadata-based, transcript-metadata-based, and hybrid-metadata-based techniques. Each is described below.

For annotation-based techniques, manual or automatic methods are used for extraction of information contained in video data. Image processing is commonly used for information extraction in the automatic techniques. Techniques include automatic partitioning of video based on information within video data [4], extraction of camera and object motion [5, 18], and object, face, texture, visual text identification [6, 10, 11, 13, 14, 15, 17]. The metadata describing large digital video libraries can also be extracted off-line and stored in a database for fast query processing and retrieval [6].

Transcripts associated with video data can provide an additional source of metadata associated with video segments. Brown et al. [8] use transcript-metadata to deliver pre-composed news data. Wachman [19] correlates transcripts with the scripts of situation comedies. The Informedia project [20] uses a hybrid-metadata approach to extract video segments for browsing using both the visual and transcript metadata.

In the above works, keyword searching is either used to retrieve a pre-assembled news item or the segments associated with the query keywords. In this work, our objective is to search for segments that belong to the various instances of the same event and to cover various time periods (e.g., retrieve information about Albright's trip to the Middle East). Therefore, we seek to maximize the availability of information to support the creation of a cohesive video piece. For this purpose we require, in addition to the the segments matching a query, any segments that are related via a transitive or structural relationship. In this manner, segments belonging to various instances of a news event can be merged to create a new composition. Our technique uses a four-step approach applied to both annotation-based and transcript-based (unstructured) metadata. We use a transitive search on transcripts and the union operation on structural metadata to retrieve related video segments.

5.3 THE PROPOSED FOUR-STEP HYBRID TECHNIQUE

The four-step hybrid retrieval technique is based on establishing transitive relationships among segment transcripts and the use of annotated metadata. After introducing our terminology (symbols used throughout the paper are summarized in Table 5.4), we describe the different types of metadata and how they are used to support the four-step process.

Table 5.4: Symbols Used to Define the Retrieval Technique

Symbols	*Descriptions*
s	A video segment
S	Universe of video segments
N	Size of the universe S
R_f	A binary relationship on S for transitive search
R_u	A binary relationship on S for related segment search
tf_i	Frequency of a concept (term) i in unstructured metadata
N_i	Number of unstructured metadata components with term i
$w1_i$	Intermediate weight assigned to a concept i for query match
$w2_i$	Final weight assigned to a concept i for query match
$w3_i$	Final weight assigned to a concept i for transitive search
q	A query
S_q	A set of segments returned as a result of a query
$d(a, b)$	The similarity distance between two sets of keywords
QS	A subset of S_q
T_c	Cluster cut-off threshold
CL_i	A cluster
$q(s)$	A query comprised of unstructured metadata component
s_t	A segment retrieved as a result of a query $q(s)$
$S_{q(s)}$	Set of segments s_t retrieved as a result of a query $q(s)$
TCL_i	An extended cluster CL_i resulting from a transitive search
S_a	A candidate set resulting from cluster TCL_i

5.3.1 *Preliminaries*

Metadata described in this paper include unstructured metadata, such as free-form text and annotation metadata. The former is used for transitive search. The latter is comprised of content metadata and structural metadata.

Unstructured Metadata and Transitivity. Transcripts originating from closed-caption data (audio transcripts), when available, are associated with video segments when the segments enter the content universe S. These transcripts comprise the unstructured metadata for each segment.

Unstructured metadata are used for indexing and forming keyword vectors for each semi-structured metadata segment. Indexing is the process of assigning appropriate terms to a component (document) for its representation. Transitivity on the unstructured data is defined below.

Let $\mathcal{R}_f$ define a binary relationship f on the universal set of video segments S (i.e., $(s_a, s_b) \in R_f \iff s_a$ is *similar* to s_b). If similarity distance, defined as $d(s_a, s_b)$ for segments s_a and s_b, is greater than an established value then the two segments are considered to be similar. The transitive search satisfies the following property (for all $s_a \in S, s_b \in S, s_c \in S$):

$$(s_a, s_b) \in \mathcal{R}_f \wedge (s_b, s_c) \in \mathcal{R}_f \Rightarrow (s_a, s_c) \in \mathcal{R}_f$$

Therefore, in a transitive search we first match a query with unstructured metadata in the universe S. The results are applied as a query to retrieve additional unstructured metadata (transcripts) and associated segments, increasing the the recall of the process.

Annotated Metadata. Annotated metadata consist of content and structural metadata as described in Section 5.1. Structural metadata exist if segments are annotated as such when they enter the segment universe S, either as video shot at a single event (e.g., a sporting event) or as decomposed segments originating from preassembled news items (as is the case for our dataset). We call such segments ***siblings*** if they posses either of these relationships.

A shortcoming of the aforementioned transitive search is that it may not retrieve all segments related via siblings. This can be achieved by the following.

Let $\mathcal{R}_u$ define a binary relationship u on the universal set S (i.e., $(s_a, s_b) \in R_u \iff s_a$ and s_b are part of the same same news event). The final step expands the set of segments as a union operation as follows:

$$S_a \leftarrow S_a \cup \{s_b \mid \exists s_a \in S_a : (s_a, s_b) \in \mathcal{R}_u\},$$

where, S_a represents the candidate set of segments used as a pool to generate the final video piece (or composition set) [1]

Hierarchical structure of related segments is stored as structural metadata that are utilized in the proposed hybrid retrieval technique (Table 5.3).

Table 5.5: Sample Unstructured Metadata

.idDoc:
cnn2.txt/O193
.videoFile:
d65.mps
.textData:
Justice correspondent Pierre Thomas looks at the long-awaited decision. After months of intense pressure, attorney general Janet Reno has made a series of decisions sure to ignite a new round of political warfare. Regarding fund raising telephone calls by Mr. Clinton at the White House: no independent counsel. On vice president Gore's fund raising calls: no independent counsel. Controversial democratic campaign fund-raiser Johnny Chung has alleged he donated 25,000 to O'Leary's favorite charity in exchange for a meeting between O'Leary and a Chinese business associate. Three calls for an independent counsel. All three rejected.

5.3.2 *Segment Keyword Analysis and Weighting*

We use text indexing and retrieval techniques proposed by Salton [16] and implemented in SMART [9] for indexing the unstructured metadata. To improve recall and precision we use two sets of indices, each using different keyword/term weighing. In the remainder of the paper we use s interchangeably to represent a video segment or its associated unstructured metadata. The similarity distance of a segment with a query or a segment is measured by the associated unstructured metadata.

The selection process is comprised of an initial segment weighting followed by a clustering step.

Initial Segment Weighting. Initially, a vector comprised of keywords and their frequency frequency (term frequency *tf*) is constructed using the unstructured metadata of each segment without stemming and without common words. The frequency of a term or keyword indicates the importance of that term in the segment. Next, we normalize the *tf* in each vector with segment (document) frequency in which the term appears by using Eq. 5.1.

$$w_{1_i} = tf_i \times log\left(\frac{N}{N_i}\right)^2, \tag{5.1}$$

where N is the number of segments in the collection, and N_i represents the number of segments to which term i is assigned. The above normalization technique assigns a relatively higher weight w_{1_i} to a term that is present in smaller number of segments with respect to the complete unstructured metadata. Finally, w_{1_i} is again normalized by the length of the vector (Eq. 5.2). Therefore, the influence of segments with longer vectors or more keywords is limited.

$$w_{2_i} = \frac{w_{1_i}}{\sqrt{\sum_{j=0}^{n}(w_{1_j})^2}} \tag{5.2}$$

Clustering and Transitive Weighting. Here we use word stemming along with stop words to make the search sensitive to variants of the same keyword. In segments belonging to a news item, the same word can be used in multiple forms. Therefore, by stemming a word we achieve a better match between segments belonging to the same news item. For the transitive search and clustering, we use the complete unstructured metadata of a segment as a query, resulting in a large keyword vector because we want only the keywords that have a high frequency to influence the matching process. Therefore, we use a lesser degree of normalization (Eq. 5.3) as compared to the initial segment weighting.

$$w_{3_i} = tf_i \times log\left(\frac{N}{N_i}\right) \tag{5.3}$$

Table 5.6: Weight Assignment

Doc ID	*Concept*	*Scheme 1*	*Scheme 2*
146	barred	0.62630	4.04180
146	weapons	0.15533	2.50603
146	iraqi	0.21202	
146	u.n	0.18075	2.72990
146	continues	0.31821	2.58237
146	standoff	0.36409	3.87444
146	iraq	0.13211	2.71492
146	sights	0.50471	4.04180

Table 5.6 shows a comparison of the weighting schemes for the same unstructured metadata. The two concepts "Iraq" and "Iraqi" in the second scheme are treated as the same and hence the concept "Iraq" gets a higher relative weight.

For the purpose of a query match we use the cosine similarity metric (Eq. 5.4) proposed by Salton. The metric measures the cosine or the measure of angle between two unstructured metadata segment vectors. The product of the length of the two segment vectors divides the numerator in the cosine metric. The longer length vectors produce small cosine similarity. In Eq. 5.4, n is the number of terms or concepts in the universe.

$$\text{cosine}(\vec{A}, \vec{B}) = \frac{\sum_{k=1}^{n}(a_k \times b_k)}{\sqrt{\sum_{k=1}^{n}(a_k)^2 \times \sum_{k=1}^{n}(b_k)^2}} \tag{5.4}$$

The proposed query processing technique is a bottom-up approach in which the search starts from the unstructured metadata. We describe the details next.

5.3.3 The Selection Mechanism

The four-step selection mechanism is illustrated Figure 5.2. A query enters the system as a string of keywords. These keywords are matched against the indices created from the unstructured metadata. The steps of this process are query matching, clustering the results, retrieval based on the transitive search, and sibling identification. These are described below.

Query Matching. This stage involves matching of a user-specified keyword vector with the available unstructured metadata. In this stage we use indices that are obtained as a result of the initial segment weighting discussed in the previous section. As the match is ranked-based, the segments are retrieved in the order of reduced similarity. Therefore, we need to establish a cut-off threshold below which we consider all the segments to be irrelevant to the query. Unfortunately it is difficult to establish an optimum and static query cut-off threshold for all types of queries as the similarity values obtained for each query are different. For example, if we are presented with a query with

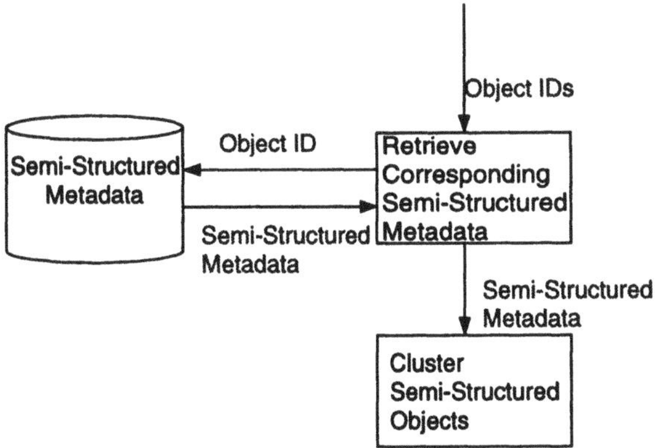

Figure 5.3: Process Diagram of the Clustering Process

keywords belonging to multiple news items then the similarity value with individual object in the corpus will be small. If the query has all keywords relevant to single news item then the similarity value will be high. Because of this observation, we establish a dynamic query cut-off threshold ($D \times max\{d(s,q)\}$) and we set it as a percentage D of the highest match value $max\{d(s,q)\}$ retrieved in set S_q. The resulting set is defined as:

$$QS \leftarrow \{s \in S_q \mid d(s,q) \geq (D \times max\{d(s,q)\})\},$$

where s is the segment retrieved and $d(s,q)$ is the function that measures the similarity distance of segment s returned as a result of a query q.

Results Clustering. In this stage, we cluster the retrieved segments with each group containing yet more closely related segments (segments belonging to the same event). We use the indices acquired as a result of the transitive scheme (Fig. 5.3). During the clustering process, if the similarity ($d(s_a, s_b)$) of the two segments is within a cluster cut-off threshold T_c, then the two segments are considered similar and have a high probability of belonging to the same news event. Likewise, we match all segments and group the segments that have similarity value within the threshold, resulting in a set

$$\{CL_1, CL_2, CL_3, ..., CL_k\},$$

where CL_i are a clusters (sets) each consisting of segments belonging to a single potential news item. An algorithm for forming the clusters is as follows:

$k \leftarrow 1$	Index on clusters
For each $s_a \in QS$	Loop on segments in QS
$CL_k \leftarrow s_a$	Assign segment to the cluster
For each $s_b \in QS$	Loop on remaining segments

If $d(s_a, s_b) \geq T_c$	Segments similar to the reference?
$CL_k \leftarrow CL_k \cup \{s_b\}$	Assign segment to the cluster
$QS \leftarrow QS - CL_k$	Remove the elements from the set QS
$k \leftarrow k + 1$	Next cluster
End	

This algorithm, although fast, is neither deterministic nor fair. A segment, once identified as similar to the reference, is removed from consideration by the next segment in the set. An alternative approach does not remove the similar element from QS but results in non-disjoint clusters of segments. We are exploring heuristic solutions that encourage many clusters while maintaining them as disjoint sets.

Transitive Retrieval. We use the transitive search (Fig. 5.4). The transitive search increases the number of segments that can be considered similar. During query matching, the search is constrained to the similarity distance (d_1) and segments within this distance are retrieved. During the transitive search we increase the similarity distance of the original query by increasing the keywords in the query so that segments within a larger distance can be considered similar. In the transitive search we use unstructured metadata of each object in every cluster as a query, $q(s)$, and retrieve similar segments. Again, we use item cut-off threshold that is used as a cut-off point for retrieved results and the retained segments are included in the respective cluster.

The transitive cut-off threshold ($T \times max\{d(s_t, q(s))\}$) is set as the percentage (T) of the highest similarity value retrieved $max\{d(s_t, q(s))\}$. For example, the distances d_{21}, d_{22}, and d_{23} (Fig. 5.4) fall within the transitive cut-off thresholds of respective segments.

Consider a cluster $CL_i = \{s_1, s_2, s_3, ..., s_N\}$ formed in the results clustering step. The extended cluster resulting from the transitive search can be defined as:

$$TCL_i \leftarrow \bigcup_{\forall s \in CL_i} \{s_t \in S_{q(s)} \mid d(s_t, q(s)) \geq (T \times max\{d(s_t, q(s))\})\},$$

where, s_t is a segment returned as a result of a transitive search of a segment $s \in CL_i$, $d(s_t, q(s))$ is the function that measures the similarity value of a segment s_t to query $q(s)$.

Sibling Identification. To further improve recall we use the structural metadata associated with each news item to retrieve all other related segments (Fig. 5.5). We find siblings of a segment s in set TCL_i from the structural metadata and incorporate them into the set TCL_i. Likewise, each original segment in set TCL_i is inspected for its siblings. If any are found, they are incorporated into the set.

Next we discuss the quantitative analysis of the retrieval, clustering, and proposed transitive search process.

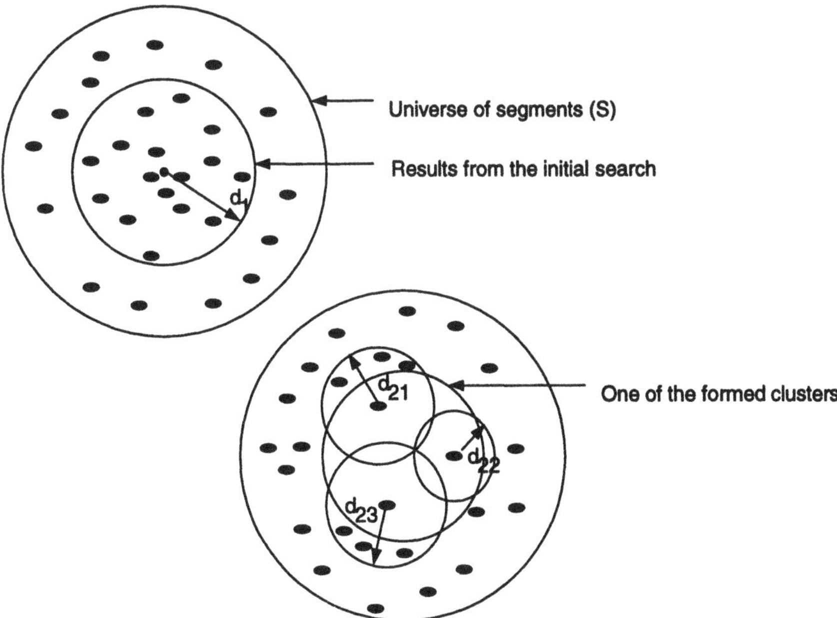

Figure 5.4: Similarity Measure based on the Transitive Search

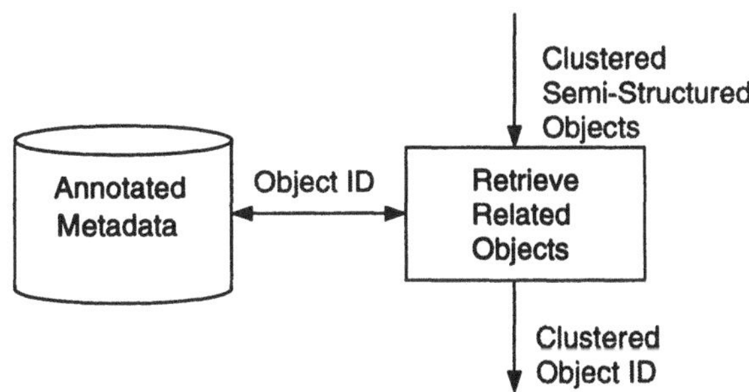

Figure 5.5: Process Diagram for Retrieving Related Segments

5.4 ANALYSIS OF THE PROPOSED HYBRID TECHNIQUE

We evaluated the performance of our technique based on 10 hours of news video data and its corresponding closed-caption data acquired from the network sources. Our results and analysis of the application of our techniques on this data set are described below.

Because the objective of our technique is to yield a candidate set of video segments suitable for composition, we focus on the inclusion-exclusion metrics of recall and precision for evaluating performance. However, subsequent rank-based refinement on the candidate set yields a composition set that can be ordered for a final video piece [1].

The data set contains 335 distinct news items obtained from CNN, CBS, and NBC. The news items comprise a universe of 1,731 segments, out of which 537 segments are relevant to the queries executed. The most common stories are about bombing of an Alabama clinic, Oprah Winfrey's trial, the Italian gondola accident, the UN and Iraq standoff, and the Pope's visit to Cuba. The set of keywords used in various combinations in query formulation is as follows:

race relation cars solar planets falcon reno fund raising
oil boston latin school janet reno kentucky paducah rampage
santiago pope cuba shooting caffeine sid digital genocide
compaq guatemala student chinese adopted girls isreal netanyahu
isreal netanyahu arafat fda irradiation minnesota tobacco trial
oprah beef charged industry fire east cuba beach varadero
pope gay sailor super bowl john elway alabama clinic italy
gondola karla faye tuker death advertisers excavation Lebanon
louise woodword ted kaczynski competency

The number of keywords influences the initial retrieval process for each news item used in a query. If more keywords pertain to one news item than the other news items, the system will tend to give higher similarity values to the news items with more keywords. If the query cut-off threshold is high (e.g., 50%), then the news items with weaker similarity matches will not cross the query cut-off threshold (the highest match has a very high value). Therefore, if more than one distinct news item is desired, a query should be composed with equal number of keywords for each distinct news item. All the distinct retrieved news items will have approximately the same similarity value with the query and will cross the query cut-off threshold.

For the initial experiment we set the query cut-off threshold to 40% of the highest value retrieved as a result of a query, or $0.4 \times max(S_q)$. The transitive cut-off threshold is set to 20% of the highest value retrieved as a result of unstructured metadata query, or $0.2 \times max(S_q(s))$. The results of 29 queries issued to the universe are shown in Fig. 5.6. Here we assume that all the segments matched the query (we consider every retrieved segment a positive match as the segments contain some or all keywords of the query).

Not all the keywords are common among the unstructured metadata of related segments, nor are they always all present in the keywords of a query. Therefore, to enhance the query we use a transitive search with a complete set of unstructured metadata. The probability of a match among related segments increases with the additional keywords; however, this can reduce precision.

As the result of the transitive search the recall of the system is increased to 48% from 25% (another level of transitive search may increase it further). The precision of the results due to this step is reduced to 89% from 100%.

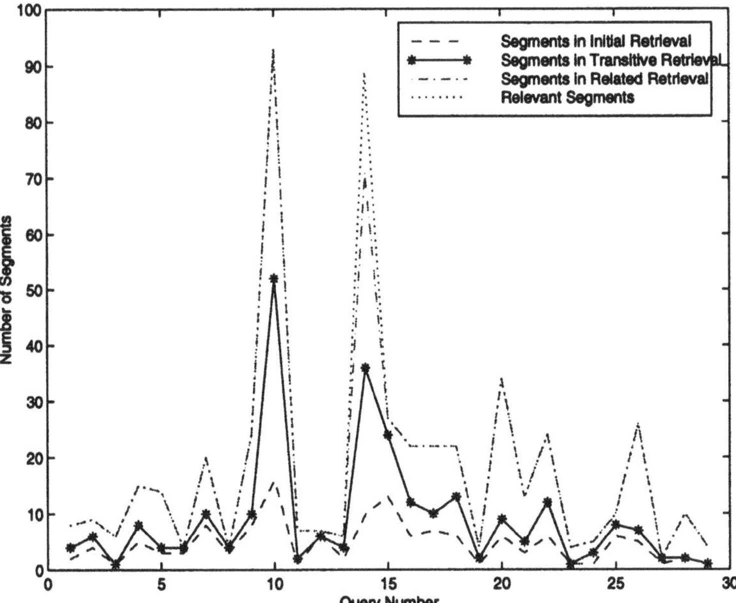

Figure 5.6: Summary of Performance of Different Retrieval Techniques

Table 5.7: System Performance

Search Technique	*Total Segments Retrieved*	*Relevant Segments Retrieved*	*Recall*	*Precision*
Query Match	137	137	25%	100%
Transitive Search	293	262	48%	89%
Sibling Identification	517	517	96%	100%

A cause of such low recall of the initial retrieval and subsequent transitive search is the quality of the unstructured metadata. Often this quality is low due to incomplete or missing sentences and misspelled words (due to real-time human transcription).

Using the structural hierarchy (Section 5.3.1) we store the relationships among the segments belonging to a news item. Therefore, if this information is exploited we can get an increase in recall without a reduction in precision (as all segments belong to the same news item). In the last step of the query processing we use structural metadata to retrieve these additional segments.

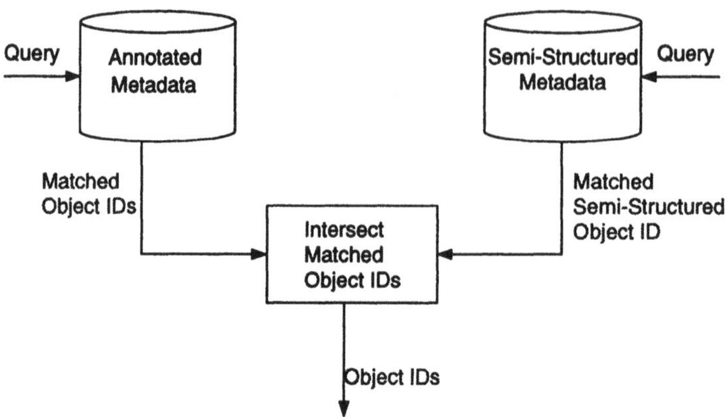

Figure 5.7: Process Diagram for Using Visual Metadata to Increase Precision

As observed from the above results, the recall is then increased to 96%. The remaining data are not identified due to a failure of the prior transitive search.

The results demonstrate that the combination of different retrieval techniques using different sources of metadata can achieve better recall in a news video composition system as compared to a the use of a single metadata set.

5.5 OBSERVATIONS

To emulate news items which encompass multiple foci (i.e., concepts from each are associated with many segments), it becomes difficult to balance the clustering of segments for these foci with our techniques. For example, the query "State of the Union Address" applied to our data set will yield foci for the address and the intern controversy. However, there are many more segments present in the data set for the intern controversy.

The query precision can also be increased by forming the intersection of the keywords from the content and unstructured metadata sets.

For example, consider the scenario for composing a news item about Clinton speaking in the White House about the stalemate in the Middle East. From the content metadata, we might be able to retrieve segments of type Speech for this purpose. However, many of the returned segments will not be associated with the topic. In this case an intersection of the query results of the salient keywords applied to the unstructured metadata will give us the desired refinement (Fig. 5.7).

If a query retrieves a set of new items based on a date or period then access can be achieved directly from the content metadata. For the process of composition, the broader set of metadata need to be used.

5.6 CONCLUSION

In this paper we proposed a four-step hybrid retrieval technique that utilizes multiple metadata sets to isolate video information for composition. The technique relies on the availability of annotated metadata representing segment content and structure, as well as segment transcripts that are unstructured. The retrieval applies a conventional approach to identifying segments using the segment content metadata. This is followed by clustering into potential news items and then a transitive search to increase recall. Finally, creation-time relationships expand the final candidate set of video segments.

Experimental results on our data set indicate a significant increase in recall due to the transitive search and the use of the creation-time relationships. Additional work will seek a heuristic clustering algorithm that balances performance with fairness.

References

[1] Ahanger, G. and Little, T.D.C. (1998). Automatic Composition Techniques for Video Production. *IEEE Trans. on Knowledge and Data Engineering* to appear.

[2] Ahanger, G. and Little, T.D.C. (1998). A Language to Support Automatic Composition of Newscasts. *Computing and Information Technology* to appear.

[3] Ahanger, G. and Little, T.D.C. (1997). A System for Customized News Delivery from Video Archives. *Proc. Intl. Conf. on Multimedia Computing and Systems*, Ottawa, Canada, pages 526-533.

[4] Ahanger, G. and Little, T.D.C. (1996). A Survey of Technologies for Parsing and Indexing Digital Video. *Visual Communication and Image Representation*, 7(1):28-43.

[5] Akutsu, A. and Tonomura, Y. (1994). Video Tomography; An Efficient Method for Camerawork Extraction and Motion Analysis. *Proc. ACM Multimedia '94*, San Francisco, CA, pages 349-356.

[6] Ardizzone, E. and La Casia, M. (1997). Automatic Video Database Indexing and Retrieval. *Multimedia Tools and Applications*, 4(1):29-56.

[7] Branigan. E. (1992). Narrative Schema. In *Narrative Comprehension and Film*, pages 1-32. New York: Rutledge.

[8] Brown, M.G., Foote, J.T., Jones, G.J.F., Jones, K.S., and Young, S.J. (1995). Automatic Content-Based Retrieval of Broadcast News. *Proc. ACM Multimedia '95*, San Francisco, CA, pages 35-43.

[9] Buckley, C. (1985) Implementation of the SMART Information Retrieval System. Computer Science Department, Cornell University, No. TR85-686.

[10] Chang, S.-F., Smith, J.R., Beigi, M., and Benitez, A. (1997). Visual Information Retrieval from Large Distributed Online Repositories. *Communications of the ACM*, 40(12):63-72.

[11] Hafner, J., Sawney, H., Equitz, W., Flickner, M., and Niblack, W. (1995). Efficient Color Histogram Indexing for Quadratic Form Distance Functions. *IEEE Trans. Pattern Anaylis and Machine Intelligence*, 1(7):729-736.

[12] Klippgen, W., Little, T.D.C., Ahanger, G., and Venkatesh, D. (1998). The Use of Metadata for the Rendering of Personalized Video Delivery. In Amit Sheth and Wolfgang Klas, eds., *Multimedia Data Management: Using Metadata to Integrate and Apply Digital Media*, pages 287-318, Ney York: McGraw Hill.

[13] Lienhart, R., Pfeiffer, S., and Effelsberg, W. (1997). Video Abstracting. *Communications of the ACM*, 40(12):55-62.

[14] Ogle, V.E., and Stonebreaker, M. (1995). Chabot: Retrieval from a Relational Database of Images. *Computer*, 28(2):49-56.

[15] Picard, R. and Minka, T. (1995). Vision Texture for Annotation. *Multimedia Systems*, 3(3):3-14.

[16] Salton, G. and McGill, M.J. (1983). *Introduction to Modern Information Retrieval.* New York: McGraw-Hill Book Company.

[17] Santini, S. and Jain, R. (1997). Similarity is a Geometer. *Multimedia Tools and Applications*, 5(3):277-306.

[18] Sclaroff, S. and Isidoro, J. (1998). Active Blobs. *Proc. Intl. Conf. on Computer Vision*, Mumbai, India.

[19] Wachman, J.S. (1997). A Video Browser that Learns by Example. *Master Thesis*, Technical Report #383, MIT Media Laboratory, Cambridge, Massachusetts.

[20] Wactlar, H., Kanade, T., Smith, M.A., and Stevens, S.M. (1996). Intelligent Access to Digital Video: The Informedia Project. *Computer*, 29(5):46-52.

6 SYNTACTICAL AND SEMANTICAL DESCRIPTION OF VIDEO SEQUENCES

N. Luth, A. Miene, P. Alshuth

Center for Computing Technology
Image Processing Department
University of Bremen
{nluth,andrea,petera}@tzi.de

Abstract: Archiving, processing, and intelligent retrieval of digital video sequences can be efficiently solved by a high-level representation of video sequences. We describe a complete system for encoding the contents of video sequences based on their syntactical and semantical description. Our techniques are built on two phases: analysis and synthesis. The analysis phase involves the automatic generation of a syntactical structure using image and image-sequence analysis, image understanding as well as text recognition. Moreover, the syntactical description of images will be completed by a semantical understanding of video sequences. The full representation of video sequences will be generated during the synthesis phase by combining results from the analysis phase. Our developed prototype system is planned to be integrated into the co-operative work of a TV-team of the TV-station *"Radio Bremen"*. Additionally, we describe some special functionality: scene analysis by clustering of video sequences with the aim of identifying a typical video genre. The latter is an useful approach for automatic trailer generation and for intelligent video editing as add-on for a video-cut-system.

6.1 INTRODUCTION

The last years have been significant for the rapid growth of multimedia technology. The process was especially accelerated by the fast development of hardware, and the increased use of Internet-communication. In this context vast amount of video data needs to be archived, browsed, and retrieved using a structure that allows to carry out an efficient access and retrieval of video sequences. The content-based analysis and retrieval of video data is important, but not yet suitable integrated in current video database systems. A great amount of research work has been done on the analysis, indexing, and retrieval of still images in image databases. The image retrieval paradigm is a keyword annotation, mostly done manually. There are three main difficulties with this approach:

1. a great deal of manual effort to annotate interactively every video sequence,

2. different interpretation of image content because of human subjectivity, and

3. inconsistency of the keyword assignments among different archivists.

An automatic, content–based annotation is an additional way to overcome these difficulties. Surveys and discussions of approaches and systems for image retrieval have been published by [4] [23, 13]. The ImageMiner™[1] was developed by the Image Processing Group at the University of Bremen [10] and realizes content–based retrieval of still images through an appropriate combination of methods for image analysis and understanding. The system has been applied to two domains: landscape images and technical drawings. The system provides an automatic generation of object–based image description.

Our early work on indexing MPEG videos extended the same approach used for still images by treating video sequences as collections of still images – extracting representation frames and their indexing using tested image database techniques [17]. With ImageMiner™, the representation frames are used to process color, texture, and contour detection. To support MPEG videos in an image retrieval system, a special mechanism is needed to reduce the high number of frames of a video. A first step is the automatic shot detection. In a second step the amount of frames is reduced by choosing a representational frame for each shot. This frame should represent the entire content of a shot.

In this paper we concentrate on a complex content–based representation of the video sequences, including the syntactical and semantical description of images and recognized text. A special algorithm for a fast shot detection to index a video by image processing based on single images was developed. The parameters of the frame sequence to still image conversion are useful to describe camera parameters for a shot. This is done by a mosaicing technique. The structure of a given video is useful to efficiently and automatically index long video sequences. A comparison between shots gives an overview about cut frequency, cut pattern, and scene units. After a shot detection, the shots are grouped into clusters based on their visual similarity.

We further address the problem of automatic image analysis and appropriate use of application uncertain domain knowledge using stochastic grammars. The image analysis approach taken in this paper combines color, texture, contour, and information of shots for a robust description of video and image structures.

[1]ImageMiner is a trademark of IBM Cooperation.

By using domain knowledge, our approach for object recognition is able to identify primitive objects and complex scenes on basis of various regions extracted during the image analysis. The resulting content descriptions will be stored in a textual form for automatic retrieval which could be carried out by any text retrieval algorithm.

6.2 APPLICATIONS

The developed system supports and facilitates the archiving process, especially the content–based video annotation and retrieval and the non–sequential access to video sequences. Part of the system is intended to be used in the daily work of the archivists and editorial staff at "Radio Bremen" TV-station for archiving and retrieval of a local TV–programm *"buten un binnen"*. The archiving procedure includes the automatical digitalization and annotation of the programm as described in Sec. 6.4. Most of the video analysis algorithms are performed in real time. After that the archivist is able to add additional information to the automatical descritption if needed. The retrieval performance is very high because the search is done over the textual annotations without any necessity of time expensive image processing within the retrieval process.

The automatic identification of video genre in combination with expert knowledge makes it possible to extend the functionality of the system to automatic trailer generation.

Additionally, it is possible to extend a commercial cut system, like AVID [3], by the functionality for intelligent support during the configuration of a new video film or document similar to a genre chosen from an available case–base.

6.3 RELATED WORKS

6.3.1 Retrieval of still images

One of the first image retrieval projects was QBIC [24]. With a visual query interface an user can draw a sketch to find images with similar sketches, or find images with specific positioned color, texture, or formulate object motion for the video domain. Some systems are developed to perform retrieval systems on both sides: formulating an user query by finding useful techniques, like hierarchical representation of icons, objects, or keywords, and representing the results in a graphical view to collect similar objects together and to navigate for additional information. ART MUSEUM [12] is used to find images from a data base which contains artistic paintings and photos only. The algorithm of sketch retrieval and similarity retrieval is based on graphical features. An user can formulate a query by using sketches – from a template or drawn free–hand. The PHOTOBOOK system is a set of interactive tools for browsing and searching single images and sequences [26]. A query is based on image content rather than using text annotations.

Another example for an interactive content-based retrieval is based on user's relevance feedback (URF) [27]. The URF is generated by capturing dynamically updated weights during user's query and perception subjectivity.

6.3.2 Video Retrieval

Last years image retrieval systems have been extended to video retrieval systems by addition of shot detection and representing shots by still images (key–frame or mosaic).

The VIRAGE VIDEO ENGINE uses several video–specific data, like motion, audio, closed caption, etc., to build an information structure and content information about a video [9]. The user can formulate a query to find commercials, scenes with special camera motion, e.g. a talking head, or just a scene with some given words. In most of the systems only limited information, like color– and texture–vectors or cut detection, is calculated automatically. None of them is able to build objects.

The extraction of spatially reduced image sequences from MPEG–2 compressed video sequences is investigated in [31]. Comparing to MPEG–1, MPEG–2 has an extended functionality and additional syntax; many different options can be mixed into a video sequence, making the task of analysis very complicated. The method is based on a new class of DCT domain operations. The reduced images extracted from MPEG–2 video are useful for video processing and fast low–cost browsing.

The task of similarity detection between video sequences is described in [18]. Their approach is based on the matching of frames, shots, scenes and videos, as a multiresolution method. At each level the features of the level of higher temporal resolution are considered. A similarity measure of video sequence matching is defined.

The Informedia-system [6, 7] aims to handle effectively about 1000-hour digital video library supporting content-based indexing and retrieval of video segments. Image processing, powerfull speech recognition tool Sphinx-II, and natural language processsing techniques were applied to the video data for content extraction and temporal segments. Moreover, a novel techniques for the automatic generation of video skims, consisting from significant audio and video components, was developed. This allows to produce automatically best abstracts of video sequences [5].

6.4 OVERVIEW OF THE APPROACH

We consider video annotation as a complex content representation, consisting of syntactical and semantical description of video sequences. The whole system architecture is shown in Fig. 6.1. The syntactical description is a result of video dividing into primitives, which constitute a video sequence. For example a video consists of shots and image frames, every image consists of color or gray level, texture, contour, and maybe textual information. The syntactical description is generated from low–level information. The semantical description is a result of dividing syntactical description into units, which are similiar to the human perception of the contents. For example, an image consists of green forest, blue sky and so on.

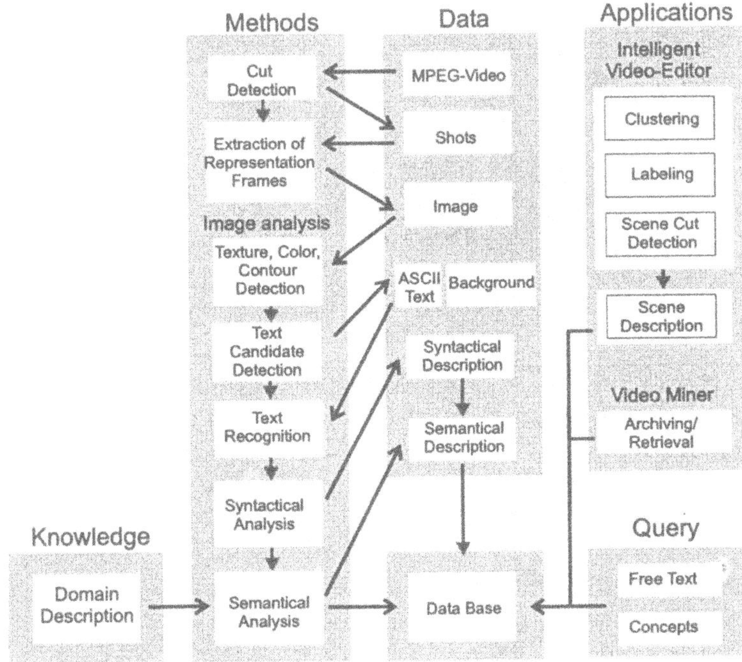

Figure 6.1: System architecture

6.4.1 Extraction of Low-Level Information

6.4.1.1 Shot Analysis. Our first step to extract syntactical information is a shot analysis based on MPEG-1 video streams. That means dividing the complete video stream into single shots to be analyzed separately. The developed method for shot detection is based on the difference of the chrominance and luminance values. The color values U and V of the chrominance are treated separately. If the difference reaches a certain threshold, a shot boundary is detected [8]. The difference is calculated for every two succeeding frames. This guarantees precise shot boundaries, which are essential for our approach because all further analysis is done on single shots. In the same step we analyze the camera motion within the shot. For this task we use the motion estimation part of the MPEG format [8], with the aim of automatically detecting camera pans or tilts in a shot.

One way to visualize the results of a shot detection is a video icon as shown in Fig. 6.2.

Figure 6.2: Shot detection

6.4.1.2 Still image generation from single shots. In a second step every detected shot is reduced to one representative still image by key–frame extraction or mosaicing of images. The choice of the method depends on the results of the camera motion analysis. If the shot contains one dominant camera motion direction, i.e. a pan or a tilt, mosaicing is usefull to join the whole information included in the pan or tilt in one single mosaic image. The mosaicing process is described in section 6.4.1.2.

If no dominant camera motion direction is detected one representative key–frame will be extracted. Some ideas how to obtain representative key–frames are introduced in section 6.4.1.2.

Both key–frames and mosaicing of images will be considered as a still image. Therefore the analyis of frame sequences in shots is reduced to a still image analysis described in section 6.4.1.3.

The mosaicing procedure. For a detailed shot representation it would be perfect to view a shot as a still image that contains all single frames based on the camera movements. The first step is to calculate the camera movements between each frame. Using this information it is possible to combine the frames within one mosaicing image.

The motion parameters are included in a continuous equation for the optical flow. Camera movements like tilt, pan, and zooms are detected with a projective model using only pixel information. The model contains eight parameters that can be used for the transformation equation, $[x, y]^T$ describes the pixel coordinate at time t, the vector $[x', y']^T$ at time t'.

$$X' = [x', y']^T = \frac{A[x, y]^T + \vec{b}}{\vec{c}^T[x, y]^T + 1} = \frac{Ax + \vec{b}}{\vec{c}^T x + 1} \tag{6.1}$$

The 2×2 matrix describes the rotation of the image, $\vec{b}$ and $\vec{c}$ are the parameters to describe the transformation. This transformation can be used for deriving the model flow components. Minimizing the sum of the squared differences between flow velocity and model velocity, and expanding the results into a Taylor series using only the first three terms, this leads to a formula corresponding to the bilinear model [21].

This approach is well suitable if there exists only a global motion. Particular motion of objects inside a shot destroys the global motion property. A special segmentation of the frames and their movements can extract a moving object and a background image. With the dominant mosaicing technique [29], two images are generated: one that contains the motion objects in the foreground and one those in the background.

Figure 6.3: Mosaic image

Extraction of representative key–frames. An easy way to extract key–frames is to take every nth frame of the sequence or to take the first or the middle frame of every shot detected. But such methods do not necessary come up with the frames which are most important for the understanding of the content of the scene. As mentioned before our further content analysis is based on the still image analysis done on the key–frames extracted from each shot.

To obtain best results with the still image analysis we need key–frames which represent the key information included in the shot. Provided that the camera holds on objects or on parts of the scene which contain key information we use a heuristic to obtain significant key–frames: for each shot take the frame where the camera motion as well as the difference in chrominance and luminance to the neighboring frames is minimal.

In some cases it is not necessary to extract one frame for each shot. In an interview, for example, one shot shows the interviewer and the next one shows the interview partner and so on. In such a case one can use the results of the video clustering algorithm described in section 6.4.3 to detect such scenes and extract one key–frame for each cluster instead of one for each shot.

If the shot contains text inserts, a frame with the insert visible would be a good key–frame because the textual information often supplies an additional description of the content.

Further work has to be done to expand the set of rules mentioned above for extraction of representative key–frames. For example, as proposed in [30] the audio signal may also give some useful hints where to find important scenes within a video sequence.

6.4.1.3 Still image analysis. The still image analysis consists of three modules, each extracting one of the low level features color, texture, and contour. Three modules work independent of each other.

Color segmentation. First the image is transformed from RGB to HLS color space. HLS defines the color space by three parameters: hue, lightness and saturation. The main idea of our approach is to group the pixels of the image into regions with equal color, using certain thresholds for the difference between the color values H, L, and S of neighboring pixels. Then we calculate the circumscribing rectangle for each of the color segmented regions. The result of the color analysis consists of the color, the coordinates of the circumscribing rectangle, and its center of gravity for each color region that was found.

Texture classification. Our approach for texture segmentation is based on a region– and edge–oriented method to detect regions of homogeneous texture [16]. A rectangle is cropped out of every texture region found within the image. These texture segments are analysed by a texture analysis system [22, 11], which calculates the value of characteristics for seven visual texture properties (see Fig. 6.4). The visual texture properties are called shape of primitives, line–likeness, coarseness, regularity, directionality, contrast and softness, and allow a domain–independent description of textures [2].

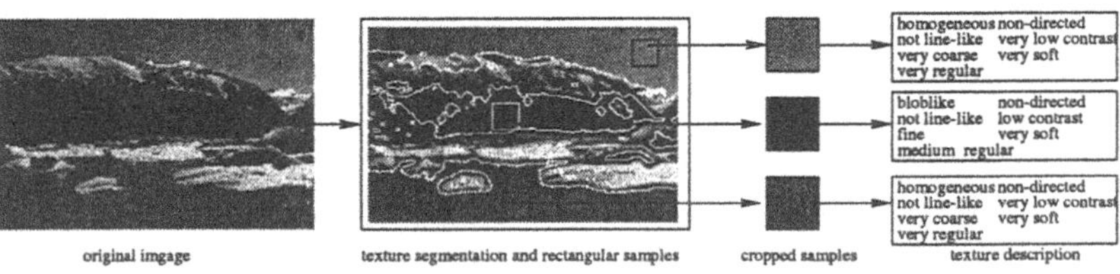

Figure 6.4: Texture analysis.

We performed a significance analysis to find the most suitable statistical feature for each visual property to compute its value of characteristics from a digital grayscale image [11]. The setting of the parameters of the statistical features were evaluated in this significance analysis, too. An overview of all seven properties and the corresponding statistical features is given in Tab. 6.1. For example, to find out whether the shape of primitives of a given texture is homogeneous, multi–areas or blob–like, we use the statistical feature roughness F_{rgh}, as proposed in [33]. To estimate the roughness of a texture a statistical feature matrix is used, which calculates the difference of the gray levels for pairs of pixels having a certain distance. The maximum distance is specified by the parameters L_c and L_r. To calculate the line–likeness, coarseness, regularity, and directionality of a texture we use the statistical features F_{lin}, F_{crs}, F_{reg}, and F_{dir} defined by [32]. The main idea for the calculation of the line–likeness of a texture is based on an edge detection and a counting of edges appearing as lines. The parameter t is a threshold for the gray level difference used for edge detection. The directionality is derived from using a histogram measuring the direction of edges in the image. If the histogram has a single peak the texture has a main direction. The value of directionality is given by the height of the peak. The regularity of a texture is calculated by measuring the variation of a certain feature over the whole texture region. The region is divided into s^2 subregions. Then the feature is calculated for each subregion and the difference of the results is used as a measure for regularity. The feature calculated for the subregions to estimate the regularity is the gray level variance. It measures the contrast of a texture. The algorithm for the calculation of coarseness is described in detail in [32, 11].

The value of the statistical feature symbolizes that of the visual propertie, except for softness, where a high value for complexity (f_{com}) implies a non-soft texture whereas a low value implies a soft one. The parameter d specifies the width of the local neighborhood the neighborhood gray–tone difference matrix is calculated for. This matrix is used to estimate the statistical feature complexity [1].

Table 6.1: Significant statistical features

Visual Property	Statistical Feature	Parameter
shape of primitives		
homogeneity	F_{rgh} – Wu & Chen	$L_c = L_r = 2$
bloblikeness ↔ *multiareas*	F_{rgh} – Wu & Chen	$L_c = L_r = 8$
linelikeness	F_{lin} – Tamura et al.	$t = 32$
coarseness	F_{crs} – Tamura et al.	$d = 2$
regularity	F_{reg} – Tamura et al.	$s = 4$
directionality	F_{dir} – Tamura et al.	–
contrast	graylevel variance	–
softness	f_{com} – Amadasun & King	$d = 12$

All statistical features are calculated on the original gray scale images of the textures, with the exception of directionality, where a linear histogram scaling is performed to pre–process the image before calculating the statistical feature.

The result of our texture analysis is an automatically generated texture description based on visual properties of textures. The main advantage of this approach lies in its usability for several texture domains.

Contour approximation. The detected contours are boundaries of extracted regions as results of the texture and color segmentation process. The contours are represented by a pixel sequence which will be transformed in approximated polylines:

$$\{(x_i, y_i)\}_{i=0}^{N} \to \{p_j\}_{j=1}^{K}, K << N. \tag{6.2}$$

Our approximation method of pixel sequence to polylines is based on the detection of Digital Straight Segments (DSS).

The main problem is to find an optimal DSS with

- minimal distance between every DSS and pixel sequence, and
- minimal number of DSS for a given pixel path.

The process is designed in two steps:

1. detection of DSS considering local pixel constellation $\{p_j\}$, and
2. approximation of polylines $\{p_j\}$ considering curvature's criterions.

6.4.1.4 Text string extraction. Additional information about the contents of a video stream is contained in text inserts superimposed on some frames.

To extract this information the following steps are necessary:

- to localize the frames with superimposed textual inserts,
- to separate text candidates from background, and
- to recognize the detected text candidates.

Problems are caused by the low resolution of the characters and the often very complex background. Lately, a number of methodes have been proposed for text string extraction and character recogition for videos. One method introduced by [28] uses an interpolation filter, multi-frame integration and a combination of four filters to solve the problems addressed above. Another method proposed by [25] is based on adaptive thresholding to segment the image first in regions. Character candidate regions are then detected by observing gray level differences between adjacent regions. Another way to segment character candidate regions is to treat text as a distinctive texture. Subsequently strokes are extracted from the segmented text regions. Using heuristics on the appearance of text strings like for example height similarity and character as well as line spacing, the strokes are processed to form tight rectangular bounding boxes around the corresponding text strings. In a last step the background is cleared up and the text is binarized [34]. Both approaches use grayscale images as input. An approach which uses color images was proposed by [19]. It is based on a split and merge algorithm which first splits the image into segments of homogeneous color and then merges adjacent segments if their color difference is less than a threshold.

Our approach combines some of the ideas mentioned before. On the assumption that an insert has to be displayed for a certain minimum time to be read by the viewer, we first examine every nth frame for text inserts. If a certain frame to seems to contain an insert, we examine a surrounding sequence of frames, in order to support or neglect this hypothesis.

After localizing the sequence of frames with imposed inserts, we have to separate the text strings from the background. We analyze a sequence of succeeding frames showing the same insert and combine the results to enhance the recognition.

To find the text candidate regions in a frame we make use of our color analysis algorithms described in section 6.4.1.3. The algorithm detects the characters as homogeneous color regions. In a next step we concatenate these separate regions to text strings and the strings to text blocks using the following heuristics about the appearance of text:

- all characters within one image are of the same color, and the contrast to the colors appearing in the background behind the text is high,
- the spacing between the characters of one word is always the same,
- the spacing between all words of a text string is the same,
- characters are aligned on horizontal lines, and
- the line spacing between two lines of text is constant.

After that, the image is binarized by setting all pixels belonging to text candidates to black and the background pixels to white.

The final step, i. e. the recognition of the characters in the binarized image, is done by a commercial OCR software.

6.4.2 Semantical description with graph grammars

To analyze the semantics of a video or an image we use the syntactical information extracted with the previously described methods for object recognition. In a first step we have to combine all the quantitative, syntactical informations we got until now from the different low level analysis methods to recognize atomic entities. These atomic entities are on a qualitative, semantical level, i. e. primitive objects, e.g. grass or forest on a landscape image.

The results build hypotheses related to the primitive objects. In a second step we combine the hypotheses about the primitive objects according to the compositional semantics of more complex objects by means of which the hypotheses becomes a thesis [15]. For both steps we use neighborhood–controlled node–labeled and node–attributed feature graph grammars (1-NRCFGG) as specified in [14]. The edges of the feature graph represent the topological neighborhood *nr* relations between the different image segments resulting from the image analysis, for example certain color or texture regions detected within the image. An example of a feature graph is shown in Fig. 6.5. These neighborhood relations are for example *meets*, *overlaps* or *contains*. The fundamental assumption for our object recognition is, that these relations restrict the recognition of objects, i.e. a kind of *nr*–inheritance is guaranteed. The process of object recognition can be treated as a process of graph transformation. This step is performed by a graph parser - the so called *GraPaKL* [14]. Two graph grammars are used: one to bridge the gap between lower–level information and primitive objects, and a second to combine the primitive objects in order to recognize complex objects.

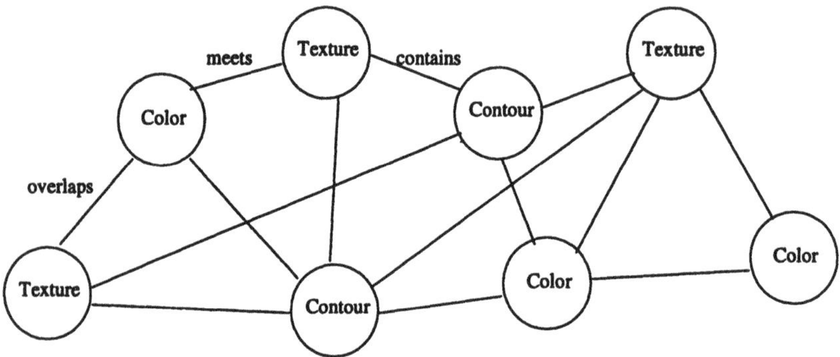

Figure 6.5: Feature graph

To detect a forest scene, for example, one has to combine the primitive objects grass and forest. The primitive object forest consists of a texture, a color, and a contour segment which must hold certain conditions. The derivation from a complex object on the highest level of abstraction via primitive objects down to the low-level features is called a path through the feature graph. An example is shown in Fig. 6.6.

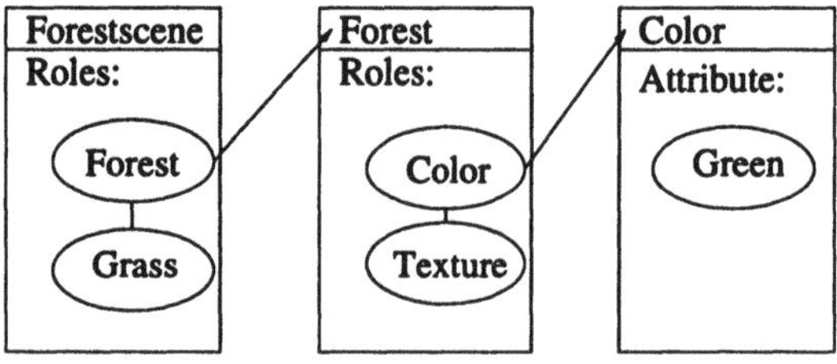

Figure 6.6: A path from high to low level of abstraction

6.4.2.1 1–NRCF Graph Grammars and GraPaKL. In this section we introduce 1–NRCF Graph Grammars and GraPaKL as described in detail in [10].

A finite undirected node attributed and node labeled graph, short *feature graph*, is a 6–tuple $(V, E, \mathcal{A} \cup \mathcal{R}, \psi, \pm, \varphi)$, where:

- V is a finite, not empty set of attributed and labeled nodes,
- $E \subseteq V \times V$ is a finite set of undirected edges,
- $\mathcal{A}, \mathcal{R}$ are finite sets of attribute–value pairs, where $\mathcal{A} \cap \mathcal{R} = \emptyset$,
- $\psi : V \rightarrow 2^{\mathcal{A} \cup \mathcal{R}}$ is an attribute function,
- Σ is a finite not empty alphabet of node labels, and

- $\varphi : V \to \Sigma$ is a label function.

As mentioned before, the interpretation of the edges is restricted to the topological neighborhood (*nr*).

A neighborhood–controlled node labeled and node attributed feature graph grammar (1–NRCFGG) is a 10–tuple $(V_{NT}, V_T, P, S, \mathcal{A} \cup \mathcal{R}, \psi, \mathcal{AGL}, \xi, \pm, \varphi)$, where:

- V_{NT} is a finite, not empty set of nonterminals, where $\forall v \in V_{NT} : \psi(v) \cap \mathcal{R} \neq \emptyset$,
- V_T is a finite, not empty set of terminals, where $\forall v \in V_T : \psi(v) \cap \mathcal{R} = \emptyset$,
- P is a finite set of productions,
- $S \in V_{NT}$ is the start node,
- $\mathcal{A} \cup \mathcal{R}, \psi, \pm, \varphi$ as previously defined,
- $\mathcal{AGL}$ is a set of conditions, so called dependency relations, for example equations or predicates etc., and
- $\xi : P \to 2^{\mathcal{AGL}}$ is a condition function.

The productions left–hand side (lhs) is described by one single node and the productions right–hand side (rhs) is given by any graph. Additional conditions, called ***dependency relations*** are used for proving, passing, or generating information by calculating attributes. The global embedding specification is given by the *nr*–inheritance.

The chart parser GraPaKL is described in detail in [14]. The main algorithm consists of the rules `initialize`, `choose` and `combine`. The input for the GraPaKL is a terminal feature graph, which contains the low–level features as terminal nodes and a 1-NRC graph grammar representing the productions. Starting from this terminal feature graph complex objects are detected.

6.4.2.2 Extension of the 1–NRCF Graph Grammar to a stochastic grammar. In object recognition there are often several alternatives to combine the low–level information in order to achieve primitive objects and later on the primitive objects in order to achieve complex objects. These different alternatives may have different probabilities. The idea is to extend the 1-NRCFG grammar in a way that for each production a certain probability is specified [20]. The probability for each parse is calculated by multiplying the probabilities of the productions that were applied to achieve parse. The probability calculated for a parse is the probability that the corresponding (primitive or complex) object has been recognized.

For each production rule of the form

$$A_j \to \beta_{j,i} \quad 1 \leq i \leq u \tag{6.3}$$

associated with it exists a probability $p_{j,i}$, and u is the number of productions with premise A_j.

A stochastic grammar is proper if

$$\sum_{i=1}^{u} p_{j,i} = 1 \quad \text{for all} \quad A_j \in N. \tag{6.4}$$

The grammatical word function generated by G is defined as

$$\begin{aligned} f(v) &= \sum_{n=1}^{N(v)} \prod_{k=1}^{K(v,n)} p_{n,k}(v) && \text{if} \quad v \in L(G) \\ &= 0 && \text{if} \quad v \notin L(G) \end{aligned} \tag{6.5}$$

where:

- $L(G)$ Language defined by G,
- $N(v)$ is the number of distinct leftmost derivations of v,
- $K(v,n)$ is the number of steps in the nth derivation, and
- $p_{n,k}(v)$ is the probability of the production used at the kth step of the nth derivation.

Following this approach, by defining a mapping function δ, we extend the previously defined 1-NRCFGG, which serves the conditions above given. The likeliness of the alternative productions has to be observed by empirical analysis of the domain.

The automatically estimation of $p_{j,i}$ will be calculated by the formula:

$$p_{j,i} = \frac{2 \cdot (u - i + 1)}{u \cdot (u + 1)}, 1 \leq i \leq u \tag{6.6}$$

$$\sum_{i=1}^{u} p_{j,i} = \frac{2}{u(u+1)} \sum_{i=1}^{u} (u - i + 1) \tag{6.7}$$

The image illustrated in Fig. 6.7 represents a forest scene combined with a see scene. The seewater reflects the sky with clouds, located in lower part of the whole scene, that is not typical for a sky scene. This picture would be never found using only 1-NRCF Graph Grammar, because the sky location is defined in upper part of the picture. By extending the corresponding rule by additional rules considering these spatial location and smoothed texture it is possible to capture these scene as forest-sky scene.

6.4.3 Cluster analysis of videos

After a shot detection the shots are grouped into clusters based on their visual similarity. A time-constraint clustering procedure is used to compare only those shots that are located inside a time range. Shots from different sections

Figure 6.7: forest-sky scene.

of the video (e.g., begin/end) are not compared. With this cluster information that contains a list of shots and their clusters, it is possible to calculate scene bounds. Labeling of all clusters gives a description of cut pattern. It is now easy to distinguish a dialogue from an action scene.

Consecutive shots in a scene are in a close semantical relation. A dialogue can be characterized by one or two opening shots followed by at least two alternating shots until the end, which adds another shot. An action scene usually contains many short shots. The same used within the cut detection algorithm can be used for the grouping procedure of shots. A cluster contains all shots with similar visual properties. An additional parameter can be used as a time constraint. Only those clusters are compared with the current one that fit into a fixed time interval [35].

A histogram of a key–frame is taken from each shot and compared with the histogram of the previous key–frames of the clusters. In the initial phase the first shot is assigned to the first cluster, the second shot to the second cluster. All succeeding shots will be compared to all previous shots of the clusters except the first previous one, because two consecutive shots are never taken from the same position or contain the same visual content. Therefore they cannot belong to the same cluster. If there is no cluster found which matches the histogram a new cluster will be generated containing the current shot. To minimize computing time only the last shot of a cluster will carry the current histogram. An example for the clustering is shown in Fig. 6.8. Each row represents the shots belonging to the same cluster.

After all shots are grouped into clusters all clusters should be checked for a scene cut. All clusters between two scene cuts are called a scene unit. Clusters are represented in a hierarchical scene transition graph. Nodes represent the clusters that contain the shots with visual similarity under a time constraint. Edges represent the connection corresponding to the story flow. Only one key–frame from a shot of each cluster will be shown in the graph.

There are three different kinds of edges:

- a directed edge that connects two scene units,
- a directed edge inside a scene unit which connects two clusters in one direction, and

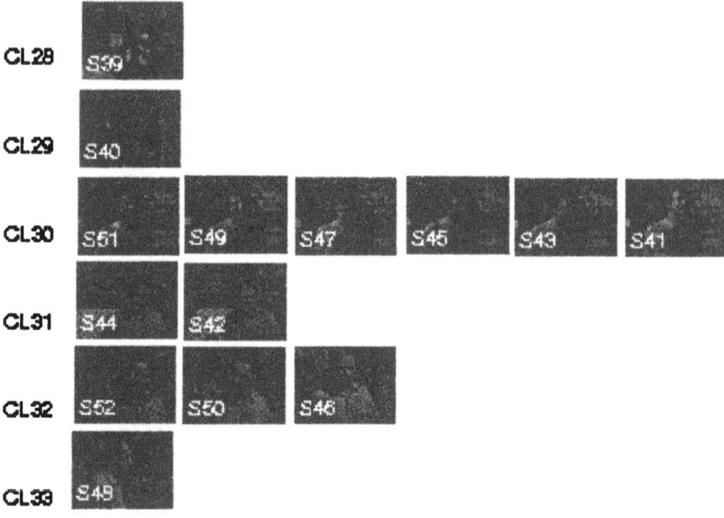

Figure 6.8: Clustering of shots

- a bidirectional edge inside a scene unit which connects two clusters in both directions.

This kind of representation makes it easy to sum up the entire video at a glance. Individual scene units can be easily recognized through the clustering. Action scenes and scenes with only a few shots are represented by special patterns.

A scene contains a number of shoots that are cut into shots. These shots are found inside a start and end sequence in which the viewer of a video focuses towards a new situation. The algorithm of the clustering procedure cannot sort these separate shots into one scene unit because of the visual dissimilarity. The scene transition graph representation of a video still abstracts from the dynamic flow of the single cuts. Therefore, it is desirable to start a classification of the shot order which would it make easy to distinguish an action scene from a dialogue between a sequence of starting and a sequence of ending shots [36].

6.5 CONCLUSION

In this paper we investigate the generation of a syntactical and semantical description of video sequences as full process from low–level to high–level representation. The important advances of our system lie in the extension of uncertain domain–knowledge representation using stochastic grammars.

The use of uncertainty provides us with the possibility to estimate how sure is the object recognition and scene interpretation. Additionally, the bidirectional inference process makes it possible to continue a parser in case of deadlocks.

The syntactical analysis involves the image analysis and text recognition.

From our current experiences with audio processing and speech recognition we plan to integrate an audio analysis in our system.

The syntactical description as a time–consuming process can be created only once, since the results are deterministic and non–subjective. Therefore they are reuseable for the generation of an updated version of semantical description. If novel objects or synonyms are inserted into a domain representation, the semantical description, in its turn, can be created repeatedly according to the possibly extended domain knowledge. The manual adaptation of domain knowledge is everytime allowable, especially for information updating.

Acknowledgements
This work is being supported in part by the German Research Association (DFG, contract no. HE 989/4-1)

References

[1] M. Amadasun and R. King. Textural Features Corresponding to Textural Properties. *IEEE Transactions on Systems, Man, and Cybernetics*, 19(5):1264–1274, 1989.

[2] G. Asendorf and T. Hermes. On Textures: An Approach For A New Abstract Description Language. In *Proceedings of IS&T/SPIE's Symposium on Electronic Imaging: Science & Technology*, pages 98–106, San Jose, CA, USA, 29 January - 1 February 1996.

[3] Avid Technology GmbH. *Cutter Guide - AVID*. Hallbergmoos, 1997.

[4] A. Cawkell. Imaging systems and picture collection management: a review. In *Information Services & Use 12*, pages 214–220, 1992.

[5] M. G. Christel, M. A. Smith, C. R. Taylor, and D. B. Winkler. Envolving Video Skims into Useful Multimedia Abstractions. In *Proceedings of the ACM CHI'98 Conference on Human Factors in Computing Systems*, Los Angeles, USA, April 1998.

[6] M. G. Christel, S. Stevens, T. Kanade, M. Mauldin, R. Reddy, and H. Wactlar. Techniques for the Creation and Exploration of Digital Video Libraries. In B. Furht, editor, *Multimedia Tools and Applications, Vol. 2.* Kluwer Academic Publishers, Boston, MA, USA, 1996.

[7] M. G. Christel, D. B. Winkler, and C. R. Taylor. Improving Access to a Digital Video Library. In *Human–Computer Interaction: INTERACT97, the 6. IFIP Conference on Human–Computer Interaction*, Sydney, Australia, July 14–18 1997.

[8] A. Dammeyer, W. Jürgensen, C. Krüwel, E. Poliak, S. Ruttkowski, T. Schäfer, M. Sirava, and T. Hermes. Videoanalyse mit DiVA. In *Proceedings of KI-98 Workshop Inhaltsbezogene Suche von Bildern und Videosequenzen in digitalen multimedialen Archiven*, Bremen, Germany, 16 - 17 September 1998.

[9] A. Hampapur. Virage Video Engine. In *Proceedings of IS&T/SPIE Symposium on Electronical Imaging Science & Technology*, San Jose, CA, USA, February 1997.

[10] T. Hermes, C. Klauck, J. Kreyß, and J. Zhang. Content–based Image Retrieval. In *Proc. of CASCON '95 (CD-ROM)*, Toronto, Ontario, Canada, 7-9 November 1995.

[11] T. Hermes, A. Miene, and O. Moehrke. On Textures: Analysis and Description. *Image and Vision Computing (submitted to)*, 1998.

[12] K. Hirata and T. Kato. Query by visual example. In *Proceedings of Third Intern. Conf. on Extending Database Technology*, pages 56–71, Vienna, Austria, March 1992.

[13] B. R. Jain. NSF Workshop on visual Information Management Systems, Workshop report. Technical report, Computer Science and Engineering Division, The University Michigan, Ann Arbor, Mich., 1992.

[14] C. Klauck. *Eine Graphgrammatik zur Repräsentation und Erkennung von Features in CAD/CAM.* PhD thesis, University of Kaiserslautern, vol. No. 66 of DISKI, infix-Verlag, St. Augustin, 1994.

[15] C. Klauck. Graph Grammar Based Object Recognition for Image Retrieval. In *Proc. of the 2th Asian Conference on Computer Vision (ACCV'95)*, Singapore, Republic of Singapore, December 1995.

[16] P. Kreyenhop. Textursegmentierung durch Kombination von bereichs– und kantenorientierten Verfahren. Master's thesis, University of Bremen, 1998.

[17] J. Kreyß, T. Hermes, P. Alshuth, and M. Röper. Video Retrieval by Still Image Analysis with ImageMiner. In *IS&T/SPIE Symposium on Electronical Imaging Science & Technology (Storage and Retrieval for Images and Video Databases II)*, volume 3022, pages 36–44, San Jose, CA, Feb. 1997.

[18] R. Lienhart, W. Effelsberg, and R. Jain. VisualGREP: A systematic method to compare and retrieve video sequences. In *Proceedings of IS&T/SPIE Symposium on Electronical Imaging Science & Technology (Storage and Retrieval for Images and Video Databases)*, volume 3312, pages 271–282, San Jose, CA, USA, January 1998.

[19] R. Lienhart and F. Stuber. Automatic Text Recognition in Digital Videos. In *Proceedings of SPIE Image and Video Processing IV*, volume 2666, pages 180–188, September 1996.

[20] S.Y. Lu and K.S. Fu. Stochastic Tree Grammar Inference for Texture Synthesis and Discrimination. *Computer Graphics and Image Processing*, 9(3):234–245, 1979.

[21] S. Mann and R.W. Picard. Video Orbits of the Projective Group: A New Perspective on Image Mosaicing. Technical Report 338, MIT Media Laboratory Perceptual Computing Section, 1996.

[22] A. Miene and O. Moehrke. Analyse und Beschreibung von Texturen. Master's thesis, University of Bremen, 1997.

[23] G. Nagy. Image Databases. *Image and Vision*, 3(3):111–117, 1985.

[24] W. Niblack, R. Barber, W. Equitz, M. Flickner, E. Glasman, D. Petkovic, P. Yanker, C. Faloutsos, and G. Taubin. The QBIC Project: Querying Images By Content Using Color, Texture, and Shape. In *IS&T/SPIE Symposium on Electronical Imaging Science & Technology*, San Jose, CA, USA, Feb. 1993.

[25] J. Ohya, A. Shio, and S. Akamatsu. Recognizing Characters in Scene Images. *IEEE Transactions on Pattern Analysis and Machine Intelligence*, 16(2):214–220, 1994.

[26] A. Pentland, R. W. Picard, and S. Sclaroff. Photobook: Content-based manipulation of image databases. In *Proceedings of IS&T/SPIE Symposium on Electronical Imaging Science & Technology (Storage and Retrieval for Images and Video Databases II)*, San Jose, CA, USA, Feb. 1994.

[27] Y. Rui, T. S. Huang, and S. Mehrotra. Relevance Feedback Techniques in Interactive Content-Based Image Retrieval. In *Proceedings of IS&T/SPIE Symposium on Electronical Imaging Science & Technology (Storage and Retrieval for Images and Video Databases)*, volume 3312, pages 25–36, San Jose, CA, USA, January 1998.

[28] T. Sato, T. Kanade, E. Hughes, and M. Smith. Video OCR for Digital News Archives. In *IEEE Workshop on Content-Based Access of Image and Video Databases (CAIVD'98)*, Bombay, India, January 1998.

[29] H.S. Sawhney, S. Ayer, and M. Gorkani. Dominant and Multiple Motion Estimation for Video Representation. In *IEEE International Conference on Image Processing, ICIP'95*, pages 322–325, Washington, D.C., Oct. 1995.

[30] M. Smith and T. Kanade. Video Skimming and Characterization through the Combination of Image and Language Understanding. In *IEEE International Workshop on Content-Based Access of Image and Video Databases*, Bombay, India, 1998.

[31] J. Song and B.-L. Yeo. Spatially Reduced Image Extraction from MPEG-2 Video: Fast Algorithms and Applications. In *Proceedings of IS&T/SPIE Symposium on Electronical Imaging Science & Technology (Storage and Retrieval for Images and Video Databases)*, volume 3312, pages 93–107, San Jose, CA, USA, January 1998.

[32] H. Tamura, S. Mori, and T. Yamawaki. Textural Features Corresponding to Visual Perception. *IEEE Transactions on Systems, Man, and Cybernetics*, SMC-8:460–473, 1978.

[33] C.-M. Wu and Y.-C. Chen. Statistical Feature Matrix for Texture Analysis. *CVGIP: Graphical Models and Image Processing*, 54(5):407–419, 1992.

[34] V. Wu, R. Manmatha, and E.M. Riseman. Finding Text In Images. In *20th ACM SIGIR Conference on Research and Development in Information Retrieval*, pages 3–12, Philadelphia, USA, 1997.

[35] M.M. Yeung and B.L. Yeo. Time-constrained Clustering for Segmentation of Video into Story Units. In *International Conference on Pattern Recognition*, August 1996.

[36] M.M. Yeung and B.L. Yeo. Video Content Characterization and Compaction for Digital Library Applications. In *IS&T/SPIE Conference on Storage and Retrieval for Image and Video Databases*, volume 3022, pages 45–58, San Jose, CA, Feb. 1997.

7 A MULTI-MODEL FRAMEWORK FOR VIDEO INFORMATION SYSTEMS

Uma Srinivasan, Craig Lindley, and Bill Simpson-Young

CSIRO Mathematical and Information Sciences
North Ryde, NSW, Australia

Abstract: In order to develop Video Information Systems (VIS) such as digital video libraries, video-on-demand systems and video synthesis applications, we need to understand the semantics of video data, and have appropriate schemes to store, retrieve and present this data. In this paper, we have presented an integrated multi-model framework for designing VIS application that accommodates semantic representation and supports a variety of forms of content-based retrieval. The framework includes a functional component to represent video and audio analysis functions, a hypermedia component for video delivery and presentation and a data management component to manage multi-modal queries for continuous media. A metamodel is described for representing video semantic at several levelss. Finally we have described a case study - the FRAMES project - which utilises the multimodel framework to develop specific VIS applications.

7.1 INTRODUCTION

Video information systems (VIS) such as digital video libraries, video-on-demand systems, and video synthesis applications introduce new challenges in the management of large collections of digital video and audio data with associated texts, images, and other objects. In order to manage digital videos, we need to understand the semantics of video data, and have appropriate schemes to store, retrieve and present it. Researchers have studied video data from different perspectives. The pattern recognition community has largely concentrated on image data in video and has come up with algorithms that can detect patterns in the data at the visual level (Aigrain *et al*, 1996). The database community has focussed on logical structures that facilitate indexing of video sequences for retrieval purposes. In order to manage large digital collections, we need a video[1] management strategy that can exploit the research outcomes of both of these groups, and at the same time manage the complex semantics of continuous visual media where interpretations are subjective and domain dependent. A conceptual model for such applications must address a number of issues.

It should be capable of representing the high level semantics of a visually rich medium such as a video.

(i) It should support operators and constructors that allow manipulation of a continuous (temporal) medium such as video.

(ii) It should be able to represent low level visual features such as shot boundaries, camera operations, and object tracking, which can be extracted from video data streams.

(iii) It should be capable of modelling audio features such as distinct sound patterns present in the audio stream of a digital video.

(iv) It should be supported by a storage model that supports storage and delivery of video sequences, based on their features.

(v) It should include presentation functions that can provide navigation and browsing facilities to view videos.

(vi) It should provide video composition functions to generate virtual videos.

In section 7.2 of this paper we explore the semantics of video data and present a metamodel with 8 semantic levels, in section 7.3 we identify the requirements of a typical VIS application, and in section 7.4 we present an integrated modelling framework for designing VIS applications. The primary purpose of this framework is to present a unified approach for video management, which includes functions for creating, storing, managing and presenting video applications. In section 7.5, we present a case study - the FRAMES project - to illustrate the application of the proposed multi-model framework in developing an experimental environment to provide access to video material.

Much of the work on developing conceptual models for multimedia data has resulted in models that address specific issues of multimedia data such as representation of image features (Gupta 1997, Flickner, et al. 1995), synchronisation and presentation (Adjeroh and Lee 1996), video navigation and browsing (Simpson-Young and Yap 1996, Arman et al 1994) and models for video management, (Zhang, Low and Smoliar 1995, Hjelsvold, Midstraum and Sandsta 1996). While each of these functions is essential, focussing on only one model is not sufficient to address all aspects of delivering an interactive video application. This paper takes a more holistic approach to modelling and presents a multi-model approach for developing VIS applications. While many of the individual modelling levels have been demonstrated by other research groups, FRAMES is unique in that it

---

[1] When using to the term *video*, we include audio and video components unless the context dictates otherwise.

integrates these into a comprehensive overall framework. The FRAMES project has developed most of the elements of this framework, together with appropriate processing modules and interfaces. Ongoing research is addressing the specific content of the different models.

7.2 SEMANTICS OF VIDEO INFORMATION SYSTEMS

The conceptual model of any information system has to represent objects and relationships well understood by users in a given application domain. For VIS applications, in addition to application domain objects, a conceptual model has to include video objects, meanings associated with those video objects, and other associated objects and attributes that are derived from video data. Film semiotics, pioneered by the film theorist Christian Metz (1974), has identified five levels of cinematic codification that cover visual features, objects, actions and events depicted in images together with other aspects of the meaning of the images. These levels, all of which can be represented within a VIS metamodel, are:

1. the *perceptual level*: the level at which visual phenomena become perceptually meaningful; the level at which distinctions are perceived by a viewer within the perceptual object. This level includes perceptible visual characteristics, such as colours and textures. This level is the subject of a large amount of current research on video content-based retrieval (see Aigrain *et al*, 1996).
2. the *cinematic level*: the specifics of formal film and video techniques incorporated in the production of expressive artefacts ("a film", or "a video"). This level includes camera operations (pan, tilt, zoom), lighting schemes, and optical effects. Automated detection of cinematic features is another area of vigorous current research activity (see Aigrain *et al*, 1996).
3. the *diegetic level*: at this level the basic perceptual features of an image are organised into the four-dimensional spatio-temporal world posited by a video image or sequence of video images, including the spatiotemporal descriptions of agents, objects, actions, and events that take place within that world. An example of an informal description at this level may be "Delores Death enters the kitchen, takes a gun from the cutlery drawer and puts it into her handbag". This is the "highest" level of video semantics that most research to date has attempted to address, other than by associating video material with unconstrained text (allowing video to be searched indirectly via text retrieval methods, eg. Srinivasan *et al*, 1997).
4. the *connotative level*: metaphorical, analogical, and associative meaning that the denoted (ie. diegetic) objects and events of a video may have. The connotative level captures the codes that define the culture of a social group and are considered "natural" within the group. Examples of

connotative meanings are the emotions connoted by actions or the expressions on the faces of characters, such as "Delores Death is angry and vengeful", or "Watch out, someone's going to get a bullet!".

5. the *subtextual level*: more specialised meanings of symbols and signifiers. Examples might include feminist analyses of the power relationships between characters, or a Jungian analysis of particular characters as representing specific cultural archetypes. For example, "Delores Death violates stereotypical images of the passivity and compliance of women", or "Delores Death is the Murderous Monster Mother".

Lindley and Srinivasan (1998) have demonstrated empirically that these descriptions are meaningful in capturing distinctions in the way images are viewed and interpreted by a non-specialist audience, and between this audience and the analytical terms used by film-makers and film critics. Modelling "the meaning" of a video, shot, or sequence requires the description of the video object at any or all of the levels described above. The different levels interact, so that, for example, particular cinematic devices can be used to create different connotations or subtextual meanings while dealing with similar diegetic material.

Despite their importance, the connotative and subtextual levels of video semantics have generally been ignored in attempts to represent video semantics in computing science research to date, despite being a major concern for film-makers and critics[2]. Perhaps one reason for this is that these are not levels of annotation that can be expected to be automated in the short term (in the longer term, memory- and case-based approaches may make some degree of automation feasible). The requirement for the provision of these descriptive annotations changes the production model for interactive video systems (compared with the production model for tradition linear video productions). Authorship is no longer limited to the assembly of the video data, but extends to the generation of descriptive annotations that facilitate and constrain the ways in which the video data can be interactively and dynamically reused. Authorship also extends to high level virtual video prescriptions upon which virtual video generation is based (see below).

All of the above five levels concern the description of the visual and auditory content of video data. We can also identify a level of descriptive information that describes a video production or component without describing its visual and auditory content:

6. the *bibliographic* level is concerned with information about the video such as production details (production crew and principle creative authors, year, etc.), inventory information such as original film gauge or type of tape, standard and format, etc.

---

[2] This may be due to video semantics work being closely aligned with automated video analysis work with its origins in robotics and industrial/manufacturing applications.

Finally, in addition to these six levels, for digital video systems we can identify two additional levels concerned with the semantics of digital video data representation and presentation:

7. the *system* level, concerned with operating systems and networked data file storage and manipulation. This is the level at which the video data is simply "a file" that can be moved, copied, etc.
8. the *video data* level, concerned with the interpretation of the contents of a video data file as a time-ordered series of frames, each substructured as an array of colour values corresponding to a grid of pixels. This level also includes various video compression and encoding models.

An orthogonal way of modelling a video sequence[3] is to distinguish a set of its attributes representing those patterns (features) in the data that can be automatically detected from the bit streams from those attributes that must be manually defined. We shall call the former attributes the *data-driven attributes* of a video sequence. Patterns or features that can be detected so far mostly belong to the perceptual level and cinematic level of codification. By this definition, we recognise that the data-driven attributes that can be determined will change (in particular, increase in number and type) with evolving feature detection technology. The second set of attributes of a video sequence in this orthogonal scheme contains authored models/descriptions of a video. These attributes are manually annotated descriptions of video content, including descriptions of automatically detectable features. In this paper we shall refer to such attributes as *authored -description attributes.*

Some important aspects of video semantics cut across multiple content levels. For example, issues concerned with temporal sequencing of video include elements at the video data level (frames), the cinematic level (shots), and the diegetic level (a scene as a sequence of shots implied by location and time of day). Hence the time order of a video sequence can be subdivided at various levels of granularity. Figure 7.1 shows the different abstraction levels of this subdivision. These levels of subdividing a sequence represent different sizes of video object on which search and retrieval can be conducted; ideally all of these levels should be accommodated in the conceptual schema of a VIS application.

[3] Video sequence here is a generic term that represents any level of video abstraction such as clip, scene and shot.

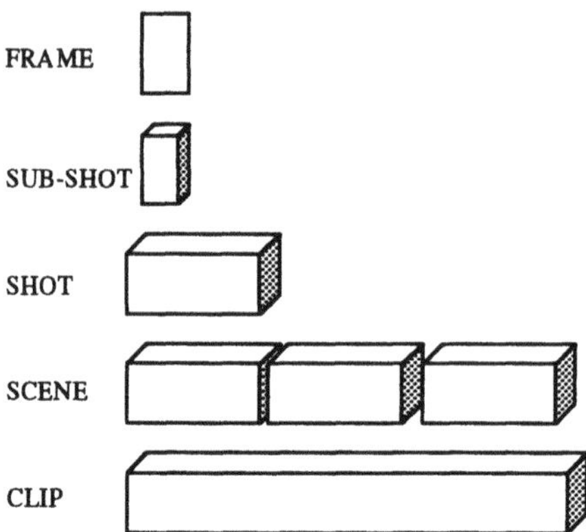

Figure 7.1: Levels of abstraction of a video sequence

Different representations may be used to model these descriptions, with each representation supporting different forms of query or computational operation upon the description. Alternate representations may include textual descriptions or structured database models, such as relational or object models. Text descriptions support search by ranked text retrieval routines using free text descriptions as queries. Relational models support search by SQL queries. Complex object models can depict object hierarchies, allowing search on (or via) subtype/supertype relationships, and can include object encapsulation to represent different abstraction levels of video sequences. The attributes of complex video objects represented in the model could be attributes that are generated automatically by video analysis tools.

7.3 FUNCTIONAL REQUIREMENTS OF A TYPICAL VIS

A typical VIS requires some component sub-systems to manage and present video data. A few key modules are described here. User requirements will have to determine which of these modules are essential for a given application.

7.3.1 Video Analysis

In order to manage digital video sequences, we need video analysis tools to partition the video into the various levels of temporal grouping described above. A shot is usually indexed by a key frame, ie., a still image that represents the shot. Key frames can be further indexed by content-based features such as colour, texture and shape, using image analysis software such as (Gupta 1997). Additionally, shots can also be characterised by camera work such as pan and zoom operations (Aigrain, *et al*, 1996, Gu, *et al*, 1997).

7.3.2 Audio Analysis

The audio signals available in digital videos can provide valuable information when analysing video programs. Although speech recognition has proved to be a difficult problem, other aspects of audio analysis such as aligning speech with textual transcripts (Robert-Ribes and Mukhtar 1997) has been found to be very useful. In some cases audio signals can provide valuable information about non-audio events; for example in the sports domain, loud sound bursts such as a crowd cheer indicate the highlights of a sporting event. Other tools for audio content processing and analysis are reported in (Pfieffer *et al*, 1996).

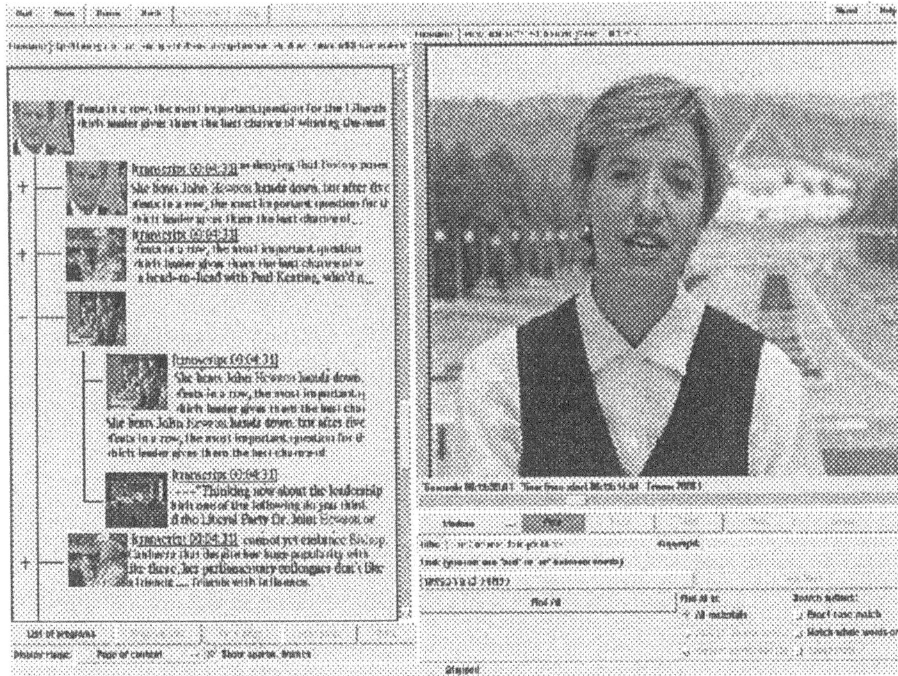

Figure 7.2: Hierarchical browsing using multiple representations (images © Australian Broadcasting Corporation)

7.3.3 Interaction and Presentation

As video is a visually rich medium, users often need to browse through a video before saving a required video sequence. Navigation and browsing tools, therefore, form an important component of a VIS application. Effective browsing through video material requires a combination of actual video material and other available alternate representations of the material such as shotlists containing descriptions of the sequence, transcripts of audio content, and sets of key frames (Yap, Simpson-Young and Srinivasan, 1996). Figure

7.2 shows an example of such an interface using the FRANK client (Simpson-Young and Yap 1996).

7.3.4 Video Composition

Although conceptual models augmented with video analysis tools can be used directly for search and retrieval of video content, applications such as automatic video generation and virtual video synthesis require specific video composition rules as criteria for generating virtual videos from an archive of video clips. Virtual videos can be specified by an author in the form of virtual video prescriptions (Lindley and Vercoustre, 1998). A virtual video prescription is a high level description of the structure of a (possibly interactive) video program. Interpretation of a prescription involves the interpretation engine reading queries embedded in the prescription and sending them to appropriate query processors that will return references to video components that satisfy those queries. The references are then sent by the interpreter to a video server for execution, thereby generating the dynamic virtual video presentation for the user of the system. Although a virtual video prescription contains embedded database queries expressed in terms of both data-driven attributes and authored-description attributes of the video, the prescription itself is also a data structure that can be searched and queried upon. The overall VIS schema may therefore accommodate the representation of virtual video prescriptions, either as generic (searchable) text files, or structured according to specific document type definitions (DTDs).

7.3.5 Data Management

As video information is a combination of visual, audio and text material, a VIS application should be capable of handling multi-modal queries, where each mode or media traditionally has a different indexing mechanism. For example, a sports channel may wish to retrieve a video sequence that shows 'a *close-up* of *Davidson's play* accompanied by a *loud cheer*'. In this query the *close-up* is a framing characteristic (cinematic level) defined on a diegetic object (character), the *loud cheer* is an audio signal and the description about *Davidson's play* could be textual information[4]. That is, a single query may involve accessing data represented by multiple data types. The data management function has to offer support for managing video objects whose attributes could be audio/video feature extraction functions, text documents and key frame images.

Traditional database management systems that store multimedia data as binary large objects (BLOBS) are no longer adequate to handle functional

[4] A close-up could be represented as a manual annotation or automatically detected, either on demand or during a prior video analysis operation.

attributes that may be generated in real-time. A database management system to store video objects requires the ability to extend traditional data types with suitable operators for manipulating video sequences, constructors for video composition and delivery mechanisms for presentation. The requirements of a multimedia database management system have been discussed in a number of recent papers (Nwosu *et al* Eds 1996). The Object-relational model is well suited to be the logical model for VIS applications as it supports derived data types and abstract data types to represent video, audio and image data (Subrahmanyam 1997).

The requirements specified thus far need a modelling approach that can model complex video objects, generate functional attributes, support specification of video composition rules within a virtual video prescription and provide presentation capabilities that can support navigation and browsing.

7.4 A FRAMEWORK FOR DESIGNING VIDEO APPLICATIONS

In order to develop VIS applications, we need a modelling framework that is rich enough to support the video semantics described in section 7.2, and robust enough to meet the demands of evolving technology in the areas of video content analysis and automatic video generation, as described in the previous section.

Video analysis requires extensive computation of digital data. While the objects involved in the computation could be represented within an object-oriented model (or any semantic model), the emphasis in this case lies in describing the computations involved. This calls for a thrust towards a functional component, as the functional modelling approach is well suited for non-interactive programs, where the main purpose is to compute a function. By contrast, databases often have a trivial functional model, since their purpose is to store and organise data, not to transform them.

In the case of the video presentation, the emphasis is on accessing information in a structured way, which is a typical hypermedia application requirement. Design of hypermedia applications involves capturing and organizing the structure of complex domain and making it clear and accessible to users (Tomas *et al* 1995). The hypermedia model provides a control structure that supports navigation through data based on its content. While this is ideal where nodes consist of persistent data such as text, finding a general way to indicate dynamic media such as a portion of video or audio is a difficult problem. This requires augmenting a hypermedia model with a storage model that supports multimedia data types and complex temporal relationships among data items that support high level presentation semantics. (Hardman, *et al* 1994).

A VIS application model therefore has to draw from both (functional and hypermedia) modelling approaches in order to meet the VIS requirements.

These models need to be supported by a storage model that supports operations on complex data types and temporal relationships.

Given these requirements, now we present an integrated multimodel framework to support the complex environment of a VIS application.

7.4.1 The Integrated Multi-model Framework

Figure 7.3 shows the proposed integrated framework for developing VIS applications. The framework illustrates the different modelling components that are appropriate for delivering the functional modules of a VIS application. The modelling components are described in greater detail in the rest of this section.

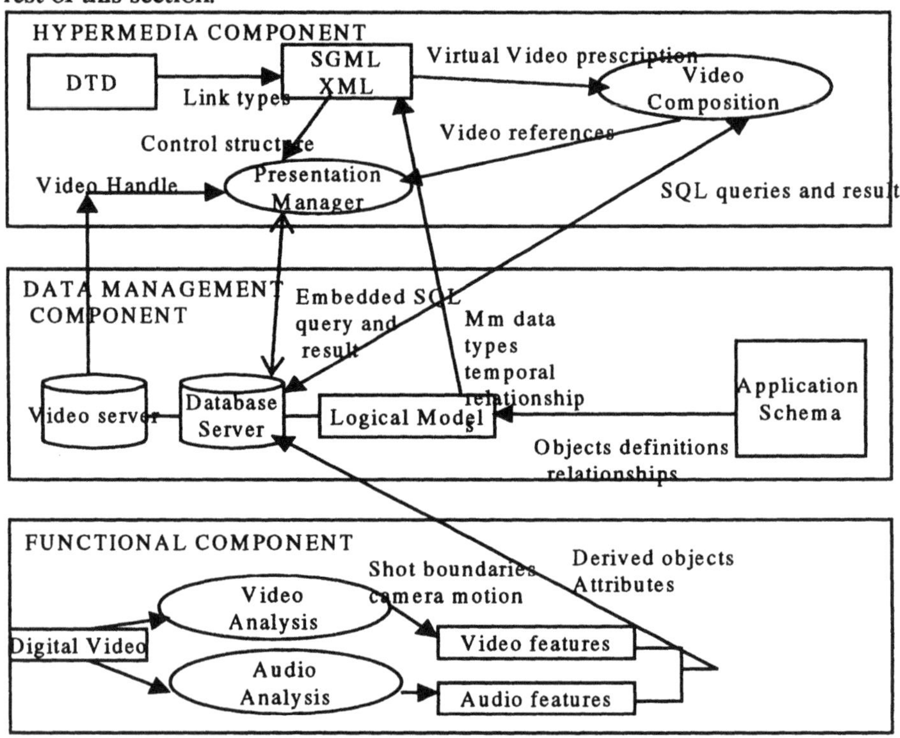

Figure 7.3: An Integrated Framework for VIS applications

In figure 7.3, the functional component of the application deals with the modules that are computation-intensive, such as video analysis and audio analysis. The features automatically generated by the video analysis and the audio analysis components are stored as derived objects and attributes in the database. The hypermedia component deals with the presentation manager that uses an SGML or XML document to support video navigation and browsing. (In a web-based environment environment, the presentation manager could have components on the server side eg, CGI script, and/or on the client side eg, a Java applet or a Java script code.) A video composition process within the hypermedia component reads queries from a SGML/XML document and uses them to query the contents of the database. The complex data types used to represent video data are available to the presentation manager from the logical database model. The logical model is created from the VIS application schema. The application schema represents video semantics at the different levels discussed in section 7.2.

7.4.1.1 Functional Component. Digital video data forms the input to the video analysis module. The video analysis module identifies features determined by patterns in the video data. The type of features could be camera shots, camera type such as pan, zoom, object identification etc. Many algorithms are available for shot detection, ie, parsing videos into distinct shots (Arman, Hsu and Chiu 1993, Feng, Meng, Juan and Chang 1995, Zhang, Low and Smoliar 1995, Gu, Tsui and Keightley 1996). Such algorithms that deal with the non-trivial data structures are best specified as part of the functional component in the integrated framework. Similarly the audio processing module also forms part of the functional component.

Video parsing and audio analysis are usually performed before the video is made available for browsing, navigation and querying. Both video analysis and audio analysis functions produce derived objects and attributes that are stored in the database.

While a camera shot could form a fundamental browsing unit, a group of shots may also be aggregated into a meaningful unit or 'scene' for querying video content. What constitutes a scene has to be determined by the user-requirements of the video application.

7.4.1.2 Hypermedia Component. The hypermedia design approach is well suited for presentation of videos as it offers control structures well suited for navigation and browsing. The presentation manager has to support navigation through a video at several levels of abstraction, and also allow navigation across multiple videos in applications such as digital video libraries and virtual video generation. Management of these functions is facilitated by the use of structured documents.

A structured document basically separates the presentation style from logical structure and content. A DTD or Document Type Definition provides a framework for the elements that constitute a structured document and also specifies the rules and relationships between the elements that constitute a document. Using a standard such as SGML or XML it is possible to define a structured document that has elements to describe the semantic structure of a video. In FRANK (Simpson-Young and Yap 1996) this is achieved by using the Text Encoding Initiative (TEI) DTD which supports a semantically rich document structure.

The presentation manager uses the control structures and the links in a structured document to facilitate authoring as well as querying contents of the Video database. Using SGML-compliant tags it is possible to embed SQL queries within a document. The results of the query are displayed through the presentation manager.

In applications that require video composition, the video composition module utilises a standard such as SGML or XML to specify virtual video prescriptions which are read by the video composition component of the application. The video composition component directs queries represented in a prescription to appropriate query processors and sends the video components returned from the queries to the presentation manager. This generates a virtual video program from various levels of sequences, possibly within separate video data files.

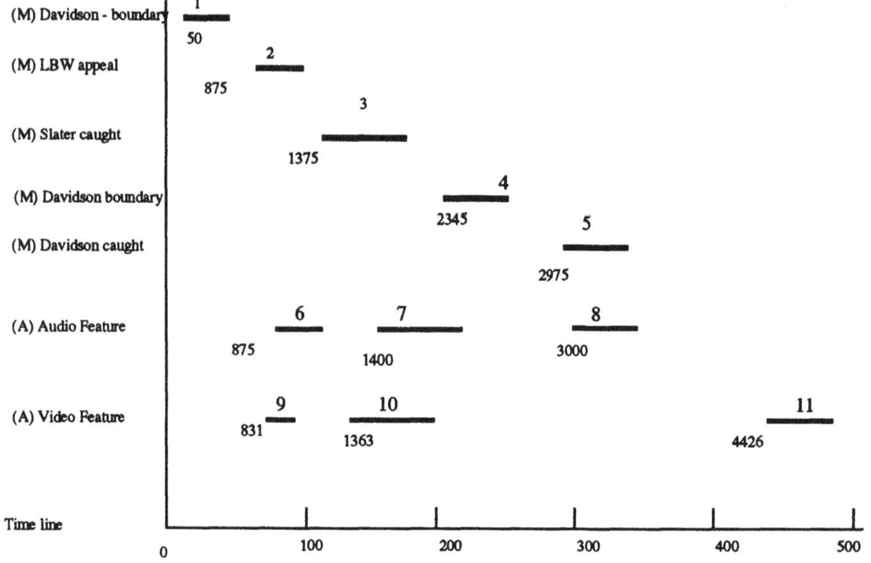

Figure 7.4: A Sports Sequence

7.4.1.3 Data Management Component. The object definitions and relationships are represented in the VIS application schema, which in turn is mapped onto the logical model of the database server. The logical model defines the multimedia data types and temporal relationships needed to represent video sequences. For VIS applications, the database server is usually connected to a media server to manage the high volume video data and deliver continuous video in a synchronised manner to the presentation manager.

Video data has temporal requirements that have implications on storage, manipulation and presentation. In the storage model, the logical representation of a video sequence is a time-ordered sequence of frames and operations on video sequences are temporal operations on time intervals. The following example illustrates the need for a temporal mapping of video objects.

A video sequence may spread over an interval of 5000 frames i.e., 3 mins and 20 secs. (A video in PAL format delivers 25 frames per second.) The objects and/or events of significance may occur at different intervals in the sequence. Temporal attributes of a video sequence such as startOffset and endOffset map the data storage pattern onto a temporal presentation order. Figure 7.4 shows some significant events in a sports sequence. Events marked (M) are manually annotated events and events marked (A) are automatically detected events. In this example, the audio feature is a loud burst of sound, and the video feature is an automatically generated camera zoom-in operation. The automatically detected camera shot boundaries (not shown in the diagram) are present at different points within this interval.

A query to retrieve Davidson's play accompanied by a close-up camera operation would require operations on time intervals 1, 4, 5, 9 and 10. In order to satisfy a comprehensive range of temporal ordering requirements in queries, we need a number of set operations on time intervals in order to reconstruct total time sequence that encapsulates all and only those subsequences that satisfy a query. In this case the subsequence order is (1⊕9⊕10⊕4⊕5). The ⊕operation here is defined as follows: the ⊕ operator takes two intervals and returns a new interval such that the start-time of the new interval is the lesser of the start-times of the two intervals and the end-time of the new interval is the greater of the two end-times. This definition ensures that any overlapping intervals or intersections (as in 1 and 9) are not duplicated and gaps between two intervals (as in 9 and 10) are included in the returned sequence. The ⊕ operator defined here is only one example of a temporal operator. Allen (1983) has shown that there are thirteen disjunct relationships that can exist between two temporal intervals. In the context of videos, a comprehensive set of temporal operators have to be defined to handle a variety of queries incorporating specific temporal constraints.

The video application should have the capability to manage such temporal data and its associated relationships. Spatial relationships can also be represented in detail, supporting dedicated spatial query forms. However, the FRAMES project has not yet addressed spatial data in this level of detail.

Table 1 presents a summary of the essential components and the factors that need to be considered while developing a conceptual model for a VIS application. Column 1 shows the required components of a VIS application. Column 2 shows the services provided by these components. Column 3 shows the data structures and functions involved in delivering the type of services shown in column 2. Coulmn 4 shows the appropriate modelling methodology or formalism suited to deliver the component shown in col. 1.

The next section describes the FRAMES architecture that utilises the multimodel framework presented in this section.

7.5 THE FRAMES ARCHITECTURE

The functional architecture being used in the FRAMES[5] project utilises this multimodel framework to develop video content models for VIS applications.

Table 7.1. Summary of Data structures and Modelling Formalism

Requirement	Services	Data Structures and Functions	Modelling Formalism
Video analysis	Camera-shot boundary detection Categorisation of camera operations Video indexing by low level features	Derived objects and attributes, Complex computation functions to generate video objects and attributes	Functional Model
Audio Analysis	Detection of interpretive classes characterised by distinct sound patterns	Complex computation functions to generate audio objects and attributes	Functional Model
Video composition	Virtual video generation	Video composition functions, SGML/XML DTDS for presentation	Object relational model Hypermedia model - DTD
Video Interaction and presentation	Presentation generation Web-friendly navigation and browsing facility	SGML/XML DTDs for user interaction Document interpretation and management functions	Hypermedia Model -DTD
Data management	Database functions,	Object relational tables, complex objects, abstract data types, temporal mapping of video sequences Object-relational operations	Storage model to support mm data types

A core component of the architecture is a video semantics metamodel, which is a model of the different ways in which video semantics can be expressed. The metamodel represents video semantics based on film semiotics described in section 7.2. The primary hypothesis is that modelling the meaning of a video sequence can involve description of the video object

[5] The FRAMES project is being carried out within the Cooperative Research Centre for Research Data Networks established under the Australian Government's Cooperative Research Centre (CRC) Program.

at one or more of these levels. The metamodel is used as the canonical basis for the definition of specific content models for a given VIS application. Since all specific video content models are expressed in terms of objects, attributes and relationships that are predefined in the metamodel, and all queries on video data are also expressed in terms of the same metamodel, the system guarantees a commonality of language during the search process.

7.5.1 Video Semantics Metamodel

5.1.1 The Cinematic Level of Video Semantics. The cinematic level of video semantics is concerned with the specifics of how formal film and video techniques are incorporated in the production of expressive artefacts ("a film", or "a video") in such a way as to achieve artistic, formal, and expressive integrity. The process is complex, partially codified within various stylistic conventions, and tightly linked to other levels of meaning. Common examples of cinematic techniques (extracted from Arnheim, 1971) include shot characteristics, (eg. effect of angles, size, and relative placement on how one object is interpreted in relation to others in the diegetic space, etc.), mobile camera, shot speed (frame rate), optical effects, and principles of montage (eg. long strips for quiet rhythm, short strips for quick rhythm, climactic scenes, tumultuous action).

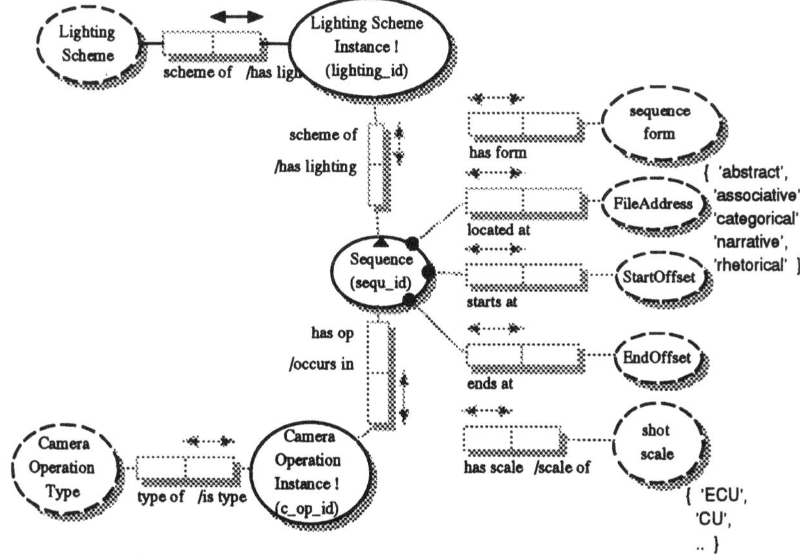

Figure 7.5: Schema for the Cinematic Level of Video Semantics

The initial FRAMES demonstrator includes very simple cinematic annotations, shown on the conceptual model of Figure 7.5. The model has been developed using the Object Role Modelling Formalisam (Halpin 1995). The model includes the file address and start and end offsets of a modelled video segment. A shot scale label can be used for sequences that correspond with single shots. The sequence is also classified as having one of five primary sequence forms ie, abstract, associative, categorical, narrative, and rhetorical (described in Bordwell and Thompson, 1997). The FRAMES project has developed extensions to this model that include camera operations, lighting schemes, and other cinematic characteristics.

7.5.1.2 The Diegetic Level of Video Semantics. *Diegesis* designates the sum of a film's denotation: the narration, the fictional space and time dimensions implied in and by the narrative, the characters, locations, events, and other narrative elements considered in their denoted aspect (Metz, 1974). Based upon this definition, we define the diegetic meaning of video data as the four-dimensional spatio-temporal world that it posits, including agents, objects, actions, and events that take place within that world.

Davis (1994) considers a number of specific ontological issues in the representation of video semantics that address the diegesis of video data as a spatio-temporal world. The sequencing of shots allows the construction of many types of space (including real, artificial, and impossible spaces). For real locations it is possible to distinguish the actual location of the recording, the spatial location inferred by a viewer of an isolated shot, and the spatial location inferred when a shot is viewed in the context of a shot sequence. The virtual spaces created by videos require the use of relative three-dimensional spatial position descriptions. Video requires techniques for representing and visualising the complex structure of the *actions* of characters, objects, and cameras. For representing the action of bodies in space, the representation needs to support the hierarchical decomposition of units, spatially and temporally. Conventionalised body motions (walking, sitting, eating, talking, etc.) compactly represent motions that may involve multiple abstract body motions (represented according to articulations and rotations of joints). Much of the challenge of representing action is in knowing what levels of granularity are useful. *Time* (analogously to space) requires the representation of actual time and both possible and impossible visually-inferred time.

The initial FRAMES conceptual model includes five primary diegetic entity types, as shown on Figure 7.6: characters, objects, locations, speech acts, and actions. Diegetic modelling is an area of considerable ambiguity, since it can extend to arbitrary degrees of complexity in modelling the structure of any of these basic types and their interrelationships. A major modelling consideration is whether to include various details within the structure of the conceptual model, or to include them within more generic and unconstrained descriptive fields. For example, if a character performs an action upon another primary entity type, could this be modelled as an instance of a structural relationship with the other entity type, or could alternatively be incorporated into the "action description" associated with an action. Including the substructure of actions within the conceptual model supports more direct forms of processing upon action descriptions. If the detail is held within generic description fields, access to that detail requires more complex and time-consuming processing of the internal content of descriptions. Processing the text of descriptions is made more difficult if the format of the text is not constrained; if it is constrained, then it is simpler to break this format information out into the conceptual model.

Decisions regarding the complexity of the conceptual model involve a trade-off between increasing the complexity of creating models on the one hand, and being able to process the models with more discrimination on the other. It is a major aim of the FRAMES project to gain an understanding of how much complexity is required in order to synthesise coherent video sequences of different types, and to develop tools and techniques for creating models having appropriate detail as efficiently as possible.

7.5.1.3 The Connotative and Subtextual Levels of Video Semantics. The connotative level of video semantics is the level of metaphorical, analogical, and associative meaning that the denoted (ie. represented diegetic) objects and events of a video may have. The connotative level captures the cultural codes that define the culture of a social group and are considered “natural” within the group.

The subtextual level represents a range of possible 'readings' or interpretations of video content, and hence is an important level of video semantics. The level of *subtext* corresponds to the level of hidden and suppressed meanings of symbols and signifiers, preceding and extending the immediacy of intuitive consciousness. The subtextual level is more specifically concerned with the levels of meaning that may *not* be immediately apparent to a reader (ie. viewer).

For both the connotative level and the subtextual levels, a definitive representation of “the meaning” of video content is in principle impossible. The most that can be expected is the development and representation of a body of evolving interpretations and their interrelationships.

An ideologically neutral content-based search and retrieval system must not restrict the range of possible interpretations of images. If such a system uses content representations, it must represent and support different views of content.

The FRAMES conceptual model accommodates connotations and subtext associated directly with video sequences, or indirectly with sequences via characters, locations, and objects.

7.5.1.4 Interactions Between Semantic Levels. Interaction between interpretation paradigms at the different levels of meaning are highly complex, which makes a universal film syntax impossible. The current version of the FRAMES schema includes very simple interconnections between levels (eg. Figure 7.7 shows interconnections between the cinematic and diegetic levels. Ongoing research will address the development of more systematic knowledge and information models to represent semantic interactions within specific film styles and genres. Interdependencies between levels create the need to protect schema and data integrity. For example, if a diegetic entity is deleted, and it has connotations associated with it, there should be a systematic way of managing the referential dependency (it cannot be assumed that all deletions should cascade to dependent entities). Tools for managing data integrity are an area for ongoing research. The elements of FRAMES architecture are shown on Figure 7.8.

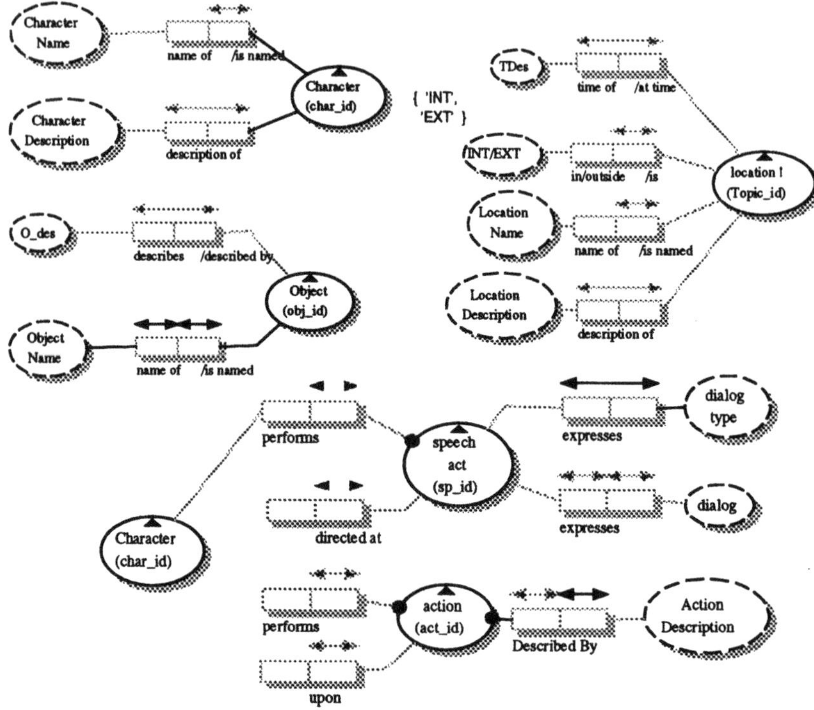

Figure 7.6: Schemas for the Diegetic Level of Video Semantics.

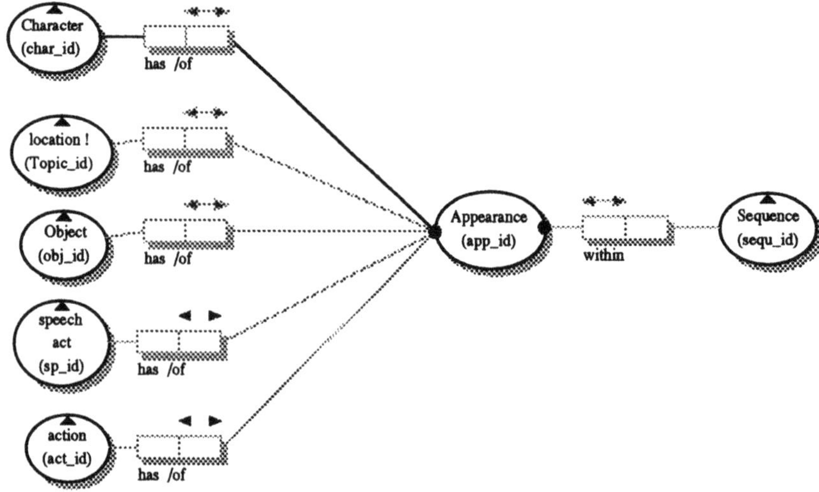

Figure 7.7: Schema Associating Diegetic Level Objects with the Cinematic Level of Video Semantics

7.5.2 Components of the FRAMES Architecture

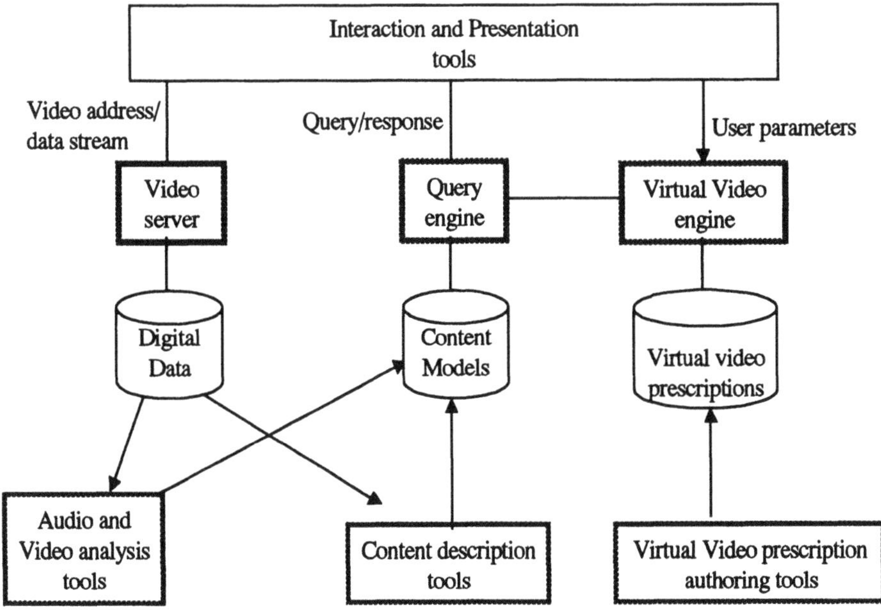

Figure 7.8: The FRAMES Architecture

7.5.2.1 Content description tools. The content description tool provides a way of developing a conceptual model for a specific VIS application. This model (also referred to as the content model) is developed using the semantics represented in the metamodel. The content model provides an integrated environment (section 7.4) and describes the video sequences, associated objects and operations on the objects as per the requirements of a given VIS application. Applying constraints on the conceptual model generates the logical model for the DBMS. The data model allows access and retrieval of video data by supporting appropriate indexing mechanism required during query processing. Queries can be specified directly by users using a *query authoring tool* (which is part of the interaction and presentation tools of figure 7.8) that provides structured interfaces for expressing queries in terms of components specified by the metamodel. Well-formulated queries (ie. those expressed in terms of the metamodel and according to the syntax of the query language) are dispatched to a *query processor*. The query processor performs matching of queries against content models in order to find references to video objects in the video database that satisfy each query. Since queries can be expressed at various levels of abstraction, it is possible for a sequence of video components , rather than a primitive video data object, to satisfy a query. An answer to a query may then be a list of references to primitive video objects, or a list including sequences of such objects.

7.5.2.2 Virtual Video Prescription Tools. Virtual video composition is carried out by a virtual video engine. The virtual video engine is used when the video data is to be delivered to users in the form of highly structured and coherent video productions. In this case, a *virtual video prescription authoring tool* is used to specify the high level structure of the virtual video in the form of a *virtual video prescription.* A virtual video prescription includes embedded queries that are executed by a *virtual video prescription interpreter* in order to synthesise a complete *virtual video* having content tuned to specific user requirements at the time of interpretation. Virtual videos are specified and presented using the hypermedia modelling approach.

7.5.2.3 Automated Video/Audio analysis tools. The *automated video analysis tools* include algorithms for characterising video data in terms of visual features (eg. using colour histograms and texture measures), in terms of automatically detectable camera operations (eg. pan, tilt, and zoom), and basic object and shape detection. Automated cut detection is incorporated for parsing video data streams that extend beyond a single cut (ie. sequences or complete productions). The audio analysis tools include algorithms for detecting distinct loud sounds and characterisation of audio events such as music, voice, etc.

7.5.2.4 Presentation Tools. The presentation tools include the user interaction component, which includes query, navigation and browsing. Experience with the FRANK navigation and browsing tool (Simpson-Young and Yap, 1996) suggests that a web-based browsing tool provides an appropriate interface for searching, navigating and browsing through video material.

7.6 CONCLUSION AND ONGOING WORK

In this paper, we have presented a multi-model framework for designing VIS applications. The framework includes a functional component to represent video and audio analysis functions and a hypermedia component for video delivery and presentation. Modelling video data involves understanding the semantics of visual information. Towards this end, we have described the various levels at which video data can be interpreted. We have then presented a metamodel for modelling video content. Finally we have described a case study - the FRAMES project - which utilises the multimodel framework to develop specific VIS applications.

We plan to extend our research in two areas; query languages for continuous visual media, and virtual video generation. We will continue to develop tools and infrastructure to allow specialists to articulate interpretive models at different levels and then use these models in support of video search, retrieval, browsing and synthesis. On the application side, work will involve developing systems for specific domains such as the sports domain, which will include multi-modal queries to query sports highlights.

Acknowledgments

The authors wish to acknowledge that this work was carried out within the Cooperative Research Centre for Research Data Networks established under the Australian Government's Cooperative Research Centre (CRC) Program and acknowledge the support of the Advanced Computational Systems CRC under which the work described in this paper is administered.

References

ADJEROH AND LEE (1996): Synchronisation and User Interaction in Distributed Multimedia Presentation Systems, *Multimedia Database Systems, Kluwer Academic publishers, 1996* .

AIGRAIN, P. ZHANG, H. and PETKOVIC, D. (1996): Content-Based Representation and Retrieval of Visual Media, *Multimedia Tools and Applications,* 3, 179-202.

ALLEN, J.F. (1983): Maintaining knowledge about temporal intervals, *Communications of the ACM, vol.26 No.11*, 882-843.

ARMAN, DEPOMMIER, HSU, CHIU (1994)*: Content-based Browsing of Video Sequences, Proceeedings of ACM international Conference on Multimedia '94, California, 1994.*

ARMAN, F., HSU, A., and CHIU, M.Y. (1993): Image processing on compressed data for large video databases, *Proc. ACM Multimedia 93, Anaheim, California, August 1993*, pp 267-272.

ARNHEIM, R., (1971): *Film as Art*, University of California Press.

BORDWELL, D. and THOMPSON,K. (1997): *Film Art: An Introduction, 5th edn.*, McGraw-Hill.

DAVIS, M., Knowledge Representation for Video", *Proceedings of the 12th National Conference on Artificila Intelligence*, AAAI, MIT Press, pp. 120-127, 1994.

FENG, J., LO, K-T. and MEHRPOUR, H. (1996): Scene change detection algorithm for MPEG video sequence, *IEEE International Conference on Image Processing (ICIP96)*, September 1996.

FLICKNER, SAWHNEY, NIBLACK, ASHLEY, HUANG, DOM, GORKHANI, HAFNER, LEE, PETKOVIC, STEELE AND YANKER (1995): Query by image and video content: The QBIC system, *IEEE Computer*, 28(9), pp 23-32.

GORKY (1994): Multimedia Information Systems, *IEEE Multimedia* , Spring 1994.

GRIFFIEON, J., YAVATKAR, R. and ADAMS, R. (1996): Automatic and Dynamic Identification of Metadata in Multimedia.

GU, L., TSUI K. AND KEIGHTLEY D. (1997): Dissolve detection in MPEG compressed video, *Proceedings of IEEE International Conference on Intelligent Processing Systems, October 1997.*

GU, L., TSUI, K. and KEIGHTLEY D. (1996): Camera shot boundary detection in MPEG compressed video, *Technical Report, CSIRO Mathematical and Information Sciences, December 1996.*

GUPTA, A. (1997): Visual Information Retrieval: A Virage Perspective, *Visual Information Retrieval White Paper, http://www.virage.com/wpaper.*

HALPIN (1995): Conceptual schema and Relational database Design, 2nd edition, Prentice Hall, Sydney, Australia.

HARDMAN, L., BULTERMAN.D.C.A, VAN ROSSUM, G., The Amsterdam Hypermedia Model, Communications of the ACM, Vol.37, No.2, February, 1994.

HJELSVOLD,MIDSTRAUM AND SANDSTA (1996): *Searching and Browsing a Shared Video Database, Multimedia Database Systems*, Kluwer Academic publishers, 1996 .

ISAKOWITZ, T, STOHR, E, and BALASUBRAMANIAN , P., (1995): *RMM: A Methodology for Hypermedia Design*, Communications of the ACM vol. 38, No. 8, August 1995.

KIM M., CHOI J. G. AND LEE M. H. (1998): Localising Moving Objects in Image Sequences Using a Statistical Hypothesis Test, *Proceedings of the International Conference on Computational Intelligence and Multimedia Applications, Churchill, Victoria, 9-11 Feb., 836-841.*

LINDLEY C. A. & VERCOUSTRE A. M. (1998): *Intelligent Video Synthesis Using Virtual Video Prescriptions*, International Conference on Computational Intelligence and Multimedia Applications, Churchill, Victoria, 9-11 Feb.

LINDLEY C. A. 1997 A Multiple-Interpretation Framework for Modeling Video Semantics, *ER-97 Workshop on Conceptual Modeling in Multimedia Information Systems.*

LINDLEY C. A. AND SRINIVASAN U. 1998 "Query Semantics for Content-Based Retrieval of Video Data: An Empirical Investigation", Storage and Retrieval Issues in Image- and Multimedia Databases, August 24-28, in conjunction with 9th International Conference DEXA98 Vienna, Austria.

METZ C. 1974 *Film Language: A Semiotics of the Cinema*, trans. by M. Taylor, The University of Chicago Press.

NWOSU, K. THURAISINGHAM, B. and BRUCE BERRA, P. (1996): *Multimedia Database Systems,* Kluwer Academic Publishers, 1996.

PFEIFFER, S. FISCHER, S. and EFFELSBERG ,W. (1996): Automatic Audio Content Analysis, *Proceedings of ACM Multimedia, Boston, 1996.*

ROBERT-RIBES, J. and MUKHTAR, R.G., (1997): Automatic Generation of Hyperlinks between Audio and Transcript, *Fifth European Conferenceon Speech Communication and Technology,* September 1997.

SIMPSON-YOUNG, W. and YAP, K. (1996): FRANK: Trialing a system for remote navigation of film archives, *SPIE International Symposium on Voice and Video Communications, Boston, November 1996.*

SRINIVASAN, GU, TSUI AND BILL SIMPSON-YOUNG (1997): A Data Model to support Content-based Search on Digital Video Libraries, *Australian Computer Journal, Vol.29, No 4, November 1997.*

SUBRAHMANYAM V.S., *Principles of Multimedia Database Systems,* Morgan and Kaufmann, 1998.

YAP, K., SIMPSON-YOUNG, W, and SRINIVASAN, U. (1996): Enhancing Video Navigation with existing alternate Representations, *First International Conference on Image Databases and Multimedia Search, Amsterdam, August 1996.*

ZHANG, H., LOW, C.Y. and SMOLIAR S.W. (1995): Video parsing and browsing using compressed data, *Multimedia Tools and Applications,* 1(1), pp 89-111.

8 COSIS: A CONTENT-ORIENTED SHOEPRINT IDENTIFICATION SYSTEM

Mohamed Tahar Meharga, Corinne Plazanet, and Stefano Spaccapietra

Database Laboratory
Computer Science Department
Ecole Polytechnique Fédérale de Lausanne (EPFL)
CH-1015 Lausanne, Switzerland*

{mohamed.meharga, corinne.plazanet, stefano.spaccapietra}@epfl.ch

Abstract: COSIS is a content-based image retrieval system designed for the shoeprint identification. It consists of a matching-based query tool, an attribute-based query tool and an icon-based browser. The matching-based tool considers the complete and partial shoeprints as query images. The complete-shoeprint query tool is fully-automatic whereas the partial-shoeprint one is user-driven. The development of the matching-based query tool is inspired from the template-matching approach largely used in pattern recognition. This paper presents COSIS by focusing, in particular, on its main component: the Matching-based Query Tool.

8.1 INTRODUCTION

Several products providing the content-based image retrieval (CBIR) functionalities are already available in the marketplace, but since they lack accuracy and the query result is not completely guaranteed, one can never have complete confidence in their conclusions, notably in strategic domains such as identification for access control, forensic science, or medical applications. The main problem is to improve both their efficiency and effectiveness. Further solutions

*This project is partially funded by the Swiss National Science Foundation.

and advances in indexing and matching efficiency are needed to handle large image databases.

The problem of the similarity perception is complex and depends on the context, the interest and the observer. Query by example is only possible if a constrained view of what is meant by "similar" is defined. Tracking efficiency, our research work has been set up in a concrete application framework, which, at least in a first step, would provide a defined environment as well as a chance to work in close cooperation with users having application expertise and capable of giving us a precise definition of their requirements and direct feedback on our suggestions and results. Thanks to an interesting opportunity, this application domain is the one of criminal investigation, for which the local police maintains a database of images of shoeprints. These black and white binary images also represent a good starting point for such a project: they have reduced, although not minimal, complexity, and allow to focus on shape and texture issues, rather than the more conventional color issues. Moreover, the fact that the number of images is not that large, the relevance of search criteria, similarity measurements and appropriateness of results is easier to assess.

From the user point of view, in our application, each image contains one semantic object: a shoeprint, which can be complete or partial. A semantic object here is defined as an object of the real world, identified by its name in an univocal way.

In object recognition and image understanding, the template matching approach is widely used. To detect the presence of an object in an image, a template of the object is convolved with each pixel of the image and the region that responds the best could correspond to the searched object. The conclusions of the application specification analysis suggested us to investigate this approach and this gave rise to the COSIS system.

In this paper, the Content-Oriented Shoeprint Identification System (COSIS) is described, in particular, its approach to perform the content-based querying. COSIS has three main components. Section 8.2 presents the shoeprint application, the data as well as the retrieval needs and requirements. Section 8.3 exposes a survey of relevant efforts in content based retrieval in general and in forensic science in particular. Section 8.4 discusses the proposed approach for the content-based querying of shoeprint images. Section 8.5 presents the COSIS components. Finally, the Section 8.6 reveals the possible extensions of COSIS to cope with other applications and our future work.

8.2 APPLICATION AND PROBLEM STATEMENT

8.2.1 The data

One form of physical evidence in judicial investigations is the **shoeprint identification**. The shoeprints are often encountered at the scene of burglaries and other kinds of crimes. The shoeprints are important for different reasons. They can be found at most of the crime scenes, they are the fastest way to solve a crime, and they are the best way to link crime scenes.

In a typical situation of police investigations by shoeprints, three main collections of shoeprints are considered: (1) those from shoes of commerce, (2) those from shoes of suspects and (3) impressions gathered from the crime scenes.The main purpose is, using shoeprints from the third category, to look for possible suspects, by getting models and brand names of shoes and to link crime scenes.

For our experiments, our database is composed of more than 800 shoeprints of the category (1). The second category is considered equivalent to the first category. However, the images of the third category are obtained from scanned and binarised grey-level photographs of real impressions.

8.2.2 Retrieval needs and requirements

Basically, we have to answer the following query: giving a shoeprint as input, the system has to retrieve similar ones contained in the database. This has to be done with the following considerations:

- Every image (shoeprint) of the database similar to the query one has to be returned by the system. More details are given in the section 8.4 about the meaning of the similarity in this application.
- Invariance is required under translation, scaling, rotation and mirroring.
- The retrieval approach has to be robust to overcome the noise and the artifacts affecting the input images because of the wear of the shoes, the crime scene state, and the conditions under which the impressions are captured. In the gathered impressions, some regions can be absent, dilated, eroded or collapsed with other regions. Moreover, the partial shoeprints have to be taken into account. In several situations, only parts of shoe impressions are gathered from the crime scenes.

8.3 RELATED WORK

In the plethora of the proposed CBIR systems (research prototypes or products), we find domain-dependent systems and domain-independent ones. If the first systems lack flexibility and openness, they are more effective and more efficient than the latter ones, since they take advantage of a context (meta-knowledge) which is very helpful for the identification of the similarity criteria.

As examples of the first category, we quote ARTISAN [4] and TODAI [5]. ARTISAN is a prototype shape retrieval system for trade mark images (logos). ARTISAN is intended to be a powerful tool for the UK Patent Office Trade Marks Registry. TODAI (Typographic Ornament DAtabases and Identification) is a CBIR system based on the orientation radiograms to describe the content of images. TODAI is used by researchers, working in the area of old books, to consult an International Bank of Printers' Ornaments on the Web.

In the second category, QBIC [6, 7], Virage [8] and Excalibur occupy the head of the list. Virage is perhaps the most interesting. Unlike its rivals, it is designed as a series of independent modules, which can be incorporated within existing database management products to extend their image-handling capabilities to content-based retrieval, e.g. VIR datablade in Illustra. In [9], a CBIR system for ophthalmological images is presented. Based on the Virage Incorporated framework, Gupta and al. have designed a number of primitives extracted from ocular fundus images in order to define their similarity for automatic indexing.

Concerning the forensic science community, most (if not all) of the proposed methods (systems) are *classification based* [10, 13]. With respect to a specific rules, for each shoeprint in the database is linked a set of geometric shapes (alphanumeric data) as metadata. These metadata are manually introduced by a restrictive group of users who are more experienced and well trained on the system. The classification process requires a coding system which associates for each geometric shape a specific code. The classification codes are divided into main groups and these groups into sub-features. In [12], the major groups are Bars, Circles, Design, Mesh, Pattern, Studs, Waves and Zig-Zags. Each shoeprint is partitioned into four distinct areas of Toe, Ball, Instep and Hill. A set of metadata is associated for each area. Using a graphical interface for questioning the system, the user has to describe the input shoeprint (introduce the metadata). After codification of the geometric shapes proposed by the user and by mean of index the system returns the result (a list of shoeprints the most similar to the proposed one).

Classifying shoeprints is not an easy task because of the incalculable number of various geometric shapes that are constantly being changed. The manual acquisition of features asks for more objectivity from the group of users responsible of the databases updates which is not an easy task too. It has been also difficult to design a multi-user classification system and a system which perform identification of partial shoeprints.

Among the pertinent research results, conducted by forensic science researchers, obtained up-to-date, the most important one is REBEZO [14]: the first system (in this application) which after segmenting the picture, analyses the geometric shapes (two-dimensional shape analysis with FFT) but the codification is still user-assisted, i.e. the system make only suggestions of the shapes which it recognizes.

8.4 PROPOSED APPROACH

8.4.1 Approach motivations

Digital image analysis techniques use features (metadata) to classify an image or to segment it. Experience shows that designing appropriate features for a pattern recognition application is the most critical effort to be invested in the course of design. We estimate that, in this project, this step is at least as crucial as in the classical pattern recognition problem, which is related to the issues we want to investigate: binary image retrieval.

One of the key problems in content-based image retrieval is the resolution of the correspondence or similarity between images (or regions) in the both images (query image and database image). There are two broad classes of techniques for similarity measurement: *matching-based* (area-based) and *feature-*

based (indexing-based). In matching-based approach, the intensity of a region around each pixel is taken as the feature and is used so that the regions in both images match. Thus, a local similarity for a region can be found based on measures such as sum of absolute difference of pixel intensity. In the indexing-based approach, features such as the average amount of red, green, and blue in color images (3 features per image: R_{avg}, G_{avg} and B_{avg}), instead of intensity arrays, derived from two images are tested for a similarity.

There are some advantages of indexing-based systems. They are usually faster than matching-based methods since only the features of the target image are calculated at the querying time. The features of the database images are derived at insertion time and stored in indexes which avoids the systematic sweeping of all the database images. They are also less sensitive to photometric variations since they represent (in general) global geometric properties of a scene.

In some cases (particularly when images contain only one semantic feature), the matching-based techniques are more efficient than indexing-based ones since they work directly on the images. However, as they require a sequential scanning of the image database, the system performance is considerably reduced.

After the analysis of an exhaustive sample of the images (the shoeprints , more than 800), we noticed that it is difficult to consider a shoeprint (for about 38% of the shoeprints) as collection of objects (geometric shapes) with some properties and a specific spatial relationships (Figure 8.1). Furthermore, the use of global features which capture global properties of the picture, as the maxima of orientation radiograms [5], are not appropriate because they are designed for grey-level images. It is better to use information spatially distributed over the object shape rather than at localized portions of the shape. Another aspect

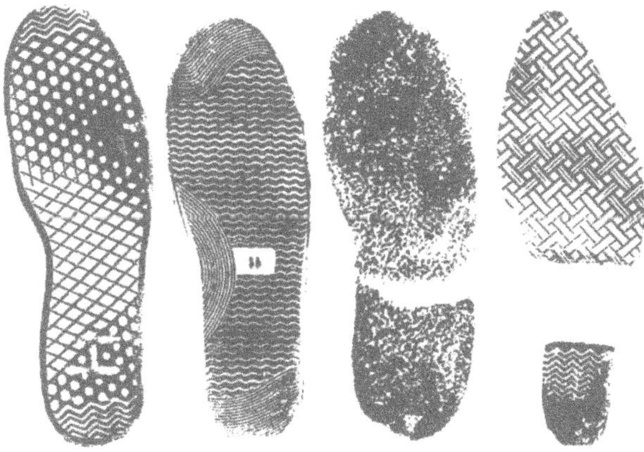

Figure 8.1: Examples of shoeprints.

motivating the proposed approach is that the goal of the retrieval process here is the identification: the images of interest are those corresponding exactly to the query one with tolerance of some degree of noise and artifacts. In the example of the Figure 8.2a, the user is interested by the image of the Figure 8.2b and not by the image of the Figure 8.2c even it is also similar to the query image.

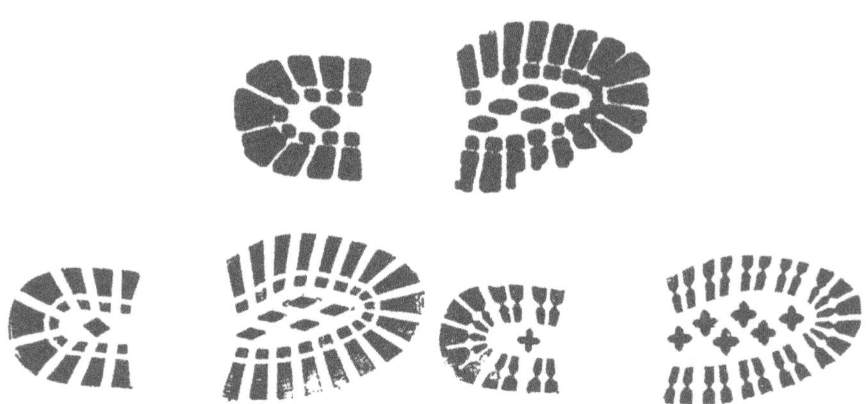

Figure 8.2: Retrieval requirements.

We can distinguish the two kinds of CBIR:

- Similarity oriented retrieval: Among the images of the database, we search images presenting some properties similar to the query image: $I_{db} \cap I_q \neq \emptyset$.
- Identification oriented retrieval: The images of interest are those containing or "equal" to the query image: $I_q \subseteq I_{db} \pm \Delta I$.

Our application falls mainly in the second category.

8.4.2 *The approach*

All the specifications listed above have conducted us to investigate a matching-based approach. The main idea is to match the two images to compare, by a logical operation, and analyse the difference, i.e. after normalizing the query image (same scale, same position and same direction as the database image), apply a logical difference between the two images and analyse the resulting image. As a simple decision criteria, we can say that the database image the more similar to the query one is the one which has the less number of pixels in the resulting image.

The querying algorithm involves three main steps: 1) preprocessing of the query image, 2) logical operation between the query image and the database images, and 3) analysis of the resulting images.

Algorithm:

1st Step: Preprocessing of the query image (I_q)

- Shoeprint localization in the image and cropping.

- Standard orientation: the slope of the line of the least squares ($y = A + B * x$) is used to bring back the shoeprint to a standard orientation,

$$B = \frac{n\sum x_i y_i - (\sum x_i \sum y_i)}{n\sum x_i^2 - (\sum x_i)^2} \tag{8.1}$$

$$A = \frac{\sum y_i - (B\sum x_i)}{n} \tag{8.2}$$

n: number of black pixels, (x_i,y_i): coordinates of the ith black pixel.

- Standard dimensions: As explained above, as the goal of the querying is to retrieve the images that match exactly the query one, this operation doesn't damage the retrieval process since the database images and the query one undergo the same effect of this operation (the same distortion). The database images ($IDB = \{I_{db}\}$) are preprocessed at insertion time (off-line).

2nd Step: Logical operation

- An exclusive OR operation is applied between the query image and each image of the database ($I_d = I_{db} \oplus I_q$) to obtain a set of difference images ($ID = \{I_d\}$).

3rd Step: Analysis of the difference images

- The difference images are analyzed to be ranked by their descending similarity degree to the query image. One simple similarity criteria can be the number of pixels in the difference images. The I_d that has the less number of pixels could correspond to the I_{db} which is the most similar to I_q and so on. A more sophisticated criteria is the analysis of the connected components (eight connectivity) of the difference images. For each I_d, the two following parameters are considered:

  - *NBCC*: the number of the connected components that have the size greater than defined threshold,

  - *SLCC*: the size of the largest connected component.

  The I_{db} the most similar to I_q corresponds to the I_d which has the smallest ($NBCC$, $SLCC$).

8.5 COSIS COMPONENTS

COSIS aims at providing various ways to access and retrieve the database images by offering the three following functionalities:

- an Icon-based Browser,
- an Attribute-based Query Tool,
- and a Matching-based Query Tool.

COSIS is accessible from any platform via its Web User Interface. Its interface can be any WWW navigator with JAVA facilities.

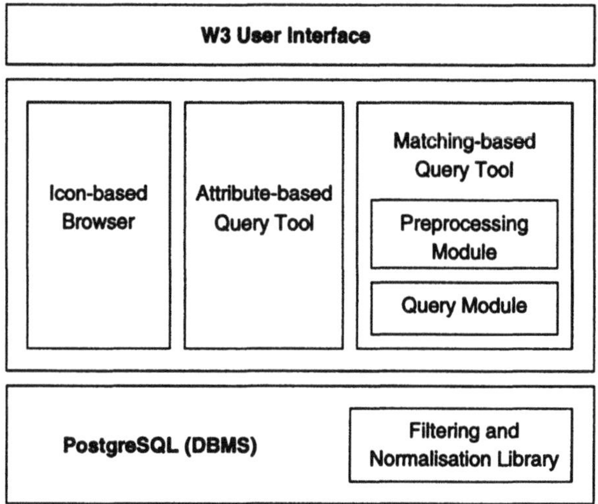

Figure 8.3: COSIS Architecture.

8.5.1 The Icon-based Browser

The originality of the Icon-based Browser is that the user, throw his Web Interface, can configure the display of the icon array (the size and the number of icons horizontally and vertically he wants to see at one time). This is performed without causing any distortion to the images. The images are correctly resized to hold within the icon box defined by the user. By clicking on an icon, the corresponding image is displayed in a new window with the list of its attributes (Figure 8.4). Three types of attributes are possible: `INTEGER`, `TEXT` and `SLIDER`. The last attribute was introduced to express the properties that are difficult to specify manually by a number or a string (subjective properties) such as the image luminosity described by an operator. A SLIDER is materialized by a value (1 to 100) contained between two bounds (ex. min and max, low and high, etc.). The names of the two bounds are given by the Database Administrator at the creation of the image database.

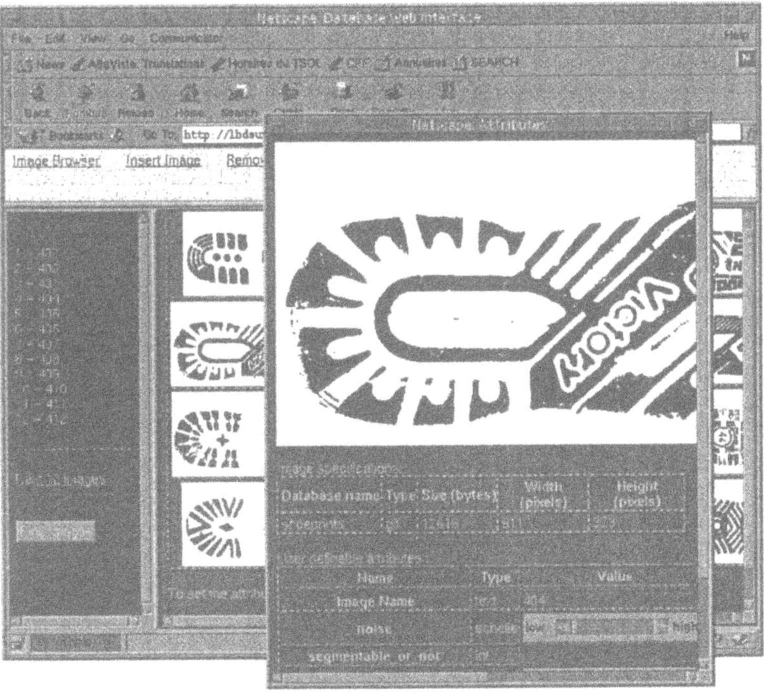

Figure 8.4: The Icon-based Browser.

8.5.2 *The Attribute-based Query Tool*

In the Attribute-based Query Tool, the user is invited to introduce the attributes of the images he is searching. Among the attributes describing the images, for each attribute he is interested by, the user specifies the corresponding value as shown on the Figure 8.5. The result is returned in the Icon-based Browser. As the result consists of a list of images verifying the properties indicated by the user, it would be better viewed by this tool.

8.5.3 *The Matching-based Query Tool*

The Matching-based Query Tool implements the proposed approach presented in section 8.4. The interface uses the file dialog box of the navigator to read the name of the file containing the query image. After the upload of the image, the retrieval process is performed following the algorithm described in the section 8.4 and the result is, as in the Attribute-based Query Tool, returned in the Icon-based Browser. In the example of the Figure 8.6, the query image corresponds to the first image (high-left corner in Figure 8.6b) which has undergone artificially some changes: a spread algorithm, a scaling of factor 0.5 and a rotation of 90 degrees.

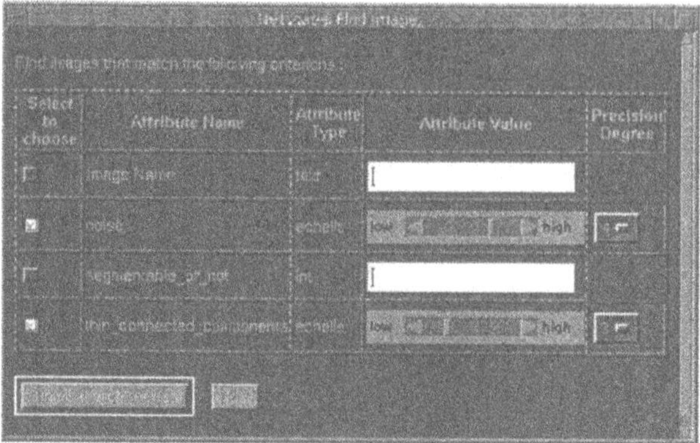

Figure 8.5: Example of attribute-based query.

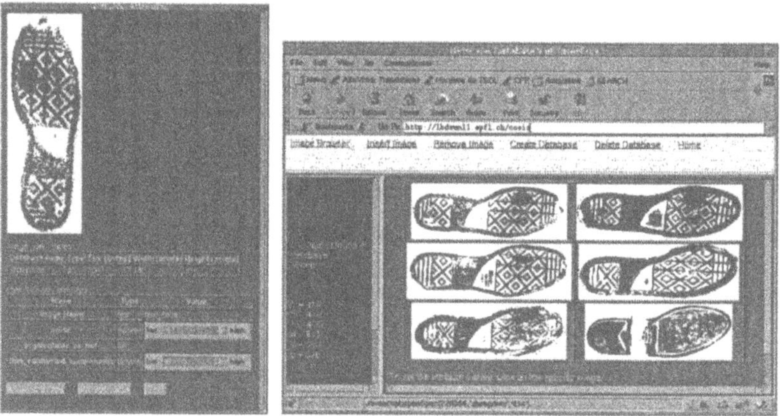

Figure 8.6: Example of matching-based query.

A sample of ten shoeprints is chosen from the database and used as query images in the experiment phase. The images are artificially modified by a graphical editor. They have undergone several changes simultaneously: scaling, rotation and spreading operation (the black uniform regions are split). The Table 8.1 shows the difference between the query image and the returned images for the first images of the result. We clearly see the jump between the first image which is similar to the query one and the rest of the images.

8.5.3.1 Partial shoeprint case. As indicated before, the impressions or the query shoeprints can be only part of shoeprints. The use of the proposed algorithm for these images is obviously not convenient, i.e. we can't convolve a partial object with a complete object as the possible location of the first one

Table 8.1: Difference between the result images and the query one (average).

Result image	*Difference with the query image ($^0/_{00}$)*
1st	12.4
2nd	76.1
3rd	80.2
4th	87.3
5th	89.3
...	...

in the second one is unknown. For the querying by partial shoeprints we have developed a user-driven algorithm. The idea is to identify first the position of the partial shoeprint in an outline of shoeprint, apply the same algorithm as for the complete shoeprint and using binary mask ignore the rest of the shoeprint.

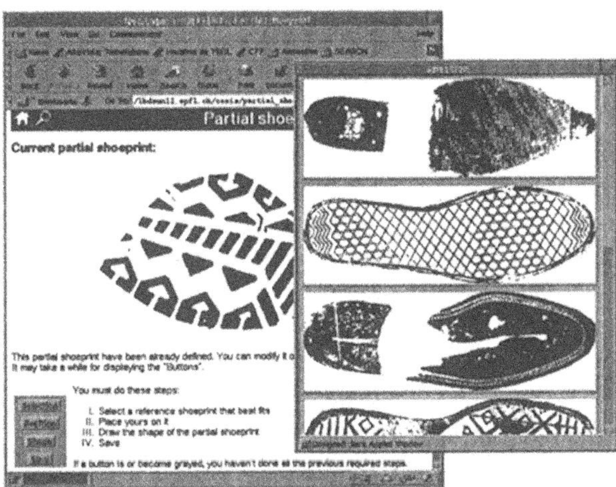

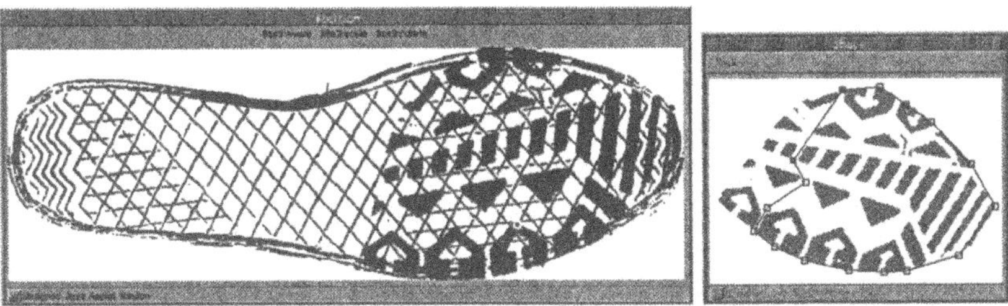

Figure 8.7: Querying with partial shoeprint.

For the position identification, rather than to scan all the database image (pixel per pixel) to detect which region of the image matches the best the partial shoeprint (as in the template-matching approach in image processing which is very time consuming), this task is delegated to the user. This has been decided after discussion with the concerned users who specified us that, in the majority of the cases, the position of the partial shoeprint in the global outline of a shoeprint is known. This choice is also articulated on the following consideration [6]: "let computers do what they do best - computing - and let humans do what they do best - the positioning in this case which is a quick and non-hard task".

Helped by a user-friendly editor, the user selects first the shoeprint (from a list of representative shoeprints) that the outline may correspond to the searched shoeprint by examining the partial shoeprint (Figure 8.7a). In a second step, he puts the partial shoeprint in the right place of the example-shoeprint (Figure 8.7b) after what he delimits the region of the partial shoeprint he is interested by (Figure 8.6c) and finally lets the system perform the retrieval.

As the user positioning of the partial shoeprint is not perfect (not trivial task) the results were not as expected. To remedy to this limitation, the input image is convolved ten times with different displacements from the position specified by the user and the position that responds the best is retained. The results were highly improved but still lack accuracy.

8.6 CONCLUSIONS AND FUTURE WORK

A matching-based approach to the problem of the shoeprint identification has been proposed. The preliminary results of this approach seems to be very encouraging especially for the complete shoeprints. Normalization is a critical stage of the retrieval process, in particular, invariance to rotation. But the experiments led to very satisfactory results. The benefit to using this approach is that it is still robust for the case where some objects of the query shoeprint are fragmented.

The method may be extended to other applications (binary images) having one semantic object (such as the leaf identification) or considering only one spatial disposition of the image objects. It is developed in our prototype system COSIS. COSIS is implemented on top of the object-relational DBMS PostgreSQL, and its interface can be any WWW browser with JAVA facilities. Users of COSIS may access and retrieve shoeprint images in three different ways.

The matching-based query tool takes for about 2mn 20" per retrieval in a database of 200 shoeprints. This has to be improved and the future work will include the design of an indexing-based retrieval method to obtain an efficient two-step approach taking advantage of the two concepts: indexing-based and matching-based: 1) coarse retrieval by an indexing-based method to discard the amount of non-candidate images and 2) refinement of the resulting set of images by a matching-based method to maintain only the effective similar images.

References

[1] S. Ravela and R. Manmatha. *Retrieving Images by Similarity of Visual Appearance.* In the Proc. of the IEEE Workshop on Content Based Access of Image Databases, Puerto Rico, June 20, 1997

[2] Stan Sclaroff, Leonid Taycher and Marco La Cascia. *ImageRover: A content-based image retrieval browser for the world wide web.* Proc. IEEE Workshop on Content-based Access of Image and Video Libraries, 6/1997

[3] Brian Scassellati, Sophoclis Alexopoulos and Myron Flickner. *Retrieving images by 2D shape: a comparison of computation methods with human perceptual judgements.* Proceedings of the International Society for Optical Engineering (SPIE), "Storage and Retrieval for Image and Video Databases II". February, 1994

[4] Eakins J P, Boardman J M and Shields K. *Retrieval of trade mark images by shape feature - the ARTISAN project.* presented at IEE Colloquium on Intelligent Image Databases, London, May 1996

[5] S. Michel, B. Karoubi, J. Bign and S. Corsini. *Orientation radiograms for indexing and identification in image databases.* in European Conference on Signal Processing (Eupsico), Trieste, 10-13 septembre 1996, pp. 1693-1696

[6] Wayne Niblack, R. Barber, W. Equitz, M. Flickner, E. Glasman, D. Petkovic, and P. Yanker. *The QBIC project: Querying images by content using color, texturē, and shape.* In Proc. SPIE Electronic Imaging: Science 8 Technology, San Jose, CA February 1993. SPIE

[7] Christos Faloutsos, Ron Barber, Myron Flickner, Jim Hafner, Wayne Niblack, Dragutin Petkovic and Will Equitz. *Efficient and Effective Querying by Image Content.* Journal of Intelligent Information Systems, 3, 3/4, pp. 231-262, July 1994

[8] Jeffrey R. Bach, Charles Fuller, Amarnath Gupta, Arun Hampapur, Bradley Horowitz, Rich Humphrey, Ramesh Jain, and Chiao-fe Shu. *The Virage Image Search Engine: An open framework for image management.* Virage, Inc., 1996

[9] Amarnath Gupta, Saied Moezzi, Adam Taylor, Shankar Chatterjee, Ramesh Jain, Michael H. Goldbaum, and S. Burgess. *Content-based retrieval of ophthalmological images.* In IEEE International Conference on Image Processing, November 1996

[10] Sirkka Mikkonen, Vesa Suominen, and Pia Heinonen. *Use of footwear impressions in crime scene investigations assisted by computerized footwear collection system.* National Bureau of Investigation, Crime Lab., Finland. Elsevier Science Ireland Ltd, Vol. 82, Issue 1, Sept. 1996

[11] Ch. Belser, M. Ineichen, and P. Pfefferli. *Evaluation of the ISAS system after two years of practical experience in forensic police work.* Zurich Cantonal Police, Forensic Science Division, Switzerland. Elsevier Science Ireland Ltd, Vol. 82, Issue 1, Sept. 1996

[12] Wayne Ashley. *What shoe was that? The use of computerized image database to assist in identification.* Crime Scene Section, Victoria Forensic Science Centre, Forensic Drive, Australia. Elsevier Science Ireland Ltd, Vol. 82, Issue 1, Sept. 1996

[13] Alexandre Girod. *Computerized classification of the shoeprints of burglars soles.* Police Cantonale Neuchteloise, Service d'Identification Judiciaire, Switzerland. Elsevier Science Ireland Ltd, Vol. 82, Issue 1, Sept. 1996

[14] Zeno Geradts and Jan Keijzer. *The image database REBEZO for shoeprints with developments on automatic classification of shoes outsole designs.* National Forensic Science Laboratory of the Ministry of justice in the Netherlands, The Netherlands. Elsevier Science Ireland Ltd, Vol. 82, Issue 1, Sept. 1996.

9 A USER INTERFACE FOR EMERGENT SEMANTICS IN IMAGE DATABASES

Simone Santini[†], Amarnath Gupta[‡], and Ramesh Jain[†]

[†]Visual Computing Laboratory, University of California, San Diego.
{ssantini,jain}@cs.ucsd.edu

[‡]San Diego Supercomputer Center*
gupta@sdsc.edu

Abstract: In this paper, we discuss image semantics and the repercussions that its correct definition have on the design of image databases. We start by rejecting the simplistic notion that the meaning of an image is a function of the objects that the image contains, and show that meaning can only be defined in the context of a query, and can only be revealed in the context of the whole database.

With our definition, meaning is no longer a characteristic of the image that is extracted and compared in the querying process. Meaning is a product of the query process. In particular, meaning is *emergent* from the interaction of the user with the database. This state of affairs makes the interface one of the most crucial components in the database, since it is through the interaction that takes pace in the interface that the meaning of images is extracted. We propose a new model for interfaces that takes into account the necessity for the user to *explore* the database rather than passively asking questions and waiting for answers.

9.1 INTRODUCTION

In this paper we propose a new theory of image semantics, and study some of the consequences of the new definition on image databases. Most current image databases follow a model derived from traditional databases according to which

*This work was partially supported by NSF under grant NSF IRI-9610518

the meaning of a record is a compositional function of the syntactic structure of the record and of the meaning of its elementary constituents. We show that this definition and its obvious extensions are inadequate to capture the real meaning of an image. Even if we could do perfect object recognition (which we can't), this would still not be enough to assign to images a semantics that satisfies the user of the database. The reason for this state of affair is that images are designed to convey a certain message, and the message is concealed in the whole organization of the image, and is not possible to divide it syntactically into smaller parts.

We propose that the meaning of an image is characterized by the following properties:

- It is *contextual.* The meaning of an image depends on the particular conditions under which the query is made, and the particular user that is querying the database.

- It is *differential.* The meaning of an image is apparent if the image is placed in the context of other similar images.

- It is *grounded in action.* The database can establish the meaning of an image based on the actions of the user when the image is presented. In a database situation, the only action allowed to the user is asking a query. Therefore, the meaning of an image will be revealed to the database by interpreting the sequence of queries posed by the user.

These ideas lead to the design of a different type of image database. In our system the semantics is not an intrinsic property of the images, but an *emergent* property of the interaction between the user and the database. The interface between man and machine assumes a preponderant role in this new organization.

This paper is organized as follows. In Section 9.2, we present an analysis of the meaning of records in traditional databases and show that this analysis cannot be extended to the meaning of images. Moreover, we present an alternative analysis of the meaning of an image and show how it depends on the actions of the user and on the relation between an image and the rest of the database. In Section 9.3 we present a formalization of the meaning of an image, and show how the meaning is altered by a certain class of operations on the feature space. In Section 9.4 we introduce informally our database interface based on a *direct manipulation* model. Our interface is directly related to our definition of meaning. In Section 9.5, we formalize the interface introduced in Section 9.4, and define it as a number of operators on three image spaces. In Section 9.6, we present an implementation of this interface in our system El Niño, and present some examples of extraction of meaning from a collection of images. Conclusions and future directions of research are presented in Section 9.7.

9.2 MEANING

In most databases, the meaning of a record is a simple function of the syntactic structure of the record and of the meanings of its components. In other words, the meaning of a record is compositional. We have already pointed out in the previous section that, according to our point of view, the meaning of a stimulus in a given situation must be related to the set of possible actions of an actor in that situation. In a database situation, the only possible actions are asking queries and answering them. Then, if Q is the set of all possible queries, the meaning of a record, or a fragment of a record R, can be defined as a function

$$[R] : Q \rightarrow \{\text{yes}, \text{no}\} \tag{9.1}$$

such that $[R](q) = \{\text{yes}\}$ if the record r satisfies the query q. Compositionality implies that, if a record is produced by a rule like

$$j : R \rightarrow \alpha_1 R_1 \alpha_2 \cdots \alpha_n R_n \alpha_{n+1} \tag{9.2}$$

where α_i are terminal symbols of the record language, and R_i are non terminal symbols, and j is the label of the production rule, then the meaning of R is:

$$[R] = f_j([R_1], [R_2], \dots, [R_n]). \tag{9.3}$$

The meaning of the whole record depends on the production rule and on the meaning of the non terminals on the right side of the production, but not on the syntactic structure of the non terminals.

This property makes the analysis of the meaning of records in traditional databases but, unfortunately, it does not hold for images. As [2] puts it:

> The most naïve way of formulating the problem is: are there iconic sentences and phonemes? Such a formulation undoubtedly stems from a sort of verbocentric dogmatism, but in it ingenuousness it conceals a serious problem.

The problem is indeed important and the answer to the question, as Eco points out, is "no." It is true that we can find certain semantic units in images in the form of objects, but there are two factors that prevent us from equating images and language sentences: objects are not further decomposable using linguistic means, and they do not fully represent the meaning of images.

In language we find the presence of verbal rules and discrete units at all levels. A tree defines the deep structure of a sentence (at least if we follow Chomsky's theory); a grammar transforms the deep structure into a series of words; phonetic rules govern the articulation of phonemes into words. On the iconic level, however, we face a much more complicated situation. We should regard images as "weak" codes [2], as opposed to the "strong" code represented by language. Although some images contain syntactical units in the form of objects, underneath this level it is no longer possible to continue the subdivision.

In addition to this, objects are not sufficient to encode the meaning of an image. Consider the two images of Fig. 9.1, both of which contain essentially

Figure 9.1: Two images responding to the query "image of a woman" with very different semantics.

a single object that can be characterized as "a woman." According to the simplistic interpretation, these two images have the same semantics. However, if looked in the context of our culture and society, they are very different. One of these two images conveys a sense of activity: it is obvious that the woman in the first image has very little time to waste, and is attending some important and urgent business. The second image conveys a certain bucolic tranquillity. We can imagine that the woman in the second image can make an excellent tea

Semantic level beyond the objects are used very often in evocative scenarios, like art and advertising [1]. There is, for instance, a fairly complex theory of the semantics associated with color [5], and with certain representational conventions [3].

The full meaning of an image depends not only on the image data, but on a complex of cultural and social conventions in use at the time and location of the query, as well as on other contingencies of the context in which the user interacts with the database. This leads us to reject the somewhat Aristotelean view that the meaning of an image is an immanent property of the image data. Rather, the meaning arises from a process of interpretation and is the result of the image data and the perceptual processes of the observer. The process of querying the database should not be seen as an operation during which images are filtered based on the illusory pre-existing meaning but, rather, as a process in which meaning is *created* through the interaction of the user and the images.

This example also reveals another aspect of the image-sign: its *conventionality*. Although the contents of an image are not arbitrary in the way in which the Saussurean sign is [12], they are still produced through a convention: they are *cultural* manifestations [2].

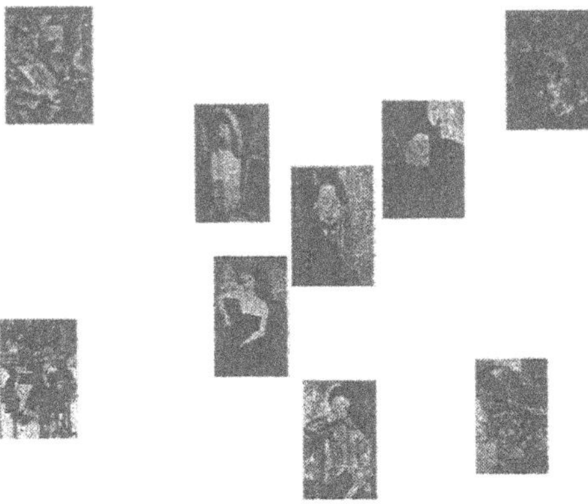

Figure 9.2: A Modigliani portrait placed in a context that suggests "Painting."

Figure 9.3: A Modigliani portrait placed in a context that suggests "Face."

Consider the images of Fig. 9.2. The image at the center is a Modigliani portrait and, placed in the context of other 20th century paintings (some of which are portraits and some of not), suggests the notion of "painting." If we take the same image and place it in the context of Fig. 9.3, the context suggests the meaning "Face."

We are now caught in the middle between two tractable but unattainable opposites. On one hand, images are not linguistic signs that is, their meaning can't be described by a grammar and resolved using standard parsing techniques.

On the other hand, semantics is not a simple function of image contents at all. In particular, we can't hope to find intrinsically determined units of meaning in the image data. The meaning of the image data can only result from the interaction with the user. The user will provide the cultural background in which meaning can be grounded. We call this concept *emergent semantics*. The semantics of an image is not a property of the image per se, but something that emerges from the interaction of the user with the database. This concept has important consequences for our query model and, ultimately, for the architecture of image databases.

In traditional database, the assumption that the meaning is a property of the image leads us to the the query process as a filter. We take all the records, filter out those that don't have the required meaning, and show the others. If meaning is the result of user interaction, this approach is no longer possible. Rather, querying should be seen as a process of *exploration* and *reorganization* of the database.

In this approach, the interface between the user and the database is of primary importance. The interface is no longer the place where questions are asked and answers are obtained, but it is the tool for active manipulation of the database as a whole. We present our approach to interfacing, called *direct manipulation* in Sect. 9.4. Before that, in the next section, we will briefly formalize the definition of meaning that we have outlined in this section.

9.3 MEANING. A FORMAL MODEL

As discussed in the previous section, the meaning of an image is a set of relations between that image and the other images in the database. These relations are expressed as *dissimilarity*, or distance between two images. The distance function in the image space, on the other hand, is determined by the specific query that the user is asking. As we will see more in detail in the next section, a query q endows the feature space in which images are described with a metric $g(q) = \{g_{ij}(q)\}$ which, in turn, can be described by a finite number of parameters ξ^{μ}, $\mu = 1, \ldots, m$. The metric g determines the distance and the relation between images.

Let $\mathcal{I}$ be the set of images in the database, and $\mathcal{Q}$ the set of queries. Image $I \in \mathcal{I}$ is described by a feature vector x_I. Given the metric $g(q)$, the distance between two images is a function

$$f(x_I, x_J; g(q)) = \int_{x_I}^{x_J} \left(\sum_{ij} g_{ij}(q) \dot{x}^i \dot{x}^j \right)^{\frac{1}{2}} dt \tag{9.4}$$

where the integral is computed along a curve $x(t)$ which is a geodesic between x_I and x_J [7]. The semantic difference between images I and J is a function

$$m_{I,J} : Q \to \mathbf{R}^+ : q \mapsto \frac{f(x_I, x_J; \xi^\mu(q))}{f(0, x_I; \xi^\mu(q))} \tag{9.5}$$

We can generalize our definition and make it independent on the particular contents of the database. We can imagine that every point in $\mathbf{R}^n$ contains an image, and define the difference in meaning between points x and y as

$$m_{xy} : Q \to \mathbf{R}^+ : q \mapsto \frac{f(x, x; \xi^\mu(q))}{f(0, x; \xi^\mu(q))} \tag{9.6}$$

The meaning of point $x \in \mathbf{R}^n$ is a function $m_I \in L^2(\mathbf{R}^n \times Q, \mathbf{R}^+)$ defined as:

$$m_x(y, q) = m_{xy}(q) \tag{9.7}$$

and the meaning assignment operator is

$$\mu : \mathbf{R}^n \to L^2(\mathbf{R}^n \times Q, \mathbf{R}^+) : x \mapsto m_x \tag{9.8}$$

With these definitions, the meaning of an image is no longer a "thing" contained in the image or a function of the image data alone. The meaning depends on the whole distribution of images in the database (via the image y in (9.7) and on the metric induced by the current query (via the parameters ξ^μ in (9.6)).

The meaning of an image depends on the query that is being asked. Once a query has been specified, the meaning can be grounded to that query by the operator $\gamma : Q \to L^2\left(L^2(\mathbf{R}^n \times Q, \mathbf{R}^+), L^2(\mathbf{R}^n, \mathbf{R})\right)$ defined as:

$$\gamma(q)(m_x) = f(x, \cdot; \xi^\mu) \tag{9.9}$$

The operator Γ is the grounded meaning assignment. Given a query q, the meaning of an image x with respect to q is

$$\Gamma_{q,x} = \Gamma(q, x) = f(x, \cdot; \xi^\mu(q)) \tag{9.10}$$

We also call this function the *configuration* of the images with respect to the point x and query q.

This definition of meaning is an important step to understand the inadequacy of the traditional query model when applied to image database. Most of the problems come from the different definitions that apply in the two cases. The theory of meaning presented here forms a basis for the concept of *emergent semantics* that will lead to the definition of *direct manipulation interfaces* in the following section.

Semantics is emergent in the sense that it can only be defined with respect to the distribution of images induced by a particular query. Therefore, the process of query making is not just a filter that selects some of the images based on a pre-existing meaning, but a "conversational" activity during which the meaning of the images is created. The following section will introduce informally our interface and, hopefully, make this concept clearer.

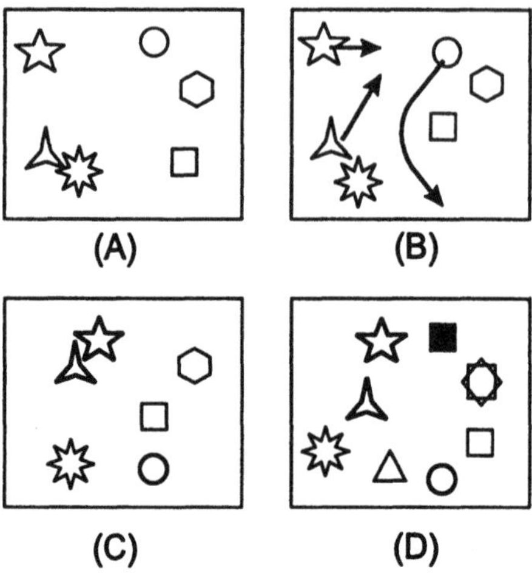

Figure 9.4: Schematic description of an interaction using a direct manipulation interface.

9.4 EMERGENT SEMANTICS: AN INTERFACE PROPOSAL

From the considerations of the previous two sections it appears that the user plays an essential role in determining the meaning of an image in a specific situation and the similarity between two images. In the example of the two women above, the user should provide the context to decide whether the "woman" aspect of the images is prevailing (in which case the two images should be considered fairly similar) or the "business" aspect should prevail (in which case the two images would not be considered similar.)

Based on this principle, we replaced the query-answer model of interaction with *direct manipulation*. In our model, the database gives information about the status of the whole database, rather than just about a few images that satisfy the query. Whenever possible, the user manipulates the image space directly by moving images around, rather than manipulating weights or some other quantity related to the current similarity measure. The manipulation of images in the display causes the creation of a similarity measure that satisfies the relations imposed by the user. Rather than the user trying to understand the properties of the similarity measures used by the database, the database should use the user categorization to develop new similarity measures.

An user interaction using a direct manipulation interface is shown schematically in Fig. 9.4. In Fig. 9.4.A the database proposes a certain distribution of images (represented schematically as colored rectangles) to the user. The distribution of the images reflects the current similarity interpretation of the database. For instance, the green image is considered very similar to the orange one, and the brown to the purple. In Fig. 9.4.B the user moves some images around to reflect his own interpretation of the relevant similarities. The result

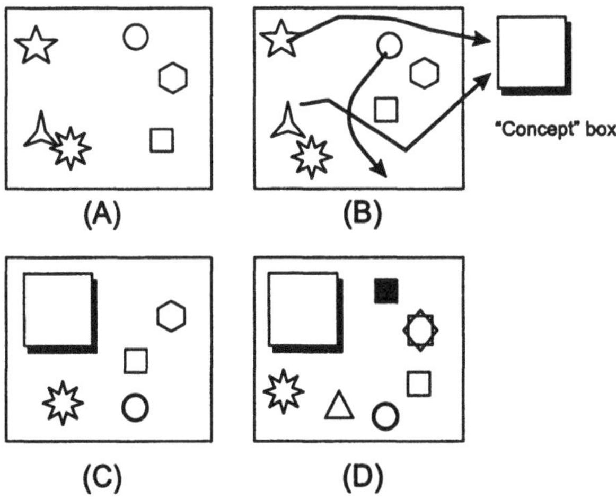

Figure 9.5: Interaction involving the creation of concepts.

is shown in Fig. 9.4.C. According to the user, the red and green images are quite similar to each other, and the brown image is quite different from them.

As a result of the user assessment, the database will create a new similarity measure, and re-order the images, yielding the configuration of Fig. 9.4.D. The red and the green images are in this case considered quite similar (although the green image has been moved from its intended position), and the brown quite different. Note that the result is not a simple rearrangement of the images in the interface. For practical reasons, an interface can't present more than a small fraction of the images in the database. Typically, we display the 100-300 images most relevant to the query. The reorganization consequent the user interaction involves the whole database. Some images will disappear from the display (the purple image in Fig. 9.4.A), and some will appear (the yellow, gray, and cyan images in Fig. 9.4.D).

A slightly different operation on the same interface is the definition of *visual concepts*. In the context of direct manipulation, the term concept has a more restricted scope than in the common usage. A visual concept is simply a set of images that, for the purpose of the current application, can be considered as equivalent or almost equivalent. Images forming a visual concept can be dragged into a "concept box" and, if necessary, associated with some text (the text can be used to retrieve the concept and the images similar to it). The visual concept can be then transformed into an icon and placed on the screen like every other image.

Fig. 9.5 is an example of interaction involving the creation of visual concepts. Fig. 9.5.A contains the answer of the database to a user query. The user considers the red and green images as two instances of a well defined linguistic concept. The user opens a *concept box* and drags the images inside the box. The boxes then used as an icon to replace the images in the display space.

From the point of view of the interface, a concept is a group of images that occupy the same position in the display space. In addition, it is possible to attach meta-data information to a concept. For instance, if a user is exploring an art database, he can create a concept called "medieval crucifixion." The words "medieval" and "crucifixion" can be used to replace the actual images in a query. This mechanism gives a way of integrating visual and non visual queries. If an user looks for medieval paintings representing the crucifixion, she can simply type in the words. The corresponding visual concept will be retrieved from memory, placed in the visual display, and used as a visual query (see below for a more detailed introduction to the use of visual concepts for the integration of meta-data).

It is interesting to note that the distinction between the role of the user and the role of the database is blurred in this model. In very general terms, the role of the database is to *focus* the attention of the user on certain relations that, given the current interpretation of meaning in the database, are deemed relevant. The database does this by displaying a subset of relevant images and their relations in the similarity criterion that is used to define the meaning.

The role of the user is exactly the same. By displacing images in the interface plane, the user focuses the attention on the database on certain relation between images that, given the user interpretation of the meaning of the displayed images, are relevant. Both systems, the database and the user, will adjust their similarity measure based on the response of the other system. The fact that we expect more flexibility from the database rather than from the user (i.e. the database should adapt its similarity measure, while the user has a relatively stable idea of what he/she wants) makes the difference between the two a matter of degree rather than a categorical distinction.

Direct manipulation requires a different and more sophisticated organization of the database:

1. Manipulation of a contextual representation a formal definition of one or more *display spaces*, in which manipulation takes place. The display space should present images in a usable format, while retaining as much as possible the distance induced by the query.

2. The database must accommodate arbitrary (or almost arbitrary) similarity measures, and must automatically determine the similarity measure based on the user interface.

In the following section we describe in greater details the principles behind the design of direct manipulation interfaces. The focus of this paper is in interfaces, so we will not consider point 2 above in any detail. We will just make the necessary assumption about the similarity measures used by the system without explaining how these measures are implemented. The reader should refer to [10, 11] for more details.

9.5 DIRECT MANIPULATION INTERFACE

The direct manipulation interface is composed of three spaces and a number of operators [4]. The operators can be transformations of a space onto itself or transformations from one space to another. The three spaces on which the interface is based are:

- The *Feature space* $\mathcal{F}$. This is the space of the coefficients of a suitable representation of the image. The feature space is a topological space, but not a metric one. There is in general no way to assign a "distance" to a pair of feature vectors.

- The *Query space* $\mathcal{Q}$. When the feature space is endowed with a metric, the result is the query space. The metric of the query space is derived from the user query, so that the distance from the origin of the space to any image defines the "dissimilarity" of that image from the current query.

- The *Display space* $\mathcal{D}$ is a low dimensional space (0 to 3 dimensions) which is displayed to the user and with which the user interacts. The distribution of images in the display space is derived from that of the query space. We will mainly deal with two-dimensional display spaces (as implemented in a window on a computer screen.) For the sake of convenience, we also assume that every image in the visualization space has attached a number of *labels* λ_i drawn from a finite set. Examples of labels are the visual concepts to which an image belongs. The conventional label α is assigned to those images that have been placed in their position by the user.

The feature space is a relatively fixed entity, and is a property of the database. The query space, on the other hand, is created anew with a different metric for every new query. Note that the feature space is not completely immutable. Some of the operators presented in the following operate on the feature space. This is usually done for reasons of convenience (some queries may be faster on some particular transformation of the feature space), a concept not dissimilar from the formation of "stored views" in databases.

9.5.1 *Operators in the Feature Space*

A feature is an attribute obtained applying some image analysis algorithm to the image data. Features are often collected in a feature vector, an immersed in a suitable vector space, although this is not always the case. In El Niño an image is represented by a set of coefficients, each belonging to a relatively low dimensional space [10].

We make a distinction between the raw, unprocessed vector space and spaces that are adapted from it for reasons of convenience. This distinction is not fundamental (all feature spaces are the result of some processing) but it will be useful to describe the operators. The *raw feature space* is the set of complete feature vectors, as they come out of the image analysis algorithm. In many cases, we need to adjust these vectors for the convenience of the database operations. A very common example is dimensionality reduction [8]. In this case, we will say that we obtain a *view* in the feature space. The operators that operate on the feature space are used for this purpose. The most common are:

Projection.. The feature vector is projected on a low dimensional subspace of the raw feature space, obtaining a low dimensional view. Operators like Singular Value Decomposition, projection of Zernike moments, and of statistical moments belong to this class.

Quantization.. These operators are used in non-vector feature spaces like the set of coefficients used in El Niño. In this case, we reduce the dimensionality of the feature space by representing an image with a limited number of coefficients (e.g. 50 or 100). This is done by vector quantization of the image coefficients.

Apply Function.. Applies the function F to all the elements of a set of numbers to create another set of numbers of the same dimension. Filtering operations applied to color histograms belong to this class.

These operators "prepare" the feature space for the database operations. They are not properly part of the interaction that goes on in the interface, since they are applied off-line before the user starts interacting. We have mentioned them anyway for the sake of completeness.

9.5.2 The Query Space

The feature space, endowed with a similarity measure derived from a query, becomes the query space. The "score" of an image is determined by its distance from the origin. The determination of the geometry of the query space is in general quite complicated, and is beyond the scope of this paper. We will just assume that every image is represented as a set of n number (which may or may not identify a vector in an n-dimensional vector space, as discussed in the previous section) and that the query space is endowed with a distance function that depends on m parameters.

The feature sets corresponding to images x and y are represented by x^i and y^i, $i = 1, \ldots n$, and the parameters by ξ^μ, $\mu = 1, \ldots, m$. Also, to indicate a particular image in the database we will use either different Latin letters, as in x^i, y^i or an uppercase Latin index. So x_I is the I-th image in the database ($1 \le I \le N$), and x_I^j is the corresponding feature vector. Since this notation can be quite confusing, we will try to avoid it whenever possible, and use x^i, y^i instead.

The parameters ξ^μ are a representation of the query, and are the values that determine the distance function.

Given the parameters ξ^μ, the distance function in the query space can be written as

$$f : \mathbf{R}^n \times \mathbf{R}^n \times \mathbf{R}^m \to \mathbf{R}^+ : (x^i, y^i, \xi^\mu) \mapsto f(x^i, y^i; \xi^\mu) \tag{9.11}$$

with $f \in L^2(\mathbf{R}^n \times \mathbf{R}^n \times \mathbf{R}^m, \mathbf{R}^+)$. Depending on the situation, we will write $f_\xi(x^i, y^i)$ in lieu of $f(x^i, y^i; \xi^\mu)$.

As stated in the previous section, the feature space per se is topological but not metric. Rather, its intrinsic properties are characterized by the functional

$$L : \mathbf{R}^m \to L^2(\mathbf{R}^n \times \mathbf{R}^n, \mathbf{R}^+) \tag{9.12}$$

which associates to each query ξ^μ a distance function:

$$L(\xi^\mu) = f(\cdot, \cdot; \xi^\mu). \tag{9.13}$$

A query q, characterized by a vector of parameters ξ^μ, can also be seen as an operator q which transforms the feature space into the query space. If L is the characteristic functional of the feature space, then $qL = L(\xi)$ is the metric of the query space.

Once the feature space $\mathcal{F}$ space has been transformed into the metric query space Q, other operations are possible [4], like:

Distance.. Given a feature set x^i, return its distance from the query:

$$D(x^i) = f(0, x^i; \xi^\mu) \tag{9.14}$$

Select by Distance.. Return all feature sets that are closer to the query than a given distance:

$$S(d) = \{x^i : D(x^i) \leq d\} \tag{9.15}$$

***k*-Nearest Neighbors..** Return the k images closest to the query

$$N(k) = \{x^i : |\{y^i : D(y^i) < D(x^i)\}| < k\} \tag{9.16}$$

It is necessary to stress again that these operations are not defined in the feature space $\mathcal{F}$ since that space is not endowed with a metric. Only when a query is defined does a metric exist.

9.5.3 The Display Space

The display operator ϕ projects image x^i on the screen position X^Ψ, $\Psi = 1, 2$ in such a way that

$$d(X^\Psi, Y^\Psi) \approx f(x^i, y^i; \xi^\mu) \tag{9.17}$$

In El Niño, we use a simple elastic model to determine the position of images in the display space. First, we query the database so as to determine the P images closer to the query. The display space will be concerned only with these images. In general, we use $100 \leq P \leq 300$. A few hundred images are in general sufficient to give the user a fair idea of the distribution of images, and don't clutter the display with irrelevant information. Let $f(x_I^k, x_J^k; \xi^\mu)$, $I, J \leq P$ be the distance between the I-th and the J-th image in the database, with $0 \leq f(x_I^k, x_J^k; \xi^\mu) \leq 1$. Also, let X_I^Ψ be the coordinates of the I-th image in the display space, and $d(X_I^\Psi, Y_I^\Psi)$ the Euclidean distance between images I and J in the display space. We imagine to attach a spring of length $d(X_I^\Psi, Y_I^\Psi)$ between images I and J. In a given configuration $\{X_I^\Psi, i = 1, \ldots, P\}$ the energy of the system is proportional to:

$$E = \sum_{i,j=1}^{Q} \left(d(X_I^\Psi, Y_I^\Psi) - f(x_I^k, x_J^k; \xi^\mu)\right)^2 \tag{9.18}$$

We can use standard optimization techniques to solve this optimization problem and find the optimal configuration of the display space. More sophisticated methods can be used depending on the situation. The result is an operator that we write:

$$\Psi(x_I^k; f_\xi) = (X_I^\Psi, \emptyset). \tag{9.19}$$

The parameter f_ξ reminds us that the projection that we see on the screen depends on the distribution of images in the query space which, in turn, depends on the query parameters ξ^μ. The notation $(X_I^\Psi, \emptyset)$ means that the image x_I is placed at the coordinates x_I^Ψ in the display space, and that there are no labels attached to it (that is, the image is not anchored at any particular location of the screen, and does not belong to any particular visual concept).

A configuration of the display space is obtained by applying the display operator to the whole query space:

$$\phi(\mathcal{Q}) = \phi(\mathcal{F}; f_\xi) = \left\{(X_I^\Psi, \aleph_I)\right\} \tag{9.20}$$

where $\aleph_I$ is the set of labels associated to image I. As we said before, it is impractical to display the whole database. More often, we display only a limited number P of image. Formally, this can be done by applying the P-nearest neighbors operator to the space $\mathcal{Q}$:

$$\phi(N(P)(\mathcal{Q})) = \phi(N(P)(\mathcal{F}; f_\xi)) = \left\{(X_I^\Psi, \aleph_I), i = 1, \ldots, P\right\} \tag{9.21}$$

where $\aleph_I$ is the set of labels associated to the I-th images. The display space $\mathcal{D}$ is the space of such configurations.

With these definitions, we can describe the operators that manipulate the display space.

The Place Operator. The place operator moves an image from one position of the display space to another, and attaches a label α to the images to "glue" it to its new position. The operator that places the I-th image in the display is $\zeta_I : \mathcal{Q} \to \mathcal{Q}$ with:

$$\zeta_I \left\{(X_J^\Psi, \aleph_J)\right\} = \left(\left\{(X_J^\Psi, \aleph_J)\right\} - \left\{(X_I^\Psi, \aleph_I)\right\}\right) \cup \left\{(\tilde{X}_I^\Psi, \aleph_I \cap \alpha)\right\} \tag{9.22}$$

where $\tilde{X}$ is the position given to the image by the user.

Visual Concept Creation. A visual concept is is a set of images that, conceptually, occupy the same position in the display space and are characterized by a set of labels. Formally, we will include in the set of labels the keywords associated to the concept as well as the identifiers of the images that are included in the concept. So, if the concept contains images $I_1, \ldots, I_k$, the set of labels is

$$\lambda = (W, \{I_1, \ldots, I_k\}) \tag{9.23}$$

where W is the set of keywords. We call Λ the set of concept, and we will use the letter λ to represent a concept.

The creation of a concept is an operator $\kappa : \mathcal{D} \to \Lambda$ defined as:

$$\kappa\left\{(X_J^\Psi, \aleph_J)\right\} = W \cup \{I_1, \ldots, I_k\} = \lambda \tag{9.24}$$

Visual Concept placement. The insertion of a concept in a position Z^Ψ of the display space is defined as the action of the operator $\eta : \Lambda \times \mathbf{R}^2 \times \mathcal{D} \to \mathcal{D}$ defined as:

$$\eta\left(\Lambda, Z^\Psi, \{(X_J^\Psi, \aleph_J)\}\right) = \left(\{(X_J^\Psi, \aleph_J)\} - \{(X_{I_k}^\Psi, \aleph_J)\}\right) \cup \left\{Z^\Psi, \alpha \cup \lambda\right\} \tag{9.25}$$

Meta-data Queries. Visual concepts can be used to create visual queries based on semantic categories. Suppose a user enters a set of words A. It is possible to define the distance from the set A to a visual concept λ using normal information retrieval techniques [9]. Let $d(A, \lambda)$ be such a distance. Similarly, it is possible to determine the distance between two concepts $d(\lambda_1, \lambda_2)$. Then the textual query A can be transformed in a configuration of the display space

$$\left\{X_I^\Psi, \alpha \cup \lambda_I\right\} \tag{9.26}$$

where

$$\left[\sum_\Psi \left(X_I^\Psi\right)^2\right]^{\frac{1}{2}} \approx d(A, \lambda_I) \tag{9.27}$$

and

$$\left[\sum_\Psi \left(X_I^\Psi - X_J^\Psi\right)^2\right]^{\frac{1}{2}} \approx d(\lambda_I, \lambda_J) \tag{9.28}$$

In other words, we can use the distance between the concepts and the query, as well as the distances between pairs of concepts, to place the corresponding images in the display space, thus transforming the textual query in a visual query.

9.5.4 *Query Creation*

When the user moves images around the interface, he or she imposes a certain number of constraints of the form $d(x^I, y^I) = d_{xy}$. Assume that the user takes a set T of images and places them in certain positions of the interface, so that, for all pairs $(x,y) \in T \times T$, the value d_{xy} is given. The query can then be determined by solving the system of equations:

$$f(x^i, y^i; \xi^\mu) = d_{xy} \quad x, y \in T \tag{9.29}$$

in the unknown ξ^μ.

Depending on the number of images that the user has placed (that is, the number of elements in T) the system (9.29) can be under-determined or over-determined. Even if the system is under-determined, the particular form of the function f might prevent us to find an exact solution. In these cases, it is useful to determine a least squares solution.

In any case, the creation of a query can be seen as an operator

$$\chi : \mathcal{D} \to \mathbf{R}^m : \{(X_I^\Psi, \aleph_I)\} \mapsto \xi^\mu. \tag{9.30}$$

In general, we require that a query depends only on the images that have been anchored by the user, so, if $C = \{(X_I^\Psi, \aleph_I)\}$ and $C' = \{(X_I^\Psi, \aleph_I) \in C : \alpha \in \aleph_I\}$ we have $\chi(C) = \chi(C')$.

9.6 THE INTERFACE AT WORK

We have used these principles in the design of the interface for our database system El Niño. As we mentioned in the previous section, the interface that we described requires the support of a suitable engine and data model. In particular, the engine must be able to

- Understand the placement of images in the display space.
- Be able to create a similarity criterion "on the fly" based on the placement of samples in the display space.

The engine that we use in El Niño satisfies these requirements using a purely geometric approach. The feature space is generated with a multi-resolution decomposition of the image. Depending on the transformation group that generates the decomposition, the space can be embedded in different manifolds. If the transformation is generated by the two dimensional affine group, then the space has dimensions x, y, and scale, in addition to the three color dimensions R, G, B. In this case the feature space is diffeomorphic to $\mathbf{R}^6$.

In other applications, we generate the transform using the phase space of the Weyl-Heisenberg group [10], obtaining transformation kernels which are a generalization of the Gabor filters [6]. In this case, in addition to the six dimensions above we have the direction θ of the filters, and the feature space is diffeomorphic to $\mathbf{R}^6 \times S^1$.

An image is represented as a set of coefficients in this six (or seven) dimensional space. The raw feature space of El Niño is the space of such sets of coefficients. Each image is represented by a set of about 30,000 coefficients. In order to reduce the memory occupation of each image and make the distance

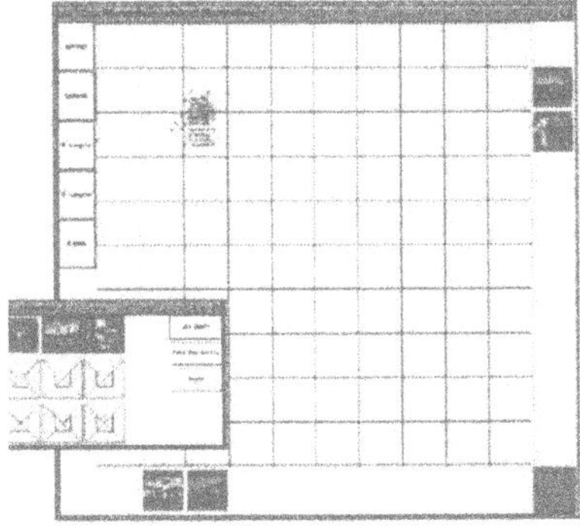

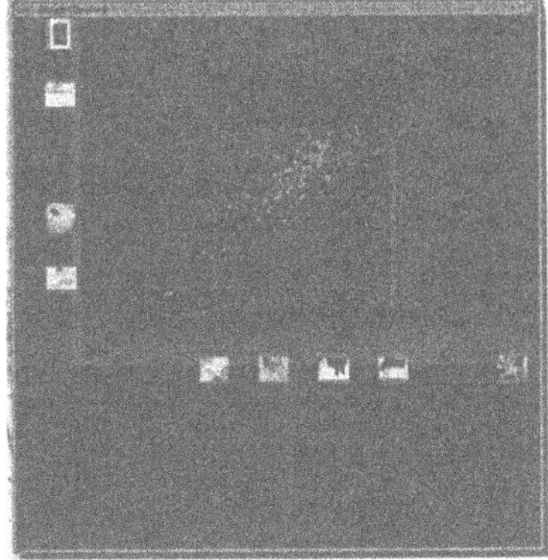

Figure 9.6: Two and three dimensional embodiments of the display space.

computations more efficient, we create a *view* in this space by a vector quantization operation that reduces an image to a number of coefficients between 50 and 100 (depending on the particular implementation of El Niño).

The query space is created endowing the view on the feature space with a metric. One of the characteristics of El Niño is that the metric is not a simple Minkowski metric, but a more general Riemann metric. This fact allows us to create endless similarity criteria based on the query choices of the user. The description of the engine of El Niño goes beyond the scope of this paper. The interested reader can find a full description in [10].

The display space in El Niño can be visualized using a number of two-dimensional displays, and some three dimensional displays. Fig. 9.6 shows a two dimensional display of El Niño. The user can zoom in and out, and see a sample of the images in the display along the two axes (at higher magnification the dots inside the display also are displayed as images). The small window on the left is a visual concept being formed. Other possible displays include a "checkerboard" display, in which images are displayed in a fixed grid a three dimensional display (Fig. 9.6.b).

To give an example of a typical interaction session with El Niño, consider a query in which we are looking for some old cars. At the beginning our ideas are quite fuzzy, and we set to explore the database. We have a few cars in our "labeled" subset of the database, and we start defining the concept of car as in Fig. 9.7. The result of a query using this concept is shown in Fig 9.8 This answer is not satisfactory, but it contains the seeds from which we can proceed towards more interesting areas of the image space. We select a few of the cars in the display and add them to the concept of car. We go through the stage of Fig. 9.9 until, at the end of our query, our concept of "car" has become that of Fig. 9.10. During this interaction, our idea of what would be an answer to the

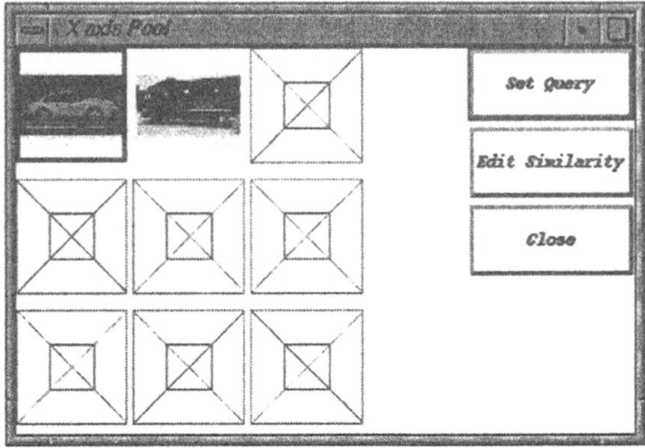

Figure 9.7: The initial concept of car that we use.

Figure 9.8: The result of a query with our first "car" concept.

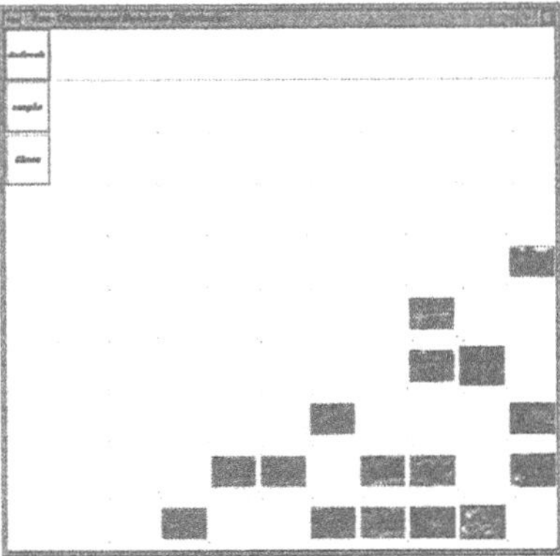

Figure 9.9: The result of a query with our second "car" concept.

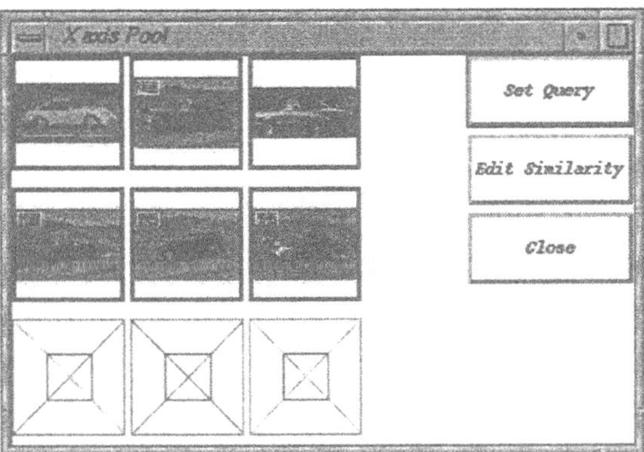

Figure 9.10: The final concept of car after the interaction.

query changed continuously as we learned what the database had to offer, and redefined our goals based on what we saw.

9.7 CONCLUSIONS

In this paper we have defined a new model of interface for image databases. The motivation for the introduction of this model comes from an analysis of the semantics of images in the context of an image database. In traditional databases, the meaning of a record is a function from the set of queries to a set of truth values. The meaning of an image, on the other hand, is a function from the Cartesian product of the feature space times the set of queries to the positive real values. This definition embodies the observation that the meaning of an image can only be revealed by the comparison of an image with other images in the feature space.

These observations led us to define a new paradigm for database interfaces in which the role of the user is not just asking queries and receiving answers, but a more active *exploration* of the image space. The meaning of an image is *emergent*, in the sense that it is a product of the dual activities of the user and the database mediated by the interface.

We have proposed a model of interface for active exploration of image spaces. In our interface, the role of the database is to *focus* the attention of the user on certain relation that, given the current database interpretation of image meanings, are relevant. The role of the user is exactly the same: by moving images around, the user focuses the attention of the database on certain relations that, given the user interpretation of meaning, are deemed important.

Our future plans are to include different access modalities to the data into a single interface. Images accessed by keywords can be placed in the interface just like images accessed by visual features. Also, we plan on building more perceptually comprehensive interface, in which aural and haptic clues play are used to supplement visual clues.

References

[1] Caliani, M., Pala, P., and Del Bimbo, A. (1998). Computer analysis of TV spots: The semiotics perspective. In *Proceedings of the IEEE International Conference on Multimedia Computing and Systems, Austin, TX.*

[2] Eco, U. (197). *A Theory of Semiotics.* Indiana University Press, Bloomington.

[3] Gombrich, E. H. (1965). *Art and Illusion. A study in the pshychology of pictorial representation.* Pantheon Books.

[4] Gupta, A., Santini, S., and Jain, R. (1997). In search of information in visual media. *Communications of the ACM*, 40(12):35–42.

[5] Itten, J. (1961). *The art of Color.* Reinhold Pub. Corp., New York.

[6] Kalisa, C. and Torrésani, B. (1993). N-dimensional affine Weyl-Heisenberg wavelets. *Annales de L'Instut Henri Poincarè, Physique thèorique*, 59(2):201–236.

[7] Lovelock, D. and Rund, H. (1975, 1989). *Tensors, Differential Forms, and Variational Principles.* Dover Books on Advanced Mathematics, 63. Dover Publications, Inc, New York.

[8] Ravi Kanth, K., Agrawal, D., and Singh, A. (1998). Dimensionality reduction for similarity searching in dynamic databases. In *Proceedings of the 1998 ACM SIGMOD conference*, pages 166–175.

[9] Riloff, E. and Hollaar, L. (1996). Text databases and information retrieval. *ACM Computing Surveys*, 28(1):133–135.

[10] Santini, S. (1998). *Explorations in Image Databases.* PhD thesis, Univerity of California, San Diego.

[11] Santini, S. and Jain, R. (1997). Similarity is a geometer. *Multimedia Tools and Applications*, 5(3). available at http://www-cse.ucsd.edu/users/ssantini.

[12] Saussure, F. D. (1960). *Cours de linguistique generale.* Payot, Paris.

10 DESIGN, IMPLEMENTATION, AND EVALUATION OF TOOMM: A TEMPORAL OBJECT-ORIENTED MULTIMEDIA DATA MODEL

Vera Goebel[†], Ilan Eini[‡], Ketil Lund[†], Thomas Plagemann[†]

[†]University of Oslo, UniK - Center for Technology at Kjeller
{goebel,ketillu,plageman}@unik.no

[‡]Avenir ASA, Oslo
ilan.eini@avenir.no

Abstract: Multimedia database systems (MMDBSs) must be able to handle efficiently time dependent and time independent data, and to support Quality-of-Service. Based on the requirements of the DEDICATION project, i.e., building a MMDBS for asynchronous distance education, we have designed the data model TOOMM (Temporal Object-Oriented MultiMedia data Model). TOOMM is a novel data model that integrates temporal concepts into an object-oriented multimedia data model. TOOMM supports three time dimensions: valid time, transaction time, and a new time dimension specifically tailored for multimedia data types called *play time*. In this paper, we describe the concepts, implementation, and evaluation of TOOMM for the distance education scenario of the University of Oslo.

10.1 INTRODUCTION

Distributed multimedia applications like News-on-Demand, digital libraries, and asynchronous interactive distance education will be an important part of the future information society. These applications must be able to handle efficiently complex, continuous, and time dependent data types like video and audio as well as time independent data types like integer and text. The management of the complex structures of multimedia objects is one of the most challenging research issues for multimedia database management systems

(MMDBMSs). Today, object-oriented database systems (OODBSs) are used to handle multimedia data types (MMDTs). However, current object-oriented data models are not able to model all the temporal and spatial aspects of complex multimedia objects [18, 21]. Both these aspects are essential for presenting multimedia objects. Therefore, several features such as synchronization mechanisms, temporal and spatial relationships between objects, decomposition and re-combination of objects, and corresponding specification languages need further research.

In order to overcome the lack of an appropriate data model, we have developed a temporal object-oriented multimedia data model called TOOMM (Temporal Object-Oriented MultiMedia data Model). In addition to existing temporal concepts of transaction and valid time, TOOMM supports the so-called *play time* dimension. The play time dimension places multimedia data elements, such as video frames or audio samples, into a temporal structure for multimedia presentations. Furthermore, the *logical data model*, i.e., classes (object types) and instances (objects) containing multimedia data, and the *presentation model*, i.e., specifying how multimedia data should be presented, are separated in TOOMM. This separation is in accordance with the basic data modeling concept of independence between the way the data is stored in the database, and how it is presented to the user. The advantage of this separation and explicit combination is that multiple specialized presentations based on the same multimedia data can be created without the need for replication.

The remainder of this paper is structured as follows: Section 10.2 describes the distance education scenario and related projects at UniK in order to illustrate the usage and benefits of TOOMM in MMDBSs. Section 10.3 presents background and related work. In Section 10.4, the concepts of TOOMM are presented. In Section 10.5, we summarize the most important implementation issues. Section 10.6 presents an evaluation of TOOMM for the distance education scenario presented in Section 10.2. Section 10.7 concludes this paper and gives an outlook on future work.

10.2 DISTANCE EDUCATION SCENARIO

10.2.1 Synchronous Distance Learning

Distance education refers to all types of studies in which students are separated by space and/or time. The electronic classrooms [3] at the University of Oslo overcome separation in space by exchanging digital audio, video, and whiteboard information between two sites of the University of Oslo and one of the University of Bergen. Since 1993, the electronic classrooms are regularly used for teaching graduate level courses as well as for research on Quality-of-Service (QoS) support in distributed multimedia systems [17]. The main parts of each electronic classroom are:

- **Electronic whiteboard:** at each site there is at least one electronic whiteboard (100") that is used to display lecture notes and transparencies written in Hypertext Markup Language (HTML) format. Transparencies consume about 200 KB (per transparency) and must be kept in the buffer while displayed at the whiteboard. When a section is displayed, the lecturer can write, draw, and erase comments on it by using a light-pen.

- **Document camera and scanner:** can be used from the whiteboard application to capture the contents of printed materials, e.g., a page of a book, and present it on the whiteboard.

- **Audio system:** microphones are mounted evenly distributed on the ceiling in order to capture the voice of all the participants. Audio is PCM encoded and is digitized using a 16 bits/16 MHz sampler, which results in a constant data stream of 32 KB/s.

- **Video system:** one camera focuses on the lecturer, and two further cameras focus on the students. A video switch selects the camera corresponding to the microphone with the loudest input signal. Two monitors are placed in the front, and two monitors are placed in the back of each classroom displaying the incoming and outgoing video information. A H.261 codec is currently used to digitize and (de-)compress video data.

Today, only synchronous teaching is supported, that means the lectures are transferred in real-time over an ATM-based network to the peer classroom(s) and vice versa. Consequently, all students have to be physically present in one of the classrooms during a lecture.

10.2.2 Asynchronous Distance Learning

In the DEDICATION (Database Support for Distance Education) project at UniK, we extend the functionality of today's electronic classroom to support asynchronous teaching by using a MMDBS to store the lectures for graduate level courses. To allow maximum flexibility, all transparencies and scanned images that are used in the lecture, the interactions with the whiteboard in the classrooms, as well as video and audio streams from the different classrooms are separately stored in a MMDBS. The separate modeling and storing of different MMDTs enables independent retrieval of data, e.g., reading the transparencies of the first hour of a certain lecture. Furthermore, the entire lecture, i.e., all multimedia data types and according data elements, can be reproduced: audio and video streams from all classrooms are continuously retrieved and their presentation to the user is synchronized with retrieval and presentation of transparencies and interactions with the whiteboard.

In such a MMDBS, students are able to retrieve lectures at any time. They may search for interesting topics, and play back only parts of lectures. Depending on the student's end-system, network connections, and requirements of the students, different QoS specifications have to be supported. For example, one student might work at home and is connected via ISDN, i.e., 2 x 64 Kbit/s, to the server. The student has followed the lecture, has a hardcopy of the transparencies, and wants only to recapitulate the explanations of the teacher. Thus, the student retrieves the audio stream of the particular lecture with maximum quality and the video stream with low quality, i.e., low frame rate. Another student might have missed the lecture and retrieves the full lecture, i.e., audio, video, whiteboard, and document camera, in maximum quality from a terminal that is connected via Fast Ethernet, i.e., 100 Mbit/s, to the server.

10.3 BACKGROUND AND RELATED WORK

In this Section, we shortly survey the most important concepts and approaches for temporal and multimedia DBSs which provide the basis and related work for TOOMM.

10.3.1 Temporal Data Models

Conventional temporal data model concepts [14] such as temporal dimensions, temporal domains, multiple granularities, and temporal relationships are the temporal basis of MMDTs. TOOMM provides a formal temporal framework for MMDTs solving many problems related to time management of multimedia presentations. For temporal DBSs, there exist many suggestions to realize temporal capabilities in the data model for relational DBSs [22] and OODBSs [4, 8, 19]. Multimedia data models such as SGML/HyTime [15] and Mediadoc [12] are more concerned with MMDTs and do not have the precise semantics of time, like pure temporal data models. A number of scheduling and synchronization techniques have been introduced for authoring multimedia presentations such as interval-based, axes-based, control flow-based, and event-based models. TOOMM includes many parts of these models and combines their advantages.

Various models of time have been proposed, e.g., discrete, dense, or continuous time [11, 14]. The time values of time dimensions can either be discrete or continuous. The discrete time domain model assumes that each time value in the time domain is mapped to a natural number, and for any member of a discrete time domain, there is a unique successor and predecessor. MMDTs like video and audio are called time dependent data types since the abstractions of the real world they model are continuous. However, when we capture video or audio data, we only capture data for discrete instants of time.

In the real world, we assume generally that there is only one time dimension. In the context of temporal DBSs [6], two time dimensions are of general interest: *valid* and *transaction time*. Valid and transaction time are orthogonal, meaning they can coexist in a DBS (bitemporal DBS) without interfering with each other while increasing expressiveness. Valid time denotes the time a fact is true in reality. Transaction time is the time during which the fact is stored in the database.

Conventional DBSs support time values as date and time of the day. Dealing with time values of different granularities creates certain problems such as how to handle the semantics of operations with operands of different granularities, and how to convert one granularity into another. Another important issue is the choice of the master time unit. All other time value granularities must be related to the master time unit either directly or transitively by mapping functions [9].

10.3.2 Multimedia Data Models

Many of the earlier works on MMDBSs are done in the context of multimedia document systems or as multimedia extensions for existing DBSs [7, 18]. More recent works on multimedia modeling mostly concentrate on developing models for dynamic elements of multimedia data presentations associated with continuous multimedia data. Three of the most relevant related multimedia data models for TOOMM are AMOS [1, 23], SGML/HyTime [15], and LMDM [20]. These systems support conventional alphanumeric data types (e.g., integer and real), *time independent data types* (like images, graphics, and text), and *time dependent data types* where we distinguish between two categories based on temporal characteristics: (1) *streams*, i.e., arrays of data elements that are intended for sequential presentation (e.g., audio, speech, and video), and (2) *computer generated multimedia data* (CGM), i.e., sets of operation specifications that a computer can execute over a period of time (e.g., animations and music).

An important aspect in all MMDBSs which is not sufficiently solved today is synchronization. Synchronization refers to the temporal relationships within multimedia objects and between multimedia objects. A presentation object can contain several multimedia objects which must be synchronized when multiple MMDTs are presented in parallel. Synchronization must be examined on many different levels. There exist two types of synchronization: (1) *intra-object synchronization*, i.e., temporal relationships within a time dependent multimedia object, and (2) *inter-object synchronization*, i.e., synchronization between multimedia objects.

In temporal reasoning, relationships between time intervals have been identified [2]. Little and Ghafoor [13] expand these temporal relationships to include n-ary relationships, although they are only of the same type. However, temporal relationships between objects of different types are additionally needed.

In a complex multimedia presentation, the start and stop times of the playback interval of one object can depend on the start and stop times of another object. When dealing with user interactions, this is especially useful since it takes into account operations and interrupts with unpredictable duration. Start and stop times of objects can either be expressed as delays relative to the global start time of the presentations, or as delays relative to other presentation objects. If events like start of a video playback are timestamped with delays relative to the global presentation start time, then after an edit operation that shortens or extends the entire multimedia presentation, the timestamps following the edit will be incorrect. Using temporal relationships the actual playback time is calculated at run-time.

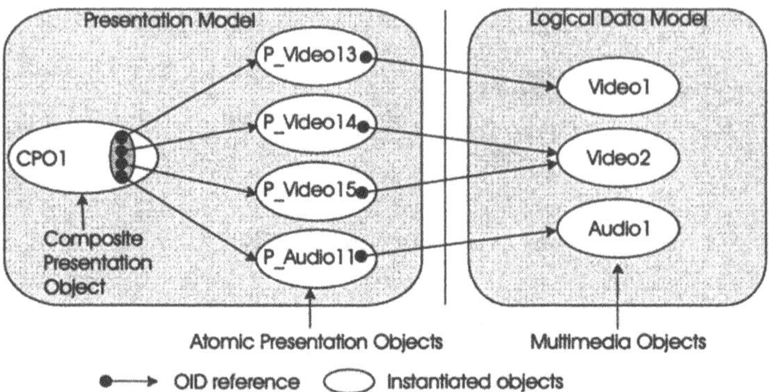

Figure 10.1: Relationships between logical data model and presentation model.

10.4 CONCEPTS OF TOOMM

TOOMM is a novel data model that integrates temporal concepts into an object-oriented multimedia data model. Objects in TOOMM comprise the properties of traditional object-oriented data models and three different time dimensions: valid time, transaction time, and play time. The play time dimension places *logical data units* (LDUs) of multimedia data, such as frames or audio samples, into a temporal structure for multimedia presentations. Furthermore, TOOMM is based on the following two principles:

- *Separation of multimedia data from its presentation specification:* This principle is in accordance with the basic data modeling concept of independence between the way data is stored in the database, and how it is presented to the user. Objects containing multimedia data are instances of object types from the logical data model. Objects instantiated from the presentation model specify how multimedia data should be presented. We differentiate between *atomic presentation objects* (APOs), that describe the presentation of single multimedia objects, and *composite presentation objects* (CPOs), that contain collections of presentation objects and metadata [5, 10], and support the correctly synchronized playback of multimedia data. Fig. 10.1 gives an example how the objects from the logical data model and presentation model are related. Summarizing, this principle supports multiple specialized presentations that are based on the same multimedia data which is only stored once in the MMDBS.

- *Separation of multimedia data from its temporal information:* Time dependent multimedia data include inherently temporal information, like a video that has a particular frame rate. In TOOMM, we detach the temporal information from the data, e.g., video frames, in order to enable reuse of data in contexts with other timing constraints. For example, a video frame might also be used as an image in another multimedia presentation. Therefore, each video frame object - or generally each MMDT object - is associated with a timestamp via a *time associator* (TA) *object*. Fig. 10.2 illustrates the schema definition of a single video object.

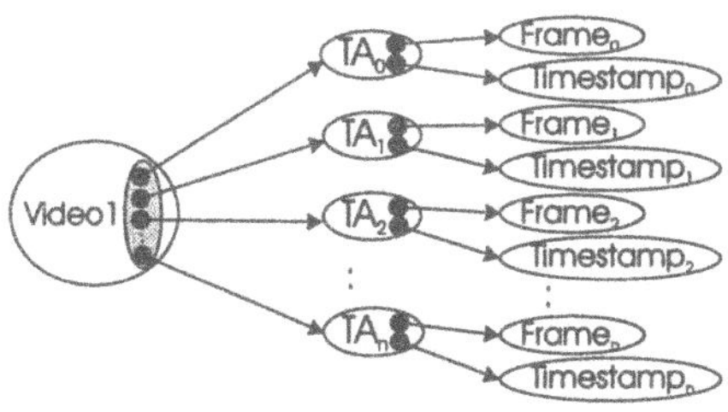

Figure 10.2: Modeling a single video object in TOOMM.

The following sections give a detailed description of the main elements of TOOMM, i.e., logical data model, play time, and presentation model.

10.4.1 Logical Data Model

The logical data model consists of an extensible class hierarchy of the most common MMDTs such as video, audio, animation, music as well as basic abstract data types (ADTs). In this hierarchy, we differentiate between the following three main categories of MMDTs:

- *play time independent multimedia data types* (PTI_MMDTs),
- *play time dependent multimedia data types* (PTD_MMDTs), and
- *components of PTD_MMDTs,* which are for simplicity denoted later on as *components.*

ADTs that have static appearance during their presentation are said to belong to the PTI_MMDT category (see Fig. 10.3). Basic ADTs such as integer, real, boolean, character, and long also belong to the PTI_MMDT category. Additionally, TOOMM supports PTI_MMDTs with temporal characteristics: each PTI_MMDT can be extended with valid time and transaction time dimensions. Such an extension of time independent ADTs and PTI_MMDTs with temporal characteristics enables TOOMM to model data history and versions.

Unlike PTI_MMDTs, PTD_MMDTs comprise all types that have dynamic appearance during their presentation. In Fig. 10.3, the object types audio, video, music, and animation are shown as examples of PTD_MMDTs. Based on the PTD_MMDTs temporal characteristics, these object types are further

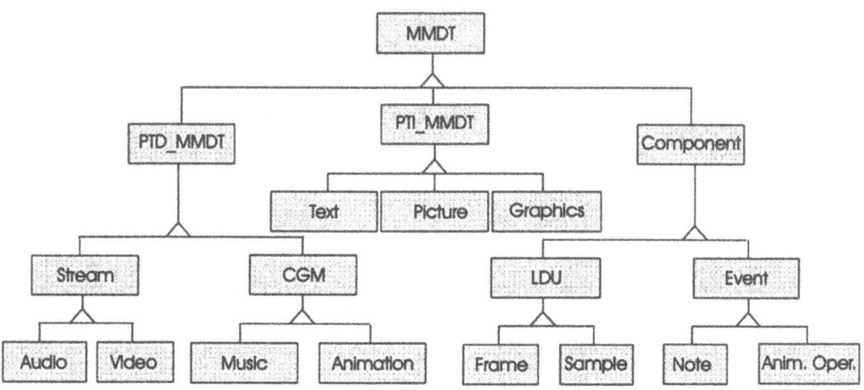

Figure 10.3: Logical data model type hierarchy.

classified into either *stream* or *CGM* sub-category. Stream objects are always related to a discrete time domain and are of periodic nature. Its components have to be presented at a constant rate and each single component has to be presented for a fixed duration. For example, all frames of a video object have to be presented with a rate of 30 frames per second (fps), and each frame has to be presented 1/30 seconds (s). In contrast, components of CGM objects are related to continuous time domains and can be presented in an arbitrary manner, i.e., they are a-periodic. The presentation duration of components is not fixed, and components can be presented sequentially or concurrently. For example, an animation of the space probe Voyager traveling through the solar system and adjusting its antennas might be composed out of three animation operations: one that generates the moving planets of the solar system, one that moves Voyager, and one for the adjustment of the antennas. The solar system and Voyager movements will be performed during the entire animation, but the antennas will only be adjusted from time to time for a short duration.

Component object types are classified according to the sub-category of the PTD_MMDTs they belong to. Component object types of stream object types are denoted LDU object types and component object types of CGM object types are denoted event object types (see Fig. 10.3). In other words, a stream object like video includes a set of references to LDUs and a CGM object like an animation includes a set of references to events. By placing components on the same level in the MMDT hierarchy as PTI_MMDTs and PTD_MMDTs, we achieve data independence and data reuse. All the object types in the PTD_MMDT category have corresponding object types in the Component category. This relationship exists for the PTD_MMDT object types introduced in this paper, because of their inherent temporal nature based on Components. Since the PTD_MMDT category in TOOMM can be extended with new object types, the temporal nature of each new object type that is added must be investigated to decide whether it needs a new corresponding Component object type or not. For example, a video that has been originally stored with 30 fps can be easily (and without redundancy) provided with different frame rates, e.g., 10 fps, by creating a video object that contains only references to every third frame and adjusting the LDU_duration to 1/10 s. The provision of different frame rates in turn enables us to adjust the presentation and the amount of data to be retrieved to the user's QoS requirements.

The logical data model of TOOMM comprises in addition to this MMDT hierarchy two further important features: (1) metadata to describe the contents of multimedia data and (2) temporal information. PTI_MMDT objects and PTD_MMDT objects can contain references to metadata, i.e., text, that describes the contents of the multimedia object. For PTD_MMDT objects, two play time timestamps are used to relate the content description of a certain interval, e.g., a scene in a video, to the data of this interval. The following five types of temporal information are supported in TOOMM: (1) duration needed to present multimedia data; (2) duration needed to present the smallest LDU of multimedia data, which is not further decomposable; (3) data types may also contain additional time dimensions such as valid and transaction time; (4) object versions; (5) QoS information such as resolution, frame rate, and picture quality for video.

10.4.2 Play Time Dimension

The valid and transaction time dimensions are not sufficient to model the temporal nature of multimedia objects and its diversity in time granularities. For example, the video standards NTSC and PAL work with different frame rates (NTSC 30 fps and PAL 25 fps) and time granularities of 1/30s and 1/25 s respectively. Audio is generally based on a much finer time granularity, e.g., the sampling rate of PCM coded audio is 8 kHz and CD-quality audio has a sampling rate of 44.1 kHz, which means time granularities of 1/8000 sec and 1/44100 sec. Therefore, we have introduced the play time dimension to handle the temporal nature of time dependent data and different time granularities in a media independent manner. Play time is used in the logical data model and in the presentation model; it can be seen as the glue between the two models. In the presentation model, play time is used as a means to map different time granularities of various multimedia objects to the global time granularity. In the logical data model, the play time dimension is used to define a temporal order between all components of multimedia objects. Based on this temporal order, we calculate the relative playback times of all components. Since streams and CGMs have different temporal characteristics, we look at the play time dimension for these MMDTs separately.

Streams contain a finite set of LDUs that have to be presented with a fixed rate and each for a fixed duration. Each stream object has to specify the default duration an LDU has to be presented (at normal rate), which is called *LDU_duration*. LDU_duration defines the time granularity of the multimedia object, because it is the play time dimensions equivalent to a chronon [11]. For streams it defines the interval between the presentation of two consecutive LDUs and is inverse proportional to the LDU rate. All LDUs of a stream object are ordered according to the normal playback mode by associating each single LDU with a play time timestamp via a TA (see Fig. 10.2). The moment a user initiates the playback of a multimedia object, the play time values of the LDUs are bound to the actual time.

CGMs contain a finite set of events that might be presented in an arbitrary manner, sequentially or concurrently, and all with possibly different presentation durations. Thus, CGMs cannot be associated with duration specification for all its components (as it is done in streams). However, each CGM requires the specification of a chronon, because the theoretically continuous time domain of CGMs cannot be implemented in reality, and it is necessary to relate all its temporal specifications to one specific time scale. These temporal specifications are actually start and stop times of events and are related via a TA to each event. Fig. 10.4 compares the usage of play time in streams and CGMs.

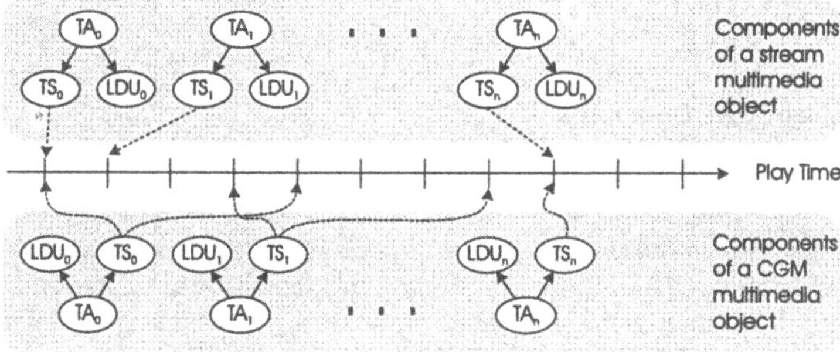

Figure 10.4: Usage of play time in streams and CGMs.

A major benefit of TOOMM is to combine streams and CGMs in a presentation in a uniform and flexible way. This is achieved through mechanisms for management of mixed granularities, and construction of CPOs for handling the presentation information of different MMDTs. The time scale used in the temporal specifications of a CGM is the play time dimension of that CGM. One granule in that time scale corresponds to a chronon.

10.4.3 Presentation Model

The logical data model supports temporal information for single multimedia objects, like LDU_duration, because this (default) temporal information belongs inherently to the data. However, a single multimedia object might be presented in different ways, independent of its default temporal information.

For example, a video with 30 fps might be presented with the default rate or in slow-motion. Thus, we have to differentiate between the default temporal information of multimedia objects and temporal information that is used for a particular presentation of the object. Furthermore, temporal relationships between multimedia objects are not included in the logical data model to support unconstrained combination of multimedia objects in presentations. For instance, a particular video sequence might be presented with audio sequences (speech) and sub-titles in different languages. In order to promote data reuse in TOOMM, all temporal relationships that are relevant for presentations are part of the presentation model. Different presentations that use the same data can be independently stored, and the multimedia data is only stored once.

We differentiate between two object types in the presentation model: APO types and CPO types. APOs are the atomic building blocks of a complex multimedia presentation that is specified in a CPO. Each APO specifies the presentation of a part, or entire single multimedia object. Thus, for each multimedia object type, TOOMM provides one APO type. APOs typically contain information about:

- References to multimedia data in terms of play time using the global play time dimension that is defined in the corresponding CPO. APOs that refer to a PTD_MMDT object must specify a continuous sequence of LDUs that have to be presented via start and stop time. In this way, the APO can select a part of, or the entire data set of the multimedia object. APOs that refer to a PTI_MMDT object must specify the time when the PTI_MMDT object should be presented. For instance, a presentation object referring to a picture object should specify the time interval within the multimedia presentation the picture should be shown.

- QoS specification for multimedia data presentation. The QoS of the presentation can differ from the maximal quality of the stored multimedia data. The presentation model enables us to specify different (lower) QoS for a presentation. For example, a video that is captured and stored with 30 fps might be presented at 25 fps. Network QoS parameters such as throughput requirements, jitter threshold, skew tolerance, error tolerance, and synchronization requirements can be extracted from the data and metadata stored with TOOMM, and used to negotiate QoS requirements and guarantees by the presentation execution module. For example, presentation parameters such as frame rate or frame resolution can be reduced to satisfy limitations in the available resources for a specific presentation.

- Effects on the multimedia data, such as, fade in, fade out, or change in volume.

CPOs specify the structure of complex multimedia presentations. The main elements of a CPO are a set of APOs and a set of temporal relationships among these APOs. Additionally, it contains the definition of a master chronon, termed *Master Time Unit Duration* (MTU_duration). The MTU_duration sets the granularity of the global play time which all the presentation objects must relate to. CPOs typically contain:

- Temporal relationships among multimedia data presentations. This is done through ***temporal relationship objects*** (TROs) which connect presentation objects, and specify their mutual temporal dependencies.
- Alternate multimedia data. For instance, if a video sequence has audio sequences in different languages available then the user should be able to choose between them.

Fig. 10.5 illustrates structure and usage of the presentation model. The extended entity-relationship diagram shows the type hierarchy of the presentation model and how the objects in the different parts of the data model relate to each other. The MMDT object type is the same as depicted in Fig. 10.3 but its sub-type hierarchy is omitted because of space limitations.

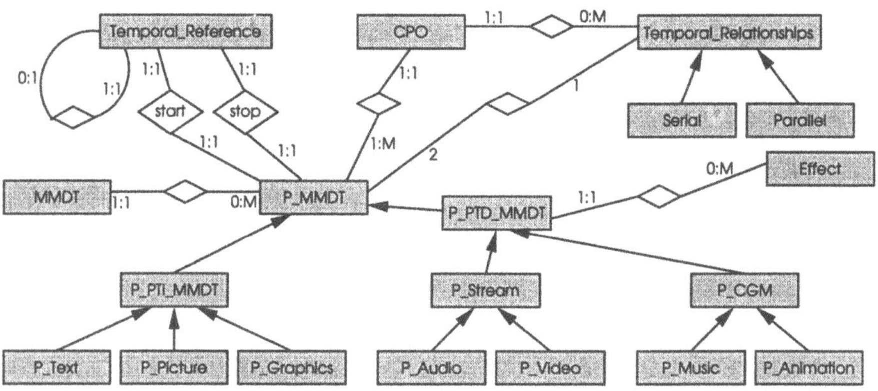

Figure 10.5: Extended entity-relationship diagram.

10.4.4 Comparison of TOOMM with Related Approaches

TOOMM integrates and extends well known concepts from object-oriented, temporal, and multimedia data models to provide better DBMS support for multimedia applications. Especially, TOOMM utilizes concepts from T_Chimera [4] and TIGUKAT [16] temporal object models, and the News-on-Demand [15] multimedia object model. The T_Chimera object model provides the temporal (T) construct, which extends the type T with temporal capabilities. In TOOMM, we use this construct to add temporal capabilities to MMDTs. It provides us with a concept to structure the temporal information of both data history and data presentation.

Presentation of multimedia data can be performed in many different ways. Hence it is beneficial to separate the logical data model of multimedia data from the presentation model similar to the view model of traditional DBSs. This is also done in the SGML/HyTime data model through their event schedule.

10.5 IMPLEMENTATION ISSUES

TOOMM is implemented on top of the OODBS ObjectStore. We have implemented a C++ class library that utilizes ObjectStore and provides DBMS support for common MMDTs. This implementation of TOOMM is based on the object definition language (ODL) of ObjectStore. The important advantage of using ODL is that the ODL definition can be used to produce the class implementations of the TOOMM object types in different programming languages by applying ODL preprocessors. The TOOMM object model is implemented in a client-server architecture where the server side is implemented in C++ (ObjectStore), and the client side can for instance be implemented as Java-applets that access the DBS over a network. In order to use TOOMM, an application developer must include the TOOMM C++ library files in the application programs, and an ObjectStore server must be available. In this section, we briefly review the most important implementation issues of TOOMM by illustrating object types that are necessary to present video.

10.5.1 Logical Data Model

10.5.1.1 Organizing Temporal Information. In addition to the object types in the logical data model, we need the object type time values, timestamps, and the construct Temporal (T,M) to manage temporal issues (see Fig. 10.6). Time value object types are modeled like the T_discreteDeterminate Instant object type of the TIGUKAT temporal object model [8]. The Timestamp object type is abstract and never instantiated. Sub-types of type Timestamp can model time entities such as instants or intervals. Furthermore, they can contain as many time dimensions as desired.

```
interface Play_Time (
     attribute T_discreteDeterminanteInstant time;
);
interface Timestamp (
     ....
);
interface Temporal (T,M) (
     attribute Set<struct<T Timestamp, M MMDT>> m_history;
);
```

Figure 10.6: Time value, timestamp, and Temporal (T,M) interface specification.

In the Chimera Temporal Object Model [4], T_Chimera, data types are extended with temporal capabilities through the construct Temporal (T). In TOOMM, we extend the basic idea of the T_Chimera model with various temporal characteristics of MMDTs. The object type Temporal (T,M) is used to attach Timestamp objects of category T to MMDT objects of category M.

Object types in the Component category are normally associated with the LDU_Timestamp or the Event_Timestamp objects containing the Play_Time attributes. The structure in the Temporal (T,M) definition corresponds to the TA objects in Fig. 10.3.

10.5.1.2 Type Hierarchy. The type hierarchy of the logical data model comprises for video the following specifications (see Fig. 10.7): MMDT, PTD_MMDT, component, stream, LDU, LDU_Timestamp, and video. The type MMDT is an abstract super-type of all the MMDTs. When non-empty, the default_presentation attribute specifies how the content of the MMDT object should be presented if no other specification exists. The PTD_MMDT abstract object type is meant to be sub-classed by time dependent MMDTs such as audio, video, music, and animation. It contains general information for all MMDTs that need a temporal extent to be played out meaningfully.

The Component object type is sub-typed by all the PTD_MMDT components. The belongs_to attribute inherited by all object types in the Component category is used to reach the PTD_MMDT object that the Component object is a component of.

The Stream object type contains general information for data types having a constant LDU rate such as audio and video. The m_data (multimedia data) attribute is a set of pairs of LDU_Timestamps and LDU object types. In the m_data attribute the LDU instances are always instances of a sub-type of the object type LDU. For instance, the m_data attribute of the Video object type is realized by a set of (LDU_Timestamp, Frame) pairs.

LDU is an abstract super-class, which must be sub-classed by the specific Component type of the PTD_MMDT. Since streams usually are recordings of real events it can be meaningful to register their valid times and transaction times. The LDU_Timestamp must at least contain the play time attribute pt, which places its corresponding LDU on the play time dimension. In addition, the LDU_Timestamp object type can be defined with other time values. The user of TOOMM may create user-defined timestamps through sub-classing the Timestamp super-class.

The object type Video inherits the m_data attribute from the object type Stream. The LDU_duration attribute is inherited from the PTD_MMDT. These characteristics, globally described by the Video object type attributes, are shared by all frames belonging to the same Video object. The Frame object type is a component of the Video object type. It represents an image that during presentation of a Video instance must be displayed at a given time for a certain duration.

```
interface MMDT {
     attribute P_MMDT default_presentation;
};
interface PTD_MMDT:MMDT {
     attribute Temporal (CD_Timestamp, Text) content_description;
     /* A textual description of the content of multimedia data */
     attribute float LDU_duration;
     attribute integer duration;
};
interface Component:MMDT {
     attribute belongs_to;
     ....
};
interface Stream:PTD_MMDT {
     attribute Temporal<LDU_Timestamp, LDU> m_data; /* TA! */
     ....
};
interface LDU:Component {
     ....
};
interface LDU_Timestamp:Timestamp {
     attribute Play_Time pt;
     attribute Valid_Time vt;
     attribute Transaction_Time tt;
};
interface Video:Stream {
     attribute Compression_Scheme cs; /*Specifies how all the frames are compressed */
     attribute Coding c;              /*Specifies how the frames are coded */
     attribute Resolution res; /*Specifies horizontal and vertical resolution */
     attribute Color_Depth cd; /*Specifies how many colors the frames consist of */
};
interface Frame:LDU {
     attribute Bit_String Frame_data;
};
```

Figure 10.7: Interface specification of logical data model.

10.5.2 Presentation Model

10.5.2.1 Temporal Issues. The definition of temporal references and temporal relationships is necessary to handle the temporal issues of the presentation model (see Fig. 10.8). Temporal reference objects refer to other temporal reference objects, but an invariant is that the references cannot be cyclic. In addition, the last temporal reference object in a list must point to the global play time dimension of a CPO object. It must be ensured that these invariants are maintained during the creation and updates of a Temporal_Reference object. If the value of reference is false, the object is a time point and the play time relative to the CPO presentation is found in the time_point attribute. Otherwise, the actual time point of the reference is as follows: deviation + ref.get_time_point(). The function get_time_point() is a recursive function that traverses a list of references and accumulates their deviation values. The function terminates as soon as it runs into the first Temporal_Reference instance that has the reference value set to false. The return value of get_time_point() can be expressed by the equation:

$$[reference = FALSE \implies get\_time\_point() = time\_point]$$
$$\wedge \ [reference = TRUE \implies get\_time\_point() = deviation + ref.get\_time\_point()]$$

```
interface Temporal_Reference {
     attribute boolean reference;
     attribute Play_Time time_point;
     attribute Temporal_Reference ref;
     attribute CPO the_presentation;
     attribute long deviation; /*In units of the_presentation.MTU_duration */
     Play_Time get_time_point();
};
interface Temporal_Relationship {
     attribute P_MMDT m1;
     attribute P_MMDT m2;
     relationship CPO belongs_to inverse CPO::Temporal_Relationships;
     boolean integrity_test();
};
interface Sequential:Temporal_Relationship {
     attribute enum sequential_rel_type (before, after, meets, met_by);
     boolean integrity_test();
};
interface Parallel:Temporal_Relationship {
     attribute float skew_toleranse;
     attribute enum parallel_rel_type (equal, starts, started_by, finishes,
                         finishes_by, overlaps, overlapped_by, during, contains);
     boolean integrity_test();
     ....
};
```

Figure 10.8: Interface specification of temporal issues.

Fig. 10.9 gives an example of how temporal references can be utilized. The resulting start times are: 10 for both P_Video1 and P_Audio2, and 15 for P_Text3.

We look now at the practical realization of temporal relationships from the data model. We create object types whose instances function as edges in an object graph where the nodes are multimedia objects. This approach supports only binary temporal relationships. The two P_MMDT attributes m1 and m2 are references to the two presentation objects whose temporal relationship we want to model. The belongs_to relationship relates the Temporal_Relationship to a CPO instance. The integrity_test() method must be reimplemented in the sub-types of the Temporal_Relationship object type. This test must basically check that the start and stop endpoints of the multimedia object referred to by m1 and m2 are according to the relationship type and that they belong to the same presentation.

The Sequential object type models all the serial temporal relationships [2]. The Sequential_rel_type attribute value must be set to the type of the serial temporal relationship that the instance of Sequential models.

The Parallel object type models all the temporal relationships where multimedia objects are played back in parallel. The parallel_rel_type attribute value must be set to the type of the parallel temporal relationship that the instance

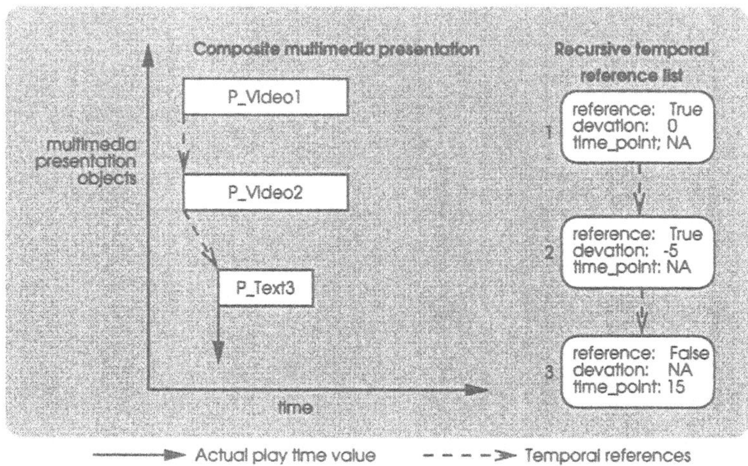

Figure 10.9: Example of temporal reference usage.

of Parallel models. The skew_tolerance attribute is an essential QoS parameter. The skew_tolerance unit is milliseconds. The skew between the presentation of two temporally related objects must be monitored at all times during presentation to avoid overstepping the skew tolerance limit.

10.5.2.2 Presentation Multimedia Data Types. Based on the previous specifications, we define the presentation multimedia data types that are necessary to present video objects: P_MMDT, P_PTD_MMDT, and P_Video (see Fig. 10.10). The presentation model (P_MMDT) consists of object types describing how the data should be displayed. The P_MMDT interface can be further sub-typed into object types used to present different MMDT data. An MMDT instance can be referred to by many P_MMDT instances. This accurately models the fact that a multimedia object can be presented in many ways.

The *presentation play time dependent MMDT* (P_PTD_MMDT) object type contains presentation information applicable to all play time dependent MMDTs. The start and stop attributes are relative to the start-time and stop-time of the MMDT instance referred to by mm_ref. If start equals zero and stop equals mm_ref.duration then the entire referred object is included. The speed attribute defines the speed of the presentation of the PTD_MMDT instance.

The Effects attribute is a set of (Effect_Timestamp, Effect) pairs. Some effects are global and can be executed by all play time dependent MMDTs such as hide, show, fade in, fade out, loop, and stretch. To include a new effect on a multimedia object we have to sub-type the abstract Effect object type. The effects must be executable in real-time. For completion, we define the skeleton of the abstract object type Effect. The Effect_Timestamp object type

```
interface P_MMDT:MMDT {
     attribute MMDT mm_ref; /*Reference to its corresponding MMDT object */
     Relationship CPO belongs_to inverse CPO::multimedia_objects;
     attribute Temporal_Reference p_start;
                         /*Refers to time point on the global play time scale */
                         /*of the CPO referred to by the belongs_to relationship */
     attribute Temporal_Reference p_stop;
};
interface P_PTD_MMDT:P_MMDT {
     attribute Play_Time start;
     attribute Play_Time stop;
     attribute double speed;
     attribute Temporal<Effect_Timestamp, Effect> Effects;
};
interface Effect {
     ....
};
interface Effect_Timestamp:Timestamp {
     attribute Temporal_Reference start;
     attribute Temporal_Reference stop;
};
interface P_Video:P_Stream {
     attribute position x;
     attribute position y;
     attribute float width;
     attribute float height;
     attribute boolean color_mode;
     attribute resolution res;
     ....
};
```

Figure 10.10: Interface specification of temporal issues.

is basically an interval. The Temporal_Reference pointers start and stop must refer to the global time line of the CPO instance that the Effect_Timestamp instance belongs to.

The temporal characteristics of the presentation of all the play time dependent MMDTs has been taken care of by the abstract super-types P_MMDT and P_PTD_MMDT. The object type P_Video is concerned with other aspects of the presentation information for their corresponding MMDT. Fig. 10.11 illustrates how a P_Video object relates multimedia data to a multimedia presentation. In particular, it shows the relationship between start and stop Play_Time attributes, and p_start and p_stop Temporal_Reference attributes of the P_Video object.

10.6 EVALUATION OF TOOMM

In this Section, we examine how a lecture given in the electronic classroom can be modeled with TOOMM and stored in a MMDBS (see Section 10.2). We explain the used MMDTs based on an example shown in Fig. 10.12. The Audio object named PMC_Lecture_hour1_clip1 has the smallest LDU_duration, which is the duration of one sample. Hence, it is reasonable to use this LDU_duration as the MTU_duration for the CPO object named Lecture_19_2_1998. The p_start and p_stop values of all the APO instances in the presentation are set

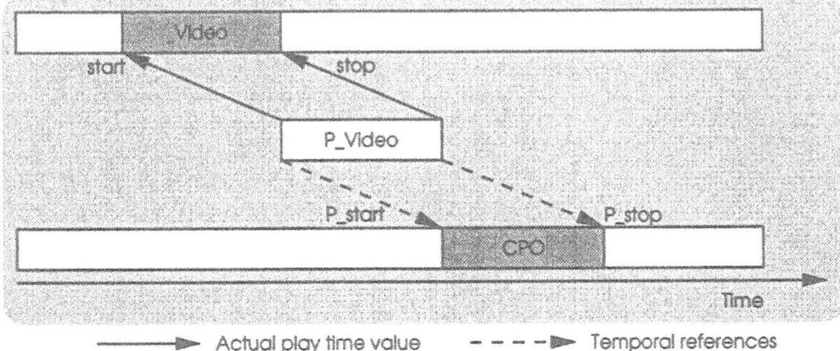

Figure 10.11: P_Video relates multimedia data to a multimedia presentation.

in units of the MTU duration. The Temporal Relationship object TR1 specifies through the Parallel_rel_type attribute that the presentation of P_Video1 and P_Audio1 must start at the same time and stop at the same time. The skew_tolerance attribute specifies that the skew during the concurrent presentation of P_Video1 and P_Audio1 must not exceed 80 ms. The Light_Pen object named Drawing_objects contains two operations which draws a box and a dot during the presentation of the HTML document object called FileSystem. It should be noted that Fig. 10.12 only displays a subset of the objects required to model an entire lecture.

- **Audio and video:** The quality of audio in this application must be very high. The Audio MMDT in TOOMM can be used directly to model the audio in the electronic classroom application. The presentation object type of audio P_Audio can also be used directly. The MMDT Video and its corresponding presentation object type P_Video can also be used directly in this application.

- **Document camera and scanner:** The application program responsible for capturing the events of the lecture can store the data received by the document camera as text if optical character recognition (OCR) tools are available. Alternatively, the data can be stored as a picture using the Picture MMDT. The data coming from the scanner can also be stored using the Picture MMDT.

- **HTML documents (electronic whiteboard):** HTML documents are stored in the MMDBS containing lectures given in the electronic classroom. The HTML document structure is modeled with TOOMM. The electronic whiteboard is the output device for the transparencies similar to a monitor. This implies that the presentation object types of the relevant MMDTs must recognize the electronic whiteboard as an output

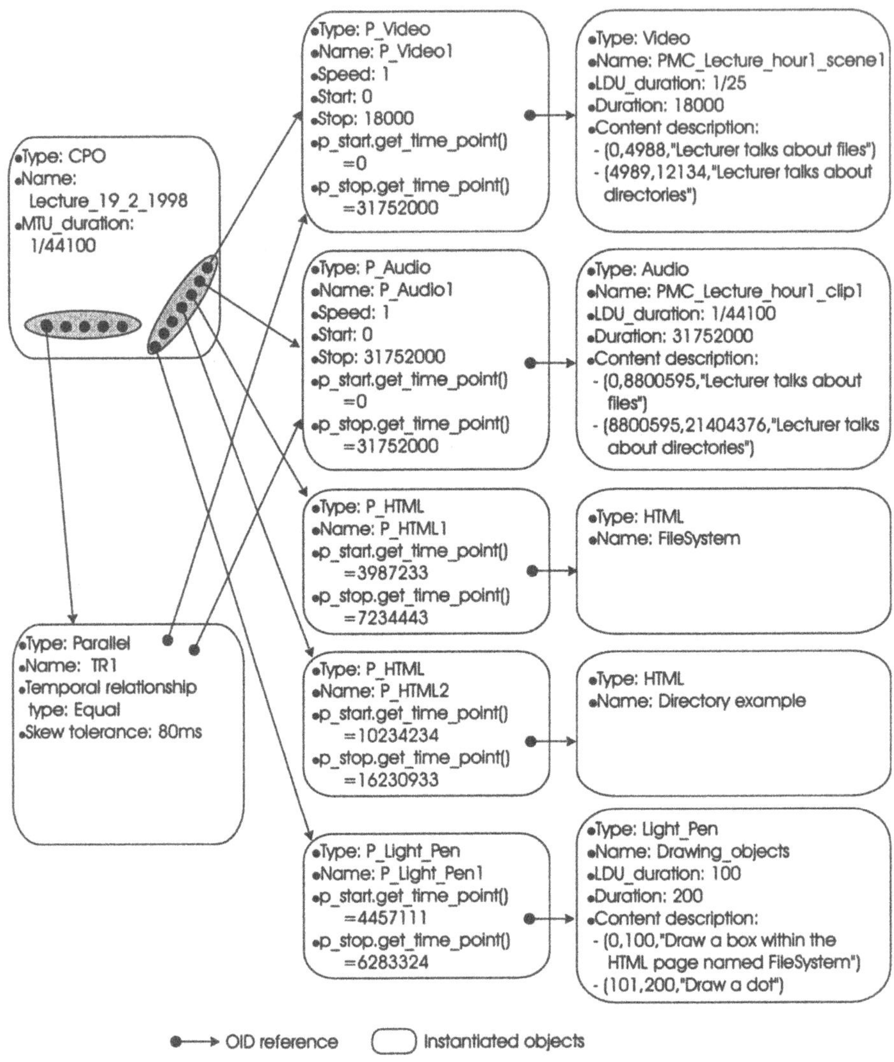

Figure 10.12: Modeling a lecture with TOOMM.

unit. This can be achieved by sub-classing the appropriate presentation object type.

- **Metadata:** The data types needed to model metadata about courses are only basic data types such as numbers and text. These basic data types can be easily modeled with TOOMM and associated with the complex multimedia objects.

- **Light-pen and other input devices:** The light-pen is used on the electronic whiteboard to issue commands within a browser-like application environment hereafter called browser. We also need to capture what the browser does in response to the actions invoked by the light-pen in order to capture and replay the actions of the light-pen. An application accessing the MMDBS and retrieving a previously recorded lecture must be able to invoke operations, just as if the lecturer using the light-pen issued them in order to properly replay the lecture. During a lecture the actions of the light-pen can also be supplemented with input from the keyboard and mouse attached to the computer running the browser. To model the light-pen, the keyboard, and the mouse using TOOMM, we must find out where the input units fit into the logical data model type hierarchy. Since the actions from the input units happen at irregular intervals with random duration, the CGM MMDT matches the temporal characteristics most accurately.

10.7 CONCLUSIONS

In this paper, we present TOOMM, a temporal object-oriented multimedia data model which integrates and extends well known concepts from object-oriented, temporal, and multimedia data models to provide better DBMS support for multimedia applications. We describe the concepts, implementation, and evaluation of TOOMM for the distance education scenario of the University of Oslo.

TOOMM has several advantages compared to other multimedia object models such as a formal structure for representing time in MMDTs, temporal relationships, and structured synchronization information. The separation of presentation information from the actual multimedia data in the SGML/HyTime model lead us to create the logical data model and the presentation model as two separate modules. The logical data model type hierarchy in TOOMM is structured as a tree classifying different MMDTs according to their temporal characteristics. Moreover, each multimedia object in the logical data model can have many corresponding presentation information objects in the presentation model, making it possible to view the data elements in many different ways. Hence, multimedia objects that are used for different purposes need only to be stored once, reducing redundancy and preserving integrity in the DBS. Many multimedia application level QoS parameters are present in both the object types of the logical data model and the presentation model of TOOMM. Temporal relationships contain synchronization requirements between multimedia objects and information on deadlines.

TOOMM provides an advanced framework for creating multiple specialized multimedia presentations based on the same multimedia data without the need for replication. The object types in the presentation model correspond to the

MMDTs in the logical data model. Each presentation object type provides an easy way of specializing the presentation of a MMDT. Sets of presentation object types can be combined with temporal relationships to form complete and highly specialized multimedia presentations.

Adding a new object type to the logical data model in TOOMM requires the developer to choose which of the three categories (PTD_MMDT, PTI_MMDT or Component) the new object type belongs to. However, it is possible that other categories exist which the new object type belongs to, making it worth while to investigate other possible categories and how to include these categories into TOOMM.

Some temporal concepts are not included in TOOMM, but deserve further investigation. For instance, a study on how indeterminate timestamp values can help to model and support user interactions should be performed. The concept of periodicity is also of interest in the context of multimedia data. The presentation of stream MMDTs is strongly periodic, making it suitable for data modeling using periodicity. An investigation on how branching time can help to model multimedia presentations taking alternate routes is also of interest. Another concept that should be investigated is temporal relationships of higher order than two for use with multimedia presentations. Such relationships can model the temporal dependence of the presentation of many multimedia objects, but they can get very complex. In [13] temporal relationships of higher order are investigated, but only for relationships of the same type and not for multimedia applications.

References

[1] Aberer K., Klas W., Supporting Temporal Multimedia Operations in Object Oriented Database Systems, Proc. of IEEE Multimedia Computing and Systems Conf., Boston (USA), May 1994, pp. 352-361

[2] Allen J. F., Maintaining Knowledge About Temporal Intervals, Communication of the ACM, Vol. 26, No. 11, 1983, pp. 823-843

[3] Bakke, J. W., Hestnes, B., Martinsen, H., Distance Education in the Electronic Classroom, Televerkets Forskningsinstitutt, report TF R 20/94, 1994

[4] Bertino E., Ferrari E., Guerrini G., A Formal Temporal Object-Oriented Data Model, P. Apers, (Ed.), Proc. Fifth International Conference on Extending Database Technology, Avignon (France), March 1996

[5] Böhm K., Rakow T. C., Metadata for Multimedia Documents, ACM SIGMOD Record, Vol . 23, No. 4, December 1994, pp. 21-26

[6] Clifford J., Isakowitz T., On The Semantics of (Bi) Temporal Variable Databases, Proc. of Fourth Int. Conf. on Extending Database Technology, Cambridge (England), March 1994, pp. 215-230

[7] Gibbs S., Breiteneder C., Tsichritzis D., Data Modeling of Time-Based Media, Proc. of ACM SIGMOD Conf., May 1994, pp. 91-102

[8] Goralwalla I., Lentiev Y., Özsu M. T., Szafron D., A Uniform Behavioral Temporal Object Model, University of Alberta, TR 95-13, July 1995

[9] Hjelsvold R., Midtstraum R., Sandstå O., A Temporal Foundation of Video Databases., Proc. of the International Workshop on Temporal Databases, Zürich (Switerland), 1995

[10] Jain R., Hampapur A, Metadata in Video Databases, ACM SIGMOD Record, Vol . 23, No. 4, December 1994, pp. 27-33

[11] Jensen C. S., Clifford J., Elmasri R., Gadia S.K., Hayes P., Jajodia S. (Eds.), A Consensus Glossary of Temporal Database Concepts, ACM SIGMOD Record, Vol. 23, No. 1, March 1994, pp. 52-64

[12] Karmouch A., Emery J., A Playback Schedule Model for Multimedia Documents, IEEE Multimedia, Vol. 3, No. 1, Spring 1996

[13] Little T. D. C., Ghafoor A., Interval-Based Conceptual Models for Time-Dependent Multimedia Data, IEEE Trans. Knowledge and Data Engineering, Vol. 5, No. 4, 1993 pp. 551-563

[14] Özsoyoglu G., Snodgrass R. T., Temporal and Real-Time Databases: A Survey, IEEE Trans. on Knowledge and Data Engineering, Vol. 7, No. 4, August 1995, pp.-513-532

[15] Özsu M. T., Szafron D., El-Medani G., Vittal C., An Object-Oriented Multimedia Database System for a News-on-Demand Application, Multimedia Systems, Vol. 3, 1995, pp. 182-203

[16] Özsu M. T., Peters R. J., Szafron D., Irani B., Lipka A., Munoz A., TIGUKAT: A Uniform Behavioral Objectbase Management System, The VLDB Journal, Vol. 4, 1995, pp. 100-147

[17] Plagemann, T., Goebel, V., Experiences with the Electronic Classroom - QoS Issues in an Advanced Teaching and Research Facility, Proceedings of 5th IEEE Workshop on Future Trends of Distributed Computing Systems (FTDCS'97), Tunis (Tunesia), October 1997, pp. 124-129

[18] Prabhakaran B., Multimedia Database Management Systems, Kluwer Academic Publishers, 1997

[19] Rose E., Segev A., TOODM - A Temporal Object-Oriented Model with Temporal Constraints, Entity-Relationship Conf., 1991, pp. 205-230

[20] Schloss G., Wynblatt M., Building Temporal Structures in a Layered Multimedia Data Model, ACM Multimedia Conf., October 1994, pp. 271-278

[21] Subrahmanian V. S., Jajodia S. (Eds.), Multimedia Database Systems - Issues and Research Directions, Springer, 1996

[22] Tansel A. U., Clifford J., Gadia S., Jajodia S., Segev A., Snodgrass R. T., Temporal Databases: Theory, Design and Implementation, Database Systems and Application Series, Benjamin/Cummings, Redwood City, CA (USA), 1993

[23] Thimm H., Klas W., Playout Management in Multimedia Database Systems, in: Nwosu K. C., Thuraisingham B., Berra P. B. (Eds.), Multimedia

Database Systems - Design and Implementation Strategies, Kluwer Academic Publishers, 1996, pp. 318-376

11 SPATIOTEMPORAL SPECIFICATION & VERIFICATION OF MULTIMEDIA SCENARIOS

I. Kostalas, T.Sellis, M. Vazirgiannis

Abstract: A Multimedia Application (MAP) consists of a set of media objects ordered in the spatial and temporal domains. In this paper we present an authoring & verification methodology for MAP documents development. We capitalize on a solid theoretical model for spatiotemporal compositions. The tool may be used both for prototyping and verification of multimedia presentations or spatiotemporal compositions in general. Regarding the authoring phase, emphasis was put on the flexible definition of spatial and temporal relationships of the participating entities. The verification procedures are supported by multiple tools allowing designers to preview their applications, in various ways: spatial layouts of the application window, temporal layouts, indicating the temporal duration and relationships among the participating objects and animation of the application.

11.1 INTRODUCTION

A Multimedia Application (MAP) involves a variety of individual media objects, called *actors*, presented according to the MAP scenario. The term *scenario* covers two areas: i. the spatial and temporal ordering of actors within the application context and the relationships among them and ii. the way that the user will interact with the application as well as how the application will treat application or system events.

Another relevant issue is that the actors participating in a MAP, are transformed either spatially and/or temporally in order to be presented according to the author's requirements. For instance, we may want to present part of a video clip faster or slower at a bigger or smaller window.

The authoring procedure for complex MAPs, that involve a large number of actors, may be a very complicated task, having in mind the large set of possible events that may be encountered in the application context, the number of actors and relationships as well as the various potential combinations of these factors.

A MAP specification should describe both the temporal and spatial ordering of actors in the context of the MAP. In the past, the term "synchronization" has been widely used to describe the temporal ordering of actors in a MAP. The spatial ordering issues (i.e. absolute position and spatial relationships among actors) have not adequately been addressed up to now. We claim that the term synchronization is poor for MAPs. Instead we propose the term "*composition*" to represent both the temporal and the spatial composition of actors.

The potential high complexity of MAPs, results in substantial effort required for design and development. In real-life applications, usually only programmers are able to develop MAP scenarios since current authoring tools provide rather low level specification languages. Moreover, these languages are inadequate for the complete description of the scenario aspects mentioned before. Therefore, the lack of an integrated mechanism for high level complete specification of a MAP scenario arises as a main issue. Moreover, in current MAP development tools the MAP script is mixed with the application content (actors). This prevents the explicit reusability of scenarios in other MAPs with different content but similar functionality.

Another important aspect is the verification of MAP scenarios during MAP development. The term verification in this context implies the various procedures that will allow the author to review the result of their authoring effort prior to the production and execution of the MAP. This will enable revisiting the application and adjusting the spatiotemporal specification in order to align to the document style the authors has in mind or to fix specification errors that result in spatial and or temporal exceptions.

In this paper we present an authoring & verification methodology for MAP documents development supported by a full implementation. The MAP design is based on a theoretical model for spatiotemporal compositions in the context of multimedia presentations (Vazirgiannis et al, 1998). The tool may be used both for *prototyping* and *verification* of multimedia presentations or spatiotemporal compositions in general.

Regarding the authoring phase, emphasis was put on the flexible definition of spatial and temporal relationships of the participating entities. In other words, the authoring phase consists mainly of declarative specifications of the spatial and temporal ordering of participating multimedia objects based on their spatial and temporal relationships.

The *verification* procedures are supported by multiple tools allowing designers to preview their applications, in various ways: *spatial layouts* of the application window, *temporal layout* of parts (or the whole application), indicating the temporal duration and relationships among the participating objects and *animation (rendering)* of the application (i.e. what would the execution of the application like) in three modes (real time, manual and snapshots of the application at regular temporal intervals).

The paper is organized as follows. In the next section we present related research and industrial products in the area of multimedia application modeling and synchronization. In section three, we briefly present the theoretical model (Vazirgiannis et al, 1998) that served as the basis for the authoring and verification tool, which is presented in section four. There, we present the authoring procedures as spatiotemporal specification of multimedia objects and the verification tools provided by the system. In the last section, we conclude by presenting our contributions and discussing on further research and extensions of the tool.

11.2 RELATED WORK AND BACKGROUND

The specification of a multimedia application is essentially the definition of the composition of the participating media objects in space and time along with the appropriate transformations of the media object.

In the literature there is a confusion among the concepts of *synchronization* and *temporal specification.* They are used interchangeably. Existing multimedia document standards (MHEG, HyTime) propose Object-Oriented approaches for modeling the structure and behavior of multimedia documents. The proposed standards, however, do not provide means for the complete specification of spatial and temporal composition of actors. Moreover, the issues of storage, retrieval, execution and sharing of application scripts are not addressed, while event modeling and composition schemes are inadequate to cover the requirements for the variety of events that may occur in an MAP. Finally, there are no large scale implementations of these standards to prove their credibility and usability.

Regarding commercial authoring tools (Assymetrix/ToolBook, Macromedia/MacroMind Director) for MAP development, they adopt mostly Object Oriented authoring models, providing high-level script languages. These tools do not adequately fulfill requirements regarding:

- Declarative Spatiotemporal composition schemes and modeling of the actor transformations
- Event representation and composition: only a limited repertoire of events is supported, while no composition of events is feasible. They mostly manipulate events related to mouse and to the actors' state (start, stop, active, idle, etc.).
- Database support for the application scripts (multimedia data and scripts are bundled together in most cases)

Many existing models for temporal composition of multimedia objects in the framework of a multimedia application are based on Allen's relations (Allen, 1983). However, these relations are not suitable for composition description since the are descriptive (they do not reflect causal dependency between intervals), they depend on interval durations and they may lead to temporal inconsistency. More specifically, the problems that arise when trying to use these relations are the following (Duda et al, 1995):

The relations are designed to express relationships between intervals of fixed duration. In the case of multimedia applications it is required that a relationship holds independently from the duration of the related object (i.e. the relationship does not change when the duration changes). Their descriptive character does not convey the cause and the result in a relationship.

Other models for multimedia composition representation may be classified in two categories: point-based and interval-based. In point-based models, the elementary units are points in time and space. Each event in the model has its associated time point. The time points arranged according to some relations such as "precede", "simultaneous" or "after" form complex multimedia presentations. An example of the point-based approach is timeline. Interval based models consider elementary media entities as time intervals ordered according to some relations. Existing models are mainly based on the relations defined by Allen for expressing the knowledge about time.

An interesting mechanism for temporal composition is presented in (Duda et al, 1995). This work presents a model that takes into account the semantics of temporal relationships between objects. A set of operators is defined expressing the causal relations between intervals. In (Hirzala et al, 1995), a temporal model for interactive scenarios is presented. This model is based on the timeline approach and provides the primitives for specification of synchronous and asynchronous interactive and temporal multimedia compositions. The timeline approach is extended to a tree of timelines. Each branch of timelines represents the different scenarios that may be selected by the user.

Other approaches use Allen's relations to specify a multimedia database schema. In (Little et al, 1993) an OCPN (Object Composition Petri Nets) model equivalent to Allen relationships is proposed. This approach, though, does not take into account the possible unknown durations of intervals. Thus, in order to prepare an instantiated presentation the tree of interval relations must be traversed to get deadlines to be used in the presentation schedule. In (Iino et. al, 1994) a model for spatiotemporal multimedia presentations is presented. The temporal composition is handled in terms of Allen relationships whereas spatial aspects are treated in terms of a set of operators for binary and unary operations.

The model lacks the following features: i. There is no indication of the temporal causal relationships (i.e. what are the semantics of the temporal relationships between the intervals corresponding to multimedia objects); ii. The spatial synchronization essentially addresses only two topological relationships: overlap and meet, giving no representation means of the directional relationships between the objects (i.e. Object A is to the right of object B) and the distance information (i.e. object A is 10 cm away from object B); iii. The modeling formalism is rather oriented towards execution and rendering of the application rather than authoring. This means that the specifications are closer to the logic of the presentation scheduling rather that to the author's declarative requirements.

There are other approaches based on interval temporal logics (King, 1994). Although such formalisms have a solid mathematical background, the specification of multimedia presentations is awkward since the specification does not correspond explicitly to the author's perception of the multimedia composition.

Related work has been published in (Karmouch et al, 1996). Although it copes with multimedia objects, it models a smaller part of the MAPs that relate to multimedia documents and not to multimedia applications. Thus, taking for granted that the document will be based on textual resources, the model tries to make an interactive multimedia book containing some form of multimedia objects like images, sound and video. The book is divided in chapters and the screen layout is similar to the one of word processors, along with their temporal information. The temporal relationships are taken into account, but not the spatial ones since it is assumed that they are solved depending on the text flow on the page. An interesting survey on authoring models and approaches may be found in (Jourdan et al, 1998).

11.3 THE COMPOSITION MODEL

The "action" concept is related to the presentation of actors (multimedia objects) participating in MAPS. A multimedia application specification should describe both temporal and spatial ordering of actors in the context of the application. The spatial ordering (i.e. absolute positioning and spatial relationships among actors) issues have not been adequately addressed. We claim that the term "*synchronization*" is poor for multimedia applications and, instead, we propose the term "*composition*" to represent both the temporal and the spatial ordering of actors. In the current modeling effort we made a fundamental assumption by considering objects that appear and after some time they disappear from the presentation context without changing their position during their lifetime. Thus, here we do not consider motion. We also assume that the spatial features of the media objects are defined by the rectangle that bounds them.

11.3.1. Temporal Relationships

The topic of relations between temporal intervals has initially been addressed in (Allen, 1983). We exploit the temporal composition scheme as defined in (Vazirgiannis et al, 1998). We briefly introduce that scheme for representing the temporal composition of multimedia objects that also captures the causality of the temporal relationships. In that scheme the start & end points of a multimedia instance are exploited as events. The end of a multimedia object presentation is either *natural* (i.e. when the media objects finishes its execution) or *forced* (i.e. when an event explicitly stops the execution of a multimedia object). Moreover, the well-known *pause* (temporarily stop of execution) and *resume* procedures (start the execution from the point where the pause operation took place) are also taken into account.

An important concept is the temporal instance: we consider it as an arbitrary temporal measurement that is relative to some reference point (i.e. the application temporal starting point in our case, hereafter T).

Based on the above descriptions we define the following operators attached to the corresponding events:

Definition: Let A be a multimedia instance, then A> represents the start of the multimedia instance, A< the natural end of the instance, A! the forced stop, A|| the pause and A|> the resume actions.

Definition: Let A, B two multimedia instances, then the expression: Aop1 t Bop2 represents all the temporal relationships between the two multimedia instances, where op1∈ {>,<,||,|>} and op2∈ {>,!,||,|>} and t is a vacant temporal interval.

Definition : Let A be a multimedia instance, we define as t_{Aop} the temporal instances corresponding to the events Aop, where op ∈ {>,<,!,||,|>}.

Definition : Let A be multimedia instance, we define as d_A the temporal duration of the multimedia instance A.

11.3.2 Spatial Relationships

Another aspect of composition of multimedia objects in MAPs is related to the spatial layout of the application, i.e. the spatial arrangement and relationships of the participating objects. The spatial composition aims at representing three aspects:

- The topological relationships between the objects (*disjoint*, *meet*, *overlap*, etc.)
- The directional relationships between the objects (*left*, *right*, *above*, *above-left*, etc.)
- The distance characteristics between the objects (*outside* 5cm, *inside* 2cm, etc.)

We will exploit the scheme presented in (Vazirgiannis et al, 1998]. We will briefly present this scheme for clarity reasons.

Regarding directional relationships, there is a complete set of relationships defined in (Papadias et al, 1995). This set of 169 (13^2) relationships $R_{i\,j}$ ($i = 1, ..., 13$ and $j = 1, ..., 13$) arises from the exhaustive combination of the relationships defined in (Allen, 1983) regarding relationships between temporal intervals. It is evident that in the case of MAPs these relationships have to be grouped in sets of relationships to assist the authoring procedure.

11.3.3 Spatiotemporal composition model

In this section we present briefly the theoretical foundations we use for our spatiotemporal verification framework. We exploit the model introduced in (Vazirgiannis et al, 1998) aiming at representation of the spatiotemporal composition of media objects in the context of a MAP. The model we propose will translate spatiotemporal relationships among multimedia objects into minimal and uniform expressions, as imposed by the requirements for correct and complete representations.

For uniformity reasons, we define an object named Θ, that corresponds to the spatial and temporal start of the application (i.e. upper left corner of the application window and the temporal start of the application). Another assumption we make is that the objects that are included in the composition include their Spatiotemporal presentation characteristics (i.e. size, temporal duration, etc.)

Definition : Assuming two spatial objects A, B, we define the generalized spatial relationship between these objects as: S_R = (r_{ij}, v_i, v_j, x, y) where r_{ij} is the identifier of the topological-directional relationship between A and B , v_i, v_j are the closest vertices of A and B respectively (as defined in Vaz98) and x, y are the horizontal and vertical distances between v_i, vj.

Hereafter, we define a generalized operator expression to cover the spatial and temporal relationships between objects in the context of a multimedia application. It is important to stress the fact that in some cases we do not need to model a relationship between two objects but to declare the spatial and / or temporal position of an object relative to the application spatial and temporal start point Θ (i.e. object A to appear at the spatial coordinates (110, 200) on the 10th second of the application).

Definition: We define a composite Spatiotemporal operator that represents absolute spatial/temporal coordinates or Spatiotemporal relationships between objects in the application: `ST_R(sp_rel, temp_rel)`, where `sp_rel` is a spatial relationship (`S_R`) as defined above, and `temp_rel` is a temporal relationship.

The Spatiotemporal composition of a multimedia application consists of several independent fundamental compositions. The term "independent" implies that actors participating in them are not related explicitly (either spatially or temporally) except from their implicit relationship to the start point Θ. Thus, all compositions are explicitly related to Θ. We call these compositions *composition_tuples* and these include spatially and/or temporally related objects.

Definition: We define the composition_tuple in the context of a multimedia application as : `composition_tuple = Ai [{ ST_R Aj}]`, where

`Ai, Aj` are objects participating in the application, `ST_R` is a Spatiotemporal relationship (as defined above).

Definition: We define the composition of multimedia objects in the context of multimedia applications as a set of `composition_tuples`: `composition = Ci {,Cj}`, where `Ci, Cj` are `composition_tuples`.

The EBNF definition of the Spatiotemporal composition based on the above definition follows:

```
composition ==:
        composition_tuple{[,composition_tuple]}
composition_tuple ==:
        Θ {[spatio_temporal_relationship actor |
        composition]}
spatio_temporal_relationship ==:
    "[("[spatial_operator | spatial_instance")" ,
    "("temporal_operator | temporal_instance")]"
temporal_operator ==: Θ | t_event t_interval
                      TAC_operation
t_event ==: ">" | "<" | "!" | "|>" | "||"
spatial_operator ==: (rij, Vi, Vj, x, y)
x ==: INTEGER
y ==: INTEGER
```

where `rij` denotes a topological- directional relationship between two objects and `vi, vj` denote the closest vertices of the two objects (see definition above).

11.3.4 A Sample Multimedia Composition

In this section we describe a MAP corresponding to TV news clip in terms of spatio-temporal relationships as defined above. The high level scenario of the application is the following:

"*The **News** clip starts with presentation of image A (located at point 50,50 relatively to the application origin Θ). At the same time a background music E starts. 10 sec after a video clip B starts. It appears to the right side (18cm) and below the upper side of A (12cm). Just after the end of B, another MAP starts. This MAP(**Fashion_clip**) is related to fashion. The Fashion_clip consists of a video clip C that showing the highlights of a fashion show and appears 7cm below (and left aligned to) the position of B. 3 sec after the start of C, a text logo D (the designer's logo) appears inside C, 8cm above the bottom side of C, aligned to the right side. D will remain for 4 sec on the screen. Meanwhile, at the 10th sec of the News clip, the TV channel logo (F) appears at the bottom-left corner of the application window. F disappears after 3 sec. The application ends when music background E ends.*"

The spatial composition (screen layout) appears in **Figure 11.1**, while the temporal one appears in Figure 11.2. The objects to be included in a composition tuple of a MAP are those that are spatially and/or temporally related. In our example (News clip), A and B and Fashion clip should be in the same composition tuple since A relates to B, B relates to Fashion clip. On the other hand, F is not related to any other object, nor spatially neither temporally, so it composes a different tuple.

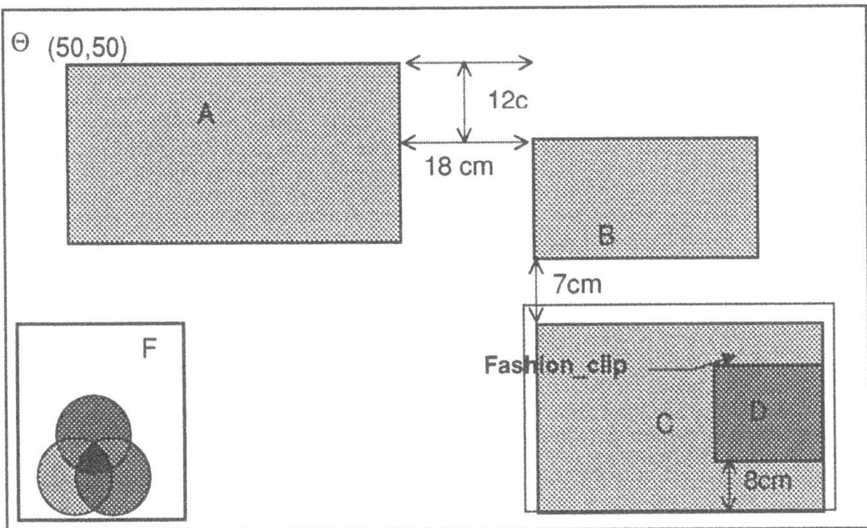

Figure 11.1: The spatial composition of the News MAP

The above spatial and temporal specifications defined by the author in a high level GUI are transformed into the following representation according to the model primitives defined:

```
// News Clip
    composition = {r1, r2}
    r1 = Θ [(_, _, _, _,_), (>0>)]
         E [(_, _, _, _,_), (<0!)]
         News
    r2 = Θ [(r1_1, _,v2, 5, 5), (>0>)]
         A [(r11_13, v3, v2,18,12),(>10>)]
         B [(r13_6, v1, v2, 0,-7), (>0>)]
         Fashion_clip
    r3 = Θ [(_, _, v1, 0, 300), (>10>)]
         F
// Fashion clip
    composition = {r4}
    r4 =  Θ [(_, _,v2,0,0), (>0>)]
         C [(r9_10, v4, v4, 0, 8), (>3>)]
```

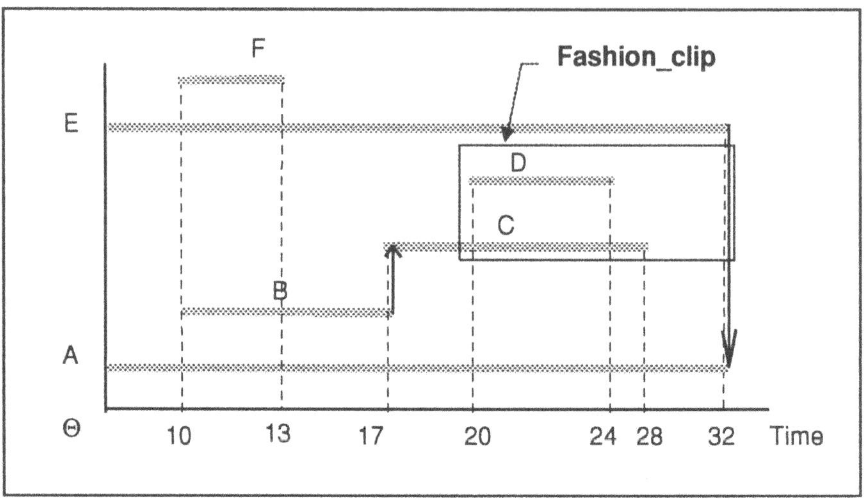

Figure 11.2: The temporal composition of the News MAP

11. 4. AUTHORING SPATIOTEMPORAL COMPOSITIONS FOR MAP DOCUMENTS

The authoring methodology we present hereafter is based on the model introduced in the previous section. A MAP document contains objects composed in space and time according to a set of spatial and temporal relationships. The scenario is build in a stepwise procedure. The first step is the specification of the objects that participate in the application along with their spatial and temporal transformations (i.e. which spatial and/or temporal part of the object will participate in the MAP, under what spatial/temporal scaling etc.). The second step is to define the actors' spatial and temporal position in the MAP document in terms of absolute or relative coordinates. The authoring tool transforms these specifications and produces the spatiotemporal scenario, i.e. when, where and for how long each object will be presented.

We distinguish the actors in four main categories: text, sound, image and video. We assume that each object (except sound) has some spatial extent so it can be represented by a rectangle in which the image text/video information is presented. On the other hand, sound objects have only temporal aspects.

11.4.1. Authoring environment

The authoring interface supports to a great extend visual definition of the multimedia scenario. Conceptually the scenario specification should start at the temporal start of the MAP. Thus, the authoring procedure starts at the beginning of the application (time = 0) and specifies the participating actors in a more or less increasing temporal order.

Composition Specifications. Initially the author(s) may insert or remove media objects from the actors list. Each actor object is further defined by assigning values to its spatial and temporal attributes.

Each actor includes its identification data such as name, media type and media file corresponding to the actor, the temporal and spatial coordinates of the object in the application context. The name of an actor must be unique name in the MAP context. Though, the tools allows the definition of different actors based on the same media object. The data that the user enters (*external*) are transformed into absolute coordinates (*internal*) in order to produce the scenario. The external data mostly relate the spatial and temporal coordinates of the new object to those of other objects, previously defined.

The methodology supports incremental authoring by adding new actors to the existing spatiotemporal composition and relating it to them spatially and/or temporally.

Temporal attributes specification. The *temporal attributes* of the object include its temporal start and end points (see Figure 11.3). The author may define the beginning of an object in relation to another object that is already, or will be, active. Thus, the starting time be relate to the temporal application origin **T**, or to the start/end point of another object (in this case, we do not distinguish between the *pause* and the *stop* events or between the *start* and the *resume* event). The same applies to the definition of the *end* time of the object as long as the object does not have an internal (natural) duration (like video and sound do).

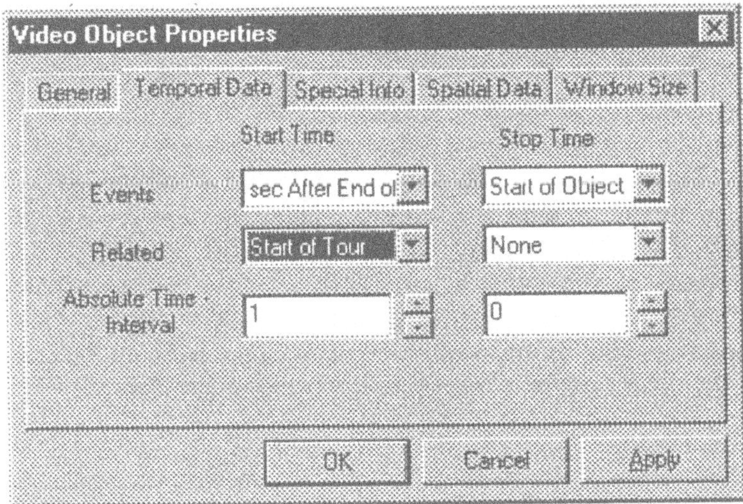

Figure 11.3: The Properties of an object to participate in the MAP (temporal data).

If the object has a natural length, then the user can either let it end naturally or force it to end before its natural end. That event can be a stop or a pause event. As mentioned before, the author may define the temporal data of the actor in question in relation to the starting/ending point of another actor. We have to distinguish here between the events *pause, restart* that are also included in our design. The pause event may be considered as a temporary *stop* event, whereas a *restart* event may be considered as a start event. This may be adjusted by the author using the property sheet appearing in Figure 11.4.

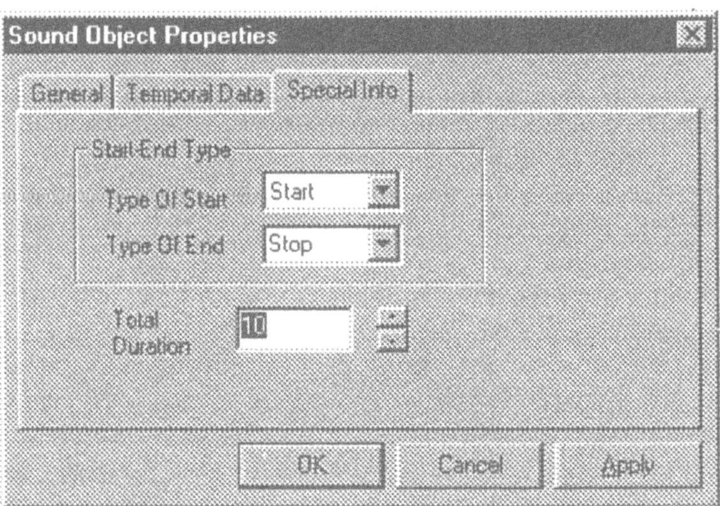

Figure 11.4: Specification of the start and stop events of an actor

Spatial attributes specification The issue of spatial features of actors in MAPs has been rather under-addressed in the multimedia literature. The authoring tools enable specification of the spatial features of an actor, either as absolute coordinates or in relation to other objects. We assume that each object is bounded by a rectangle (whose dimensions may be changed by the author) and the author may define its position. The actor's upper left corner is related either to the origin of the MAP (T) or to any vertice (Upper Left, Upper Right, Lower Left, Lower Right) of any other actor already defined. It is important to stress that it is possible to relate the actor under concern to different actors as regards the X and Y axis. In the case of absolute coordinates, we define the position of the upper left corner of the actor related to the top left corner of the application window (see Figure 11.5).

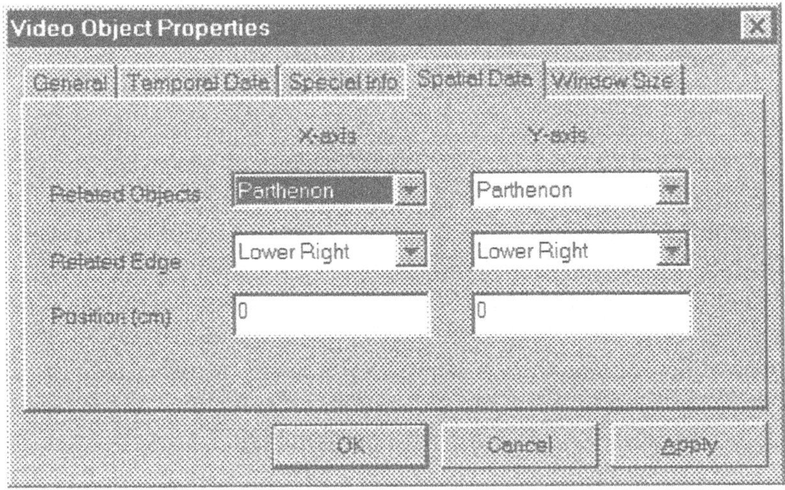

Figure 11.5: The spatial properties of an actor.

11.5. VERIFICATION OF MAP DOCUMENTS

During the authoring procedure it is probable/anticipated that the author(s) might want to query the scenario, especially if it is extended and complicated in terms of interactions and composed presentation actions. This can be helpful in order to:

- Inform the author(s) about the underlying spatiotemporal constraints of the scenario,
- Modify the scenario and, in this way, create, correct or improve the scenario in an incremental way.

In this last case, the author, depending on the answer of the query, can do the modification on the scenario, currently under creation. The queries may be classified into the following categories:

- *Point queries*, which are useful when the author is interested in finding relationships between events. For instance: "Does actor Starting Logo start before Tour video?" or "which objects appear at the position (50,50) before the 5th second of the MAP"?
- *Relationship queries*: In this category we are interested in relationships among the temporal intervals that represent the presentations of actors or alternatively the relationships between the spatial extents of the actors. Such a queries would be: "Are the presentations of objects "tour_video" and "agora"simultaneous?" or "Is "tour_video" overlapping with "agora"?".
- *Layout queries*. They result in graphical representations, depicting the spatial and temporal relationships among presented objects. Such kind of

queries is a necessity that is recognized among the authoring community (Vazirgiannis et al, 1998]. An example can be: "Show the temporal layout of the IMD between the 2nd and 10th second of the presentation".

It is evident that handling such queries can enhance the flexibility and quality of the authoring procedure through verification of the MAP under development. In the sequel we present the tools and methodologies we have developed to tackle the above set of requirements.

A multimedia scenario may be very complicated if we consider the multitude of objects and the spatiotemporal relationships among them. Thus, it is essential for a consistent MAP development procedure to allow the preview of several aspects of the application previous to the final implementation. In this section we introduce a set of techniques to verify a MAP document during authoring and prior to its execution. The verification is related to temporal & spatial aspects and may fulfill requirements such as viewing MAP snapshots at any temporal point, finding out the temporal relationships between actors, viewing an animation of the MAP, etc.

11.5.1. Temporal layout tool

The first verification tool is the *temporal layout* that displays, in a graphical form, the temporal order and the duration of the actors (see **Figure 11.6**). This facility gives an overview of the temporal configuration of the MAP and, moreover, provides support to queries of the type: "which objects are active at a specific time?" or "which objects are active at a specific period of time?" (i.e. during the temporal interval in which another object is active). The temporal layout may refer to a part of the temporal duration of the MAP (e.g. from the 5th to the 20th second of the MAP) or to its total duration. The list of objects (in absolute temporal coordinates) is sorted according to their starting time. This list is exploited in the rest of the verification tools, more specifically in the execution table and in the spatial layout tool that are described hereafter.

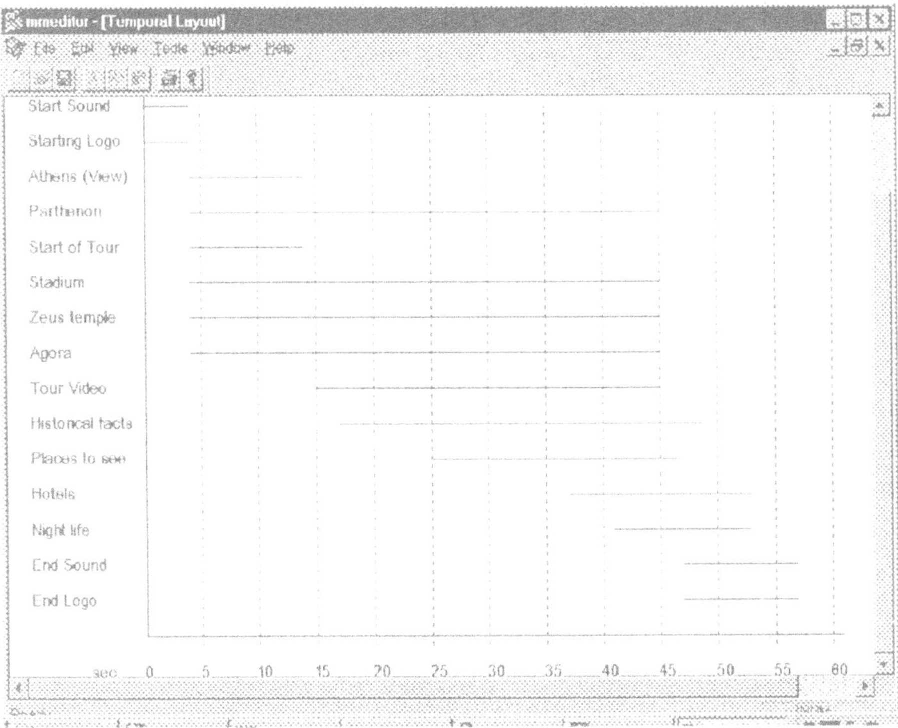

Figure 11.6: The temporal layout of the MAP

11.5.2. Spatial Layout

The term "spatial layout" implies the appearance of the MAP application window, conveying information about the position and dimensions of the actors participating in the MAP. It is important for MAP authors to be able to preview the MAP Spatiotemporal layout at any time during the development, so that the appropriate modification may take place. The spatial layout tool makes possible for the author to view how the application window will look like at any temporal point during a potential MAP execution (e.g. which objects and where on the application window, appear on the 20th sec. of the MAP). The temporal duration of each object is derived from the temporal layout.

The author may set the desired time point (see Figure 11.7) through the *timer* and then with *update display* option get the layout of the screen. Thus, the display may be checked before a new object is inserted and find *if* and *where* it should be placed.

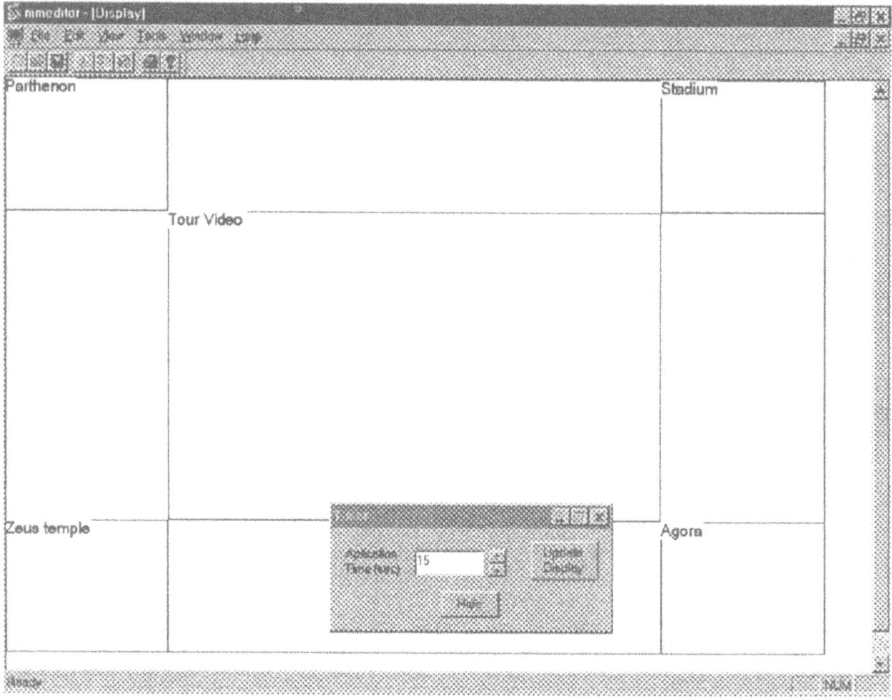

Figure 11.7: The spatial layout of the MAP at any time using the "Timer" tool.

11.5.3. Scenario animation tool

The most appealing feature of the verification tool is the opportunity to render (animate) the application. In other words, to have an animated view of the spatiotemporal specifications of an IMD in terms of spatial snapshots of the IMD evolving through time. This is accomplished through the "play" tool (see **Figure 11.8**). In this chapter we use the terms "rendering" and "animation" interchangeably. The animation is a simulation of an IMD execution session using consecutive snapshots of the application updated at regular time intervals. The author may change the value of this interval. The default temporal granularity is one second. This kind of animation enables the author notice any mistakes or misplacements and to mend them later.

The author has the opportunity to change the time limits of the animation and animate only a temporal part of the MAP (i.e. for the 5th to the 25th second). The animation may be interrupted at any time, while changes in the scenario may be done and then resume again into animation to verify the changes. The default values of the time limits are: 0 (for "Start Time") and the last second of the MAP (for the "End Time").

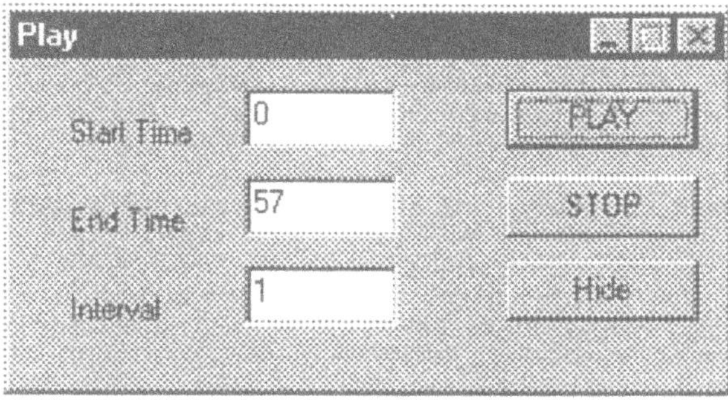

Figure 11.8: Scenario rendering tool.

In order to be able to manage large numbers of actors, we exploit the functionality of the previous tools (the spatial layout and). The animation is initiated by a list of objects that appear on the screen at start time, and is created by the spatial layout tool. This list is updated at time intervals imposed by the time granularity set by the author using the execution table and performing the actions it describes. Searching in the execution table is carried out by an algorithm of the family of the "divide and conquer" algorithms, in order to locate the actions of the corresponding to a specific temporal point (e.g. 10th sec). The time is measured by internal system timers.

11.5.4. Execution table

A common requirement is that the authors need to have an overview of the IMD structure in ascending temporal order. This need is fulfilled by the execution table tool. This table, that may be generated at any time during the authoring session, includes the temporal and spatial coordinates of each start and stop event in the IMD (see **Figure 11.9**). The table contents are listed in ascending temporal order (i.e. start or stop events for actors along with their position and size in the IMD). The execution table is filled with the appropriate data resulting from the sorted list of objects, and sorted again depending on the time that each event occurs (two events, start/stop for each object). It is feasible to have the execution table in text file by pressing the save button when the execution table window is active.

The MAP becomes persistent by saving it to a file. The file is in binary format and can be interpreted only by the tool. Another type of output is the "script". This is adopted for compatibility between authoring tools. The script, however, contains the declarative script representing the spatiotemporal relationships among the participating actors as the user has defined them.

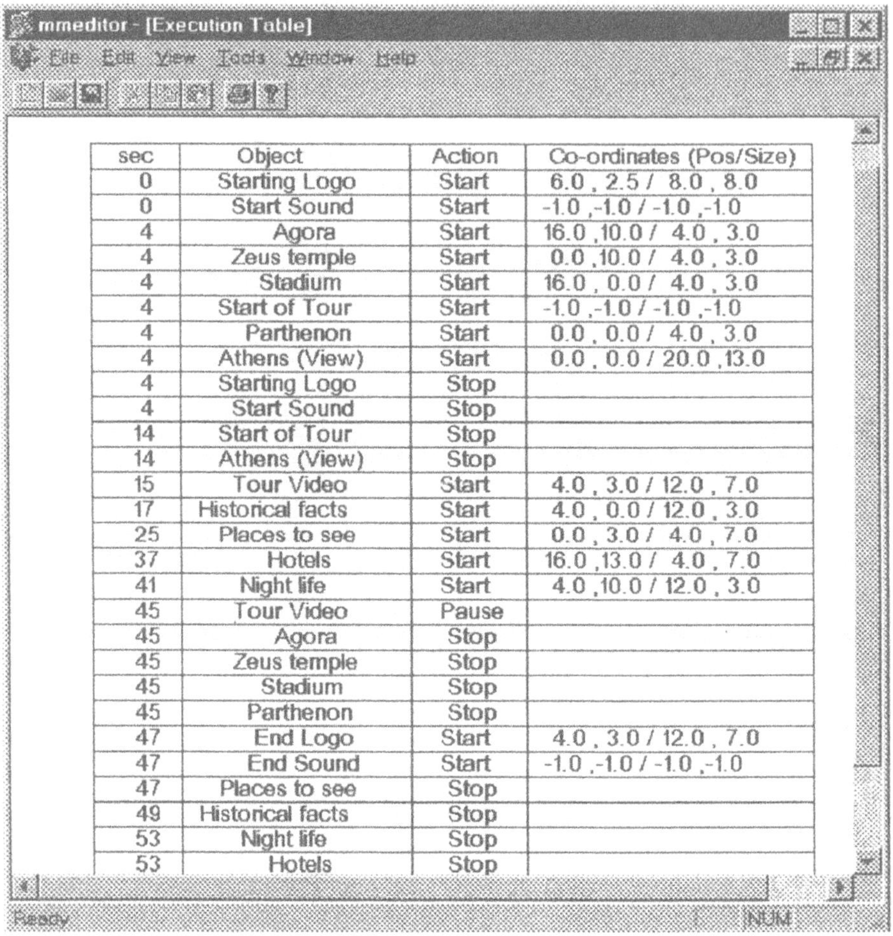

mmeditor - [Execution Table]

sec	Object	Action	Co-ordinates (Pos/Size)
0	Starting Logo	Start	6.0 , 2.5 / 8.0 , 8.0
0	Start Sound	Start	-1.0 ,-1.0 / -1.0 ,-1.0
4	Agora	Start	16.0 ,10.0 / 4.0 , 3.0
4	Zeus temple	Start	0.0 ,10.0 / 4.0 , 3.0
4	Stadium	Start	16.0 , 0.0 / 4.0 , 3.0
4	Start of Tour	Start	-1.0 ,-1.0 / -1.0 ,-1.0
4	Parthenon	Start	0.0 , 0.0 / 4.0 , 3.0
4	Athens (View)	Start	0.0 , 0.0 / 20.0 ,13.0
4	Starting Logo	Stop	
4	Start Sound	Stop	
14	Start of Tour	Stop	
14	Athens (View)	Stop	
15	Tour Video	Start	4.0 , 3.0 / 12.0 , 7.0
17	Historical facts	Start	4.0 , 0.0 / 12.0 , 3.0
25	Places to see	Start	0.0 , 3.0 / 4.0 , 7.0
37	Hotels	Start	16.0 ,13.0 / 4.0 , 7.0
41	Night life	Start	4.0 ,10.0 / 12.0 , 3.0
45	Tour Video	Pause	
45	Agora	Stop	
45	Zeus temple	Stop	
45	Stadium	Stop	
45	Parthenon	Stop	
47	End Logo	Start	4.0 , 3.0 / 12.0 , 7.0
47	End Sound	Start	-1.0 ,-1.0 / -1.0 ,-1.0
47	Places to see	Stop	
49	Historical facts	Stop	
53	Night life	Stop	
53	Hotels	Stop	

Ready NUM

Figure 11.9: The MAP execution table, presentation actions in temporal ascending order including spatial information (position and size)

11.6. CONCLUSIONS

In this paper we presented an implemented authoring & verification methodology for MAP documents development. The MAP design is based on a theoretical model for spatiotemporal compositions in the context of multimedia presentations (Vazirgiannis et al, 1998). The tool may be used both for *prototyping* and *verification* of multimedia presentations or spatiotemporal compositions in general. As for the authoring phase, emphasis was put on the flexible definition of spatial and temporal relationships of the participating entities. The authoring phase consists mainly of declarative specifications of the spatial and temporal ordering of participating multimedia objects based on their spatial and temporal relationships.

The *verification* procedures give multiple tools to designers, preview their applications, in various ways: *spatial layouts* of the application window, *temporal layout* of parts (or the whole application), indicating the temporal duration and relationships among the participating objects and *animation (rendering)* of the application (i.e. what would be the execution of the application like)..

The *advantageous features* of the proposed tools are the following:

Regarding authoring:

- Declarative & visual authoring methodology
- Integrated Spatiotemporal MAP specification, taking into account the temporal and spatial features of the participating objects along with their spatiotemporal relationships. The methodology is based on a sound theoretical framework.
- Relative actor positioning in spatial and temporal domains. Moreover, the object under concern may be related to different objects (i.e. "Object A to appear 10cm to the right of the bottom right corner of object B and 4 cm above the upper-left corner of object C" or "Object A to start 10sec after object B and 4 sec before object C").

As for *verification*, we provide a set of tools that enable the authors verify multiple aspects of their scenario and answer queries related to the spatiotemporal configuration of the MAP. The tools include spatial/temporal layouts and MAP animation tools.

The most important advantage of our design is that the authoring and the verification process are well integrated and interleaved so as the author is able to verify the authoring specification within the authoring procedure and environment.

The tool presented above may be extended towards the following directions:

- *Interactive scenario integrity checking:* The scenario integrity issue is crucial when designing a complex interactive scenario. The multitude of events and the related interactions that may occur in a MAP session may create a lot of potential evolution paths which are difficult to follow at authoring time, considering all potential implications.
- *Connection to other authoring tools.* It will be feasible that the specification will be exported to various authoring tools scripts (i.e. Assymetrix/Toolbook, Mac/Director, Hytime etc.). This would require translation of the tool proprietary script into the authoring tool script language. The specific mappings would be required.

References

J. F. Allen. (1983). "Maintaining Knowledge about Temporal Intervals". *Communications of the ACM*, 26(11)

A. Duda, C. Keramane. (1995)."Structured Temporal Composition of Multimedia Data", in the proceedings of the *IEEE-MMDBMS '95 workshop.*

N. Hirzalla, B. Falchunk, A. Karmouch. (1995). "A Temporal Model for Interactive Multimedia Scenarios". *IEEE Multimedia Magazine, Fall 1995.*

M. Iino, Y. F. Day, A. Ghafoor. (1994). "An Object - Oriented Model for Spatiotemporal Synchronization of Multimedia Information", *in the proc. of the IEEE Multimedia Conference*, pp. 110-119.

M. Jourdan, N. Layaïda, C. Roisin. (1998). A survey on authoring techniques for temporal scenarios of multimedia documents, *to be published in Handbook of multimedia , CRC Press.*

Karmouch. A, Emery J. (1996), "A playback Schedule Model for Multimedia Documents", *IEEE Multimedia, v3(1), pp. 50-63.*

P. R. King. (1994). "Towards a temporal logic based formalism for expressing temporal constraints in multimedia documents". *Technical Report 942, LRI, Universite de Paris-Sud, Orsay*, France.

T. Little, A. Ghafoor, (1992)."Interval-Based Conceptual Models for Time Dependent Multimedia Data", *IEEE Transactions on Knowledge and Data Engineering, vol. 5(4), pp. 551-563.*

D. Papadias, Y. Theodoridis, T. Sellis, M. Egenhofer. (1995). "Topological Relations in the World of Minimum Bounding Rectangles: a Study with R-trees", *Proceedings of ACM SIGMOD '95.*

M. Vazirgiannis, Y. Theodoridis, T. Sellis. (1998)."Spatiotemporal Composition and Indexing for Large Multimedia Applications", *to appear in ACM/Springer-Verlag Multimedia Systems Journal.*

12 ZYX — A SEMANTIC MODEL FOR MULTIMEDIA DOCUMENTS AND PRESENTATIONS

Susanne Boll, Wolfgang Klas

Database and Information Systems (DBIS)
University of Ulm, Computer Science Department, Ulm, Germany
{boll,klas}@informatik.uni-ulm.de

Abstract: Existing languages, formats, and multimedia document models such as HTML, MHEG, SMIL, HyTime, SGML, and XML, do not provide the appropriate modeling primitives needed to provide adequate support for *reusability*, *interaction*, *adaptation*, and *presentation-neutral description* of the structure and content of multimedia documents as required in the Cardio-OP project. Since each of these models lacks some significant concepts and does not meet all of the requirements, we propose a new approach for the semantic modeling of multimedia content, the ZYX model, which we implemented on the basis of an object-relational database system. The approach taken allows for fine-grained representation and retrieval of structures and layout of multimedia material, for flexible on-the-fly composition of multimedia fragments in order to create individualized multimedia documents, and for the realization of adaptation and personalization of multimedia presentations depending on the user environment specified by means of user profiles.

12.1 INTRODUCTION

Application fields that make dedicated use of various types of media most often require a well-organized and sound representation of the many semantic components and relationships defined between the different types of media. Depending on the requirements of such applications, one can choose from a variety of "data models" for modeling multimedia content, e.g., proprietary formats given by commercial products, or standards like HTML, MHEG [11, 10, 9], SMIL [6], and document models constructed by applying HyTime [8, 15], SGML [7], or XML [4]. All of these formats are quite open with regard to the formats of the "atomic" constituents like MPEG or JPEG they allow to build on. However, the various formats and document models differ significantly in various aspects: support for semantic modeling, interaction, reusability, flexible composition, adaptation and individualization for presentation, presentation-neutral storage, and Internet applicability. This is mainly due to the fact that the development of these formats took place in viewpoint of particular types of applications. HTML was developed for the WWW, which basically follows the hypertext approach, i.e., an interlinking of individual pages which do not form an integrated multimedia presentation. The development of MHEG-5 was mainly driven by the set-top-box type of application which resulted in a model that tries to organize the world by means of a collection of interconnected scenes. The HyTime development was driven by the idea of extending SGML toward support for multimedia documents, but it was based on a notion of documents which does not include user interaction. SMIL [6] has been developed for synchronized multimedia presentations in the Internet.

Background for our work is the project "Gallery of Cardiac Surgery" (Cardio-OP[1]). The overall goal is to develop a network-based and database-driven multimedia information system for physicians, medical lecturers, students, and patients in the domain of cardiac surgery. The system will serve as a common information and education base for its different types of users in the domain of cardiac surgery. The users are provided with multimedia information according to their specific request, their different understanding of the selected subject, their geographic location and technical infrastructure.

Within this project context, our group is developing concepts and prototypical implementations of a database-driven multimedia repository that integrates *modeling*, *management*, and *content-based retrieval* of multimedia content with flexible dynamic multimedia presentation services that *deliver* and *present* the multimedia content according to the user context. Major project requirements are the support for *interaction*, *reusability*, *adaptation*, and *presentation-neutral description* of the structure and content of multimedia documents.

As the information system is shared by different user groups it will be designed to support flexible re-use of the multimedia material in different context, with different communication media (on-line, CD-ROM, print media), and at different locations (university campus, hospitals, at home). The repository will contain pre-orchestrated reusable multimedia document fragments which can be composed on-the-fly to final multimedia documents. This calls for a presentation-neutral representation of multimedia content in the database allowing to store modular multimedia documents independent of the final presentation format. The quality of a presentation still is a parameter for such a

[1]Partially funded by the German Ministry of Research and Education, grant number 08C58456. Our project partners are the University Hospital of Ulm, Dept. of Cardiac Surgery and Dept. of Cardiology, the University Hospital of Heidelberg, Dept. of Cardiac Surgery, an associated Rehabilitation Hospital, the publishers Barth-Verlag and dpunkt-Verlag, Heidelberg, FAW Ulm, and ENTEC GmbH, St. Augustin. For details see also URL www.informatik.uni-ulm.de/dbis/GH/

composition of multimedia document fragment and will be determined by the output channel chosen by the user, e.g., at the university campus or at home.

Given these requirements, we face serious problems concerning the support for modeling the content given in the project by existing document models based on formats like HTML, MHEG, SMIL, HyTime, SGML/DSSSL, or XML. In this paper, we present the ZYX model, which forms the core for the modeling of the multimedia data in our repository. In comparison to existing models, it provides more adequate support for *semantic modeling*, *interaction*, *reusability* and *flexible composition*, *adaptation* and *individualization* for presentation, *presentation-neutral storage*, and *Internet applicability*.

The paper is organized as follows: Section 12.2 first provides a better understanding of the requirements, which leads to a metric that we used to analyze existing models. Second, the result of the analysis is summarized. Section 12.3 presents the basic ideas and design considerations of our model and gives a formal framework for a more detailed understanding. Section 12.4 summarizes our work and gives an outlook to future work.

12.2 BASIC REQUIREMENTS AND ANALYSIS OF EXISTING MODELS

In order to support modular and context-dependent composition of multimedia documents from media objects and parts of multimedia documents, we have to provide a data model which meets the following criteria:

Reusability. Reusability of document components should be supported along three dimensions: (1) *granularity* of the components, i.e., reuse of complete multimedia documents, fragments of multimedia documents, or individual atomic media objects, (2) *kind* of re-usage, i.e., identical reusage including all temporal, spatial, design and interaction relationships as given by the author, or structural reusage by means of separating layout and structure and reusing only structural parts, and (3) *selection* and *identification* of components, which calls for mechanisms for classifying, indexing, and querying components.

Interaction. Cardio-OP users should be able to interact with presentations in terms of three types of interaction: (1) *Navigational interactions* determining the user-defined flow of a multimedia presentation, (2) *design interactions* influencing the visual and audible layout of a presentation, and (3) *movie interactions* affecting the temporal course of the *entire* presentation. Navigational and design interactions should be specified within multimedia documents, whereas movie interactions are expected to be offered by the presentation engine.

Adaptation. Cardio-OP presentations should be adaptable to *user-specific characteristics*, i.e., personal interest of a user by means of professional level, degree of details, or user preferences, and by means of a user's technical infrastructure like kind of network connection, on-campus or off-campus locations. Adaptation of multimedia presentations should take place at the *client* and/or at the *server*, whatever is most suitable for the kind of adaptation needed.

Presentation-neutral Representation. The multimedia material available in the Cardio-OP repository has to be presentable in a heterogeneous software and hardware environment. As a consequence, the multimedia material has to be stored presentation-neutral, i.e., independent of the actual realization of a presentation at a client. This calls for converting a presentation-neutral representation of multimedia content into a presentation-specific format used for playout of the multimedia material. It is desirable that this conversion is lossless. The presentation-neutral representation of multimedia content should — besides the coverage of rich multimedia functionality — take place on a high level of semantics. The presentation-neutral model should be open in the sense that it allows for later integration of multimedia functionality expected to be developed in the future.

Figure 12.1 summarizes the analysis of the most relevant existing approaches and shows to which extent MHEG-5/6, HyTime, and SMIL, fulfill the specific requirements. Due to the limitation of space we can not present the comprehensive discussion how they meet the specific requirements in this paper but refer the reader to specific literature for a detailed description of the standards and data models. The analysis of existing standards, defacto standard formats, and

	MHEG-5 / MHEG-6	SMIL	HyTime
Reusage			
Granularity			
atomic media objects	+	+	+
document parts	-	-	+
complete documents	+	+	+
Kind of re-usage			
identical	+	+	+
structural	-	-	+
Identification/Selection	-	o	+
Interaction			
Navigational interactions	+	+	-
Design interactions	+	-	-
Adaptation			
User-specific Adaptation			
to personal interest	- / +	-	-
to technical infrastructure	- / +	o	-
Location of Adaptation			
Server-based	-	-	-
Client-based	- / +	+	-
Presentation-neutral representation			
Presentation-neutral	-	-	+
High semantic level	-	o	+

Figure 12.1: Summary of the support of the requirements by MHEG-5/6, SMIL, and HyTime (+ support, o partial support, — no support)

models shows that, although, individual formats and models are strong with respect to particular features, they are not capable to meet all the requirements identified in the Cardio-OP project. This led to the design and implementation of the ZyX model which tries to exploit the features of existing formats and models, especially also recent developments in the area of Internet-applicable models driven by the development of XML and SMIL.

12.3 THE ZyX MODEL

In the following, we first sketch some design considerations of our model and the points of contact with other approaches in the field in Section 12.3.1. In Section 12.3.2, we introduce the reader into the basic concepts of our ZyX data model before we present a formal framework in Section 12.3.3.

12.3.1 Design Considerations

For the design of the new model we considered the semantic level of the data model, the underlying temporal and spatial model, interaction capabilities, adaptation modeling and presentation neutral representation.

Semantic level. The semantic level of the data model is important for the support of both reusability of multimedia documents and fragments of multimedia documents and presentation-neutral representation of multimedia documents. We decided to develop a data model that describes a multimedia document on a high semantic level. This allows us a (lossy) *export* of our multimedia documents into data models like MHEG-5, SMIL, and HTML.

Document structure. For the structure of the document we consider a hierarchical organization of the document as can be found with SMIL documents. However, the modeling capabilities of our data model extends those of SMIL by the aspects of reusability and the possibilities for modeling adaptation to users interests.

Temporal model. We decided to use an interval-based temporal model. One important requirement to the temporal model hereby is its capability to describe the temporal dimension of interaction. Existing interval-based temporal models are mainly based on some or all of the 13 binary temporal relations between time intervals as defined by Allen [1]. These models, however, do not support time intervals of unknown duration that occur, e.g., in the context of user interaction in multimedia presentations (e.g., Object Composition Petri Nets (OCPN) [13]). With the Interval Expressions [5] we find a temporal model for multimedia presentations on the level of intervals with a set of temporal operators to relate time intervals which possibly have an unknown duration, that also overcomes the problem of temporal inconsistencies by construction. The Interval Expressions form the basis of the underlying temporal model of the ZyX data model.

Spatial model. We constrain ourselves to a simple spatial model as we emphasize the modeling of the temporal course, interaction, adaptation and reusability with our ZyX model. We decided to support the spatial layout by a point-based description of each visual media entity in a multimedia document. Each visual media entity has assigned 2-dimensional extension plus a third dimension to specify overlapping of visual media entities. We do not consider the specification of spatial relationships between media entities like *right-of* or *besides*. The ZyX data model, however, allows to be extended by a more sophisticated spatial model later.

Interaction. Our model supports the two interaction types navigational/ decision interactions and design interactions. This means that our model provides a comprehensive support for these two interaction types comparable with the interaction capabilities of MHEG-5, but more sophisticated than HyTime and SMIL.

Adaptation. Our model supports adaptation mechanisms like can be found with SMIL but that go far beyond the adaptation capabilities of SMIL. In SMIL adaptation is limited to the exploitation of a set of discriminating attributes of a `switch` element, like system-bitrate and system-language to select one out of a set of alternatives by evaluating these attributes. Our support for adaptation within the data model of the multimedia document is twofold — at selection time of the document and at presentation time of the document. Adaptation at selection time means that the document itself is adjustable to the user's interest and system environment before it is executed for presentation. Adaptation at presentation time means that in a client/server environment the presentation engine exploits information of the multimedia document to adjust, e.g., the quality of the selected media elements to cope with a lower network bandwidth.

Presentation-neutral representation. The presentation neutral representation of multimedia documents is strongly related to our requirement of reusability at different levels of granularity. We developed a generic representation that comprises the different granules: media elements, document fragment, and entire documents. The design allows to reuse and to compose these building block in an arbitrary fashion.

12.3.2 Basic Concepts of the ZyX Model

In this section, we present the terminology and the basic concepts of the ZyX model. The ZyX model describes a multimedia document by means of a tree. The nodes of the tree are the *presentation elements* and the edges of the tree *bind* the presentation elements together in a hierarchical fashion. Each presentation element has one *binding point* with which it can be bound to another presentation element to it. It also has one or more *variables* with which it can bind other presentation elements. Figure 12.2 shows the graphical representation of these basic elements of the model.

Presentation elements are the generic elements of the model. They can be mere media elements or hold the place for *fragments*. They can also be elements that represent the temporal, spatial, layout, and interactive semantic relationships between the elements of a multimedia document. Consider the example in Figure 12.3. A temporal element, e.g., the sequential element *seq*, binds the media elements $slide_1$, $slide_2$ and $slide_3$ to its variables v_2, v_3, and

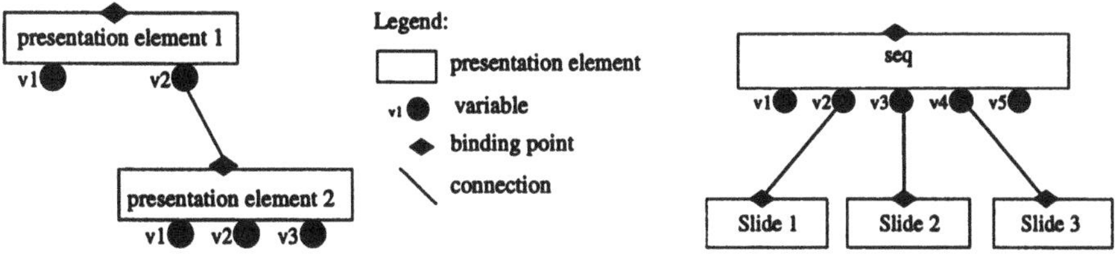

Figure 12.2: Graphical representation of the basic document elements

Figure 12.3: Simple document tree with seq element

v_4. This represents the semantic relationship of the sequential presentation of the three slides. With the *seq* element's binding point this sequential slide presentation can be bound to another presentation element in a more complex multimedia document tree.

We now explain the modeling capabilities of our model with regard to our specific requirements of reusability, interaction, adaptation and presentation-neutral representation.

Reusability. In the ZYX model, not all of the variables of a presentation element must be bound at authoring time. In Figure 12.3 the variables v_1 and v_5, e.g., the title and the summary of the slide presentation are still unbound. This means that the slide sequence can later be completed by binding presentation elements to the *free variables.* The simple sample tree in Figure 12.3 hence forms a "template". This is an important feature for building reusable *fragments* that can be reused in different multimedia documents by binding the free variables differently corresponding to the context.

It is also possible to form more complex fragments like the one shown in Figure 12.4. Here, on different "levels" of the specification tree variables are left unbound. To make later composition of such fragments easier a fragment can be *encapsulated* by a *complex media element.* This means that a fragment appears like a single presentation element in the specification tree with one binding point and a set of free variables. The free variables of the fragment are *exported.* Figure 12.4 illustrates how a complex media element encapsulates a complex fragment. The complex media element somehow is the black box view to a complex presentation fragment. Analogously, an *external media element* encapsulates a specification of a fragment that was composed in another *external* document format. This allows that the inclusion of existing documents into our model. What, however, is encapsulated by the external media element is dependent of the external document format. The concepts of free variables and complex media element guarantee reusability on the level of presentation fragments. External media elements allow for document format comprehensive reusability.

Reusability on the level of media elements is supported by means of *selector elements.* These are presentation elements that determine *what,* that is which

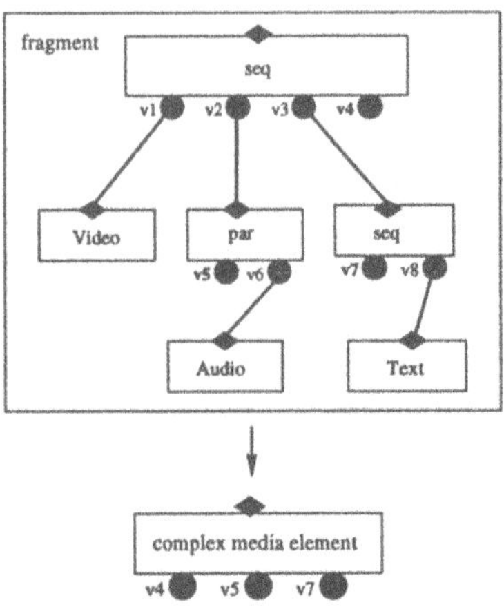

Figure 12.4: Complex fragment encapsulated in a complex media element

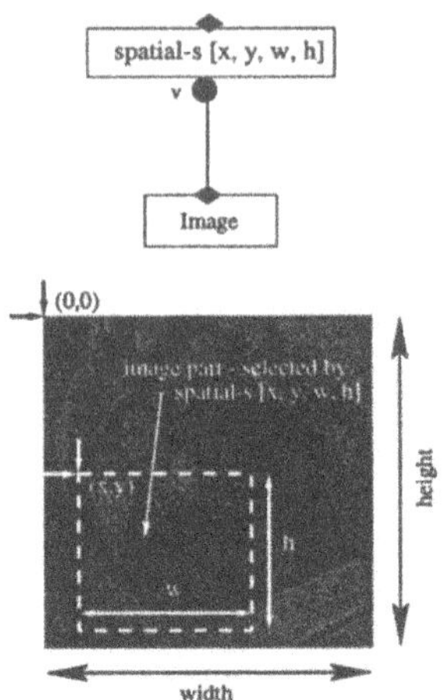

Figure 12.5: Spatial selector element — *spatial-s* $[x, y, w, h]$ and its semantics

part of a media element is presented. They can be used to select a specific part of an audio or a specific area of an image. Figure 12.5 illustrate such a usage and semantics of a spatial selector element. Here, a spatial selector is applied to an image media element to select a rectangular area from the image. The selectors can be applied to both media elements as well as to fragments, e.g., a temporal selector to select two minutes of an existing slide presentation. The selectors can be organized in a hierarchy so that, e.g., one can select a part of a video element with a certain duration by means of a temporal selector and use only a specific detail by means of a spatial selector.

Besides the selector elements the ZYX data model offers *projector elements* that influence the visual and audible layout in a presentation of a multimedia document. Projector elements determine *how* a media element or a fragment is presented. They determine for example the presentation speed of a video or the spatial position of a video on the screen. Projectors can only be bound to *projector variables* of media elements and fragments. Each presentation element can have one or more projector variables to which projectors can be bound. Figure 12.6 illustrates the usage of projector elements and their semantics when the document is presented. In this example a fragment defines the sequential presentation of two text elements and a video. Two projector elements are bound to the sequential element, a spatial projector and a typographic projector. A projector applies not only to the presentation element it is bound to but also to its subtree. However, a projector applies only to those elements in the same tree that can be affected by it. A spatial projector affects the layout of an image but not that of an audio. The semantics of the spatial projector is to define the position of all three visual elements for a presentation. The typographic projector applies to the two text elements and sets their font, size and style for presentation. The appearance of an audio by an acoustic projector element and so on. By means of the projector elements one can add two layouts to the same document. This allows for reusability of the same document in different presentation contexts.

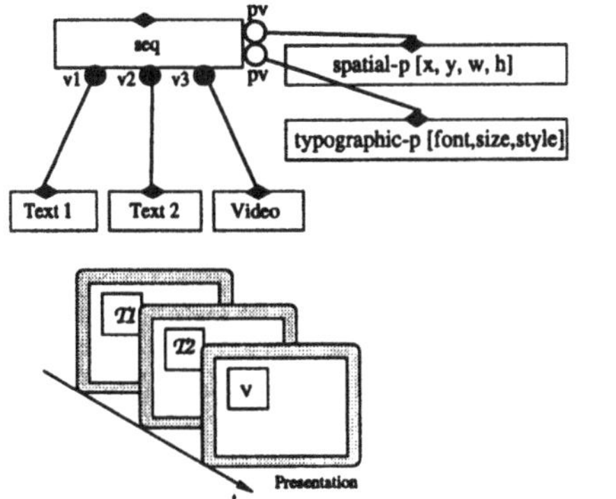

Figure 12.6: Simple fragment with spatial and typographic projector elements — *spatial-p* $[x, y, w, h]$ *typographic-p* $[font, size, style]$ and their semantics

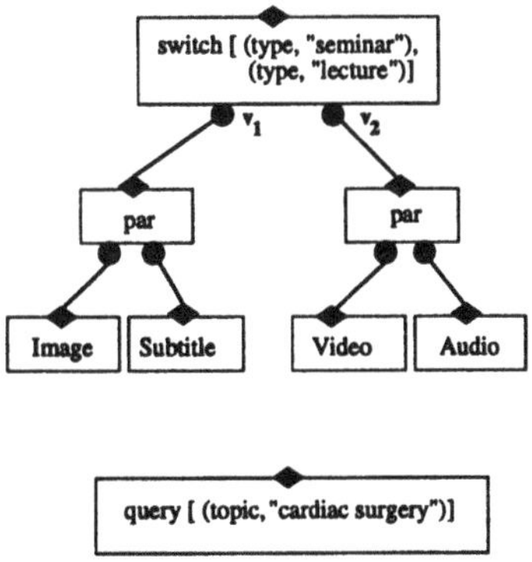

Figure 12.7: Specification of presentation alternatives with the switch and the query element

Adaptation. Adaption in the context of the ZyX model means that the multimedia document delivered to a user for presentation in respond to a user query should match the user's interest and the user's system environment collected in a user *profile.* Therefore, each fragment is assigned a set of meta data that describes its content. In addition to the multimedia document a user profile, also meta data, is defined to capture values that describe a user, topics of interest, presentation system environment, network connection characteristics and the like. *Meta data* that describes users and fragments is organized as key-value pairs.

The ZyX data model offers presentation elements to support adaptation to a user's profile by means of *switch elements* and the *query elements.*

The switch elements allows to specify different alternatives for a part of the document. One of the alternatives is selected corresponding to the user profile. An illustration of the switch element is given in Figure 12.7. When the document is presented depending of the type of teaching either the left or the right subtree is presented. A switch element is used if all alternatives are known to the author of the fragment.

However, there might be the case that the selected alternative can be determined only at selection time. For example, an author wants to determine that at a specific point in the presentation about "cardiac surgery" a digression to physiology is to be made but does not specify which fragments are relevant to this. This can be specified with a *query* element. The query is represented by a set of meta data. When the document is selected for presentation the query element is evaluated and replaced by the fragment best matching the meta data. An illustration of the query element is given in Figure 12.7. The sample query element is the place holder for the fragment best matching the query with topic "cardiac surgery". The more meta data tuples are used the more specific the query is.

Interaction. The requirement to support the modeling of interactive multimedia presentations is met by the data model's *interaction elements.* The model offers two types of interaction elements, *navigational interactive elements* and *design interactive elements.* Example for a navigational elements is the *link* element that allows to specify hypertext structure. A *menu* element supports to interactively follow of one presentation out of a set of presentations paths. The design interactive elements are the interactive version of the projector elements. For example, for the typographic projector that allows to specify font, size and style of a text, the *interactive typographic selector element* specifies that these settings can be carried out interactively when the document is presented.

Presentation-neutral representation. The usage of projectors does not mean that the layout is statically anchored in the document. As outlined before not all variables of a presentation element must be bound in the first place. They can be bound when the document is selected for presentation. This is also the point in time when the projector variables of a document can be bound to a set of projectors. This follows the idea of separating structure from layout information as can be found with SGML and XML and complies with our requirement for presentation-neutral representation of the documents.

12.3.3 Formal Framework of the ZyX Model

12.3.3.1 Basic Terminology. The *presentation elements* are the generic elements of the ZyX model. Each presentation element p has assigned exactly one *binding point* b_p. This is the connector with which a presentation element can be bound to another presentation element. A presentation element has furthermore 0 to n *variables* v which are used to bind other presentation elements to it. To add layout information to a presentation element it optionally can have 0 to n *projector variables* pv that can be used to bind *projector elements* to the element. Projector variables can be seen just as "normal" variables, that is $v \equiv pv$. The projector variables are separated due to separating structure and layout (see Section 12.3.3.3). In the following definitions, let denote B the set of all binding points, VAR the set of all variables, $PVAR$ the set of all projector variables, T the set of all element types, MT the set of media types, M the set of all raw media data, $OT \subseteq T$ the set of all operator element types. A presentation element p can therefore be defined as follows:

Definition 12.3.1 (Presentation element)
A presentation element p is a tuple $p : [t_p, b_p, V_p, PV_p]$ with $t_p \in T$ denoting the type of p, $b_p \in B$ denoting the binding point of p, $V_p \subseteq VAR$ denoting the set of variables of p, and $PV_p \subseteq PVAR$ denoting the set of projector variables of p. p can be augmented with further tuple elements depending on its type t_p.

A presentation element p can be an atomic media element, a complex media element, an external media element, or a specific element to build up the temporal, structural and interactive relationships of a multimedia presentation.

The basic units of a multimedia document are the *atomic media elements.* An atomic media element is an instantiation of a *media type.* The atomic media element in our model abstracts from the raw media data and just represents the media element and its media specific characteristics.

Definition 12.3.2 (Atomic media element)
An atomic media element $am : [t_{am}, b_{am}, V_{am}, PV_{am}, m]$ is a presentation element with $t_{am} \in MT = \{Audio, Video, Image, Text\} \subseteq T$, $V_{am} = \emptyset$, and $m \in M$ denoting the media data represented by am.

Presentation elements are interconnected via the variables and binding points. In the graphical representation connections are represented by edges between presentation elements (see Figure 12.2). A *connection* is defined as:

Definition 12.3.3 (Connection)
A connection $c = [v, b_{p'}]$ connects the (projector) variable $v \in V_p \cup PV_p$ of a presentation element p with the binding point $b_{p'}$ of presentation element $p' \neq p$.

The result of interconnecting presentation elements is a specification tree that describes a *fragment.* A fragment encapsulates a reusable part of a multimedia document be it a single media element, a part, or an entire multimedia document. The formal description of a valid fragment is given in Definition 12.3.4.

Definition 12.3.4 (Fragment)
A fragment $f = (P, C)$ is an acyclic, undirected graph that describes a part or an entire multimedia document with:

- *P the set of presentation elements that are part of the tree.*
- *$C \subseteq \{[v, b_{p'}] \mid p, p' \in P, p \neq p', v \in V_p \cup PV_p\}$ the set of connections in the tree.*

For a valid fragment $f = (P, C)$ the following conditions must hold:

1. *If $c_1, c_2 \in C$, $c_1 = [v_1, b_p], c_2 = [v_2, b_p], p \in P$ then $v_1 = v_2$, i.e., each binding point can be bound to only one variable.*
2. *If $c_1, c_2 \in C$, $p, p' \in P$ and $c_1 = [v, b_p], c_2 = [v, b_{p'}]$ then $p = p'$, i.e., each variable can be bound to only one binding point.*

3. $Unbound_f = \{p \in P | \neg \exists v \in \bigcup_{p' \in P} V_{p'} : [v, b_p] \in C\}$ *and* $|Unbound_f| = 1$, $root_f = p \in Unbound_f$
There is exactly one presentation element $p \in P$ *of the fragment* f *that is not bound to any other presentation element. This unbound presentation element is called the root element, denoted* $root_f$*, of the fragment and has the binding point* b_{root_f} *that forms the "entry point" of the fragment.*

4. There is no sequence of connections $c_1, \ldots, c_n$*, such that* $c_i = [v_i, b_{p_i}], i = 1 \ldots n-1$*, with* $v_{i+1} \in V_{p_i}$*, and* $v_1 \in V_{p_n}$*. This means that* f *is acyclic.*

Fragments form the building blocks of a multimedia document. They are the units that can be reused and recomposed in different multimedia documents. Therefore, the definition of a *complex media object* is needed. A complex media object *cm* encapsulates a fragment $f = (P, C)$ so that a fragment can simply be reused like a presentation element in any other fragment. A complex media element *cm* can be characterized as follows:

Definition 12.3.5 (Complex media element)
A complex media element cm : $[t_{cm}, b_{cm}, V_{cm}, PV_{cm}, f]$ *is a presentation element with* $t_{cm} = Complex \in T$, $f = (P, C)$ *denoting the fragment encapsulated by cm,* $b_{cm} = b_{root_f}$, $V_{cm} = \{v \in \bigcup_{p \in P} V_p \mid \forall q \in P : [v, b_q] \notin C\}$*, and* $PV_{cm} = \{pv \in \bigcup_{p \in P} PV_p \mid \forall q \in P : [pv, b_q] \notin C\}$.

The binding point of the root of the encapsulated fragment f is also the binding point of the complex media object *cm*. All variables and all projector variables in the fragment f that are not bound are *exported* and form the unbound variables and projector variables of the complex media object. For an illustration see Figure 12.4.

As complex media objects encapsulate fragments of multimedia documents, they offer a means of abstraction. Complex media objects can be treated like presentation elements and can be used in any other fragment, arbitrary complex. The export of unbound variables also allows for a later specialization of complex media objects. Hence, by complex media elements document templates can be encapsulated.

To encapsulate fragments that are specified in an external format we define, *external media elements*. An external media element *em* is also a complex media element. It encapsulates, however, not a fragment specified in ZyX , but the specification of an external fragment available in another data model. Like the complex media element, the external media element has assigned a set of variables V_{em}, projector variables PV_{em}, and one binding point b_{em}. However, the meaning of the variables and projector variables depends on the external document format.

With the definitions given so far it is possible to arrange presentation elements in certain relationships by means of connections. Though the connections of variables to binding points bring presentation elements in a relationship, the semantics of this relationship is not yet defined. Therefore, our data model offers different types of operator elements which relate presentation elements with a certain semantics.

In the following, we present the element definitions of several groups of *temporal operators*, *projectors*, *selectors*, *interaction elements*, and *adaptation elements*. These elements determine the semantics that have to be interpreted by a presentation environment and mapped into the spatial, temporal, structural, interaction, and adaptive domain of a multimedia presentation. In the following definitions, only the domains of those tuple elements that characterize the element specific semantics are explicitly given.

12.3.3.2 Temporal Operator Elements. The *temporal operator elements* determine the temporal relationships between the presentation elements. As outlined above, our temporal model is based on Interval Expressions [5]. In the following, we present the definition, specific parameters, and semantics of the temporal operator elements *par*, *seq*, *loop*, and *delay*. For an illustration of the temporal operator elements see Figure 12.8.

The semantics of the *par operator element* is that the presentation elements bound to its variables are to be presented in parallel by a presentation engine. The element is defined as follows:

Definition 12.3.6 (Temporal operator element — *par*)
The temporal operator element par : $[t_{par}, b_{par}, V_{par}, PV_{par}, finish, lipsync]$ *is a presentation element with* $t_{par} = Par \in OT$, $V_{par} = \{v_1, \ldots, v_n\} \subseteq VAR$, $finish \in \{1, \ldots, n, min, max\}$, *and* $lipsync \in \mathcal{N}_0$.

The *par* operator element offers two parameters to control the synchronization of parallel presentation. The parameter $finish$ determines which one of the n presentation elements terminates the parallel presentation, i.e., the one with the minimal presentation time by setting $finish = min$, the maximum presentation time by setting $finish = max$, or a dedicated presentation element bound to v_i, by setting $finish = i, i \in \{1, \ldots, n\}$. If the parameter $lipsync = 0$ no lip synchronization is specified. If the value of $lipsync = i$, $i > 0$, the presentation of the presentation elements bound to $v_1, \ldots, v_n$ is carried out in lip synchronization and the presentation element bound to v_i forms the master of the synchronization.

The semantics of the *seq operator element* is that a presentation engine presents the presentation elements that are bound to it in sequence. The presentation of a *seq* operator element starts the sequential presentation of the presentation elements that are bound to the variables $v_i, i = 1 \ldots n$ in the order of $v_1, v_2, \ldots, v_n$. The presentation of the *seq* operator element ends with the end of the presentation of the element bound to v_n. The *seq* operator element is defined as:

Definition 12.3.7 (Temporal operator element — *seq*)
The temporal operator element seq : $[t_{seq}, b_{seq}, V_{seq}, PV_{seq}]$ *is a presentation element with* $t_{seq} = Seq \in OT$, *and* $V_{seq} = \{v_1, \ldots, v_n\} \subseteq VAR$.

The semantics of a *loop operator element* is that its presentation starts the repeated presentation of the single presentation element bound to $v \in V_{loop}$. The presentation is repeated r times and stops after the rth presentation of the presentation element.

Definition 12.3.8 (Temporal operator element — *loop*)
The temporal operator element loop : $[t_{loop}, b_{loop}, V_{loop}, PV_{loop}, r]$ *is a presentation element with* $t_{loop} = Loop \in OT$, $|V_{loop}| = 1$, *and* $r \in \mathcal{N}$.

The *delay* operator element models a temporal delay of t milliseconds. It can be seen as an "empty" media element that is presented for t milliseconds.

Definition 12.3.9 (Temporal operator element — *delay*)
The temporal operator element delay : $[t_{delay}, b_{delay}, V_{delay}, PV_{delay}, t]$ *is a presentation element with* $t_{delay} = Delay \in OT$, $V_{delay} = \emptyset = PV_{delay}$, *and* $t \in \mathcal{N}$.

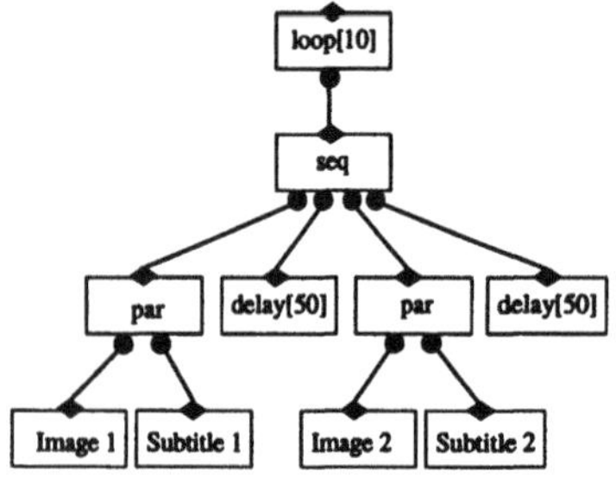

Figure 12.8: Fragment illustrating the usage and semantics of the temporal operator elements

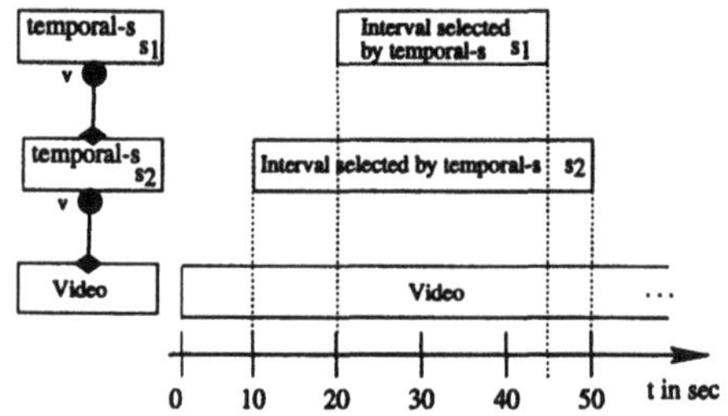

Figure 12.9: Sample fragment illustrating the usage and semantics of the temporal selector element *temporal-s*

12.3.3.3 Projectors. To add "layout" information to a presentation element, it can have 0 to n projector variables pv that can be used to bind *projector elements* to the presentation element. The projector elements can be statically bound to projector variables at authoring time or just before the presentation of a document. Projector elements are also presentation elements that determine *how* presentation elements are presented. A projector element can not bind other presentation elements and, therefore, for all projector elements $V_{proj} = \emptyset$ and $PV_{proj} = \emptyset$. The model offers four different projector elements, *spatial-p*, *temporal-p*, *acoustic-p*, and *typographic-p*, some of which we define in the following.

First, an auxiliary definition of the notion of a *successor* in a fragment needed for subsequent definitions is given:

Definition 12.3.10 (Successor)
Let $\mathcal{F}$ *denote the set of all fragments. We then define a function expand* : $\mathcal{F} \to$

$\mathcal{F}$ that computes for a fragment f the fragment that is semantically equivalent to f but does not contain any complex media element. expand(f) recursively replaces each complex media element in f by the fragment that the complex media element encapsulates.

Be $f \in \mathcal{F}$ a fragment, $expand(f) = (P, C)$, and $p, p' \in P$ presentation elements. Then the following direct and indirect successor relationships hold:

1. *p' is direct successor of $p \iff \exists [v, b_{p'}] \in C : v \in V_p$.*
2. *p' is indirect successor of $p \iff p'$ is not a direct successor of p and there exists a sequence $succ_1, \ldots, succ_n, n \in \mathcal{N}$ with $succ_1$ is direct successor of p, $succ_i$ is direct successor of $succ_{i-1}, i = 2, \ldots, n$, and p' is direct successor of $succ_n$.*
3. *p' is successor of $p \iff p'$ is direct or indirect successor of p.*

For example, in Figure 12.4 the video media element and the parallel element are direct successors of the root sequential element. The audio element is an indirect successor of the root sequential element and a direct successor of the parallel element. There is no successor relationship between video and the audio media element.

The presentation semantics of the *spatial projector element spatial-p* (Definition 12.3.11) bound to a presentation element p is that the presentation engines "projects" the visual presentation of p on a rectangular presentation area, which is defined by the projector element. The parameters x and y define the position of the upper left corner of a rectangle with the given *width* and *height*. The parameter *priority* defines the order of the overlapping of visual objects so that an object with a higher priority value covers objects with a lower priority value. The parameter *unit* defines the measurement unit to specify whether the values $x, y, width, height$ are given in pixel or in percent of a presentation window.

Definition 12.3.11 (Spatial projector element — *spatial-p*)
The spatial projector element spatial-p : $[t_{spatial-p}, b_{spatial-p}, V_{spatial-p}, PV_{spatial-p}, x, y, width, height, priority, unit]$ is a presentation element with $t_{spatial-p} = \text{Spatial-P} \in OT$, $V_{spatial-p} = PV_{spatial-p} = \emptyset$, x, y, $priority \in \mathcal{N}_0$, $width$, $height \in \mathcal{N}$, and $unit \in \{pixel, percent\}$.

A spatial projector applies not only to the presentation element it is bound to but to all successors of this presentation element. If the projector is bound to a media object then the media object is scaled to the presentation area defined by the projector's parameters. If the *spatial-p* element of a presentation element p defines a presentation rectangle, the spatial coordinates and extensions of the successors of p are seen in the context of that rectangle and not of the entire presentation window.

The presentation semantics of the *temporal projector element temporal-p* (Definition 12.3.12) bound to a presentation element p is that a presentation engine presents the element p with the given playback direction and speed. The parameter *direction* specifies, whether the presentation element (and its subtree) is presented in forward (1) or in backward direction (−1). The actual playback speed is computed by multiplying the original playback speed with the factor given by the speed parameter.

Definition 12.3.12 (Temporal projector element — *temporal-p*)
The temporal projector element temporal-p : $[t_{temporal-p}, b_{temporal-p}, V_{temporal-p}, PV_{temporal-p}, direction, speed]$ *is a presentation element with* $t_{temporal-p}$ = *Temporal-P* $\in OT$, $V_{temporal-p} = PV_{temporal-p} = \emptyset$, *direction* $\in \{-1, 1\}$, *and speed* $\in \Re^+$.

Like the spatial projector element a temporal projector element applies not only to the presentation element p it is bound to but to all successors of that presentation element. If, for example, the *temporal-p* projector of a presentation element p defines *speed* = 2 and a successor p' of p has a temporal projector that also defines *speed* = 2 then in fact the successor p' is presented at a speed factor of 4.

In the same way an acoustic projector element and a typographic projector element are defined. The acoustic projector element *acoustic-p* affects the, e.g., volume, balance, base, and treble of the presentation of a presentation element p, while the typographic projector element *typographic-p* affects parameters like the font, size, and style of the presentation of p.

12.3.3.4 Selectors. The model offers *selector elements* to reuse parts of media elements and fragments, i.e., spatial regions, temporal intervals. A *temporal selector element temporal-s* (Definition 12.3.13) is a presentation element that can bind one other presentation element p. The presentation semantics of this element is that the presentation of the direct and indirect successors of p is started *start* milliseconds after the original starting point of the fragment and lasts for *duration* milliseconds.

Definition 12.3.13 (Temporal selector element — *temporal-s*)
The temporal selector element temporal-s : $[t_{temporal-s}, b_{temporal-s}, V_{temporal-s}, PV_{temporal-s}, start, duration]$ *is presentation element with* $|V_{temporal-s}| = 1$, $t_{temporal-s}$ = *Temporal-S* $\in OT$, *and start, duration* $\in \mathcal{N}_0$.

A *spatial selector spatial-s* (Definition 12.3.14) element can bind one other presentation element p, which can be a visual media element like an image or a video but also a complex media element. The spatial selector selects a spatial area from p. The presentation semantics is that the presentation engine presents only those visual parts of p and its successors that are visible in the rectangular area that is specified with the element's parameters x, y, *width*, and *height*.

Definition 12.3.14 (Spatial selector element — *spatial-s*)
The spatial selector element spatial-s : $[t_{spatial-s}, b_{spatial-s}, V_{spatial-s}, PV_{spatial-s}, x, y, width, height]$ *is a presentation element with* $t_{spatial-s}$ = *Spatial-S* $\in OT$, $|V_{spatial-s}| = 1$, x, $y \in \mathcal{N}_0$, *and width, height* $\in \mathcal{N}$.

The application of selector elements is context sensitive. That is, it applies to the entire subtree of the presentation element bound to it. Selector elements can be organized in a hierarchy. Then, each selector element is applied relatively to the context of the subtree bound to it. Consider for example two temporal selector elements s_1 and s_2, $s_1 = [\textit{Temporal-S}, b_{s_1}, \{v_{s_1}\}, \emptyset, 10000, 25000]$ and $s_2 = [\textit{Temporal-S}, b_{s_2}, \{v_{s_2}\}, \emptyset, 10000, 40000]$. Let s_2 be a direct or indirect successor of s_1 then the selected temporal interval defined by s_1 is defined relative to the temporal interval specified by s_2 (see Figure 12.9).

12.3.3.5 Interaction Elements. To support the requirement of interactive multimedia presentations, the model offers different *interaction elements.*

The *link* interaction element (Definition 12.3.15) can be used to model navigational interactions between multimedia documents. Herewith hypertext structures can be modeled.

Definition 12.3.15 (Interaction element — *link*)
The interaction element link : $[t_{link}, b_{link}, V_{link}, PV_{link}]$ *is a presentation element with* $t_{link} = Link \in OT$, $V_{link} = \{v_1, \ldots, v_n, t_1, \ldots, t_n\}$, *and* $n \in \mathcal{N}$.

The *link* interaction element defines a set of links between the presentation elements bound to $v_i \in V_{link}, i = 1 \ldots n$, and the presentation elements bound to $t_i \in V_{link}$. Each presentation element bound to v_i represents the anchors of a link while the presentation element bound to the variable t_i specificies the target of the link. The presentation semantics of the *link* element is that a user interaction, e.g., a mouse click, with a presentation element bound to v_i, e.g., an image, starts the presentation of the target presentation element bound to t_i, e.g., a slide show. The presentation of the link element terminates when an interaction with one of the anchor elements occurred or the presentation of all anchor elements is terminated.

While a *link* interaction element is intended for the navigation *between* documents, the *menu* interaction element (Definition 12.3.16) is provided to allow for navigation *within* a document, i.e., the selection of one out of a set of presentation paths.

Definition 12.3.16 (Interaction element — *menu*)
The interaction element menu : $[t_{menu}, b_{menu}, V_{menu}, PV_{menu}, mode]$ *is a presentation element with* $t_{menu} = Menu \in OT$, $mode \in \{vanish, prevail\}$, $V_{menu} = \{v_1, \ldots, v_n, t_1, \ldots, t_n\}$, *and* $n \in \mathcal{N}$.

Similar to the *link* interaction element, the *menu* interaction element defines a set of selectable presentation elements bound to $v_i \in V_{menu}, i = 1 \ldots n$. The presentation elements bound to $t_i \in V_{menu}, i = 1 \ldots n$ represent the corresponding target elements of the selection. The presentation semantics of the *menu* element is that on presentation of the *menu* element, the engine starts in parallel the presentation of the elements bound to $v_i \in V_{menu}, i = 1 \ldots n$. On selection of a presentation element bound to v_i, the engine presents the target element of the selection bound to t_i. That is, a selection of the element bound to v_i corresponds to the presentation of the target bound to t_i. If parameter $mode = vanish$, the engine finishes the presentation of all presentation elements bound to $v_j, j = 1 \ldots n$, and starts the presentation of the presentation element bound to t_i. If parameter $mode = prevail$, the engine "merges" the presentation of the presentation element bound to t_i with the currently running presentation. If no element is selected, the presentation of the *menu* element stops as soon as the presentation of all presentation elements bound to $v_i, i = 1 \ldots n$, is finished.

We have also defined two further types of interaction elements, ***interactive projector elements*** and ***interactive selector elements***. These elements comply in general with the projector and selector elements presented before, but they have an additional "interactive" component. For each projector element and selector element, a corresponding interaction element is offered. With these interactive elements design interactions of multimedia presentations can be modeled.

For example, an interactive projector element *temporal-pi* is an interactive variant of the *temporal-p* projector element. Its presentation semantics is that, in addition to the specified temporal projection, the presentation engine offers a user to interactively adjust the parameters *direction* and *speed*.

12.3.3.6 Adaptation elements. Our model offers the two elements *switch* and *query* which allow for the adaptation of a multimedia presentation according to the user's interest and system environment that are described in a ***global profile GP*** by means of attribute value pairs. The *switch* adaptation element (Definition 12.3.17) serves the purpose to specify different presentation alternatives with regard to GP.

Definition 12.3.17 (Adaptation element — *switch*)
The adaptation element switch : $[t_{switch}, b_{switch}, V_{switch}, PV_{switch}, M_1, \ldots, M_n]$ *is a presentation element with* $t_{switch} = Switch \in OT$, M_i *denoting sets of attribute-value pairs,* $V_{switch} = \{v_1, \ldots, v_n, v_{default}\}$, *and* $n \in \mathcal{N}$.

The semantics of the *switch* element is that upon its presentation the presentation engine sequentially evaluates the metadata given with the GP against the sets of metadata $M_i, i = 1 \ldots n$. Let $M_j, j \in \{1, \ldots, n\}$ be the set of metadata which matches best GP. Then, the fragment bound to v_j is presented. If there is no suitable set of metadata among $M_1, \ldots, M_n$, the presentation element bound to $v_{default}$ is selected for presentation. The presentation of the *switch* element terminates when the presentation of the selected presentation element is finished.

In cases in which the presentation alternatives of a document are not known at authoring time, the *query* element (Definition 12.3.18) is provided. The *query* element is a placeholder for a fragment. It specificies a "query" which selects a fragment at presentation time from all available fragments. Therefore, we enhance the definition of a fragment such that it includes metadata, i.e., $f = (P, C, M)$ with M being a set of attribute-value pairs. This metadata describes both the content of a fragment f and technical features of the fragment like the network bandwidth needed for its presentation.

Definition 12.3.18 (Adaptation element — *query*)
The adaptation element query : $[t_{query}, b_{query}, V_{query}, PV_{query}, M]$ *is a presentation element with* $t_{query} = Query \in OT$, M *denoting a set of attribute-value pairs, and* $V_{query} = \emptyset$.

The semantics of the *query* element is that the presentation engine evaluates the metadata specified with $M \cup GP$ against the metadata given with all fragments known to the system. Then the fragment with the best match with respect to M and the profile GP is selected for presentation. This allows to dynamically select the most suitable fragment at presentation time taking into account the actual user interest and system environment. The presentation of the *query* element terminates when the presentation of the selected fragment is finished.

12.4 CONCLUSION AND FUTURE WORK

Starting out with the requirements of the Cardio-OP project, which calls for the support of ***reusability***, ***interaction***, ***adaptation***, and ***presentation-neutral description*** of the structure and content of multimedia documents, we sketched our analysis of existing relevant multimedia document models. As these models do not meet the project's requirements, we introduced our new ZYX model that gives the necessary support. We outlined the design considerations and the basic concepts followed by a formal framework of the ZYX primitives.

The ZYX model has been implemented as a DataBlade module for the object-relational database system Informix Dynamic Server/Universal Data Option under Sun Solaris, following the architectural framework initially presented in [12, 3]. Ongoing work includes the identification and realization of possible optimizations of the implementation of the DataBlade.

The formal description served as the basis for the definition of an XML DTD for the ZYX model[2]. This will enable access to content stored in the Cardio-OP repository by future XML-capable browsers and we can also think about storing ZYX documents in an SGML/XML-capable database system in the future, following the approach taken in [2].

Furthermore, we are working on a generic presentation engine for ZYX documents which includes support for continuous MPEG video streams based on an extension of the L/MRP buffer management technique [14].

Further work is needed to extend the representation of meta data, its usage for querying the Cardio-OP repository taking into account the various approaches discussed in, e.g., [16], and to exploit appropriate indexing techniques.

[2]The element definitions for a very first version of an XML DTD is available under URL www.informatik.uni-ulm.de/dbis/Cardio-OP/cardioopxml.dtd

Acknowledgments

We would like to thank Utz Westermann for his contributions to the design and implementation of the ZyX model and to preparing the final version. We would also like to thank Christian Heinlein for his valuable comments on the paper.

References

[1] Allen, J. (1983). Maintaining Knowledge about Temporal Intervals. *Communications of the ACM*, 26(11):832–843.

[2] Böhm, K., Aberer, K., and Klas, W. (1997). Building a Hybrid Database Application for Structured Documents. In *Multimedia - Tools and Applications, Accepted for Publication*, Dordrecht. Kluwer Academic Publishers.

[3] Boll, S., Klas, W., and Löhr, M. (1996). Integrated Database Services for Multimedia Presentations. In Chung, S., editor, *Multimedia Information Storage and Management*. Kluwer Academic Publishers, Dordrecht.

[4] Bray, T., Paoli, J., and Sperberg-McQueen, C. (1998). *Extensible Markup Language (XML) 1.0 – W3C Recommendation 10-February-1998*. W3C, URL: http://www.w3.org/TR/1998/REC-xml-19980210.

[5] Duda, A. and Keramane, C. (1995). Structured temporal composition of multimedia data. In *Proc. IEEE International Workshop on Multimedia-Database-Management Systems*, Blue Mountain Lake.

[6] Hoschka, P., Bugaj, S., Bulterman, D., et al. (1998). *Synchronized Multimedia Integration Language – W3C Working Draft 2-February-98*. W3C, URL: http://www.w3.org/TR/1998/WD-smil-0202.

[7] ISO/IEC (1986). *Information processing - Text and Office Systems - Standard Generalized Markup Language (SGML)*. ISO/IEC IS.

[8] ISO/IEC (1992). *Information Technology - Hypermedia/Time-based Structuring Language (HyTime)*. ISO/IEC IS.

[9] ISO/IEC (1995). *Information Technology – Coding of Multimedia and Hypermedia Information – Part 5: Support for Base-Level Interactive Applications, ISO/IEC IS 13522-5*. ISO/IEC IS.

[10] ISO/IEC (1996). *Information Technology – Coding of Multimedia and Hypermedia Information – Part 6: Support for Enhanced Interactive Applications, ISO/IEC IS 13522-6*. ISO/IEC IS.

[11] ISO/IEC (1997). *Information technology – Coding of multimedia and hypermedia information – Part 1: MHEG object representation ISO/IEC 13522-1*. ISO/IEC IS.

[12] Klas, W. and Aberer, K. (1997). Multimedia and its Impact on Database System Architectures. In Apers, P., Blanken, H., and Houtsma, M., editors, *Multimedia Databases in Perspective*. Springer, London.

[13] Little, T. D. C. and Ghafoor, A. (1993). Interval-based conceptual models for time-dependent multimedia data. *IEEE Transactions on Knowledge and Data Engineering*, 5(4).

[14] Moser, F., Kraiß, A., and Klas, W. (1995). L/MRP: A Buffer Management Strategy for Interactive Continuous Data Flows in a Multimedia DBMS. In *Proceedings VLDB 1995*, USA. Morgan Kaufmann.

[15] Newcomb, S., Kipp, N., and Newcomb, V. (1991). HyTime – The Hypermedia/ Time-Based Document Structuring Language. *Communications of the ACM*, 34(11).

[16] Sheth, A. and Klas, W. (1998). *Multimedia Data Management - Using Metadata to Integrate and Apply Digital Media.* McGraw-Hill, New York.

13 FUZZY LOGIC TECHNIQUES IN MULTIMEDIA DATABASES QUERYING: A PRELIMINARY INVESTIGATION OF THE POTENTIALS

Didier Dubois
Henri Prade
Florence Sèdes

Institut de Recherche en Informatique de Toulouse
(IRIT) - CNRS
Université Paul Sabatier, 118 route de Narbonne
31062 Toulouse Cedex
France

{dubois, prade, sedes}@irit.fr

Abstract: Fuzzy logic is known for providing a convenient tool for interfacing linguistic categories with numerical data and for expressing user's preference in a gradual and qualitative way. Fuzzy set methods have been already applied to the representation of flexible queries and to the modelling of uncertain pieces of information in databases systems as well as in information retrieval. This methodology seems to be even more promising in multimedia databases which have a complex structure and from which documents have to be retrieved and selected not only from their contents but also from their appearance, as specified by the user. This paper provides a preliminary investigation of the potential applications of fuzzy logic in multimedia databases. Querying issues are more particularly emphasized. We distinguish two types of request, namely those which can be handled within some extended version of an SQL-like language, and those for which one has to elicitate user's preference through examples and which have an incremental nature. Moreover, the particular case of semi-structured documents is briefly discussed. Lastly, potentials of flexible constraint satisfaction problems in document production are pointed out.

13.1 INTRODUCTION

With the advent of the multimedia age, new functionalities and capabilities are needed for managing new kinds of data: images, sounds, texts, video data, and their combination into composite objects. The spatial, temporal, storage, retrieval, integration and presentation requirements of multimedia data differ significantly from those for traditional data. A multimedia DBMS (Adjeroh and Nwosu, 1997) must address many requirements such as:

- traditional DBMS capabilities,
- huge capacity storage management,
- information retrieval,
- media composition, integration and presentation,
- query support,
- interface and interactivity,
- performance and QoS (Quality of Service).

The full use of such information systems raises new issues, specially for the access and the manipulation of information in a more intuitive, less formalized and human-friendlier way. It poses new challenges from data indexing to querying and retrieval; due to the richness of multimedia data content, querying systems must have extended capabilities: providing high-level abstractions in order to model multimedia data and their presentation, querying them by the appearance rather than by their content, querying by example and allowing for flexible queries.

It is well-known that fuzzy logic provides a framework for modelling flexibility and vagueness in the interface between human conceptual categories and data. Such capabilities have been already developed in the database field, specially for handling flexible queries. There has been only a few very preliminary and very specialized papers on the use of fuzzy logic in multimedia databases systems (Bosc, Connan and Rocacher, 1998; Connan and Rocacher, 1997). In this paper, discussing some emerging but promising applications, we suggest that this methodology might be even more necessary and useful for multimedia applications, although no specific systems are surveyed.

In the next section, we explain multimedia databases specificities and features, versus "classical" (relational) databases requirements. Then, in Section 13.3, we restate and synthesize the contributions of fuzzy approaches to database and information retrieval systems. In the last section, we examine what functions, traditionnally allocated to DBMSs, still make sense in a multimedia environment, what new ones would be useful, and how fuzzy set-based techniques make it actually possible to improve multimedia systems capabilities. We specially investigate the querying step, by considering representative examples in the following.

13.2 MULTIMEDIA DATABASES

To meet the requirements we have mentioned, the multimedia DBMS must address a number of issues, including: data modelling, object storage, indexing, retrieval and browsing, query support, multimedia objects integration and presentation. A multimedia DBMS should provide tools for the efficient storage and manipulation of multimedia data in all its varied forms (Pazandak and Srivasta, 1997). We can view a multimedia database as a controlled collection of multimedia data items, such as text, images, graphic objects, sketches, video and audio. The multimedia DBMS should accommodate these special requirements by providing high-level abstractions in order to manage the different data types, along with a suitable interface for their presentation.

Some multimedia data types such as video, audio, and animation sequences also have temporal requirements, which have implications on their storage, manipulation and presentation. Images, graphics and video have spatial constraints in terms of their contents, and objects in an image present some spatial relationships between them. Representing multimedia information such as pictures or image sequences poses some problems for information retrieval due to the limitations of high level textual descriptions, and the massive information available according to the context, interpretation, user's profile, etc. The lack of standard structure of potential information means that it can be difficult to express precise queries from the beginning. The limitations of textual descriptions associated to a document imply the need for content-based access to multimedia information, referring for instance to shape, color, texture, etc.

On the whole, characteristic features of multimedia data are: lack of structured information, inadequacy of textual descriptions, multiplicity of data types, spatial and temporal characteristics, and huge volumes of data. Besides, the problems of heterogeneity of formats and of inconsistency between pieces of information, commonly encountered in multiple source databases, are still present in multimedia systems, but will not be addressed in the following since they are specific to them.

13.2.1 Indexing

Queries in relational systems are exact match queries: the system is able to return exactly those tuples a user is precisely asking for and nothing more. To specify the resulting relation, conditions concerning known attributes of known relations can be formulated.

From the Information Retrieval area, we know how difficult it is to characterize the contents of textual objects. Problems are encountered on the one hand in specifying the contents of the objects, and on the other hand, for describing the objects one is looking for. In multimedia databases, the question is thus how to characterize the 'contents' of image, audio or video data. Indeed, we must face the problem of giving an interpretation to a photo or a song, for which many interpretations exist in general, according to the context, the user's point of view (Apers et al., 1997).

Multimedia data must be preferably interpreted before they can be queried, in order to generate content descriptions (otherwise it might be more costly to make it on line). Multimedia information can be retrieved using identifiers, attributes, keywords,... Keywords are by far the predominant method used for indexing multimedia data. These keywords are metadata, since they are data about multimedia data. A user is supposed to select keywords from a set of words belonging to a prescribed vocabulary (specialized or not) or thesaurus. This method is simple and intuitive, but depends on the subjectivity of the person who makes the indexation or on the underlying hypotheses of an automatic indexation system, and obviously depends on the given vocabulary. Thus, indexing is context-dependent. Introducing abstractions allows the user to refer to the data in terms of high level features, which constitute his model of the application domain. For the retrieval and organization of the multimedia data, it should be possible to provide several layers of abstractions.

By contrast, low level representation of multimedia data encodes the physical reality. Automated indexing based on this representation uses features such as color, shape, texture, spatial information, symbolic strings, for indexing images; for instance (Flickner et al., 1995). For audio data (Wold et al., 1996), describing can involve analysis of the signal or speech recognition followed by keyword-based indexing; other perceptual and acoustic features are used for music data, such as note, tone, duration, or rhythm signature, chord and melody.

However, it is difficult to completely automate indexing: while the computer can easily analyze a picture containing works of art in terms of colors, textures, and shapes (Martinez, 1998), it is almost impossible to automatically determine interpretive or aesthetical features of an art object (e.g., is the red circle a rising sun on the landscape or the brim of a hat ?).

13.2.2 Querying and information retrieval: content-based query and retrieval

Roughly speaking, we can distinguish between queries aiming at retrieving one document from some distinctive pattern, and topically-oriented requests aiming at collecting a family of related documents. For instance, searching for data which contains specific audio samples or spoken parts, such as broadcasted news about a specific issue specified by some terms. In addition to single media based search, one may want to access data on the basis of a multiple media specification. In this case, a query usually involves different multimedia data types, various attributes, possibly keyword-based or content-oriented, or even contextual information. Retrieval algorithms must support content and context-based retrieval and multimedia DBMS should offer support for spatial and temporal queries.

Extensions of conventional concepts of query languages - all the retrieved objects exactly match to the query - will require that these characteristics be taken into account. It requires approaches that can deal with the temporal and spatial semantics of multimedia data, or query languages that can incorporate flexibility in the expression of requests. Indeed, queries are usually imprecise, so, relevance feedback and meaning similarity, rather than exact matching, and mechanisms for displaying ranked results are important. This is particularly important in combination with content-based access, where the specifications are often approximate and imprecise.

Besides, since information extracted from the data or from the queries might contain errors or might be inconsistent, query interpretation should accommodate uncertainties. Thus, facilities are needed in order to support incomplete information. Moreover, multimedia querying should offer support for new requirements such as querying by examples (from an existing image), querying spatial or temporal data, flexible querying using fuzzy predicates.

13.3 FUZZY DATA BASES

Research on "Fuzzy databases" (see Bosc and Kacprzyk, 1995; Petry, 1996) has been developed for about twenty years by a few small groups of scholars, with only marginal connections to the main trends of database research. If we except the more recent use of fuzzy techniques in data mining, these works have been mainly concentrating on three issues:

- flexible querying in classical languages (e.g., Kacprzyk and Ziolkowski, 1986 ; Bosc and Pivert, 1995), and in object-oriented languages (DeCaluwe, 1997);
- handling of imprecise, uncertain, or fuzzy data (e.g., Prade and Testemale, 1984; Dubois and Prade, 1997a);
- defining and using fuzzy dependencies (e.g., Raju and Majumdar, 1988; Bosc et al., 1998).

An introduction to these different issues may be found in a recent survey by Bosc and Prade (1997).

These tasks involve the three basic semantics which can be naturally attached to a fuzzy set (Dubois and Prade, 1997b), namely : preference, uncertainty and similarity. Indeed, the flexibility of a query reflects the preferences of the end-user. Using a fuzzy set representation, the extent to which an object described in the database satisfies a request then becomes a matter of degree. Besides, the information to be stored in a database may be pervaded with imprecision and uncertainty. Then ill-known attribute values can be represented by means of fuzzy sets viewed as possibility distributions. Moreover, a query may also allow for some similarity-based tolerance: close values are often perceived as similar, interchangeable (e.g., Buckles and Petry, 1982). Indeed, if for instance an attribute value v satisfies an elementary requirement, a value "close" to v should still somewhat satisfy the requirement. The idea of approximate equality, of similarity plays a key role also in the modelling of fuzzy dependencies. However, this last research trend will not be reviewed in the following, since this issue does not seem to be immediatly relevant for multimedia databases.

An advantage of fuzzy set-based modelling, is that it is mainly qualitative in nature. Indeed in many cases, it is enough to use an ordinal scale for the membership degrees (e.g., a finite linearly scale). This also facilitates the elicitation of (context-dependent) membership functions, for which it is enough in practice to identify the elements which totally belong and those which do not belong at all to the fuzzy set.

Fuzzy set-based techniques have been also raising interest in information retrieval for a long time (see Kraft and Buell, 1983; Miyamoto, 1990; Bordogna et al., 1995). In these approaches, degrees of relevance can be attached to each pair (key word, document). Besides, we may also think of fuzzy thesauri; but then we have to distinguish between a statistical degree which reflects the co-occurrence of non-interchangeable keywords in the description of documents belonging to the same corpus, and a degree of (approximate) synonymy between keywords (or a technical key word used for indexation and a user word). The analysis of relevance might be further refined by distinguishing, for a given vocabulary, between keywords which more or less certainly pertain to the document, and others which are relevant but somewhat optional (Prade and Testemale, 1987).

13.3.1 Advantages of flexible querying

Fuzzy set membership functions (Zadeh, 1965) are convenient tools for modelling user's preference profiles and the large panoply of fuzzy set connectives can capture the different user attitudes concerning the way the different criteria present in his/her query compensate or not; see (Bosc and Pivert, 1992) for a unified presentation in the fuzzy set framework of the existing proposals for handling flexible queries.

Thus, the interest of fuzzy queries for a user are twofold:

i) A better representation of his/her preferences. For instance, "he/she is looking for an apartment which is not too expensive and not too far from downtown". In such a case, there does not exist a definite threshold for which the price becomes suddenly too high, but rather we have to differentiate between prices which are perfectly acceptable for the user, and other prices, somewhat higher, which are still more or less acceptable (especially if the apartment is close to downtown). Obviously, the meaning of vague predicate expressions like "not too expensive" is context/user dependent, rather than universal. The large panoply of fuzzy set connectives can capture the different user's attitude concerning the way the different criteria present in his/her query compensate or not. Moreover in a given query, some part of the request may be less important to fulfil; this leads to the need for weighted connectives. Elicitation procedures for membership functions and connectives are thus very important for practical applications.

ii) Fuzzy queries, by expressing user's preferences, provide the necessary information in order to rank-order the answers contained in the database according to the degree to which they satisfy the query. It contributes to avoid empty sets of answers when the queries are too restrictive, as well as large sets of answers without any ordering when queries are too permissive.

13.3.2 Flexible queries and their evaluation

13.3.2.1 Enlarging a pattern by a tolerance relation

Two values u_1 and u_2 belonging to the same attribute domain U may be considered as approximately equal even if they are not identical. For instance if the pattern requires somebody who is 40 years old, an item corresponding to a person who is 39 may be considered in some cases as approximately matching the request. An approximate equality can be conveniently modelled by means of a fuzzy relation R which is reflexive (i.e. $\forall$ u $\in$ U, $\mu_R(u,u) = 1$) and symmetrical (i.e. $\forall$ $u_1 \in$ U, $\forall$ $u_2 \in$ U, $\mu_R(u_1,u_2) = \mu_R(u_2,u_1)$). The closer u_1 and u_2 are, the closer to 1 $\mu_R(u_1,u_2)$ must be. The quantity $\mu_R(u_1,u_2)$ can be viewed as a grade of approximate equality of u_1 with u_2. R is then called a proximity or a tolerance relation. When the query pattern is represented by a subset P of U (P may be fuzzy) but the retrieved item is a (precise) constant d, the tolerance R can be taken into account in the degree of matching by replacing P by the enlarged subset P ô R, defined by

$$\mu_{P\hat{o}R}(d) = \sup_{u \in U} \min(\mu_P(u), \mu_R(u,d)) \geq \mu_P(d). \quad (1)$$

Note that when P is fuzzy, $\mu_P(d) = 1$ still means total compatibility with P and $\mu_P(d) = 0$ means total incompatibility with P. Intermediary degrees of matching account for partial compatibility.

13.3.2.2 Weighted combination of matching degrees

In case of the *logical* conjunctive combination of several requirements P_i, which corresponds to an egalitarist view between the different requirements, the elementary degrees of matching are aggregated by the min operation which might be weighted for taking into account the importance of each requirement (min is the largest associative aggregation operation which extends ordinary conjunction; it is also the only idempotent one). Thus, for a piece of information $d = (d_1, \ldots, d_n)$, we obtain the global matching degree

$$\min_{i=1,\ldots,n} \max(1 - w_i, \mu_{P_i}(d)). \quad (2)$$

with $\mu_{P_i}(d) = \mu_{P_i}(d_i)$ where u_i is the precise value of the item d for the attribute pertaining to P_i, and where the following condition should be satisfied by the weights w_i:

$$\max_{i=1,n} w_i = 1, \qquad (3)$$

if there is at least one requirement that is imperative and thus can eliminate an item d when it is violated. Clearly when $w_i = 0$, the degree of matching $\mu_{P_i}(d)$ is ignored in the combination, then P_i has absolutely no importance; the larger w_i, the smaller the degrees of matching concerning P_i which are effectively taken into account in the aggregation. The normalization (3) expresses that the most important requirement has the maximal weight (i.e., 1) and is compulsory.

In the above model, each weight of importance is a constant and thus does not depend upon the value taken by the concerned attribute for the considered object d. This limitation may create some unnatural behaviour of the matching procedure. For instance, the price of an object you are looking for may be of a limited importance only within a certain range of values; when this price becomes very high, this criterion alone should cause the rejection of the considered object, in spite of the rather low importance weight. To cope with this limitation it has been proposed (Dubois et al., 1988) that the weight of importance become a function of the concerned attribute value.

Recently, Fagin and Wimmers (1997) have advocated the use of another weighted aggregation mode , namely

$$\Sigma_i (w_i - w_{i+1}) * i * f(x_1, \ldots, x_i)$$

$$\text{where } \Sigma_i w_i = 1 \text{ and } w_1 \geq \ldots \geq w_i \ldots \geq w_n,$$

and f is an aggregation function. The advantage of this scheme is its generality; moreover, it enjoys a restricted linearity property w.r.t. to the weights w_i which makes it similar to a Choquet integral (see, e.g., Grabisch et al., 1995). However this framework requires a *numerical* scaling, while (2) requires an *ordinal*, linearly ordered scale only (1- (·) being the order - reversing map of the scale). Indeed, since the numerical meaningfulness of degrees of relevance of documents, or of degrees of importance of keywords is debatable, qualitative aggregation schemes are more desirable.

We may think think that in some cases, min based aggregation leads to a ranking of retrieved items that is insufficiently discriminating because it relies on the comparison of the least satisfied properties. This can be greatly improved by the use of refinements of the min ordering (Dubois, Fargier, Prade, 1996b).

13.3.3.3 Hierarchical requirements

This framework also allows for conditional requirements. A conditional requirement is a constraint which applies only if another one is satisfied. This notion will be interpreted as follows: A requirement P_j conditioned by a hard requirement P_i is imperative if P_i is satisfied and can be dropped otherwise. More generally, the level of satisfaction $\mu_{P_i}(d)$ of a fuzzy conditioning requirement P_i for an instance d is viewed as the level of priority of the conditioned requirement P_j, i.e., the greater the level of satisfaction of P_i, the greater the priority of P_j is. A conditional constraint is then naturally represented by a fuzzy set $P_i \rightarrow P_j$ such that:

$$\mu_{P_i \rightarrow P_j}(d) = \max(\mu_{P_j}(d), 1 - \mu_{P_i}(d)) \quad (4)$$

where $P_i \rightarrow P_j$ is a prioritized constraint with a variable priority.

Nested requirements with preferences, of the form "P_1 should be satisfied, and among the solutions to P_1 (if any) the ones satisfying P_2 are preferred, and among those satisfying both P_1 and P_2, those satisfying P_3 are preferred, and so on", where P_1, P_2, P_3..., are hard constraints (Lacroix and Lavency, 1987), can be understood in the following way: satisfying P_2 if P_1 is not satisfied is of no interest; satisfying P_3 if P_2 is not satisfied is of no use even if P_1 is satisfied. Thus, there is a hierarchy between the constraints. One has to express that P_1 should hold (with priority 1), and that if P_1 holds, P_2 holds with priority α_2, and if P_1 and P_2 hold, P_3 holds with priority α_3 (with $\alpha_3 < \alpha_2 < 1$). Thus, this nested conditional requirement can be represented by means of the fuzzy set P*

$$\mu_{P*}(d) = \min(\mu_{P_1}(d), \max(\mu_{P_2}(d), 1 - \min(\mu_{P_1}(d), \alpha_2)), \max(\mu_{P_3}(d), 1 - \min(\mu_{P_1}(d), \mu_{P_2}(d), \alpha_3)). \quad (5)$$

Another type of sophisticated flexible queries which can be handled in the fuzzy set framework are those which call for an extended division, e.g., «find the items which satisfy at a sufficienly degree all the important requirements» (Bosc et al., 1997; Dubois et al., 1997).

13.3.3.4 Logical and compensatory ANDs

Queries are usually compound, and this raises the issue of finding the appropriate aggregation operation for combining the elementary degrees of matching. Even if the combination is linguistically expressed by the conjunction AND, it may correspond to very different aggregation attitudes ranging from logical to compensatory ANDs. Logical ANDs are modelled by weighted min operations as explained above. Many other (weighted) operations exist (for example, weighted averages correspond to an utilitarist view where compensation makes sense). Procedures for the practical elicitation of the right AND operator can be based on the ranking by the user of a few prototypical examples presented to him in order to identify what kind of aggregation he implicitly used (Dubois and Prade, 1988). More generally, examples can be used for identifying an operator in a parametered family.

13.3.3 Robust querying

As we already said, flexible queries are often motivated by the expression of preferences or tolerance, and of relative levels of importance. However, the use of queries involving fuzzily bounded categories may be also due to an interest for more robust evaluations. This is the case in a query like "find the average salary of the *young* people stored in the database", where the use of a predicate like "young" (whose meaning is clearly context-dependent) does not here refer to the expression of a preference; here, it is rather a matter of convenience since the user is not obliged to set the boundaries of the category of interest in a precise and thus rather arbitrary way. In such a case, a range of possible values for the average salary instead of a precise number will be returned to the user. This range can be viewed as bounded by the lower and the upper expected values of a fuzzy number; see (Dubois and Prade, 1990). It is a robust evaluation which provides the user with an idea of the variability of the evaluation according to the different possible meanings of 'young' (in a given context).

Another important class of flexible requests oriented toward robustness are those involving linguistic quantifiers such as 'most', e.g., «do most of the international trains leave on time?». In such a query, 'most' should be understood as a potential proviso for exceptions rather than as the approximate specification of a proportion to be checked (Bosc , Liétard and Prade, 1998).

13.3.4 Uncertain data

Viewing tuples as lists of attribute values, fuzzy data are associated with lists of fuzzy sets. Such lists contain possibly ill-known attribute values pertaining to the description of objects. Namely, a component in a list refers to only one (ill-located) element of the scale or domain of the concerned attribute; the corresponding fuzzy set which restricts the possible values of this attribute is called a possibility distribution.

The basic dissymmetry of the pattern-data matching is preserved by this modeling convention. Indeed, a fuzzy pattern represents an ill-bounded class of objects, while a fuzzy item represents an ill-known object whose precise description is not available. Namely let P and D be respectively a pattern atom and an item component pertaining to the same single-valued attribute, which are to be compared. P and D refer to the same scale U conveying their meanings. Let μ_P be the membership function associated to atom P and π_D

be the possibility distribution attached to D. Both are mappings from U to [0,1], but $\pi_D(u)$ is the grade of possibility that u is the (unique) value of the attribute describing the object modelled by the item. D is a fuzzy set of *possible* values (only one of which is the genuine value of the ill-known attribute), while P is a fuzzy set of *more or less* compatible values. For instance $\pi_D(u) = 1$ means that u is totally possible, while $\pi_D(u) = 0$ means that u is totally impossible as an attribute value of the object to which the item pertains. In the following μ_P and π_D are always supposed to be normalized, i.e., there is always a value which is totally compatible with P, and a value totally possible in the range D.

Two scalar measures are used in order to estimate the compatibility between a pattern atom P and its counterpart D in the item list, namely a degree of possibility of matching $\prod(P ; D)$ and a degree of necessity of matching N(P ; D) which are respectively defined by (see Zadeh (1978), and Dubois and Prade (1988)):

$$\prod(P ; D) = \sup_{u \in U} \min(\mu_P(u), \pi_D(u)), \quad (6)$$

$$N(P ; D) = \inf_{u \in U} \max(\mu_P(u), 1 - \pi_D(u)). \quad (7)$$

The limiting cases where $\prod(P ; D)$ and N(P ; D) take values 0 and 1 are useful to study in order to lay bare the semantics of these indices. For any fuzzy set, F on U, let $F^\circ = \{u \in U \mid \mu_F(u) = 1\}$ be the core of F, and $s(F) = \{u \in U, \mu_F(u) > 0\}$ its support. Then it can be checked that

(i) $\prod(P ; D) = 0$ if and only if $s(P) \cap s(D) = \emptyset$,

(ii) $\prod(P ; D) = 1$ if and only if $P^\circ \cap D^\circ \neq \emptyset$,

(iii) $N(P ; D) = 1$ if and only if $s(D) \subseteq P^\circ$,

(iv) $N(P ; D) > 0$ if and only if $D^\circ \subset s(P)$ (strict inclusion).

Note that $\prod(P ; \{d\}) = N(P ; \{d\}) = \mu_P(d)$ in case of a precise data ($\pi_D(d) = 1$ and $\pi_D(u) = 0$ if $u \neq d$).

Besides, fuzzy relations R on the real line can be used to grasp such usual notions as "much-before", "closely after", etc that can be applied to the comparison of (fuzzy or non-fuzzy) time-points and time-intervals. Thus, $\prod(D_1 \hat{o} R ; D_2)$ and $N(D_1 \hat{o} R ; D_2)$ evaluate respectively to what extent it is possible and certain that the fuzzy point D_1 be in relation R with the fuzzy point D_2. See (Dubois and Prade, 1989) for an extension of Allen(1983)'s temporal relations to the case of fuzzy data and/or fuzzy relations.

13.4 FUZZY SETS TECHNIQUES IN MULTIMEDIA SYSTEMS QUERYING

Making the most open form of querying possible addresses the need for a richer mixing of DB and IR in terms of predicates. New operators must be integrated into queries that often refer to the document appearance rather to its content. The notion of "content" already exists in classical IR through keywords, but not in classical DB.

As we already said, audio data, for example, can be indexed by signal analysis or speech recognition followed by keyword-based indexing. So, the fuzzy set techniques referred to in the previous section can be applied in multimedia data querying. We can also imagine audio records segmented and classified according to the speaker, or the musical atmosphere, with an assessment of level of similarity.

The previous section deals with "classical" flexible queries, that can also work on an abstract representation (metadata) of the objects, via indexes for instance. Indeed, the next sub-section deals with multimedia-oriented extensions of SQL/OQL. We will then consider queries implicitly specified through examples.

13.4.1 SQL/OQL like queries

It seems that one of the main differences between a multimedia database and an ordinary one from a querying point of view, is that in the first case the request may refer to a document[1] in terms of its appearance (e.g., in terms of features such as size, color, shape of pictures included in it) and not only in terms of its information contents. The lack of standardized structure of the document(s) to be retrieved calls for the use of flexible queries. e are going to illustrate these different points by several examples.

Q1. Retrieving an already seen document . The request refers to characteristic details in terms of appearance (spatial constraints).

"Find **THE** paper published in the *early 90's* which deals with 'x...' and 'y...', and *maybe* also with 'z...', with two pictures on the first page, of which the red one is *rather on the right*"

An extended OQL translation of this query could be (Ogle and Stonebraker, 1995):

```
select q
from q in doc_lib
where
q.creation_date in early_90() /*on-line process, expression of fuzzy set */
and q.description#'x....' and q.description#'y...'
and (maybe) q.description#'z...'
and count(meets_criteria(q.first_page(), picture))=2
and exists p1 in picture where meets_criteria(q,p1)
and meets_criteria(p1.histogram, «Red»)
and exists p2 in picture where meets_criteria(q,p2)
and meets_criteria(p1, (rather) right p2)
```

in which the features pertaining to the uncertainty of the description are highlighted.

[1] The notion of composite object is covered by the notion of "document".

early_90() is a fuzzy predicate expression which will be used for estimating the plausibility that a current document be the document we look for. **maybe** will be understood in the following way: the overall relevance of a document which does not deal with 'z...' will be discounted with respects to the ones which deal with 'x...', 'y...' and 'z...' (in other words, the latter documents are hierarchically preferred, see section 13.3.2 equation (5)). The evaluation of the fuzzy predicate expression '**rather** on the right' exploits the HTML description of the structure of the document.

Q2. Retrieving an already seen document (temporal constraints)
"Find **THE** video sequence which comes after a scene in which there's a man waiting *close to* a tree during *about 30 seconds* and where *a little after* we hear the sound of an engine"

```
select q
from q in video_lib
where
exists s where (
exists m where m.class#human and meets_criteria(s,m)
and exists o where o.class#.... and meets_criteria(m,(close_to) o)
and meets_criteria(s.length(), (about) 30 s))
and (exists sound where sound.class=engine
and meets-criteria(sound, (little_after) s))
and meets_criteria(q, after s)
```

about 30 s and **little_after** are temporal fuzzy predicates which can be evaluated from the story board.

The evaluation of **close_to** presupposes either a very precise indexation or an online evaluation of the image. If it is not possible (e.g., the indexation only mentions a man and a tree without distance information), the evaluation process should not reject the document even if it discounts it. This is a very general issue in such a problem where due to the lack of known structure of the document we cannot know if some feature is available or not. In such a case, the relevance of the current document will depend on the number of available features of the description (a document mentioning a man and a tree will be preferred to a document mentioning only a man or only a tree, etc).

Q3. Looking for a collection of never seen documents.

Visual display.
"find the documents dealing with 'x...' in which *most* pictures are from the 90's"

```
select q
from q in doc_lib
where
q.description#'x....'
and exists p in picture where meets_criteria(q,p)
and (most) p.creation_date in 90()            /* extended division */
```

This supposes that the detailed description of the picture includes its creation date.

This is an example where most is a proviso for exceptions (a document will be all the more preferred as it includes less photos before 1990 and more photos of the 90's).

"find the paintingS with *warm* colors"

```
select q
from q in photo_lib
where
q.class#art_object
and q in warm_colors()
```

By contrast with the previous example, here, warm_colors rather reflects user's preferences. warm_colors is a fuzzy set of colours whose definition may be context-dependent (see 4.2).

Auditory display

"find the pieceS where cellos *dominate*"

```
select q
from q in audio_lib
where
q.class#music
and cello.duration%q.duration in dominate()
```

The evaluation of a document supposes that it is known when cellos play and when they don't.

13.4.2 Incremental building of queries from examples

The user is not always able to easily express his request even in a flexible way. First, it may be more convenient for him to express what he is looking for from examples. Second, since he may have absolutely no a priori knowledge of the amount of retrievable documents (for a given request), it may be useful if the system is able to guide him about what exists.

Querying based on examples, for elicitating user's preferences, can provide the necessary information for building a query. Thus, the user may say to what extent a few examples of documents are similar to what he is looking for by using some (finite) similarity scale. Then, relevance of current documents is evaluated in terms of their similarity with respect to these examples. Issues are then close to fuzzy case-based reasoning (Dubois et al. 1998).

A first request, if it is too general, may retrieve too large a number of documents. Many techniques (fuzzy or not) exist for clustering such a set of documents. Then, these clusters have to be summarized in terms of prototypical elements (e.g. implicit keywords in an abstract) which are provided to the user. Once the user has chosen a cluster, he can refine his specification by means of a more accurate flexible query. This specification can be expressed in term of weighted keywords (and in term of similarities with other words).

13.4.3 Flexibility and semi-structured information

An important class of multimedia documents are semi-structured documents. The idea is here to allow for flexibility in exploiting semi-structured information (Abiteboul 1997), like HTML documents (Chrisment and Sedes, 1998). More precisely, we may like to refer to the structure in a flexible way.

Indeed, the request may refer to the description of a document structure (e.g. title, author(s), probably an abstract, maybe key-words, a body structured in sections and sub-sections, certainly followed by references, among which we preferably may find some author's name...).

Thus, a first level of querying, already exemplified in 4.1, is to retrieve an already seen document where the description refers to its structure (Djennane and Sedes 1996) in a flexible way.

Another example of this type of query is: 'find the paper including imperatively keywords 'x...', and preferably keywords 'y...', and which refers mostly to good papers in the domain'. The retrieving of relevant paper requires (i) to identify keywords and references in the document, (ii) to check if most of the authors belong to a set of 'good' authors on the domain associated with the present keywords.

Another type of query is to ask for "similar" documents, in terms of structure, from the previous sample structure.

13.5 OTHER RELATED ISSUES

Multimedia document editing environments mainly aim at enriching the representation of spatial placement and temporal layout (e.g., "the 2 sequences at the same time" in video). Modelling composition between objects and their synchronisation (intra/inter component) must express temporal relationships and spatial ones. One of the problems of multimedia document modelling is the specification of relationships and constraints: "this object finishes more or less at the same time as this other one". The display of multimedia objects must be coordinated so that the display meets prespecified and dynamic temporal and spatial constraints. For instance, Madeus (Jourdan et al., 1997) is a multimedia authoring and presentation tool that takes into consideration the four dimensions of multimedia documents: logical, spatial, temporal and hyperlinking. The temporal organisation of the document is called scenario. The temporal constraint networks formalism has been chosen to represent the set of temporal relations used to relate objects. Its advantage is to be easily interfaced with a declarative symbolic representation based on a set of quantified Allen operators together with a set of causal operators. In such a context, it may be useful to express flexibility in the adjustment constraints (e.g., beginning *nearly* at the same time) as well as in spatial ones (this object should *be rather on the right* of the other one). For that purpose, works on flexible constraint satisfaction problems (e.g., Dubois, Fargier and Prade, 1996a) are relevant.

It is worth pointing out that the handling of flexible queries may also require the evaluation of features at the signal level. For instance, in a remote image database, queries may for instance refer to the "average surface area of the large parcels". For such a query, the first step is a matter of image processing: detecting boundaries of parcels, computing their surface. The second one consists in entering, via the interface, what the user means by "large" (1 or 10 ha ?). The relative position of two objects in an image can be also computed at the pixel level using fuzzy set methods (Matsakis, 1998).

The intended purpose of this paper is to provide a preliminary investigation of the potential applications of fuzzy logic techniques in multimedia databases. Emphasis has been put on querying issues. However it is worth pointing out that these techniques could be also fruitful in other multimedia problems that we just briefly described above. Several different uses of fuzzy logic techniques in relation with multimedia systems have been surveyed. Among them, the application of these tools to semi-structured documents seems to be particularly promising and could be developed in a near future. Indeed, the current information systems technology is widely available and provide the support on which fuzzy specifications can be based. Some other applications clearly requires advanced indexation or on-line content analysis of the documents, which maybe still partially beyond the current available technology.

References

Abiteboul S. (1997), Semi-structured information, Proc. of ICDT'97, International Conference on Database Theory, Invited talk.

Allen J. F. (1983) Maintaining knowledge about temporal intervals. Communications of the ACM, 26, 832-843

Adjeroh D. A., Nwosu K. C. (1997) Multimedia Database Management Requirements and Issues, IEEE Multimedia, Vol. 4, n 3, pp. 24-33.

Apers P. et al (1997) Multimedia Database in Perspective, Springer-Verlag, 1997.

Bordogna G., Carrara P. and Pasi G. (1995) Fuzzy approaches to extend Boolean information retrieval. In Fuzziness in Database Management Systems (P.Bosc and J. Kacprzyk , eds.) Physica-Verlag, 231-274.

Bosc P., Connan F., Rocacher D. (1998) Flexible querying in multimedia databases with an object query language. Proc. 7th IEEE Int. Conf. on Fuzzy Systems, Anchorage, May 5-10, 1308-1313.

Bosc P., Dubois D., Pivert O., Prade H. (1997) Flexible queries in relational databases —The example of the division operator— Theoretical Computer Science, 171, 281-302.

Bosc P., Dubois D., Prade H. (1998) Fuzzy functional dependencies and redundancy elimination. J. Amer. Soc. Infor. Syst, 217-235.

Bosc P., Kacprzyk J. (Eds.) (1995) Fuzziness in Database Management Systems. Physica-Verlag, Heidelberg.

Bosc P., Liétard L., Prade H. (1998) An Ordinal Approach to the Processing of Fuzzy Queries with Flexible Quantifiers. in: Uncertainty in Information Systems (A. Hunter, S. Parsons Eds.). Springer Verlag LNCS series to appear.

Bosc P., Pivert O. (1992) Some approaches for relational databases flexible querying. J. of Intelligent Information Systems, 1, 323-354.

Bosc P., Pivert O. (1995) SQLf: A relational database language for fuzzy querying. IEEE Trans. on Fuzzy Systems, 3(1), 1-17.

Bosc P., Prade H. (1997) An introduction to the fuzzy set and possibility theory-based treatment of soft queries and uncertain or imprecise databases. In: Uncertainty Management in Information Systems: From Needs to Solutions (A. Motro, Ph. Smets, eds.), Kluwer Academic Publ., Chapter 10, 285-324.

Chrisment C., Sèdes F (1998). Bases d'objets documentaires. Tutoriel, INFORSID 98.

Connan F., Rocacher D. (1997) Gradual and flexible Allen relations for querying video data. Proc. 5th Europ. Cong. on Intelligent Techniques and Soft Computing (EUFIT'97), Aachen, Germany, Sept. 8-11, 1132-1136.

De Caluwe R. (ed.) (1997) Fuzzy and Uncertain Object-Oriented Databases. Concepts and Models. World Scientific, Singapore

Djennane S., Sedes F.(1996) Audio facilities for hypermedia consultation. 2nd Int. Workshop on Natural Language and Databases, Amsterm, IOS Press, 91-101.

Dubois D., Esteva F. , Garcia P., Godo L., Lopez de Mantaras R. and Prade H. (1998). Fuzzy set modelling in case-based reasoning. Int. J. of Intelligent Systems, 13, 301-374.

Dubois D., Fargier H., Prade H. (1996a) Possibility theory in constraint satisfaction problems: handling priority, preference and uncertainty. Applied Intelligence, vol. 6, 287-309.

Dubois D., Fargier H., Prade H. (1996b) refinements of the maximin approach to decision making in fuzzy environments. Fuzzy Sets and Systems, 81, 103-122.

Dubois D., Nakata M., Prade H. (1997) Find the items which certainly have (most of) important characteristics to a sufficient degree. Proc. 7th IFSA World Cong. Prague, Academia publ., 243-248.

Dubois D., Prade H. (1988) Possibility Theory — An Approach to Computerized Processing of Uncertainty. Plenum Press, New York.

Dubois D., Prade H. (1989) Processing fuzzy temporal knowledge. IEEE Trans. on Syst., Man and Cyber., 19, 729-744.

Dubois D., Prade H. (1990) Measuring properties of fuzzy sets: A general technique and its use in fuzzy query evaluation. Fuzzy Sets and Systems, 38, 137-152.

Dubois D., Prade H. (1996) Semantics of quotient operators in fuzzy relational databases. Fuzzy Sets and Systems, 78, 89-93.

Dubois D., Prade H. (1997a) Valid or complete information in databases. Possibility theory-based analysis. DEXA'97, LNCS n° 1308, 603-612.

Dubois D., Prade H. (1997b) The three semantics of fuzzy sets. Fuzzy Sets and Systems, 90, 141-150, 1997

Dubois D., Prade H., Testemale C. (1988) Weighted fuzzy pattern matching. Fuzzy Sets and Systems, 28, 313-331.

Fagin, R., Wimmers, E. (1997) Incorporating User Preferences in Multimedia Queries, Proc. of International Conference on Database Theory ICDT'97, 247-261.

Faloutsos C., Barber R., Flickner M., Hafner J., Niblack W., Petkovic D., and Equitz W. Efficient and effective querying image by content, J. Intell. Inf. Syst. 3, 4, pp. 231-262.

Flickner M., Sawhney H., Niblack W., Ashley J., Huang Q., Dom B., Gorkani M., Hafner J., Lee D., Petkovic D., Steele D., Yanker P. (1995) Query by Image and Video Content: the QBIC system, IEEE Computer, 28(9), pp. 23-32.

http://wwwqbic.almaden.ibm.com/

Grabisch M., Nguyen H.T., Walker E.A. (1995). Fundamentals of Uncertainty Calculi with Applications to Fuzzy Inference, Kluwer Academic, Dordrecht.

Grosky W.I. (1997) Managing Multimedia Information in Database Systems, Communications of the ACM, Vol. 40, n 12, pp. 73-80.

Jourdan M., Layaida N., Sabry-Ismail L. (1997). Time representation and management in MADEUS: an authoring environment for multimedia documents. Multimedia Computing and Networking 1997, Proc. SPIE 3020, pp. 68-79.

Kacprzyk J., Ziolkowski A. (1986) Data base queries with fuzzy linguistic quantifiers. IEEE Trans. on Systems, Man and Cybernetics, 16(3), 474-478.

Kraft D.H. and Buell D.A. (1983) Fuzzy sets and generalized Boolean retrieval systems. Int. J. Man-Machine Studies, 19, 45-56.

Lacroix M., Lavency P. (1987) Preferences: putting more knowledge into queries. Proc. 13th Int. Conf. on Very Large DataBases, Brighton, 217-225.

Martinez J., Guillaume S. (1998). Colour image retrieval fitted to "classical" querying. Ingenierie des Systemes d'Information, 6(1), 1-12.

Matsakis P. (1998). Relations spatiales structurelles et interprétation d'images. PhD thesis, Université P. Sabatier, Toulouse.

Miyamoto S. (1990) Fuzzy sets in information retrieval and cluster analysis. Kluwer Acad. Publ.

Ogle V. and Stonebraker M. (1995) Chabot: Retrieval from a Relational Database of Images, 28(9), IEEE Computer.

Pazandak P., Srivasta J. (1997) Evaluating Object DBMS for Multimedia, IEEE Multimedia, Vol. 4, n 3, pp. 34-49.

Petry F.E. (1996) Fuzzy Databases: Principles and Applications. Kluwer Acad. Pub., Dord.

Prade H., Testemale C. (1984) Generalizing database relational algebra for the treatment of incomplete/uncertain information and vague queries. Information Sciences, 34, 115-143.

Prade H., Testemale C. (1987). Application of possibility and necessity measures to documentary information retrieval. Uncertainty in Knowledge Based Systems, (B. Bouchon, R. Yager, Eds.) LNCS n° 286, 265-274.

Raju K.V.S.V.N., Majumdar A.K. (1988) Fuzzy functional dependencies and lossless join decomposition of fuzzy relational database systems. ACM Trans. on Database Systems, 13(2), 129-166.

Wold W., Blum T., Keislar D., Wheaton J. (1996) Content-Based Classification, Search and Retrieval of Audio, IEEE Multimedia, Vol. 3, n 3, pp. 27-36.

Zadeh L.A. (1965) Fuzzy sets. Information and Control, 8, 338-353.

Zadeh L.A. (1978) Fuzzy sets as a basis for a theory of possibility. Fuzzy Sets and Systems, 1, 3-28.

14 DEFINING VIEWS IN AN IMAGE DATABASE SYSTEM *

Vincent Oria, M. Tamer Özsu, Duane Szafron and Paul J. Iglinski

Department of Computing Science - University of Alberta
Edmonton, Alberta, Canada T6G 2H1
{oria, ozsu, duane, iglinski}@cs.ualberta.ca

Abstract: A view mechanism can help handle the complex semantics in emerging application areas such as image databases. This paper presents the view mechanism we defined for the DISIMA image database system. Since DISIMA is being developed on top of an object-oriented database system, we first propose a powerful object-oriented view mechanism based on the separation between types (interface functions) and classes that manage objects of the same type. The image view mechanism uses our object-oriented view mechanism to allow us to give different semantics to the same image. The solution is based on the distinction between physical salient objects which are interesting objects in an image and logical salient objects which are the meanings of these objects.

14.1 INTRODUCTION

Views have been widely used in relational database management systems to extend modeling capabilities and to provide data independence. Basically, views in a relational database can be seen as formulae defining virtual relations that are not produced until the formulae are applied to real relations (view materialization is an implementation/optimization technique). View mechanisms are useful in other newly emerging application areas of database technology. In this paper, we discuss a view mechanism for one of those areas, image databases. This work is conducted within the context of the DISIMA (DIStributed Image database MAnagement system) prototype which is under development at the

*This research is supported by a strategic grant from the Natural Science and Engineering Research Council (NSERC) of Canada.

University of Alberta. Since DISIMA uses object-oriented technology, we deal with object-oriented views.

Despite several research efforts in the object-oriented community [4, 1, 14, 16], the objective of a view mechanism, as defined for the relational model, has not yet been achieved. The problem is more complex and may be too general in the object-oriented environment. Assume that a virtual class is defined from an existing schema. Will each virtual object in this virtual class get a new OID each time the view is activated? This violates object-oriented principles. Can this virtual class be considered as a normal class? In this case, what is its place in the class hierarchy?

Due to the volume and the complexity of image data, image databases are commonly built on top of object or object-relational database systems. Image databases, in particular, can benefit from a view mechanism. Specifically, an image can have several interpretations that a view mechanism can help to model. The DISIMA system [11] defines a model that is capable of handling an image and all the meta-data associated with it, including syntactic characterization (shape, color and texture) of *salient objects* contained in the image. The level at which the syntactic features are organized and stored is called the physical salient object level. Each physical salient object can then be given a meaning at the logical salient object level. How do we get this information? In general, salient object detection and annotation is a semi-automatic or a manual process.

Given the fact that we can manually or automatically extract meta-data information from images, how do we organize this information so that an image can be interpreted with regard to a context? That is, if the context of an image changes, the understanding of the image may change as well. Consider an electronic commerce system with a catalog containing photographs of people modeling clothes and shoes. From the customer's point of view, interesting objects in this catalog are shirts, shorts, dresses, etc. But the company may want to keep track of the models as well as clothes and shoes. Assume the models come from different modeling agencies. Each of the agencies may be interested in finding only pictures in which their models appear. All these users of the same database (i.e. the catalog) have different interpretations of the content of the same set of images.

Defining an image content with regard to a context helps capture more semantics, enhances image modeling capabilities, and allows the sharing of images among several user groups. Our mechanism of image views, currently being implemented in the DISIMA system, allows users to virtually create an image interpretation context that includes salient object semantics and representations.

Our class derivation mechanism is general enough to be applied to any object-oriented application and is presented in Section 14.2. Section 14.3 describes the DISIMA model and extends it to support views on images, Section 14.4 presents the image view definition language and describes the current implementation of the image views, Section 14.5 discusses the related work and Section 14.6 concludes.

14.2 DERIVED CLASSES

We separate the definition of object characteristics (a *type*) from the mechanism for maintaining instances of a particular type (a *class*) for several well known reasons [9]. A *type* defines behaviors (or properties) and encapsulates hidden behavioral implementations (including state) for objects created using the type as template. We use the term behaviors (or properties) to include both public interface functions (methods) and public state (public instance variables). The behaviors defined by a type describe the *interface* for the objects of that class. A *class* ties together the notion of *type* and *object instances*. The entire group of objects of a particular type, including its subtypes is known as the *extent* of the type and is managed by its class. We refer to this as *deep extent* and introduce *shallow extent* to refer only to those objects created directly from the given type without considerating its subtypes. For consistency reasons all the type names used in this paper start with $T\_$.

Let C be the set of class names. If C is a class name, $T(C)$ gives the type of C and $\Gamma(C)$ denotes the extent of the class C. We denote by $\mathcal{T}$, the graph representing the type hierarchy. We consider two types of derived classes: simple derived classes (derived from a single class called *the parent class*) and composed derived classes (derived from two or more parent classes). We will use the term root class to refer to a non-derived class. In the same way, a root object refers to an object of a root class. The derivation relationship is different from the specialization/generalization one in the sence that the objects and properties introduced are obtained from data previously stored in the database.

14.2.1 Simple Derived Class

A simple derived class is a virtual class derived from a single parent class.

Definition 1 *A* **derived class** C_d *is defined by* (C, Φ, Ψ) *where:*

- C *is the parent class*
- Φ*, the filter, is a formula that selects the valid objects from* C *for the extent of* C_d
- Ψ*, the interface function, defines the type of* C_d *by combining the functions* A: Augment *and* H: Hide *such that* $\Psi = A \circ H$*, where* A *maps a set of objects of a particular type to a set of corresponding objects in a type with some addtional properties. Similarily* H *hides some properties.*
- $\Gamma(C_d) = \Psi(\Phi(\Gamma(C)))$

As defined, Ψ, A and H have to be applied to sets of objects of a certain type to return sets of objects of another type. To avoid introducing news terms, we will extend their applications to types.

If $\alpha, \beta, \gamma, \delta$ are properties defined in T_C, $H(T\_C, \{\alpha, \beta\})$ will create a new type (let us call it $T\_restricted\_C$) in which only the properties γ, δ are defined. Hence $T\_restricted\_C$ is a supertype of T_C.

$A(T\_C, \{(\mu : f_1), (\nu : f_2)\})$ will create a type ($T\_augmented\_C$) with the additional properties μ and ν, where f_1 and f_2 are functions that implement them. $T\_augmented\_C$ is a subtype of T_C.

$A(H(T\_C, \{\alpha, \beta\}), \{(\mu : f_1), (\nu : f_2)\})$ defines the type T_C_d for a class C_d derived from a class C with the properties α, β of T_C hidden and μ, ν as new properties.

In general, the type $T(C_d)$ of a class C_d derived from the class C, is a sibling of $T(C)$. However, if no properties are hidden, $T(C_d) \leq T(C)$, where $\leq$ stands for a subtyping relationship and $\geq$ for a supertyping relationship. Alternatively, if no properties are added, $T(C_d) \geq T(C)$. The notion of sibling generalizes the notion of subtyping and supertyping. The most general case where some properties are removed and new ones are added is illustrated by Figure 14.1. In this example, we assume that the following properties are defined for the different types:

- T_Person(SIN: int, LastName: string, FirstName: string, Sex: char, DateOfBirth: date)
- T_Restricted_Person(SIN: int, LastName: string, FirstName: string, Sex: char)
- T_Augmented_Restricted_Person(SIN: int, LastName: string, FirstName: string, Sex: char, Age: int)

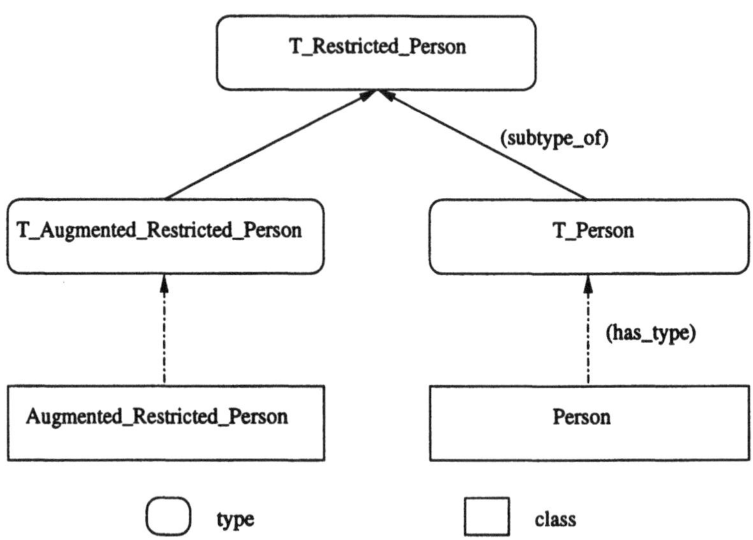

Figure 14.1: An Example of a Derived Class and its Type

In Figure 14.1, the extent of *Augmented_Restricted_Person* is a subset of the extent of *Person* with a different interface defined by the type *T_Augmented_Restricted_Person.*

14.2.2 Composed Derived Class

Assume that the type *T_Person* has two subtypes *T_Student* and *T_Faculty.* Some of the students teach and some faculty do only research. The Type *T_Student* has the properties *(Year: int)* and *(Teach: boolean)* while the properties *(HiringDate: date)* and *(Teach: boolean)* are defined for *Faculty.* We would like to derive a class *Teacher* of all the persons who teach with the property *(TimeServed: int)* obtained either from *HiringDate* or from *Year* depending on the type of the root object. The class *Teacher* cannot be directly derived from the class *Person* since the useful properties are not defined in *T_Person.* In the following, we propose a way (composed derived class) to solve this problem.

Definition 2 *Let* $(C_1, C_2) \in \mathcal{C}^2$ *be a pair of classes. Then:*

- $C_d = C_1 * C_2$ *with a filter* Φ *and an interface* Ψ *is a composed derived class with* $\Gamma(C_d) = \Psi(\Phi(\Gamma(C_1) \cap \Gamma(C_2))$
- $C_d = C_1 + C_2$ *with a filter* Φ *and an interface* Ψ *is a composed derived class with* $\Gamma(C_d) = \Psi(\Phi(\Gamma(C_1) \cup \Gamma(C_2))$
- $C_d = C_1 - C_2$ *with a filter* Φ *and an interface* Ψ *is a composed derived class with* $\Gamma(C_d) = \Psi(\Phi(\Gamma(C_1) - \Gamma(C_2))$

with $T(C_d)$ *a sibling of* $Anc(T(C_1), T(C_2))$ *where* $Anc(T(C_1), T(C_2))$ *is a function that returns the first common ancestor of* $(T(C_1), T(C_2))$ *in the type hierarchy* $\mathcal{T}$.

The semantics of the constructive operations $\{*, +, -\}$ are respectively based on the basic set operations $\cap, \cup$ and $-$. As defined, $\{*, +, -\}$ are binary operations but the formulae obtained can be seen as terms and be combined for more complex ones. Note that C_1 and C_2 can be derived classes as previously defined. The ancestor function *Anc* works fine when $\mathcal{T}$ is rooted. When this is not the case, a common supertype *T_C* is created for $T(C_1), T(C_2)$. In the worst case, *T_C* will not have any properties in it.

The problem of deriving a class *Teacher* can be solved by defining a simple derived class *Student_Teacher* whose extent is a subset of all the students. In the same way, we derive the class *Faculty_Teacher* from *Faculty*. *Teacher* is then defined as $Teacher = Student\_Teacher + Faculty\_Teacher$. The type *T_Teacher* is a subtype of *T_Person* which is the common ancestor (Figure 14.2).

14.2.3 Identifying and Updating a derived object

A derived object is always derived from one and only one root object although its properties can be totally different from the properties of the root object.

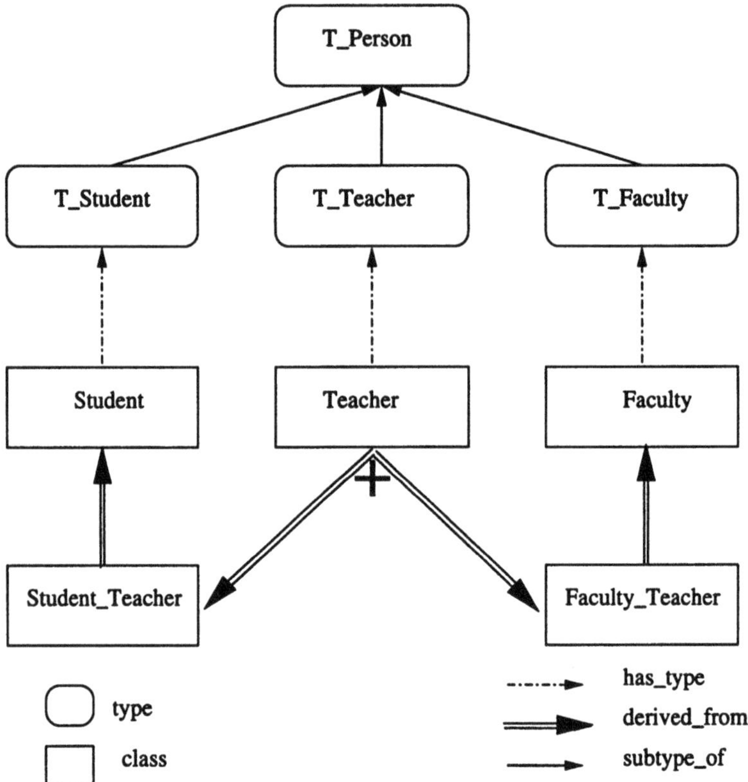

Figure 14.2: An Example of a Composed Derived Class and its Type.

This happens when all the properties of the root class are hidden and new ones are defined for the derived class. Hence, a derived object can be seen as a root object viewed from another angle (the interface function of the derived class). Both the derived object and its corresponding root object can be identified by the OID of the root object (ROOT_OID). If we redefine the notion of OID as follows: OID= $< class\_name, ROOT\_OID >$ then the root object can be differentiated from the derived one. This OID defines a logical idenfier for any object including the derived ones independently from any view implementation technique. In the case of view materialization with incremental maintenance, an active research area [3, 6, 12, 2], the derived object OID is a key candidate and can be directly used as identifier.

A derived object knows its root object. Therefore, updating a property inherited from the root type can easily be propagated to the root object. Creating new objects for a derived class should first create the objects in the root class with some possible unknown property values.

14.3 DEFINING IMAGE VIEWS IN DISIMA

The mechanism of image views presented in this paper is based on the DISIMA image DBMS, which is a research project for developing a distributed interoperable DBMS for image and spatial applications. The DISIMA model aims at organizing the image and associated meta-data to allow content-based queries.

14.3.1 The DISIMA Model: Overview

The model provides efficient representation of images and related data to support a wide range of queries. The DISIMA model, as depicted in Figure 14.3, is composed of two main blocks: the image block and the salient object block. We define a *block* as a group of semantically related entities.

14.3.1.1 The Image Block. The image block is made up of two layers: the *image* layer and the *image representation* layer. We distinguish an image from its representations to maintain an independence between them, referred to as *representation independence.*

At the *image* layer, the user defines an image type classification. Figure 14.4 depicts a type hierarchy for an electronic commerce application that represents the catalogs as classes. The general *T_Catalog* type is derived from the root type *T_Image*, the root image type provided by DISIMA. The type *T_Catalog* is specialized by two types: *T_ClothingCatalog*, and *T_ShoesCatalog.*

14.3.1.2 The Salient Object Block. The *salient object* block is designed to handle salient object organization. A simple example of a salient object hierarchy, corresponding to the image hierarchy defined in Figure 14.4, is given in Figure 14.5.

DISIMA distinguishes two kinds of salient objects: physical and logical salient objects. A *logical salient object* is an abstraction of a salient object

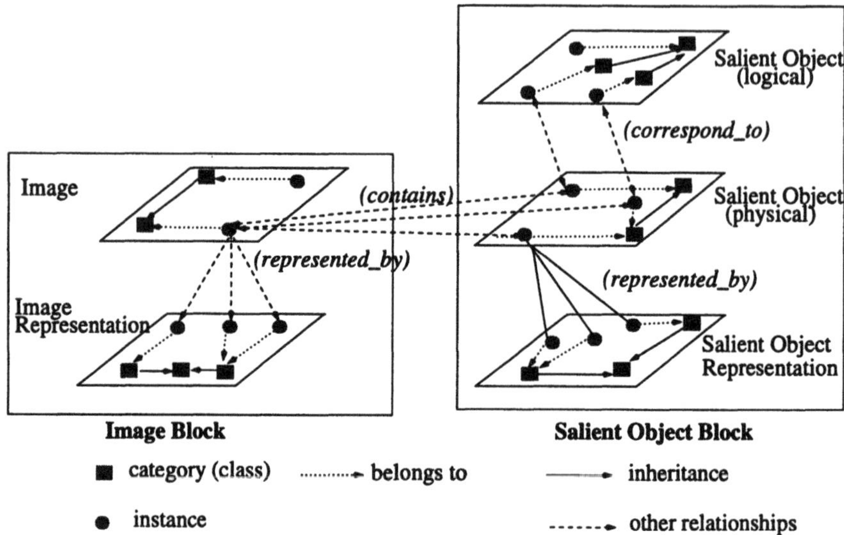

Figure 14.3: The DISIMA Model Overview.

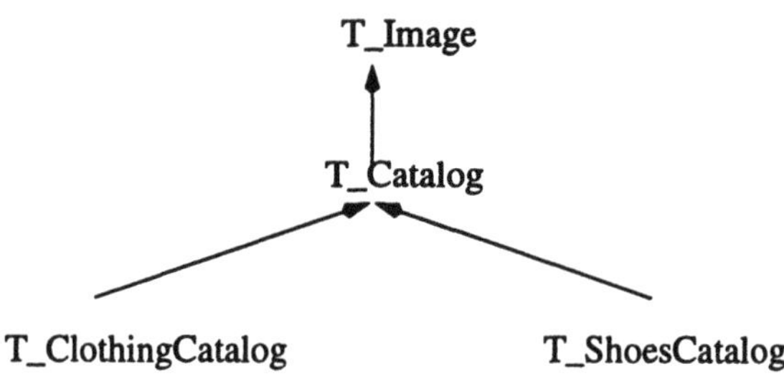

Figure 14.4: An Example of an Image Hierarchy.

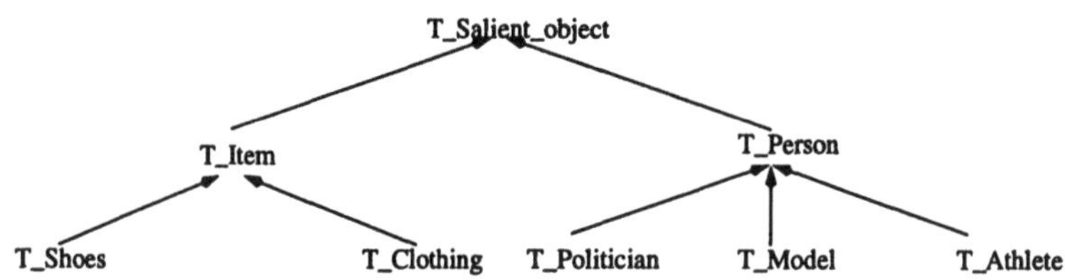

Figure 14.5: An Example of Logical Salient Object Hierarchy.

that is relevant to some application. For example, an object may be created as an instance of type *Politician* to represent President Clinton. The object "Clinton" is created and exists even if there is yet no image in the database in which President Clinton appears. This is called a *logical salient object*; it maintains the image independent generic information that might be stored about this object of interest (e.g., name, position, spouse). Particular instances of this object (called *physical salient objects*) may appear in specific images. There is a set of information (data and relationships) linked to the fact that "Clinton appears in an image". The data can be the colors of his clothes, his localization, or his shape in this image.

We now give a formal definition of the content of an image, using physical and logical salient objects.

Definition 3 *A* **physical salient object (PSO)** *is a region of an image, that is, a geometric object (without any semantics) in a space (defined by an image) with the following properties: shape, color, and texture.*
A **logical salient object (LSO)** *is the interpretation of a region. It is a meaningful object that is used to give semantics to a physical salient object.*

Definition 4 *Let $\mathcal{L}$ be the set of all logical salient objects and $\mathcal{P}$ be the set of all physical salient objects. The* **content of an image** *i is defined by a pair $Cont(i) = < \mathcal{P}^i, s >$ where:*

- $\mathcal{P}^i \subseteq \mathcal{P}$ is a set of physical salient objects,
- $s : \mathcal{P}^i \longrightarrow \mathcal{L}$ maps each physical salient object to a logical salient object.

An image is a basic unit in the DISIMA model and is defined as follow:

Definition 5 *An* **image** *i is defined by a triple <Rep(i), Cont(i), Desc(i)> where:*
- Rep(i) is a set of representations of the raw image in a format such as GIF, JPEG, etc;
- $Cont(i)$ is the content of the image i;
- $Desc(i)$ is a set of descriptive alpha-numeric data associated with i.

Color and texture characterizing the whole image are part of the $Desc(i)$.

14.3.1.3 How to Recognize the Salient Objects of an Image. Despite progress in the computer vision field, automatic detection of objects is "hard" and application-dependent. The state of the art in computer vision does not permit automatic recognition of an arbitrary scene [15].

Assume an object is detected by the image analysis software. In the general case, this object is a syntactic object without any semantics. That is, it is a region of an image with properties such as color, shape and texture. Another challenge is to provide syntactic objects with semantics. Assume the object detected is a person. How can a computer assign a name to this person? This example explains why, in most cases, the image analysis is semi-automatic or manual.

One component of the DISIMA project is in charge of image processing and object detection. Our first concern was images with people. The image processing software detects the faces contained in the image with a minimum bounding rectangle (useful for spatial relationships) and a human-annotator assigns a logical salient object to the face. In addition, an image has some descriptive properties such as date and photographer that have to be provided. In the remainder of the paper, we assume that the information at the two levels of salient objects is provided.

The two levels of salient objects ensure the semantic independence and multi-representation of salient objects. The idea of image views is based on this semantic independence and the class derivation mechanism presented in Section 14.2.

14.3.2 Extending the DISIMA Model to Support Image Views

A DISIMA schema is composed of two sub-schemas: the image type hierarchy and the salient object type hierarchy. An image view can be defined by a derived image class or by giving different semantics to the salient objects an image contains using derived logical salient object classes.

Derived classes can be defined for both image and salient-object classes. Derived salient object classes are illustrated by examples shown in Section 2. The aim of a derived image class is to filter salient objects or to redefine their semantics through derived logical salient object classes.

14.3.2.1 Defining Image Views Using Derived Image Classes. A derived image class, in addition to defining a new type, converts some salient objects of a parent image class into non-salient in a derived one.

Definition 6 *A* **derived image class** *is a class derived from an image class that specifies the valid logical salient objects for images in its extent. If i_d is an image derived from an image i, then the set of physical salient objects contained in i_d is a subset of the set contained in i. The physical salient objects in i_d are those for which the corresponding logical salient objects belong to one of the valid logical salient objects.*

In addition to redefining the type, a derived image class redefines the content of the images it contains. For example, from the *ClothingCatalog* class defined in Figure 14.4, we can derive two different catalogs giving different interpretations of the images in the *ClothingCatalog* image class: the customer catalog class (*CustomerCatalog*) and the clothing company catalog (*CompanyCatalog*). The customers are interested in finding clothing from the catalog. Therefore, the valid logical salient object class is *Clothing*. In addition to the clothing, the company may be interested in keeping some information about the models.

A composed derived image class can also be created. For example, from *ClothingCatalog* we can derive the class *FemaleClothingCatalog*. We can also derive *FemaleShoesCatalog* from *ShoesCatalog*. *FemaleClothingCatalog* and *FemaleShoesCatalog* can be combined using the + operator to derive a class *FemaleApparelCatalog*. The common ancestor of *FemaleClothingCatalog*, and *FemaleShoesCatalog* is *Catalog*. Therefore the type of *FemaleApparelCatalog* has to be a sibling of the type of *Catalog* (Figure 14.6).

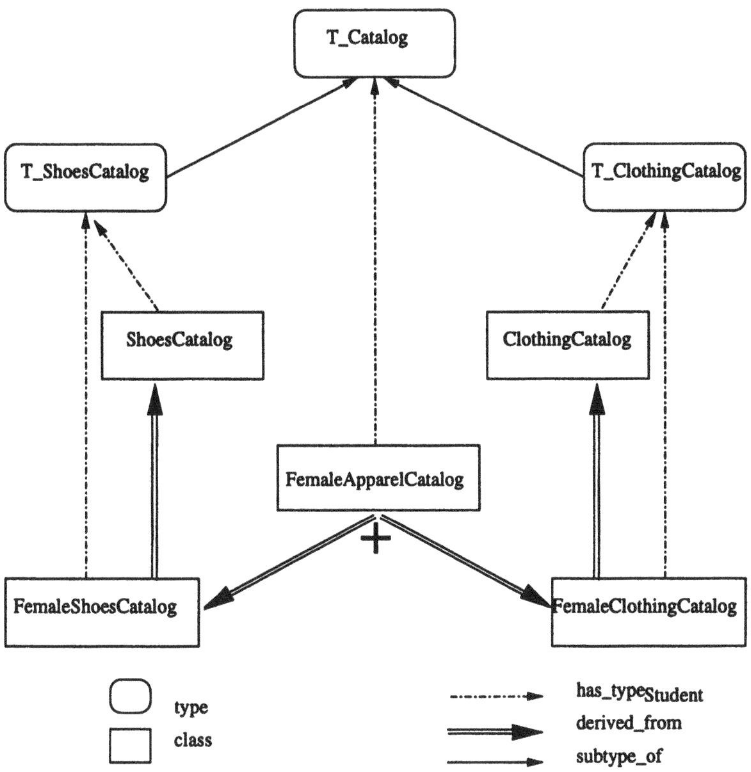

Figure 14.6: An Example of a Composed Derived Image Class

14.3.2.2 Defining Image Views Using Derived Logical Salient Object Classes. Definition 5 defines the content of an image i as a pair $Cont(i) =< \mathcal{P}^i, s >$ where $\mathcal{P}^i$ represents the physical salient objects and the function s maps each physical salient object to a logical salient object. An image i_d can be derived from i and $Cont(i_d) =< \mathcal{P}^i, s_d >$. Assume we derived a logical salient object class L_1 from the logical salient object class L and that all the physical salient objects in $\mathcal{P}^i$ are mapped to objects of L. If we note by f the interface function that transforms an object of L to an Object of L_1, and we define $s_d = s \circ f$, then i_d is a derived image that contains L_1 objects.

For example, the classes *FemaleClothing* and *FemaleShoes* can be respectively derived from *Clothing* and *Shoes* (Figure 14.5). A composed derived class *FemaleApparel* can be derived from the two previously derived classes and the derived image class *FemaleApparelCatalog* can be defined as images containing female apparels. Of course, *T_FemaleClothing* and *T_FemaleShoes* can respectively be different from *T_Clothing* and *T_Shoes*. *T_FemaleApparel* is then, a sibling of *T_Apparel*.

Definition 7 *An* **image view** *is defined by:*

- *a derived image class*
- *redefining the semantics of the physical salient objects an image contains through derived logical salient object classes.*

14.4 THE IMAGE VIEW DEFINITION LANGUAGE

The view definition language allows us to define derived classes. Queries in the view definition are expressed in MOQL (Multimedia Object Query Language) [10], the query language defined for DISIMA. MOQL extends the standard object query language, OQL [5] with predicates and functions to capture temporal and spatial relationships. Most of the extensions have been introduced in the *where* clause in the form of new predicates including the *contain* predicate to check if a salient object belongs to an image. The convention used in the language definition is: [ ] for optional, { } (different from **{}** which are part of the language) for 0 to n times, and | for one and only one among different possibilities. The view language allows us to create and delete derived classes.

- Create a derived class

```
derive { <derived class name> from <class definition >
    [ augment {<virtual property name> as <query> |
              <function name> ;}]
    [ hide    < property list>]
    {cast     < property> into <derived type> }
    [ content < valid salient object class list>]
    extent    <extent name > [as <query>]
};

    <class definition> := <class name> |
    (<class definition > union | intersect | minus <class definition>)
```

- Delete a derived class

```
    delete <derived class name>
```

The *derive* clause is used to define a derived logical salient object class, as well as derived image classes. The classes that the *derived classes* are derived from can be ordinary or derived classes. The query in the *extent* clause defines the derived class extent and must return a unique subset of the combination of the parent class extents. The *augment* clause is used to define new properties. A query can invoke an existing property. In this case, the keyword *this* is used to refer to the current object. If $(\alpha : T(C))$ is a property and C_d is a class derived from C, then the clause *cast* can be used to cast the type of α into $T(C_d)$.

The *content* clause allows us to define the valid logical salient objects. This clause is used only for derived image classes and does more than hide the previous image content and redefine a new one. It implements the image views using derived logical salient object classes. If the logical salient object class mentioned is a derived class, then it changes the semantics of the physical salient objects from parent to derived objects. Assume a salient object class S_d is derived from class S and an image i (element of the image class I) contains a salient object of type $T(S)$. If we derive an image class I_d from I with the clause *content* S_d, image i_d derived from i will contain a salient object of type $T(S_d)$ instead of $T(S)$. For example, in the image view *CustomerClothing* that follows, an image of *CustomerCatalog* contains elements of *CustomerClothing*, rather than *Clothing* as salient objects.

14.4.1 Examples of Image Views

In the following, we give some examples of image views derived from the catalog database. The corresponding schema expressed in the ODMG object model [5] is given in the Appendix. The schema given in the Appendix can be seen as the view of the company: each image contains models and clothes. The examples correspond to the Customer View, the Female Clothing Catalog View, and the Female Aparel Catalog view.

Image View 1 The CustomerCatalog view

```
derive   {CustomerClothing from Clothing
augment  inStock as this.inStock();
         avgPriceForType as
         avg(Select c.price
         From Clothes c
         Where c.type = this.type);
hide     stock, lastOrderDate, lastArrivalDate, nextArrivalDate
extent   CustomerClothes};

derive   {CustomerCatalog from ClothingCatalog
hide     photographer, date, time, place
cast     accessories into Set<Ref<CustomerCatalogs>>
extent   CustomerCatalogs
content  CustomerClothing};
```

The derived class *CustomerClothes* redefined *Clothes* for the customers' use. Attributes *stock, lastOrderDate, lastArrivalDate, nextArrivalDate* are hidden and the virtual attribute *avgPriceForType* returns the average price for this type of clothing.

The image view *CustomerCatalog* uses the image class *Catalog* renamed as *CustomerCatalog* with *CustomerCatalogs* as its extent name. All the images are available but their content will be limited to objects of type *CustomerClothes* which redefines *Clothing.* Attributes ***photographer, date, time, place*** are hidden. The attribute ***accessories*** was defined as a set of images from *Catalog.* Its type has to be changed to set of *CustomerCatalogs* to ensure consistency.

Image View 2 The FemaleClothingCatalog view

```
    derive    {FemaleClothing from CustomerClothing
    extent    FemaleClothes as
              Select c
              From CustomerClothes c
              Where c.sex = 'female' or c.sex = 'unisex'};

    derive    {FemaleClothingCatalog from ClothingCatalog
    hide      photographer, date, time, place
    cast      accessories into Set<Ref<CustomerCatalogs>>
    extent    FemaleClothingCatalogs
    content   FemaleClothing};
```

Only images containing female items are selected from the clothing catalog. The salient objects are restricted to female clothing.

Image View 3 The FemaleApparelCatalog view

```
    derive    {FemaleShoes from Shoes;
    augment   inStock as this.inStock();
              avgPriceForType as
              avg(Select s.price
              From Shoes s
              Where s.type = this.type);
    hide      stock, lastOrderDate, lastArrivalDate, nextArrivalDate
    extent    FemaleShoesExtent as
              Select s
              From ShoesExtent c
              Where c.sex = 'female' };

    derive    {FemaleShoesCatalog from ShoesCatalog
    hide      photographer, date, time, place
    extent    FemaleShoesCatalogs
    content   FemaleShoes};

    derive    {FemaleApparelCatalog from FemaleClothingCatalog union
              FemaleShoesCatalog
    extent    FemaleApparelCatalogs};
```

The *FemaleApparelCatalog* combines the *FemaleClothingCatalog* and the *FemaleShoesCatalog* into a new derived catalog.

14.4.2 Implementing Derived Classes in DISIMA

The distinction between types and classes is not supported by most object-oriented languages in current use. DISIMA is being implemented on top of ObjectStore [8] using C++. DISIMA provides types for image and logical salient objects that can be subtyped by the user. The implementation we describe in this section simulates the idea using C++. We implement all our types as C++ classes. We call these C++ classes *type classes* and their names start with *T_*. For example *T_Person* will be a type class for the class *Person*. Our classes are objects of the C++ class *C_Class*. *C_Class* has a subclass *D_Class* for derived classes. The properties defined for *C_Class* are:

- Name: name of the class
- Type: type class name
- SuperclassList: list of the superclasses
- SubClassList: list of the subclasses
- ShallowExtent (virtual function): The shallow extent of the class
- DependentList: list of classes derived depending on this one

The properties defined for *D_Class* are:

- RootClassList: list of the classes it is derived from
- Filter: filter function
- ShallowExtent: redefined
- MaterializationFlag: set when the ShallowExtent is up-to-date
- Change: function used to unset the MaterializationFlag

The *DependentList* in the class *C_Class* contains all the classes derived from that class and also all the derived classes for which an augmented property is computed using objects of that class. Since the type of a derived class can be different from the type of its root class we choose to materialize the derived class extent. An object of *C_Class* represents a user's class and the extent (*ShallowExtent*) property returns objects of the type class (*Type*). The *SubClassList* can be used to recursively compute the deep extent. To simplify the materialization process, we only store one level of root class. That is, the *RootClassList* of a derived class contains only non-derived classes. A derived class extent is materialized the first time the class is referred to and the materialization flag is set. Each time new objects are created, modified or deleted in a root class, a change message is sent to each of the classes in the *DependentList* to unset the materialization flag. If the materialization flag is unset when a derived class is accessed, the derived class extent is recomputed and the materialization flag is reset.

When the augmented properties of a derived object are computed from the single root object without any aggregate, the management algorithm for incremental view maintenance can easily be implemented as follows. An object of a derived class contains the OID of the root object it is derived from. The *Change* method passes the OID of the changed root object (new, deleted or updated) to the derived class object where it is kept in the *ChangeList* of the derived class object. The *ChangeList* can then be visited to update or create the derived objects for modified or new root objects and to delete derived objects corresponding to deleted root objects.

14.5 RELATED WORK

To the best of our knowledge, there is no other view mechanism defined for image which can be compared to our solution. DISIMA, as well as most multimedia products and prototypes, is being developed on top of an object-oriented database system. We defined an object-oriented view mechanism used in the image view solution. This section will focus on two of the most representative object-oriented view solutions: O_2View and Multiview.

14.5.1 O_2View

O_2View is the view mechanism defined for the O_2 system. O_2View distinguishes two kinds of derived classes: virtual and imaginary classes. The main ideas are the following:

- A virtual class (1) selects through a query, objects existing in the root database; (2) is connected to the root hierarchy; and (3) provides a name for the extension of the virtual class. Its interface can be modified for hiding an attribute or adding a virtual one.
- An imaginary class (1) selects and restructures through a query data from the root database or the view, (2) turns them into objects, (3) is not connected to the root hierarchy, and (4) provides an extension.
- A virtual attribute attaches (possibly restructured) data to an object in the view, through a query on the root database or the view. It augments the original interface of virtual objects.
- An attribute hiding restricts the original interface of root objects. It hides the attributes of a virtual object not to be visible to the end-user

14.5.2 Multiview

Multiview [7] is a research prototype developed at the University of Michigan on top of the GemStone system. Multiview provides updatable materialized object-oriented database views. The main features of the system are:

- Integration of both virtual and base classes into a unified global schema. This is done through a classification algorithm [13] that restructures the whole class hierarchy. Hence, virtual classes participate in the inheritance hierarchy and can be used in the same way base classes are used.

- Generation of schemata composed of user-selected bases and virtual classes.
- Includes incremental view maintenance algorithm for view materialization.

O_2Views [14], makes the distinction between *virtual classes* that select through queries existing objects in the database and *imaginary classes* for which the selected objects are restructured and turned into objects. Virtual classes are connected to the generalization hierarchy by a *maybe* relationship whereas imaginary classes are not. Multiview [7] integrates the derived classes into the global class hierarchy using a complex classification algorithm [13]. Our solution is simpler and yet more powerful. A virtual class can be derived from one or several classes with its type integrated into the type hierarchy without any modification of the user-defined root classes. In addition to having the object-oriented views features, an image view should provide a semantic independence. That is, the content of the same image can be different from one view to another.

14.6 CONCLUSION

Several object view mechanisms have been proposed since the early 90s [4, 1, 14, 16, 7]. In general, the main problems with these views are [16] (i) expressive power (restrictions on queries defining views), (ii) reusability and modeling accuracy (insertion of the views into the generalization hierarchy), and (iii) consistency (stability in OID generation).

Problems (i) and (ii) are somewhat related. For example, using the view mechanism in [14], if the user wants the view class to be linked to the generalization hierarchy, the query that generates the view class has to be restricted. In addition, the problem (ii) raises a typing problem (how is the type of the virtual class related to the type hierarchy?) and a classification problem (how is the extent of a virtual class related to the existing ones?). Finding an answer to these two questions in an environment where the only relationship is the *is-a* relationship can lead to contradictions. The distinction between the derivation hierarchy and the generalization hierarchy in our proposal, based on the distinction between type and class, provides an elegant solution to problems (i) and (ii). In addition, the object-oriented view mechanism presented in this paper allows us to derive classes from several existing ones. Problem (iii) is also solved by the fact that a derived object is seen as a root object with a different interface function. A derived object and its root class share the same OID but are uniquely identified by the pair $< class\_name, OID >$ which is invariant even if the derived object is recomputed.

The DISIMA model separates the objects contained in an image (*physical salient objects*) from their semantics (*logical salient objects*). Using our object view mechanism, we proposed an image view mechanism that allows us to give different semantics to the same image. For example, a derived image class can be defined by deriving new logical salient object classes that give new semantics to the objects contained in an image or by hiding some of the objects by directly defining a derived image class.

The main contributions of this paper are the proposal of a powerful object-oriented view mechanism based on the distinction between class and type, a proposal of an image view mechanism based on image semantics and the image view implementation using a language that does not intrinsically support the distinction between class and type.

References

[1] S. Abiteboul and A. Bonner. Objects and views. In *Proceedings of ACM SIGMOD International Conference on Management of Data*, pages 238—247, Denver, Colorado, May 1991.

[2] B. Adelberg, H. Garcia-Molina, and J. Widom. The STRIP rule system for efficiently maintaining derived data. In *Proceedings of ACM SIGMOD International Conference on Management of Data*, pages 147—158, Tucson, Arizona, May 1997.

[3] D. Agrawal, A. El Abbadi, A. Singh, and T. Yurek. Efficient view maintenance at data warehouse. In *Proceedings of ACM SIGMOD International Conference on Management of Data*, pages 417—427, Tucson, Arizona, May 1997.

[4] E. Bertino. A view mechanism for object-oriented databases. In *Proceedings of International Conference on Extending Data Base Technology*, pages 136—151, Viena, Austria, March 1991.

[5] R. G. G. Cattell, D. Barry, D. Bartels, M. Berler, J. Eastman, S. Gamerman, D. Jordan, A. Springer, H. Strickland, and D. Wade, editors. *The Object Database Standard: ODMG 2.0.* Morgan Kaufmann, San Francisco, CA, 1997.

[6] L. S. Colby, A. Kawaguchi, D. F. Lieuwen, I. S. Munick, and K. A. Ross. Supporting multiple view maintenance policies. In *Proceedings of ACM SIGMOD International Conference on Management of Data*, pages 405—416, Tucson, Arizona, May 1997.

[7] H. A. Kuno and E. A. Rundensteiner. The MultiView OODB view system: Design and implementation. *Journal of Theory and Practice of Object Systems (TAPOS)*, 2(3):202—225, 1996.

[8] C. Lamb, G. Landis, J. Orenstein, and D. Weinreb. The objectstore database system. *Communications of ACM*, 34(10):19—20, 1991.

[9] Y. Leontiev, M. T. Özsu, and D. Szafron. On separation between interface, implementation and representation in object DBMSs. In *Proceedings of Technology of Object-Oriented Languages and Systems 26th International Conference (TOOLS USA98)*, pages 155—167, Santa Barbara, August 1998.

[10] J. Z. Li, M. T. Özsu, D. Szafron, and V. Oria. MOQL: A multimedia object query language. In *Proceedings of the 3rd International Workshop on Multimedia Information Systems*, pages 19—28, Como, Italy, September 1997.

[11] V. Oria, M. T. Özsu, X. Li, L. Liu, J. Li, Y. Niu, and P. J. Iglinski. Modeling images for content-based queries: The DISIMA approach. In *Proceedings of 2nd International Conference of Visual Information Systems*, pages 339—346, San Diego, California, December 1997.

[12] K. A. Ross, D. Srivastava, and S. Sudarshan. Materialized view maintenance and integrity constraint checking: Trading space for time. In *Proceedings of ACM SIGMOD International Conference on Management of Data*, pages 507—518, Montreal, Canada, June 1996.

[13] E. A. Rundensteiner. A classification algorithm for supporting object-oriented views. In *Proceedings of International Conference on Information and Knowledge Management*, pages 18—25, June 1994.

[14] Casio Santos, Claude Delobel, and Serge Abiteboul. Virtual schema and bases. In *Proceedings of International Conference of extending Data Base Technology*, pages 81—94, Cambridge,UK, March 1994.

[15] A. W. M. Smeulders, M. L. Kersten, and T. Gevers. Crossing the divide between computer vision and data bases in search of image databases. In *Proceedings of 4th IFIP 2.6 Working Conference on Visual Database Systems - VDB 4*, pages 223—239, L'Aquila, Italy, May 1998.

[16] X. Ye, C. Parent, and S. Spaccapietra. Derived objects and classes in DOOD system. In *4th International Conference on Deductive and Object-Oriented Databases, DOOD 95*, pages 539—556, Singapore, December 1995.

Appendix: Sample Schema

```
class Image{
    Set<Ref<Representation>> representations;
    Set<Ref<PhysicalSalientObject>> physicalSalientObjects
            inverse image;
    // Methods
    display(); }
class Catalog: Image{
    Person photographer; Date date; Time time; String place; }
class LogicalSalientObject{
    Set<Ref<PhysicalSalientObject>> physicalSalientObjects
            inverse logicalSalientObject;
    //Methods
    Region region(Image m); // salient object's region in image m
    Color color(Image m); // salient object's color in image m
    Texture texture(Image m); // salient object's texture in image m }
class Person: LogicalSalientObject{
    String name; String occupation; Address address; }
class Model: Person{
    String : agency; }
class Apparel: LogicalSalientObject{
    String name; String type; Real price; Set<Real> size;
    Manufacturer manufacturer; Integer stock; String colors;
    Date lastOrderDate; Date lastArrivalDate; Date nextArrivalDate;
    //Methods
    Boolean inStock(); // true if the the clothing is in stock }
class Clothing: Apparel {
    Set<Ref<Catalog>> accessories;// images of items that match with the cloth
class Shoes: Apparel {
    String sole;String upper; }
class PhysicalSalientObject{
    Ref<LogicalSalientObject> logicalSalientObject
            inverse physicalSalientObjects;
    Ref<Image> image
            inverse physicalSalientObjects;
    Region region; Color color; Texture texture }
Set<Ref<SalientObject>> SalientObjects; //all salient objects
Set<Ref<Person>> Persons; //salient objects of type Person
Set<Ref<Model>> Models; //salient objects of type Model
Set<Ref<Clothing>> Clothes; //salient objects of type Clothing
Set<Ref<Shoes>> ShoesExtent; //salient objects of type shoes
Set<Ref<Image>> Images; //all images
```

15 A THREE-DIMENSIONAL REPRESENTATION SCHEME FOR INDEXING AND QUERYING IN ICONIC IMAGE DATABASES

Jae-Woo Chang

Department of Computer Engineering, Chonbuk National University
Chonju, Chonbuk 560-756, South Korea
Phone: +82-652-270-2414 (FAX: 270-2418)

jwchang@dblab.chonbuk.ac.kr

Abstract: In multimedia information retrieval applications, content-based image retrieval is essential for retrieving relevant multimedia documents. The purpose of our paper is to provide both effective representation and efficient retrieval of images when a pixel-level original image is automatically or manually transformed into its iconic image containing meaningful graphic descriptions, called icon objects. For this, we propose a new spatial match representation scheme, called 27DLT one, by extending the conventional 9DLT(Direction Lower Triangular) scheme so that we can describe three-dimensional spatial relationships between icon objects accurately. In order to accelerate image searching, we also design an efficient retrieval method using a signature file technique. Finally, we evaluate the retrieval performance of the proposed 27DLT scheme in terms of retrieval effectiveness.

15.1 INTRODUCTION

Recently, much attention has been paid to Multimedia Information Retrieval (MIR) because we have had so many applications that should be supported by handling multimedia data, such as text, image, video, audio, and animation. The applications include digital libraries, advertisements, medical information, remote sensing and astronomy, cartography, digital newspapers, and architectural design. So far, text attributes in multimedia documents have mainly been used for supporting queries by content. The approach using text content(e.g., captions and keywords) has a couple of problems. First, the original keywords do not allow for unanticipated searching. The other problem is that the caption is not adequate to describe the layout, sketch, and shape of the image. Therefore, in order to support MIR applications effectively, content-based image retrieval is essential because it plays an important role in retrieving relevant multimedia documents.

Given a pixel-level original image, various image processing and understanding techniques are used to identify domain objects and their positions in the image. Though this task is computationally expensive and difficult, it is performed only at the time of image insertion into the database. Moreover, this task may be carried out in a semi-automated way or in an automated way, depending on the domain and complexity of the images. An iconic image is obtained by associating each domain object of the original image with a meaningful graphic description, called an icon object. Thus, an iconic image representation can provide users with a high level of image abstraction. The iconic image representation has some advantages. First, the use of iconic images avoids the need for repeated image understanding tasks. Processing an original image for interactive responses to high level user queries is inefficient because the number of images tends to be large in most MIR applications. Secondly, the iconic image representation is useful in a distributed database environment where an original image is stored only at a central node and its iconic image is stored at each local node. Finally, the representation of original images into iconic images enables users to achieve domain independence and to deal with a group of icon objects in a systematic way.

In the paper, we assume that all images at the pixel level are analyzed prior to storage so that icon objects can be extracted from their content and stored into the database together with the original images. The icon objects are used to search the image database and to determine whether an image satisfies query selection criteria. Ultimately, the effectiveness of MIR systems depends on the type and correctness of image content representation, the type of queries allowed, and the efficiency of search techniques designed. The purpose of our paper is to provide both effective representation and efficient retrieval of images when a pixel-level original image is automatically or manually transformed into its iconic image including icon objects. For this, we propose a new spatial match representation schemes, called 27DLT one, to support the content-based image retrieval in an effective way. The proposed 27DLT scheme can describe three-dimensional spatial relationships between icon objects in a precise way by extending the conventional 9DLT scheme. In order to accelerate image searching, we also design an efficient retrieval method using a signature file technique.

The remainder of this paper is organized as follows. A review of related work done in the area of iconic image databases is introduced in Section 15.2. The proposed 27DLT representation scheme is described in Section 15.3. A new efficient retrieval method to accelerate image searching is presented in Section 15.4. Section 15.5 provides the performance evaluation of the proposed 27DLT scheme in terms of retrieval effectiveness. Section 15.6 shows user interfaces for iconic image indexing and querying. Finally, Section 15.7 concludes the paper with some issues for future research.

15.2 RELATED WORK

There have been many proposals for spatial match representation and retrieval in order to search symbolic images efficiently, satisfying certain spatial relationships [1, 2, 3, 4]. In particular, there have been two previous efforts on spatial match representation schemes using signature file techniques, namely the 2D(Dimensional)-string scheme [2] and the 9DLT(Direction Lower Triangular) scheme [4].

15.2.1 The 2D-string scheme

Chang, Shi and Yan [1] first proposed a 2D string to represent symbolic images. The 2D string makes use of a symbolic projection to represent a symbolic image by preserving some spatial knowledge of objects embedded in an original image. Here, a symbol in the symbolic image corresponds to an object in its original image. In addition, they defined three types (type-0, type-1, and type-2) of 2D sequence pattern matching. For type-0 matching, an arbitrary number of symbols, rows, and columns can be deleted from a symbolic image and can be merged together in order to make it the same as a pattern. Type-1 matching is the same as type-0, except that adjacent rows or columns of a symbolic image cannot be merged. Type-2 matching does not permit any rows and columns to be deleted from a symbolic image.

Lee and Shan [2] proposed a 2D-string representation scheme to express some types of spatial relationships of symbolic images. In this scheme, they generated four kinds of two-level signature files by associating each symbolic image with a record signature and by relating some images with a block signature. These signatures are retrieved by either specifying a symbol or specifying a type-i match for i=0, 1, or 2. In addition, they adopted a superimposed coding technique to use the spatial relationships among symbols in a symbolic image as well as to filter quickly for any of the four types of queries. For convenience of signature generation, they defined a spatial string to represent the pairwise spatial relationships embedded in a 2D string. A type-i 1D spatial character V^{AB} is a character describing the spatial relationship between A and B symbols in the 1D string as follows:

$$
\begin{array}{lll}
\text{(type-0)} & V^{AB} = "0" & \text{if } r(A) = r(B) \\
 & V^{AB} = "0" \text{ and } "1" & \text{if } r(A) < r(B) \\
 & V^{AB} = "0" \text{ and } "2" & \text{if } r(A) > r(B) \\
\text{(type-1)} & V^{AB} = "0" & \text{if } r(A) = r(B) \\
 & V^{AB} = "1" & \text{if } r(A) < r(B) \\
 & V^{AB} = "2" & \text{if } r(A) > r(B) \\
\text{(type-2)} & V^{AB} = "0" + str(r(A) - r(B)) & \text{if } r(A) = r(B) \\
 & V^{AB} = "1" + str(r(B) - r(A)) & \text{if } r(A) < r(B)
\end{array}
$$

$$V^{AB} = "2" + str(r(A) - r(B)) \quad \text{if } r(A) > r(B)$$

Here $r(X)$ is the rank of symbol X, "+" denotes the string concatenating operator, and str(X) is a transformation function from integer to string; for example, str(3)="3". A type-i 2D spatial string for symbols A and B when i=0, 1, and 2, S_i^{AB}, is a string formed by concatenating A, B, and type-i spatial characters V_X^{AB} and V_Y^{AB}, where V_X^{AB} is a spatial character along the X-axis and V_Y^{AB} is a spatial character along the Y-axis. Therefore, S_i^{AB} is written as $A+B+V_X^{AB}+V_Y^{AB}$. S_i is a set of S_i^{AB} for all pairs of symbols A and B in an symbolic image.

15.2.2 The 9DLT scheme

Chang [3] proposed 9DLT direction codes to describe the type-1 spatial relationship embedded in a 2D string. Therefore, nine integers(i.e., 1, 2, 3, 4, 5, 6, 7, 8, and 0) are used to represent pairwise spatial relationships embedded in a 2D string. Figure 15.1 shows the nine direction codes, where R indicates the reference symbol, 1 stands for "north of R," 2 stands for "northwest of R," and 0 stands for "at the same location as R," and so on.

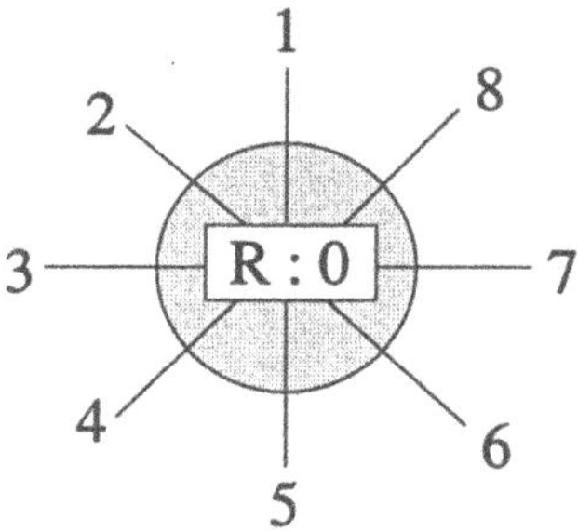

Figure 15.1: 9DLT direction codes

Chang and Jiang [4] proposed a 9DLT representation scheme to express three types of spatial strings so that they can fully support the description of type-0, type-1, and type-2 pairwise spatial relationships embedded in a 2D string. They also designed a quick-filter based signature file organization as a filter for spatial match retrieval of images. The 9DLT scheme describes a spatial representation between A and B symbols as follows.

(type-0) $ST_0^{AB} = (A, B, D'_{AB})$

$D'_{AB} = 0$	if $D_{AB} = 0$
$D'_{AB} = 0$ and 1	if $D_{AB} = 1$
$D'_{AB} = 0$ and 3	if $D_{AB} = 3$
$D'_{AB} = 0$ and 5	if $D_{AB} = 5$
$D'_{AB} = 0$ and 7	if $D_{AB} = 7$
$D'_{AB} = 0,1,2$ and 3	if $D_{AB} = 2$

$$
\begin{aligned}
& D'_{AB} = 0,3,4 \text{ and } 5 \quad \text{if } D_{AB} = 4 \\
& D'_{AB} = 0,5,6 \text{ and } 7 \quad \text{if } D_{AB} = 6 \\
& D'_{AB} = 0,1,7 \text{ and } 8 \quad \text{if } D_{AB} = 8 \\
\text{(type-1) } & ST_1^{AB} = (A, B, D_{AB}) \\
\text{(type-2) } & ST_2^{AB} = (A, B, D_{AB}, SC_X^{AB}, SC_Y^{AB}) \\
& SC_X^{AB} = 0 \text{ if } |r_X(A) - r_X(B)| \leq 1 \\
& SC_X^{AB} = 1 \text{ if } |r_X(A) - r_X(B)| > 1 \\
& SC_Y^{AB} = 0 \text{ if } |r_Y(A) - r_Y(B)| \leq 1 \\
& SC_Y^{AB} = 1 \text{ if } |r_Y(A) - r_Y(B)| > 1
\end{aligned}
$$

Here, S_i^{AB} represents the type-i spatial strings for A and B symbols, and (A, B, D_{AB}) denotes the 9DLT representation of symbols A and B. SC_X^{AB} and SC_Y^{AB} represent the spatial codes for symbols A and B in the X-axis and the Y-axis, respectively. Expression $|t|$ denotes the absolute value of t; for example, $|-2| = 2$.

15.3 A NEW THREE-DIMENSIONAL REPRESENTATION SCHEME

For image indexing, a large number of known image processing and understanding techniques [5] can first be used to identify some domain objects and their relationships in an original image. Next, we can easily obtain an iconic image by associating a meaningful icon object with each domain object in the original image. By using some spatial match representations, we can finally obtain spatial strings from spatial relationships between icon objects. For image retrieval, a user query can first be transformed into an iconic image in the same way as that used in the image indexing. Next, we can represent the query iconic image as spatial strings by using some spatial match representations. Then, we can generate a query signature from the spatial strings and can get some potential matches by comparing the query signature with all of the signatures in the signature file. By excluding some false matches from the potential ones, we can finally retrieve some iconic images to satisfy the user query. The architecture of a spatial match retrieval system is shown in Figure 15.2.

For spatial match representations, there have been two main representation schemes to search image results efficiently, satisfying certain spatial relationships [1, 3]. However, both representation schemes have a critical problem in that they can represent spatial relationships between icon objects for only the two-dimensional(2D) images. As a result, they are not suitable to expressing spatial relationships between objects for handling three-dimensional(3D) images. In order to support 3D content-based image retrieval, we propose a new three-dimensional representation scheme for iconic image indexing and querying, called 27DLT one, by extending the conventional 9DLT scheme.

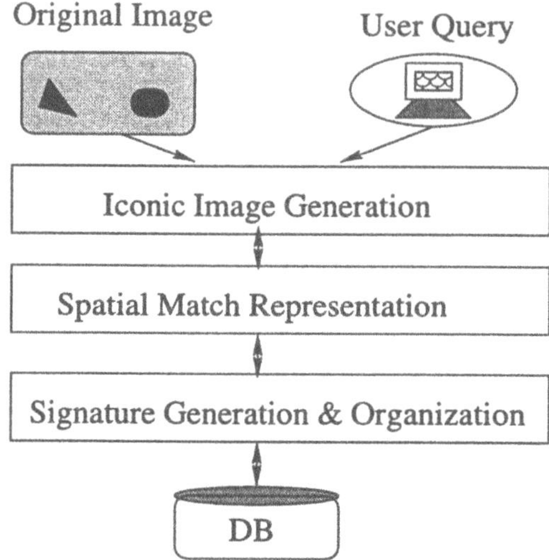

Figure 15.2: Architecture of a spatial match retrieval system

15.3.1 27DLT representation scheme

To describe the spatial relationship between icon objects for 3D images, we propose 27DLT direction codes which extends the 9DLT codes for handing relationship embeded in a 3D images. Therefore, twenty-seven integers from -8 to 18 are used to represent pairwise spatial relationships embeded in a 3D string. Figure 15.3 shows the twenty-seven direction codes, where R indicates the reference icon object. The codes from 1(North) to 8(Northeast) denote directions in a counterclockwise order on the same plane as R and 0 stands for "at the same location on the same plane as R". The codes from -1 to -8 denote the same directions as those of 1 to 8 except that they are described on the inner plane of R. The integer 0 stands for "at the same location as R on the inner plane". Similary, the codes from 11 to 18 denote the same directions as those of 1 to 8 on the outer plane of R. The integer 10 stands for "at the same location as R on the outer plane".

Thus, an exact-match direction character, RE_{AB} is a character describing the 3D spatial relationship between objects A and B when the projects of A and B are represented as a point in a 3D space, respectively. The exact-match direction character is written as the following:

RE_{AB} = 1, -1, 11	if B is north of A in the same, the inner, the outer plane, respectively.
RE_{AB} = 2, -2, 12	if B is northwest of A in the three planes
RE_{AB} = 3, -3, 13	if B is west of A in the three planes
RE_{AB} = 4, -4, 14	if B is southwest of A in the three planes
RE_{AB} = 5, -5, 15	if B is south of A in the three planes
RE_{AB} = 6, -6, 16	if B is southeast of A in the three planes

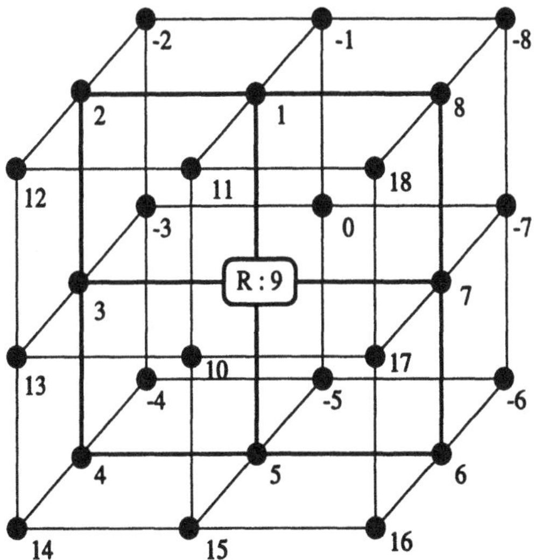

Figure 15.3: 27DLT direction codes

Table 15.1: Approximate-match direction characters

RE_{AB}	RA_{AB}	RE_{AB}	RA_{AB}	RE_{AB}	RA_{AB}
9	9	0	0	10	10
1	1 and 9	-1	-1 and 0	11	10 and 11
3	3 and 9	-3	-3 and 0	13	10 and 13
5	5 and 9	-5	-5 and 0	15	10 and 15
7	7 and 9	-7	-7 and 0	17	10 and 17
2	1, 2, 3, and 9	-2	-1, -2, -3 and 0	12	10, 11, 12 and 13
4	3, 4, 5, and 9	-4	-3, -4, -5 and 0	14	10, 13, 14 and 15
6	5, 6, 7, and 9	-6	-5, -6, -7 and 0	16	10, 15, 16 and 17
8	1, 7, 8, and 9	-8	-1, -7, -8 and 9	18	10, 11, 17 and 18

RE_{AB} = 7, -7, 17 if B is east of A in the three planes
RE_{AB} = 8, -8, 18 if B is northeast of A in the three planes
RE_{AB} = 9, 0, 10 if B is at the same location as A in the three planes

In addition, an approximate-match direction character, RA_{AB} is a character describing the 3D spatial relationship between objects A and B when the projects of A and B are represented as a point in a 3D space, respectively. The approximate-match direction character is written as Table 15.1.

Based on the 27DLT direction codes, we propose a 27DLT representation scheme to express both exact-match and approximate-match of spatial strings so that we can support the full description of pairwise spatial relationships embeded in a 3D string. The exact-match spatial string can be classified into two groups, i.e., general exact-match and distance-considered exact-match, depending on whether or not a distance between two objects is consideted in addition to a direction between them when we represent an iconic image as spatial strings. For expressing the distance, two distance degrees are used; N(near) and F(far-away). The optimal threshold value of differenciating between 'N' and 'F' can be determined by a large number of experiments, but a naive value can be determined to be the average distance between two objects. The three-dimensional distance character between objects A and B over X-,Y-, and Z-axis, D_{AB}, is shown in Table 15.2.

Table 15.2: Distance character between objects A and B

distance character	distance over X-axis	distance over Y-axis	distance over Z-axis
0	N	N	N
1	N	N	F
2	N	F	N
3	N	F	F
4	F	N	N
5	F	N	F
6	F	F	N
7	F	F	F

An approximate-match spatial string of objects A and B, STA_{AB}, a general exact-match spatial string, STE_{AB}, and a distance-considered exact-match spatial string, STD_{AB}, are expressed as follows:

- approximate-match string
  $SBA^{AB} = \{(A, B, RA_{AB}\}$
- general exact-match string
  $STE^{AB} = \{(A, B, RE_{AB}\}$
- distance-considered exact-match string
  $STD^{AB} = \{(A, B, RE_{AB}, D_{AB}\}$

15.4 AN EFFICIENT RETRIEVAL METHOD

In order to support fast searching of spatial strings for iconic images, it is necessary to construct an efficient retrieval method using a signature file technique because of its main advantages: fast retrieval time and low storage overhead [6, 7]. When an iconic image consists of both icon objects and a set of spatial strings among them, we first create an object signature for each object in the iconic image and superimpose all of the signatures by using a superimposed coding technique. Then, we create an approximate-match signature by superimposing all of the signatures, each of which is made from each approximate-match spatial string for the iconic image. In addition, we construct a general exact-match signature by superimposing all of the signatures, each of which is made from each general exact-match spatial string for the iconic image. Similarly, we create a distance-considered exact-match signature for the iconic image. Superimposing signatures leads to reducing the disk space to be accessed dramatically. Using a disjoint coding technique, we finally construct an image signature by concatenating the object signature, the approximate-match one, and the superimposing one of both the general exact-match and the distance-considered exact-match signature.

Therefore, we can offer a way to answer a variety of user queries effectively since an image signature is composed of three parts of signatures. For example, if a user query needs some image results, including icon objects A and B, we can access only a portion of object signatures, thus dramatically reducing the query processing time. Similarly, if a user query requires all relevant images satisfying a certain relationship approximately, we can access only a portion of approximate-match signatures to answer the query.

15.4.1 Signature generation

With a set of distance-considered exact-match spatial relationship strings (DESRs) corresponding to a given iconic image, we can generate a set of general exact-match spatial relationship strings (GESRs), approximate-match spatial relationship strings (ASRs), and an object list (OL). Given the OL, a set of ASRs, a set of GESRs, and a set of DESRs, we can also generate four kinds of signatures for the iconic image, i.e., object, approximate-match, general exact-match, and distance-considered exact-match ones. Then, an image signature for the iconic image is constructed by concatenating the object one, the approximate-match one, and the superimposing one of both general and distance-considered exact-match signatures. The algorithm to generate an image signature is illustrated below.

[Algorithm 1] Generation of image signature
Input: a set of DESRs for an iconic image, each being (A,B,R_{AB},D_{AB})
Output: image signature, IS
Variables:
S_{obj}, S_{app}, S_{gex}, S_{dex} : object, approximate-match, and general exact -match, distance-considered exact-match signature for an iconic image, respectively
so_k : object signature for the k-th object of the OL
sa_i, sge_i, sde_i, : approximate-match, general exact-match, and distance-considered exact-match signature for the i-th DESR, respectively
s_i^j : approximate-match signature for the j-th ASR of the i-th DESR
Begin:
$S_{obj} = 0$; $S_{app} = 0$; $S_{gex} = 0$; $S_{dex} = 0$;
Compute the OL from a set of DESRs;

while(each k-th object of the OL for some k) {
    Create so_k from the k-th object of the OL; $S_{obj} = S_{obj} \vee so_i$;
} /* while loop for k */
while(each i-th DESR for some i) {
    Create sde_i from the i-th DESR; $S_{dex} = S_{dex} \vee sde_i$;
    Determine a GESR from the i-th DESR;
    Create sge_i from the GESR; $S_{gex} = S_{gex} \vee sge_i$;
    Determine a set of ASRs from the i-th DESR; $sa_i = 0$;
    while(each j-th ASR for some j) {
        Create s_i^j from the j-th APR; $sa_i = sa_i \vee s_i^j$;
    } /* while loop for j */
    $S_{app} = S_{app} \vee sa_i$;
} /* while loop for i */
$RS = S_{obj} || S_{app} || (S_{gex} \vee S_{dex})$;

End:

15.4.2 Insertion and Retrieval

When a set of signatures for an iconic image is generated using Algorithm 1, we can store the object signature and the approximate-match signature into an object signature file and an approximate-match one, respectively. We also store the superimposing one of both general and distance-considered signatures into an exact-match signature file. Therefore, the insertion of an image signature can be easily handled because it only needs to append its three parts of signatures to those three signature files.

When a user query is given, it can be transformed into a query signature using Algorithm 1. Depending on whether the query belongs to an approximate-match or an exact-match type, we can decide in what sequence three signature files should be accessed so that we may achieve good retrieval performance. After accessing the corresponding signature files, we can obtain some qualifying signatures to satisfy the relationship strings in the query. Finally, we can find iconic image results by examining whether the iconic images corresponding to the qualifying signatures actually satisfy the query. If necessary, we can retrieve some pixel-level original images given by the iconic image results. Both the insertion and retrieval algorithms are omitted because of their simplicity.

15.4.3 Example

We assume that we have four iconic images consisting of icon objects A, B, and C as shown in Figure 15.4. A set of approximate-match, general exact-match, and distance-considered exact-match spatial relationship strings in our basic representation can be obtained as follows:

- approximate-match representation
  (Image-1) (A,B,10),(A,C,10),(A,C,17),(B,C,-7),(B,C,0)
  (Image-2) (A,B,3),(A,B,9),(A,C,0),(B,C,-7),(B,C,0)

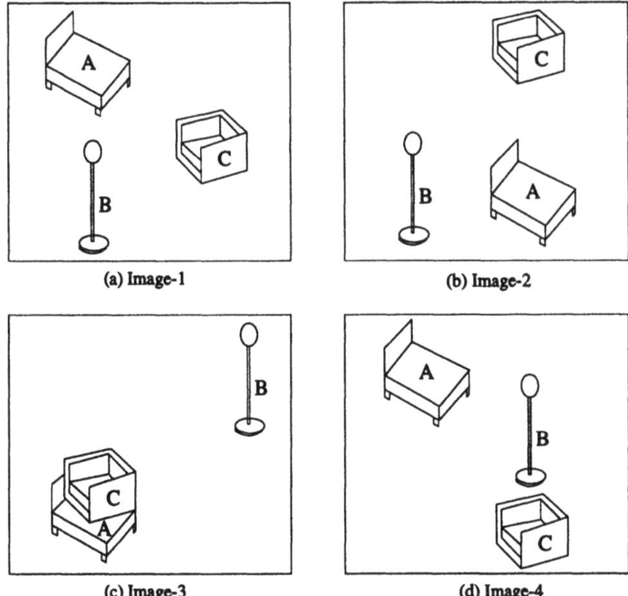

Figure 15.4: Four example iconic images

(Image-3) (A,B,-7),(A,B,0),(A,C,1),(A,C,9),(B,C,10),(B,C,13)
(Image-4) (A,B,10),(A,B,17),(A,C,10),(A,C,17),(B,C,10)

- general exact-match representation
  (Image-1) (A,B,10),(A,C,17),(B,C,-7)
  (Image-2) (A,B,3),(A,C,0),(B,C,-7)
  (Image-3) (A,B,-7),(A,C,1),(B,C,13)
  (Image-4) (A,B,17),(A,C,17),(B,C,10)
- distance-considered exact-match representation
  (Image-1) (A,B,10,1),(A,C,17,0),(B,C,-7,0)
  (Image-2) (A,B,3,0),(A,C,0,1),(B,C,-7,1)
  (Image-3) (A,B,-7,5),(A,C,1,0),(B,C,13,5)
  (Image-4) (A,B,17,0),(A,C,17,5),(B,C,10,0)

To create image signatures for the four iconic images, we assume that an object signature has 8 bits in length, an approximate-match signature has 16 bits, and each exact-match signature has 16 bits. In addition, we assume that four hashing functions are used to generate these signatures. Table 15.3, Table 15.4, Table 15.5, and Table 15.6 list the object, the approximate-match, the general exact-match, and the distance-considered exact-match signatures, respectively. Based on them, we can generate image signatures for the four iconic images as shown in Table 15.7.

Figure 15.6 illustrates a signature file structure after we insert the four image signatures in Table 15.7. Here the SRS file is the one storing a set of DESRs,

Table 15.3: Object signatures

object	object signature
A	00010001
B	00100010
C	01000100

Table 15.4: Approximate-match signatures

ASR	approximate-match signature
(A,B,-7)	00000000 00000001
(A,B,0)	00000000 00000010
(A,B,3)	00000000 00000100
(A,B,9)	00000000 00001000
(A,B,10)	00000000 00010000
(A,B,17)	00000000 00100000
(A,C,0)	00000000 01000000
(A,C,1)	00000000 10000000
(A,C,9)	00000001 00000000
(A,C,10)	00000010 00000000
(A,C,17)	00000100 00000000
(B,C,-7)	00001000 00000000
(B,C,0)	00010000 00000000
(B,C,10)	00100000 00000000
(B,C,13)	01000000 00000000

Table 15.5: General exact-match signatures

GESR	general exact-match signature
(A,B,-7)	00000000 00000001
(A,B,3)	00000000 00000010
(A,B,10)	00000000 00000100
(A,B,17)	00000000 00001000
(A,C,0)	00000000 00010000
(A,C,1)	00000000 00100000
(A,C,17)	00000000 01000010
(B,C,-7)	00000000 10000100
(B,C,10)	00000001 00001000
(B,C,13)	00000010 00010000

GESRs, and ARSs. For example, suppose that we have a query to find such an iconic image as Image-Q in Figure 15.5. To answer this query, we first generate a set of SRS for Image-Q in our basic representation as follows:

Table 15.6: Distance-considered exact-match signatures

DESR	distance-considered exact-match signature
(A,B,-7,5)	10000000 00000001
(A,B,3,0)	01000000 00000010
(A,B,10,1)	00100000 00000100
(A,B,17,0)	00010000 00001000
(A,C,0,1)	00001000 00010000
(A,C,1,0)	00000100 00100000
(A,C,17,0)	00000010 01000010
(A,C,17,5)	00000001 01000010
(B,C,-7,0)	00000000 10000100
(B,C,-7,1)	00000000 01000100
(B,C,10,0)	00000000 00100000
(B,C,10,1)	00000000 00010000
(B,C,13,5)	00000000 00001000

Table 15.7: Image signatures for the four example iconic images

Image	IS_{obj}	IS_{app}	$IS_{gex} \vee IS_{dex}$
Image-1	01110111	00011110 00010000	00100010 11000100
Image-2	01110111	00011000 01001100	01001000 11010010
Image-3	01110111	01100001 10000011	10000110 00101001
Image-4	01110111	00100110 00110000	00010001 01101000

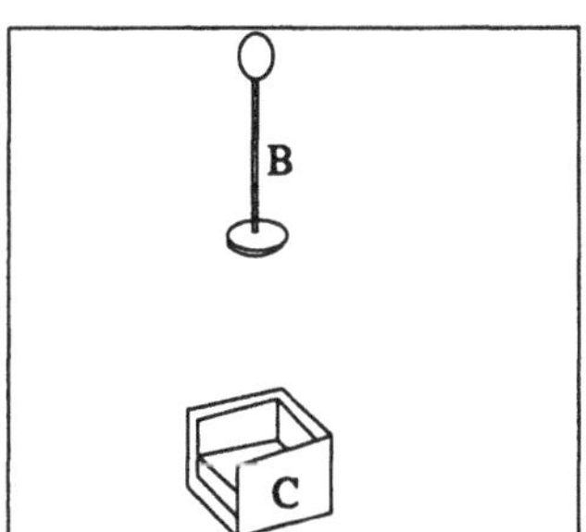

Figure 15.5: Image-Q: A query iconic image

- approximate-match representation
  (B,C,10)
- general exact-match representation
  (B,C,10)
- distance-considered exact-match representation
  (B,C,10,1)

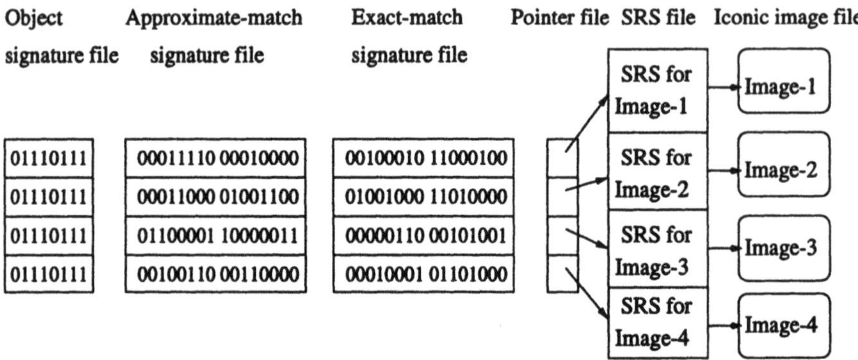

Figure 15.6: New signature file organization

Next, we create the object, the approximate-match, the general exact-match, and the distance-considered exact-match signatures for Image-Q by using Table 15.3, Table 15.4, Table 15.5, and Table 15.6 as follows:

$$IS^Q_{obj} = 01100110$$
$$IS^Q_{app} = 00100000\ 00000000$$
$$IS^Q_{gex} = 00000001\ 00000000$$
$$IS^Q_{dex} = 00000000\ 00010000$$

If we require some distance-considered exact-match answers, we can compare IS^Q_{dex} with the four signatures in the exact-match signature file. we can obtain one qualifying signature because the second signature in the exact-match signature file satisfies the bit pattern of IS^Q_{dex}. However, it is proved to be a false match because the corresponding DESRs for image-2 does not actually contain the DESR of the query. On the other hand, if we require some approximate-match answers, we can search for only the four signatures of the approximate-match signature file. We obtain two qualifying signatures, i.e., the third and the fourth of the approximate-match signature file, because they contain the bit pattern of IS^Q_{app}. Thus, we can access the ARS of iconic images corresponding to the qualifying signatures so that we can find out some false drops. As an approximate-match answer, we finally obtain two qualifying iconic images, i.e., Image-3 and Image-4, because both the ARSs of Image-3 and those of Image-4 both include the ARS of Image-Q.

15.5 PERFORMANCE EVALUATION

We assume that an iconic image consists of icon objects, each having its icon name and its position. For our experiment, we generate the following iconic databases [8].

- Icon objects have 25 different types.

- An iconic image consists of two to ten icon objects.
- The total number of iconic images used is 10,000.
- A query iconic image contains two to five icon objects.

In order to evaluate retrieval effectiveness [9], we make use of recall and precision measures. Let IRT be the number of iconic images retrieved by a given query, IRL be the number of iconic images relevant to the query, and IRR be the number of relevant iconic images retrieved. The relevant images can be determined by computing the similarity between two iconic images, based on their spatial relationship. The recall and precision measures are computed as the following:

$$Recall = \frac{IRR}{IRL}$$

$$Precision = \frac{IRR}{IRT}$$

When 1000 different queries are executed, Table 15.8 shows the retrieval effectiveness of our 27DLT representation scheme, in terms of precision measure. Here, "Exact" means a query type for the general exact match and "Approx." means one for the approximate match. Our 27DLT representation scheme achieves nearly the same retrieval precision, compared to the 9DLT scheme. When the number of icon objects in a query is small, it is shown that the precision values of the exact-match query are higher than those of the approximate-match one. As the number of icon objects is increased, the precision values of the approximate-match query are closer to those of exact-match one. This is because the number of qualifying iconic images is dramatically decreased as the number of objects in a query is increased.

Table 15.8: Precision measure of our 27DLT scheme

# of icon objects in a query	9DLT Scheme		Our 27DLT scheme	
	Approx.	Exact	Approx.	Exact
2	0.12	0.19	0.13	0.18
3	0.39	0.52	0.41	0.48
4	0.45	0.50	0.50	0.54
5	0.47	0.53	0.52	0.53
Precision	0.35	0.43	0.39	0.43

In order to verify the correctness of our experiment, we also implemented our 27DLT representation scheme using 100 real interior design images. The iconic images corresponding to the real images were obtained by manual transformation. Iconic objects forming the iconic images have 20 different types related with an interior design field, such as, bed, chair, desk, sofa, table, armchair, standard lamp, bookcase, dressing table, wardrobe, oven, refrigerator, and so forth. A query iconic image contains two to three icon objects. When a variety of ten queries are executed, Table 15.9 shows the retrieval effectiveness of our 27DLT representation scheme, in terms of precision and recall measures. Our 27DLT representation scheme shows approximately the same retrieval effectiveness results, compared to those in Table 15.8. In case of the approximate-match query, the precision values of our implementation with real images are a little lower than those of our experiment with imaginary images. This is because we don't have a large number of real images enough to obtain sufficient qualifying images to answer a given query. It is shown from the results that our 27DLT representation scheme holds about 0.3 precision value in the approximate match and about 0.5 in the exact match, while their recall values are kept one.

Table 15.9: Retrieval effectiveness of our 27DLT scheme

retrieval effectiveness	9DLT Scheme		Our 27DLT Scheme	
	Approx.	Exact	Approx.	Exact
Precision	0.2	0.38	0.22	0.44
Recall	1.0	1.0	1.0	1.0

15.6 USER INTERFACES FOR ICONIC IMAGE GENERATION

As shown in Figure 15.2, some original images are transformed into their iconic images through the iconic image generation step, prior to their storage to the database. In addition, a user query can be transformed into its iconic image query through this step so that we search for qualifying iconic images to satisfy the query. In order to make this step easy-to-use, we implemented user interfaces for both image indexing and querying.

15.6.1 User interface for image indexing

For image indexing of a pixel-level original image, a large number of known image processing and understanding techniques [5] can be used to identify some domain objects and their positions in the original image. For example, the MBR(Minimum Bounding Rectangle) technique can represent the positional relationships among domain objects in a precise manner because it can preserve the size of the domain objects. Though the image processing and understanding task is computationally expensive and difficult, it is performed only at the time of image insertion into the database. We provide a user interface where a pixel-level original image can be transformed into an iconic image by manually associating each domain object in an original image with a meaningful icon object. Figure 15.7 shows the user interface for image indexing. A set of domain objects surrounded by the six rectangles of the original image in Figure 15.7(a) can be transformed into their corresponding iconic objects by using this interface. In Figure 15.7(b), the iconic objects of the upper left, the upper right, and the bottom left indicate those appeared in the inner plane, the same plane, and the outer plane, respectively. Therefore, an iconic image of the bottom right in Figure 15.7(b) is made by combining all the iconic objects in the three planes.

a

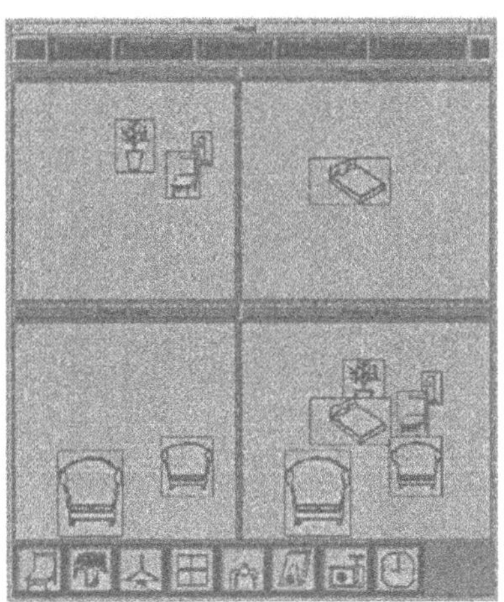
b

Figure 15.7: Image indexing interface

15.6.2 User interface for image querying

For image retrieval, a user query can first be transformed into an iconic image in the same way as the image processing and understanding techniques. The traditional user interface is not appropriate for users to retrieve relevant images in a convenient way. Thus, it is necessary to make a visual user interface where users can easily construct their query being expressed as icon objects. Therefore we impliment a query-by-iconic image interface in order to provide users with a more convenient tool for writing their query. In Figure 15.8(a), the query consists of three iconic objects each of which comes from the inner, the same, and the outer plane, respectively. As shown in Figure 15.8(b), we obtain only one qualifying image to satisfy the query since we use a small database with 100 real interior design images.

15.7 CONCLUSIONS AND FUTURE WORK

Recently, much attention has been paid to Multimedia Information Retrieval (MIR) because there are so many applications which require multimedia data. In order to support MIR in an effective way, content-based image retrieval is essential for retrieving relevant multimedia documents. For this, we proposed our 27DLT spatial match representation scheme so as to support three-dimensional content-based image retrieval in an effective way. Our representation scheme accurately described three-dimensional spatial relationships between icon ob-

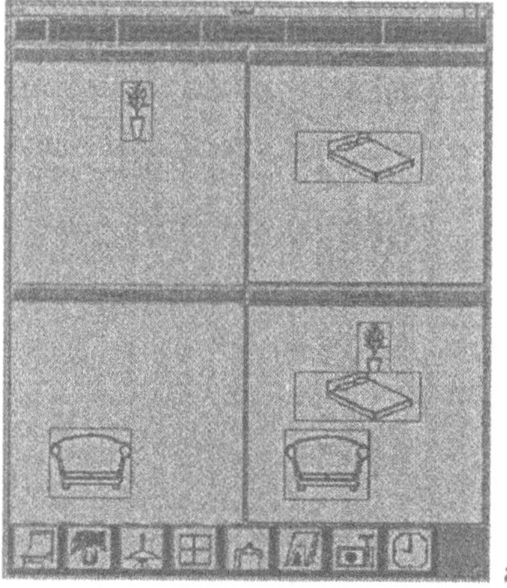
a

b

Figure 15.8: Image querying interface

jects because they could make use of 27DLT direction codes. To accelerate searching, we also designed our efficient retrieval method based on a signature file technique.

In order to prove the superiority of our 27DLT scheme on retrieval effectiveness, we evaluated its retrieval performance in terms of both precision and recall measures. We showed from our experiment that our 27DLT scheme holds about 0.3 precision value in the approximate match and about 0.5 in the exact match, while its recall values are kept one. As further work, our 27DLT representation scheme should be applied to real application areas using three-dimensional iconic images, proving the efficiency of our scheme in these areas.

References

[1] S. K. Chang, Q. Y. Shi, and C. W. Yan. Iconic indexing by 2d strings. *IEEE Transactions on Pattern Recognition and Machine Intelligence*, 9(3):413–428, 1987.

[2] S. Y. Lee and M. K. Shan. Access methods of image databases. *International Journal of Pattern Recognition and Artificial Intelligence*, 4(1):27–44, 1990.

[3] C. C. Chang. Spatial match retrieval of symbolic pictures. *Information Science and Engineering*, pages 142–145, 1991.

[4] C. C. Chang and J. H. Jiang. A fast spatial match retrieval using a superimposed coding technique. In *Proc. of the Int'l Symposium on Advanced database Technologies and Their Integration*, pages 71–78, Nara, Japan, 1994.

[5] C. Faloutsos et al. Efficient and effective querying by image content. *Journal of Intelligent Information Sysyems*, 3:231–262, 1994.

[6] C. Faloutsos and S. Christodoulakis. Signature files: An access methods for documents and its analytical performance evaluation. *ACM Transactions on Database Systems*, 2(4):267–288, 1984.

[7] J. W. Chang, J. H. Lee, Y. J. LEE. Multikey Access Methods Based on Term Discrimination and Signature Clustering. In *ACM 12th International Conference on Research and Development in Information Retrieval*, pages 176-185, Cambridge, Massachusetts, Jun, 1989.

[8] V. N. Gudivado. Tessa - an image testbed for evaluating 2d spatial similarity algorithms. *ACM SIGIR Forum*, pages 17–36, Fall 1994.

[9] G. Salton. *Automatic Text Processing.* Addison-Wesley, 1989.

16 MULTIMEDIA INFORMATION RETRIEVAL FRAMEWORK: FROM THEORY TO PRACTICE

F. Moelaert EL-Hadidy, H.J.G. de Poot, and D.D. Velthausz

Telematica Instituut
P.O. Box 589, 7500 AN, Enschede, the Netherlands,
Phone: +31-53-4850485, Fax: +31-53-4850400,
E-mail: {moelaert,poot,velthausz}@telin.nl

Abstract: Easy access to multimedia information is important as the amount of information is exponentially growing. Content-based retrieval is a viable approach. Extensibility and flexibility of data models is another important issue as the field is constantly evolving. The ADMIRE framework applied in this paper satisfies both criteria. This we show in two practical cases, one in the field of clinical assessments of measurement data, the other in the field of video directory services. ADMIRE offers a uniform solution for structuring these data. Content disclosure is supported by labelling of these data structures. This is done by automatic, semi-automatic or manual labelling.

16.1 INTRODUCTION

The aim of multimedia IR systems is to handle general queries such as "find outdoor pictures or videos of an interview with James Cameron discussing the making of the Titanic film". Answering such queries requires intelligent exploitation of both speech and visual content. For multimedia retrieval, the combination of multiple integrated media types increases the performance of content-based retrieval, to overcome mismatches and missing matches. Available content analysis and retrieval techniques tailored to a specific media are therefore not adequate for queries as the one mentioned above. From the above example it is clear that multimedia IR is a very broad area covering both infrastructure issues (e.g. framework models, efficient storage criteria, networking, client-server models) and intelligent content analysis and retrieval. This all needs to be integrated as a seamless whole. That involves expertise from a wide variety of fields and lots of research.

The infrastructure issues are closely related to information supply. The way information is structured has a direct impact on the retrieval strategies. So for example if a slide show presentation and a corresponding audio track are stored as two loose information objects, it is difficult to retrieve the sound related to a certain slide in the presentation. On the other hand if the system allows the definition of relationships between different media then retrieval becomes more easy. Multimedia models have thus to allow for a uniform way to represent different media and the relationships between media.

Here the need emerges for a heterogeneous framework for representing all types of media in a uniform manner. This paper contributes to the infrastructure issues with a general framework for representing multimodal information.

Existing multimedia models focus mostly on a single aspect of multimedia information, like presentation (e.g. PREMO [ISO94]), or exchange of documents, or on a particular format (e.g. HyTime [ISO97]). Models that do facilitate content-based information retrieval in general are for example MORE [TYH+91], VODAK [GuNe93], CORE [WNM+95] and AIR [GuRV96]. These models either do not support a layered definition of information objects (e.g. MORE and VODAK) or can only represent the content of specific unstructured media types (e.g. AIR). MPEG7 which is currently being developed as a general multimedia standard for content representation for information disclosure [MPEG98] is promising, but it is still in an early stage. The model in [CMF96] for representing digitised document and the Amsterdam Hypermedia Model (AHM) [Hard98] is directed to modelling and authoring of Hypermedia documents.

This paper presents a general framework called ADMIRE [VeBE96]. It resembles the CORE model but offers more flexibility in modelling object relationships. ADMIRE emphasises on the disclosure of all kinds of forms and types of existing digital information [Velt98]. It uses an object-oriented modelling technique together with a layered definition of information objects. It is thus suitable for representing multimedia information. The basic difference between these models and ADMIRE lies in the ability to represent features and concepts at every level in the information hierarchy. Features are context independent functions operating on the data (e.g. shape). Concepts are context dependent interpretations of the data (e.g. goal).

The intelligent content analysis and retrieval of multimedia IR are related to information demand. Unlike traditional databases, an exact matching between demand and supply in multimedia databases is frequently not possible since the information is differently structured. This requires, besides an accurate and comprehensive model of the available information, specific functionality to handle the queries and the presentation of the (intermediate) results.

In content-based retrieval, information should be extracted from features, concepts or a combination of both. This should be possible across all media. To retrieve a statement that James Cameron made in the interview, a combination of pattern recognition (feature) in video material for lip movement and the concept "Oscar" in the audio material can be combined. Such queries are strongly dependent on the context where they are used. Therefore, the choice of features and concepts and extraction rules depend on the context. This paper shows how the ADMIRE framework supports extraction of multimedia information in general. Further more, two cases are presented to demonstrate context specific matters one in the medical field and the other in the field of video directory services (VDS).

In the clinical information case patients' movement disorders are recorded and monitored using multiple techniques. This results in huge files with multimedia data. To support data analysis data disclosure techniques are used. The VDS case covering the soccer domain offers an interactive way to retrieve (fragments of) content that the user is interested in. To support queries in that domain we need to disclose soccer related information.

In section 16.2 the ADMIRE framework is briefly explained. A general guideline for content-based retrieval using the ADMIRE framework is presented in section 16.3. This has been applied in two cases that are presented in sections 16.4 and 16.5. Finally, some conclusions are given in section 16.6.

16.2 ADMIRE FRAMEWORK

As the field of multimedia is constantly developing, we advocate a generic approach to multimedia modelling. Our ADMIRE framework, presented in [VeBE96], provides an information object hierarchy on the one hand and an abstraction hierarchy on the other hand. The information object hierarchy makes sure that every piece of multimedia information, from loose pictures or soundbites to elaborated reports, coverages etc. can be described. The abstraction hierarchy distinguishes respectively raw data, computable features of this data and context and interpretation dependent concepts. See Figure 16.1. All properties in the data layer (format and attribute properties) are stored since they convey information that cannot be determined differently. The feature and concept layers contain information that can be determined using the properties of the lower layers, and extraction algorithms for features and (domain) inference rules for concepts. As opposed to features, concepts are context dependent: Different concepts can be inferred from the same data and features, Figure 16.1.

We go through some simple examples of multimedia information to demonstrate how the ADMIRE framework works. Figure 16.2 is an image containing three objects. This image can be modelled in ADMIRE as an information object (IO) as shown in Figure 16.1. At the data level this IO consists of an array of pixels or, depending on the format, a set of vectors and areas. At the feature level functions can be defined that operate on this data, e.g., the percentage green, the presence of sharp edges, and the such. At the concept level interpretations and meaning is given to the data, e.g., the fact that there is a tree, a sun and a partially visible car.

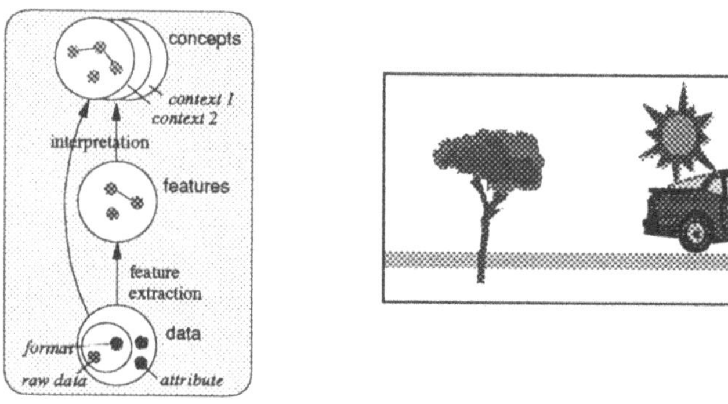

Figure 16.1: Illustration of an IO **Figure 16.2**: an example of an IO.

We distinguish between retrievable and non-retrievable IOs. The smallest retrievable IO we call a *basic* IO e.g. a frame in a video and is defined by the designer. A collection of basic IOs we call composite IO. In this paper when we mention IO we mean retrievable IO. A non-retrievable IOs where further decomposition of an IO is unfeasible, e.g. individual words or pixels, but still useful for extraction, we call *pseudo IOs*. Pseudo IOs are part of the information hierarchy. They are also characterised by features and concepts, but the data possesses a function that specifies the subset of the raw data and format of an accompanying IO. It is comparable to the non-materialised nature of 'scripted objects' [ScWy95] and 'anchor values' used in hypermedia models [HaSc94]. Examples of pseudo IOs are: sequence of characters within a textual fragment; a specific region in a pixel based image (frame), e.g. rectangle 1 indicating a 'car' as illustrated in frame 1 in Figure 16.3 or a person's voice within an audio fragment.

In pseudo IOs, features and concepts are strongly linked. E.g. in pseudo video IO B, colours and shapes are features from which the concept "tree" can be inferred. Also the sound feature of an audio IO, if present, of a high frequency white noise could reflect the wind blowing through the leaves, adding to the concept "tree". Therefore, any feature from any modality can contribute to the concepts that are being inferred.

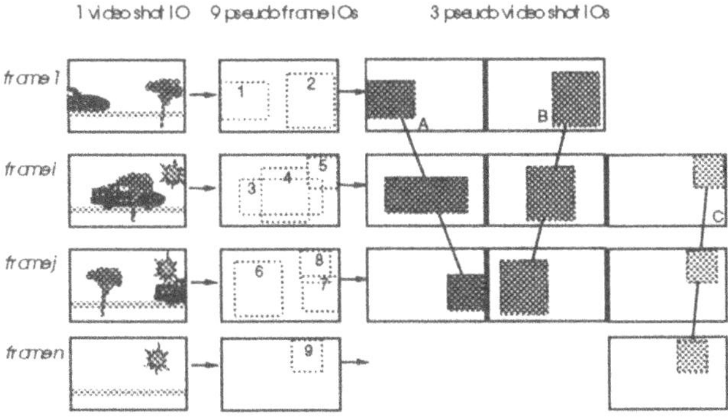

Figure 16.3: Four sample frames of a video shot with the corresponding nine pseudo frame IOs and three pseudo video shot IOs

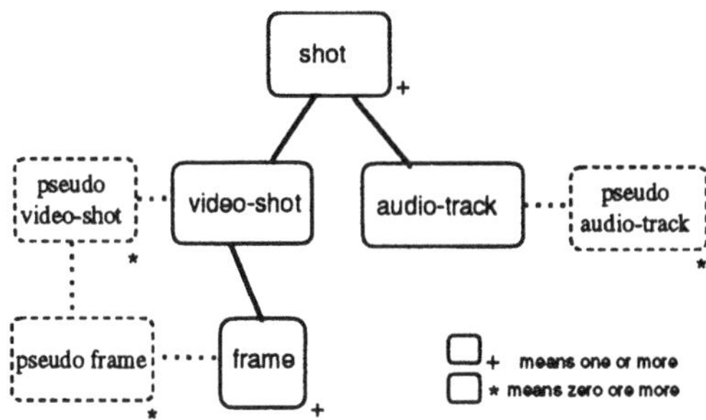

Figure 16.4: The information hierarchy of our sample movie shot

In the ADMIRE framework, this integration of media is modelled in hierarchical relations which exist for IOs as well as their pseudo IOs. The example of Figure 16.2 is frame j in the video shot IO in Figure 16.3. In the centre nine corresponding pseudo *frame* IOs are shown. Related pseudo *frame* IOs in successive frames are linked forming a pseudo video shot IO. See A,B and C in Figure 16.3. The information hierarchy for this cxample for a movie shot is given in Figure 16.4. It includes images (frames) from the video shot and sound tracks from audio. The data layer of the pseudo video shot object allows new features to be extracted, e.g., concerning a more completed shape of an object as some occlusions in individual frames are resolved or concerning rotation (viz. of the wheels). These features may then support concepts like "wheels", "fast", "car" etc.

Motion between objects, is part of the feature layer of the video shot IO. At the concept layer, these motions can be interpreted, e.g. using world knowledge that the camera rather than a tree moves, and that cars do not fly. From this the motion of the car may be inferred. Each feature and concept has to take its suitable place in the information hierarchy.

In Figure 16.5 the ADMIRE information structure for the example is given. The frames are *basic IOs*. The shot is a *composite IO* as it contains sub IOs of type frame. The contents of the (pseudo)IOs can be read as follows: At the pseudo frame IO level colour and shape are extractable features and objects are extractable concepts. At the frame level new features and concepts arise. Positions of and relations between pseudo-objects are features and states are concepts At the pseudo video shot level similar features can be combined to new features and concepts, either to extract static aspects (shape, paint) or to extract dynamic aspects (wheels turning). At the video shot level motion is an extractable feature and action verbs and changes are extractable concepts.

A formal approach to do concept inference is presented in section 16.3, while practical examples of concept inference presented in section 16.4 and section 16.5.

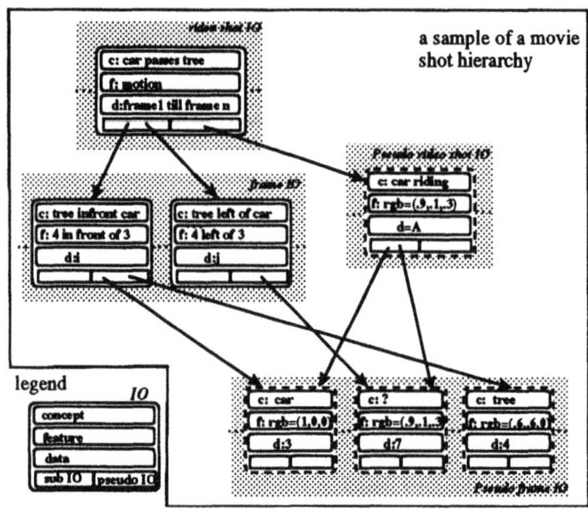

Figure 16.5: The hierarchy between (pseudo) IOs (arrows) and within IOs (layers)

16.3 PROPERTY DERIVATION

As we have seen, information in the ADMIRE framework can be modelled at multiple levels of granularity. Not just data, but also features and concepts of basic IOs can be aggregated forming composite IO. Figure 16.6 is an extended version of Figure 16.1. It shows that a concept associated to a composite IO can be inferred in multiple ways: entirely on the basis of features and concepts of the same composite IO, i.e., within the composite IO, or entirely on the basis of concepts of its sub-IOs, or anywhere between. This depends on the quality of features and concepts.

Two alternatives are illustrated in Figure 16.7. On the left all necessary features are aggregated to a feature within the composite IO which we call feature aggregation. On the right concepts of sub IOs are aggregated to infer a new concept. This we call concept aggregation.

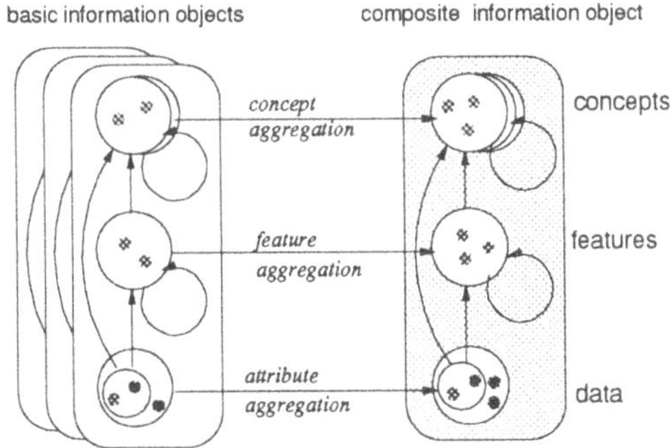

Figure 16.6: Property aggregation operations

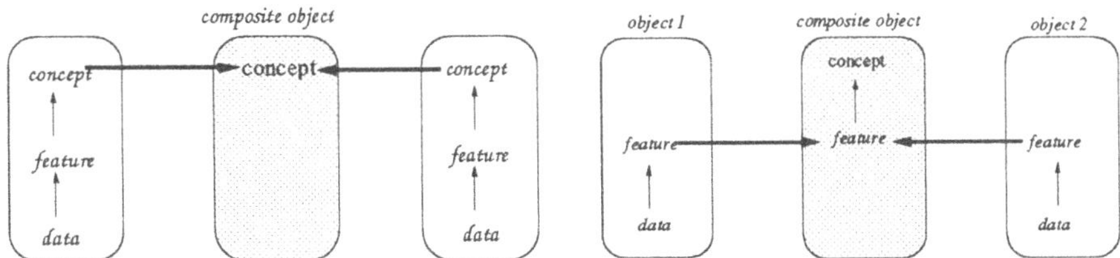

Figure 16.7: Composite IOs concept derivation using feature aggregation (left) and concept aggregation.(right)

As the two examples show, concept inference initially requires features. Concepts can also be labelled manually. But that depends on the interpretation of the labeller. When concepts are automatically inferred, the features must be explicit. Features are mathematical functions. E.g. the feature greenness is a function of an object's RGB value. How high need a greenness be, to call something "green"? This is the process of concept inference: In what range must function values lie to infer a concept? And how certain are we about this concept? Therefore, many researchers have associated *belief values* to concept labels and so do we. The concept inference is twofold: How are belief values estimated when features are evaluated and concepts are inferred and How are belief values combined? (multiple knowledge rules applying to one concept, multiple concepts being aggregated, concept as premises in a knowledge rule). The estimation of belief values is not addressed here. We apply the definition of *precision* as in [Rijs79]. High precision as a search key justifies high belief.

The combination of belief values has been extensively addressed in literature. Some well known methods to do automatic inference of computer supported evidence were considered, namely rule based systems ([BuSh84]), Bayesian Belief networks ([LaSp88], [Pear90]), and Dempster-Shafer sets

([Shaf78]). Below we characterise these methods and the method we propose by their pros and contras (for an extensive review, see [KrCl93]):

method	pros	contras
rule based	simple, allowing belief & disbelief	causality & its inverse mixed up [KrCl93, p63], order effect & no semantics [Heck86]
BBN	causality made explicit, anything is computable	closed world assumption, lot of input needed [WiEd88]
DS sets	notion of ignorance, semantic soundness, no order effect, idempotence	strange renormalisations due to closed world assumption [Zade84], [Clar88]
our approach	the above pros	none of the above contras

As a basic building block we adopt knowledge rules of the kind $P[c/e]=p$, i.e., The belief (elicited probability) that the concept c applies, given evidence e is p, where $0 \leq p \leq 1$. When in an IO the criterion e is met, the triple $\langle c, e, p \rangle$ is added to the "bunch" of evidence, i.e., the set of instantiated knowledge rules, e.g. $\{\langle c, e, p \rangle\}$ when $\langle c, e, p \rangle$ is the first piece of evidence. Working with sets of evidence commutativity (unimportance of order of pieces of evidence) and idempotence (unimportance of double instances of pieces of evidence) are assured.

Suppose that concept c has a priori belief c_0, and that there would be k independent pieces of evidence, $B=\{ \langle c, e_1, p_1 \rangle, \ldots, \langle c, e_k, p_k \rangle \}$, then the belief in concept c given bunch of evidence B would be $P^+[c/B]=1-(1- c_0)^{1-k}\Pi(1-p_i)$. The a priori correction factor is necessary because it is implicitly included in each of the p_i's. The + in P^+ denotes that only positive evidence is combined here. This is comparable to DS theory, but with an open world assumption and without re-normalising belief values.

Similarly counter evidence may be combined where $P_-(c) \equiv P^+(\neg c)$, where we propose a conservative combination $P(c)=P^+(c)\times(1-P_-(c))$.

If pieces of evidence for a concept are not independent, the joint conditional belief values must be known e.g., $\langle c, e_m, . \rangle, \ldots, \langle c, e_n, . \rangle$ being reduced to $\langle c, \{e_m, \ldots, e_n\}, P[c/e_m, \ldots, e_n] \rangle$.

When concepts are evidence to other concepts, their uncertainty is propagated into the knowledge rule: E.g., concept X, with belief value $P[X]=p$ is used to infer concept Y with conditional belief value $P[Y|X]=q$, this is equivalent to a piece of evidence $\langle Y, X, r \rangle$ with belief value $r= P[Y|X]\times P[X]=p\times q$, i.e., the belief in both X and Y given X.

With Bayesian belief networks our approach has in common that knowledge rules are chosen with care: We use feature and concept information only in a bottom-up fashion, and attribute information only in a top-down fashion. For example a concept of an IO can be inferred on the basis of concepts of its sub-IOs, but not on the basis of concepts of its containing super IO. On the other hand, an attribute of an IO is inherited by its sub-IOs. Because of this strictness, a sequence of inferred concepts cannot be dependent on itself across different IOs. Circular or *mutual* dependencies between concepts within a single IO are easily avoided by checking the knowledge rules operating on that IO.

We emphasise that our method is pragmatic allowing easy integration in the case studies. Experience with this approach will show its usability.

16.4 CASE 1: CLINICAL ASSESSMENT

At the Roessingh Research & Development rehabilitation clinic (The Netherlands) large amounts of data are collected of patients suffering from movement disorders (e.g., cerebral palsy). Data include muscle activity (EMG), motion, force (viz. of the feet on the ground), and video recordings, as well as ordinary patient data. In Figure 16.8 the processes leading to body movement is drawn: First there must be an intention for body movement, then the central nervous system executes a motor program, activating the muscles, then the muscles start to contract changing the angles between joints. This leads to body movement as we observe it. The EMG, force and motion recordings give information about the last three phases of this process. With the advent of multimedia it is now possible to view these data on a computer and share data with colleagues, cf. Figure 16.9. Furthermore automated searches are possible, e.g. finding patients with similar movement disorders.

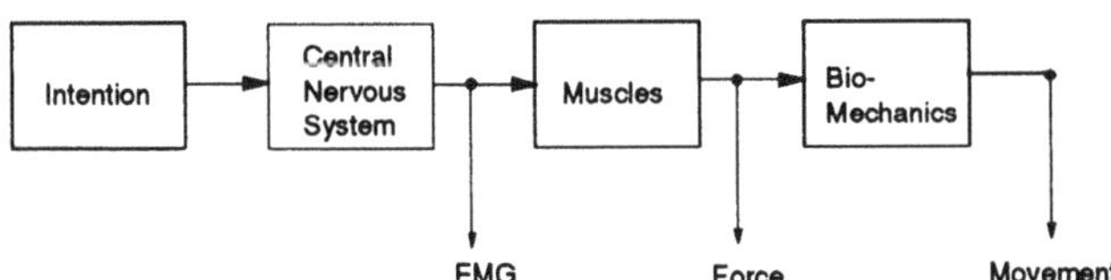

Figure 16.8: Different measurements at a functional motion chain

The ADMIRE framework is used to structure all patient information. The information hierarchy is given in Figure 16.10. It facilitates content-based retrieval of folders of patients with similar disorders: From the data recordings, features can be defined like the phase lag between EMG and kinetic extremes. These features enable limited patient similarity searching. For sophisticated searches concepts are needed, as we will illustrate using a 'stiff legged knee' case.

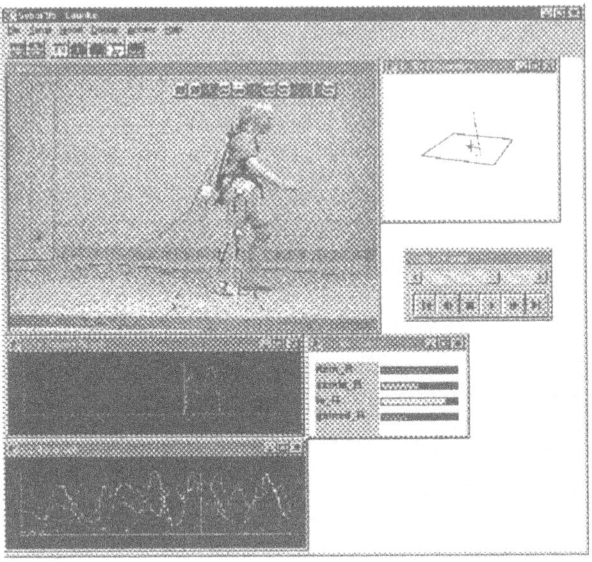

Figure 16.9: The Sybar system [Haut97] is used for quantitative monitoring and teleconsulation between Roessingh and AZVU in the MESH project [HoLu98].

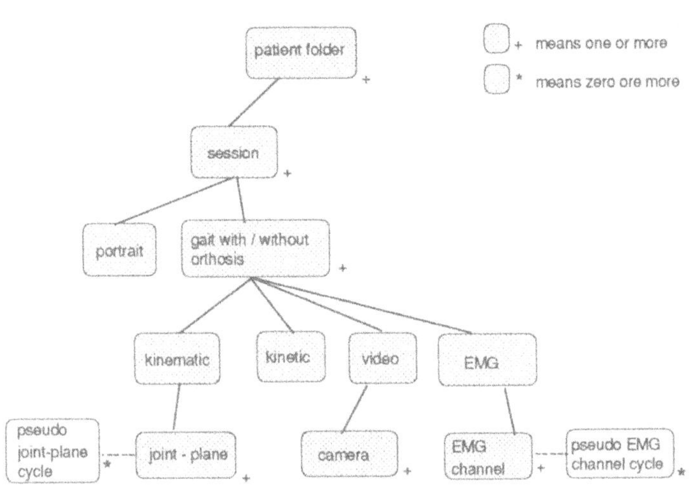

Figure 16.10: Information objects hierarchy structure.

Property extraction

Matching features is not just matching graphs of measurement data. The suitability of a method depends on its domain. For example, for a 'stiff-legged knee', the knee motion range during the swing phase is an important criterion. Looking at the sagittal plane, the marked dots of Figure 16.11 indicate where abnormal knee function is most significant [Perr92]. So the *knee motion range feature* (max - min, during swing phase) can be used as a degree of 'stiffness'. Such choices should be made by a domain expert. These features can be used to find similar 'stiff legged' patients, but also to extract the concept 'stiff legged knee', e.g. using the rule that the absolute motion range is less than 20 degrees. Features from different modalities have been used to classify patient's gait, e.g. using EMG [BCP+79], and EMG in combination with photographed marker trajectories in [KnRi79] or kinematic data [WiGH87]. The ADMIRE framework applied to the Roessingh case enables a multitude of feature combinations that can be used for feature similarity searching and even more important concept extraction.

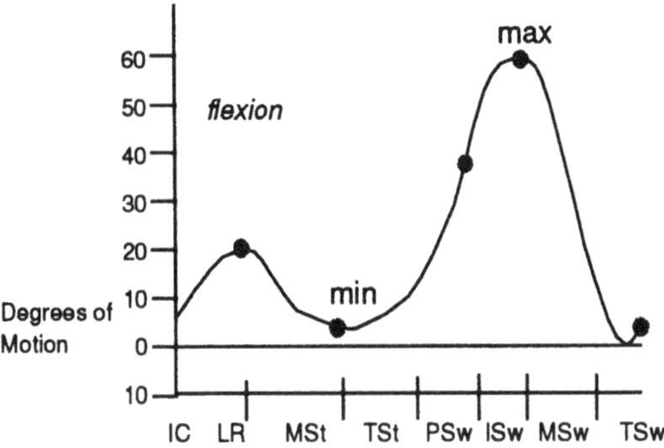

Figure 16.11: Knee motion, the marked dots indicate where most abnormal knee function can be observed.

Property aggregation

As explained in section 16.3, two types of aggregation can be applied to infer concepts. Feature aggregation results in the inference of a single concept while concept aggregation combines already inferred concepts. Now let us look at the subobjects of the gait IO. During a single gait measurement multiple cycles are measured. A cycle within a gait, i.e. the period between two successive initial heel floor contacts of the same foot, can be automatically identified. So gait cycles form important pseudo IOs. On the other hand the sub IOs of the gait IO, as Figure 16.10, could lead to concepts. As timing relationships between different measurements, like joint angles and EMG signals, are important for gait analyses, the gait pseudo IO are most important.

As explained before the concept 'stiff legged knee' can be inferred for individual cycles, hence pseudo gait IOs. Aggregating these concepts will result in concepts for the gait IO (cf. Figure 16.7). In addition, features from multiple successive cycles (pseudo gait IO) would typically result in an aggregated feature from which a concept for the gait IO is inferred (cf. Figure 16.7). Thus the identification and extraction of properties for pseudo IOs is important for the inference of concepts of IOs. Furthermore this enables a better and finer-grained similarity search.

Following the query by example paradigm, the measured patient's gait is used as the similarity search key. Searching for similar patients can be done through by comparing properties of any of the IOs in the object hierarchy. For example using concepts to eliminate the non relevant gait IOs while using features of e.g. the pseudo gait IOs to determine a more finer quantitative similarity. The above indicates that using concepts are more appropriate to search in the information hierarchy in a top-down fashion while features are suitable at lower levels in the information hierarchy.

There is an ongoing research effort between the Telematica Instituut and Roessingh Research Center to apply the methods described above. From the Mesh project [HoLu98], which is a general framework for computer supported co-operative work, a telemedicine pilot is currently running. Here a need has been identified for a multimodal patient database. Also a query language and a feature database are necessary.

Collaborative aspects for multimedia databases are also being addressed. The advantage of using the ADMIRE model in the above research lies mainly in two aspects, the possibility to query concepts as well as features, and being able to combine the evidence of different media to obtain higher accuracy in queries.

16.5 CASE 2: VIDEO DIRECTORY SERVICE

Here we present a video directory service (VDS) for soccer matches. Different from the medical case in section 16.4, the users of a VDS are typically ordinary consumers that do not want to be bothered with the rather technical feature properties. So the challenge is to label these concepts (semi)automatically.

Quite a few studies were centred around analysis of soccer games. There are generally two possible, an elaborated off-line video and live video. The approach presented here is mainly designed for live broadcast, like e.g. [AnHR94]. In live broadcast there is no look ahead.

Although soccer seems easily understandable, with players wearing a number, teams wearing specific colours, and the ball being clearly visible, the images from video material are quite difficult to interpret with a computer algorithm. This is due to limited TV image resolution and the camera focus at one depth at a time.

There are many studies dealing with translation of different media into language, e.g. languages for the description of images [Okad79], video [Badl75], etc. These languages can be used for disclosure of the media. An example used in the soccer game can be found in [AnHR94]. There a system is built that automatically generates textual comments to soccer videos in real-time. Here one stationary camera was used for recording.

In [InBo95] the source material is a normal recording as opposed to the fixed camera in the previous study. Here a football game is used for disclosure using video data only. The complexity here lies in tracking objects. Domain knowledge is used to solve uncertainties.

The paper [GSC+95] focuses on labelling of video shots. It is assumed that relevant objects are present in the first two frames of the video shot. Here only a subset of soccer related features is supported such as detection of edges to identify the soccer court, colour detection of a team's uniform etc. This allows the identification of concepts as corner kicks.

As presented in section 16.2, our approach distinguishes between the data model and the retrievable properties. This allows the disclosure of concepts across different media. Therefore disclosing information from multimedia rather than mono-media offers a better disclosure. The price is increased complexity. This work has been partly done in co-operation with the Dutch telecommunications provider KPN. A prototype has been built [WVP+98].

Figure 16.12 shows how the ADMIRE model is applied to soccer coverages. Every soccer match, summaries and complete (= 'live-taped') coverages may exist. Within a TV-coverage we distinguish the following IO classes: *scene* (semantic coherence), *shot* (continuous sequence), *video shot* (shot's video part), *audio track* (shot's audio part), *text title* (e.g. actual score, play time, name of player that received a yellow card), and *frame* (a 2-dimensional image sample).

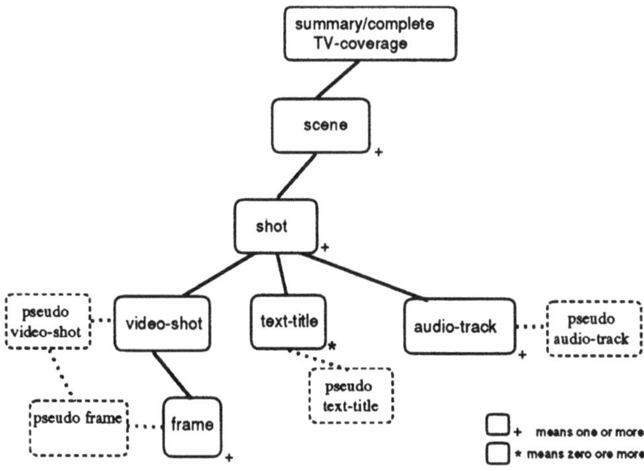

Figure 16.12: Hierarchy of IOs within a TV-coverage composite IO

Property extraction

Like was described in section 16.3, inference percolates through the information hierarchy in a bottom-up manner. We start with the extraction of features from basic IOs, frames, text and audio track. However, many phenomena are not present at the basic IO level. E.g. changes in scores in the text domain and long sentences in the audio domain. So at higher aggregation levels new features are extractable. A user friendly system must links these features, like roundness, to concepts like "ball" or "head". Some of these concepts may be extracted at a basic IO level. In general, concepts become more pronounced at higher levels of abstraction with an increasing spatial and temporal window. The inference of, e.g. the concept 'ball', should thus be delayed. This is illustrated by Figure 16.13, with two candidate pseudo frame IOs, '1' and '2', that share features at the frame level, but differ in their motion features at the video shot level. '1' moves and is actually a ball, while '2' is a spot on the camera lens.

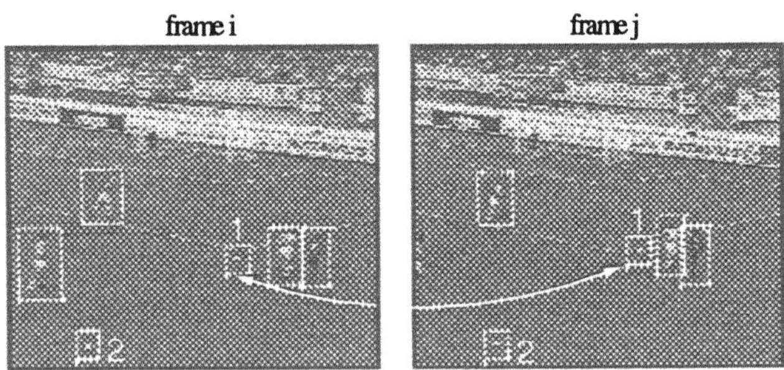

Figure 16.13: A video shot IO consisting of two successive frame IOs. The frame IOs contain multiple pseudo frame IOs. Corresponding pseudo frame IOs, e.g. indicated by '1', form pseudo video-shot IOs.

Property aggregation

Now we show how this process is supported quantitatively as introduced in section 16.3. A shape feature, circularity, is a piece of evidence for the concept 'ball' that is equally strong for the four pseudo frame IOs *pfio i.1*, *pfio i.2*, *pfio j.1*, *pfio j.2* belonging to the frames *i* and *j* in Figure 16.13. So their bunches of evidence *B* contain the same piece of evidence e.g., *pfio i.1.B* ∋ ⟨'ball',circularity,0.6⟩.

The motion features differ for the two pseudo video shot IOs, *pvsio 1* and *pvsio 2*, and so do their bunches of evidence, e.g., *pvsio 1.B*={⟨'ball',*frame*,0.6⟩,⟨'ball', moving ,0.3⟩} and *pvsio 2.B*={⟨'ball',*frame*,0.6⟩,⟨'spot on lens', sticking to lens ,0.9⟩,⟨¬'ball', 'spot on lens',1⟩}

Suppose a priori belief for an *arbitrary* pseudo video shot IO is P[ball]= 0.01. Then the belief values for the concept ‘ball’ for the pseudo video shot IOs 1 and 2 diverge: P[‘ball’ | *pvsio 1.B*] = 1 - (1-0.6)(1-0.3)/(1-0.01)= 0.72 > P[ball | *pfio i.1.B*] whereas P[‘ball’ | *pvsio 2.B*] = 0.6×(1-0.9)=0.06 << P[ball | *pfio i.2.B*] and so do the belief values for the concept ‘spot on lens’: P[‘spot on lens’| *pvsio 1.B*]=0 and P[‘spot on lens’| *pvsio 2.B*]=0.9.

Eventually queries like ‘show all corners that lead to a goal’ must be addressed. Such a query can be formulated in SQL-like expression in terms of high level properties:

SELECT <scene> FROM <TV-coverage> WHERE
<scene.‘Approved_Goal’ AND shot.‘Corner_Event’> ORDERED BY <
Function(P[‘Approved_Goal’|scene.*B*], P[‘Corner_Event’|scene.*B*])>

The wanted scenes in this query have an approved goal and a shot with a corner event. We show how the concept ‘Approved _Goal’ is inferred. First of all evidence for the concept ‘Approved_Goal’ comes from shot y1 in scene-x where this goal shot is visible:

scene-x.*B* ∋ ⟨‘Approved_Goal’, shot-y1.‘Approved_Goal’, 1⟩

But also other evidence might add to the belief in the concept ‘Approved_Goal’ e.g. ‘replay’, ‘close-up’, ‘cheering cluster’, ‘cheering public’, ‘approved text goal’. This is visualised in the Figure 16.14.

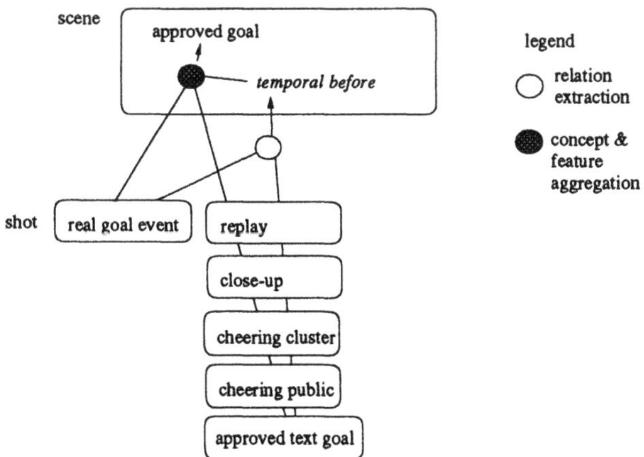

Figure 16.14: Example of evidence for extracting the concept “real-goal-opportunity”

Temporal relations between these pieces of evidence are vital. For example a referee’s whistle just before a goal shot makes the goal shot invalid. We follow the ‘Real_Goal_Event’.

shot-y.B ∋ ⟨'Real_Goal_Event', {video shot-p.'Real_Goal_ Opportunity', audio track-q.'Public_Real_Goal_Cheering'} AND video shot-p TEMPORAL WITHIN THRESHOLD AFTER audio track-q, λ⟩

In this knowledge rule two phenomena, namely a 'Real_Goal_Event' and a 'Public_Real_Goal_Cheering' are possible pieces of evidence from different media. If they occur together, the latter must follow after the first within a certain time, e.g. a few seconds. Note that the conjunction of concepts is accounted for by multiplying the belief values:

P['Real_Goal_Event'| shot-y.B]= $\lambda \times$P['Real_Goal_Opportunity'| video shot-p.B]$\times$P['Public_Real_Goal_Cheering'| audio track-q.B]

We follow the 'Real_Goal_Opportunity' concept:

video shot-p.B ∋ ⟨'Real_Goal_Opportunity', pseudo video shot-x.'Ball' AND pseudo video shot-y.'Goal_Area' AND SPATIO TEMPORAL OVERLAP DURATION (pseudo video shot-x, pseudo video shot-y) Threshold, λ_2⟩

So two pseudo video shot IOs must be identified as 'Ball' and 'Goal_Area' respectively, and they must share the same spatial position over a certain minimal period of time. So a ball passing by quickly does not make the system infer a 'Real_Goal_Event'.

Finally we arrive at a concept we inferred already, 'ball'. In this brief overview it is evident that information from different media is easily combined in one framework.

The prototype is implemented as a client/server application using the Informix Universal Server (IUS) as the object-relational database platform. The clients are implemented on Windows NT 4.0 machines using Delphi and IUS query tools. All Soccer data is stored at the server side. The clients contain several applications for manipulating the data. The Universal Server is extended with a number of software libraries called DataBlades that provide data storage and management functionality. The prototype uses DataBlades for video (Informix), image (Excalibur), audio information retrieval (AIR by Musclefish) and text (Excalibur) as presented in [WVP+98].

The current prototype implementation supports inference. Automated tracking of corresponding frame IOs is supported. Also, several features have been predefined in the software libraries for instance audio features others have been specially defined for the prototype. At the moment missing algorithms are replaced by manual annotation. Improving this inference is one of the major topics we currently work on.

16.6 CONCLUSIONS

We have shown the importance of structuring multimedia information (information supply) and its effect on content analysis and retrieval (information demand). The ADMIRE framework was presented where all types of media can be modelled in a uniform way. Beside the three level structure of information within an Information Object, the information object it self is part of a hierarchical structure that is imposed by the application domain. There are three types of Information Object, namely basic, composite and pseudo. Further, a set of relations are defined between Information objects. This is explained in section 16.2. There are different ways to label concepts in an Information Object. This may vary anywhere between fully-automated and manual. The ADMIRE framework offers the freedom to chose the appropriate labelling method. Labels generated automatically or semi-automatically should include uncertainty measures as algorithms have finite precision. Our approach using uncertainty was presented in section 16.3.

We have also demonstrated that structuring the information depends on the context. This has been shown in the two cases presented in sections 16.4 and 16.5 where the ADMIRE framework has been applied. In the first case, data from patients with movement disorders was modelled. Here the medical practice was used for defining the hierarchical structure, property extraction and property aggregation. In the second case, a soccer VDS, the hierarchical structure was easier to identify. This structure is a general VDS. Yet property extraction and aggregation needs some insight in the soccer domain.

For this soccer VDS case we wanted to reach two goals, first we wanted to mingle manual labelling and automated labelling. At the moment many algorithms that extract features are still under development while they improve every moment. Scene detection for example is already common in MPEG editing software. For these algorithms manual labelling was used in the prototype.

In the two cases presented in this paper we have gained field experience which is recapitulated below.

Modelling hierarchical structure was relatively straightforward compared to defining features and concepts. For example, in the clinical assessment case domain expertise is necessary to identify the proper features to be extracted from measurement data and to infer the proper concepts combining these features.

Combining multimodal information is important. Uni-modal information is frequently incomplete and sometimes error prone. Combining different modalities may solve these problems. In the clinical case we saw that EMG graph and motion information are both required for generating analysis information of a patient.

Extensibility of the model is an advantage for supporting new forms of content disclosure. For example extending the hierarchical model of the VDS with Tele-text information should be a straightforward operation. Further, reuse of information for other purposes is supported. For example, methods to recognise a player in a soccer game can be used for volleyball games as well.

Answering queries is a top-down process where concepts are first identified high in the hierarchy in combination with pruning mechanisms. Whereas concepts and feature extraction is a bottom up processes. From our experience it is advisable to infer concept higher-up in he hierarchy to guarantee higher certainty.

Up till now the ADMIRE framework has been shown to be widely applicable. For example it has also been applied in the hypermedia domain. In [VeEe98], and [Velth98] a retrieval service for the web is presented where users can specify time and/or cost constraints over their queries.

Future challenges are to investigate scaleable and generic aspects of the ADMIRE framework. This a topic for future research at our institute. Think for example of applications for large user groups where collaboration between members is supported on very large distributed databases.

Acknowledgements

The authors would like to thank René Bakker and Henk Eertink for reviewing this paper. The KPN is acknowledged for the contribution in the soccer VDS case. The Roessingh and the faculteit der geneeskunde from the AZVU are acknowledged for the contribution in the medical case study.

References

[AnHR94] André, E., Herzog, G. & Rist, T. Multimedia Presentation of Interpreted Visual Data, *Proceedings of the AAAI Workshop on "Integration of Natural Language and Vision Processing"*, Seattle, WA, 1994

[Badl75] Badler N.I., Temporal Scene Analysis: Conceptual Description of Object Movements, Technical Report 80, Computer Science Department, University of Toronto, 1975

[BCP+79] Bekey G.A., Chang C.W., J. Perry, and M.M. Hoffer. Pattern-Recognition of Multiple EMG Signals Applied to Description of Human Gait. In *Proc. Institut. Electrc. And Electron. Eng.* Vol. 65, 1979, pp 674-681

[BuSh84] Buchanan, B.G. and E.H. Shortliffe,., 1984, *Rule-Based Expert Systems: The MYCIN experiments of the Stanford Heuristic Programming Project*, Reading, Massachusetts, Addison-Wesley

[Clar88] Clarke, M.R.B., 1988, Discussion to "Belief Functions" by Smets, P., In: Smets, P., et al (eds.) *Non Standard Logics for Automates Reasoning*, London, Academic Press

[CMF96] Chiaramella,Y. P. Mulhem, F. Fourel, Clips: A Model for Multimedia Retrieval, internal report, IMAG, Grenoble.

[GuRV96] Gudivada V.N., V.V. Raghavan, and K. Vanapipat, A Unified Approach to data Modelling and Retrieval for a Class of Image database applications. In *Multimedia Database Systems*, Springer, pp37-78, 1996

[GuNe93] Gu J., and E.J. Neuhold, A data model for multimedia information retrieval. *Proc. Multimedia Modeling*, Singapore, 1993, p. 113-127

[GSC+95] Gong Y., L. T. Sin, C. H. Chuan, H. Zhang, and M Sakauchi, Automatic parsing of TV soccer programs, *Proc. Of IEEE ICMCS'95*, International conference on multimedia computing and systems, pp. 167-174, 1995

[Hard98] Hardman, L., Modelling and Authoring Hypermedia Documents, Ph.D. Thesis, University of Amsterdam, 1998.

[HaSc94] Halasz, F. And M. Schwartz, (1994), The Dexter Hypertext Reference Model, *Communications of the ACM*, 37 (2), Feb, pp 30-39.

[Haut97] Hautus E., Sybar A Human Motion Analaysis System for Rehabilitation Medicine. PhD Thesis TU Eindhoven, November 1997

[Heck86] Heckerman, D., 1986, Probabilistic Interpretation of Mycin's Certainty Factor Model, In Kanal, L. N., & Lemmer, J.F. (eds) *Uncertainty in Artificial Intelligence*, Elsevier Science Publishers (North Holland)

[HoLu98] Houtsma M.A.W. and H.J. van der Lugt, Applying advanced multimedia concepts in health and education. In *Advances in Information Technologies:* In Proc. of *EMMSEC97*, Florence, November 3-5, 1997

[InBo95] Intille, S. and A. Bobick, Visual, Tracking Using Closed-Worlds, *Proc. of the Fifth International Conference on Computer Vision*, MIT, Cambridge, MA, pp. 672-678, 1995.

[ISO94] International Standards Organisation, *Presentation Environment for Multimedia Objects (PREMO)*, ISO/IEC 14478, 1994

[ISO97] International Standards Organisation, *HyTime Hypermedia/Timebased Structuring Language*, ISO/IEC 10744, 1997

[KnRi79] Knutsson E., and C. Richards. Different types of Disturbed Motor Control in Gait of Hemiparetic Patients. In *Brain*, Vol. 102: pp 405-430, 1979

[KrCl93] Krause, P.J. and Clark, D.A., 1993, *Representing Uncertain knowledge, An Artificial Intelligence Approach*, Dordrecht, Kluwer Academic Publishers

[LaSp88] Lauritzen, S.L. and Spiegelhalter, D.J., 1988, Local computations with probabilities on graphical structures and their application to expert systems (with discussion), *Proc. Royal Stat. Society*, B.50, 157-224

[MPEG98] MPEG Requirements Group, "MPEG-7 Requirements Document", Doc. ISO/MPEG N2083, MPEG San Jose Meeting, February 1998.

[Okad79] Okada N., SUPP: Understanding Moving Picture Patterns Based on Linguistic Knowledge, In *Proc .IJCAI*, Tokio, Japan, 1979, pp 690-692

[Pear90] Pearl, J., Bayesian and Belief-Function Formalisms for Evidential Reasoning: a Conceptual Analysis, In: Shafer G. And Pearl, J., *Readings Uncertain Reasoning*. San Mateo, Morgan Kaufmann, 540-574.

[Perr92] Perry J., Gait Analysis, Normal and Pathelogical Function. SLACK inc. Thorofare NJ. 1992

[Rijs79] Rijsbergen, C.J. van, *Information Retrieval*, Butterworth, 2nd edition. London 1979.

[ScWy95] Schloss G.A., and M.J. Wynblatt, *Providing definition and temporal structure for multimedia data*. Multimedia Systems. vol. 3, no. 5/6, 1995, p. 264-277

[Shaf78] Shafer, G. *Non-additive probabilities in the work of Bernoulli and Lambert*. Archive for History of Exact Sciences, 19, pp. 309-370, 1987.

[TYH+91] Tsuda K., and K. Yamamoto, M. Hirakawa, and T. Ichikawa, *MORE: An object-oriented data model with a facility for changing object structures*. IEEE on Knowledge and Data Engineering, vol. 3-4, '91, p. 444-460

[VeBE96] Velthausz, D.D., C.M.R. Bal, and E.H. Eertink, A Multimedia Information Object Model for Information Disclosure. *MMM'96 proceedings of the Third International Conference on MultiMedia Modelling*, Toulouse, France, 12-15 November 1996,pp 289-304

[VeEe98] Velthausz D.D., H. Eertink, Meta-data for resource-limited retrieval, paper submitted to *ACM the SIGIR'98 workshop on Hypertext Information Retrieval for the web*, Melbourne, Australia, August 28, 1998.

[Velth98] Velthausz D.D., *Cost-effective networked based multimedia information retrieval*. PhD. thesis to be published in 1998.

[WiEd88] Winterfeldt, J. von and W. Edwards, 1988, *Decision Analysis and Behavioural Research*, London, Cambridge University Press

[WiGH87] Winters T. F., J.R. Gage and R. Hicks. Gait patterns Spastic Hemiplegia in Children and Young Adults. In *Journal of Bone and Joint Surger* , Vol. 69, No. 3, March 1987 pp. 437-441

[WNM+95] Wu J.K., A.D. Narasimhalu, B.M. Mehtre, A.P. Lam and Y.J. Gao, CORE: a content-based retrieval engine for multimedia information systems. In *Multimedia Systems*, Vol. 3, No. 1, 1995, p. 25-41

[WVP+98] Woudstra A., D.D. Velthausz , H.J.G. de Poot, F. Moelaert El-Hadidy, W. Jonker, M.A.W. Houtsma, R.G. Heller, J.N.H. Heemskerk, Modelling and Retrieving Audiovisual Information: *A Soccer Video Retrieval System. MIS'98*, September 24-26, 1998, Istanbul, Turkey.

[Zade84] Zadeh, L.A., 1984, Review of Shafer's "A Mathematical Theory of

17 CLASSIFICATION BASED NAVIGATION AND RETRIEVAL FOR PICTURE ARCHIVES

Sean Bechhofer, Carole Goble

Information Management Group
Department of Computer Science
University of Manchester
Oxford Road
Manchester M13 9PL
UK
seanb@cs.man.ac.uk

Abstract: Current state of the art in image retrieval and indexing doesn't meet all the needs of users of electronic picture collections. Content based retrieval provides little support for *semantic metadata*, in particular descriptions of what the image contains or represents. We present the approach being taken by the STARCH project, which is using a Description Logic (DL) for semantic metadata. The structured representation of the DL can assist in providing more powerful environments for retrieval, through the support of browsing, navigation and the serendipitous discovery of information. The conceptual space can also prove useful for defining notions of similarity and semantic closeness. We illustrate these claims with a series of examples taken from our prototype system.

17.1 INTRODUCTION

Museums and other cultural organisations increasingly make use of electronic resources in the form of on-line public catalogues, on-line databases and CD-ROMS. This move to electronic management of archives is reflected by the emergence of Digital Libraries. Digital picture archives use metadata to provide flexible descriptions of the images within them in order to index and consequently retrieve those images. Metadata standards such as the Dublin Core

[9] are concerned largely with devising minimum and uniform data sets of cataloguing information, for example, the author, title, and date of acquisition. Other metadata represents content based information which can be classified at various levels [12]:

1. syntactic information, concerned with the primitive image features, e.g. colour or texture;
2. descriptions of objects of a particular type, corresponding to Panofsky's [29] pre-iconographic level of picture description e.g. pictures of a train crossing a bridge or of Nelson's column in the sunshine;
3. descriptions of named events or types of activity (e.g. English folk dancing), or concepts of emotional or symbolic significance (e.g. "happy" pictures). Subdivisions correspond roughly with the ideas of iconography and iconology.

Retrieval on the basis of syntactic metadata is frequently referred to as Content Based Retrieval (CBR), exemplified by systems such as QBIC [14]. Although CBR has attracted considerable research interest, the images are not assigned any sense of meaning, limiting their use when indexing and retrieving on the conceptual, abstract or icongraphical information in levels 2 and 3; such activities need human indexers. For users who need retrieval based on abstract notions, such as *freedom* or *joy* [5], this semantic metadata is essential.

17.1.1 Representing the Semantic Metadata

There are a variety of solutions to the problem of representing metadata. Free text has the advantage of flexibility and expressiveness in terms of the information that can be represented. However, querying such information is difficult and may require rather sophisticated natural language processing.

An alternative has been to use keywords. This makes querying simpler, but different cataloguers and users may use inconsistent sets of keywords. A controlled vocabulary classification schema seeks to alleviate this imprecision by constraining the indexer and searcher to use only terms from the vocabulary. The art and museum communities have invested considerable effort in the production of such restricted subject thesauri, for example AAT [16].

Certain kinds of controlled vocabularies, known as coding schemes are a collection of terms arranged in a hierarchy that is usually intended to represent the "subsumption" or specialisation/generalisation relation, for example Iconclass [38] and SHIC [33].

The classification forms a semantic index space [7] which can be used to cluster pictures associated with concepts in the same class. Querying the picture's content descriptor retrieves those that are conceptually similar according to some specification of what is meant by similarity. The intention is that the user can not only retrieve objects annotated with a specific term but also pose general queries – an essential requirement for a system where the user may not have a clear initial idea of what she is looking for.

For example, an image of cats will be classified as about domestic animals and animals in general. Images about dogs are similar to those about cats in that they are both about domestic animals.

The difficulties in using such models include: coherent reasoning over the model of terms; organisation of the model and the classification of documents as the model changes or as they are associated with more concepts. Coding schemes in particular suffer from several problems.

- They are often too big, as a term must be introduced for each concept required to be represented in the scheme;

- They are mostly single-axial – each term has at most one immediate parent in the hierarchy. Some systems do provide a certain degree of multi-axial classification (for example the "roof terms" or macros of [5]), but this is generally done on a rather ad-hoc basis. Multi-axial classifications can provide more expressive querying.

- The construction and maintenance of a collection of terms can be problematic, requiring the positioning of new terms in the "right" place. In the presence of multiple-axial classification this difficulty increases.

- The semantics of the "kind-of" relationship used to build hierarchies are often overloaded. In traditional thesauri the hierarchy is devised on the basis of "broader/narrower", though this means relationships can be unclear.

17.1.2 Retrieval from Picture Collections

There are various tasks that we might wish to support, placing requirements on the framework used for the cataloguing and the choice of metadata representation scheme. We consider a spectrum of users ranging from the "Joe Public" user, who has no in depth knowledge of the organisation of the collection or its content, to the expert who has specific questions about particular objects.

Tasks undertaken by experts such as art historians will often involve specific information that is best dealt with by traditional database systems. We target users who have vague queries about general subjects and may not have specific predetermined entry points from which to begin searching [15].

17.1.2.1 Focused Retrieval and Filtering. In a traditional query formulation system the user seeks and filters; i.e. the user looks for images that fit a particular description and filters out those that are not relevant from the result collection. Requests can range from the highly specific – *find Van Gogh's Sunflowers* to the vague and indicative – *find a picture of a stately home*. Enser [13] characterises requests made to image collections according to two orthogonal notions:

- Unique vs. non-unique e.g. *Prince Charles* as opposed to *Royal*;

- Refined vs. un-refined e.g. *Prince Charles holding Trophy* as opposed to *Prince Charles.*

Modes of query and index can also be characterised as being either linguistic or visual. Where both catalogue and query are couched in linguistic terms, Enser concludes that matching query terms with catalogue terms will only adequately support unrefined unique subjects, and thus "offers little promise as an effective pictorial information retrieval procedure". This conclusion is made in the context of simple keyword or coded index terms. We hope to show that, with further structure in the representation, support for refined queries can be provided and the hierarchical nature of the representation helps in bridging the gap between unique and non-unique queries. The fact that *Prince Charles* is a *Royal* ensures that images indexed as containing *Prince Charles* will be retrieved when the query is for a picture of *Royals.*

17.1.2.2 Semi-focused retrieval: Similarity-based Searching and Query By Example. A common question with image collections is *find me an image like this one.* An exemplar is presented and the system is asked to find those that are similar. The issue of what is meant by similar is discussed in Section 4.5.

17.1.2.3 Unfocused retrieval: Browsing. If the user has no predefined specific idea of what she wants, being able to browse serendipitously through a collection while discovering similar pictures can be useful, particularly if that browsing is guided by some underlying structure.

17.1.3 Similarity-based Semantic Retrieval

The STARCH (Structured Terminologies for ARCHives) project proposes a similarity based semantic retrieval system using controlled vocabularies to describe and classify the semantic content of pictures. We use a Description Logic (DL) of limited expressivity to represent the terminology, harnessing the expressive and powerful classification reasoning powers of this technology. Our work differs from [25] in that we do not extend the DL with extra reasoning power and expressivity. In addition we concentrate simply on content without attempting to incorporate reasoning about the syntactic structure of images. We have developed an intelligent model-driven interface to navigate the conceptual model, construct and manipulate elaborate queries and retrieve instances similar to another through a model of similarity based on subsumption.

The project is in collaboration with Getty Images Ltd and our case study uses a small subset of their Hulton Getty collection, a photographic archive indexed using an in-house collection of keywords. Our case study conceptual model uses the collection's keywords along with a subset of AAT concerning People. Consequently, we do not directly use one coding scheme but develop an ontology based on a number of schemes, plus cataloguing information and user information.

Our concern is with the management and cataloguing of a particular collection, as is the case with cultural heritage organisations such as museums or galleries, where the contents are known and human driven cataloguing is feasible, although if the collection is large, some automated assistance will be required. This is as opposed to the activity of *discovering* images, often performed with respect to the World Wide Web.

The emphasis of this paper is on the retrieval and navigation though the collection using the catalogue. The approach has the cost of constructing the conceptual model and cataloguing the archive with respect to this model which we do not discuss here.

Section 17.2 introduces our Description Logic approach for describing metadata. Section 17.3 describes the retrieval capabilities through the use of an example scenario using our model-driven interface. Section 17.4 cites related work, and Section 17.5 concludes the paper with a discussion of the issues raised and pointers towards future areas of investigation.

17.2 DESCRIBING METADATA USING A DESCRIPTION LOGIC

Description Logics (DLs) are a family of knowledge representation languages that allow reasoning with compositional structured information. In particular, a DL supports hierarchical classification through the use of a well-defined notion of subsumption. For a full description of DLs and their uses, see [6].

A DL models an application domain in terms of *concepts* (classes), *roles* (relations) and *individuals* (objects). The domain is a set of individuals, and a concept is a description of a group of individuals that share common characteristics. Formally, a concept is interpreted as a subset of the individuals which make up the domain. Roles model relationships between, or attributes of, individuals. Formally, a role is interpreted as a set of binary tuples relating pairs of individuals. Compositional concept descriptions can then be built up using recursive term constructors, where terms are concepts or roles. Individuals can be asserted to be instances of particular concepts and pairs of individuals can be asserted to be instances of particular roles.

Using the basic concrete syntax from [2], we can define a small piece of model as shown in Table 17.1. We can now construct compositions of these primitive concepts, for example the concept of a person holding a cup:

(and Person (some holding Cup)).

The and operator conjoins two descriptions (formally, it is interpreted as set intersection), while the construction (some R C) is a concept representing those individuals which are related to an instance of the concept C by an instance of the role R. New expressions can also be defined:

(defconcept HatWearer (and Person (some wearing Hat))).

This is a different mechanism from the introduction of new primitives, and is essentially a kind of naming which allows easy access to commonly used compositions. Construction of DL expressions is further discussed in Section 17.3.

Primitive Concepts	Roles
Thing	holding
(defprimconcept Trophy Thing)	wearing
(defprimconcept Cup Trophy)	
(defprimconcept Shield Trophy)	
(defprimconcept Person Thing)	
(defprimconcept Hat Thing)	
Individuals	**Assertions**
(Person TomWhittaker)	(holding TomWhittaker CharityShield)
(Person BillyWright)	(holding BillyWright FACup)
(Person PrinceCharles)	
(Cup FACup)	
(Cup AmateurCup)	
(Shield CharityShield)	

Table 17.1: A sample DL Model

17.2.1 Reasoning Services

DLs provide a variety of services [2] that make them particularly attractive as models for describing semi-structured and complex information [6].

17.2.1.1 Subsumption. The power of DLs is derived from the automatic determination of subsumption between compositional descriptions. Given two conceptual definitions A and B, we can determine whether A subsumes B, in other words whether every instance of B is necessarily an instance of A.

Formally, subsumption is defined as an implicit subset/superset relationship between the interpretations of the two concepts.

17.2.1.2 Classification. A collection of conceptual definitions can be organised into a partial order based on the subsumption relation. This provides a multi-axial hierarchy of definitions, ranging from the general to the specific. Primitive concepts have no characterising attributes and must be explicitly placed in the hierarchy by the system designer, but new, composed definitions have their position determined automatically. Thus classification is a *dynamic* process where new compositions can be added to an existing hierarchy.

17.2.1.3 Retrieval. Given a concept definition, we can retrieve all the instances of that concept (which of course includes all instances of subsumed concepts). For example, the collection {FACup, CharityShield} are the instances of Trophy.

17.2.1.4 Realization. Given an individual, we can provide the most specific concepts (w.r.t. subsumption) that the individual is an instance of. So we can determine that TomWhittaker is an instance of (and Person (some holding Shield)).

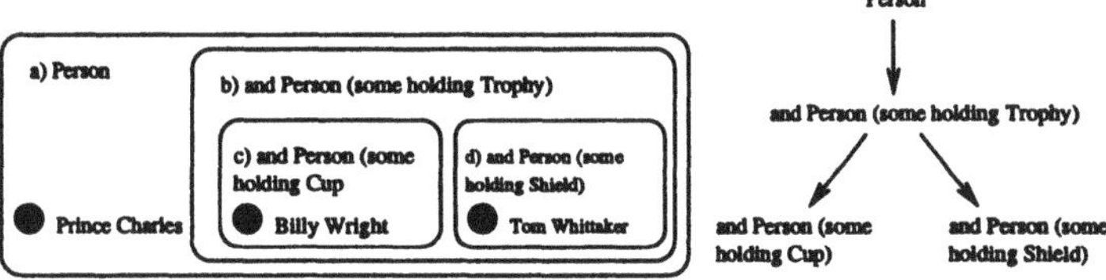

Figure 17.1: Query Inclusion

Subsumption and classification are the key services related to the construction, maintenance and use of an ontology (or conceptual model), while retrieval and realization are concerned with the tasks of indexing and cataloguing a collection using that ontology. The concept hierarchy forms an ontology that can be browsed, queried and can drive interfaces (see Section 17.3).

17.2.2 Coherent Semantics for the Concept Model

A DL has a well-defined semantics. If terms are placed in a child-parent relationship in the concept hierarchy, they are in this relationship because of subsumption. This contrasts with systems such as coding schemes, where the classification is often *ad-hoc*, leading to difficulty in interpreting the hierarchy in a consistent manner.

17.2.3 Query Inclusion

In DLs the definition language and the query language are the same thing. To retrieve the individuals satisfying a concept, or to find the subsuming or subsumed concept descriptions of a concept, one describes the concept in the same way as one would define it. The subsumption, classification and retrieval reasoning services do the rest. Consequently, it is possible to interpret the whole DL model as a classification of queries. Figure 17.1 shows the individuals included in a series of queries and how those queries are included within one another. Tom Whittaker is included in the answer to query d), while both Billy Wright and Tom Whittaker are included in the answer to query b).

17.2.4 Incremental reclassification

A DL can deal with incremental addition of knowledge. New assertions made about individuals will result in their reclassification – thus individuals can initially be given general descriptions, which are refined when further information becomes available. This is essential as cataloguing can be an incremental process, with descriptions being refined and changed.

17.2.5 A Generative Model

The DL used in the project is a derivative of GRAIL [31], a DL with the addition of a constraint mechanism known as sanctioning which controls the formation of composite concepts. Generally in DLs, role restrictions can be used to express the fact that, for example, if a person is wearing something, it must be an item of clothing. In our language, sanctions perform this task, with the composition of any two concepts using a role being explicitly forbidden until it is sanctioned.

Sanctions play several roles:

- They restrict the formation of compositions and ensure that only semantically viable compositions are built. Thus we can prevent the formation of nonsensical concepts such as Cup wearing Person.
- They provide an answer to the question "what can I say about this concept?" This facilitates the building of interfaces allowing construction of query expressions without having to explicitly deal with the raw DL expression.
- Using a collection of primitive concepts and roles and some sanctions, we can *generate* and automatically fill-in sections of composed models. The asserted model can thus be relatively sparse, but still allow the potential representation of many composed concept definitions.

Although the language used here is inexpressive – sitting somewhere between $\mathcal{FL}^-$ and $\mathcal{FL}'$, and lacking many of the constructors provided in other DLs – we believe it is sufficient to demonstrate the principles.

17.2.6 A Demonstrator Application

For our early demonstrator we have developed a simple application using a small database of pictures taken from the Hulton Getty collection and indexed with a collection of DL terms. This is a preliminary to a larger pilot providing more functionality. The application is built using Smalltalk and uses a client-server architecture for the interaction with the conceptual model [4]. The prototype is limited and only provides retrieval based on a single concept description – this could easily be extended to allow boolean operations such as AND and OR.

It is unreasonable to expect users to express complex DL expressions directly – we have instead developed a forms based interface, dynamically driven by the ontology which guides the user, integrating model browsing and query formulation [3]. The interface is described further in Section 17.3.

17.3 THE RETRIEVAL AND NAVIGATION PROCESS

There are several key aspects to the retrieval process.

- How does the user find a starting point for the query or navigation?
- How does the user know what's in the model?

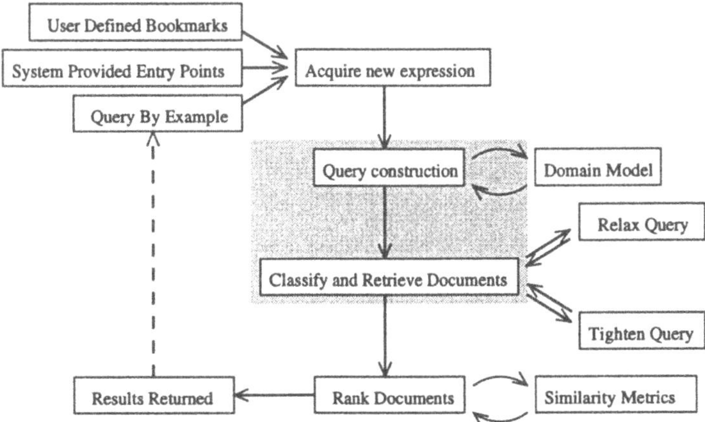

Figure 17.2: The Query Construction Process

- How can we use knowledge about the conceptual model to provide the user with feedback?

Figure 17.2 illustrates how the steps of the retrieval process fit together. For the initial query expression, the system can provide a number of common concept entry points or "lead-ins" as they are called in the traditional thesaurus literature. These could be supplied by the system designer, gleaned from examining user profiles and usage or user-defined "bookmarks" or favourites. Alternatively, the description applied to an exemplar may be used, providing support for Query By Example as discussed in Section 4.3.

Adjustments are made to the query, and once the user is satisfied with the query expression, documents are retrieved. Based on the results of that retrieval, further manipulations can be applied to the query, for example tightening the query if too many results are being returned. Finally, the retrieved documents are ranked and presented to the user.

17.3.1 Refining Requests

We can perform a variety of query manipulations or reformulations.

17.3.1.1 Specialization. Further role-role filler pairs (*criteria*) can be added to the description applied to the topic of the query. A request for Person could be specialized to a request for Person holding Cup. Alternatively, the base concept of the query could be replaced by a more specific subclass. Specialization is equivalent to narrower term navigation in the thesaurus tradition and is providing *refinement* as discussed in Section 17.1.

17.3.1.2 Generalization. Queries can be relaxed by the removal of criteria or the replacement of the base concept. We could move from a request for Person holding Cup & wearing Hat to Person wearing Hat. This is equivalent to broader term navigation in the thesaurus tradition.

17.3.1.3 Sub-query Replacement. We can allow replacement of subqueries with sibling concepts, say moving from Person holding Cup to Person holding Shield. This is an example of one kind of related term navigation in the thesaurus tradition.

These manipulations are controlled and guided by information in the model particularly the sanctions, restricting the options presented, and ensuring that only reasonable queries are built. This provides a flexible and powerful mechanism for navigation through the conceptual model, allowing the incremental construction of queries. This process is *dynamic* – as adjustments are made, the classifier can indicate the current position of the query within the hierarchy and its relationship with neighbouring concepts, providing the user with feedback on the query. The phases of query construction and document retrieval can be combined as shown by the shaded area in the diagram, providing tighter coupling between manipulation and retrieval. In this way, the user can make greater use of feedback in guiding the construction of the query. Query construction is thus an iterative, interactive process, with the user involved in a dialogue with the ontology.

17.3.2 Feedback

An important aspect of dynamic querying is the provision of feedback informing the user of the progress of the query and guiding her towards the possible actions that can be performed. Feedback can be at a metadata level, constraining and guiding the user based on knowledge about the information model – for example offering suitable options for specialization of a query, while preventing the formation of queries about Hat wearing Cup. Alternatively, we can provide feedback at the data level, say providing the user with a count of the number of instances to be returned.

17.3.3 Query By Example

Another common technique used for database query is that of Query By Example (QBE), where a particular instance is presented as a representative of a class of instances in which the user is interested. By using the described instances of a description logic along with realization services, the description applied to the instance is used as the starting point for a query, providing not only the values instantiating the form, but also the structure of the form itself. For example, if we presented BillyWright as the exemplar, the query would be for Person holding Cup.

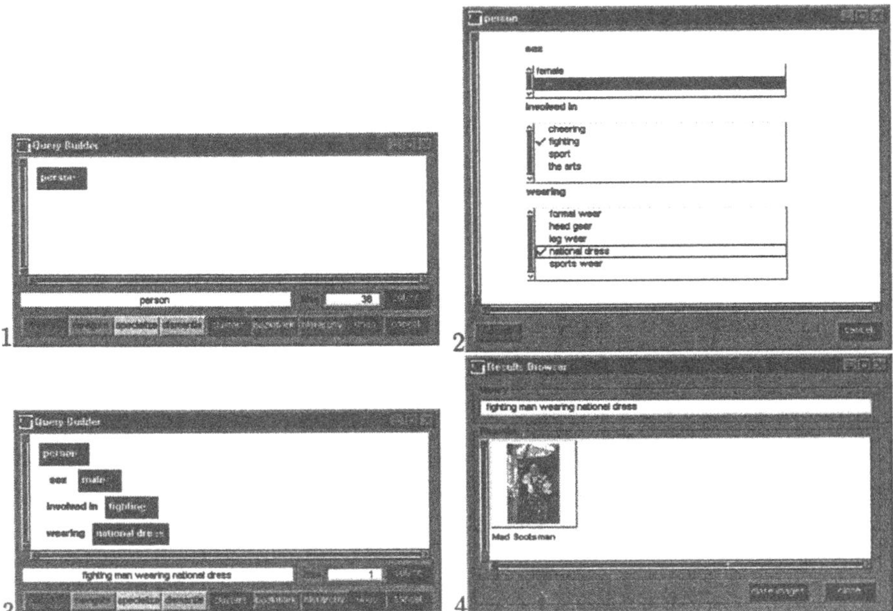

Figure 17.3: Query Construction

17.3.4 Example Query Manipulations

Figure 19.3 shows a simple query for images described as featuring a person (1). We elect to specialize this, and are given possible criteria that could be used to further elaborate on the concept (2). Three have been chosen, producing a query for a man wearing national dress involved in fighting (3). This results in a single image being retrieved – a man with a sword wearing a kilt (4).

In Figure 19.4 we manipulate the query (1), replacing the value of a particular relationship. We are offered a number of alternative fillers – the interface displays these as a small segment of the concept hierarchy, with more general terms above, more specific terms below and siblings alongside (2). We have selected music, a different kind of activity resulting in a query (3) returning an image of a piper wearing a kilt (4).

Query By Example is illustrated in Figure 17.5. The description applied to a particular picture (a male member of the royal family wearing a suit and holding a cup (1)) is used to form the initial query (2). This results in two pictures (including the original) being returned (3). By successively removing specializing criteria, we retrieve more images which share some content, but with increasing differences – a female member of the royal family holding a cup (4,5), then a member of the royal family not holding a cup (6,7).

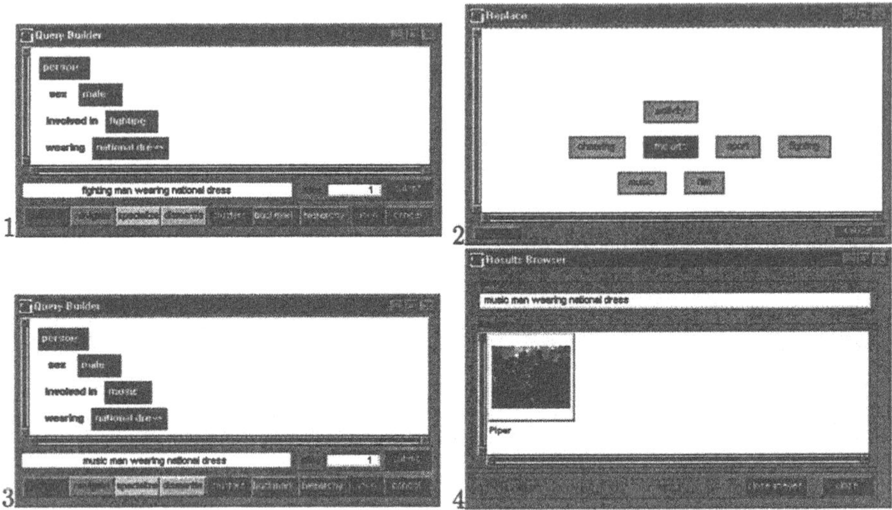

Figure 17.4: Query Replacement

Further operations that can be performed are discussed in [3].

17.3.5 Similarity

Similarity metrics are essential if we are to rank results of a query. Similarity can also be used during browsing, allowing the user to move to related or relevant concepts. Approaches such as those described in [11, 34] use metrics defined over semantic networks essentially based on distances (or number of links) between terms. The measures are controlled and fine-tuned through the use of weights. This approach works well with static models where the terms are *fixed* in a topology, but is less appropriate with the dynamic classification of a DL. The "distance" or number of links between terms may vary depending on the compositions that have been constructed.

To overcome these problems, we must investigate a model of similarity that is based on subsumption. The basic premise is that two terms are similar if they share a number of parents in the concept hierarchy. This fits with the ideas of similarity described in [37], where metrics are defined based on common and distinguishing features. Shared parents encapsulate the notion of a shared feature, while a parent that is not shared indicates a distinguishing feature.

The measure can be controlled by the user through the use of "view-points" – the important features which are to be used when considering similarity. Given a collection of views $V = \{V_1, \ldots, V_n\}$ and weights $W = \{w_1, \ldots, w_n\}$,

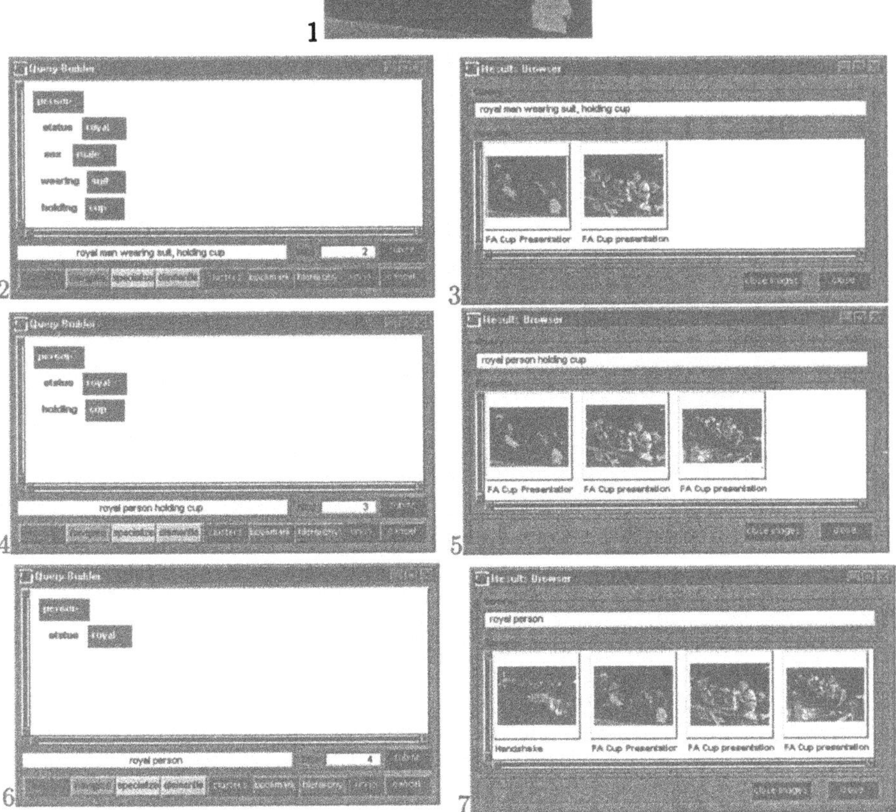

Figure 17.5: Query By Example

we define the similarity of two concepts X and Y as :

$$Sim_{V,W} = \sum_{i=1}^{n} \sigma_i(X,Y)w_n - \alpha\tau_i(X,Y)w_n - \beta\tau_i(Y,X)w_n$$

where α, β are arbitrary constants (determined through experiment) and

$$\sigma_i(X,Y) = \begin{cases} 1, & \text{if } X \text{ and } Y \text{ are subsumed by } V_n \\ 0, & \text{otherwise} \end{cases}$$

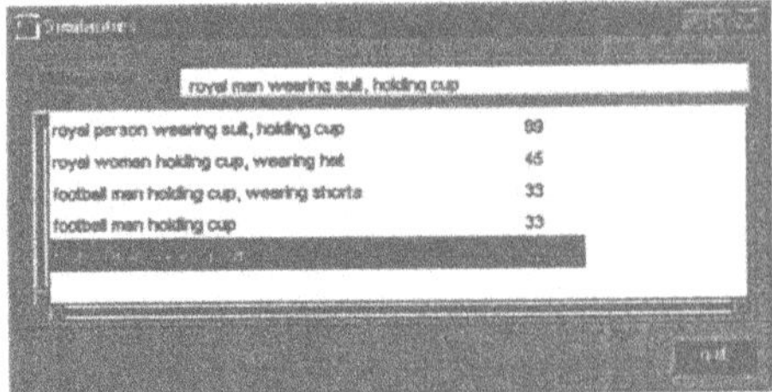

Figure 17.6: Similarity Example

$$\tau_i(X,Y) = \begin{cases} 0, \text{ if} X \text{ is subsumed by } V_n \text{ and } Y \text{ is not} \\ 0, \text{ otherwise} \end{cases}$$

The numbers produced by this algorithm can be normalised by comparing with the similarity value given by comparing a concept with itself. Thus

$$NormSim_{V,W}(X,Y) = \frac{Sim_{V,W}(X,Y)}{Sim_{V,W}(X,X)}$$

An interesting effect of the normalisation is that the measure is no longer symmetric. However, as discussed in [37], similarity is not necessarily a symmetric relation.

In our example, we have provided views specifying that the interesting characteristics of the descriptions (in decreasing order of importance) include: what they are holding; what they are wearing; their status; and their sex. This provides us with results as shown in Figure 17.6 (The descriptions use a primitive form of natural language generated from the DL expressions and the measure is given out of 100). A closely related description is that of a royal woman wearing a hat and holding a cup, while a footballer simply wearing a suit is less similar.

17.4 RELATED WORK

WebSEEk [35] and [1] are systems which scour the web, deriving conceptual terms through analysis of URLs and HTML text. However, the conceptual model used is very simple. The Art Museum project [21] attempts to derive relationships between colour histograms of pictures with terms such as "charming", "romantic", "wild" through the use of a training set.

Commercial providers of visual content, such as CORBIS and Getty Images, use large keyword or term collections to index collections. Another common approach is to encode semantic metadata in some type structure. Examples include [27] where *salient objects* (interesting objects that appear in images) are modelled and classified using an object-oriented framework. Although OO systems provide many suitable features for multimedia database systems [23], Oomoto and Tanaka [28] in particular make the criticism that OODB type systems are generally static and do not support schema evolution well. They propose a descriptive schema that is evolutionary but within the framework of a conventional OO approach that doesn't support automatic classification. DL expressions can be added to or refined anytime, effectively re-typing the document. The retyping (i.e. reclassification) is automatically managed. This is especially important as no description could ever be complete and hence needs to be extended. Lahlou [24] shares many of our aims and uses a Semantic Data Model to describe images; however his model doesn't appear to support automatic class classification. [19] use an object-based representation of semantic and spatial information to support content-based image navigation.

Several approaches [36, 17, 32] have used some form of knowledge base, usually based on semantic nets or frames, to describe images, drive image interpretation systems or to automatically label features with a semantic description. However they have not directly exploited the imprecise querying and automatic classification possible through the use of a DL or used the knowledge descriptions directly as an instance annotation mechanism.

Close work in terms of the application area is that of Glamorgan's Semantic Hypermedia system [11]. This work uses weighted spreading activation to determine links, and describe browsing scenarios similar to those for STARCH (query based navigation by moving around the conceptual hierarchy). However, their semantic network is represented using a binary-relation store, so they do not have terminological reasoning capabilities and do not support automatic, dynamic classification.

Many authors [26, 7] refer to the use of semantic networks or term classification systems to underlie hypertext linking or to support the typing of documents and links [26]. Others refer to the implementation of hypermedia systems in an object-oriented model, for example HyperStorM [39] and Multicard [10].

DLs have been used in the field of Information Retrieval to describe and classify documents. [22] employ conceptual graphs to unify structural knowledge about documents and link semantics, and use this to underlie a unified querying and browsing interaction model. Meghini [25] adopts a DL for information retrieval. Their work differs from ours in that they intend modelling both form (syntactic metadata) and content (semantic metadata) using one unified system. There is little focus on interaction with the metadata representation or how queries might be constructed. Their approach also includes the extension of the description logic with special predicate symbols for particular concrete domains and fuzzy reasoning. In contrast, we are interested in how much added value we can obtain through the "simple" application of a DL, although there are DL research issues as discussed in Section 6.4.

17.5 DISCUSSION

Although still in its preliminary stages, we believe that the approach described here holds some promise. DLs offer a principled and powerful way of expressing, indexing and retrieving annotations. The hierarchical structure helps support abstraction and general queries. Retrieval of objects fitting a general description can be performed without having to explicitly catalogue using those general terms.

New, complex terms can be built on the fly, freeing the modeller from the need to include all eventualities in the term collection, while the automated classification reduces the work required in building and maintaining the ontology. These complex, composite terms can support query refinement.

A browsable ontology is an aid to navigation and serendipitous browsing, supporting semi- focused or unfocused retrieval. However, there are limitations in both the specific language we are using and the use of DLs in general. The major issues are outlined below.

17.5.1 The Ontology

Crucial to our approach is the provision of an ontology – the collection of basic concepts and relationships that are being used to represent the domain. The construction of such an ontology is a non-trivial task. Experiences in the Tambis [18] and GALEN [30] projects suggest large ontologies of thousands of concepts require several man-years to produce.

While the production of domain models cannot be fully automated, help can be provided for modellers. When coding schemes and controlled vocabulary keyword collections already exist, the keywords give a starting point for the ontology, which can be enriched with the addition of subsumption relationships and compositional terms. Automatic thesaurus construction has long been the subject of research. Techniques generally require comprehensive document sets (in our case picture captions and museum catalogues) and produce constructed thesauri based on the syntactic relationships between terms. The combination of both strategies augmented with an interactive modellers toolset is high on our agenda.

17.5.2 Cataloguing vs. Query

Although in the paper we have focussed on the query process, cataloguing is of equal importance. Tools are required which allow those maintaining collections to select and compose terms that describe the images. The requirements for indexing tools will differ from those for query. While querying makes use of general or abstract terms, cataloguing descriptors should use the most specific terms which are appropriate, allowing the classification to do the work when retrieval is being performed.

The question of automated cataloguing is also important, particularly when existing collections have already been catalogued using some keyword terms or a coding scheme. Two issues are raised here – the production of a new ontology based on the existing terms and the mapping of the old terms to the new hierarchy.

17.5.3 Conceptual vs. Specific Queries

The DL representation provides support for querying at the conceptual level – requests for Person holding Trophy. However, if users are interested in specific queries, e.g. looking for pictures of Prince Charles, it is likely that a traditional database system will be more suited to answering the query. When the query involves elements of both, e.g. Prince Charles holding Trophy, a combination of classification reasoning and database retrieval is required.

17.5.4 Fundamental DL Research

The support offered for model construction and maintenance allows the construction of more complicated models than would otherwise be possible. However, this is not without its costs. With large, complex models and collections of individuals, the tasks of retrieval and realization become computationally expensive when compared to the retrieval task using a traditional thesaurus. The reclassification of individuals as further information is added can be difficult, particularly when many inter-relationships are present between the individuals. These are active areas of research in the DL community.

The interaction between roles and subsumption is an important issue, particularly for partitive or locative relationships. For example, a Man sitting on the Bonnet of a Car is a kind of Man sitting on a Car, even though the Bonnet of a Car is not a *kind* of Car, but instead is a *part* of it. DL formalisms supporting this kind of reasoning are under investigation [20].

17.5.5 Concept-based linking and similarity

Conceptual hypermedia systems complement conventional static linking with links generated through the used of a conceptual domain model of the contents of the hypermedia nodes; the concept model acts as a hyperindex [7] to the nodes. Links and concept-based queries are considered to be synonymous. TourisT [8] supports similarity-based linking through a DL-based ontology; we plan to incorporate STARCH into an Open Hypermedia System as a link resolution service. TourisT has a particular information-seeking task, and consequently supplements its ontology with a task model. In a similar way [26], supplement their semantic network (k-level), with a task model, using scripts to control complex task-oriented link generation. Hence the notion of similarity-based linking is extended across the subsumption relationship to other relationships. For example, given a picture of a royal holding a trophy a similarity-navigation might be oriented around the trophy rather than the royal, but the classification is always oriented around the base concept. To link to related sporting events we have to re-focus the query. Our graphical interface allows this refocusing.

Our approach to similarity navigation is still experimental, and interesting questions remain – in particular the selection of the view points. Is it possible to infer appropriate viewpoints based on the past behaviour of the user? If particular criteria are repeatedly added this may suggest that they are considered to be important; repeated removal may suggest irrelevance.

Acknowledgments

This work was supported by EPSRC grant GR/L71216. The authors would like to thank Getty Images for their collaboration in providing a sample collection of images and keyword tags. We would also like to thank Joe Bullock for his ideas and stimulation, David Phillips and Richard Giordano for their guidance and Ian Horrocks for advice on Description Logics.

References

[1] Amato, G., Rabitti, F., and Savino, P. (1998). Supporting Image Search on the Web. In *The Challenge of Image Retrieval*, University of Northumbria, Newcastle.

[2] Baader, F., Brckert, H.-J., Heinsohn, J., Hollunder, B., Mleer, J., Nebel, B., Nutt, W., and Profitlich, H.-J. (1991). Terminological Knowledge Representation: A Proposal for a Terminological Logic. Technical Memo TM-90-04, Deutches Forschungszentrum fr Knstliche Intelligenz (DFKI).

[3] Bechhofer, S. and Goble, C. (1997). Using a Description Logic to Drive Query Interfaces. In *DL97, International Workshop on Description Logics*, Gif sur Yvette, France.

[4] Bechhofer, S. K., Goble, C. A., Rector, A. L., Solomon, W. D., and Nowlan, W. A. (1997). Terminologies and Terminology Servers for Information Environments. In *Eighth International Workshop on Software Technology and Engineering Practice - STEP97*, pages 484 - 497, London, UK. IEEE Computer Society.

[5] Bjarnestam, A. (1998). Description of an Image Retrieval System developed by Getty Images for the Tony Stone Images collection. In *Workshop on Image Retrieval, University of Northumbria*, University of Northumbra, Newcastle.

[6] Borgida, A. (1995). Description Logics in Data Management. *IEEE Transactions on Knowledge and Data Engineering*, 7(5):671–782.

[7] Bruza, P. D. (1990). Hyperindices; a novel aide for searching in Hypermedia. In *Proceedings of the ACM European Conference on Hypermedia Technology*, pages 109 - 122.

[8] Bullock, J. and Goble, C. (1998). TourisT: The Application of a Description Logic based Semantic Hypermedia System for Tourism. In *HT98.*

[9] Cathro, W. (1997). Metadata: An Overview. In *Standards Australia Seminar.*

[10] Christophides, V. and Rizk, A. (1994). Querying Structured Documents with Hypertext Links using OODBMS. In *ECHT 94: European Conference on Hypertext Technology*, pages 186–197, Edinburgh.

[11] Cunliffe, D., Taylor, C., and Tudhope, D. (1997). Query-based Navigation in Semantically Indexed Hypermedia. In *Hypertext '97*.

[12] Eakins, J. P. (1996). Automatic image content retrieval – are we getting anywhere? In *3rd International Conference on Electronic Library and Visual Information Research, ELVIRA3*.

[13] Enser, P. G. B. (1995). Pictorial Information Retrieval. *Journal of Documentation*, 51(2):126–170.

[14] Flickner, M., Sawhney, H., Niblack, W., Ashley, J., Huang, Q., Dom, B., Gorkani, M., Hafner, J., Lee, D., Petkovic, D., Steel, D., and Yanker, P. (1995). Query by Image and Video Content: The QBIC System. *IEEE Computer*, 28(9).

[15] Garber, S. R. and Grunes, M. B. (1992). The Art of Search: A Study of Art Directors. In *CHI '92: Conference on Human factors in computing*, pages 157–163, Monterey, CA.

[16] Getty Information Institute (1998). Art and Architecture Thesaurus. `http://www.ahip.getty.edu/aat_browser`.

[17] Goble, C., O'Docherty, M., Crowther, P., Ireton, M., Oakley, J., and Xydeas, C. (1992). The Manchester Multimedia Information System. In *Advances in Database Technology EDBT '92, Third International Conference on Extending Database Technology*, pages 39–55, Vienna.

[18] Goble, C., Paton, N., Baker, P. G., Brass, A., Bechhofer, S., and Stevens, R. (1998). TAMBIS: Transparent Access to Multiple Bioinformatics Information Sources. An Overview. Submitted to the Journal of Intelligent Information Systems.

[19] Hirata, K., Mukherjea, S., Okamura, Y., Li, W., and Hara, Y. (1997). Object-based navigation. An intuitive navigation style for content-oriented integration environment. In *Hypertext '97*, pages 75–86, Southampton, UK.

[20] Horrocks, I. and Sattler., U. (1998). A Description Logic with Transitive and Inverse Roles and Role Hierarchies. In *Collected Papers from the International Workshop On Description Logics, DL'98*.

[21] Kato, T. (1992). Database architecture for content-based image retrieval. In *SPIE Vol. 1662 Image Storage and Retrieval Systems*.

[22] Kheirbek, A. and Chiaramella, Y. (1995). Integrating hypermedia and information retrieval with conceptual graphs. In *HIM '95*, pages 47–60, Konstanz.

[23] Klas, W., Neuhold, E., and Schrefl, M. (1990). Using an Object-Oriented Approach to Multimedia Data. *Computer Communications*, 13(4):204–216.

[24] Lahlou, Y. (1995). Modelling complex objects in content-based image retrieval. In *Proceedings of Stprage and Retrieval for Image and Video Databases III*, volume Vol. 2420, pages 104–115, San Jose, CA.

[25] Meghini, C., Sebastiani, F., and Straccia, U. (1997). The Terminological Image Retrieval Model. In Bimbo, A. D., editor, *Proceedings of ICIAP-*

97, 9th International Conference on Image Analysis and Processing, volume LNCS 1311, pages 156–163, Firenze, Italy. Springer Verlag.

[26] Nanard, J. and Nanard, M. (1993). Should Anchors Be Typed Too? An Experiment with MacWeb. In *ACM Hypertext '93*, pages 51–62.

[27] Niu, Y., Özsu, M., and Li, X. (1997). 2D-h Trees: An Index Scheme for Content-Based Retrieval of Images in Multimedia Systems. In *IEEE International Conference On Intelligent Processing Systems (IEEE ICIPS'97)*, pages 1710–1715, Beijing, China.

[28] Oomoto, E. and Tanaka, K. (1993). OVID: Design and Implementation of a Video-Object Database System. *IEEE Transactions on Knowledge and Data Engineering*, 5(4):629–643.

[29] Panofsky, E. (1974). *Meaning in the Visual Arts.* The Overlook Press, Woodstock, New York.

[30] Rector, A., Rogers, J., and Pole, P. (1996). The GALEN High Level Ontology. In *MIE 96*, Copenhagen.

[31] Rector, A. L., Bechhofer, S. K., Goble, C. A., Horrocks, I., Nowlan, W. A., and Solomon, W. D. (1997). The GRAIL Concept Modelling Language for Medical Terminology. *Artificial Intelligence in Medicine*, 9:139–171.

[32] Rostek, L. and Möhr, W. (1994). An Editor's Workbench for an Art History Reference Work. In *ECHT'94*, pages 233–238, Edinburgh.

[33] SHIC Working Party (1983). *Social History and Industrial Classification: A Subject Classification for Museum Collections (2 vols).* Centre for English Cultural Tradition and Language, University of Sheffield, UK.

[34] Smeaton, A. F. and Quigley, I. (1996). Experiments in Using Semantic Distances Between Words in Image Caption Retrieval. In *19th International Conference on Research and Development in Information Retrieval*, Zürich.

[35] Smith, J. R. and Chang, S.-F. (1996). Searching for Images and Videos on the World Wide Web. Technical Report 459-96-25, Columbia University Department of Electrical Engineering and Center for Image Technology for New Media.

[36] Srihari, R. K. (1995). Automatic Indexing and Content-Based Retrieval of Captioned Images. *IEEE Computer*, 28(9).

[37] Tversky, A. (1977). Features of Similarity. *Psychological Review*, 34(4).

[38] Waal, H. v. d. (1985). *ICONCLASS: An Iconographic Classification System.* Koninklijke Nederlandse Akademie van Wetenschappen.

[39] Wäsch, J. and Aberer, K. (1995). Flexible Design and Efficient Implementation of a Hypermedia Document Database System by Tailoring Semantic Relationships. In *Sixth IFIP Conference on Data Semantics (DS-6)*, Atlanta, Georgia.

18 Searching Distributed and Heterogeneous Digital Media: The VisualHarness Approach[1]

Amit Sheth, Kshitij Shah, Krishnan Parasuraman, Srilekha Mudumbai
Large Scale Distributed Information Systems (LSDIS) Lab
Computer Science Department, University of Georgia,
415 GSRC, Athens GA 30602-7404 USA
amit@cs.uga.edu, http://lsdis.cs.uga.edu

18.1 CHALLENGES IN RESOURCE DESCRIPTION AND DISCOVERY FOR DIGITAL MEDIA

Current Web-based search engines do a reasonable job when dealing with primarily textual and in some cases semi-structured data. Web-based interfaces to traditional databases also allow us to exploit structured databases. However, there is little help when we wish to find relevant information in visual and so-called new digital media (with significant temporal and spatial components), which are being put on the Internet at an exponential rate. Today, usually a user needs to know the specific repository and use the specific access mechanisms and interfaces that have been provided by the repositories of such information. There is also little help when we wish to deal with a broad variety of heterogeneous media. What if we don't know which type of digital media we need to target the query to? What if the response to the query is best satisfied by a collection of artifacts of different media? Thus one challenge in the current Internet environment is to have the ability to search and access information in various media, including visual media.

The second challenge is to have different ways of describing information of interest. The current Web-based search engines do reasonably well to exploit keyword-based search techniques, primarily derived from the field of

[1] Research reported here is funded in part by "InfoHarness: A System for Scalable Search of Heterogeneous Information" in the Massive Digital Data initiative managed by the Office of Research and Development under contract No. 95 - F138400 – 000.

information retrieval. But, any user is well aware of the lack of precision, selectivity or quality of results, and the resulting information load when too many hits are returned. The users' own lethargy in picking good keywords and a good set of keywords connected using advanced query options is partly to blame. The concept-based searches that exploit statistical techniques, the human-developed concept hierarchies, and information categorization, provide good improvements in certain situations. However, additional techniques involving ontology supported attributed search and content-based search techniques need to be exploited, especially when dealing with new media types.

The third challenge is to be able to have semantic-level modeling of related and relevant information. How do we describe semantically related distributed and heterogeneous information (e.g., a "person portfolio" consisting of his structured database records, his/her articles or articles about him/her in semi-structured form, software that s/he has created, his/her photograph, and a video of his/her talk)? How do we describe information at a logical or semantic level that may be independent of media or may involve multiple media? How do we describe the context of his/her information search such that the system can distinguish between medical instruments when the term instrument appears in his/her portfolio?

This paper deals with some of the aspects of the first two challenges. It presents the VisualHarness system developed at the LSDIS lab that supports a customizable search involving keywords, attributes and (visual) content of heterogeneous data (currently text, structured databases and image repositories). The third challenge is being addressed in our InfoQuilt project. Section 18.2 presents the background, while section 18.3 discusses metadata that play key roles in the VisualHarness system. Section 18.4 presents a brief overview of the VisualHarness including its extensible architecture. Section 18.5 presents the novel black box approach for supporting content based access of images using third party visual information retrieval engines. Section 18.6 provides a summary and outlines some of the ongoing research. The Appendix at the end presents early results showing efficacy of the novel black box approach when using a naïve strategy.

18.2.1 REQUIREMENTS FOR RESOURCE DESCRIPTION AND DISCOVERY

The challenges discussed earlier translate into the following set of emerging requirements for Web-based information searches (as well as associated information management functions involving access, filtering and integration):

- support for heterogeneous digital media,

- support for complimentary access strategies involving keyword-, attribute- and content-based access, preferably with an ability to combine these components with different weights, or to use them iteratively,
- specification of media independent queries,
- specification of information correlation at a logical level, and
- support for semantics, including context of a query and available information, possibly supported by use of ontologies and profiles

A key to our approach is to exploit the metadata to a much fuller extent than was perhaps done before. The approach involves
- identification of a broad variety of metadata,
- extraction of these types of metadata,
- logical correlations involving any type of metadata (for different types of media) [Sheth and Kashyap 96, Shah and Sheth 98], and
- specification of customizable (with different weights or sequences) information requests, involving keyword-, attribute- and content-based engines, and associated metadata-driven information request processing

The run-time system exploits and adapts a number of well-known and emerging technologies, including
- modified Web-server technology to utilize the broad variety of metadata in processing information requests,
- use of multiple (third-party) indexing techniques for textual data as well as other digital media,
- database management systems to manage metadata, and
- object-oriented modeling and software management, distributed object management

Our system that supports the above is called the VisualHarness system. Although it shares a number of similar features and capabilities with other contemporary systems that support integration of heterogeneous information, such as GARLIC [GARLIC], HERMES [HERMES], InfoHarness [I-HARNESS], Information Manifold [I-MANIFOLD], InfoSleuth [I-SLEUTH], SIMS [SIMS], TSIMMIS [TSIMMIS], and several others, it also has a number of differences. The features we focus on in this paper that are by and large different or unique are (a) use of a broader variety of metadata, (b) support for multiple third party indexing including a black-box approach to adapting visual information retrieval engines to capture metadata from visual information, and (c) integrated and customizable support for keyword, attributed *and* content-based access to distributed and heterogeneous information. While individual techniques used are not novel, except for the black-box approach to using visual information retrieval engines, their integration and the issues related to integration are what we believe is novel.

A part of this paper focuses on the content-based retrieval of images. Here the related work includes (a) systems for content-based retrieval called Visual Information Retrieval (VIR) systems such as Virage's VIR [Gupta 95], MIT Media lab's Photobook [Pentland et al 96], IBM's QBIC [Ashley et al 95], among several others, and (b) content-based image retrieval using metadata and relaxation techniques [Chu et al 98]. VisualHarness system complements and significantly extends the current VIRs to support a broader search strategy over a broader variety of distributed and heterogeneous data. In fact, for its black-box approach it uses Virage's VIR technology [Virage] for computing the image properties. Our approach can be seen as a metadata based approach that is extensible such that any metadata type for multiple domains can be obtained using extractors, the corresponding access method for that metadata can be supported, and different access strategies can be combined to achieve better quality results. More detailed comparison can be found in [Mudumbai 97].

18.3 METADATA FOR HETEROGENEOUS DIGITAL MEDIA

Metadata represent information about the data. Metadata can be regarded as an extension (albeit a significant one) of, the concept of a schema in structured databases. They may describe, or be a summary of the information content of the individual databases in an intentional manner. They typically represent constraints between the individual media objects that are implicit and not necessarily represented in the databases themselves. Some metadata may also capture content-independent information like location and time of creation. Examples of what we consider media types are structured data (data in relational or object-oriented databases), textual data (of different formats, such as Word files, source code, etc.), images (of possibly different modalities such as X-Ray, MRI scan), audio (of possibly different modalities such as monaural, stereophonic) and video.

Although there are a number of ways to classify metadata (e.g., see [Boll et al 98] for a more detailed discussion), the criteria we use to classify the metadata [Kashyap et al 95] is the extent to which they are successful in capturing the (data and information) content of the artifacts or documents represented in various media types. The level of abstraction at which the content of the documents is captured is very important. We believe that to capture the semantic content (i.e., at a level of abstraction closer to that of humans), it is important for the metadata to model application domain-specific information.

Thus, we classify the various kinds of metadata depending on whether they are based on the (data or information) content of the artifacts/ documents or not. The basic kinds of metadata we identify are:

- content-dependent metadata,
- content-descriptive metadata, and
- content-independent metadata.

Content-dependent metadata, as the name suggests, depends only on the content of the original data. A text index, like the document vectors in the LSI [Deerwester et al 90] index and the complete inverted WAIS [Kahle and Medlar 91] index (among many others) are examples of metadata that is determined by the content, i.e. the frequency and position of text units in the document. This kind of metadata is referred to as content-dependent metadata for textual data. When we associate metadata with the original data, which describes the contents in some way, but cannot be extracted automatically from the contents themselves, we call it content-based metadata. This kind of metadata could be determined exclusively by looking at the content, or is derived intellectually by automatic or semi-automatic means. However, it could not have been derived on the basis of content alone.

Table 18.1: Metadata for different digital media[2]

Metadata	Data Type	Metadata Type
Q-Features [Jain and Hampapur]	Image, Video	Domain Specific
R-Features [Jain and Hampapur]	Image, Video	Domain Independent
Meta-Features [Jain and Hampapur]	Image, Video	Content Independent
Impression Vector [Kiyoki et al.]	Image	Content Descriptive
NDVI, Spatial Registration [Anderson and Stonebraker]	Image	Domain Specific
Speech Feature Index [Glavitsch et al.]	Audio	Direct Content Based
Topic Change Indices [Chen et al.]	Audio	Direct Content Based
Document Vectors [Deerwester et al.]	Text	Direct Content Based
Inverted Indices [Kahle and Medlar]	Text	Direct Content Based
Content Classification Metadata [Bohm and Rakow]	MultiMedia	Domain Specific
Document Composition Metadata [Bohm and Rakow]	MultiMedia	Domain Independent
Metadata Templates [Ordille and Miller]	Media Independent	Domain Specific
Land Cover, Relief [Sheth and Kashyap]	Media Independent	Domain Specific
Parent Child Relationships [Shklar et al.]	Text	Domain Independent
Contexts [Sciore et al., Kashyap and Sheth]	Structured	Domain Specific
Concepts from Cyc [Collet et al.]	Structured	Domain Specific
User's Data Attributes [Shoens et al.]	Text, Structured	Domain Specific
Domain Specific Ontologies [Mena et al.]	Media Independent	Domain Specific

Content-descriptive metadata can be both domain-dependent and domain-independent. Domain-dependent metadata uses domain-specific concepts as a basis to determine the actual metadata created. Domain-independent metadata, on the other hand, relies on no such domain-specific concepts. A typical

[2] The citations in the table appear in [Klas and Sheth 94, Sheth and Klas 98].

example of a domain-independent metadata would be the one that describes the structure of a multimedia document.

Content-independent metadata, on the other hand, does not depend on the content. This kind of metadata can be derived independently from the content of the data. This is like attaching a tag to the data irrespective of the data contents. Examples of content-independent metadata of a document are its date of creation and location. Table 18.1 lists a few examples of different kinds of metadata.

18.4 VISUALHARNESS

The VisualHarness system is aimed at providing rapid access to huge amounts of heterogeneous data available over the World Wide Web. Our work so far has explicitly dealt with repositories of a variety of textual data, relational databases, and images, although this paper primarily focuses on the support for image data by this system. The VisualHarness system uses the components of the InfoHarness (IH) [Shklar et al 95, I-HARNESS] platform that supports textual data, with extensions to deal with visual data (using the ZEBRA system for supporting image data). Its metabase, that is the database of metadata, can consist of indices (e.g., full text index for textual data, feature based index for image data), and attribute value pairs used to support attribute based access as well as content-based access of visual data using a novel black-box approach that converts feature vectors into structured metadata. The VisualHarness system maintains metadata about the information space without restructuring, reformatting or relocating the original information enabling access to information by logical units of interest. An object-oriented layer (using InfoHarness Objects - IHOs) supports logical structuring of the metadata objects and thus allows arbitrary relationships amongst the represented information artifacts. VisualHarness is built using the IH integration platform. The VisualHarness system architecture is open and extensible. It provides hooks using which different third party indexing engines for textual data, and third party VIR engines, such as the Virage's VIR for image content based access, can be integrated.

Figure 18.1 shows a high level view of the VisualHarness architecture. VisualHarness supports comprehensive querying that is performed as follows. The IH server accepts a user query as a client request from a browser. The Query Engine module of the Query Processing Unit (QPU) creates subrequests for the relevant search components. The search components use metadata—both precomputed and stored in metabase, as well as that computed at run-time, to determine references to the relevant data and provide them to the result composition module of the QPU. QPU performs normalization, rescaling and formatting of the result. The IH server then displays the result to the user. When the user selects one or more data objects to be displayed, the IH server accesses the appropriate repositories directly to retrieve data. Table 18.2 lists some sample image metadata used by the VisualHarness system. Similar metadata classification can be given for other digital media accessible by the system.

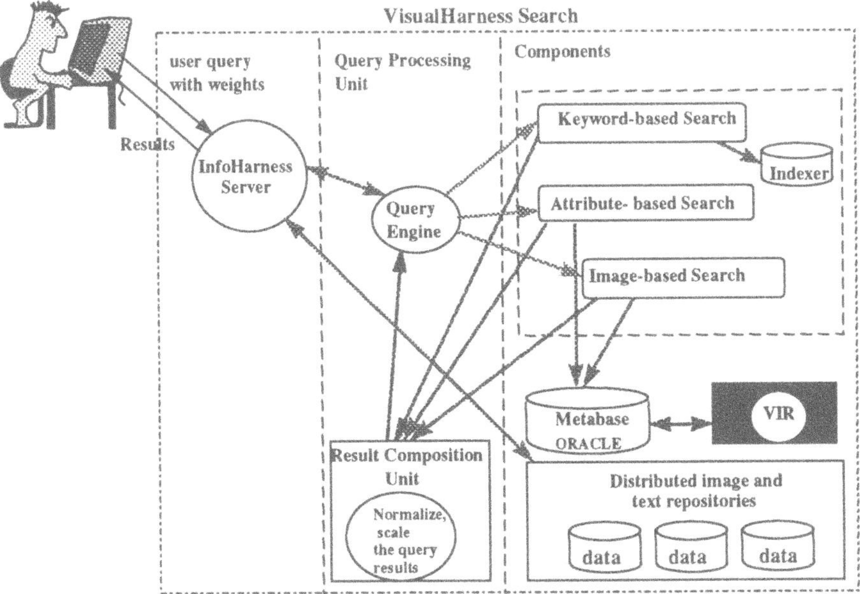

Figure 18.1: The VisualHarness architecture

The query processing subsystem uses weighting strategies to provide a scalable approach. By scalable approach, we mean that a user can assign different weights to different properties on which the similarity is based. Information retrieval from the database is restricted according to the user assigned weights. For example, if we have three properties say, P_1, P_2, and P_3, supported by the VIR engine, then the user can assign different weights i_1, i_2 and i_3 to each of these properties so that the retrieval by the VIR is based on

$$i_1P_1 + i_2P_2 + i_3P_3 \text{ where } 0.0 <= i_1,i_2,i_3 <= 1.0$$

The resulting values are normalized and scaled in order to give a ranking to each of the objects retrieved from the database.

Property weights in the VisualHarness system refer to the user weights assigned for different properties of the image via the user interface. The property weights vary between 0 and 1.0. If O_1, O_2,..,O_n are the objects in the image database, P_1, P_2,..,P_n are the different properties supported for an object O_i and Q is the input query object, the score S, obtained for each retrieved object O_i for the user assigned property weights i_1, i_2, i_3 and i_4 would be

$$S = i_1z_1 + i_2z_2 + i_3z_3 + i_4z_4$$

where z_1 = abs(P_1 value of O_i - P_1 value of Q) and similarly for z_2, z_3 and z_4. Scaling of property weights is done by multiplying the property weights into the appropriate difference in the property values z_1, z_2, z_3 and z_4. The normalization is performed by giving the highest ranking with value 1.0 to the object that has the highest score. For all other objects retrieved, we normalize them by dividing the score of that object by the score of the highest ranked object (prior to giving it the value of 1.0). This gives the overall ranking of the objects that are retrieved from the image database.

Table 18.2: Some of the image feature metadata in the VisualHarness system

Metadata classification	Requires processing raw data	Uses semantic (domain-specific) knowledge	Typical Format	Examples from image data
Content-independent	No	No	attribute values	height, width, size, date of creation etc.
Content-dependent	Yes	No	feature vectors or attribute values	color, composition, texture, structure etc.
Content-based	No	Yes	attribute values	color, height, fragrance, hybridizer of a flower; model, category etc. of an aircraft
Content descriptive	Maybe	Either	text and/or keywords	Descriptions of a flower, an x-ray, an air-craft (domain-specific); General descriptions related to the image (domain-independent)

Figure 18.2 shows an example of the comprehensive search screen. A user could focus on any one of the three search strategies, keyword-based, attribute-based and content-based, or combine the three using relative weights. Within the content-based search, it is possible to use additional features, such as color, structure, texture and composition in the case of images, as shown in Figure 18.2. Iterative refinements are also possible.

The access method mentioned above will apply to any of the VIR engines if one has knowledge about, and access to, the feature vectors of the image objects in the database. For systems such as the VisualHarness system that do not know about the internals of the VIR engine, this access method might not be applicable. An alternative, in cases where we either do not have access to the actual feature vectors or have no way of interpreting them, is the Black Box Approach (BBA) originally introduced in [Shah et al 97]. In this we try to compare the objects based on their differences with a reference image rather than a direct comparison between the objects themselves. We now describe the original BBA that involved use of what are terms as null images as reference images [Shah et al 97], followed by our recent improvements.

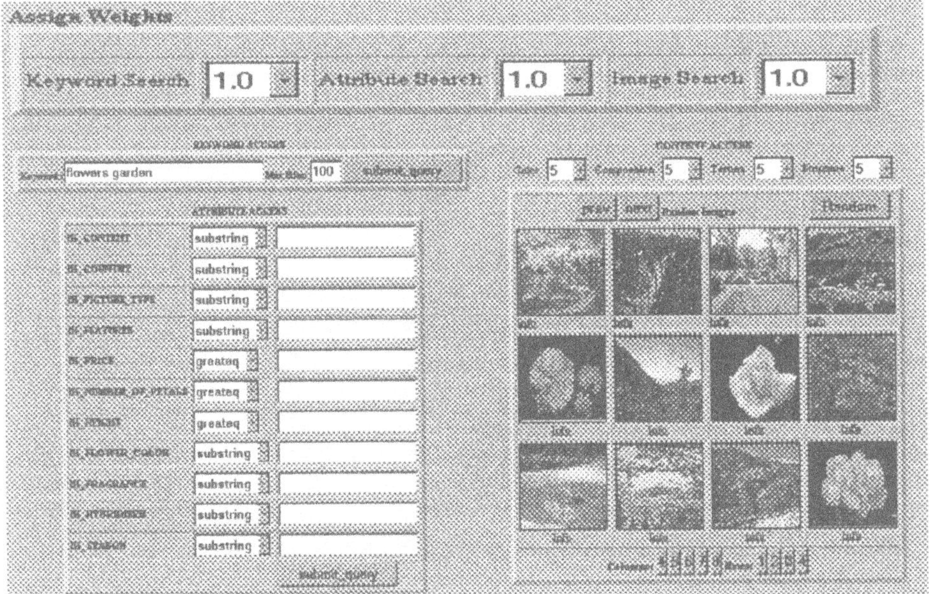

Figure 18.2: Comprehensive search in VisualHarness

18.5 THE BLACK BOX APPROACH FOR CONTENT-DEPENDENT METADATA

Feature vectors from an image refer to the features extracted from different topological spaces. Distances between the objects and the input query object are required in order to obtain a ranking of the objects similar to the given query object. As discussed above, since the VisualHarness system does not have access to the actual feature vectors of an image object or has no way of interpreting them, it uses the VIR engine as a black box. The BBA tries to compare objects based on their differences with a reference image rather than a direct comparison between the objects themselves.

If R is a reference image and the objects in the database are $O_1, O_2, \ldots, O_n$ then the feature distance

$$D(O_1,O_2) = abs(D(O_1,R) - D(O_2,R))$$

i.e., the distance between any two objects O_1 and O_2 in the feature space would be equal to the absolute value (or the Euclidean distance) of the difference between each object compared with the reference image for a particular property. Feature vectors of the object sequence in the database based on different properties of an image are mapped to a point in the feature space; a query with tolerance *e* becomes a sphere of radius *e*. This process is shown in Figures 18.3 and 18.4.

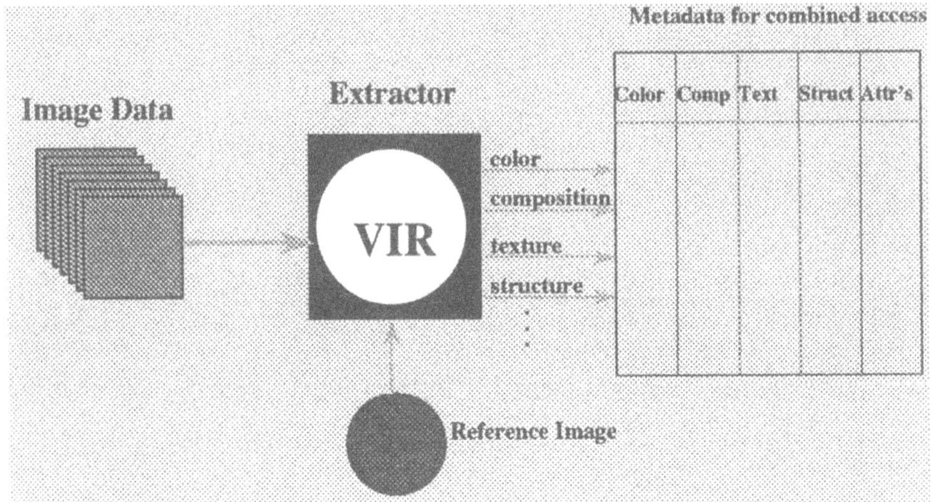

Figure 18.3: Image feature extraction in VisualHarness' Blackbox approach using a reference image

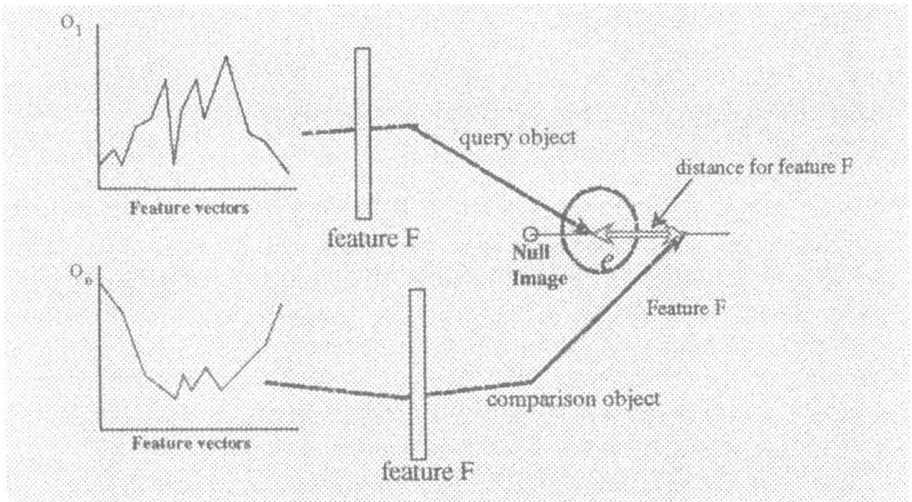

Figure 18.4: Translating n dimensional image feature vector spaces to Euclidean distances

The BBA allows the VisualHarness system to be very scalable since the information retrieval is not limited to a particular VIR engine and its corresponding image database. Any engine can be hooked up into our search system and multiple databases at different locations can be accessed. Runtime computation is not expensive as we pre-compute the distance between each object and the reference image for each of its properties and store it in a database. Run time computation basically involves retrieving the appropriate results from the database by converting the user query image, Q, into a database query D(Q,R). Without this approach, we would have to compute the distance between the query image and each image object in the databases during runtime in a sequential manner. This would be computationally very expensive. With our BBA, we can also employ different weighting strategies to combine the distances obtained in comparing each object with the reference image in that topological space. We can also try and combine features computed using different engines since we are using normalized distances. Our ongoing work studies the effectiveness of the black-box approach. The early results using a naïve strategy of using null images as reference images are reasonably good as compared to the VIR's results as the target set in most situations as discussed in the next subsection and as demonstrated in the Appendix.

18.5.1 Selecting a Reference Image

Our initial BBA strategy was to use a ***null image*** as a reference image. We chose an entirely black or an entirely white image as a null image, hypothesizing that such an image does not have any specific feature and hence no properties of its own. Using this naïve choice for a reference image, we received quite decent results as shown in the appendix. However, we continued to look for a better strategy for choosing a reference image so as to obtain more accurate results compared with the ones obtained by directly using the VIR engine.

18.5.2 Problems with Null image and the strategy based on centroid of the feature space

Consider three image objects O_1, O_2 and O_3 in a feature space. Let O_{null} be the null object and d_1, d_2 and d_3 be the respective distances between the objects and the null image. Figure 18.5 represents relative positions of the objects in the feature vector space. The feature distance between O_1 and O_2 is computed as:

$$D(O_1,O_2) = \text{abs}\,(D(O_1, O_{null}) - D(O_2, O_{null})), \text{ i.e., } D(O_1,O_2) = \text{abs}(d_1 - d_2)$$

The spatial distribution of the objects in the feature space suggests that O_1 is closer to O_2 than O_3. The VIR would have given us $D(O_1,O_2) < D(O_1,O_3)$. The distance between O_1 and O_2 is less than the distance between O_1 and O_3 and this would have led one to conclude that O_1 is more similar to O_2 than O_3.

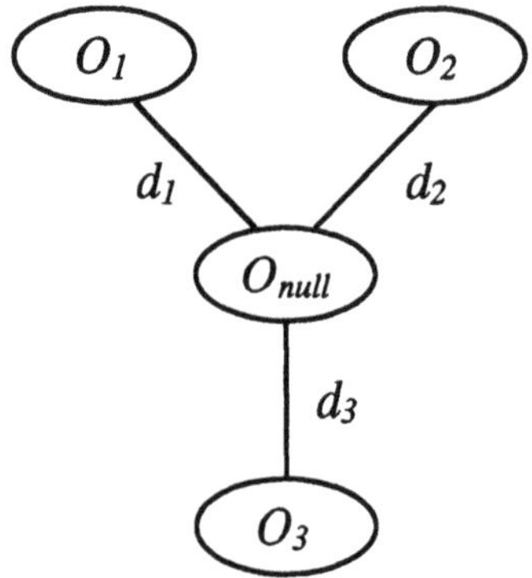

Figure 18.5: Objects in Feature Space.

Suppose the VIR had given distances $D(O_2, O_{null}) < D(O_3, O_{null})$ i.e., $d_2 < d_3$. If $d_1 > d_3$, then using the BBA, we would have concluded that the $D(O_1,O_2) > D(O_1,O_3)$. This is contradictory to VIR results! This shows that the null image may not be the ideal reference image. Theoretically a null image should be devoid of any features, but in practice even a plain black or plain white image has certain inherent features, which adds a certain amount of bias to the feature space.

In this case the null object was more or less a random object. The null object was not a part of the initial object collection and it was added such that it was at a random location in the feature space. As it was shown earlier, this might lead to contradictory results. In our second strategy, a better reference image, rather than being a random object, is the "centroid" in the feature space. Ideally it should be equidistant from all the other objects. But such an object would be difficult to construct, so we choose an existing object that is close to the "centroid" (see Figure 18.6).

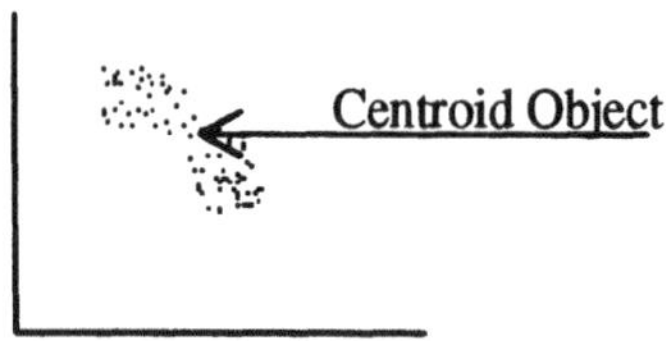

Figure 18.6: Centroid Object in Feature Space.

Finding an existing object that has the minimum distance from every other object is computed as follows:

Suppose there are n objects in the database, $O_1, O_2, O_3, \ldots, O_n$ then $D(O_i,O_j)$ is the distance metric returned by the VIR for objects O_i and O_j. For two objects to be similar $D(O_i,O_j)$ has to be minimum and to find the reference object our objective is to minimize the difference metric.

We calculate $D(O_i,O_j)$ for all objects O_i and O_j in the database and then SD_I, the standard deviation of an object O_i with respect to every other object in the database. `min(SD)` returns the object with the minimum standard deviation, which would be our reference image. A potential weakness of this strategy is the cost of recomputing the reference image every time the image database changes.

We have compiled quantitative data using the centroid based reference object that shows noticeable improvement over the null image strategy. These results, while not included here, due to time and space limitation, will be presented at the next available opportunity and at our Web site. Next we discuss a more speculative strategy that is currently being investigated, and for which quantitative results have not been obtained.

18.5.3 Reference image based on semantic correlation of objects

Our objective in this third strategy is to improve the quality of results by semantically correlating various objects into semantic groups. Members of such a group would have some binding feature and objects could belong to multiple semantic groups (i.e., we could "thread" objects based on some predefined semantics). By semantically correlating the objects we make an effort towards trying to better understand the intent of the user submitting the query.

18.5.3.1 Correlation Strategies

We outline two methods that can be use to correlate the objects. These are content semantics and context semantics. Grouping based on content semantics is purely based on statistical principles and can be mathematically formulated whereas context based grouping might be automated, manual or knowledge driven.

18.5.3.2 Content semantics

In content semantic grouping, the objects are correlated or grouped together based on their contents. We extract *n* features from an image object and map it on to *n*-dimensional feature spaces as points. If we then run any standard clustering algorithms on these points, we would be able to group the points into *clusters* (see Figure 18.7). Each member in a cluster would be correlated with one another based on content semantics.

Objects could also be correlated based on context. For instance, the objects that represent similar context could form one semantic group. As the simplest case we could use some qualifying attribute of the object and group all objects having a common value for that object. We could also use an ontology and group all objects with terminological differences resolved for a particular attribute value or user domain knowledge, and group object within the same domain.

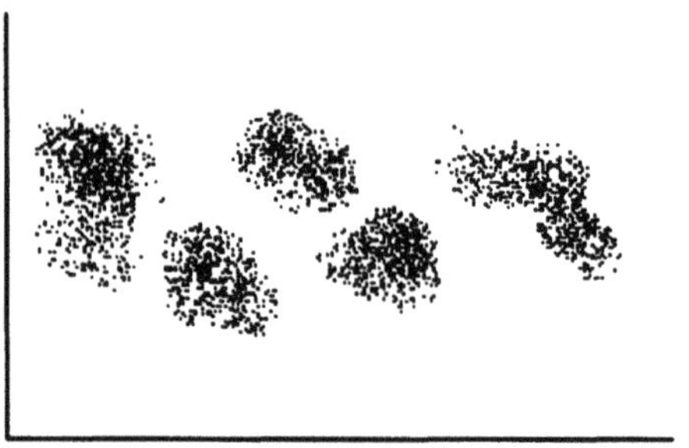

Figure 18.7: Clustering of objects in the Feature space

The query processing that involves semantic correlation involves the following strategy. Information retrieval from the database is restricted according to user assigned weights. If the VIR supports three properties, say P_1, P_2 and P_3, then the user can assign different weights, w_1, w_2 and w_3, to each of these properties and the overall weight of the retrieval w would be

$$w' = w_1P_1 + w_2P_2 + w_3P_3 \text{ where } 0.0 <= w_1,w_2,w_3 <= 1.0$$

Apart from assigning individual weights to properties, the user can also assign a value f, which is the scaling factor. The scaling factor imparts relevance to the semantic groups.

All the objects retrieved from the query object's semantic group have their overall weight w' multiplied by the scaling factor. If the scaling factor f had a value of 1.0, all the objects in the collection, whether they belong to semantic groups or not, will have the same relevance. If the scaling factor is greater than 1.0, then the objects in the querying object's semantic group have a higher preference.

As indicated earlier, quantitative evaluations for a semantic correlation based approach are yet to be performed.

18.6 SUMMARY

In this paper we discussed a metadata-based approach to search heterogeneous digital media accessible on the Internet and Intranets. Through the extensive use of metadata, we can support keyword-based, attribute-based and content-based searches, as well as their combinations. The content based search is particularly facilitated by the black-box approach that can use third party engines to deal with specific types of digital media, coercing them to extract metadata. Once we are able to extract the metadata, the Web-based VisualHarness server can provide access to any Web-accessible data using any combination of the three search alternatives and allow us to combine access to data of heterogeneous media. Extensible metabase and open architecture allow for adding or extending metadata extractors at any time for existing and new media types, allowing the system to grow with new data, new types of media and new ways of processing data of different media. The second version of VisualHarness is implemented in Java.

While this paper focused on image data, we have used a similar approach and architecture to support access to textual, structured and video data. A related project at the LSDIS lab, VideoAnywhere, focuses on a variety of video data and can be seen as a Web search engine for video data.

Another relevant on-going work at the LSDIS lab is on supporting the concept of information correlation involving heterogeneous digital media (called MREF) [Sheth and Kashyap 96] and corresponding information request processing techniques. RDF and XML have been exploited for MREF representation and implementation [Shah and Sheth 98].

References

Ashley, J., Flickner, M., Hafner, J., Lee, D., Niblack, W., and Petkovic, D. (1995). The Query By Image Content (QBIC) System. *Proc. of the ACM SIGMOD Intl. Conf. on Management of Data,* San Jose, CA.

Boll, S., Klas, W., and Sheth, A. (1998). "*Overview on Using Metadata to Manage Multimedia Data,*" in [Sheth and Klas 98].

Chu, W. W., Hsu, C., Ieong, I. T., Taira, R. (1998). "*Content-Based Image Retrieval Using Metadata and Relaxation Techniques,*" in [Sheth and Klas 98].

Deerwester, S., Dumais, S., Furnas, G., Landauer, T., and Hashman, K. (1990). "Indexing by Latent Semantic Indexing," *Journal of the American Society for Information Science*, 41(6).

The GARLIC system, http://www.almaden.ibm.com/cs/showtell/garlic

Gupta, A. (1995). *Visual information retrieval: A Virage perspective.* Technical Report, Virage, San Mateo, CA.

The Hermes system, http://www.cs.umd.edu/projects/hermes

The InfoHarness and VisualHarness systems, http://lsdis.cs.uga.edu/proj/proj.html

The Manifold system, http://www.research.att.com/~levy/imhome.html

The InfoSleuth system, http://mcc.com:80/projects/infosleuth

Kahle, B. and Medlar, A. (1991). "An Information System for Corporate Users: Wide Area Information Servers," *Connexions - The Interoperability Report*, 5(11), November.

Kashyap, V., Shah, K., and Sheth, A. (1995). "Metadata for building the MultiMedia Patch Quilt," *Multimedia Database Systems: Issues and Research Directions*, S. Jajodia and V.S.Subrahmaniun, Eds., Springer-Verlag.

Kashyap, V. (1997). "*Information Brokering over heterogeneous digital data : A metadata based approach,*" Doctoral thesis, Dept. of Computer Science, Rutgers University.

Klas, W. and Sheth, A. Eds., (1994). Metadata for Digital Media, *Special Issue of SIGMOD Record*, 23 (4), ACM Press, December.

Mudumbai, S. (1997). *ZEBRA Image Access System: Customizable, Extensible Metadata-based Access to Federated Image Repositories.* M.S. Thesis, LSDIS lab, Computer Sc. Dept., Univ. of Georgia, May.

Pentland, A., Picard, R.W., and Sclaroff, S. (1996). *Photobook: Content Based Manipulation of Image Databases*, Chapter 2, Kluwer Academic Publishers.

Shah, K., Sheth, A., and Mudumbai, S. (1997). "*Black Box Approach to Image Feature Manipulation used by Visual Information Retrieval Engines,*" The Second IEEE Metadata Conference, September.

Shah, K. and Sheth, A. (1998). "*Logical Information Modeling of Web-accessible Heterogeneous Digital Assets*", Proc. of the Forum on Research and Technology Advances in Digital Libraries (ADL'98), Barbara, CA, April.

Sheth, A. and Kashyap, V. (1996). "*Media-independent Correlation of Information: What? How?*" Proceedings of First IEEE Metadata Conference, April.

Sheth, A. and Klas, W., Eds., (1998). *Multimedia Data Management: Using Metadata to Integrate and Apply Digital Media*, McGraw-Hill.

Shklar, L., Sheth, A., Kashyap, V. and Shah, K. (1995). *InfoHarness: Use of Automatically Generated Metadata for Search and Retrieval of Heterogeneous Information* in Proceedings of CAiSE-95, June.

The SIMS system, http://www.isi.edu/sims/

The TSIMMIS system, http://www-db.stanford.edu/tsimmis

Appendix A: Results when using a null image based BBA for content-based image data access in the VisualHarness system

We show two kinds of results based on the null image strategy[3]. Even though this is a naïve strategy, the results in many cases have been good. One set of results deals with content-based retrieval focusing on the BBA retrieval compared to Virage's VIR. The second set of results shows the refinement of user queries using the combination of different access strategies to obtain better quality results.

A1: Content-based Retrieval

The first image in the sequence is the input query image. Results have been tested on the four properties of the image- color, composition, texture and

---

[3] Black and White images in the printed version of the paper may not demonstrate color-sensitive results adequately. An on-line version of the paper in color is available from the LSDIS lab's library on the Web.

structure. So far, the results have been promising and additional work with larger image repositories is in progress. The null image used for achieving the following results is a full white image.

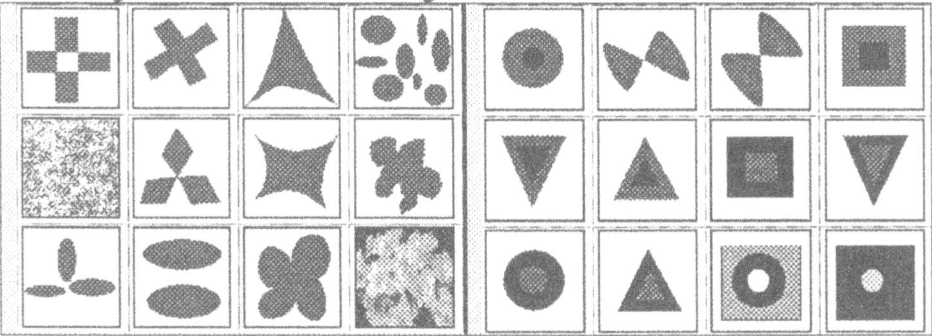

Figure A-1
COLOR (HR = 91.7%)

Figure A-2
COMPOSITION (HR = 75%)

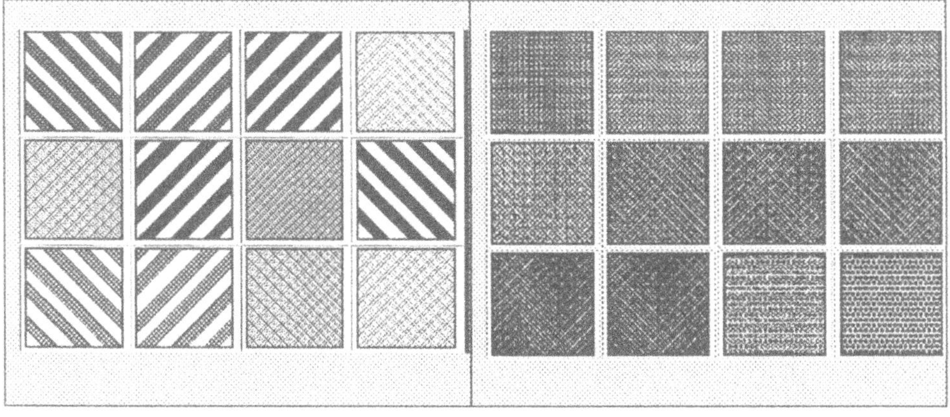

Figure A-3
TEXTURE (HR = 100%)

Figure A-4
TEXTURE (HR = 91.7%)

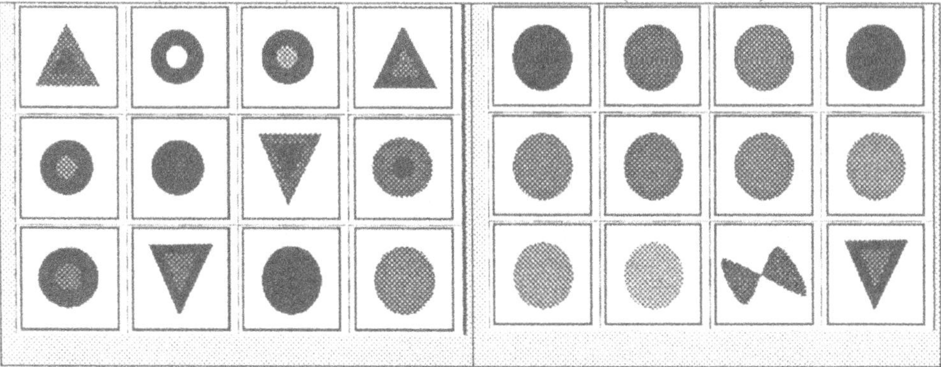

Figure A-5
STRUCTURE (HR = 91.7%)

Figure A-6
STRUCTURE (HR = 83.3%)

To compare our results with the VIR, we calculate a hit ratio which is the proportion overlap between the result set returned by VisualHarness and the VIR for n top hits. If A is the set of top n hits returned by VisualHarness and B is the set of top n hits returned by the VIR (Virage in this case) then:

Hit ratio (HR) = $((\{A\} \cap \{B\}) / n)$ where n is 12 in our examples.

A2: Combination of keyword, attribute, and image based access strategies

We now discuss some results that involve combining image based and attribute based access strategies. First a random set of images is chosen from a given collection and an icon click is done on the 10th image in the given set with all image properties having equal user weights.

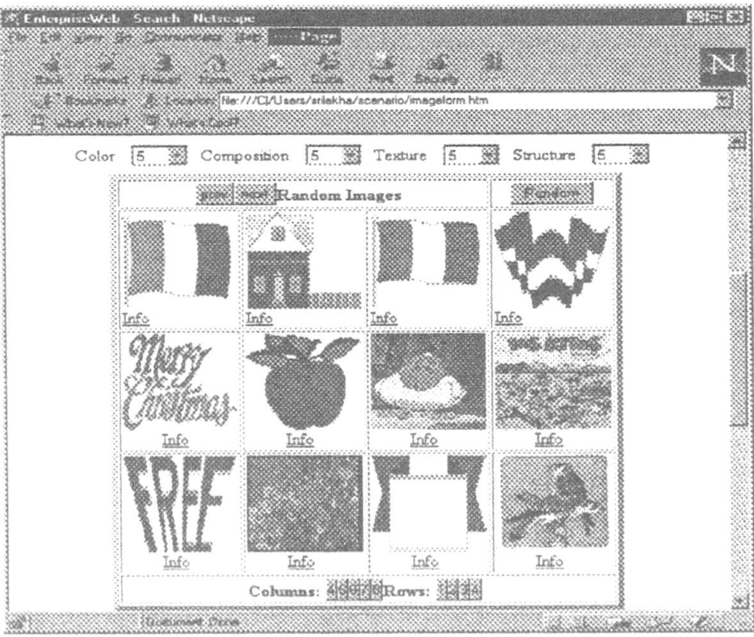

Figure A-7

Figure A-8 shows the results from choosing the 10th image in Figure A-7. Figure A-9 gives the results for the icon click on the first image of Figure A-9 in addition to attribute name, value pairs namely 'Imagename: *flowers*' and 'Color: *green*'. The results indicate how a given query can be refined using combination of different access strategies (image content based and attribute based access).

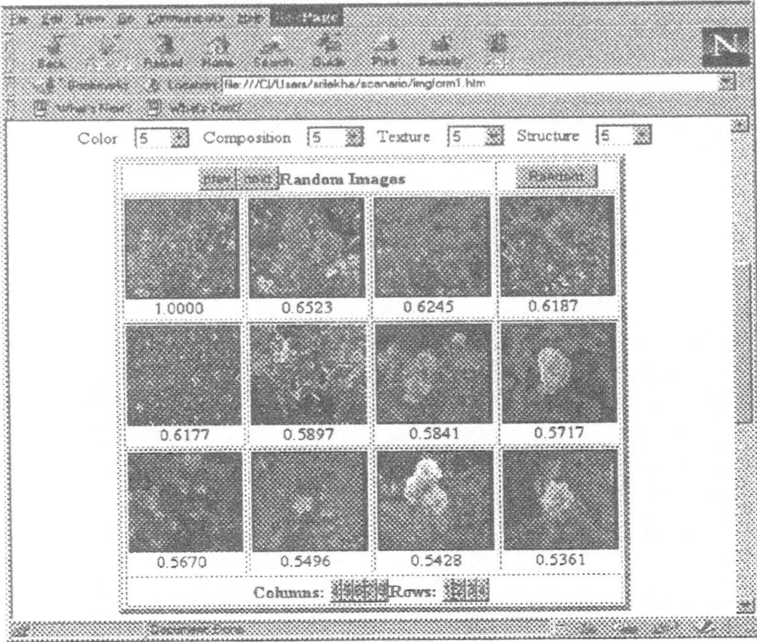

Figure A-8

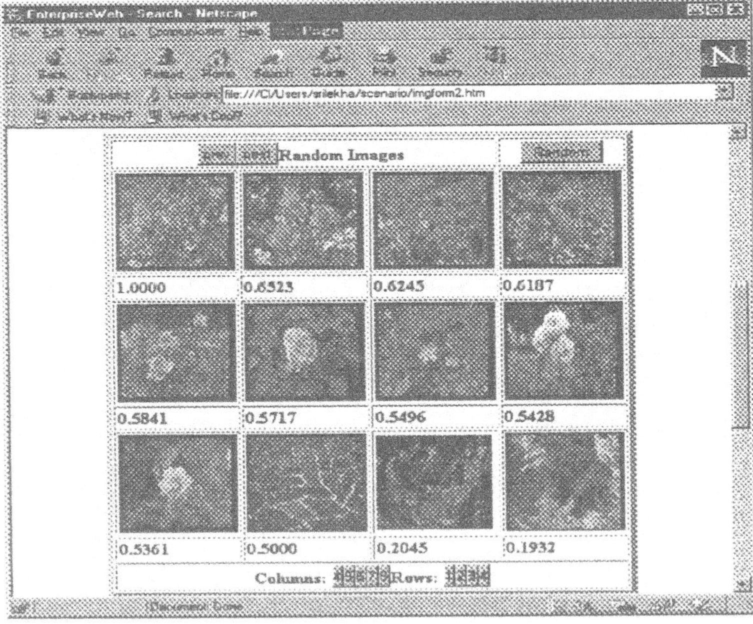

Figure A-9

Figure A-10 gives the results of only attribute based access on the attribute name, value pairs namely 'Imagename: *flowers*' and 'Color: *green*' as applied above.

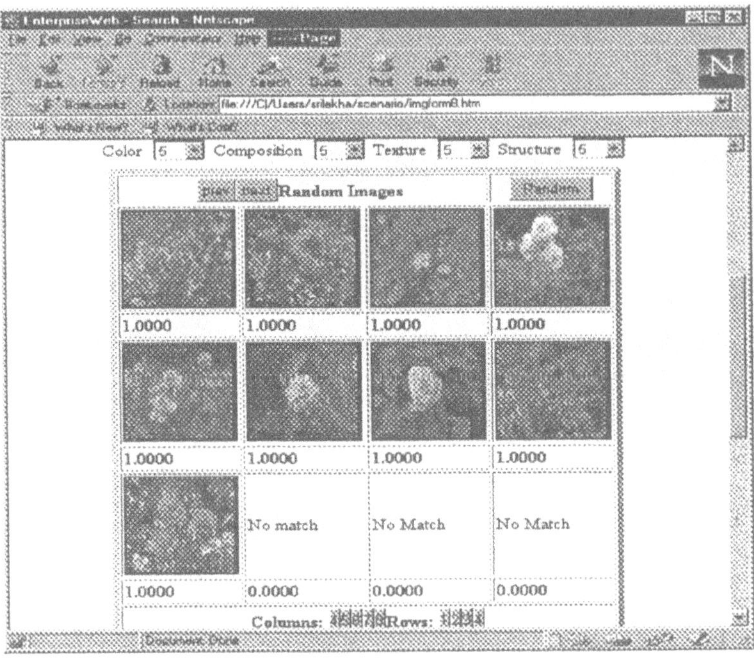

Figure A-10

A different ordering and ranking of images can be noticed at this point. This shows how a user can refine the queries and hence achieve better quality results. This is clearly indicated in the ordering of images in attribute access only and a combination of both attribute and image content based access.

19 USING WG-LOG SCHEMATA TO REPRESENT SEMISTRUCTURED DATA

E. Damiani, B. Oliboni, L. Tanca, D. Veronese

Università di Verona

edamiani@crema.unimi.it barbara@romeo.sci.univr.it

tanca@sci.univr.it davvero@romeo.sci.univr.it

Abstract: In this paper we discuss the possibility to represent synthetically semistructured information via a loose notion of schema: we say that data are *semistructured* when, although some structure is present, it is not as strict, regular, or complete as the one required by the traditional database management systems. Our proposal is based on WG-Log, a graph based language for the representation of WWW site information. We show how information encoded in a typical semistructured information model, as OEM, can be represented and queried by means of the WG-Log language, and how the TSIMMIS and WG-Log Web Query System can be integrated to allow site content exploration and exploitation by means of WG-Log.

19.1 INTRODUCTION

We say that data are *semistructured* when, although some structure is present, it is not as strict, regular, or complete as the one required by the traditional database management systems (see [1] for a survey on semistructured data).

---

* This work has been partially supported by the INTERDATA project from the Italian Ministry of University and Scientific Research, 1997.

* The WG-Log/OEM experience has been also described in a paper published in SEBD 1998 under the title "Using WG-Log to represent semistructured data: the example of OEM".

Information is semistructured also when the structure of data varies w.r.t. time, rather than w.r.t. space: even if data is fairly well structured, such structure may evolve rapidly.

Traditional database systems force all data to adhere to an explicitly specified, rigid schema, which is far less dynamic than the data itself. For many new applications involving large amounts of semistructured data there can be two significant drawbacks to the database approach:

- Data may be irregular and thus not conform to a rigid schema. In relational systems, the presence of irregular data forces the use of null values, whose appropriate handling is still a research issue in the relational database community. While complex types, object identity and inheritance in object-oriented databases clearly enable more flexibility, it can still be difficult to design an appropriate object-oriented schema to accommodate irregular data.

- It may be difficult to decide in advance on a single, correct schema. If the structure of data is in constant evolution, data element types may change, or data not conforming to the previous structure may be added.

As a first example of semistructured information we can consider data integrated from multiple, heterogeneous data sources. When data is integrated in a naïve fashion from several heterogeneous sources, there may be discrepancies among the various data representations: some information may be missing in some sources, an attribute may be single-valued in one source and multi-valued in another, or the same entity may be represented by different types in different sources. Considerable effort is typically spent to ensure that the integrated data are well structured and conforms to a single, uniform schema. Additional effort is required if one or more information sources change, or when new sources are added.

As a second example, consider data stored on the World Wide Web. At a typical Web site, data is varied and irregular, and the overall structure of the site changes often. Today, very few Web sites store all their available information in a database system; it is clear, however, that Web users could take advantage of database support, e.g., by having the ability to pose queries involving logical data relationships (which usually are known by site's creators but not made explicit).

When querying semistructured data, one can't expect the user to be fully aware of their complete structure, especially if the structure evolves dynamically. Thus, it is important not to require full knowledge of the structure to express meaningful queries.

In most schema-based systems these features cause frequent schema modifications, and for this reason a synthetic representation of the data cannot be very rigid, but should be adaptable to changes. Because of these limitations, many applications involving semistructured data are forgoing the use of a database management system, despite the fact that many strengths of a DBMS (ad-hoc queries, efficient access, concurrency control, crash recovery, security, etc.) would be very useful to those projects. Moreover, database schemata have proved to be a good mean to convey information about data semantics, and this is the reason why some kind of schema is essential in the process of query formulation. Thus, we should do as much as possible to keep this heritage from the database world.

In this paper we discuss the possibility to represent synthetically semistructured information via a loose notion of schema. As an example of application of a schema-based approach, we refer to the WG-Log project [6], a proposal that involves the use of a graph-based schema and query language for WWW information: the WG-Log proposal includes also an architecture for a Web Query System (WQS)[1].

We show how information encoded in a typical semistructured information model, as OEM [16], can be represented and queried by means of the WG-Log language, and how the TSIMMIS and WG-Log Web Query Systems can be integrated to allow site content exploration and exploitation by means of WG-Log.

In particular, we are referring to a scenario in which information about Web sites' contents represented in OEM (Object Exchange Model) is automatically translated to a WG-Log schema. Then a WG-Log user formulates a query in WG-Log; the system translates such query into LOREL [4] (an OQL-like language which queries OEM-represented information) and presents the answer to the WG-Log user. Thus, WG-Log schemata of OEM-represented sites can be kept in a schema repository, together with the other WG-Log schemata, to be queried in a transparent way by any WG-Log user.

The paper is organized as follows: next Section concerns the major research streams in this area, focusing on the TSIMMIS project [7]. After, recalling the WG-Log model and language, we present the translation of OEM representations into WG-Log schemata and the mapping of WG-Log queries on these schemata to the LOREL language. Then we describe the architecture of the WG-Log Web Query System and its integration with TSIMMIS. Finally we draw the conclusions.

19.2 RELATED WORK

To date, two main research streams can be recognized on the querying and management of WWW data:

- *program oriented:* the focus of these approaches is on the generation of *wrappers*, programs that facilitate database-like querying of semi-structured data retrieved directly from sources. The wrapper accepts queries (in a standard query language) about information in the source, fetches relevant information (hypertextual documents in the case of the WWW) and returns the results.

[1]By Web Query System we mean a set of integrated tools for the efficient and effective retrieval of information in the World Wide Web.

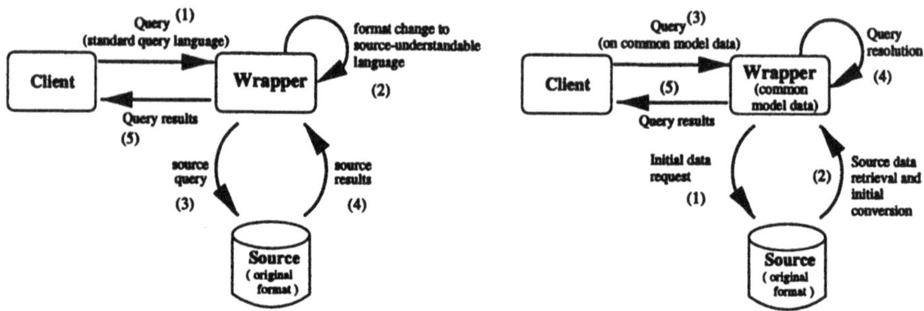

Figure 19.1: The program based approach (left) and the data-model approach (right)

An example of this approach can be found in the **SIMS** project [2], where wrappers are generated in order to provide database-like querying for semistructured WWW sources.

Another example is the **Infosleuth** project [5], developed at MCC, which uses wrappers to translate standard SQL queries to Information Retrieval expressions, with the support of a classical Entity-Relationship schema which represents the semantics of the different data sources indipendently of their actual data representations. Note that the data format remains the one internal of each data source: the E-R schema is only a conceptual representation to ease query formulation.

- *data-model oriented:* here the grounding idea is to convert semi-structured data to a representation based on a common information model, which is stored into a repository in order to be later queried via a (more or less) standard query language; this repository is kept indipendently of the original semistructured data. Queries are initially formulated over information coded into the common model; wrappers are used also here, but this time to convert (*una tantum*) the source data into the common data model, and then to answer the user queries.

  This approach to data integration is adopted in systems as Araneus [3], TSIMMIS, STRUDEL [10].

The **Araneus** project uses a representation of semantics based on a standard relational schema, where Web site crawling is employed to induce schemata of Web pages. These fine grained page schemata are later to be combined into a site-wide schema, and a special-purpose language, Ulixes, is used to build relational views over it. Resulting relational views can be queried using standard SQL, or trasformed into autonomous Web sites using a second special-purpose language, Penelope.

The **TSIMMIS** project was born at Stanford University, aimed at the development of tools that ease the rapid integration of heterogeneous information sources which may include both structured and unstructured data.

Each source of interest is endowed with a wrapper having two main functions:

- to convert the underlying data to a common information model known as OEM (Object Exchange Model). This process consists of two phases: first of all the user defines the OEM classes to be used for data representation; afterwards, an extraction technique based on a textual filter is applied (see [13]), initializing objects from the site data. OEM is a graph-structured data model where the basic idea is that each object has a label that describes its meaning. The label is used to extract information about objects that represent the underlying data.

- The second task of a TSIMMIS wrapper is to convert queries specified in a language for the common data-model, called LOREL into requests that the source can execute.

  The OEM objects obtained from the extraction process have no fixed schema; to provide usual benefits of a schema, DataGuides are introduced [12]. DataGuides are a sort of dynamic schemata generated from the OEM representation of the information sources, and are employed in order to make indexing and querying easier.

It is interesting to note that the TSIMMIS project is inspired by an instance-based representation of source data semantics, but in fact, DataGuides must be used to index and query semistructured data, since they provide the necessary facilities that are usually in charge of schemata in the database context.

STRUDEL provides a single graph data model similar to OEM in which all data sources are uniformly modeled, and a query language for data integration. At the bottom-most level, data is stored in STRUDEL's own graph data repository or in external sources which are also viewed as graphs. The communication with the data sources is done through a set of wrappers. A wrapper maps an external source's data representation into STRUDEL collections and objects and translates STRUDEL queries into queries or operations understood by the source. This approach defines a virtual loose schema and maps on it the contents of the data sources.

Under this same category we can loosely classify also two more approaches: in the Resource Description Framework (**RDF**) [14] a data model based on directed labeled graphs is proposed for representing Web sites' metadata.

RDF is a formalism that has been proposed to the W3C consortium for the Web standards, to facilitate a synthetic representation of Web sites' contents. This is interesting, since it indicates that also the industrial community has reached the conviction that Web site semistructured data must be represented in some sort of schematic way, in order to become fully accessible and understandable.

Finally, our data-model oriented approach for structuring and querying WWW data is based on the **WG-Log** language, briefly described in the following section. WG-Log is a graph-oriented description and query language specifically designed for the needs of Web sites. Based on the graph query language G-Log [17], WG-Log was extended to include some standard hypermedia design notations, thus allowing to express model entities and relationships as well as navigational concepts. The last two approaches do not require a total conversion of the semistructured data to the common data model, rather, they complement the site contents with information about their semantics.

The choice of using a graph oriented approach is not new, as we have seen observing also OEM and RDF; however, the idea of the WG-Log project is to use graphs as the formalism for a visual language unifying navigational and logical aspects of Web sites.

19.3 THE WG-LOG MODEL AND LANGUAGE

The main purpose of the WG-Log language is to support database-like querying over Web sites; differently from many of the other projects, its approach to the representation of semistructured data is *explicitly* schema-based. Indeed, a WG-Log schema can be easily derived from the design phase of a Web site, and later used for posing and answering queries. Site dinamicity is not a real issue here; as long as the schema remains the same, querying based on this schema will always give the appropriate results. However, a periodical refreshing of the schemata kept in the repository will guarantee a tolerable amount of precision in case of site evolution that affects the structure (i.e., the schema) of the site. The point here is that answers to WWW queries are themselves portions of WWW sites. Even if at some point the schema does not reflect exactly the site structure, the answer to the query will contain an access point to some of the site information, wherefrom the user can navigate through the real pages. The approach is not proposed as an alternative to the classical searching and browsing of Web sites, thus the kind of information that would be available to a normal browser is still there.

WG-Log schemata, instances and queries are depicted as directed labeled graphs, whose nodes represent objects, while the edges indicate relationships between objects. The details of the WG-Log language can be found in [9]; for our purposes we only recall that two main node types exists, indicating simple objects, or *slots* (those with an atomic, perceivable value as strings, numbers) and abstract objects, or *entities* (the ones whose properties are described by means of aggregates of simple objects, e.g. a car, a person etc). Moreover, there are other kinds of nodes to describe indexes and entry points, useful for the representation of the hypermedia structure.

Graph edges can indicate both logical and navigational relationships, the former having a label indicating the relationship name. WG-Log rules, programs and goals can be used to deduce, query and restructure the information contained in the Web site pages. Rules are themselves graphs, which can be arranged in programs in such a way that new *views* (or *perspectives*) of the Web

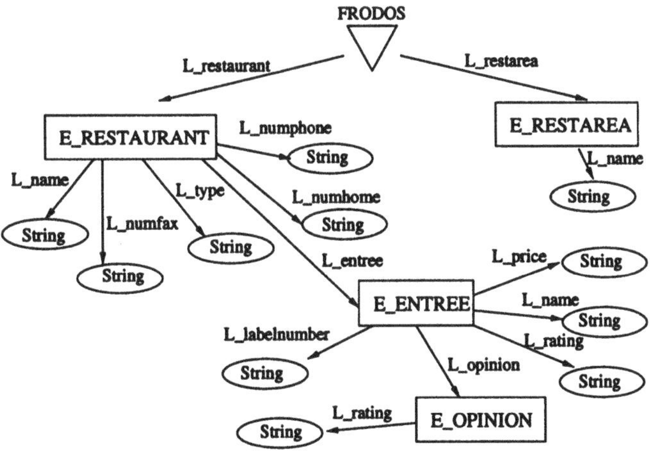

Figure 19.2: A sample WG-Log schema

site are available to the user. Goals can be applied to isolate the desired information and to arrange it in different presentation styles. Like Horn clauses, rules in WG-Log represent implications. To distinguish the body of the rule from the head in the graph P representing the rule, the part of P that corresponds to the body is colored red and the part that corresponds to the head is green (respectively thin and bold black in this paper). Queries can include *dummy* nodes, which match any type of node of the schema. This yields a great flexibility in query expression, by allowing the expression of "wildcard nodes". As an example we include a WG-Log schema representing the Frodos restaurant chain (Fig. 19.2);
the main entities are depicted as rectangles (complex objects) and indicate restaurants, rest areas and restaurant entrees. The attributes (slots) of each entity are depicted as ellipses; the Node 'Frodos', depicted as a triangle is a special WG-Log node representing pages with singleton semantics, as for example the Home Page of a site.

In Fig. 19.3 we outline a sample query aimed at selecting all the entrees of the restaurant "Blues_by_the_bay"; the green node 'Result' is used to indicate the access point to the query result. This means that the query results will be presented as a list of the selected Entrees.

It is easy to see, from this example, that the presence of a WG-Log schema does not necessarily impose the restrictions cited in Section 1: the schema

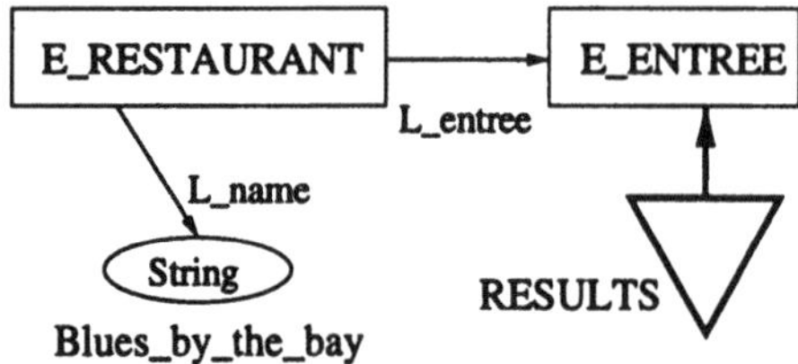

Figure 19.3: A sample WG-Log query

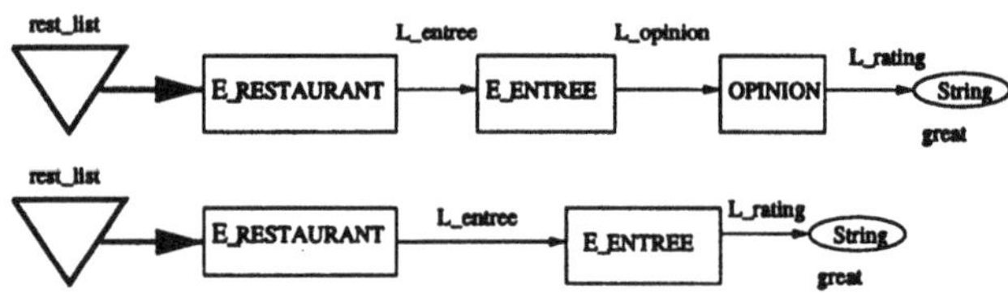

Figure 19.4: Another WG-Log query

of Fig.19.2 was deduced from an OEM data source, where irregular data are represented. Notice for example that the "Entree Rating" is expressed both as an atomic value and as a complex object ("Opinion"). In the schema this situation is depicted by introducing both a slot directly linked to the entity E_Entree via a link L_Rating and a slot linked to the entity E_Opinion which, in turn, is linked to E_Entree. Redundancy does not represent a problem here, since it is related to the schema and not to the instance.

The query of Fig. 19.4 aims at selecting all the restaurants which have an Entree rated 'Great'. Two rules are needed to capture both the situations: a query node 'Rest_list' is linked to both kinds of E_Restaurant entities, thus meaning that a unique result list is requested. Instead, if we were to select only one of the possible rating formats, we should use only the rule pertaining to it.

Note also that most of the WG-Log rules can be composed, like in this case, in a very simple way, by cutting and pasting parts of the schema with the help of a syntax-driven graphical *Query Editor*.

Our schema based approach is particularly apt for representing data which have a well-defined structure because with this method we obtain a compact data representation. However, this approach applies also to very loosely structured data or, in the worst case, to totally unstructured data: for this sort of data the schema and the instance tend to become identical. Our aim is to exploit the structure of data whenever it is possible, without losing the capability of describing unstructured data sources.

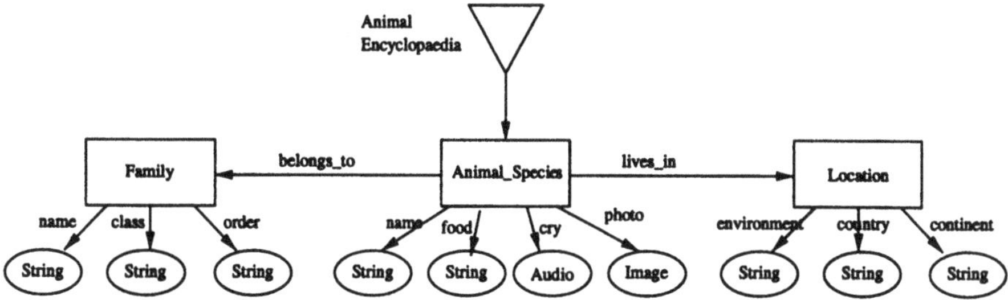

Figure 19.5: A sample WG-Log schema for the animals encyclopaedia

It is important to underline that, though WG-Log has initially been developed for the Web, it can be used also for generic semi-structured data. Consider for example the case of a CD-ROM, containing a flat file system, whose files represent data of an encyclopaedia regarding animals. The relevant information about the different species is available as text files; photos of the animals are available as image files and their cries as audio files. In this example there is a well-defined data domain (animal breeds); this knowledge has to be exploited to create a WG-Log schema (as the one in Fig. 19.5) representing the large amount of information provided in the CD-ROM.

The presence of a schema allows to refer to the data in a precise and compact way; in fact, on the instance graph representation can be added, where all multimedia files are considered just by means of a reference (file name). A software module can then take advantage of this representation to answer the queries submitted by the user, which are based on the abstract (schema) representation.

In the next section we will outline our proposal for the translation of OEM-represented data sources and DataGuides into WG-Log schemata.

19.4 EXPRESSING OEM IN WG-LOG

As seen in the first Section, the idea of representing data as a graph has inspired many projects that deal with (re)structuring and querying semistructured data. The TSIMMIS project adopts a data-model oriented approach based on OEM, whose graph based data model is currently used in other related projects, as LORE and C3 [8]. An example of OEM graph representation is shown in Fig. 19.6

The proposed standard has three main characteristics:

- *object orientation:* each OEM object has an *Object Identifier (OID)* and its representation is composed of three elements:

  – a label that describes what the object represents;

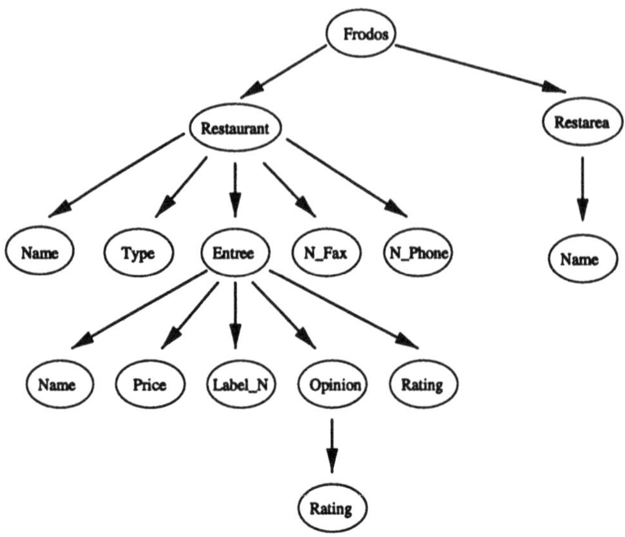

Figure 19.6: A sample OEM graph

- the data type of the object value. Any object may be atomic or complex. In the first case the type may be integer, real, string or any other data considered indivisible. The type is "set" if the object is complex.
- a value that is either the variable length value for atomic objects or, if the object is complex, a collection of one or more OEM subobjects each linked to the parent via a "descriptive textual label" .

- *representation of semantics*: the label component in OEM structure captures the semantics of the object.
- *flexibility*: the OEM structure is flexible enough to encompass all types of information.

An OEM object may be translated into a standard textual format [11]. This format keeps the information about semantics and contents and can be easily parsed by a program. An example of this format is the text in Fig. 19.7 (left).

This is the textual representation of an OEM database which contains complex (Restaurant, Entree, etc) and atomic (Name, Type, etc) objects. As in all semistructured data, in this OEM database there is no fixed schema in advance. In place of a standard schema, the LORE project uses an alternative tool to represent the time-invariant structure of an OEM database: an OEM object, called DataGuide, that is straightforwardly generated from the OEM database and dynamically maintained in order to provide several of the functions normally provided by means of a schema.

It is interesting to remark that, from the same OEM database, many DataGuides may be extracted, each of them representing a summary of the structure of the database. We are interested, in particular, to the so-called ***strong DataGuide*** [12], that induces a straightforward one-to-one correspondence between source target sets and objects in the DataGuide.

Like a WG-Log schema, a DataGuide contains no atomic values and it is essential for both programs and users to explore the OEM database and formulate queries. Since a DataGuide is an OEM object it is possible to translate it into the standard textual format: the graphical representation is depicted in Fig. 19.6.

Representing semistructured data in a synthetic way is also the basic aim of WG-Log schemata; exactly in the same straightforward way as a DataGuide is extracted, we can derive a WG-Log graph based on the OEM source data representation. Unfortunately the OEM syntax does not allow the expression of navigational and presentation-related concepts, which are very useful in the representation of Web sites: think for instance of queries involving some kind of "reachability" relationship between Web pages: this cannot be expressed over OEM or DataGuide representations.

However, even though OEM-based data lack the explicit navigational information contained in a WG-Log schema, any object in the database is either complex or atomic, both types that exist in WG-Log, so we can exploit this information to logically connect the objects.

As we outlined in Section 19.3, WG-Log schemata contain two types of nodes: *"non-printable"* representing complex object classes and *"printable"* representing atomic object classes; it is therefore possible to represent complex OEM objects via WG-Log non-printable nodes with label "E_<*complexObjectLabel*>" and atomic OEM objects by means of printable WG-Log nodes (slots) with label "string".

In an OEM representation, the binding between complex objects and their subobjects is the relationship "part_of".

This scenario is representable in WG-Log by means of logical links from the parent object to subobjects with textual label "L_<*subObjectLabel*>". If the subobject is itself complex it will have a set of labeled links to its component objects. The translation algorithm is specified in Fig. 19.8

Thus, OEM objects correspond to WG-Log objects; as an example, consider the OEM DataGuide object and its WG-Log representation in Fig. 19.9.

The textual format also provides the notion of *SymOid* (Symbolic Object Identifier) [11] to identify objects included as children of multiple complex objects. In particular, it is possible to specify that a SymOid is persistent: in an OEM database at least one persistent SymOid is required to serve as entry point. Considering this persistent SymOid as the entry point of the corresponding WG-Log schema, we can recursively apply the previous method starting from this identifier, in order to obtain a WG-Log representation of an entire OEM data source.

```
<Frodos::Frodos{
        < Restaurant {
                <Name "Blues_by_the_bay">
                <Type "Vegetarian">
                < Entree {
                        <Name "black_bean_soup">
                        <Price 10>
                } >
                < Entree {
                        <Name "asparagus_timbale">
                        <Price 2.04 >
                        < Label_Number 2 >
                } >
        } >
        < Restaurant  {
                <Name "Thai_city">
                <Number_Phone "497-4845">
                <Number_Fax "497-0000">
                <Number_Home "333-3333">
                <Type  "Thai">
                < Entree {
                        < Name "Route_9Red_curry">
                        < Opinion {
                              < Rating "Great">
                       } >
                } >
                < Entree {
                        <Name "green_curry" >
                        <Price 7.95 >
                        <Rating "Great">
                }>
         }>
        < Restarea {
                <Name "Route_9">
        } >
} >
```

Figure 19.7: OEM instance textual representation

```
WGGraph wgraph;
// symoid is the OEM database entry point's identifier
OemObject obj = *symoid;
// translate an OEM object into a WG-Log graph using
//persistent SymOid as entry point.
procedure OemToWGLog(obj) {
  while(obj.hasOtherChildren()) {
    OemObject child = obj.NextChild();
    if(obj.isComplex()) {
      // in an OEM object it's possible to create
      //some cycles using SymOid
      if(!child.alreadyVisited()) {
        // add Oem complex objects as WG-Log node
        wgraph.addNode(obj, child, child.label);
        OemToWGLog(child); // recursive procedure for
                           //complex object
      }
      // add a WG-Log link to a previously visited object
      else wgraph.addLink(obj, child);
    }
    //atomic OEM object is translated into a WG-Log slot
    else wgraph.addSlot(obj, child, child.value);
  } }
```

Figure 19.8: Algorithm to translate an OEM object into a WG-Log graph

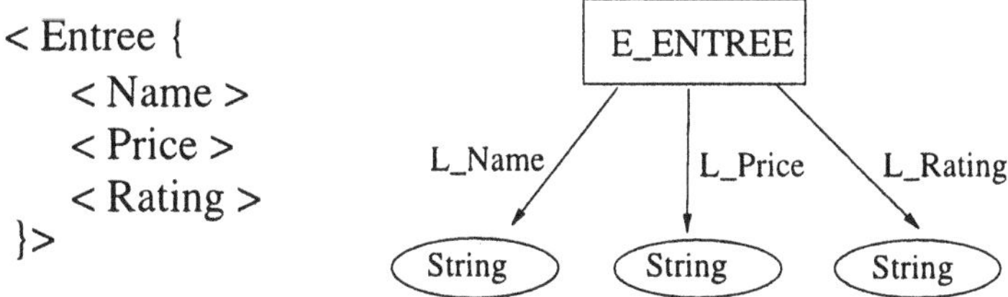

Figure 19.9: The OEM DataGuide textual format (left) and the translation in WG-Log graph

Note that Figure 19.2 depicts the WG-Log schema derived from the Data Guide textual representation of Fig. 19.7, where *Frodos* is the (unique) entry point.

The translation process outlined in this section can be applied to any OEM object and produces a WG-Log graph. DataGuides are themselves OEM objects, therefore the translation of a DataGuide will become a WG-Log schema, while the translation of a generic OEM representation will become a WG-Log instance. Consider now the translation of WG-Log queries into Lorel queries.

The query translation algorithm has to consider several particular conditions that increase its complexity and its readability. In this paper we just describe a simplified version of the algorithm showing how it works on two sample queries.

Let us consider the query depicted in Fig. 19.3, asking for a list of all the Entrees of the "Blues_by_the_bay" restaurant. The target of the operation is represented in WG-Log with a green node; therefore, in the considered query, the result is a list of Entrees. The target information has to be included in the SELECT clause of the Lorel query. The FROM clause is set by default to "root", and it is different only when more complex queries are translated.

The constraints that the result set must satisfy are expressed in the WHERE clause: in the sample WG-Log query, the only condition is that the restaurant name must be the one written in the "name" slot (i.e. "Blues_by_the_bay"). It is necessary to visit the query graph nodes to obtain the proper path expression.

The translation algorithm is specified in Fig.19.10

The Lorel translation of such a query is then:

```
SELECT Restaurant.Entree
FROM root
WHERE *.Restaurant.Name = "Blues_by_the_bay"
```

The "*" character is used here as a wildcard; in this way Lorel can indicate a variable length path starting from the root (specified in the FROM clause). Note that this is not necessary in WG-Log, where no language constraint imposes to navigate starting from the entry point.

Similarly the query depicted in Fig. 19.4 is translated into the following Lorel expression:

```
SELECT Restaurant
FROM root
WHERE *.Restaurant.Entree.Rating = "great"
OR *.Restaurant.Entree.Opinion.Rating = "great"
```

It is worth noticing that in this query we added the boolean operator OR; in this way we can express costraints on disjoint "path-expressions". This translates the WG-Log double-rule query.

19.5 INTERACTION WITH OEM DATASOURCES USING WG-LOG

Let us now use the translations we have defined. The WG-Log project is based on a distributed architecture (Fig. 19.11) whose main focus is the description

```
string WGtoLorel(WGGraph query, WGGraph schema){
   string Lorelquery;
   WGNode result = query.entry();
   // returns node to insert in SELECT
   WGNode root = schema.getroot();
   string select = result.getlabel(); //returns label
   Lorelquery.concat(select);
   string from = schema.getEntry(result);
   //returns path of the entry-node of the query
   Lorelquery.concat(from);
   WGNode node;
   string where;
   while (node = query.NextNode()){
   //returns NULL if all nodes are visited
      for i = 0 to node.numberSlot(){
         string constraint = node.getConstraint();
         //Node.link = value
         where.concat(constraint);
      }
   }
   LorelQuery.concat(where);
   return Lorelquery;
}
```

Figure 19.10: Algorithm to translate a WG-Log query into a LOREL query

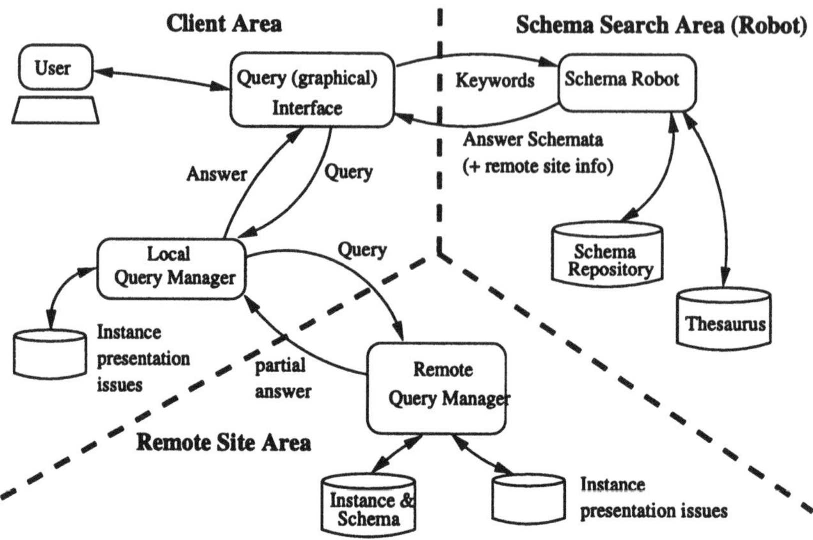

Figure 19.11: The WG-Log architecture

of Web sites by means of schemata. Schemata are made available to the user through a specialized module (Schema Robot) that keeps a repository of the known schemata and helps clients in posing the queries to the data sources more apt to the user needs, based on the information contained in the schemata.

Query execution is performed by the *Remote Query Manager* running at the target Web site, working on the internal representation of the site data. Depending on the site organization, such representation might have been extracted from the HTML pages or might exist from the beginning of the site life.

To integrate WG-Log with other Web Query Systems, the Schema Robot is replaced by a new, more general module, called the Trader, which makes WG-Log schemata describing both WG-Log and foreign data sources available to the user.

WG-Log schemata describing both WG-Log and foreign datasources are made available to the user through a specialized module, the *Trader* module also stored Translator modules as downloadable software components. Integration of OEM datasources managed by a TSIMMIS system (Fig. 19.12) in our general framework is indeed not difficult because on the TSIMMIS provides both the logical structure description (DataGuide), and the knowledge of the instance information. Since a DataGuide contains most information typical of a schema, and since it is possible to translate it from OEM to WG-Log (as described in Section 19.4), we can straightforwardly obtain the WG-Log description of OEM sites to be stored in our Trader repository. Moreover, we

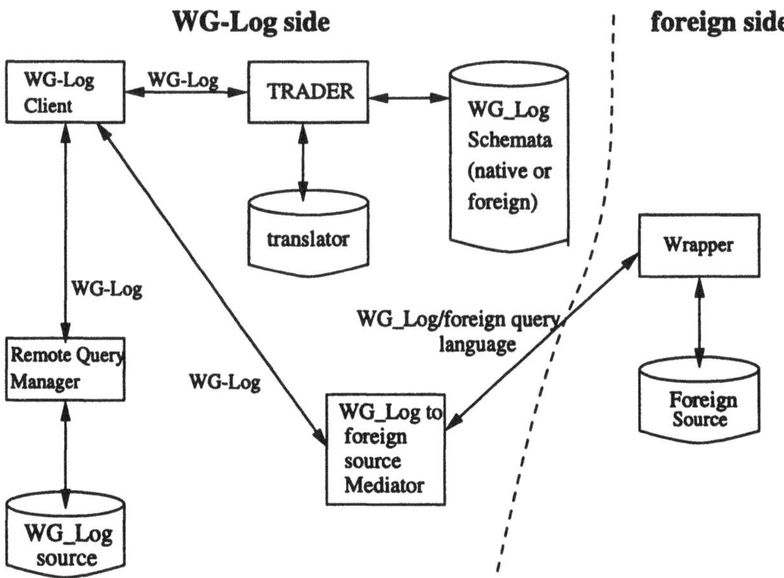

Figure 19.12: An interaction proposal

take advantage of the fact that the TSIMMIS system includes a *Mediator* component whose aim is to receive Lorel queries posed by clients and to forward them to a datasource *Wrapper*, which computes query results in terms of OEM objects that are sent back to the Mediator.

Whenever the user interacts with our Trader module, two basic usage patterns may occur.

The user selects a native WG-Log datasource, receives its schema and composes a WG-Log query. In this case, the query is sent to the remote datasource and execution is performed by the *Remote Query Manager* running at the target Web site, working on WG-Log's own internal representation of the site data.

Otherwise, the user chooses a TSIMMIS-derived schema. Then, a Translator component is tranferred to the user's machine together with the schema and the WG-Log query formulated by the user is converted to a Lorel query.

After the translation phase, the Lorel query is sent to the site Wrapper that will execute it exactly in the same way as if a TSIMMIS Mediator had sent the query. The query result produced by the Wrapper is an OEM object that is sent back to the WG-Log client and translated into a WG-Log result instance.

It is worth noticing that some kinds of WG-Log queries cannot be translated into Lorel, namely the navigational queries. However, such queries will never be issued against an OEM-represented site, since the WG-Log schema of such a site, being derived from an OEM representation, will never contain any navigational information, thus the WG-Log queries will only involve logical concepts, and be translated into Lorel without difficulty.

19.6 CONCLUSIONS AND FUTURE WORK

In this paper we have presented a technique for the representation and querying of semistructured data, which can be effectively coupled with other approaches for querying the World Wide Web. In particular, we have shown the feasibility of this integration on the example of the Tsimmis/Lorel projects, which are based on the representation of site contents via the Object Exchange Model (OEM). This experience can be easily transferred to other data-model based Web Query Systems, like Araneus and Strudel, thus allowing the WG-Log environment to seamlessly manage information about site contents derived from different approaches.

Acknowledgments
The authors wish to thank A. Dovier, M. Baldi and F. Insaccanebbia for many useful discussions on the subject. Thanks are also due to H. Garcia-Molina and R. Goldman for their assistance with the TSIMMIS system.

References

[1] Serge Abiteboul, Querying Semi-Structured Data, ICDT'97, 6th International Conference on Database Theory, Vol. 1186, pp. 1-18, Springer, 8-10 Jan 1997.

[2] N. Ashish, C. Knoblock. Wrapper generator Semi-structured Internet Sources, Proceedings of the ACM SIGMOD International Conference on Management of Data.

[3] P. Atzeni, A. Masci, G. Mecca, P. Merialdo, and E. Tabet. ULIXES: Building relational views over the Web. In Proceedings of the 13th International Conference on Data Engineering (ICDE'97), pages 576–576, Washington - Brussels - Tokyo, April 1997. IEEE.

[4] S. Abiteboul, D. Quass, J. McHugh, J. Widom and J. Wiener. The Lorel query language for semistructured data. Journal of digital Libraries, November 1996.

[5] R. J. Bayardo, Jr. and W. Bohrer and R. Brice and A. Cichocki and J. Fowler and A. Helal and V. Kashyap and T. Ksiezyk and G. Martin and M. Nodine and M. Rashid and M. Rusinkiewicz and R. Shea and C. Unnikrishnan and A. Unruh and D. Woelk, InfoSleuth: Agent-Based Semantic Integration of Information in Open and Dynamic Environments, Proceedings of the ACM SIGMOD International Conference on Management of Data, Vol. 26,2, pp. 195-206, ACM Press, May 13-15 1997.

[6] M. Baldi, E. Damiani, and F. Insaccanebbia. Structuring and querying the Web through graph-oriented languages. In *Proc. of SEBD 1997*, SEBD Conferences, Verona, Italy, June 1997.

[7] S. Chawathe, H. Garcia-Molina, J. Hammer, K. Ireland, Y. Papakonstantinou, J. Ullman, J. Widom. The TSIMMIS project: Integration of heterogenous information sources. In proceedings of IPSJ, Tokyo, Japan, October 1994.

[8] S. Chawathe and H. Garcia-Molina. Meaningful Change Detection in Structured Data.Proceedings of the ACM SIGMOD International Conference on Management of Data.Tuscon, Arizona, May 1997.

[9] E. Damiani, L. Tanca. Semantic Approach to Structuring and Querying the Web Sites. In *Proceedings of 7th IFIP Work. Conf. on Database Semantics (DS-97)*, 1997.

[10] M. Fernandez, D. Florescu, J. Kang, A. Levy, D. Suciu, STRUDEL: A Web Site Management System, Proceedings of the ACM SIGMOD International Conference on Management of Data, Vol. 26,2, pp. 549-552, ACM Press, May 13-15 1997.

[11] R. Goldman, S. Chawathe, A. Crespo, J. McHugh. A Standard Textual Interchange Format for the Object Exchange Model (OEM). Manuscript available from http://www-db.stanford.edu

[12] R. Goldman and J. Widom. DataGuides: Enabling Query Formulation and Optimization in Semistructured Databases, VLDB'97, Proceedings of 23rd International Conference on Very Large Data Bases, pp. 436-445, 1997.

[13] J. Hammer, H. Garcia-Molina, J. Cho, R. Aranha, A. Crespo. Extracting Semistructured Information from the Web. Paper available at http://www-db.stanford.edu

[14] E. Miller, B. Schloss, O. Lassila, and R. Swick. Resource description framework model and syntax. Technical report, W3 Consortium, oct 1997. Revision 1,02, `http://www.w3.org/TR/WD-rdf-syntax/`.

[15] B.Oliboni, L.Tanca and D.Veronese. Using WG-Log to represent semistructured data: the example of OEM. In *Proceedings of SEBD 1998*, Ancona, Italy, Jun 1998.

[16] Y. Papakonstantinou and H. Garcia-Molina and J. Widom, Object Exchange Across Heterogeneous information Sources, Proceedings of the 11th International Conference on Data Engineering, pp.251-260, IEEE Computer Society Press, Mar 1995.

[17] J. Paredaens, P. Peelman, L. Tanca. G-Log: A Declarative Graphical Query Language. IEEE Trans. on Knowledge and Data Eng., vol.7, 1995 pp. 436-453

[18] D. Quass, J. Widom, R. Goldman, K. Haas, Q. Luo, J. McHugh, S. Nestorov, A. Rajaraman, H. Rivero, S. Abiteboul, J. D. Ullman, J. L. Wiener, LORE: A Lightweight Object REpository for Semistructured Data, Proceedings of the 1996 ACM SIGMOD International Conference on Management of Data, p. 549, 4-6 Jun 1996.

20 ONTOBROKER: ONTOLOGY BASED ACCESS TO DISTRIBUTED AND SEMI-STRUCTURED INFORMATION

Stefan Decker, Michael Erdmann, Dieter Fensel and Rudi Studer

University of Karlsruhe, Institute AIFB, D-76128 Karlsruhe, Germany

{decker, erdmann, fensel, studer}@aifb.uni-karlsruhe.de

http://www.aifb.uni-karlsruhe.de/WBS/broker

Abstract: The World Wide Web (WWW) can be viewed as the largest multimedia database that has ever existed. However, its support for query answering and automated inference is very limited. Metadata and domain specific ontologies were proposed by several authors to solve this problem. We developed Ontobroker which uses formal ontologies to extract, reason, and generate metadata in the WWW. The paper describes the formalisms and tools for formulating queries, defining ontologies, extracting metadata, and generating metadata in the format of the Resource Description Framework (RDF), as recently proposed by the World Wide Web Consortium (W3C). These methods provide a means for semantic based query handling even if the information is spread over several sources. Furthermore, the generation of RDF descriptions enables the exploitation of the ontological information in RDF-based applications.

20.1 INTRODUCTION

In more and more application areas large collections of digitized multimedia information are gathered and have to be maintained (e.g. in medicine, chemical applications or product catalogs). Therefore, there is an increasing demand for tools and techniques supporting the management and usage of digital multimedia data. Especially the World Wide Web (WWW) can be regarded as the largest multimedia database that ever existed and every day more and more data is available through it. Its support for retrieval and usage is very limited because its main retrieval services are keyword-based search facilities carried out by different search engines, web crawlers, web indices, man-made web catalogs etc. Given a keyword, such services deliver a set of pages from the web that use this keyword. *Ontologies* and metadata (based on ontologies) are proposed as a means for retrieving and using multimedia data [4] [32]. They provide "an explicit specification of a conceptualization" [16] and are discussed in the literature as means to support knowledge sharing and reuse [9] [14]. This approach to reuse is based on the assumption that if a modeling scheme – i.e. an ontology— is explicitly specified and agreed upon by a number of agents, it is then possible for them to share and reuse knowledge. Clearly, it is unlikely that there will be a common ontology for the whole population of the WWW and every subject. This leads to the *metaphor of a newsgroup* or *domain specific ontology* [19] [26] to define the terminology for a group of people which share a common view on a specific domain. Using ontologies for information retrieval has certain advantages over simple keyword based access methods: An ontology provides a shared vocabulary for expressing information about the contents of (multimedia) documents. In addition, it includes axioms for specifying relationships between concepts. Such an ontology may then in turn be used to formulate semantic queries and to deliver exactly the information we are interested in. Furthermore, the axioms provide a means for deriving information which has been specified only implicitly.

These advantages come with the price of having to provide information in a more formal manner. Since a large portion of the WWW is formulated using HTML, which is not an entirely formal language, the following questions arise:

- How can information be represented (in a sufficiently formal way) in the WWW?
- How can this information be extracted and maintained in the WWW?
- How can we reason with it and what inferences are possible?

To answer the first question, we have to look at the effort toward standardizing data, metadata, and ontologies. XML based languages [38] are becoming standard formats for representing data in the WWW (even for multimedia data, see e.g. Precision Graphics Mark-up Language [28] or the Synchronized Multimedia Integration Language [34]. Based on XML, the metadata standard RDF (Resource Description Framework [29]) and the RDF schema language [30], which can be used to express ontologies, are under development and will probably be widely used in the near future. The use of these standards allows to access a variety of data in the WWW in a more formal way than today.

For answering the other two questions, we developed a system called ONTOBROKER [10] [27] with the following core elements (see Figure 20.1):

- The most central part are the ontologies. They are used in several components of the system. They are expressed in a representation language based on Frame-Logic [20].
- The Ontocrawler extracts formal knowledge from HTML pages. This is done in two different ways: for large collections of web pages with a similar structure a *wrapper* [37] generates formal descriptions of the

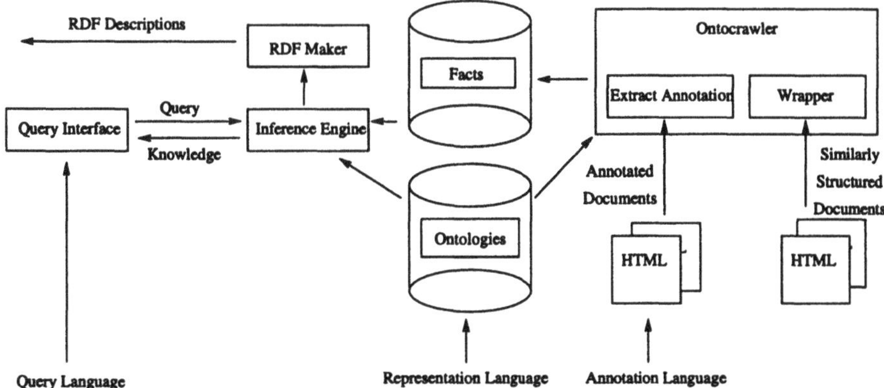

Figure 20.1: The architecture of ONTOBROKER.

content of the pages in relation to a certain ontology. Often the effort for constructing specialized wrappers is too high: in this case an annotation language is used for enabling providers to enrich web documents with ontological information in an integrated, maintenance-friendly manner.

- The inference engine exploits the formal semantics of the representation language and enables well defined automatic reasoning.

- The RDF-Maker exploits the inference engine and generates an RDF representation of information inferable from the ontology and the facts with respect to a given web resource.

- The query interface enables the interactive formulation of queries while browsing the ontology and selecting the terms constituting the query.

Thus ONTOBROKER is an integrated, comprehensive system to extract, reason and generate domain specific metadata. According to the metadata classification of [19] our approach deals with *domain-specific metadata* that is *content-descriptive* and utilizes a domain specific ontology. Additionally the metadata we generate is also *direct content-based*, thus allowing semantic-based access to web information. In addition, the reasoning service provides a means for deriving information which has been specified only implicitly in the web sources. The system is fully implemented and can be accessed via [27]. For a brief introduction of the system cf. [10].

The paper is organized as follows. In section 20.2, we will present the representation languages and the inference engine used in ONTOBROKER. Section 20.3 introduces some basics about the Resource Description Framework and the web standards developed by the W3C and relates these developments with the ONTOBROKER approach. We conclude with related work, future work, and a brief summary.

20.2 THE LANGUAGES AND INFERENCE ENGINE OF ONTOBROKER

In this section we discuss the formalisms used by ONTOBROKER. After describing the representation language used to define ontologies we discuss the query formalism that is used by a client asking for information. Then we present the inference engine that computes the answers to queries. And finally an extension to HTML is presented that allows the smooth integration of ontological annotation in existing web pages.

20.2.1 The Representation Formalism for Ontologies

The basic support we want to provide is answering queries using instances of an ontology. This ontology may be described by taxonomies and rules. Since there are effective and efficient query evaluation procedures for Horn-logic-like languages we based our inference engine on Horn-logic. However, simple Horn-logic is not appropriate from an epistemological point of view for two reasons:

1. The epistemological primitives of simple predicate logic are not rich enough to support adequate representations of ontologies.

2. It is often very artificial to express logical relationships via Horn clauses.

We will subsequently discuss how we overcame both shortcomings.

20.2.1.1 Elementary Expressions. Usually, ontologies are defined via concepts or classes, is-a relationships, attributes, further relationships, and axioms. Therefore an adequate language for defining the ontology has to provide modeling primitives for these notions. Frame-Logic [20] provides such modeling primitives and integrates them into a logical framework providing a Horn-logic subset. Furthermore, in contrast to Description Logic, expressing the ontology in Frame-Logic allows queries that directly use parts of the ontology as first class citizens. That is, not only instances and their values but also concept and attribute names can be provided as answers via variable substitutions.

We use a slightly modified variant of Frame-Logic, which suits our needs. Principally the following elementary modeling primitives are used:

- Subclassing: `C1::C2`, meaning that class `C1` is a subclass of `C2`.

- Instance of: `O:C`, meaning that `O` is an instance of class `C`.

- Attribute declaration: `C1[A =>> C2]`, meaning that for the instances of class `C1` an attribute `A` is defined whose value must be an instance of `C2`.

- Attribute value: `O[A->>V]`, meaning that the instance `O` has an attribute `A` with value `V`.

- Part-of: `O1 <: O2`, meaning that `O1` is a part of `O2`.

- Relations: predicate expressions like `p(a1,...,a2)` can be used as in usual logic-based representation formalisms, except that not only terms can be used as arguments but also object expressions.

20.2.1.2 Complex Expressions. From the elementary expressions more complex ones can be built. We distinguish between the following complex expressions: facts, rules, double rules, and queries. Facts are ground elementary expressions. A rule consists of a head, the implication sign <-, and the body. The head is just a conjunction of elementary expressions (connected using AND). The body is a complex formula built from elementary expressions and the usual predicate logic connectives (implies: ->, implied by: <-, equivalent: <->, AND, OR, and NOT). Variables can be introduced in front of the head (with a FORALL-quantifier) or anywhere in the body (using EXISTS and FORALL-quantifiers). A double rule is an expression of the form:

```
head <-> body
```

where the head and body must be conjunctions of elementary expressions. Examples of double rules are given in Table 20.1. An EBNF syntax description of the complete representation language is given in [12].

20.2.1.3 An Illustration. Ontologies defined with this language mainly consist of three parts:

- The concept hierarchy defines the subclass relationship between different classes.

- For classes attribute definitions are given.

- A set of rules defines relationships between different concepts and attributes.

This illustration is taken from the $(KA)^2$-Initiative [3] where a community of researchers agrees on an ontology about relevant aspects of a research community. Table 20.1 provides part of that ontology. The concept hierarchy consists of elementary expressions declaring subclass relationships. The attribute definitions declare attributes of concepts and the valid types which values of these attributes must have. The first rule ensures symmetry of cooperation and the second rule specifies that whenever a person is known to have a publication, then the publication also has an author who is that particular person and vice versa. This kind of rule completes the knowledge base with information that is distributed and incomplete and thus reduces development as well as maintenance effort. Especially the double rules are very useful, since they explicate e.g. a connection between two object-attribute-value triples. The third rule uses the ontology itself to complete the knowledge base. Based on the schema information missing type information for attribute values are deduced.

Concept Hierarchy	Attribute Definitions

`Object[].`
 	
`Person :: Object.`
 	
`Employee :: Person.`
 	
`Researcher :: Employee.`
 	
`Publication :: Object.`
	`Person[`
	` firstname =>> STRING;`
	` lastName =>> STRING;`
	` eMail =>> STRING;`
	` publication =>> Publication;`
	` ...].`
	
	`Employee[`
	` affiliation =>> Organization;`
	` ...].`
	
	`Researcher[`
	` researchInterest =>> Topic;`
	` cooperatesWith =>> Researcher;`
	` ...].`
	
	`Publication[`
	` author =>> Person;`
	` title =>> STRING;`
	` year =>> NUMBER;`
	` abstract =>> STRING].`

Rules

`FORALL Person1, Person2`
`  Person1:Researcher[cooperatesWith ->> Person2] <-`
`    Person2:Researcher[cooperatesWith ->> Person1].`
 	
`FORALL Person1, Publ1`
`  Publ1:Publication[author ->> Person1] <->`
`    Person1:Person[publication ->> Publ1].`
 	
`FORALL O,C,A,V,T`
`  V:T <- C[A=>>T] AND O:C[A->>V].`

Table 20.1: A part of an example ontology

20.2.2 The Query Formalism

The query formalism is oriented towards the syntax of Frame-Logic that defines the notion of instances, classes, attributes, and values. The generic schema for this is:

```
O:C[A->>V]
```

meaning that the object `O` is an instance of the class `C` with an attribute `A` that has a certain value `V`. Variables, constants or arbitrary expressions can be used at each position in the above scheme. Furthermore, because the ontology is part of the knowledge base itself the ontology definitions can be used to validate the knowledge base. In the following we will provide some queries as examples to illustrate our approach.

If we are interested in information about researchers with certain properties. e.g. we want to know the home page, the last name and the email address of all researchers with first name Richard, we achieve this with the following query:

```
FORALL Obj, LN, EM <-
  Obj:Researcher[firstName->>"Richard";
                 lastName->>LN;email->>EM].
```

In our example ONTOBROKER gives the following answer (actually, there is only one researcher with first name Richard in the knowledge base.

```
Obj = http://www.iiia.csic.es/richard/index.html
LN = Benjamins
EM = mailto:richard@iiia.csic.es
```

Another example asks for the home page of all researchers who cooperate with the researcher with last name Motta:

```
FORALL Obj, CP <-
  Obj:Researcher[lastName ->>"Motta"; cooperatesWith->>CP].
```

The interesting point in this query is that the ontology contains a rule specifying the symmetry of cooperation. That means, even if the researcher with last name Motta did not specify a cooperation with any researcher, ONTOBROKER could deduce such a cooperation, if another researcher stated that he cooperates with Mr. Motta.

Another possibility is to query the knowledge base for information about the ontology itself, e.g. the query

```
FORALL Att, T <- Researcher[Att=>>T]
```

asks for all attributes of the class Researcher and their associated types.

These queries can be posed via a web interface, but since average web users cannot be expected to be familiar with F-Logic a graphical substitution exists that is much more comprehensive. It visualizes the ontology and hides a lot of the unnecessary syntax. A description of this interface can be found in [10].

20.2.3 *Providing Input for* ONTOBROKER

To be able to answer queries, ONTOBROKER needs facts which are stored in its knowledge base. The knowledge base contains knowledge collected from scattered web sources. [1] distinguish three classes of web sources:

- *Multiple-instance sources* share the same structure but provide different information, e.g. the CIA World Fact Book [5], provides information about more than 200 different countries stored on more than 200 similarly structured pages (one page per country).
- *Single-instance sources* provide large amounts of data in a structured format.
- *Loosely structured pages* have no generalizable structure, e.g. personal home pages.

All these sources contain knowledge that should be made accessible by ONTOBROKER. To allow an integration of this knowledge into the knowledge base it has to be formalized. This can be done in two ways:

Sources falling into the first two categories allow us to implement wrappers [37] that automatically extract factual knowledge from these sources. If the structure of the pages is known and stable over time these wrappers can automatically create parts of the knowledge base of ONTOBROKER and thus allow inferencing and query answering about the provided information. We applied this approach to the CIA World Fact Book using a simple ontology about countries and their characteristics.

The second way to provide a formal representation of unstructured information is based on manual work. Since formalization in the third case mentioned above can hardly be achieved automatically we chose a manual annotation approach to capture loosely structured information. Large amounts of the information provided in the WWW are formulated using the Hyper-Text Mark-up Language (HTML) on hardly structured pages. We developed a minor extension to the HTML syntax (the onto-attribute) to enable ontological annotation of web pages. Annotating resources with semantic information has certain advantages over simple meta-tagging of resources, i.e.:

- The embedded annotations are located physically close to the rendered information they belong to.
- The semantic information is in part represented as the informal text of the resource, i.e. the text can be reused in a formal way, e.g. as the value of attributes.
- In the same way hyper links contained on web pages can be reused to establish formal relations between concepts.

The general idea behind our approach (see [12] for more details) is to take an HTML page as a starting point and to add only few ontologically relevant

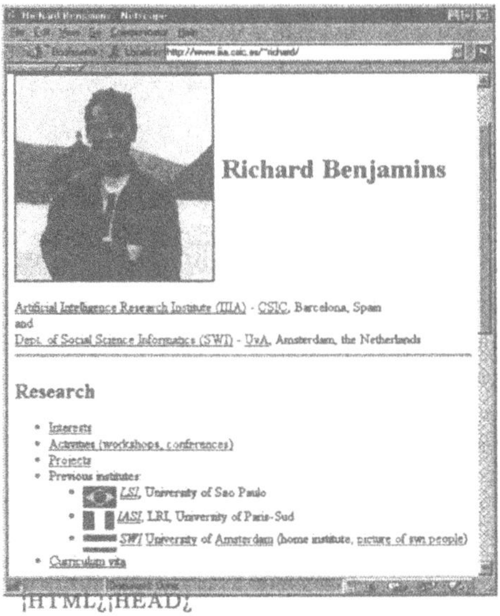

```
¡HTML¿¡HEAD¿
¡a onto="page:Researcher"¿ ¡/a¿
¡TITLE¿ Richard Benjamins ¡/TITLE¿
¡/HEAD¿
¡H1¿ ¡A HREF="pictures/id-rich.gif"¿
¡IMG SRC="pictures/richard.gif"¿¡/A¿
¡a onto="page[photo=href]"
   HREF="http://www.iiia.csic.es/richard/
             pictures/richard.gif" ¿¡/a¿

¡a onto="page[firstName=body]"¿Richard¡/a¿
¡a onto="page[lastName=body]"¿Benjamins¡/a¿
¡/h1¿ ¡p¿

¡A onto="page[affiliation=body]"¿
Artificial Intelligence Research Institute
(IIIA)¡/A¿ -
¡a href="http://www.csic.es/"¿CSIC¡/a¿,
Barcelona, Spain ¡br¿
```

Figure 20.2: An example of an annotated web page.

tags to its mark-up. By these minor changes the information contained in the page is annotated and made accessible as facts to ONTOBROKER. This approach allows providers to annotate their web pages gradually, i.e. they do not have to completely formalize the knowledge contained therein. Further, the pages remain readable by standard browsers. Thus, there is no need to keep several different sources up-to-date and consistent which reduces development as well as maintenance effort considerably. All factual ontological information is contained in the HTML mark-up itself.

We provide three different epistemological primitives to annotate ontological information in web documents:

1. An object identified by a URL (Uniform Resource Locator) can be defined as an instance of a certain class.

2. The value of an object's attribute can be set.

3. A relationship between two or more objects may be established.

All three primitives are expressed by using an extended version of a frequent HTML tag, i.e. the anchor tag.

Typically a provider of information first defines an object. This is done by stating which class of the ontology it is an instance of. For example, if Richard Benjamins (his home page and a part of its sources are depicted in Figure 20.2) would like to define himself as a researcher, he would say the URL of his home page is an instance of the class researcher. To express this in our HTML extension he uses the following line on his home page.

```
<a onto=" 'http://www.iiia.csic.es/richard' : Researcher">
```

The identifier `'http://www.iiia.csic.es/richard'` denotes an object, namely an instance of class researcher. Actually this id is the URL of Richard Benjamins' home page, thus, from now on he as a researcher is denoted by the URL of his home page (see Figure 20.2).

Each class is associated with a set of attributes. Each instance of a class can define values for these attributes. To define an attribute value on a web page the knowledge provider has to list the object, the attribute, and the value. For example, the ontology contains an attribute email for each object of class researcher. If Richard Benjamins wants to provide his email address, he uses this line on his home page.

```
<a onto=" 'http://www.iiia.csic.es/richard'
              [email='mailto:richard@iiia.csic.es'] ">
```

This line states that the object denoted by the handle has the value `'mailto: richard@iiia.csic.es'` for the attribute email.

Several objects and attributes can be defined on a single web page, and several objects can be related to each other explicitly. Given the name of a relation `REL` and the object handles `Obj1` to `Objn` this definition looks like this:

```
<a onto= "REL(Obj1, Obj2, Obj3, ..., Objn)" >
```

The listed examples look rather clumsy, esp. because of their long object handles and the redundancy due to writing information twice, once for the browser and a second time for ONTOBROKER. So the annotation language provides some means to ease annotating web pages and get rid of a big share of the clumsiness and redundancy [12]. A set of keywords with special meanings is allowed as part of the annotation syntax. The keyword *page* represents the whole web page where the ontological mark-up is contained. This is useful when looking at the page as a representative of an object. For example, a home page of a researcher might represent that person in the knowledge base. This can be defined by the following kind of annotation:

```
<a onto= "page:Researcher">
```

Table 20.2: Principle mechanism for translating F-Logic to predicate logic

Frame Logic	Meaning	Predicate Logic
`C1 :: C2`	class C1 is a subclass of C2	$sub(C1, C2)$
`O : C`	O is an instance of class C	$isa(O, C)$
`C1[A=>>C2]`	for the instances of C1 an attribute A is defined, whose value must be an instance of C2	$att\_type(C1, A, C2)$
`O[A->>V]`	the instance O has an attribute A, whose value is V	$att\_val(O, A, V)$
`O1 <: O2`	O1 is a part of O2	$part\_of(O1, O2)$

The following annotation defines the affiliation attribute of the object denoted by the URL of the current page and takes the value from the anchor-tag's href-attribute.

```
<a onto="page[affiliation=href]"
   href="http://www.iiia.csic.es/">
```

The *href* keyword allows us to establish relations between objects without a lot of typing, because the hyper-links can be reused within the ontological mark-up.

Not only hyper-links can be directly integrated as semantic information, the text that is rendered by a browser can also become a part of the formal knowledge, e.g.

```
<a onto="page[firstName=body]> Richard </a>
```

defines Richard (contained between `<a ...>` and `</a>`) as an attribute value for firstName. The keyword *body* allows this kind of reuse. Through these conventions the annotation of web pages becomes more concise and redundancy can be nearly avoided. This tight coupling eases metadata maintenance for frequently changing resources, since changing the rendered data is automatically reflected in the semantic mark-up.

Although the technique just presented is currently tailored towards HTML, it can be easily adapted for any XML based mark-up language: the only changes required are slight modifications of the respective document type definition (DTD) of that language. This is especially important since more and more applications of XML languages are currently developed.

20.2.4 The Inference Engine of ONTOBROKER

The inference engine of ONTOBROKER has two key parts: the one that does the translation (and retranslation) process from the rich modeling language (F-Logic) to a restricted one (Horn logic) and the part that does the evaluation of expressions in the restricted language.

The input of the inference engine consists of the ontology, collected facts from the web and queries formulated in Frame-Logic. We have decided against direct evaluation of expressions of the rich modeling language. There are techniques known for evaluating Frame-Logic [15], but they do not support the whole language and the semantics we need (e.g. full first order rule bodies). Furthermore a direct evaluation approach would be very inflexible, a small change in the input language would result in changes of the whole system and building a specialized inference engine for a special semantics requires an extraordinary effort. Instead a Frame-Logic-translator translates the Frame-Logic expressions via several intermediate states to first-order logic expressions. Table 20.2 gives an idea of how this translation is performed. After several transformation steps (cf. [6], [12] for more details) we obtain a normal logic program. Techniques from deductive databases are applicable to implement the bottom-up fix-point evaluation procedure. Because we allow negation in the clause body we have to carefully select an appropriate semantics and evaluation procedure. If the resulting program is stratified, we use simple stratified semantics and evaluate it with a technique called dynamic filtering [21] [13]. But the translation of Frame Logic usually results in a logic program with only a limited number of predicates (all object expressions are compiled into the same predicate), so the resulting program is often not stratified. To deal with non-stratified negation we have adopted the well-founded model semantics [35] and compute this semantics with an extension of dynamic filtering.

20.3 WEB STANDARDS AND ONTOBROKER

20.3.1 RDF/RDFS and Frame-Logic

In the WWW the need for a standardized notation for metadata led to the development of the Resource Description Framework (RDF) by the W3C. RDF is a framework for describing general-purpose metadata that is richer than simple keyword based metadata annotations, since it introduces the notion of resources. Resources are objects that can have certain properties and can be related to other resources (cf. [29] for the current status of the framework definition). Any object that can be addressed via a URL may be a resource in the sense of RDF. Since a resource together with attached properties and values can be used again as a resource, this representation style allows us to build labeled directed graphs that resemble semantic nets.

A proposed syntax for RDF uses XML so that RDF specifications can be easily integrated in applications following the current trend towards XML as *the* language for sharing information. Due to that RDF will probably become a widely recognized language and representation formalism for metadata that can serve as an interlingua for information interchange.

RDF is complemented by a schema definition language (RDF Schema) [30]. RDFS is a format for defining the terminology that can be used to describe RDF data. It basically allows us to define classes, attributes (property types), value ranges and cardinality constraints for property types. `RDF:instanceOf` and

`RDFS:subClassOf` are examples of predefined property types, which correspond to similar notions in frame-based or object-oriented languages. So RDFS allows the definition of ontologies for RDF specifications in a way which has some similarities to F-Logic-based ontologies.

However there exist some major differences:

- Both representation formalisms support an (object, attribute, value) view on the object level, and a (class, attribute, type) view on the schema level, so both have a similar kind of representation.
- F-Logic supports inference rules which can be used to make implicit knowledge explicit, e.g. to derive attribute values of objects.
- F-Logic has a well defined semantics and proof theory, thus building an inference engine for it is a clearly defined task, whereas the semantics of RDF still has to be defined formally.
- RDF supports the reification of resource descriptions, i.e. an RDF expression (consisting of a resource, a property type, and a value) can be the resource of another description. This is not possible in F-Logic.
- The schemas of RDF allow the definition of attributes, so called property types. These property types are —in contrast to frame based languages like F-Logic— general in the sense that they do exist independently of classes. Thus, it is not possible to give the same name to different properties for several classes if they have different value ranges or cardinalities.

20.3.2 What has ONTOBROKER *to offer to RDF?*

RDFMaker. The kinds of information that can be stored in RDF metadata include concepts that are stored in the ontological annotations for ONTOBROKER. To make this information accessible to a wider community we developed a tool (RDFMaker, cf. [7] and figure 20.1) that translates these annotations (in ONTOBROKER syntax) to metadata (in RDF syntax). The tool takes an annotated web page and computes all inferable information based on the ontology and the annotated facts. Subsequently, it formulates all derived information according to the RDF definition and adds it to the source. In this way any information seeker being capable of understanding RDF (e.g. information agents) can profit from the annotation made for ONTOBROKER. Thus the advantages of ontological annotations of resources and the homogeneity, accessibility and wide dissemination (at least in the future) of RDF metadata descriptions are combined.

Maintenance and Redundancy Reduction. RDF defines a portable way of expressing metadata, but it is separated from the data. So maintenance of metadata might result in high effort: if the data change, the metadata also has to be changed to keep both in sync. A better approach is to combine both aspects. In ONTOBROKER we use annotations that are included inside the data and directly refer to the information contained in the pages, thus ontological information can be automatically extracted and therefore is always consistent and up-to-date. When using RDFMaker to automatically generate RDF descriptions from the ONTOBROKER annotations, the problem of maintaining metadata can be reduced. At the same time the degree of redundancy is lowered because information from the HTML pages is directly incorporated in the metadata by RDFMaker.

Inferencing. Although RDF/RDFS does not allow the formulation of rules, there exist useful inference tasks for RDF. The property type RDFS: subClassOf is transitive [30, section 2.2.2], thus information seekers looking for all instances of a special class c should retrieve all instances of all subclasses of c as well. Another example for a useful inference task is the deduction of implicit information. RDFS allows to restrict the ranges of property types. This information could be used to infer `RDFS:instanceOf` relations and thus explicating implicit information. For example, if the property type `cooperatesWith` has the range restriction researcher, any resource that is the value of this property type can be inferred as belonging to class researcher. This is desirable, because knowledge on the WWW is often incomplete and this is a possibility to make it more complete.

Nevertheless, there is (as far as we know) no system available that contains an inference mechanism for RDF. To be able to handle inference tasks and — more general— rules we propose to use RDF as a representation language for metadata and F-Logic as the basis for the inference engine. Thus, RDF/RDFS should be used to represent metadata within the websources and F-Logic should be used when answering queries that are based on an ontology (including rules). This combination of a generally accepted and standardized representation language and a powerful and flexible inference engine would drastically enhance the power and usability of RDF. The ONTOBROKER-system has already proved the feasibility of this combination.

20.4 CONCLUSIONS, RELATED AND FUTURE WORK

Up to now, the inference capabilities of the WWW are very limited. In essence, they are restricted to keyword-based search facilities which are offered by the various web services. This is clearly not sufficient when dealing with reusable multimedia data on the WWW. As a way to overcome these problems ontologies and metadata were proposed by several authors [10] [19] [26] [4] and led to a number of systems.

Similar approaches to ours in regard to metadata are InfoHarness [33] and Observer [25]. InfoHarness extracts metadata with a kind of wrappers. Information brokering is done primarily on the level of representation and not based on domain specific ontologies. E.g. mainly metadata like author, title, file size etc. are extracted and used for query answering. Therefore, large ontologies with rules are not supported; inferences are not possible.

The Observer system can be seen as a successor of InfoHarness: it aims at integrating multiple information sources, each with its own domain specific ontology. A user poses a query in his own user ontology. This query is translated using synonyms to queries according to the component ontology and evaluated by the component systems. Observer focuses on integrating multiple ontologies, and thus several aspects are different from ONTOBROKER. In ONTOBROKER it is possible to specify rules that express dependencies between different terms from the ontology and to complete information using the ontology itself. Because Observer uses description logics this is not possible in Observer. Furthermore, ONTOBROKER is a complete approach supporting a user with an annotation language, an inference engine and a graphical query interface, while support like this is not available for the Observer system.

Another approach similar to ours is SHOE [24] which introduced the idea of using ontologies to annotate information in the WWW. HTML pages are annotated via ontologies to support information retrieval based on semantic information. However, there are major differences in the underlying philosophy: In SHOE, providers of information can introduce arbitrary extensions to a given ontology. Furthermore, no central provider index is defined. As a consequence, when specifying a query the client may not know all the ontological terms which have been used to annotate the HTML pages and the web crawler has to visit the entire WWW to ensure to find all annotated knowledge fragments. The answers given to a query may be incomplete because the used ontologies are not entirely known and the web crawler cannot find all relevant pages.

In contrast, ONTOBROKER relies on the notion of an *Ontogroup* and domain specific ontology defining a group of web users that agree on an ontology for a given subject. Therefore, both the information providers and the clients have complete knowledge of the available ontological terms. In addition, the ontogroup is stored in a provider index used by Ontocrawler when collecting all annotated HTML pages. Thus, ONTOBROKER can deliver complete answers to the posed queries. The philosophy of ONTOBROKER is also tailored to homogeneous intranet applications, e.g. for knowledge management within an enterprise. In this context the information providers are well known and the ontology can be fixed because in the enterprise a common view on the world should exist.

SHOE and ONTOBROKER also differ with respect to their inferencing capabilities. SHOE uses description logic as its basic formalism, currently offers rather limited inferencing capabilities and does not support RDF. ONTOBROKER relies on Frame-Logic and supports more complex inferencing for answering queries (see [18] [11] for a comparison of the two representation and reasoning paradigms).

Because ontologies and metadata are means to overcome the restriction of the current capabilities to access the web the definition, representation, extraction and maintenance of metadata are questions that have to be solved. This paper presented ONTOBROKER, a system that addresses these tasks. ONTOBROKER uses F-Logic to define the ontology and to represent a knowledge base that allows inferencing. Metadata extraction from a web page is done either by wrappers or by a web crawler that identifies special semantic tagging in web pages. In ONTOBROKER this annotation information is tightly integrated into the HTML mark-up. This reduces redundancy of information and makes maintenance of metadata a simpler task since metadata can easily be generated (e.g. in RDF) when changes in the original sources occur. The techniques developed for annotations are transferable to all XML-based languages.

ONTOBROKER provides means for semantic-based query handling even if the information is spread over several sources. Furthermore, the generation of RDF descriptions enables the exploitation of the ontological information in RDF-based applications —intelligent agents can use the knowledge provided by the RDF descriptions. The system is currently the basis for realizing the Knowledge Acquisition Initiative $(KA)^2$ [3] [2] and for developing a knowledge management system for industrial designers in regard to ergonomic questions. In the latter project, the same knowledge may be used by humans and for inferences of the system. This twofold use of the same piece of knowledge is enabled through the tight coupling of semi-formal and formal knowledge in ONTOBROKER.

Acknowledgements
We thank V. R. Benjamins, A. Gomez-Perez and R. Perkuhn for their helpful comments. Special thanks to J. Angele who developed the evaluation procedure for L-KARL that is used by ONTOBROKER. The CIA World Fact Book wrapper for ONTOBROKER was developed by A. Dagasan and A. Witt.

References

[1] N. Ashish and C. Knoblock: Semi-automatic Wrapper Generation for Internet Information Sources. In Proceedings of the IFCIS Conference on Cooperative Information Systems (CoopIS), Charlston, South Carolina 1997.

[2] V. R. Benjamins, D. Fensel and A. Gomez Perez: Knowledge Management Through Ontologies. In: *Proceedings of the Second International Conference on Practical Aspects of Knowledge Management (PAKM'98)*, Basel, Switzerland, October 1998.

[3] V. R. Benjamins and D. Fensel: The Ontological Engineering Initiative (KA)2. In N. Guarino (Ed.), *Formal Ontologies in Information Systems, Frontiers in Artificial Intelligence and Applications*, IOS-Press, Amsterdam, 287-301, 1998.

[4] S. Boll, W. Klas and A. Sheth: Overview on Using Metadata to Manage Multimedia Data. In: [32], pp. 1-24, 1998

[5] CIA World Fact Book 1997, http://www.odci.gov/cia/publications/factbook

[6] S. Decker. On Domain-Specific Declarative Knowledge Representation and Database Languages In: *Proceedings of the 5th KRDB Workshop (KRDB98)*, Seattle, WA, 31-May-1998, Eds: A. Borgida, V. Chaudri, M. Staudt

[7] M. Erdmann, S. Decker, D. Fensel, and R. Studer: Combining ONTOBROKER with the Standards of the WWW. research report, Institute AIFB, University of Karlsruhe, 1998.

[8] O. Etzioni: Moving Up the Information Food Chain, *AI Magazine*, 18(2), 1997.

[9] A. Farquhar, R. Fikes, and J. Rice: The Ontolingua Server: a Tool for Collaborative Ontology Construction, *International Journal of Human-Computer Studies (IJHCS)*, 46(6):707728, 1997.

[10] D. Fensel, S. Decker,M. Erdmann, and R. Studer: ONTOBROKER: The Very High Idea. In: *11th Florida Artificial Intelligence Research Symposium (FLAIRS-98)*, Sanibal Island, Florida, May 1998

[11] D. Fensel, M.-C. Rousset, and S. Decker: Workshop on Comparing Description and Frame Logics, *Data and Knowledge Engineering* 25(3):347-352, 1998.

[12] D. Fensel, S. Decker, M. Erdmann, and R. Studer: ONTOBROKER: How to make the WWW Intelligent, research report no. 376, Institute AIFB, University of Karlsruhe, 1998. http://www.aifb.uni-karlsruhe.de/WBS/broker.

[13] D. Fensel, J. Angele, and R. Studer: The Knowledge Acquisition and Representation Language, KARL. *IEEE Transactions on Knowledge and Data Engineering*, Vol. 10, No. 4, 1998.

[14] N. Fridman Noy and C. D. Hafner: The State of the Art in Ontology Design, *AI Magazine*, 18(3):53-74, 1997.

[15] J. Frohn, R. Himmeröer, P.-Th. Kandzia, G. Lausen, and C. Schlepphorst: FLORID - A Prototype for F-Logic, In: *Proceedings of the International Conference on Data Engineering (ICDE, Exhibition Program)*, Birmingham, 1997.

[16] T. R. Gruber: A Translation Approach to Portable Ontology Specifications, *Knowledge Acquisition*, 5(2), 1993.

[17] J. Hammer, H. Garcia-Molina, J. Cho, A. Crespo, R. Aranha: Extracting Semistructured Information from the Web. In: *Proceedings of the Workshop on Management of Semistructured Data*, pages 18-25, Tucson, Arizona, May 1997.

[18] P.-T. Kandzia and C. Schlepphorst: DOOD and DL - Do We Need an Integration. In: *Proceedings of the 4th KRDB Workshop*, Athens, Greece, August 30, 1997.

[19] V. Kashyap and A. Sheth: Semantic Heterogeneity in Global Information Systems: The Role of Metadata, Context and Ontologies. In: M. Papazoglou and G. Schlageter (Eds.): *Cooperative Information Systems: Current Trends and Directions*, Academic Press, 1997.

[20] M. Kifer, G. Lausen, and J. Wu: Logical Foundations of Object-Oriented and Frame-Based Languages, *Journal of the ACM*, 42, 1995.

[21] M. Kifer, E. Lozinskii: A Framework for an Efficient Implementation of Deductive Databases. In: *Proceedings of the 6th Advanced Database Symposium*, Tokyo, 1986.

[22] B. Klein and P. Fankhauser: Error tolerant document structure analysis. *International Journal on Digital Libraries* 1:344-257, Springer, 1997

[23] L. Lamping, R. Rao, and Peter Pirolli: A Focus+Context Technique Based on Hyperbolic Geometry for Visualizing Large Hierarchies. In: *Proceedings of the ACM SIGCHI Conference on Human Factors in Computing Systems*, 1995

[24] S. Luke, L. Spector, D. Rager, and J. Hendler: Ontology-based Web Agents. In: *Proceedings of First International Conference on Autonomous Agents*, 1997.

[25] E. Mena, V. Kashyap, A. Sheth, and A. Illarramendi: OBSERVER: An approach for query processing in global information systems based on interoperation across preexisting ontologies. In: *Proceedings of the First IFCIS International Conference on Cooperative Information Systems (CoopIS'96)*, June 1996

[26] E. Mena, V. Kashyap, A. Illarramendi, and A. Sheth: Domain Specific Ontologies for Semantic Information Brokering on the Global Information Infrastructure, In: *Intl. Conf. on Formal Ontology in Information Systems (FOIS'98)*, Treno, Italy, June 1998.

[27] ONTOBROKER: http://www.aifb.uni-karlsruhe.de/WBS/broker

[28] Precision Graphics Markup Language (PGML), World Wide Web Consortium Note 10-April-1998, http://www.w3.org/TR/1998/NOTE-PGML

[29] Resource Description Framework (RDF), W3C Working Draft 19 August 1998, http://www.w3.org/ TR/1998/WD-rdf-syntax-19980819

[30] Resource Description Framework Schema (RDFS), W3C Working Draft 14 August 1998, http:// www.w3.org/TR/1998/WD-rdf-schema-19980814

[31] C. Schlepphorst: Semi-naive Evaluation of F-Logic Programs, Technical Report 85 , University of Freiburg, 1997

[32] A. Sheth and W. Klas (Eds.): *Multimedia Data Management: Using Metadata to Integrate and Apply Digital Media*, McGraw-Hill, March 1998

[33] L. Shklar, A. Sheth, V. Kashyap, and K. Shah: InfoHarness: Use of Automatically Generated Metadata for Search and Retrieval of Heterogeneous Information. In: *Proceedings of CAiSE '95*, Jyvaskla, Finland, June 1995, Lecture Notes in Computer Science 932, Springer.

[34] Synchronized Multimedia Integration Language (SMIL) 1.0 Specification, W3C Recommendation 15-June-1998, http://www.w3.org/TR/1998/REC-smil-19980615/

[35] A. Van Gelder, K. Ross, J. S. Schlipf: The Well-Founded Semantics for General Logic Programs, *Journal of the ACM*, 38(3): 620650, 1991.

[36] G. Wiederhold: Mediators in the Architecture of Future Information Systems, *IEEE Computer*, 25(3):3849, 1992.

[37] G. Wiederhold and M. Genesereth: The Conceptual Basis for Mediation Services. *IEEE Expert*, September/October, pp. 38-47,1997.

[38] Extensible Markup Language (XML), http://www.w3.org/TR/PR-xml-971208.

21 ADAPTIVE AND ADAPTABLE PRESENTATION SEMANTICS

Dick C.A. Bulterman, Lloyd Rutledge, Lynda Hardman and Jacco van Ossenbruggen

CWI: Centrum voor Wiskunde en Informatica
P.O. Box 94079, 1090 GB Amsterdam
The Netherlands

{Dick.Bulterman, Lloyd.Rutledge, Lynda.Hardman, Jacco.van.Ossenbruggen}@cwi.nl

Abstract: Having the content of a presentation adapt to the needs, resources and prior activities of a user can be an important benefit of electronic documents. The semantics involved in having hypermedia presentations adapt can be divided between *adaptive hypermedia*, which adapts autonomously, and *adaptable hypermedia*, which requires intervention external to the presentation to be adapted. This paper reflects on research and implementation approaches toward both adaptive and adaptable hypermedia and how they apply to specifying the semantics involved in hypermedia authoring and processing.

21.1 INTRODUCTION

A hypermedia presentation is a structured collection of hypermedia objects. Each object can be considered to be a static element, or it can be an element that individually or in concert with other objects, has its presentation tailored to the needs of the user. Such tailoring can be based on resource constraints (such as bandwidth) or on the semantic needs of the user.

In this paper *adaptive hypermedia* is hypermedia that adapts autonomously; that is, they can provide alternatives of individual parts of a presentation under varying circumstances based on directives contained in the presentation definition. This contrasts with *adaptable hypermedia*, in which a definition of a single abstract presentation is adapted by use of directives that are external to the base presentation's definition. Both types of adaptation in hypermedia typically account for varying circumstances including user characteristics, system characteristics and intent of the presentation when processed for the user. Different approaches for making hypermedia adapt have been taken by a number of standards and research initiatives. Each approach applies its own distinction between adaptive and adaptable semantics and how they are processed into interaction with the user. Typically adaptable hypermedia is more versatile than adaptive hypermedia but it requires a more complex processing activity to support presentation transformation.

This paper contrasts adaptive and adaptable hypermedia. In section 21.2, we present an overview of existing approaches to supporting adaptive behavior. In section 21.3, we consider adaptable hypermedia. In section 21.4, we consider the relative merits of both approaches and discuss the processing support required for implementing adaptive and adaptable presentations efficiently. Section 21.5 provides closing comments.

21.2 ADAPTIVE APROACHES

The basic problem that adaptive presentations try to solve is the alteration of the presentation's content to meet the needs of the user. At a low level of detail, this involves changing the representation of a piece of data by substituting a low-quality version of an object for a high-quality (and high-bandwidth) version at data access time. This approach typically falls under the heading of *quality of service* adaptivity. It will not be considered in detail in this paper, since the processing of alternatives is not driven by semantics but by syntax.

An intuitive approach to supporting multiple semantic encodings in a presentation is to define separate projections for each composite presentation, each of which could be configured for the alternatives available. If, for example, we wanted to support a multi-lingual presentation, we could generate one complete projection for the Dutch version of the presentation and another one for the English version. This approach is also not treated in detail, since it is an example of simple presentation substitution rather than presentation adaptivity.

There are several ways that adaptive content can be added to a presentation. These fall into two categories: programming-based and declarative. Programming-based control is perhaps the most obvious form of adaptivity control. At its heart is the notion of providing a program or script-based directives within the document that analyze the runtime situation and 'does the right thing' for each data request issued. (In this section, we only consider such processing when all alternative are defined explicitly in the source presentation.) This is the approach taken by Dynamic HTML [18].

Declarative approaches provide a set of alternatives in which the author states the alternatives available and the conditions under which each alternative is preferred, either directly or indirectly, but not the logic required to implement the choice. A simple form is the definition of explicit alternatives within the contents for each particular media object reference. This is similar to the approach used within HTML for individual media objects:

```
<img src="anchor.gif" alt="Dick's face">
```

A more complex variant is a complete dynamic creation of the entire presentation at runtime using indirect access to all possible objects stored in a database and then only rendering those objects that are required at a particular moment in the presentation [14]. Here, the database query could include sufficient semantic information so that an appropriate representation (or sub presentation could be built on demand.) A compromise approach is Transparent Content Negotiation (TCN) [9]. Here, the document contains a single reference to an object. At time of access, a process of negotiation takes place that allows the 'right' object to be extracted from the server.

Although many declarative approaches allow semantic processing of alternatives, most practical systems do not make use of this power. It is interesting to compare this approach to resource management with that used in a typical HTML browser. Many browsers give the user the ability to turn images or sounds on or off. This is done to make presentation rendering a positive experience on slow communications lines. What such browsers should probably do is to support a notion of turning off irrelevant images rather than all images. Based on the user's needs, the browser should be able to analyze the content and adjust its rendering accordingly.

21.2.1 CMIF and CMIF's Channel architecture.

One of the original goals of CWI's CMIF project [8] was the definition of an information grouping abstraction that would be useful in specifying collections of related content during authoring, and then selection one or most sets of content at runtime by the user based on that user's needs. The name given to this abstraction was the *Logical Resource Channel*, or simply the *Channel* [6].

The purpose of a channel is to be a grouping abstraction for a set of media items that share some common attributes. These may include physical attributes such as screen position or text color, or they may be logical attributes, such as natural language or presentation priority.

The channel provides a logical thread upon which media objects can be placed. This thread can be turned on or off during the presentation based on the needs of the user or the user's agent (that is, the user interface or the runtime support system). In this way, the Channel abstraction can be used to support user-centered adaptation, but it can also be used by the runtime system to select more traditional QoS adaptation of content alternatives.

CMIF channels have not only a strong logical association among media objects on that channel, they also share presentation rendering and scheduling associations as well. In CMIF, it is not appropriate to speak of *the* audio or video channel – as if there was only a single video output stream – but rather *an* audio or video or text or image channel. An application may have many different text, video, audio, image or control channels, each of which is tailored to a specific logical grouping. Ultimately, the objects on a channel may get directed to a renderer of a particular type, but such a renderer may be responsible for multiple concurrent high-level information streams.

Any media item that is activated needs to be placed somewhere on the screen or an a loudspeaker. When several objects are rendered to the same space, it may make sense to manage this space based on a set of common attributes.

Similarly, the actual rendering of a media object needs to be handled by some piece of code or device that is also constrained by a set of common properties. Finally – and most importantly – it may be that a set of media objects can be grouped not only by space and type, but also based on their semantic properties. For example, in a new broadcast, a "Dutch Audio" channel could contain all of the audio in that document that is spoken in Dutch. Alternatively, a "Anchor-Audio-Dutch" channel could be defined that contains the Dutch version of all of audio associated with the anchor. If a "Anchor-Audio-English" channel existed, a user potentially select which language they wanted at runtime.

Each channel has a header that contains channel attributes allowing the channel to support a particular type of media. This type can range from simple text, through complex composite multimedia data, to non-visible control operations. Associated with a channel is its virtual timeline; media item activation instance descriptors are placed on this timeline. The timeline is virtual in that it does not define fixed offsets within the presentation: hyperlink and/or timing control (like a loop) in a particular instance will determine a presentation's 'real time'. Associated with the virtual timeline is the presentation's computed time reference line. This timeline is computed by the scheduler based on information available in the CMIF data structure.

The current run-time environment at CWI supports sixteen channel types, each of which emphasizes the physical properties of the media type, rather than the logical association among groups of generic media objects. This reflects our experience that, from an author's perspective, there are several levels of grouping that need to be managed within an application simultaneously. These are: layout grouping, renderer grouping and semantic grouping.

While the use of timelines is fairly typical, the combination of multiple virtual timelines into a presentation timeline is not. This is shown in Figure 21.1. Here we see a presentation fragment in which one video channel, two audio channels and two text channels are shown. The runtime projection of this presentation will in all probability not have all channels active at once. Most users won't want multiple language channels active at the same time (neither for the audio or the text versions). Different mixes of active channels might be activated during a particular rendering of the presentation, depending on the requirements of the user. A Dutch-speaking blind person may not want video or text, but only the Dutch-language audio channel. An English speaking student of Dutch may want the Dutch audio and the English captions active (or vice versa), while a passenger on a crowded flight may want to see only the English captions and the video. Note that the choices do not need to be made solely by the user. If the playback environment realizes that streaming audio support is not available (or if the user has not made a micro-payment for the video), then it could itself choose to deactivate certain channels or to, say, substitute still images for the videos (assuming that such alternatives were specified by the author).

Figure 21.1: Presentation fragment containing multiple logical resource channels.

21.2.2 W3C'S SMIL

SMIL, the Synchronized Multimedia Integration Language, is a W3C Recommendation for multimedia on the Web. During the development of the SMIL language [10], the issue of selectability of content in a presentation received a great deal of attention. Early on, it was decided that a `switch` construct would form the basic selection primitive in the encoding. A `switch` allows a series of alternatives to be specified for a particular piece of content, one of which is selected by the runtime environment for presentation. An example of how a `switch` might be used to control the alternatives that could accompany a piece of video in a presentation would be:

```
...
<par>
   <video src="anchor.mpg" ... />
   <switch>
      <audio src="dutch.aiff" ... />
      <audio src="english.aiff" ... />
      <text src="dutch.html" ... />
      <text src="english.html" ... />
   </switch>
</par>
...
```

This fragment (which is pseudo-SMIL, for clarity) says that a video is played in parallel with one of: Dutch audio, English audio, Dutch text, or English text. SMIL does not specify the selection mechanism, only a way of specifying the alternatives.

The SMIL V1.0 recommendation currently supports both the notions of the `switch` and a partial mechanism for controlling adaptive behavior called the *system test attribute*. The `switch` provides a conventional branching structure that allows alternatives to be defined at authoring time. The system test attributes consist of a set of pre-defined (primarily system-related) attributes that describe dynamic aspects of the environment which can then be tested at run-time. For example:

```
<text src="cap.html" system-captions="true" .../>
```

will cause the object 'cap.html' to be rendered if *system-captions* evaluates to true.

The system test attribute mechanism is a significant extension over the `switch` because of the way that it decouples the authoring and playback associations among a set of alternatives. Even so, it only partially meets the needs for adaptive control semantics because of the static nature of the attributes themselves (they are defined as part of the language, and can't be extended easily by users).

21.3 ADAPTABLE APPROACHES

Adaptive presentations provide a basis for semantic processing of documents that are based on the alteration of individual components or components group within a portion of the presentation. Adaptable approaches provide a broader scope – they can cover an entire presentation – but typically require external processing to implementation the changes in presentation semantics. This section reviews three building-block technologies for adaptable presentations and then describes how they have been applied in the context of our Berlage environment.

21.3.1 The SGML suite of formats and the SRM.

Separation of structural and style information has long been commonplace for text, and can also be found in many hypertext models. In most hypermedia design models, including RMM [15] and HDM [7], the two types of information are designed during different phases of the design process. The primary implementation of the separation of structural and style information is found in the suite of SGML standards, which includes the suite of XML standards. The two SGML-related standards focussed on for this discussion are HyTime and DSSSL, each of which is described below. We also discuss the Standard Reference Model for intelligent hypermedia presentations, which defines a processing architecture for adaptable documents.

21.3.1.1 HyTime. The ISO standard HyTime specifies the representation of hypermedia documents in a presentation-independent format [11]. Because they are presentation-independent, HyTime documents must be processed into a presentation encoding for one particular renderer in order to be perceived by the user.

HyTime is an ISO standard for representing presentation-independent hypermedia data. HyTime is defined as a subset of Standard Generalized Markup Language (SGML) [13], which defines the structure of electronic documents in general. A related language that is also defined as an SGML subset is Extensible Markup Language (XML), which is a new format for providing a common framework for documents for different applications on the Web [4]. HyTime adds more complex structuring constructs and attaches hypermedia semantics to certain patterns of composites of this structure. The basic hypermedia semantics that HyTime represents include *hyperlinking*, which establishes descriptive relationships between document objects, and *scheduling*, which puts document objects in coordinate systems that can represent spatial and temporal structure.

HyTime and SGML are generally intended for encoding documents that are presentation-independent. They can apply to a wide variety of presentation situations but do not themselves represent particular presentations. HyTime and SGML documents typically must be processed into a different format appropriate for final presentation. HyTime and SGML are meta-languages. They encode not only individual documents but also the document sets to which they belong. A document set is defined by an SGML *document type definition (DTD)*. An individual document conforms to a particular DTD. A DTD defines a specific syntax, in terms of SGML constructs, that its documents must follow. HyTime inherits from SGML the use of DTDs to define individual document sets.

HyTime implementations often include database management systems [2]. The HyTime constructs of a document, and sometimes the semantics they represent, are represented in the database. Access to these constructs and semantics is then provided by the DBMS. Data storage layer concerns for document and document system developers involve how best to define document sets to be stored and how best to author a document within a set so that the widest possible adaptation is allowed for them. Using structures that constraint how portions or aspects of a document can be presented inhibit its adaptability. Understanding how documents can be and are typically adapted can guide the document creators in how to structure them. Insights into the different layers of adaptation are provided during this paper's discussion of the SRM and its implementation in the Berlage environment.

21.3.1.2 DSSSL. The ISO standard DSSSL (Document Style Semantics and Specification Language) encodes the transformation between document storage and presentation [12]. DSSSL defines the transformation of SGML and HyTime documents into formats that present them. The use of DSSSL with HyTime was recently made easier with the release of the second edition of HyTime, which contains new facilities for use with DSSSL. SMIL is defined as a subset of XML. Thus, DSSSL can encode transformations that output SMIL. HyTime documents are encoded to be adaptable, and DSSSL encodes how they are adapted.

DSSSL is a Scheme-like language that describes how an SGML document is transformed into another SGML document or into a non-SGML format. Because HyTime documents are SGML documents, any HyTime document can be transformed by DSSSL. A DSSSL program is typically called a *style sheet.* The separation of style from structure and content enforced with the distinction between DSSSL and SGML/HyTime facilitates the creation of particular styles by the author that can be applied to documents of the same document set. Note that although the term style sheet is used, DSSSL can be used for more general, non-style transformations.

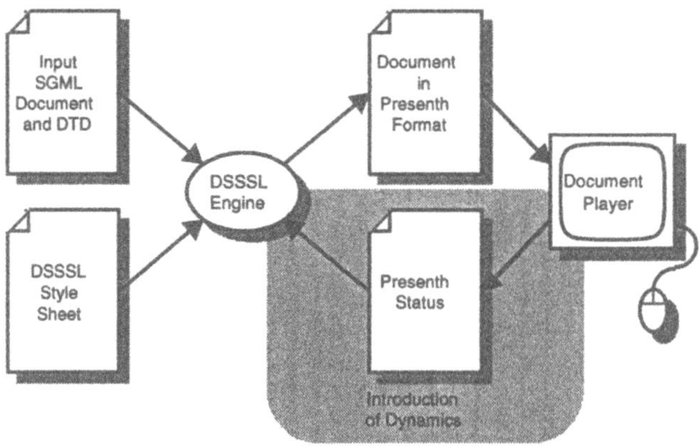

Figure 21.2: Typical usage of DSSSL and the Introduction of Dynamics.

The design of typical DSSSL usage is shown in Figure 21.2. This diagram shows how an SGML document is processed with an accompanying style sheet by a DSSSL engine. The DSSSL engine determines the mapping encoded by the style sheet and generates the appropriate transformation of the source document into the presentation format. How this typical usage was implemented in the Berlage environment is described later in this paper. Also described later in this paper are the extensions to this typical usage required to implement dynamic generation of presentation.

DSSSL style sheets can access not only the constructs encoded by HyTime but also the semantics they represent in a particular document set. This is done through the specification of *properties* in HyTime. The HyTime specification defines certain properties that are to be recognized as encoded by HyTime constructs in all documents that use those constructs. Names and descriptions of potential values for these properties are specified by the standard. These properties can be referred to directly by DSSSL style sheets. This is helpful to the style sheet author because a single property value can often be encoded with many different combinations of HyTime constructs, and thus it is easier to encode a reference to that one property and value than to each of these possible combinations.

As stated earlier, SGML and HyTime documents are often loaded into databases as part of their processing. A DSSSL engine can be provided access to such a database in its processing of an SGML or HyTime document. DSSSL has a query language for querying on SGML-defined structure and on HyTime-encoded properties. A DSSSL engine could then applies these queries to a DBMS storing a HyTime-encoded document.

With the existence of these HyTime properties, it becomes a data storage layer concern to ensure that a document set and its documents use these HyTime properties wherever appropriate. This facilitates the writing of style sheets, since they can then refer directly to these properties. It also helps make the intended semantics encoded in the document more widely accessible by ensure that all HyTime-conforming systems will recognize them as such.

HyTime also provides constructs for defining new properties for a given document set or document. With these, the creator of a document set or particular document can define properties encoded in the document that DSSSL style sheets can query directly. With this ability, it is an added data storage layer concern for document creators to specify a set of semantics properties that queries from a style sheet can use well. The HyTime and DSSSL standards do not declare a standard means of specifying how a new property is to be encoded and recognized. However, earlier work regarding the Berlage environment describes how libraries of DSSSL code to be included in style sheets can instruct a DSSSL engine on how to recognize newly-defined properties [17].

21.3.1.3 The Standard Reference Model. Intelligent Multimedia Presentation Systems (IMPS) deal with the dynamic creation of multimedia presentations optimally geared towards the needs of a user. The Standard Reference Model (SRM) specifies the decomposition of an IMPS into well-defined layers [3]. Hypermedia built based on the SRM is thus very adaptive to the user, involving a rich set of adaptive semantics.

In broad terms, the created presentation should define what is presented to the user (the content), where it is presented (the spatial layout) and when it is presented (temporal layout). Given a collection of user goals and availability of resources these three aspects leave open an immense number of possible presentations. An IMPS is a reasoning system aimed at selecting the optimal one. The SRM can be used as the basic for discussing and comparing different systems that adapt to the user. It can also be used in guiding the development of such systems.

While SRM defines a general processing model for dynamic presentation generation and adaptation, existing formats and tools based on style sheets provide an existing infrastructure for performing similar functions. The difference is that style sheet-based environments often do not have dynamic adaptation, but static presentations are often generated that are adapted to circumstances that are known at generation time.

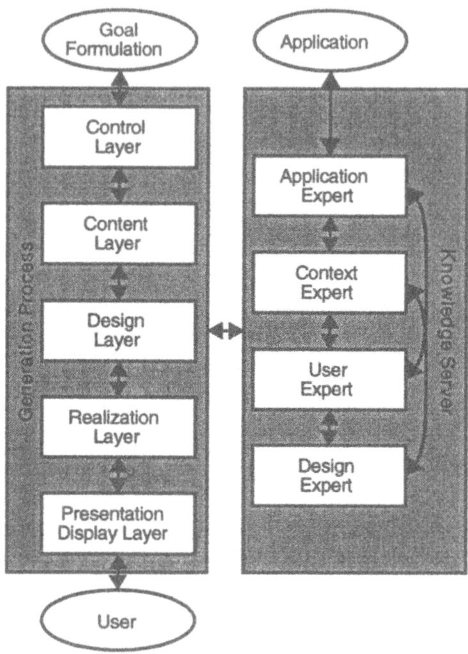

Figure 21.3: The SRM and its components.

The SRM considers the decomposition of the dynamic creation of multimedia presentations into well defined layers. The SRM components are illustrated in Figure 21.3. The SRM divides dynamic presentation generation into two areas: ***generation process*** and ***knowledge server***. The generation process performs the run-time generation of the presentation based on the user's interaction, the history of the presentation and information provided by the knowledge server. The knowledge server stores and provides long-term instructions and information that apply to multiple presentations at any point in their run. As such, the generation process is the active component of the SRM, and the knowledge server is the stable component.

What consideration of the SRM can provide the author at the data storage layer is an understanding of what type of adaptation takes place and what layers this adaptation divides into. Understanding useful and likely patterns of adaptation helps the author to specify structures and semantic properties for documents that best suit these patterns. The SRM represents the layers of adaptation one panel of experts agrees should work well. If the SRM is adopted by the presentation generation community, the adaptation of documents for presentation will tend to fall along these layers. This will result in documents being structured with these layers in mind, and in having interchangeability of document processing software components divided in terms of these layers.

21.3.2 The SRM and its implemention in the Berlage environment.

This section describes how the approaches described in this paper were applied to the design of the Berlage hypermedia authoring and browsing environment [17], which is named after H.P. Berlage, the leading 20th century architect of Amsterdam. Berlage incorporates the use of HyTime to represent hypermedia documents in a format independent of its presentation. It also incorporates the use of DSSSL to specify the different mapping of these documents to their final presentations. For the final presentation to the user, Berlage generates and hypermedia presentations encoded in SMIL. The Berlage environment consists of public domain tools to demonstrate how such environments can be readily implemented on a wide scale. The Berlage environment is designed in terms of the SRM and to specify layers of processing adaptation for the user during interaction with the presentation. A diagram of the Berlage environment design is shown in Figure 21.4.

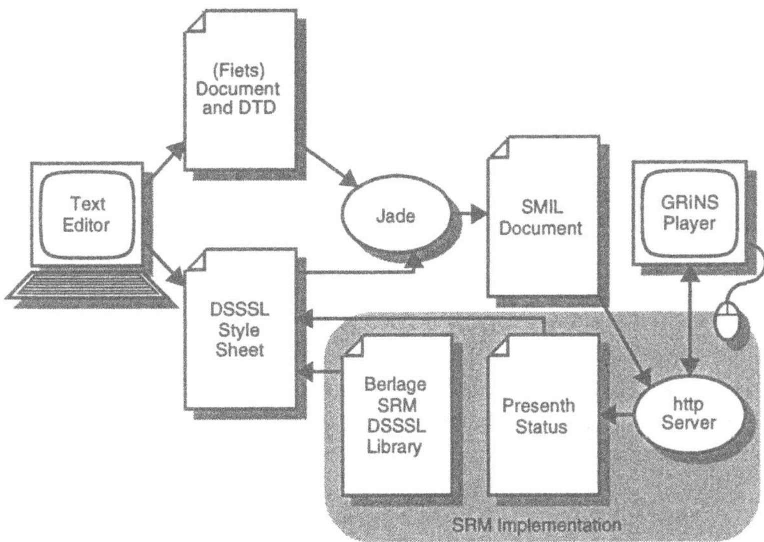

Figure 21.4: Berlage Environment Design with SRM Implementation.

Before the incorporation of the SRM, the Berlage environment created only static presentations. With the SRM incorporation performed for this paper, the Berlage environment can adapt the presentation during the presentation itself. The dynamic generation of DSSSL code required by the SRM implementation necessitated the substantial additions and modifications to the Berlage environment architecture. The primary new component added is the http server. The server enables the Berlage environment to keep track of the user's interaction with the presentation and with each interaction generate a new presentation state in the form of DSSSL code. The environment then calls the Jade DSSSL engine to again process the document with the main DSSSL style sheet, which includes by reference the newly generated presentation state code. This results in the creation of new SMIL code, which is then passed back to the SMIL player client by the http server.

To enable the Berlage http server to keep track of the user interaction, the destination of all navigational hyperlinks in the SMIL code specifies with URL code that http server. Further, these URL addresses are in the format used by HTML forms. Fields and values for those fields are set in the URL to convey to the server what the status of the presentation was and what choice among those available the user selected. The server can then update its internal data store to properly represent the presentation's state. Next it generates the DSSSL presentation state code for inclusion in the next Jade processing of the document and its presentation. This generated DSSSL code includes data that enables the style sheet to define SMIL hyperlink destination URLs so that the server will recognize them when they are activate and can respond appropriately.

The SRM's division between the generation process and the knowledge server is maintained in the Berlage environment. The data fed to the layers of the generation process, except for the presentation display layer, are represented as presentation status code. In the Berlage environment SRM extension, this code is DSSSL code that is included in the main style sheet for the document and its current presentation. The instructions for how each layer handles the data in this presentation state code are in the static main style sheet DSSSL code.

At least some of the processing of the experts can also represented by DSSSL code in the main style sheet. The code would typically reference the storage document HyTime structure code, while the generation process code references the presentation status more. DSSSL as a language has been adequate for this. More complex decisions processes may require software outside of DSSSL to complement what is provided in the Berlage environment.

21.3.2.1 Control Layer. This layer selects a goal from a set of goals which have still to be met. It influences the message to be expressed by a presentation, but does not make any decisions directly affecting the instantiation of parts of a particular presentation.

Figure 21.5 shows a fragment of a presentation called *Fiets*, which gives an adaptable tour of Amsterdam. In the view shown, the user is given a collection of Amsterdam buildings about which more detailed information can be accessed. A thumbnail image of the front of each building is shown, and each image is the starting point for a hyperlink leading to more information

Figure 21.5: GRiNS Showing a Fiets Presentation.

that building. It is a goal of the application that the user visit each of the buildings. The user is helped in this task by the changing appearance of this portion of the Fiets presentation. After the user has visited a building and returns to this screen, the visited building, and all previously visited buildings, are shown with a more lightly shaded border. The user can then see that the buildings with darker borders are ones that still need to be visited.

From the perspective of the user, the document is the presentation, and the perceived boundaries of the document are those of the presentation. What the document is to the user is a collection of related information that must be presented in full during the course of the current session. This may be part of a document as stored, or it may consist of components of several stored documents whose contents are integrated into the presentation. The control layer processes a set of goals defining what should be presented to the user during the current session, and during the presentation it tracks how many of these goals have been met.

One control layer data storage concern is that the document be structured in a way the corresponds well with the likely goals a user could have in navigating through a presentation of that document. This involves grouping together document components that are likely to be presented together as meeting a single goal. Thus, a goal can be considered as meet when all the components of the group are presented, and the system need only to refer to that one construct representing the grouping. Similar groupings can be made around components for which the presentation of any one achieves a goal. Here again, the style sheet can refer to the component as a unit and infer that the presentation of any of its children satisfies a certain goal.

21.3.2.2 Content Layer. In the SRM, the content layer takes a single goal passed on by the control layer and refines it to a list of subgoals. These are in turn transformed into a set of communicative acts and relations among these acts. This is carried out by four separate, but communicating processes-*goal refinement, content selection, media allocation* and *ordering*. Goal refinement is a task which has to be carried out before any parts of a presentation are created, so it is not discussed further here.

The content selection process communicates with the application expert, and decides on the semantic content of the presentation. In the Fiets presentation, when the user has selected a building the content of the resulting SMIL display must be determined. This display shows detailed information about a building, thus such content may include history of the building such as when it was built and whom its residents were. This display could also convey more detailed information on how the building appears on the outside and on the inside.

When the http server receives a URL request for detailed information on a particular building, it conveys in generated DSSSL code what the appropriate semantic content is to display for that building. This would typically be represented by the setting of variables similar to those used for the control layer. In the Fiets example being discussed, the main style sheet could access these settings conveying what semantic content should be in the next display. For each unit of semantic content, the main style sheet could have a set of static instructions on how to display it.

The media allocation component assigns a particular medium to a communicative act, producing a media communicative act. In the Berlage environment, this corresponds to the selection of particular media objects to display for a given semantic content. In the Fiets example, the semantic content of detailed information on a buildings exterior could correspond with particular images of its gable ornamentation and entranceway.

The instructional code for determining this media allocation would be contained in the main style sheet, not in the generated state DSSSL code. The main style sheet when given a unit of content to convey has the instructions for determining the media allocation for that content. In Fiets, such instructions often refer to the HyTime-defined structure of the stored document to determining this media allocation. For example, HyTime structures in Fiets associate images of gable ornamentation and entranceways with individual buildings. This HyTime code would be accessed by Jade as instructed by the main DSSSL style sheet to determine these image files for a particular building.

The data storage concern here is to encode enough about the relationships between document components to make possible the conclusions drawn about dividing the goals into subgoals. The concern is also to develop a good set of properties that represent these semantics and that can be readily queried for during style sheet processing.

21.3.2.3 Design Layer. The design layer allows the processes of media selection and layout design to carry on in parallel, imposing no ordering requirements for which of these should be finalized first. The design layer is split into two communicating processes: *media design* and *layout design*. The media design component makes decisions on the "look and feel" of the presentation. It can communicate with the design expert and make decisions on styles. Style information can include as color, font, background wallpaper images, and other aspects of the presentation that do not affect the actual media content or its positioning in space and time in the presentation. In the Berlage environment, the design expert can be embodied, at least in part, by code within the main style sheet.

In the Fiets example, one screen display has thumbnail images for multiple buildings. The number of thumbnail images to be displayed on a single screen is a design layer spatial layout decision. If there are too many buildings to select from, the thumbnails are distributed among multiple screen displays. Access to each of these displays is provided with hyperlinks. The number of thumbnails that can fit on a single display is determined in the SRM by the design expert. In the Berlage environment, it is code in the main style sheet that states this number, and this code corresponds to the SRM design expert.

The design layer does not provide any substantial issues for data storage because the information processed is more about the design of the presentation than the actual document information presented.

21.3.2.4 Realization Layer. In this layer the final decision is taken on the media items to be played in the presentation and their corresponding spatial and temporal layout. Again, the layer is split into two communicating processes, paralleling those in the design layer-media realization and layout realization. The media realization component ensures that appropriate media items are chosen. These may already exist, or may be generated specifically for the task.

The layout realization component calculates the final temporal and spatial layout of the presentation based on the constraints specified in the design layer. The duration in time of an atomic media object's presentation may be derived from the content for continuous media or from the storage structure. The duration of a composite portions of the presentation can be calculated on the basis of its components along with any other temporal constraints specified in the design layer. Where links define possible paths among separate multimedia presentations, there is also a duration perceived by the user when the link is followed.

In the Fiets example, the exact position of each building thumbnail would be determined. This positioning will give the building images an even distribution in the screen space. The exact font size and positioning of the associated text and hyperlink hotspots would also be determined here. The design layer determines how may building thumbnails to show at once, while the realization layer determined where on the screen to show them.

The data storage concerns regarding realization layer processing are that information be provided on which to base the choice of a particular media item and that the spatial and temporal information on the media item be available for positioning it in the presentation. To address the first concern, authors of must encode the information needed for the realization layer to understand what choices of media objects there are for presenting a unit of semantic content. Information must also be provided about each alternative on which to base the choice in a given presentation circumstance. This is similar to the adaptive concern address by SMIL with the `switch`, where a `switch` provides a set of alternatives and each alternative has attributes assigned to it on which to base a selection. To address the second concern, information on the spatial dimensions of visual media objects and on the duration of time-based media objects must be either encoded in the document or otherwise accessible by the style sheet processing mechanism.

21.3.2.5 Presentation Display Layer. In the Berlage Environment the presentation display layer is embodied by the generation of the SMIL code, which is played by GRiNS [5], that displays the presentation to the user. No data storage creation concerns arise here because the decision based on processing of the stored document have already been made.

21.4 WHERE SHOULD PRESENTATION ADAPTATION AND % ADAPTABILITY SEMANTICS BE SUPPORTED?

21.4.1 Reflections on Adaptive Hypermedia.

The primary difference between adaptive and adaptable presentations is the degree to which the adaptation process occurs autonomously. In adaptive presentations, the presentation author must account for the transformation of the presentation at author-time. As mentioned in section 2, this can happen either based on executable program code or via a declarative means.

Perhaps the most problematic aspect of using script-based control for adaptivity is that most document authors are not programmers. Even if they were, the user-centered nature of the adaptive process makes the task of integrating system- and user-needs with a single code fragment sufficiently complex that such an approach would serve as a disincentive to creating generalized alternative presentations. In the context of a full presentation, it is often difficult to define the impact of all of the various user dependencies 'up front' at author-time: if a user wanted to tailor only a special portion of a presentation or if they wanted to make unusual choices (supporting multiple languages simultaneously), this is typically difficult to predict in advance.

In general, declarative forms of adaptation control are much more flexible for the author and the runtime environment. In essence, a declarative approach provides a catalogue of needs, allowing the user and the environment to indicate which needs are relevant for any one presentation. With a declarative approach, the question is often not 'how do I support adaptivity', but rather: 'at what level in the processing hierarchy should such support take place.' This relates to the granularity of the storage model as well as the control model of the presentation.

In section 2, we discussed the use of a fully-generated presentation via a database interface, as well as simplifications on this model. In our experience, the use of database back-ends for total processing often are more appropriate for adaptable presentations than for adaptive. Inherent in the processing of adaptive presentations is the need to coordinate several concurrent streams of information, each with its own logical focus. If we add to this the inherently distributed nature of the Web infrastructure and the unpredictable semantic behavior of a hypermedia application (where rescheduling or regenerating the next presentation fragment is only a mouse-click away!), then we have yet to find a suitable information model that can effectively replace the insights of a presentation author.

Where storage-based adaptivity is appropriate is in fetching a version of a media object for which there may be many (semantic) encodings. This is the approach taken in part by Transparent Content Negotiation and similar systems. While TCN represents an improvement over the simple line-item substitution in, say, HTML, it typically hides the entire substitution process. Users have little control, since users don't get to see and evaluate the alternatives. Also, since each object is developed independently, defining common user-level grouping abstractions across these independent objects is a difficult problem.

Our experience with CMIF has led us to support the notion of author-based logical grouping of semantic alternatives for adaptive hypermedia. Constructs like CMIF's Channels provide a user-centered alternative in which a user (or user's agent) can evaluate the alternative available and select the most appropriate encoding. This has proved useful in the areas of multi-lingual presentations (where the exact combination of languages used in a single presentation can vary: some users want natural audio and customized subtitles, while others want dubbed-audio and no captions – but often, the exact choice depends on the nature of the object being viewed rather than static preferences). It has also proven useful for serving the needs to the accessibility community, where standard documents can be adapted using standard tools.

We are pleased that SMIL provides a relatively high degree of support for adaptability through the `switch` and the system test attributes. While this is a major step forward, it is still incomplete for general presentations. The `switch` has two problems. First, it restricts the resolution of a `switch` to a single alternative. (If you want Dutch audio *and* Dutch text, you need to specify a compound `switch` statement, but in so doing, you always get the compound result.) More restrictively, it requires the author to explicitly state all of the possible combinations of input streams at author time. If the user wanted Dutch audio and English text, this possibility must have been considered at authoring time. If we compare the `switch` construct with CMIF's Channels, it is true that, logically, the alternatives indicated by the channel construct could be represented as a set of `switch` statements, although the resulting size of the `switch`'s composite structure would become explosive.

We feel that the `switch` is of most use for syntactic alternatives. The test attribute option is a richer alternative, although SMIL missed an opportunity to focus on the semantic needs to the user rather than that of the encoding. Use of a Channel-like mechanism would significantly simplify the specification of user-centered alternative. The author could specify all of the individual components of a presentation at author time and then organize them in terms of their logical channel threads. The user (or user's agent) can then select which sets are active at runtime. An 'initial state' attribute can be used to define the default behavior.

21.4.2 Reflections on Adaptable Hypermedia.

The options available to supporting adaptable hypermedia can best be understood in terms of the SRM.

The role of the control layer in supporting adaptable presentations is typically restricted to processing documents (or document fragments) based on the current state of a presentation. For example, when the user selects a building in the Fiets example of section 4, the SMIL browser client sends an http request to the Berlage http server. This signals to the server that a particular building was selected. The server then generates presentation state DSSSL code that when included in the main style sheet for processing causes SMIL code to be generated that displays detailed information on that building. In this and all future presentation state DSSSL code generated, a boolean variable is set for that building indicating it has been visited. The main style sheet has instructions that access this code in determining what shade to use for the border around each building in generating the SMIL code representing the next step in the presentation. The purpose of control operation adaptability is often to reflect the navigational state in terms of the document structure rather than altering the semantics of the presentation.

At the content layer, the issues is often not one of data granularity (as was the case with adaptive substitution) but more one of ranging and ordering choices. In the Fiets example (and in Berlage, in general) the result of the ordering process is a (not necessarily linear) ordering of the media communicative acts. Navigational hyperlinks, timing relations and spatial layout are all different ways of expressing ordering relations among media items in the final SMIL presentation code. When a communicative act is to be expressed using a number of media items these methods can be traded-off against one another. For example, rather than display many items together, links can be made among smaller groups of the items, or the sequential playing of items may be a suitable alternative for laying out items next to each other at the same time. The choice among these alternatives in the Fiets application is described in other work [16]. These different ways of "ordering" the material need to be captured within the content layer, but may not be finalized until the design or realization layer. The content layer is thus restricted to specifying a structure of links, and leave the decisions on temporal and spatial layout to other layers. In the Berlage environment, specifying this link structure for a given state in the presentation means determining what to show on the display being generated and what information should instead be made accessible by links from this generated display.

While the design and realization layers have little direct influence on adaptability, a much more significant role is reserved for the presentation display layer. In nearly all previous systems, there has been a very tight coupling of presentation environment to the abstract model of the presentation domain. While HyTime and SGML provide support for decoupling the document for the presentation, the reality of most time-based (hypermedia) systems is that the development of the abstract model is often constrained by the presumed system interface. In this regard, the increasing number of options available to content developers for display of hypermedia information may provide a catalyst for developing cross-environment presentations. For example, a SMIL presentation generated for the Web domain may also be reused as part of a broadcast TV commercial, or a direct broadcast news program may be augmented with links that are only appropriate for viewing in a later on-demand mode.

In this latter case, the meaning of the presentation relative to its distribution environment, more so than its encoding, will form a fundamental requirement for including semantic-based adaptive processing of the presentation that will transcend the reliance on representation-based manipulations which form the basis of current adaptability work.

21.5 SUMMARY

This paper described various hypermedia approaches and how each handles the distinction between the semantics of adaptive and adaptable hypermedia. These approaches included primarily SMIL, CMIF, the SGML suite of standards and the SRM. Experience learned from applying these approaches to developing the Berlage environment and Fiets application was described. Conclusions were drawn from these approaches regarding when it is best to apply adaptive semantics and when it is best to apply adaptable semantics in designing hypermedia. The impact of this choice on the database performance was also described.

Acknowledgments

The GRiNS environment was implemented by Sjoerd Mullender, Jack Jansen and Guido van Rossum. The Fiets artwork and graphic design was done by Maja Kuzmanovic. The development of GRiNS was funded in part by the European Union ESPRIT Chameleon project. The images for Fiets used in this paper come from [1].

References

[1] City of Amsterdam Municipal Department for Preservation and Restoration of Historic Buildings and Sites. *Amsterdam Heritage.* `http://www.amsterdam.nl/bmz/adam/adam_e.html`.

[2] Böhm, K., Aberer, K., and Klas, W. Building a Hybrid Database Application for Structured Documents, *Multimedia Tools and Applications*, 1997.

[3] Bordegoni, M., Faconti, G., Feiner S., Maybury, M.T., Rist, T., Ruggieri, S., Trahanias, P. and Wilson, M. A Standard Reference Model for Intelligent Multimedia Presentation Systems, *Computer Standards and Interfaces* 18(6,7) December 1997, North Holland, pp. 477-496.

[4] Bray, T., Paoli, J. and Sperberg-McQueen, C.M., *Extensible Markup Language (XML).* W3C Recommendation, January 1998. `http://www.w3.org/TR/REC-xml.html`.

[5] Bulterman, D.C.A., Hardman, L., Jansen, J. Mullender, K.S. and Rutledge, L. GRiNS: A GRaphical INterface for Creating and Playing SMIL Documents, in Proc. *Seventh International World Wide Web Conference (WWW7)*, April 1998.

[6] Bulterman, D.C.A. User-Centered Abstractions for Adaptive Hypermedia Presentations, in Proc. *ACM Multimedia 98*, September 1998.

[7] Garzotto, F., Mainetti, L. and Paolini. P. Hypermedia Design, Analysis, and Evaluation Issues, *Communications of the ACM*, 38(8):74 86, August 1995.

[8] Hardman, L., Bulterman, D.C.A. and van Rossum, G. The Amsterdam Hypermedia Model: Applying Time and Context to the Dexter Model, *Communications of the ACM*, vol. 37, no. 2, February 1994.

[9] Hotlman, K. and Mutz, A. *Transparent Content Negotiation in HTTP*, IETF RFC 2295. `ftp://ftp.isi.edu/in-notes/rfc2295.txt`.

[10] Hoschka, P. (ed.). *Synchronized Multimedia Integration Language.* W3C Recommendation, June 1998. `http://www.w3.org/TR/REC-smil/`.

[11] International Standards Organization. *Hypermedia/Time-based Structuring Language (HyTime).* Second Edition. ISO/IEC IS 10744:1997, 1997.

[12] International Standards Organization. *Document Style Semantics and Specification Language (DSSSL).* ISO/IEC IS 10179:1996, 1996.

[13] International Standards Organization. *Standard Generalized Markup Language (SGML).* ISO/IEC IS 8879:1985, 1985.

[14] Kerstin, M. et al. *MONET: Extending databases for multimedia.* `http://www.cwi.nl/~monet/modprg.html`

[15] Isakowitz, T., Stohr, E.A., and Balasubramanian, P. RMM: A Methodology for Structured Hypermedia Design. *Communications of the ACM*, 38(8):34 44, August 1995.

[16] Rutledge, L., Hardman, L., van Ossenbruggen, J. and Bulterman, D.C.A. Structural Distinctions Between Hypermedia Storage and Presentation, in Proc. *ACM Multimedia 98*, September 1998.

[17] Rutledge, L., van Ossenbruggen, J., Hardman, L. and Bulterman, D.C.A. Practical Application of Existing Hypermedia Standards and Tools, in Proc. *Digital Libraries 98*, June 1998.

[18] W3C: World-Wide Web Consortium. *HTML 4.0: W3C's Next Version of HTML.* W3C Recommendation, November 1997. URL: `http://www.w3.org/MarkUp/Cougar/`

22 QUALITY OF SERVICE SEMANTICS FOR MULTIMEDIA DATABASE SYSTEMS

Jonathan Walpole, Charles Krasic, Ling Liu, David Maier, Calton Pu, Dylan McNamee, and David Steere

Department of Computer Science and Engineering
Oregon Graduate Institute*

Abstract: Quality of service (QoS) support has been a hot research topic in multimedia databases, and multimedia systems in general, for the past several years. However, there remains little consensus on how QoS support should be provided. At the resource-management level, systems designers are still debating the suitability of reservation-based versus adaptive QoS management. The design of higher system layers is less clearly understood, and the specification of QoS requirements in domain-specific terms is still an open research topic. To address these issues, we propose a QoS model for multimedia databases. The model covers the specification of user-level QoS preferences and their relationship to QoS control at the resource-management level, and is applicable to adaptive and reservation-based systems. In this paper we present the model, discuss the implications it has for multimedia database design, and describe a practical implementation of it.

* This research was supported in part by DARPA contracts/grants N66001-97-C-8522, N66001-97-C-8523, and F19628-95-C-0193, and by Tektronix, Inc., and Intel Corporation.

22.1 INTRODUCTION

Interest in QoS management has grown with the arrival of multimedia systems whose resource consumption needs often exceed the available resource capacity of the systems on which they are deployed [1]. Rather than refusing to return a presentation in such situations, multimedia systems with QoS support have the capability of returning reduced-quality presentations using the resources that are currently available. Reduced-quality presentations exhibit inaccuracy compared to perfect-quality presentations. Such inaccuracy might take the form of dropped or delayed video frames or audio samples, reduced spatial resolution, or decreased peak signal to noise ratio (PSNR), in order to allow the presentation to be made using fewer system resources [2,3,4].

High-level control over QoS management can be provided by allowing applications or users to specify their tolerance for inaccuracy in the presentations returned, or by giving them control over how such inaccuracy is introduced when resources become scarce. Essentially, QoS control gives higher system layers the ability to specify what constitutes an *acceptable* presentation generated by the lower layers, and to define what *better* means between two alternative presentations.

For systems with resource reservation capability in their lower layers, the QoS specifications generated by higher layers can be translated, together with other information into the necessary resource reservation requests [5]. Adaptive systems take a different approach and use high-level QoS information to determine the best way to adapt presentation quality in response to uncontrolled changes in available resource capacity [6,7,8,9].

Although adaptive and reservation-based systems take quite different approaches at the resource management level, both classes of system require a QoS model that allows application-level QoS requirements to be specified and then related to resource usage plans. This paper presents such an application-level QoS model and discusses its use at the resource management level.

Our QoS model allows the definition of multiple quality dimensions for multimedia presentations. Users specify their QoS requirements by defining utility functions for each dimension. Utility functions map quality to utility, define thresholds for upper and lower bounds on useful quality, and can be weighted and combined to specify overall QoS requirements. This information is then used in the derivation of resource management requirements for either reservation-based or adaptive systems.

The proposed QoS model serves a number of purposes, including its uses as a guide to system architecture, a criterion for distinguishing among presentation plans, and a control input for feedback-based QoS management. There are several semantically relevant implications of the model. QoS specifications are one way of saying what the most important elements of the data are, so they can be emphasized in both capture and retrieval. The model supports a distinction between semantics of data and semantics of query results. For example, the quality of stored data is distinct from the quality requirements for a particular instance of viewing the data. Our model also serves as a guide for deciding what meta-data should be attached to data and what information should be associated with uses of the data.

The rest of the paper is organized as follows. Section 22.2 presents our QoS model in more detail. Section 22.3 describes our use of the model in a real- world system that interactively delivers multimedia presentations from a remote storage server. We compare our model to other QoS models in section 22.4. Section 22.5 concludes the paper and discusses future work.

22.2 THE QUASAR QOS MODEL

The Quasar QoS model extends Staehli's QoS model [10,11,12]. Staehli defines the concepts of *content, view* and *quality*. Content is a composition of single-medium segments into a complete presentation, as specified by the creator of the presentation. For example, a content definition might specify 3 seconds of video source A followed immediately by 4 seconds of video source B, both proceeding in parallel with audio clip C. The view definition specifies an idealized mapping of content into a display space by a consumer of a presentation. A view might indicate that the video portion of the presentation should appear in a certain 6x8 cm rectangle on the screen or that the presentation should proceed at half normal speed.

The ability to specify view as separate from content is essential when the creator of a presentation can foresee neither all uses to which it will be put nor the environments where it will be played.

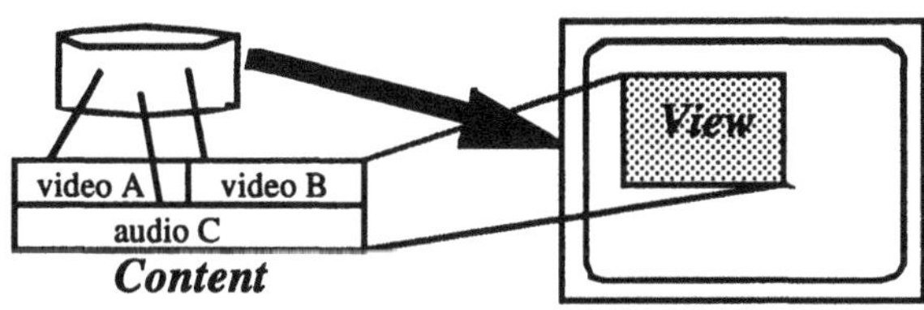

***Quality** = error in view*

Figure 22.1: Content, view, and quality

A quality definition in Staehli's model specifies the allowable divergence between the actual presentation delivered to the consumer and an ideal presentation as specified by content and view (see Figure 22.1).

Like Staehli's model, our model is based on the notion that the quality of a query result is a measure of the amount of error present in it. Our model takes the abstract view that queries return results that are approximations to real-world values, and that real-world values exist in a continuous space.

Under this model, a query returning a perfect result would return an error-free replica of this continuous space. However, computer-based storage, manipulation, and presentation requires that (a) real-world values be captured using equipment of limited accuracy, (b) they be represented digitally using a finite number of bits, and (c) computer and network resources be used to deliver the digital representation of the result to the user.

We use the term *capture error* to describe the class of errors that result from the use of inaccurate capture equipment. These errors are incidental in the sense that they depend on the characteristics of the specific capture equipment used, and may not be present when different equipment is used.

Other errors are inherent in the digital representation of continuous data. We use the terms *quantization error* and *sampling error* to describe the classes of inherent errors that result from the use of a finite number of samples and a finite number of bits per sample, respectively, to represent time- varying values from a continuous space.

We use the term *delivery error* to describe the class of errors introduced by resource management decisions that influence the delivery of query results. Delivery errors in multimedia presentations include shift, rate and jitter errors caused by, for example, page and packet-oriented data transfer, buffering delays and resource scheduling policies.

Capture, sampling, quantization and delivery errors account for the difference between the perfect continuous representation of a real-world value and the value returned by a query result that is intended to represent it. As technology advances, computers become faster and have higher precision, enabling continual improvements in the quality of the query results returned by systems. However, for a particular system, even though a query result that satisfies a user's quality requirements may be considered *as good as perfect,* from the perspective of that user, according to our model it is not possible for a system to return a truly perfect result in general, since that would require infinite resources. This concept of perfect quality provides a reference point that allows quality improvements, as well as quality degradations, to be described, and user QoS requirements, data QoS characteristics, and system QoS capabilities to be specified independently of each other.

Our model separates the QoS characteristics of delivered presentations from those of the underlying, stored, digital representation of the data. We refer to the QoS characteristics of a delivered presentation as *apparent quality*, and the QoS characteristics of the stored digital content as *latent quality*.

22.2.1 QoS as a Distance Measure

Since presentations are often used to represent reality, we model the space of possible states for a presentation as a continuous, metric space.

Definition 1 (*presentation state space*)

Let *o* denote a target object of type presentation. The space of possible states for *o*, *Sp*(*o*), is a continuous metric space with the following properties:

Distance: a distance function *distance*(*u*,*v*) is defined over every pair of states *u*,*v in Sp*. The distance function describes the absolute value of the difference between two states of a presentation.

Symmetry: for every *u*,*v in Sp*, *distance*(*u*,*v*) = *distance*(*v*,*u*).

Triangle inequality:
for every *u*,*v*,*w in Sp*, *distance*(*u*,*v*) + *distance*(*v*,*w*) >= *distance*(*u*,*w*).

The above definition of the presentation state space as a metric space is useful because it allows further definitions of quality in terms of distance measures.

Definition 2 (*relative quality*)

For two possible presentation states, *u* and *v*, in *Sp(o)*, their relative quality is defined by *distance*(*u*,v).

Definition 3 (perfect quality)

The unique, error-free state in *Sp(o)* defines perfect quality for *o*.

This definition of perfect quality provides a common reference point from which to measure the relative qualities of different presentation states.

Definition 4 (*quality-loss*)

Let *p* be the perfect quality state for object *o* in *Sp*(*o*), and *q* be another presentation state of *o*. Quality-loss is a normalization function, *quality-loss*(*q*), that maps the *distance* (*q*,*p*) to a real number in the range [0,1].

Given the properties of the presentation space, it is now possible to define a quality-loss based ordering on presentation states. The normalization of quality-loss is useful because it enables a uniform distribution of resource consumption levels across the range of quality-loss values.

Definition 5 (*latent quality*)

Let *l* be the presentation state of object *o* in *Sp*(*o*) originally captured in digital format. The latent quality of *o* is defined by *quality-loss* (*l*).

Definition 6 (apparent quality)

Let *a* be the presentation state of object *o* in *Sp*(*o*) experienced by the viewer. The apparent quality of object *o* is defined by *quality- loss*(*a*).

The latent and apparent qualities of a presentation are determined by the capture, sampling, quantization and delivery errors present in its stored and delivered representations respectively.

Definition 7 (*quality dimension*)

A quality dimension is a dimension of the presentation state space *Sp(o)*.

We use the term quality dimension to represent each distinct type of information in a presentation over which QoS control is possible. By "type of information" we mean aspects of the presentation such as its color depth, spatial or temporal resolution, which may be made available as QoS adaptation parameters.

Definition 8 (*dimensional quality-loss*)

Given the perfect quality presentation state *p* and another presentation state *s* of object *o* in *Sp(o)*, and a quality dimension *d*, the dimensional quality-loss of *s* is *distance (s,p)* along dimension d.

The use of quality dimensions and dimensional quality-loss are important for simplifying the specification of QoS requirements and the implementation of QoS control mechanisms. They allow aspects of a presentation with different degrees of importance to be distinguished from one another and insulate users and system builders from the complexity of the entire presentation state space.

Definition 9 (*quality dimension type*)

A quality dimension type is a grouping of quality dimensions with common characteristics.

Quality dimension types are defined to enable reuse and help enforce consistency among exposed quality dimensions that are similar. Quality dimensions can be categorized as being of the base types *capture*, *sampling*, *quantization* or *delivery*, or combinations thereof, according to the class of errors they introduce. To be useful in real systems, however, quality dimensions must eventually be defined in terms that are meaningful in the application domain. In our model, we allow application- specific quality dimensions to be defined as sub- types of the basic types outlined above. For example, a query result whose type is a single video stream might be described using four quality dimensions: frame rate, color-depth, horizontal and vertical resolution (see Figure 22.2)

Quality adaptations in the frame rate quality dimension can be implemented via frame dropping which reduces the temporal resolution of the video and maps to an adjustment of sampling frequency, and hence sampling error. Similarly, quality adaptations in the color-depth quality dimension can be implemented by changing the number of bits per pixel, which can be mapped to an adjustment of quantization error. Quality adaptations in the horizontal and vertical resolution dimensions can be implemented by changing the number of pixels used to represent the image, hence adjusting the spatial resolution of the image. Dropping pixels can be viewed as an adjustment of quantization in the image, or, taking the analog video display view, as a reduction in the sampling frequency along scan lines.

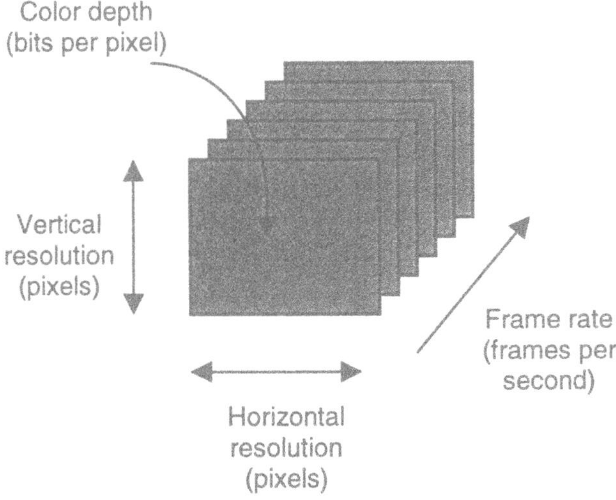

Figure 22.2: Example quality dimensions for video

Specific delivery quality dimensions include the *shift, rate* and *jitter* subtypes. Shift quantifies the amount of time a presentation is behind or ahead of schedule, rate quantifies the proximity of the actual play rate to the intended play rate of the presentation, and jitter quantifies the variation in rate of the presentation.

Some systems export quality dimensions that allow compound errors, from more than one class, to be introduced during QoS adaptation. An example in the video streaming domain includes an MPEG-1 to H.263 transcoding step, which is a lossy conversion of the video from one compressed format to another, perhaps with a new frame rate and spatial resolution. In this case, the quality dimension exported by the system combines capture, quantization and sampling errors.

22.2.2 Mapping Utility to Quality

The above definitions of the presentation state space and quality dimensions allow the quality-loss in a particular presentation state to be described either in quality dimension-specific terms, via the *dimensional quality-loss* function, or in absolute terms via the *quality-loss* function. Dimensional quality-loss functions impose a partial order on the presentation state space.

This partial order can be translated into a total order by specifying the relative importance, or weighting, of different dimensions and different values within a dimension. This assignment can be viewed abstractly as a distortion of the presentation state space. The quality-loss function, as described above, imposes a total ordering on presentation states by assuming one particular distortion of the space. In a real system, this distortion could be based, for example, on the resource consumption requirements of the various presentation states. However, different distortions are likely to be appropriate to match the requirements of different users performing different tasks.

We support the specification of user QoS requirements in our model by allowing a mapping of *utility* to dimensional quality-loss in each of the available quality dimensions.

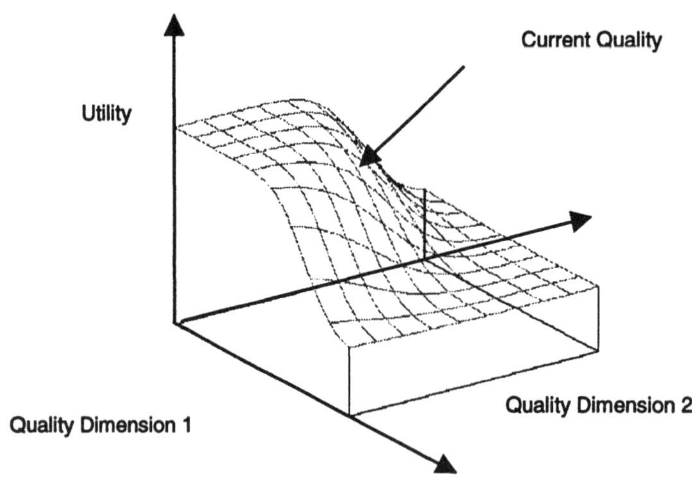

Figure 22.3: A two-dimensional quality surface

Definition 10 (*utility value*)

A utility value is a measure of usefulness, represented by real numbers in the range [0,1]. 0 represents useless, and 1 represents as good as perfect.

Conceptually, the mapping of utility to presentation states defines a multidimensional *utility surface* that describes the usefulness of all possible states in the presentation state space (see Figure 22.3).

At any instant the quality achieved by the system defines a point on the utility surface. Given such a surface, the goal of a quality adaptation strategy would be to attain the highest possible position on the surface using the currently available resources and quality adaptation options.

In practice, however, it is difficult for users to specify their requirements in terms of a multidimensional surface, therefore we use the simpler, and more restrictive, approach of defining a separate *utility function* per quality dimension. These utility functions relate particular points in that quality dimension with their utility to the user.

Definition 11 (utility function)

A utility function, U_d, is a function that maps dimensional quality-loss distances in a single quality dimension to utility values.

Associated with each utility function are two thresholds, q_{min} and q_{max}, that describe the upper and lower bounds on useful quality, respectively (see Figure 22.4).

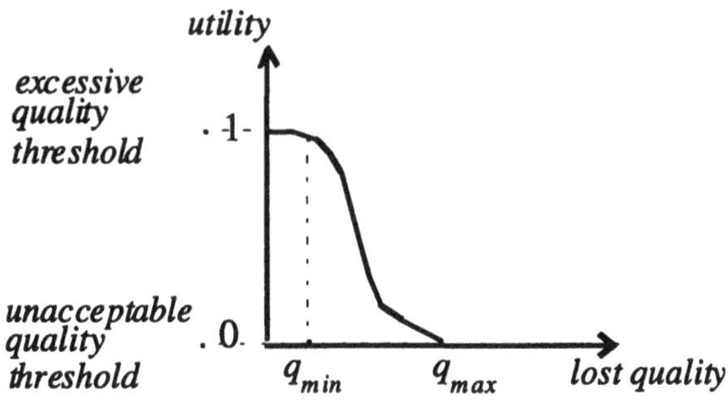

Figure 22.4: A utility function with thresholds

q_{max} defines the point at which dimensional quality-loss has grown so large that utility equals zero (i.e., its is the lower bound on useful quality). q_{min} defines the point at which further decreases in dimensional quality-loss yield no further increase in utility because utility equals 1 (i.e., it is the upper bound on uscful quality). Acccptablc quality adaptations should cnsurc that quality remains between these thresholds in each dimension.

An approximation to the true overall utility value for a presentation state can be calculated by performing a weighted combination of the values returned by the utility functions for each of the state's quality dimensions.

Definition 12 (dimensional utility)

Given a presentation state, s, of object o, in $Sp(o)$, a quality dimension, d, and a utility function, U_d over that quality dimension, the value returned by $U_d(s)$ is the dimensional utility of s in dimension d.

Definition 13 (overall utility function)

Given a presentation state, s, a set U of dimensional utilities of s, and a set W of weights, we define the overall utility function, denoted by $U_{all}(u,w)$, as follows:

$$U_{all}: U*W \rightarrow_C R$$

U_{all} takes a dimensional utility vector u in U and a weight vector w *in* W and returns a real number in R, where:

- $u = (u_1,u_2,...u_i,...,u_n)$, $1<=i<=n$, each u_i in U represents a dimensional utility,
- C is the $R =_{def} [0,1]$, and represents the weighted combination of dimensional utilities,
- constraint that if $\exists u_I$ such that $u_i = 0$ then $U_{all}(u,w) = 0$,
- $w = (w_1,w_2,...w_i,...,w_n)$, $1<=i<=n$, each w_i *in* [0,1] represents the weight that the dimensional utility u_i takes in the computation of the overall utility function.

The overall utility function described above can be used to reconstruct an approximation to the real utility surface.

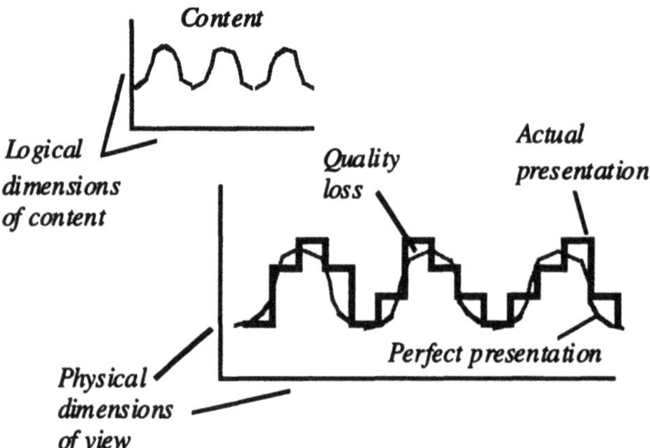

Figure 22.5: Content, quality and view concepts

22.2.3 The Quality-View Relationship

An important characteristic of the quality specification approach described above is that a user's quality requirements are not defined relative to the quality of the stored content. Instead, they are defined in absolute terms, and hence the model supports independence among viewing requirements and stored content characteristics. However, as described so far, quality requirement specifications are still somewhat ambiguous. Consider the following example.

Example 1: A user defines a utility function for the frame-rate quality dimension of a video presentation. The x axis of the function is in units of 1/(frames per second), and the upper bound on useful quality is defined to be equivalent to 30 frames per second.

The ambiguity of this specification is rooted in the use of time in the x axis of the utility function. When the user refers to 30 frames per second, whose seconds are they referring to? Do they mean seconds of playout time (viewer's time), or do they mean seconds of content time (author's time)? If the video is being viewed at normal speed, i.e., the speed the author intended it to be viewed, both interpretations are equivalent. However, in real systems viewers generally have control over play speed, through controls for fast forward, slow motion, and reverse play, etc. When such controls are used, what effect, if any, should they have on quality? Specifically, in Example 1, when a user doubles the play speed, should more than 30 frames per second ever be received? If the specification of quality requirements is based on viewer's time they should not, whereas, if it is based on author's time they should.

One reason for interpreting QoS specifications relative to viewer's time is to prevent quality parameters, such as frame rate, from surpassing the viewer's perception level and wasting resources as view parameters, such as play speed, are increased.

Conversely, a reason for interpreting QoS specifications relative to the author's time is to preserve quality when query results are stored. Consider the case of a viewer storing the result of a query instead of, or in addition to, viewing it during retrieval. The latent quality of the stored result should be independent of the speed with which it was delivered.

Because of the issues highlighted in the discussion above, our QoS model, like Staehli's, distinguishes among *view* specification and *quality* specification. View specification is concerned with mapping the logical dimensions of the content, which were specified by the author, to real world dimensions specified by the viewer (see Figure 22.5).

Example 1 only discussed the time dimension, however, view specifications can also refer to other dimensions such as window size. We refer to the default mapping for these dimensions as the *identity view*, but expect viewers to have controls to over-ride the identity view in order to define *actual views* that match their specific viewing requirements.

The discussion above illustrates that quality specifications can be interpreted relative to the identity view or the actual view. The quality requirements of query results intended for immediate viewing only should normally be interpreted relative to the actual view, whereas the quality requirements of query results intended for storage should be interpreted relative to the identity view.

22.2.4 Advantages of the Model

From a data semantics viewpoint the QoS model described above has several advantages. It identifies the data components that are important for storage and retrieval and separates quality of presentation from quality of stored representation.

The model also offers several degrees of independence that are useful in multimedia database systems. First, it supports independence among authoring and viewing concerns. At content creation time the author doesn't have to anticipate the viewer's eventual use of the presentation, or the capabilities of the system on which it will be viewed. Authors are concerned primarily with the specification of content, although they may specify default parameters for view and quality. Viewers can choose to use these defaults or over-ride them by specifying their own view and quality requirements.

Secondly, the model supports independence among viewing concerns and system capabilities. The key to providing this form of independence is the ability to specify degraded quality in order to make efficient use of scarce resources. Hence, the type of end-system the viewer has need not limit either the content or the view of the presentation. However, given a specific content and view, the capabilities of the system impose a limit on quality.

Third, since quality requirements can be specified with respect to either the identity or actual view, the model supports queries that retrieve presentations for immediate viewing as well as for storage.

Fourth, because quality is defined relative to a hypothetical perfect presentation with quality dimensions that are continuous, the model supports the quantification of the latent quality of the content. As technology advances and new capture devices, with higher precision and throughput, become available, the resultant quality improvements can also be quantified using this model. In contrast, an approach that defines quality requirements relative to the quality of the actual stored content requires a separate notion of quality to quantify the latent quality of the content. Furthermore, such an approach lacks independence between the specification of the viewer's quality requirements, the quality of the content, and the characteristics of the technology used to capture it.

The model also has the advantage of providing a basis for both hard guarantee and adaptation- based systems. Since we model requests for QoS adaptation using utility functions with upper and lower bounds on acceptable quality, a request for a hard QoS guarantee can be made simply by specifying both upper and lower bounds at the same quality level. In this case, utility functions are simple step functions.

Finally, the model illustrates a distinction between information that should be associated with data and information that should be associated with uses of data. Information describing the latent quality of the data should clearly be attached to the data itself, as meta-data. Similarly, the quality dimensions that are made directly accessible by the representation of the data (for example, a layered video encoding) should be stored as meta data associated with the data itself. QoS specifications, comprised of utility functions and parameters for combining them, should clearly be associated with uses of data, rather than associated directly with the data itself, as should view specifications.

22.3 PRACTICAL IMPLEMENTATION OF THE MODEL

22.3.1 Architecture Overview

We have implemented a prototype multimedia system based on our model

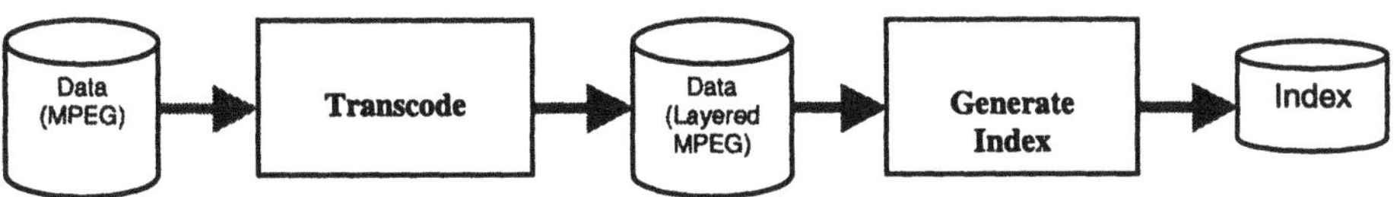

Figure 22.6-a: Off-line components of QoS adaptation prototype

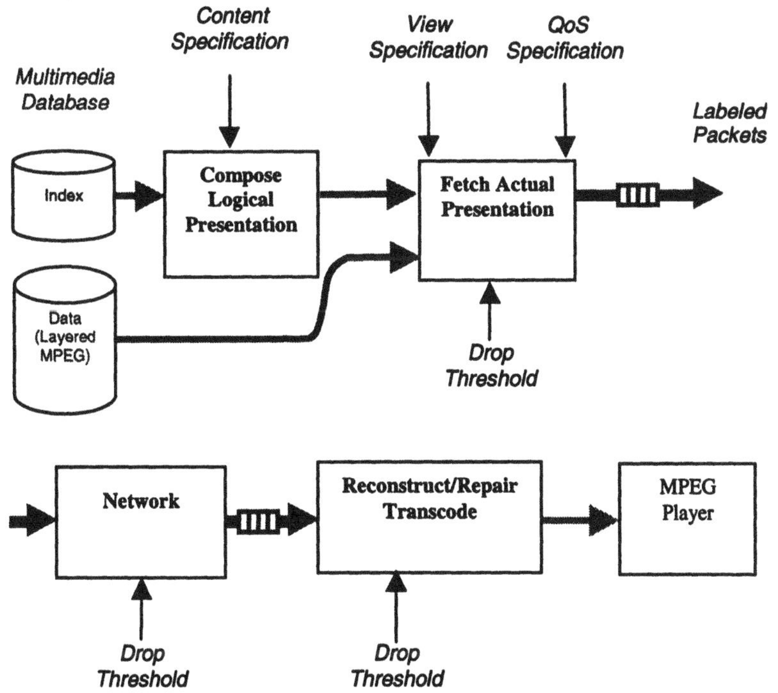

Figure 22.6-b: On-line components of QoS adaptation

(see Figure 22.6).

The basic components of the implementation are a remote storage server, a network, and a multimedia presentation client. The remote storage server supports preparation of a layered video encoding format suitable for network transport; the video format is derived from MPEG-1.

The video preparation process is divided into off-line and on-line components (see Figures 22.6-a and 22.6-b). Network filters perform prioritized data dropping to scale resource consumption. The client side includes components to reconstruct and repair data as necessary to form a standard MPEG video stream. The user is able to specify Quality of Service requirements via the client, which are used to control adaptation decisions throughout the system.

22.3.2 QoS Specification

The system allows a user to specify QoS adaptation requirements via a micro-language. The language provides constructs for expressing utility functions in the controllable quality dimensions of the multimedia system. The language also provides a construct to specify weighted combination of

```
value temporal_utility =
   let frame_rate_low =   5.0 in
   let frame_rate_high = 30.0 in
   let frames_to_lost_temporal_qos = fun fr -> 1.0 / (0.5 * fr) in
   let max_lost_temporal_qos =
                     frames_to_lost_temporal_qos(frame_rate_low) in
   let min_lost_temporal_qos =
                     frames_to_lost_temporal_qos(frame_rate_high) in
   let range = max_lost_temporal_qos - min_lost_temporal_qos in
   let user_utility = fun lq ->
                let offset = lq - min_lost_temporal_qos in
                let lq_norm = offset / range in
                let util = 1.0 - lq_norm in
                util * util
   in
                {low_thresh=min_lost_temporal_qos;
                high_thresh=max_lost_temporal_qos;
                utility_fn=user_utility}

value temporal_weight=1.0;;
value spatial_utility= ...
value spatial_weight=0.5
```

Figure 22.7: Example quality specification written in our QoS microlanguage

utility functions.

Utility functions express a mapping between lost quality levels and a normalized scale of user utility. A general utility function for a single quality dimension was shown earlier in Figure 22.4. The two thresholds indicate the points where quality becomes either excessive or inadequate, and we are primarily concerned with the shape of the function within the range defined via these thresholds. The function's shape guides the adaptation process in the multimedia system.

Figure 22.7 gives an example of a quality specification. The specification

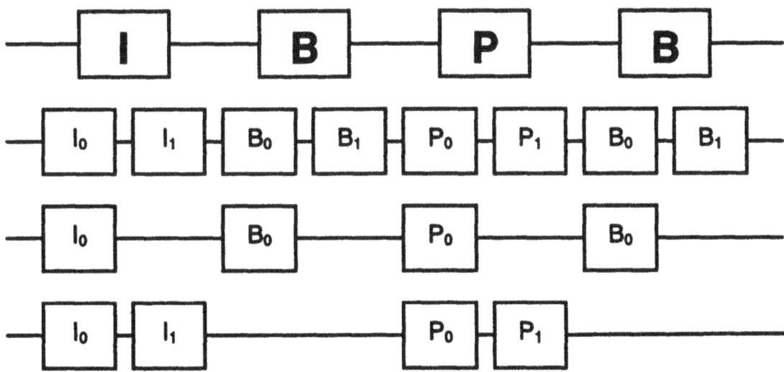

Figure 22.8: MPEG-based layered video encoding

is in the form of a micro- program which, in practice, can be produced either directly by the user, perhaps via a graphical editor, or selected from a list of prespecified defaults.

The language has the declarative style of a functional programming language, although, this style is not a hard requirement of our approach.

We model utility as it relates to quality-loss. For sampling quality dimensions we model quality-loss by 1/f, where f=frequency response. Note that this value tends to zero for perfect temporal resolution and to infinity for no frequency response. Since multimedia video involves displaying a sequence of still frames, the temporal signals are represented by discrete subsampling of the true signal. The Nyquist theorem states that maximum frequency response under discrete sampling is half the sampling rate (frame rate). In other words, lost quality is proportional to half of the sampling interval, hence the substitution of 0.5 * frame rate in the 1/f lost quality formula in Figure 22.7. The components of spatial resolution could be handled in a similar manner, but in our system we use peak signal to noise ratio (PSNR)[1] as the quality dimension for lost spatial quality.

22.3.3 Resource Management

The system delivers video as a stream of data packets, and adapts quality by selectively dropping packets. To enable this approach, the layered video encoding separates into distinct packets, data corresponding to the quality dimensions in which adaptation is possible. Figure 22.8 illustrates the selective data dropping approach. The top line depicts a sequence of four

[1]PSNR is a popular image error measurement based on the sum of the squared differences between corresponding pixels of two images.

packets, each corresponding to one MPEG picture. The second line represents a transcoding of the MPEG format where each picture has been divided into two components, denoted by the subscripts. If both level zero and level one components are decoded, the result is the same as the original MPEG picture. If level one is dropped then the result exhibits degraded PSNR compared to the original. The third and fourth lines depict different adaptation policies. In the third line, PSNR is reduced while temporal resolution is maintained. The fourth line depicts preservation of PSNR over temporal resolution.

User-provided QoS specifications are translated into a priority labeling scheme for packets in the video stream. This association of priorities with packets fixes the order in which packets will be dropped should adaptation become necessary due to resource shortages. At run time, the system adjusts the resource requirements of video delivery to match the available resources simply by adjusting the priority threshold below which packets are dropped.

In a reservation-based approach, the priority threshold would be fixed at the level corresponding to the user's maximum quality loss threshold; and admission control would ensure that adequate resources are available to process all packets with priority higher than the threshold.

22.3.4 Priority Labeling

The packet priority labeling algorithm uses utility functions to compute the cumulative utility loss of dropping each component of the layered video encoding. In our current encoding, these components are packets associated with I, B, and P pictures[2], at four PSNR levels. The computed loss is cumulative in that it accounts for the loss in the component in question and its dependencies. Dependencies are either hard, as they are implied by the structure of MPEG, or soft, as they reflect good policies for adaptation. An example of a hard dependency is that dropping an I picture implies that certain P and B frames may be dropped too. An example of a soft dependency is that dropped frames be spaced as uniformly as possible.

Hard and soft dependencies are used to define an ordering on packets within each quality dimension, which may be total or partial depending on the quality dimension in question. We then compute, for each packet and each dimension, the cumulative quality-loss when the packets and all lower-order packets in that dimension are dropped. The utility functions in the user's quality specification provide quality dimension-specific mappings from cumulative quality-loss to cumulative lost dimensional utility. The final prioritization of packets in the stream, based on lost overall utility, is then derived as follows:

---

[2]The MPEG video compression standard defines three frame types: Intra-coded (I), predictive-coded (P), and bidirectionally predictive-coded (B).

1. If in all quality dimensions the cumulative lost dimensional utility is zero, assign minimum priority.
2. If in any quality dimension the cumulative lost dimensional utility is one, assign maximum priority.
3. Otherwise, scale the weighted combination of the cumulative lost dimensional utilities into a priority in the range [minimum + 1, maximum - 1].

Minimum priority is reserved for packets that should never pass, because the cumulative lost dimensional utility of the packet in all quality dimensions does not cause quality to drop below the q_{min} threshold of any of the utility functions in the users QoS specification. Similarly, the maximum priority is reserved for packets that should always pass since in at least one of the quality dimensions, to drop the packet would cause quality to drop below the q_{max} threshold.

22.4 RELATED WORK

Sabata, et al.[13] define QoS in terms of Timeliness, Precision, and Accuracy. Roughly speaking, timeliness relates to the responsiveness of the system - how much time expires between the receipt by the system of a request, and its production of a result. Precision refers to the number of bits used to represent the result. Accuracy refers to the distance between an infinitely precise result and the real- world value it is intended to represent. These primitive QoS concepts are similar to the error classes defined in our model. Precision and accuracy error components can be applied within the quality dimensions of our model. For example, the number of frames used to represent a video presentation could be viewed as defining the precision error component of presentation states in the frame rate quality dimension. Similarly, the number of pixels per frame can be viewed as defining the precision error component of presentation states in the x and y spatial quality dimensions, and the number of bits per pixel can be viewed as determining the precision error component of presentation states in the color-depth quality dimension.

Sabata et al's accuracy component is related to our capture error class, since the capture process for obtaining video content not only imposes limits on the precision error component, but also on the accuracy due to the characteristics of the capture device.

Our utility functions are similar to Sabata et al's benefit functions. They define utility as a function of lost quality for each dimension of the result. We don't distinguish between quality lost due to imprecision or inaccuracy, since errors due to lack of precision are indistinguishable from errors due to inaccuracy as far as the user is concerned. In other words, when declaring their quality requirements, users care simply about the level of error in the result, not the source of the error. Users are capable of distinguishing among errors in different quality dimensions however. For example, they typically know the difference between low frame rate and low spatial resolution. In the lower levels of the system, however, it is useful to model sources of error. Stored data has precision and accuracy error components that define its *latent quality*. Information about these error components could be stored as meta data alongside the data itself.

Our quality adaptation machinery (the data- dropping virtual machine) introduces further error into the presentation by dropping data in various quality dimensions. The exact effect of this dropping depends on the policy for labeling/prioritizing components of the data stream, but tends to introduce precision errors, i.e., a frame dropper reduces the temporal resolution of the stream and hence is affecting the precision error component of the temporal dimension. Data droppers that drop color information are similarly affecting the precision error component in the color dimension.

Its not clear whether Sabata's notion of timeliness fits as an error component in our model. The accuracy and precision error components seem to refer to the latent quality of stored data, and could be stored as meta data. The timeliness notion seems more applicable to the apparent quality of the retrieved data. This is purely a viewing concern, not an authoring concern, and in our case this is analogous to the specification of a utility function for a new delivery quality dimension.

QoS specification, at the resource level, has received significant attention in the literature [14,15,16,17]. The token bucket model is often used to describe network traffic flows in terms of average and peak bandwidth and burstiness. The approach can be used to describe both stream characteristics and reservation requirements [14,17]. This approach to QoS specification is at a lower level of abstraction than our QoS model, but can serve as a target to map our QoS specifications into. For example, a set of utility functions that describe thresholds for video frame rate and resolution can be used, together with other video stream meta-data, to generate a token-bucket description of the video stream's resource requirements.

Thimm describes techniques for QoS adaptation in multimedia databases [8,9]. His notion of stream presentation parameter is similar to our quality dimension notion. He describes a method for varying presentation QoS using lookup tables and describes normalization functions, similar to our weighting of utility functions, for combining multiple presentation parameters. Layered above these mechanisms is an embedded QoS control system for managing QoS adaptations globally across concurrent presentations.

Rajkumar et al introduce a resource allocation model for QoS management that includes the concepts of QoS dimensions and utility surfaces [18]. The model described in [18] is somewhat more general than ours in the sense that it relates arbitrary application processes and system resources. However, the definition of content and view specifications makes our model more applicable to multimedia databases. The model described by Rajkumar et al also maps utilities directly to resource allocations, whereas our model maps utilities to dimension-specific quality measures. As a consequence, our model allows a separation between viewing concerns and system capabilities. Finally, our model introduces the concepts of latent and apparent quality, not present in the model described by Rajkumar et al.

Other researchers have proposed models for QoS contract negotiation in environments with multiple resources [19,20].

22.5 CONCLUSION

We have outlined a model for QoS control in multimedia databases. The principle concepts of the model include a separation of content, view and quality specification, the definition of quality as a distance measure in multiple quality dimensions, and the use of utility functions to capture user QoS preferences in each dimension. We demonstrated that the model can cover practically useful adaptation strategies by describing a prototype implementation in which user QoS preferences drive prioritization of an underlying data stream, enabling data to be dropped in the correct order when resources become scarce.

The model supports several degrees of independence that we believe are important in multimedia databases. In particular, it supports independence among authoring concerns, viewing concerns and system capabilities, and allows the quantification of the latent quality of content as well as the degradations in quality that result from retrieving content for viewing or storage.

In the future we plan to explore the implications of more complex content and new object-based video encoding schemes. Our definition of multiple quality dimensions, and our use of a layered stream format to implement them can be viewed as a crude form of complex content already. Our QoS model allows users to identify how important these various components of the presentation are relative to each other. This view also offers a glimpse into the future when even single video streams will have complex structure due to the independent encoding of the various objects contained in the stream. Whether to describe different objects in the video using different quality dimensions, or to define them as different points along a single quality dimension is just one of the open research questions we are interested in addressing in the future.

References

[1] "Report on the 5th IFIP International Workshop on Quality of Service (IWQoS'97)", Oguz Angin, Andrew Campbell, Lai-Tee Cheok, Raymond R-F Liao, Koon-Seng Lim, Klara Nahrstedt, ACM SIGCOMM Computer Communication Review, July 1997.

[2] "Adaptive Methods for Distributed Video Presentation", Crispin Cowan, Shanwei Cen, Jonathan Walpole, and Calton Pu, Computing Surveys Symposium on Multimedia, December 1995, Volume 27, Number 4, pages 580-583.

[3] "Design of a Multimedia Player with Advanced QoS Control", Rainer Koster, MS thesis, OGI, January 1997.

[4] "Meeting arbitrary QoS constraints using dynamic rate shaping of coded digital video," Eleftheriadis, A., and Anastassiou, D., In NOSSDAV 95, Lecture Notes in Computer Science, Springer-Verlag, vol. 1018 pp. 95-- 106, April 1995.

[5] "Resource Management in Networked Multimedia Systems," Klara Nahrstedt and Ralf Steinmetz, Computer, IEEE, pages 52-63, May 1995.

[6] "System Support for Mobile Multimedia Applications", Jon Inouye, Shanwei Cen, Calton Pu, and Jonathan Walpole, Proceedings of the 7th International Workshop on Network and Operating Systems Support for Digital Audio and Video (NOSSDAV 97), St. Louis, Missouri, May 1997.

[7] "Flow and Congestion Control for Internet Streaming Applications," Shanwei Cen, Calton Pu, Jonathan Walpole, Proceedings Multimedia Computing and Networking 1998 (MMCN98), pages 220-264, San Jose, California, January 24-28, 1998.

[8] "Optimal Quality of Service under Dynamic Resource Constraints in Distributed Multimedia Database Systems," Heiko Thimm, Ph.D. Thesis, Universitat Darmstadt, June 1998.

[9] "Managing Adaptive Presentation Executions in Distributed Multimedia Database Systems", Heiko Thimm, Wolfgang Klas, Jonathan Walpole, Calton Pu, and Crispin Cowan. Proceedings IEEE International Workshop on Multimedia Database Management Systems (IW-MM- DBMS'96), Blue Mountain Lake, NY, IEEE Computer Society Press, pp. 152-159, August 1996.

[10] "Device and Data Independence for Multimedia Presentations", Richard Staehli, Jonathan Walpole and David Maier, Computing Surveys Symposium on Multimedia, December 1995, Volume 27, Number 4, pages 640-643.

[11] "Quality of Service Specification for Multimedia Presentations", Richard Staehli, Jonathan Walpole and David Maier, Multimedia Systems, November, 1995, volume 3, number 5/6.

[12] "Quality of Service Specification for Resource Management in Multimedia Systems", Richard Staehli, Ph.D. thesis, OGI, January 1996.

[13] "Taxonomy for QoS Specifications," B. Sabata, S. Chatterjee, M. Davis, J. Sydir, T. Lawrence, In the Proceedings of the IEEE Computer Society 3rd International Workshop on Object-oriented Real-time Dependable Systems (WORDS '97), Newport Beach, CA, Feb 1997.

[14] "RSVP: A new resource reservation protocol," Zhang, L., Deering, S., Estrin, D., Shenker, S., and Zappala, D., IEEE Network 7(5), pp. 8--18, September 1993.

[15] "Integrated Services in the Internet Architecture: an Overview," R. Braden, D. Clark, S. Shenker, ISI, MIT, and Xerox PARC Internet Request for Comments 1633, June 1994.

[16] "Supporting Real-Time Applications in an Integrated Services Packet Network: Architecture and Mechanisms", Clark, D., Shenker, S., and L. Zhang, Proc. SIGCOMM '92, Baltimore, MD, August 1992.

[17] "Specification of Guaranteed Quality of Service," S. Shenker, C. Partridge, R. Guerin, Xerox/BBN/IBM, IETF Integrated Services WG, INTERNET-DRAFT, 13 August 1996.

[18] "A Resource Allocation Model for QoS Management" Raj Rajkumar, Chen Lee, John Lehoczky and Dan Siewiorek, In Proceedings of the IEEE Real-Time Systems Symposium, December 1997.

[19] "Architectural Support for Quality of Service for CORBA Objects," Zinky JA, Bakken DE, Schantz R., Theory and Practice of Object Systems, Jan 1997.

[20] "The QoS Broker," Klara Nahrstedt, Jonathan M. Smith,IEEE Multimedia, Spring 1995, Vol.2, No.1, pp. 53-67.

23 SEMANTICS OF A MULTIMEDIA DATABASE FOR SUPPORT WITHIN SYNTHETIC ENVIRONMENTS FOR MULTIPLE SENSOR SYSTEMS

Gerald Sterling
Defence Science and Technology Organisation

Elizabeth Chang, and
Tharam Dillon
LaTrobe University, Melbourne, Australia

Abstract: This paper describes work investigating the application of synthetic environment technology to sensor systems with particular emphasis on the multimedia aspects of the work. The work is being done within the Air Operations Division of the Defense Science and Technology Organisation and La Trobe University in Australia.

An analysis of the needs of the system users is carried out and a 3D synthetic environment design developed which aims to improve overall man-machine performance of the surveillance sensor systems. It is considered that the improved performance will arise from improved operator situation management system which enables the user to 'see' what his sensors detect and which assists the user in the analysis and interpretation of raw sensor data and higher level information produced by sensor system post-processing. Importantly, the interface permits a user to revisit multimedia archives that record past activity within the sensed world.

An overview of the conceptual analysis and design is presented. A conceptual model of the synthetic environment has been developed covering the knowledge base, the user interface and the sensor system interfaces. An object-oriented model of a synthetic knowledge base is used to record the sensed world and present it to the user as an analogue of the real world. The analysis of requirements of the multimedia facilities that are presented to the operator are discussed in some detail. A method of assigning meaning to segments of continues data similar to video is developed. A suitable data model to accommodate multimedia data is proposed. Finally a method if developing user interfaces for presentation of multimedia data based on the concepts of the Abstract User Interface Objects is presented.

23.1 INTRODUCTION

Synthetic Environment Systems cover a broad range of factors from displays systems, auditory and visual, through tactile interface and user interaction issues to improve generation, computing platform and other human factors aspects. This investigation considers some of these issues in the context of the concept of a 3D visual and auditory synthetic environment to portray sensor system data. Mentor is intended to improve the workload disposition of sensor system operators in the formation of some understanding of their tactical situation. To this end Mentor should help the operator assess his situation by aiding in the monitoring of the behavior of each sensor contact.

Mentor has an overall configuration as shown in Figure 23.1. In past work the structural aspects of the objects within the Mentor concept have been described (Sterling and Dillon) [[1]]. Important amongst these is the hierarchical nature of the Mentor model of the Real World Environment (RWE) that is constructed within the Mentor knowledge base. In this model the Synthetic World Environment (SWE) sensor contacts are represented as synthetic world entities (SWEs). Knowledge regarding contacts – real world entities (RWEs) – and knowledge required to reason about the RWEs is stored in this object-oriented representation of the world.

In this paper we continue to discuss the conceptual structural and behavioral analysis of Mentor. In particulate there is a focus upon those aspects of the information management that relate to multimedia issues within Mentor. Multimedia in the Mentor context deals with raw video from radar and flir sensor systems, audio recording of explanatory reasoning from operator or agents and textual record of explanatory reasoning of operator or agents as well as numerical information that indicates location, speed and duration of motion. This information is stored within a Multimedia database to provide the Mentor user the capacity to look again at the way a particular scenario developed and perhaps reinterpret the situation to take account of some previously unobserved facet of an entity's behavior.

The Multimedia information stored in the database is, therefore, primarily focused on storing information collected in real time from the sensors. It also requires putting markers on this information with respect to time, events and locations. There is also a need to retrieve information from the database not just using textual or symbolic ways but using queries that utilize image and video based information in the query. To this extent it has a somewhat different purpose to multimedia databases that might be used in conjunction with authoring systems or non time oriented information. This requires a somewhat different structure and additional semantics for the multimedia database. A key issue here is the development of the user interface to the multimedia database to assist with appropriate display of multimedia information.

In general, this display has a stronger emphasis on the dynamic aspect as well as the structural aspects normally associated with other databases. In order to facilitate an appropriate design, we introduce and define the notion of Abstract User Interface Objects which define the "external" schema to the multimedia database.

The paper will first briefly discuss the Operator's Domain and the general behavior of Mentor and its relationship to the operator. Second, the discussion revisits the conceptual model of Mentor addressing primarily the structural aspects of the knowledge base embodied within Mentor and Mentor itself. Third, some attention is paid to the nature of the SWE object representation of an entity including its attributes, methods and rule sets. Next the discussion focuses on the requirements and basis for multimedia management of video, audio and textural records of contact behavior. It examines the semantics underlying the multimedia database and defines Abstract User Interface Object which are used to define the "external schema" to the multimedia database.

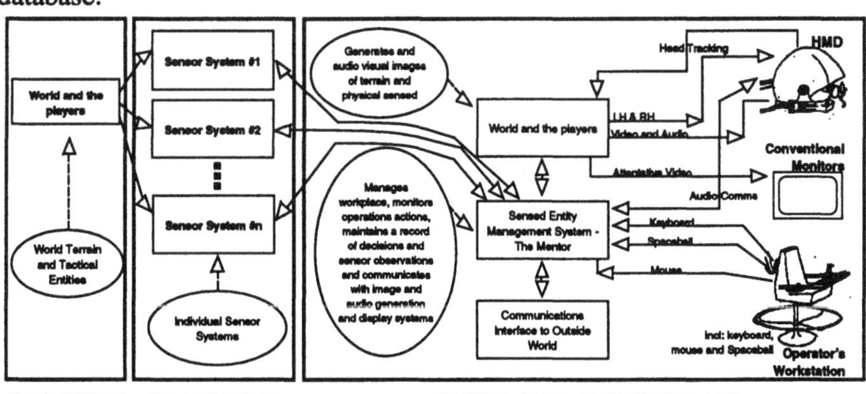

Figure 23.1: Configuration of a Sensor Platform and Mentor

23.2 BRIEF OVERVIEW OF THE MENTOR SYSTEM

We present a brief overview of Mentor in this section to create a context for the multimedia system being developed.

23.2.1 The Mentor Concept

As sensor systems become more capable many more contacts require management. Each contact requires investigation and each requires some decision making on the part of the operator/interpreter. This situation loads even more work onto already heavily loaded operators. Garner and Assenmacher [2] referred to these matters in their discussion on improving situation awareness. "Operator SA comprises detecting information in the environment, processing the information with relevant knowledge to create a mental picture of the current situation and acting on this picture to make a decision or explore further."

Mentor (see Figure 23.1) can be considered as an interface to a suite of sensors. When a sensor makes a contact, a representation is formed of an unknown entity within the existing tactical terrain environment. The spatial arrangement between the contact, the host sensor platform, the terrain, and other entities is maintained. The operator interacts with entities using this 3D perspective display. The heart of Mentor is the intelligent assistant system used in the management of these entities.

Conceptually this management system is an Intelligent Assistant System that will aid the operator to monitor the behavior of entities. Boy [3] introduces notions of Intelligent Assistants that learn in a manner similar to Rasmussen's [4] Skills Rules Knowledge model of Human Learning. Mentor will employ an object-oriented rule based approach in which intelligent assistant agents respond to rule sets devised by the operator as he deals with entity types for the first time. As these rule sets demonstrate their utility they may be retained for later application with other Synthetic World Entities (SWE's) of that class.

The long term objectives of Mentor is to investigate the use of intelligent assistant systems and multimedia database support systems and assess the utility of 3D perspective visual and auditory interfaces for Sensor management.

23.2.2 Basic Structure of Mentor

The fundamental objective of Mentor is to improve a sensor system operators understanding of what is occurring in the sensed world and ease communication of these understandings to others. To this end analysis has assumed that any final product will be distributed in nature and be of an open architecture that will readily support expansion with the addition of additional nodes to the network. However other than this underlying philosophically based assumption the analysis is not predicated on any other design consideration. The system under investigation has been described in conceptual terms elsewhere (Sterling and Dillon [[1]]) but some further attention will be paid to the issues here in particular those aspects that provide the foundation to multimedia database management objects.

The particular focus of this work has been on defence type surveillance systems. These may be airborne, seaborne or land based but for discussion purposes consider say an Airborne Early Warning & Control aircraft (AEW&C). It has many sensor systems, several with sophisticated post processing capability supporting data reduction (range bearing altitude elevation velocity) and tracking. The envisaged Mentor system will have a network interface to sensor, (say Mil Std 1553 bus interface) and it has the capacity to capture lower level raw video or audio output of such systems.

Real World Entities (RWE's) are the things that are detected by sensors and are the substance behind visual and auditory models that appear in the synthetic environment. A full sensor system has several components and these are Video, FLIR, Radar, Sonar and ESM (Electronic Support Measures). The output of all of these is continuous in the sense that video is continuous. This creates a more complex multimedia environment since there are many continuous media. Mentor's role is to provide the interface between the operator on the platform and the sensor systems.

Mentor consists of a number of component subsystems, the most important of these is the Contact Knowledge Base. The Contact Knowledge Base (CKB) is the repository of all information regarding sensed entities (contacts) and each such contact is instanced in the knowledge base as a Synthetic World Entity (SWE) – (Figure 23.2). Each SWE also acts as an agent, which using rules sets associated with each SWE reasons about the contact and informs the operator as required. Figure 23.2(b) shows one of the component objects namely Video embodiment. The other component objects excluding commentary audio have an analogous structure.

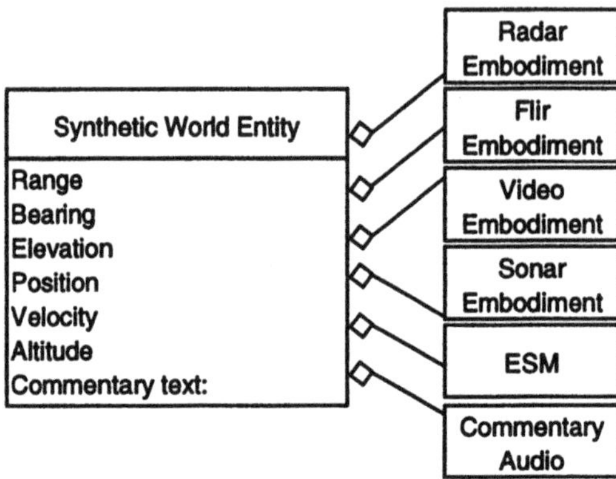

Figure 23.2(a): Synthetic World Entity

Video Embodiment

Range
Elevation
Bearing
Video Stills
Video Rush
Video Segment

[Video Rule Set]

Figure 23.2(b): Video Embodiment

The structure of the CKB is essentially hierarchical and the operator forms it as he reasons and forms inferences about a contact. An observation might first be inserted as a contact, next as an aircraft contact, next as a rotor craft, next a large rotorcraft and concludes perhaps finally as a type. However a particular operator might choose a much flatter structure and Mentor should support both approaches. At each level the context is different and for each context the operator specifies appropriate rules sets which an individual Mentor agent uses to monitor its SWE. These rules provide the action strategy to be used by each agent in its liaison with the operator, other agents, hardware systems and sensors.

An important facility provided to the operator is the capacity to replay old sensor information, that is, to revisit data to confirm that the prevailing interpretation is correct. Clearly higher level data can be stored within the knowledge base but lower level video and audio data from sensors is not so readily revisited. Also as agents reason about contacts explanatory information is produced both in auditory and textual form and the operator may himself form auditory comments that may be recorded. This is multimedia data with a strong temporal context and Mentor supports the review of such media.

Whilst the Synthetic environment itself can be replayed by looking at the temporal history of each contact and replaying it, replaying the multimedia components seems to require different handling. The requirements are analysed this way for four reasons. First, much of the multimedia data is continuous in nature. Second, it has to be viewed in the same temporal context as other media. Third, accessing the data by content is difficult and finally because of the nature of the likely multimedia archival mechanisms can be compute intensive.

With the facilities described the investigation can probe more deeply into the problems and mechanisms necessary to deliver effective sensor control and improved situation awareness using 3D perspective visual and auditory displays.

23.3 MULTIMEDIA MANAGEMENT METHODS FOR DEALING WITH MEDIA RETRIEVAL

Mentor receives sensed data in higher level form across a data bus and in lower level form as direct video or audio. It is important that the auditory comments of the operator be archived where such may be of benefit in the interpretation of a tactical situation. Further textual data reflecting intelligent assistant explanatory output should be accessible. The issue is how best to deal with this information, how best to tie it back to the synthetic world that is primary user interface to the sensor systems, and how to maintain continuity between the two.

Previous work on video management in multimedia framework was reviewed to help decide on an approach. Lieinhart, Effelsberg, Jain [5] in "Visual GREP" propose a systematic method to compare and retrieve video sequences which strives to determine similarity in video sequences. They describe techniques to compare video at the frame, shot, scene and whole video levels in an attempt to develop a query system for video files analogous to the UNIX (grep) for text files. They describe a colour coherence vector (CCV) to quantify color atmosphere, an edge change ratio (ECR) to measure motion intensity, face detectors and static and mobile framing to make similarity judgements and then use an algorithmic approach to comparing video at differing video levels. It does not seem to provide techniques that would serve especially well as an index mechanism to allow an operator a rapid search technique to review a lengthy recording that is effective for a real time system.

Wactlar, Kanade, Smith, and Stevens [6] work involves accurate connected speech recognition to automatically transcribe video sound track for later analysis. They assert the importance of image and language understanding in finding a video paragraph using camera cuts, object tracking, speaker changes and changes in audio content. They identified numerous sources of error in video transcription that must be addressed. They asserted no pressing need for real time performance. They discuss the image and language processing issues and describe the effectiveness of their combined image and language skimming techniques. However, whilst some of the image processing techniques may have some applicability in the context of our work (object presence and scene transition effects) the Imformedia Project work as a whole is not of great relevance.

Leinhart, Pfeiffer and Effelsberg [7] in "Video Abstracting" describe their work in the formation of video abstracts. They analyze a movie as a progressive aggregation of frames into shots, of shots into scenes and of scenes into the whole video. They define a "clip" as "a frame sequence selected to become an element of the abstract". Their three-step process includes video segmentation and analysis, clip selection and clip assembly. In the segementation process shots are determined by video and audio similarity (frequency and intensity spectrum) and dialog detection between consecutive shots. After segmentation the important features are extracted: e.g. actors, gunfire explosions and text. The Rowley, Buluja, Kanade face detection is used for identifying actors, audio analysis for action and OCR type text recognition. The clips are selected then on the basis of title text, action and genre. Comparison of automatically generated abstracts with man made ones did not detect a "better" product one way or the other. That being said for the purposes of our work, the interest must lie in the early segmentation work with cut detection and the use of Edge Change Ratio for that purpose. The notion using frames and clips as abstractions, is in may respects similar to our approach.

Christel, Smith, Taylor, and Winkler [8] consider that approaches of forming brief titles with individual "thumbnail" images (similar to our Stills) does not capture the temporal nature of video. Their proposal for a "video skim" presents a short video compacted by the ration 10:1 and viewed at normal playing speed. The skim preserves important audio and video component.

Our work aims to record raw material in multiple media formats and in essence the only techniques that seem applicable are either some form of visual fast forward, use of some form of cut detection and formation of a "Stills" collection or the formation of a "Rushes" collection. The other aspect of our work is the development of an appropriate user interface to support the fast review technique selected. The work at University of Mannheim and at

Carnegie Mellon University has broader applicability to video archival and retrieval particularly in a non real time framework whilst our interest is more on cut detection and image segmentation. In our technique, we abstract the meaning of the video into either stills, video rushes, temporal or textual markers.

First some preliminary discussion of the synthetic environment. As a scenario is played out a record is kept for each contact of position versus time. A trail of 'flagstones' can be switched on which trails the contact (SWE) showing where it and other entities have been in time and it also shows important event markers. By selecting a suitable flagstone or marker the synthetic environment may be regenerated and provides access to all contact data available at that point. This would include time and location and accordingly these data should be useful as an index to the multimedia recordings. Thus it should be possible to initiate replay by selection of such markers.

In recording media information the global philosophy has been to record material and maintain the context with SWE object in the process. In other words if a radar or flir maintains an ongoing focus on an entity then that video is recorded with reference to that entity. If a sensor is maintaining a general 360° sweep then a media client at the Contact Knowledge Base level manages that recording accordingly, then an operator may expect that by selecting a SWE his multimedia replay and record accesses will all pertain to that entity.

In this analysis consideration has been given to the work of Tonomura, Akutsu, Taniguchi and Suzuki [9] paper regarding structure and meaning. The approach they took in respect of browsing is of particular value with the notions they introduce of flash and rush browsers and paper video. Within Mentor after a video segment has been recorded the sequence is reviewed and searched for logical cuts and event markers. A small portion of the sequence after the cut or the marker is appended to a 'rush' file and a single frame appended to a 'still' file. The operator may then review either the 'rush' or 'still' file and commence detailed replay from that point. Checking the record time reference of the frame of interest and then replaying all media using index-time effects this. Where a media has no recorded information at the initial index-time, replay commences when data becomes available as the index-time increments during replay.

Whilst an entity is in the synthetic world there will be periods where a media record is either not necessary or not available and such breaks lead to logical formations of sequences of numbered sessions. Sessions have a start time, a duration and a start location and provide a ready access to the data in the companion media.

Video, audio and text (Media) may be received continuously or intermittently. The material will depend on the use to which the sensor is being put (it may be temporarily focused on other contacts), what the operator or agent may wish to say and what explanatory text is in fact necessary. This intermittency necessitates the provision of logical session and composite sequences.

Ultimately an operator or an agent controls a media client and recording and checking the field of view of the sensor for consistency with the bearing and elevation of the SWE and the current range of the sensor can control its termination. A facility is required such that of an SWE object is the subject of video or other media, a message is sent from the SWE object and temporary recording is started. Each recorded frame is numbered, a time recorded, a location and any event marker number and name noted.

Each reference is then be available as an index to a desired frame, audio segment or textual passage. An operator or agent may request that recording be made permanent starting at a particular time and recording continues until a stop is called or the contact moves out of focus.

Figure 23.3 depicts the logical media data format that the media units are to create that will allow the browsing of data and the replay of material from a browser selected position or from a location defined by 'flagstones' from within the synthetic environment.

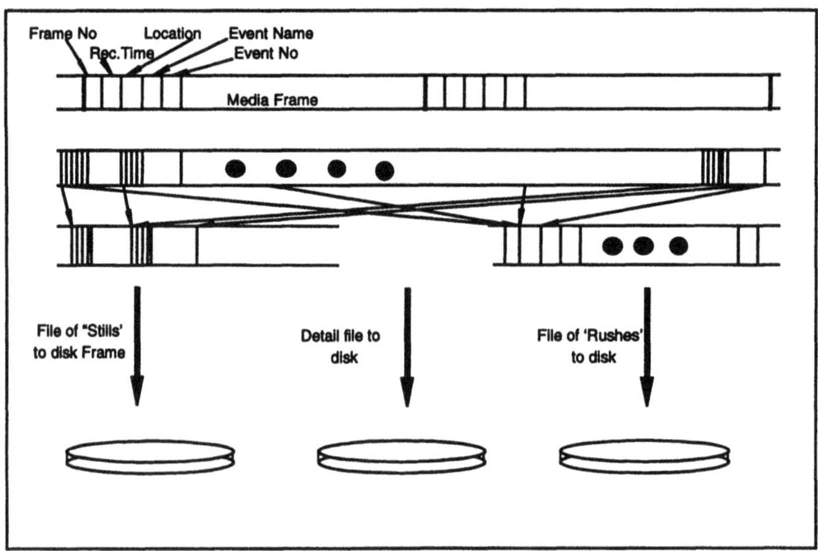

Figure 23.3: Logical Media Data Assembly

A still synopsis is to be formed by recording the location on disk of periodic frames (say every500th) interspersed with frames collected after a cut and frames that coincide with an operator or agent initiated event marker. A rush file synopsis is formed by selecting a series of say 5-second sequences of frames recording the location on disk of the start frames. Every 500th second say another 5-second interval is indexed. Interspersed within these are further 5 second frame sequences identified after a cut and 5 second frame sequences that coincide with an operator or agent initiated event marker. The formation of 'Stills' and 'Rushes' collections is less vital than real time recording and replay and is a background task that provides an important tool for the operator to find a required sequence in the archive.

23.4 MULTIMEDIA DATA MODEL

The multimedia database system is modeled using an Object-oriented Data Model, which is extended to allow for the different types of media.

In object-oriented systems, each instance object that is the value of an attribute belongs to an associated class. The associated class has a system-defined identifier, a value domain and allowed operations.

In the case of atomic instance objects, the value domain is a value set, and in the case of complex objects it is the domain construction, such as tuple type, set type, etc. If an instance object that is the value of an attribute is considered to be an element and the associated class an element type, then the value construction for instance objects and the value domain for the classes are described using a BNF-like language below.

Furthermore, the values could be complex objects. Note this forms a nested structure as the attributes associated with a class could themselves be complex objects and so on. In addition to the name and value of an attribute, it is also useful to associate semantic integrity constraints with it. These could specify the domain of the attribute (type), the range of permissible values, and admissibility of certain values.

<element>	::=	<ATOMIC element> | <COMPOSITE element>
<ATOMIC element>	::=	<INTEGER element> | <REAL element> | <BYTESTRING element> | <Image Element> | <Audio Segment element> | <Radar Segment element> | <Flir Segment element> | <Video Segment element> | <Sonar Segment element>
<COMPOSITE element>	::=	<TUPLE element> | <SET element>
<TUPLE element>	::=	$[a_1{:}E_1, \ldots, a_n{:}E_n]$ a_i : attribute name E_i : element
<SET element>	::=	$\{E_1, \ldots, E_n\}$

Figure 23.4: Value construction

```
<element type>              ::=   <ATOMIC element type> |
                                  <COMPOSITE element type>

<ATOMIC element type>       ::=   INTEGER | REAL | BYTESTRING | IMAGE | AUDIO
                                  SEGMENT | VIDEO SEGMENT | SONAR SEGMENT |
                                  Radar Segment | Flir segment

<COMPOSITE element type>    ::=   <TUPLE element type> |
                                  <SET element type>

<TUPLE element type>        ::=   TUPLE of (a1:EType1, .., an:Etypen)
                                  ai :            attribute name
                                  ETypei :   element type

<SET element type>          ::=   SET of (EType1, ...., ETypen)
```

Figure 23.5: Value domain construction

As for other object-oriented databases, an attribute in a domain object is a structure field in a tuple that gives semantics to the tuple object. It serves as a field of a tuple object that maps to an atomic object (an object which has atomic element as a value) or a set of atomic objects. Note this value which is an atomic element could belong to any of the media categories as shown in Figures 23.4 and 23.5.

As for other object-oriented databases, a relationship, like an attribute, is a field of a tuple object. Unlike an attribute which links a tuple object to an atomic object, a relationship maps a tuple object to another tuple object or a set containing at least one tuple object. That is, a relationship eventually gives an atomic object after more than one level of reference. Note here that the relationship always maps to another tuple object at the first level of mapping. It is only after this that it would map to an atomic element, drawn from different media.

As with other object-oriented databases it is important to allow hierarchical relationships and non-hierarchical relationships.

A hierarchical relationship is a relationship that links two parties in a hierarchical fashion. There are three kinds of hierarchical relationships, normally associated with object-oriented systems and these are also pertinent for multimedia databases and they are: generalisation (ISA relationship), classification (instance-of relationship) and aggregation (components-of relationship.

A non-hierarchical relationship is a relationship that links two parties in an arbitrary manner. This relationship cannot be represented in a hierarchy. These are sometimes referred to as association relationships.

The operations specified for a class and inherited by its instances are distinguished in three ways (Dittrich [10]/Dillon and Tan [11]): type specific vs generic; predefined vs user-defined; and one-level vs multi-level (composite elements). Type-specific operations are operations that are applied to the atomic values, whereas generic operations are for the composite values. Predefined operations are installed by the database developer. They are applied to some atomic value types. Generic operations are also usually predefined operations. User-defined operations, as the name suggests, are defined by the user. The existing operations can be called within the user-defined operations.

For composite elements, such as tuples and sets, operations can affect either the value only (one-level) or all levels of the whole composite element (multi-level).

Note in the case of video, to provide a handle for retrieval we often define a <labelled_video segment> as Tuple of (label: $EType_1$, duration:$Etype_2$ video_segment: VIDEOSEGMENT).

Note that the label, is of type text, image, video segment (in the case of a rush), time stamp. $Etype_2$ would be of type time duration. In a similar fashion, one could also define <labelled_audiosegment>. Note these atomic elements, labelled elements, and composite elements would be used as instance objects which form the value of attributes of domain objects.

Note that if we use a more general label to identify a video segment such as an Event label, or a label of type text, image or video segment (in the case of rush), then these would map directly to a time marker which would be used for retrieval.

With the structuring of video explained in the last section, a video segment, a radar segment or flir segment is essentially retrieved using a time marker. Event markers are mapped onto a time marker which is then used to retrieve the video segment, etc. To provide a handle for retrieval, we define a <time_labelled:video_segment> as

Tuple of (time
label:Etype1,duration:Etype2,video_segment:VIDEOSEGMENT)

Note that this time label and duration would be of type INTEGER.

23.5 ABSTRACT INTERFACE OBJECTS AS THE BASIS FOR ACCESSING MULTIMEDIA DATABASES

The user interface to a multimedia database is considerably more complex than that for a traditional database. The mechanisms used to define a user interface for a traditional database may not be adequate.

In databases, views are often used as the basis of generating particular displays for the user. A view in an object-oriented system can be thought of as a virtual class, ie. it is a class that does not contain any instances of its own. Rather, when it is invoked, a set of instances pertinent to it are generated. Since some views can be considered as specialisations of existing domain classes, the question that arises is whether these views should be incorporated into the domain ISA inheritance hierarchies. Early work on views by Scholl et al [12] and Abiteboul and Bonner [13]argued that they should be incorporated into the ISA or inheritance hierarchy of the domain. However, others such as Kim and Kelly [14] and Bertino [15] have argued that this is an inappropriate way to proceed.

It is inappropriate to include the view virtual classes in the domain inheritance hierarchies because:

(a) a view can be derived from an existing class by having fewer attributes and more methods. It would be inappropriate to treat it as a subclass unless one allowed for the notion of selective inheritance of attributes;

(b) two views could be derived from the same subclass with different groups of instances. However the instances from one view definition could be overlapping with the other and non-disjoint. An example of this would be a view A of employees that are salaried and casual employees. Consider another view B which separates employees into four different areas of Melbourne such as the Northern, Eastern, South Eastern and Western Suburbs. It is clear that both view A and view B partition the instances of class employee. However, note that one employee living in the Northern Suburbs could also be a Salaried employee. Hence, these view definitions A and B do not disjointedly partition the instances of the class employee.

(c) view definitions, while useful for examining data, might give rise to classes that may not be semantically meaningful to users Bertino [15].

(d) effects of schema changes on classes are automatically propagated to all subclasses. If a view is considered as a subclass, this could create problems Kim and Kelly [14] in requiring the changes to be propagated to the view as it might be appropriate or inappropriate.

(e) an inappropriate placement of the view in the inheritance hierarchy, could lead to violation of the semantics because of the extent of overlapping with an existing class Kim and Kelly[14].

For the above reasons, it is better that views be part of a separate inheritance hierarchy known as a view inheritance hierarchy. This view inheritance hierarchy is useful if we wish to define a view as a specialisation of another view. For example, if we wish to define the view Overtime_Permitted_Salaried_Employee as a specialisation of the view Salaried_employee. This new view is considered to be a subclass of the virtual class (view) Salaried_Employee.

Bertino [15] has essentially defined a view definition language. It is claimed that this view definition language allows one to represent both structure and behavioral features. However, it does the second only to a limited extent in the sense that it specifies the methods in the definition of a view but it does not model inter-object dynamics, such as the sequencing of messages between objects which define their dynamic interactions with one another. This feature, it must be conceded, is not of paramount importance in traditional database systems even though one still has to take cognisance of pre-conditions and post-conditions before a method in a particular object can be invoked. Kim and Kelly [14] also gave a very careful definition of views. Barclay and Kennedy [16] define three types of views: selection, projection and join. The above comments about deficiencies in modelling inter-object dynamics also apply to the work of Kim and Kelly [14] and Barclay and Kennedy [16]. While the modelling of inter-object dynamics does not loom so large in databases, it is of considerable significance when modelling multimedia systems. It is with text or numeric values of vital importance in real time systems, event driven software, simulation software and multimedia systems or in defining the navigational aspects of user interface design. In this section, we will introduce the notion of Abstract user Interface Objects, to overcome some of these deficiencies.

The primary purpose of views is three fold (Bertino [15], Kim and Kelly [14]).

(1) to allow the user to directly interact with data from a particular orientation and hence making them useful in defining queries.
(2) for content-based authorisation schemes
(3) as a basis for schema evolution

The Abstract User Interface Objects will also permit this and in addition allow the user to deal with the navigational aspects of the user interface.

Postulate 1 An Abstract User Interface Class (AUI) is a virtual class and it has
(i) attributes
(ii) methods
Since it is a virtual class, there are no stored instances; they are generated only when it is invoked. We refer to these as generated instances

Postulate2 An Abstract User Interface Class (AUI) is specified by its class specification that is a signature which consists of attributes, methods and their domains.

Postulate 3 The Abstract UI objects can generally be distinguished into two broad categories:
(i) AUI Information Objects
(ii) AUI Command Objects

Postulate 4 AUI Information Objects provide a display of information for the user, to explain and expose the system state to the user, provide help media between the user and the system. They are essentially a document which describes the knowledge of the system state to the user and is a service which the user can use for further decision making. They are more static than dynamic, because they do not have "pre-defined user operations or functions" associated with these AUI objects, which means they do not need the user to operate on them to get further processing

(Here, do not confuse predefined user operations with pre-defined object functions). All objects have their own properties such as attributes and methods. For example, 'Are you a student?' is an AUI object, which potentially will be used on screen; the 'display' of this message is a method built in with Message objects. But this is done by the system, not by the user.

Postulate 5 AUI Command Objects provide the following facilities:
(i) navigation from one window or portion of the UI to another window or another portion of UI;
(ii) moving data (ie: moving data from screen to the application program or database or vice versa);
(iii) initiating an action within the system or stopping the action being carried out by the system.

They have predefined user events or methods or functions associated with them. They need user interaction to get further processing for completing tasks. They are more dynamic in the sense they require the user to take an action during a task performance. When the user takes an action, it is seen by the system as an Event. Hence we call them Command or Event or Control Objects.

Postulate 6: An Abstract User Interface class (AUI) is a selection or a projection or contains other user-defined operations on a single domain class.

A projection consists of only some of the properties of the base domain class.

For a AUI class C' that is a projection of the base domain class C.

If $p=[p_1, p_2,.........p_n]$ is a list of properties of the base domain class C, and
$p' = [p_1', p_2',........p_3']$ is a list of properties of C', then
p' = p" U p where
p" ⊆ p''' and
p''' are the list of properties that consist of the user defined operations that are defined in the AUI class. Further p", p' and p are properties that include attributes, relationships and user defined operations.
If AUI class C' is a selection on a base domain class C, which satisfies some specified condition then C' ⊆ C. The generated instances of C' are a subset of the instances of C.

Postulate 7: An Abstract User Interface class (AUI) is a selection or a projection or other user-defined operation on two or more classes.

Postulate 8: All Abstract User Interface classes (AUI) are organised into an ISA hierarchy built by the binary ISA relationship which has a particular order. The ISA hierarchy for AUI classes is separate from the ISA hierarchy for domain classes or persistent classes (in a database). This permits an AUI class to be a specialisation of another AUI class. It also permits one to define an AUI class based on another AUI class. The reasons for separating the ISA hierarchy of the AUI classes and the domain classes or persistent classes are similar to those discussed for views in the last section.

Postulate 9: An attribute of an AUI class may be identical to that of a domain class or it could have a different definition or domain. It may also be computed from one or more attributes of domain classes.

Postulate 10: The specification of a method in an AUI class may be the same as that of the corresponding base domain classes or is redefined in the case of a method with the same name as the base class, or is newly defined in the case of an additional method name. Thus, if O is an operation or method in the base domain class C and the AUI class C' is derived from C, then an operation O' of C' where O' = O" U o. where 'o' are the user defined methods that define the AUI class C', can correspond to one of the three cases below:

(a) O" ⊆ O
(b) O" ⊇ O
(c) O" = O

Postulate 11: An AUI class C' can be a composite virtual class consisting of component AUI classes (E', F', G') where C' is derived from the base composite domain classes C and E', F' and G' are derived from domain classes E, F and G respectively where C is a composite class consisting of component classes E, F and G.

Postulate 12: If AUI classes C_1' and C_2' are derived from base domain classes C_1 and C_2 respectively.
The object messages diagram has messages between one or more of the following:

C_1' and C_1
C_2' and C_2
C_1' and C_2'
C_1 and C_2.

These Abstract Interface Objects are generalisations of the notion of views and are suitable for basing queries on Multimedia Database systems of the sort found in the Mentor system.

23.6 ILLUSTRATIVE EXAMPLE OF USE OF ABSTRACT USER INTERFACE OBJECTS

We carry out a sample design of a screen that is utilised with the multimedia database based on the notion of abstract user interface objects. For the synthetic world entity and the video embodiment given in Figure 23.2 we can derive the following abstract user interface objects shown in Figure 23.6 for use with the stills version of accessing video.

Note that these Abstract User Interface Objects have a subset of the attributes in the video embodiment object and some additional attributes and methods. A screen representation corresponding to these Abstract User Interface Objects is shown in Figure 23.7.

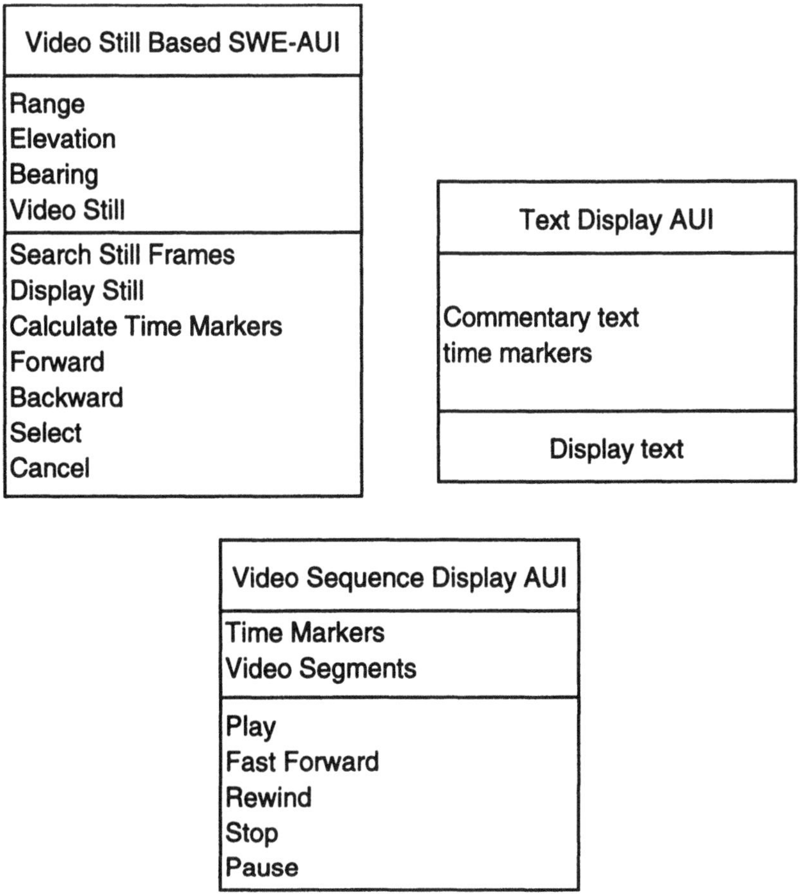

Video Still Based SWE-AUI

Range
Elevation
Bearing
Video Still

Search Still Frames
Display Still
Calculate Time Markers
Forward
Backward
Select
Cancel

Text Display AUI

Commentary text
time markers

Display text

Video Sequence Display AUI

Time Markers
Video Segments

Play
Fast Forward
Rewind
Stop
Pause

Figure 23.6: Sample Abstract User Interface Object

Figure 23.7 : Sample Window Layout

23.7 CONCLUSION

Mentor aims to create a 3D visual and auditory synthetic environment for sensor system operators. The synthetic environment will provide the operator with an interface to a knowledge base representing the contacts made in the real world environment and this knowledge base will be supported by an intermediate intelligent assistant system. The IAS in Mentor will be taught by the operator to provide him the kind of support that the particular operator values most. The operator will teach the IAS the rules sets and behaviour he finds most valuable. A data model is proposed which is the basis for video and audio segments that pertain to entities. In this paper we have described the data model and abstract interface objects that will support these multimedia facets of Mentor.

References

[1] Sterling G, Dillon T; *Analysis and Design of Synthetic Environments for Multiple Sensor Systems;* Proc. of the Second International Simtect Conference; Canberra Australia

[2] Garner K T; Assenmacher T J; *Improving Airborne Tactical Situational Awareness;* Journal of Electronic Defense; November 96 p42-45

[3] G Boy; *Intelligent Assistant Systems;* Academic Press 1991

[4] Jens Rasmussen; *Skills, Rules, and Knowledge; Signals, Signs, and Symbols, and Other Distinctions in Human performance Models*; IEEE Transactions on Systems and Cybernetics vol.SMC-13, No.3 pp.257-266

[5] Leinhart, R., Effelsberg, W., Jain, R., *Visual GREP: A systematic method to compare and retrieve video sequences*, SPIE, Vol. 3312, January, 1998

[6] Wactlar, H., Kanade, T., Smith, M., Stevens, S., *Intelligent Access to Digital Video: The Informedia Project,* IEEE Computer, Vol. 29, No. 5, May, 1996

[7] Lcinhart, R., Pfeiffer, S., and Effelsbert, W., *Video Abstracting,* Communications of ACM, Vol 40, No. 12, pp55-62, December, 1997.

[8] Christel, M.G., Smith, M.A, Taylor, C.R., & Winkler, D.B., *Evolving Video Skims into Useful Multimedia Abstraction"*, Proceeds of the CHI'98 Conference on Human Factors in Computing Systems. (Los Angeles, CA., April, 1998)

[9] Tonomura, Akihito Akutsu, Yukinobu Taniguchi, Gen Suzuki; *Structured* Yoshinobu *Video Computing;* IEEE Multimedia Fall 1994; p34-43

[10] Dittrich, K.R. *Object-oriented Database Systems for information systems of the future,* Seminar Notes, Melbourne

[11] Dillon and Tan *Object-Oriented Conceptual Modelling*, Prentice-Hall (1993)

[12] Scholl, M., etal *Object Algebra and Views for Multi-Objectbases*, Proceedings of Workshop on Distributed Object Management. Edmonton, Alberta, Aug. 1992

[13] Abiteboul, S. and Bonner, A. *Objects and Views*, Proceeds ACM SIGMOD Conference, pp 238-247 (1991)

[14] Kim, Wong and Kelly, W., *On View Support in Object-Oriented database Systems,* Marden Database Systems: The Object Model, Interoperability, and Beyond, ACM Press pp 109-129 (1995)

[15] Bertino, Elisa *A view Mechanism for Object-Oriented Databases,* Proceedings of the 3rd International Conference on Extending Database Technology (EDBT92), Vienna, Austria, March 1992 pp 136-151 (1992)

24 TWO DATA ORGANIZATIONS FOR STORING SYMBOLIC IMAGES IN A RELATIONAL DATABASE SYSTEM

Aya Soffer and Hanan Samet

Computer Science Department and
Center for Automation Research and
Institute for Advanced Computer Science
University of Maryland at College Park
College Park, Maryland 20742

aya@umiacs.umd.edu and hjs@umiacs.umd.edu

Abstract: A method is presented for integrating images into the framework of a conventional database management system (DBMS). It is applicable to a class of images termed *symbolic images* in which the set of objects that may appear are known a priori. The geometric shapes of the objects are relatively primitive and they convey symbolic information. Both the pattern recognition and indexing aspects of the problem are addressed. The emphasis is on extracting both contextual and spatial information from the raw images. A logical image representation that preserves this information is defined. Methods for storing and indexing logical images as tuples in a relation are presented. Indices are constructed for both the contextual and the spatial data, thereby enabling efficient retrieval of images based on contextual as well as spatial specifications. Two different data organizations (integrated and partitioned) for storing logical images in relational tables are proposed. They differ in the way that the logical images are stored. Sample queries and execution plans to respond to these queries are described for both organizations. Analytical cost analyses of these execution plans are given.

24.1 INTRODUCTION

Images (or pictures) serve as an integral part in many computer applications. Examples of such applications include CAD/CAM (computer aided design and manufacturing) software, document processing, medical imaging, GIS (geographic information systems), computer vision systems, office automation systems, etc. All of these applications store various types of images and require some means of managing them. The field of *image databases* deals with this problem [8]. One of the major requirements of an image database system is the ability to retrieve images based on queries that describe the content of the required image(s), termed *retrieval by content*. An example query is "find all images containing camping sites within 3 miles of fishing sites".

In order to support retrieval by content, the images should be interpreted to some degree when they are inserted into the database. This process is referred to as converting an image from a *physical* representation to a *logical* representation. The logical representation may be a textual description of the image, a list of objects found in the image, a collection of features describing the objects in the image, a hierarchical description of the image, etc. It is desirable that the logical representation also preserve the spatial information inherent in the image (i.e., the spatial relation between the objects found in the image). We refer to the information regarding the objects found in an image as *contextual information*, and to the information regarding the spatial relation between these objects as *spatial information*. Both the logical and the physical representation of the image are usually stored in the database. An index mechanism based on the logical representation can then be used to retrieve images based on both contextual and spatial information in an efficient way.

There are many image database systems (e.g., Virage [18], QBIC [11], Photobook [13], FINDIT [17] as well as others [2, 5, 6, 12]). Most systems treat the image as a whole, and index the images based mainly on color and texture. A few systems try to recognize individual objects in an image. These systems do not, however, address the issues of spatial relationship between the objects. Other systems deal with indexing tagged images (images in which the objects have already been recognized and associated with their semantic meaning) in order to support retrieval by image content.

In our work, we have chosen to focus on images where the set of objects that may appear are known a priori. In addition, the geometric shapes of these objects are relatively primitive and they convey symbolic information. Our application is the map domain where many graphical symbols are used to indicate the location of various sites such as hospitals, post offices, recreation areas, scenic areas etc. We call this class of images *symbolic images*. Other similar terms found in the literature are *graphical documents*, *technical documents*, and *line drawings*. Limiting ourselves to symbolic images simplifies object recognition enabling using well-known methods in document processing.

In this paper, we present methods for integrating symbolic images into a conventional database management system (DBMS). In our application, we make use of a relational DBMS although our ideas are applicable to other DBMS's. These methods offer solutions for both the pattern recognition and indexing aspects of the problem. We describe how to incorporate the results of these methods into an existing spatial database based on the relational model.

Our emphasis is on extracting both contextual and spatial information from the raw images. The logical image representation that we define preserves this information. The logical images are stored as tuples in a relation. Indices are constructed on both the contextual and the spatial data, thus enabling efficient retrieval of images based on contextual as well as spatial specifications. It is our view that an image database must be able to process queries that have both contextual and spatial specifications, in addition to any traditional query.

We propose two different data organizations, termed *integrated* and *partitioned*, for storing images in relational tables. They differ in how logical images are stored. All of the examples and experiments in this paper are from the map domain. However, images from many other interesting applications fall into the category of symbolic images. These include CAD/CAM, engineering drawings, floor plans, and more.

The main contribution of this work lies in demonstrating how a traditional DBMS can be used to store and retrieve images and how partitioning this data effects the performance of the database. While the database and pattern recognition techniques that we use are well-known, the novelty of this work is in adapting and integrating these techniques into one system that provides a comprehensive solution for storing and retrieving images in a DBMS. We suggest solutions for all of the steps that are involved in this integration. These steps include: image acquisition, interpretation, storage, indexing, and retrieval. The main issues that need to be resolved are:

1. finding an image interpretation procedure whose results can be stored as entries in a traditional database in such a way that both the contextual and spatial information inherent in the image will be preserved.
2. what data organization is most suitable for the types of queries that are common in this application.
3. determining what strategies to use when computing answers to queries (i.e., how to use the double indexing on both contextual and spatial data efficiently).
4. finding ways to compute their costs.

The rest of this paper is organized as follows. We first present definitions as well as the notation used. Next, we outline the image input system used to convert images from their physical representation to their logical representation as they are input to the database. We continue by describing how images are stored in a database management system using the two data organizations that we propose including schema definitions and example relations. This is followed by sample queries along with execution plans and cost estimates for these plans. We conclude with some observations as well as directions for future research.

24.2 DEFINITIONS AND NOTATIONS

Below we define some terms and the notation used in the remainder of the paper. A *general image* is a two-dimensional array of picture elements (termed *pixels*) $p_0, p_1, \ldots, p_n$. A ***binary image*** is a general image where each pixel has one of two possible values (usually 0 and 1). One value is considered the foreground and the other the background. A general image is converted into a binary image by means of a threshold operation. A ***symbol*** is a group of connected pixels that together have some common semantic meaning. In a given application, symbols will be divided into ***valid symbols*** and ***invalid symbols***. A ***valid symbol*** is a symbol whose semantic meaning is relevant in the given application. An ***invalid symbol*** is a symbol whose semantic meaning is irrelevant in the given application. A ***class*** is a group of symbols all of which have the same semantic meaning. All invalid symbols belong to a special class called the *undefined class*.

A ***symbolic image*** is a general image I for which the following conditions hold: 1) Each foreground pixel p_i in I belongs to some symbol. 2) The set of possible classes $C_1, C_2, \ldots, C_n$ for the application is finite and is known a priori. 3) Each symbol belongs to some class. 4) There exists a function f which when given a symbol s and a class C returns a value between 0 and 1 indicating the certainty that s belongs to C.

Images can be represented in one of two ways. In the ***physical image*** representation, an image is represented by a two-dimensional array of pixel values. The physical representation of an image is denoted by I_{phys}. In the ***logical image*** representation, an image I is represented by a list of tuples, one for each symbol $s \in I$. The tuples are of the form: $(C, certainty, (x, y))$ where $C \neq undefined$, (x, y) is the location of s in I, and $0 < certainty \leq 1$ indicates the certainty that $s \in C$.

24.3 IMAGE INPUT

Conversion of input images from their physical to their logical representation is performed using methods common in document analysis [9]. These methods use various pattern recognition techniques that assign a physical object or an event to one of several pre-specified classes. Patterns are recognized based on some features or measurements made on the pattern. A library of features and their classifications, termed the ***training set library***, is used to assign candidate classifications to an input pattern according to some distance metric. Each candidate classification is given a certainty value that approximates the certainty of the correctness of this classification.

We have adapted these methods to solve the problem of converting symbolic images from a physical to logical representation. Figure 24.1 is a block diagram of the image input system that we have developed for this purpose. It is driven by the symbolic information conveyed by the image. That is, rather than trying to interpret everything in the image, it looks for those symbols that are known to be of importance to the application. Any other symbol found in the image is labeled as belonging to the undefined class. This system is described in detail in [15]. In this paper we show how to integrate this system into a DBMS, thus we only give a short overview of the image input system here. A symbolic image I_{phys} is input to the system in its physical representation. It is converted into

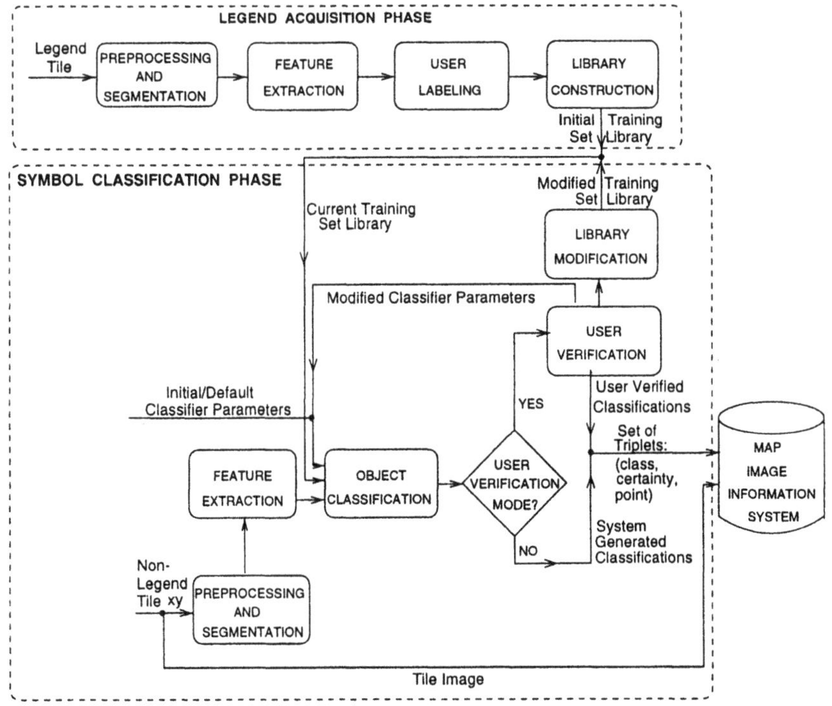

Figure 24.1: Image input system

a logical image by classifying each symbol s found in I_{phys} using the training set library. An initial training set library is constructed by giving the system one example symbol for each class that may be present in the application. In the map domain, the legend of the map may be used for this purpose.

The system may work in two modes. In *user verification mode*, users verify the classifications before being input to the database. The training set is modified to reflect the corrections that the user made for erroneous classifications. In *automatic mode*, classifications are generated by the system and input directly to the database. The user determines the mode in which the system operates. In general, the system should operate in user verification mode until the recognition rate achieved is deemed adequate. Then, the system can continue to process the input images automatically.

The output of applying the conversion process to I_{phys} is a logical image where the tuples are of the form $(C, \mathit{certainty}, (x, y))$ where $C \neq \mathit{undefined}$, $0 < \mathit{certainty} \leq 1$ indicating the certainty that $s \in C$, and (x, y) is the location of s in I_{phys}. For each image, a set of such tuples is inserted into a spatial database as described in the following section. In addition, the raw image I_{phys} (i.e., the image in its physical representation) is also stored.

24.4 IMAGE STORAGE

Images and other information pertaining to the application are stored in relational tables. The database system that we use for this purpose is SAND [1, 3] (denoting spatial and non-spatial database), developed at the University of Maryland. It is a home-grown extension to a relational database, in which the tuples may correspond to geometric entities such as points, lines, polygons, etc. having attributes which may be both of a locational (i.e., spatial) and a non-locational nature. Both types of attributes may be designated as indices of the relation. For indices built on locational attributes, SAND makes use of suitable spatial data structures. Attributes of type image are used to store physical images. Query processing and optimization is performed following the same guidelines of relational databases extended with a suitable cost model for accessing spatial indices and performing spatial operations.

We propose two different data organizations for storing the images in relational tables. They differ in the way logical images are stored. In the *integrated organization*, all tuples of the logical images are stored in one relation. In the *partitioned organization*, the tuples are partitioned into separate relations resulting in a one-to-one correspondence between relations and classes of the application. For example, tuples $(C, certainty, (x, y))$ of a logical image for which $C = C_1$ are stored in a relation corresponding to C_1. The motivation for the partitioned organization is that many queries in in an application using symbolic images need to access all symbols that are assigned the same classification. The part of the query that selects all tuples that belong to the same classification is repeated each time such a query is posed. The partitioned organization makes this repetitive selection at query time unnecessary by providing the option to partition the logical images relation. The partitioned organization is only suitable for applications in which the number of classes is relatively small, as there is one relation for each class and a proliferation of relations would make the database too complex. In the case of symbolic images, this is a reasonable assumption. The number of different symbols used to convey symbolic information (which corresponds to the number of classes) will most likely not be very large, otherwise it would be hard to keep track of or look up the semantic information that is conveyed by each symbol. For example, in the map domain this information must be contained in the legend of the map which is limited in space. Hence, the partitioned organization seems to be reasonable for a database that stores symbolic images. The partitioned organization also enables efficient use of spatial indices while processing spatial queries by using a spatial join operator (e.g., [14]).

24.4.1 Integrated Organization

The schema definitions given in Figure 24.2 define the relations in the integrated organization. We use an SQL-like syntax. The `classes` relation has one tuple for each possible class in the application. The `name` field stores the name of the class (e.g., star), the `semant` field stores the semantic meaning of

```
(CREATE TABLE classes
  name STRING PRIMARY KEY,
  semant STRING,
  bitmap IMAGE);

(CREATE TABLE physical_images
  img_id INTEGER PRIMARY KEY,
  descriptor STRING,
  upper_left POINT,
  raw IMAGE);

(CREATE TABLE logical_images
  img_id INTEGER REFERENCES physical_images(img_id),
  class STRING REFERENCES classes(name),
  certainty FLOAT (CHECK certainty BETWEEN 0 AND 1),
  loc POINT,
  PRIMARY KEY (img_id,class,loc));
```

Figure 24.2: Schemas for the relations classes, physical_images, and logical_images.

class	semantics	bitmap
S	harbor	Ⓢ
square	hotel	[filled square in circle]
scenic	scenic view	[scenic symbol]
T	customs	Ⓣ
R	restaurant	Ⓡ
P	post office	Ⓟ
M	museum	Ⓜ
K	cafe	Ⓚ
waves	beach	[waves in circle]
triangle	camping site	[triangle in circle]
B	filling station	Ⓑ
arrow	holiday camp	[arrow symbol]
cross	first aid station	[cross in circle]
fish	fishing site	[fish symbol]
H	service station	Ⓗ
inf	tourist information	[information symbol]
pi	picnic site	[π in circle]
air	airfield	[airplane in circle]
star	site of interest	[star symbol]
telephone	public telephone	[telephone in circle]
box	youth hostel	[small filled square]
U	sports institution	Ⓤ

Figure 24.3: Example instance for classes relation.

the class in this application (e.g., site of interest). The bitmap field stores a bitmap of an instance of a symbol representing this class. It is an attribute of type IMAGE. The classes relation is populated using the same data that is used to create the initial training set for the image input system (i.e., one

image_id	descriptor	raw	upper_left
image_1	tile 003.012 of Finnish road map	Fig. 24.5	(6144,1536)
image_2	tile 003.013 of Finnish road map	Fig. 24.6	(6656,1536)

Figure 24.4: Example instance for physical_images relation.

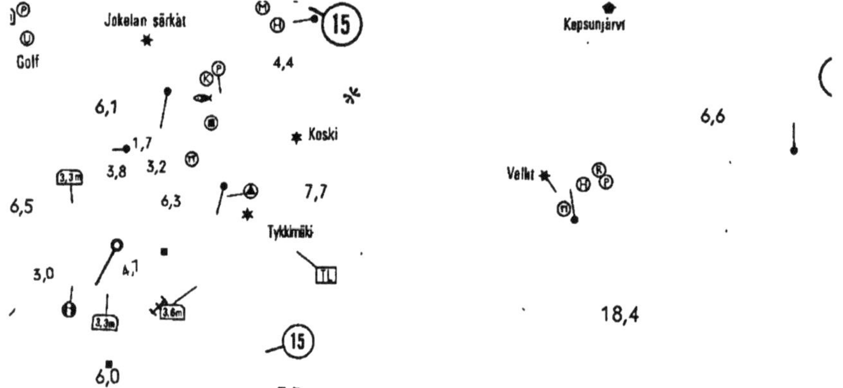

Figure 24.5: Example: image_1.

Figure 24.6: Example: image_2.

example symbol for each class that may be present in the application along with its name and semantic meaning). See Figure 24.3 for an example instance of the classes relation in the map domain.

The physical_images relation has one tuple per image I in the database. The img_id field is an integer identifier given to the image I when it is inserted into the database. The descriptor field stores an alphanumeric description of the image I that the user gives when inserting I (this is meta-data). The raw field stores the actual image I in its physical representation. It is an attribute of type IMAGE. The upper_left field stores an offset value that locates the upper left corner of image I with respect to the upper left corner of some larger image J. This is useful when a large image J is tiled, as in our example map domain. Subtracting this offset value from the absolute location of s in the the non-tiled image J yields the location of s in the tile I that contains it. It is an attribute of type POINT. Any additional meta-data that the user may wish to store about the images such as how they were formed, camera angles, scale, etc. can be added as fields of this relation. See Figure 24.4 for an example instance of the physical_images relation in the map domain.

The logical_images relation stores the logical representation of the images. It has one tuple for each candidate class output by the image input system for each valid symbol s in each image I. The tuple has four fields. The img_id field is the integer identifier given to I when it was inserted into the database.

image_id	class	certainty	location
image_1	M	1	(6493,1544)
image_1	P	0.99	(6161,1546)
image_1	H	0.99	(6513,1566)
image_1	U	1	(6167,1583)
image_1	star	0.99	(6332,1586)
image_1	P	0.99	(6432,1622)
image_1	K	1	(6416,1636)
image_1	fish	1	(6411,1661)
image_1	scenic	0.99	(6630,1662)
image_1	square	1	(6422,1693)
image_1	star	0.99	(6540,1712)
image_1	pi	0.99	(6396,1741)
image_1	triangle	1	(6475,1784)
image_1	star	1	(6474,1814)
image_1	cross	0.79	(6291,1854)
image_1	box	0.74	(6357,1862)
image_1	inf	1	(6226,1937)
image_1	box	1	(6280,2011)
image_2	arrow	0.99	(6861,1544)
image_2	scenic	0.72	(6803,1565)
image_2	pi	0.99	(6849,1756)
image_2	R	0.71	(6849,1756)
image_2	P	0.99	(6858,1771)
image_2	H	0.99	(6827,1775)
image_2	U	0.79	(6827,1775)
image_2	pi	0.99	(6800,1807)
image_2	R	0.99	(6800,1807)

Figure 24.7: Example instance for the `logical_images` relation in the map domain. The tuples correspond to the symbols in the images of Figures 24.5 and 24.6.

It is a foreign key referencing the `img_id` field of the tuple representing I in the `physical_images` relation. The **`class`** and **`certainty`** fields store the name of the class C to which the image input system classified s and the certainty that $s \in C$. The `loc` field stores the (x, y) coordinate values of the center of gravity of s relative to the non-tiled image. See Figure 24.7 for an example instance of the `logical_images` relation in the map domain for the images given in Figures 24.5 and 24.6.

Constructing Indices Indices are defined on the schemas defined above as follows (in SQL-like notation):

```
CREATE INDEX cl_sem ON classes (semant);
CREATE INDEX cl_name ON classes (name);
CREATE INDEX pi_id ON physical_images (img_id);
CREATE INDEX pi_ul ON physical_images (upper_left);
CREATE INDEX li_cl ON logical_images (class certainty);
CREATE INDEX li_loc ON logical_images (loc);
```

`cl_sem` and `cl_name` are alphanumeric indices. They are used to search the `classes` relation by `semant` and `name`, respectively. The `pi_id` index is also alphanumeric. It is used to search the `physical_images` relation by `img_id`. `pi_ul` is a spatial index on points. It is used to search the `physical_images` relation by the coordinates of the uppe. left corner of the images. `li_cl` is an alphanumeric index. It is used to search the `logical_images` relation by `class`. It has a secondary index on attribute `certainty`. Thus, tuples that have the same class name are ordered by certainty value within this index. `li_loc` is a spatial index on points. It is used to search the `logical_images` relation by location (i.e., to deal with spatial queries regarding the locations of the symbols in the images such as distance and range queries). The spatial indices are implemented using a PMR quadtree for points [10].

Observe that the file structures resulting from the integrated organization are very similar to the file structures used by inverted file methods for storing text [4]. An inverted file consists of two structures. A vocabulary list which is a sorted list of words found in the documents, and a posting file indicating for each word the list of documents that contain it and information regarding its position in the document. The vocabulary list is actually an index on the posting file, and is used to locate the record of the posting file corresponding to a given word on disk. In our organization, the `logical_images` relation corresponds to the posting file. The index `li_cl` on this relation plays the role of the vocabulary list. The main difference from text is that as we are dealing with 2-dimensional information rather than 1-dimensional information, we need more elaborate methods to store and index the locational information. In particular, just storing the location, as is done for text data, is insufficient. In order to answer spatial queries efficiently, these locations must be sorted by use of a spatial index. Figure 24.8 illustrates the file structures used following the integrated organization that correspond to similar file structures used for text data.

24.4.2 Partitioned Organization

In the partitioned organization, tuples are partitioned into separate relations resulting in a one-to-one correspondence between relations and classes of the application. For example, tuples $(C, \mathit{certainty}, (x, y))$ of a logical image for which $C = C_1$ are stored in a relation corresponding to C_1. Figure 24.9 gives schema definitions for relations of the partitioned organization corresponding to the `logical_images` relation of the integrated organization. Both the `classes` and `physical_images` definitions are identical to those in the integrated or-

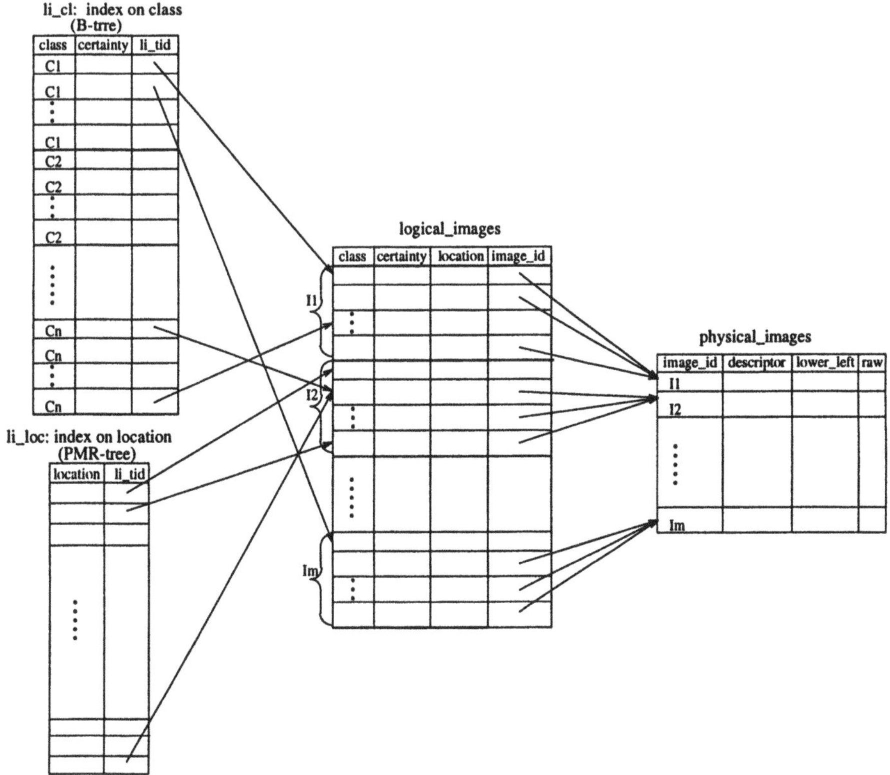

Figure 24.8: File structures for logical and physical images using the integrated organization.

ganization. The only difference between the organizations is the way the logical images are stored. In the partitioned organization, there is one relation, `cl_part` for each class *cl* in the application. Each relation `cl_part` contains the logical images tuples $(C, certainty, (x, y))$ for which $C = cl$. This is equivalent to the result of a selection operation: `SELECT FROM logical_images WHERE class =` *cl*. See Figure 24.10 for example instances of relations `star_part`, `P_part`, `scenic_part`, and `pi_part` for the images in Figures 24.5 and 24.6.

```
for each class cl in application
    (CREATE TABLE cl_part
     img_id INTEGER REFERENCES physical_images(img_id),
     certainty FLOAT (CHECK certainty BETWEEN 0 AND 1),
     loc POINT,
     PRIMARY KEY (img_id,loc));
```

Figure 24.9: Schemas for the `cl_part` relations in the partitioned organization.

star_part:

image_id	certainty	location
image_1	0.99	(6332,1586)
image_1	0.99	(6540,1712)
image_1	1	(6474,1814)

scenic_part:

image_id	certainty	location
image_1	0.99	(6630,1662)
image_2	0.72	(6803,1565)

P_part:

image_id	certainty	location
image_1	0.99	(6161,1546)
image_1	0.99	(6432,1622)
image_2	0.99	(6858,1771)

pi_part:

image_id	certainty	location
image_1	0.99	(6395,1741)
image_2	0.99	(6849,1756)
image_2	0.99	(6800,1807)

Figure 24.10: Example instances of relations `star_part`, `scenic_part`, `P_part`, and `pi_part`. The tuples correspond to the symbols in the images of Figures 24.5 and 24.6.

Constructing Indices Indices are defined on the separate class schemas of the partitioned organization as follows (in SQL-like notation):

```
for each class cl in application
    CREATE INDEX cl_cert ON cl_part (certainty);
    CREATE INDEX cl_loc ON cl_part (loc);
```

Each instance of the `cl_part` relation has an alphanumeric index on `certainty` and a spatial index on `loc`. The spatial index is used to deal with queries of the type "find all images with sites of interest within 10 miles of a picnic area" by means of a spatial join operator. Figure 24.11 illustrates the file structures for the partitioned organization corresponding to file structures used for text data.

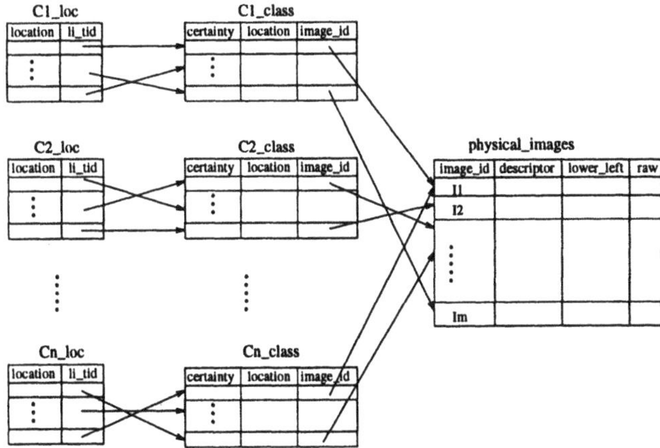

Figure 24.11: File structures for logical and physical mages using the partitioned organization.

24.5 RETRIEVING IMAGES BY CONTENT

As mentioned above, we distinguish between contextual information and spatial information found in images. Similarly, we distinguish between query specifications that are purely contextual and those that also contain spatial conditions. A *contextual specification* defines the images to be retrieved in terms of their contextual information (i.e., the objects found in the image). For example, suppose we want to find all images that contain fishing sites or campgrounds. A *spatial specification* further constrains the required images by adding conditions regarding spatial information (i.e., the spatial relations between the objects).

In order to describe the methods that we use for retrieving images by content, we first present some example queries. Next, we demonstrate the strategies used to process these queries. We conclude by analyzing the expected costs of these strategies (termed *plans*) and compare the data organizations (i.e., integrated and partitioned).

24.5.1 Example Queries

The example queries in this section are first specified using natural language. This is followed by two equivalent SQL-like queries. The first assumes an integrated organization and the second assumes a partitioned organization.

Query Q1: display all images containing a scenic view .

```
display PI.raw
    from logical_images LI, classes C, physical_images PI
    where C.semantics = "scenic view" and C.name = LI.class
        and LI.image_id = PI.image_id;

display PI.raw
```

```
    from scenic_part SC, physical_images PI
    where SC.image_id = PI.image_id;
```

Notice that in order to write SQL-like queries for the partitioned organization, the names of the relations corresponding to each partition must be known. This can easily be overcome by having the system assign names to these relations. These names are derived from the class attribute of relation classes. Two functions that perform this name conversion are provided. get_rel_name returns the name of a relation given the class name. get_class returns the class name given a relation name. Thus, there is no need for the user to know the names assigned by the system to these relations.

Query Q2: display all images containing a scenic view within 5 miles of a picnic site.

```
display PI.raw
    from logical_images LI1, logical_images LI2, classes C1,
        classes C2,  physical_images PI
    where C1.semantics = "scenic view"
        and C2.semantics = "picnic site"
        and C1.name = LI1.class and C2.name = LI2.class
        and distance(LI1.location,LI2.location) < 5
        and LI1.image_id = LI2.image_id
        and LI1.image_id = PI.image_id;
```

```
display PI.raw
    from scenic_part SC, pi_part PIC, physical_images PI
    where distance(SC.location,PIC.location) < 5
        and SC.image_id = PIC.image_id
        and PIC.image_id = PI.image_id;
```

The function distance takes two geometric objects (e.g., two points) and returns a floating point number representing the Euclidean distance between them.

24.5.2 Query Processing

The following plans outline how responses to queries Q1 and Q2 are computed using the two data organizations. These plans utilize the indexing structures available for each organization. Indices on alphanumeric attributes are capable of locating the closest value greater than or equal to a given string or number. Indices on spatial attributes are capable of returning the items in increasing order of their distance from a given point (this is termed an *incremental nearest neighbor operation*) [7]. This operation may optionally receive a maximum distance, D, and it will stop when the distance to the next nearest neighbor is greater than D. Thus, it returns all neighbors within D of a query point in increasing distance. Direct addressing of a tuple within a relation is possible by means of a tuple identifier (or *tid* for short). All index structures have an implicit attribute that stores this tid. The Xth plan, labeled $\mathrm{P}x_I$, uses the integrated organization. The Xth plan, labeled $\mathrm{P}x_P$, uses the partitioned organization.

Query Q1: display all images containing a scenic view.

Plan P1$_I$: Search using an alphanumeric index on `class`.

```
Get all tuples of logical_images which correspond to
"scenic view"
    (use index li_cl)
For each such tuple t
  display the physical image corresponding to t
```

Plan P1$_P$ Search the **scenic view** partition sequentially

```
For each tuple t of the "scenic view" partition
  display the physical image corresponding to t
```

Query Q2: display all images containing a scenic view within 5 miles of a picnic site.

Finding a suitable plan for query Q2 gives rise to many query optimization issues. Most of these issues are also applicable to spatial databases (e.g., [1]). To see the complexity of these issues, we give two different plans for computing an answer to query Q2 using each organization. The first uses only alphanumeric indices, while the second uses an alphanumeric index and a spatial index.

Plan P2A$_I$ Search picnic tuples and scenic view tuples using the alphanumeric index on `class`. For each picnic tuple, check all scenic view tuples to determine which ones are within the specified distance.

```
get all tuples of logical_images corresponding to "picnic"
    (use index li_cl)
for each such tuple t1
  get all tuples of logical_images corresponding to
"scenic view"
    (use index li_cl)
  for each such tuple t2
    if distance between t1 and t2 ≤ 5 miles
      and they are in the same image then
      display corresponding physical image
```

Plan P2B$_I$ Search for "picnic" tuples using an alphanumeric index on `class` and search for "scenic view" tuples using a spatial index on `loc`.

```
get all tuples of logical_images corresponding to "picnic"
    (use index li_cl)
```

```
    (using the incremental nearest neighbor operation)
  for each one of these points p
    if p is a ''scenic view'' and in same image then
      display the corresponding physical image
```

Plan P2A$_P$ Search both the picnic and scenic view partitions sequentially.

```
for each tuple t1 of the "picnic" partition
  for each tuple t2 of the "scenic view" partition
    if distance between t1.loc and t2.loc ≤ 5 miles
        and they are in the same image then
      display the corresponding physical image
```

Plan P2B$_P$ Search the picnic partition sequentially, and search the scenic view partition using the spatial index on `loc`.

```
for each tuple t1 of the "picnic" partition
  get all points within 5 miles of t1.loc
    in the "scenic view" partition
  for each one of these points p
    if p is in the same image as t1 then
      display the corresponding physical image
```

24.5.3 Cost Analysis

Name	*Meaning*
c_r	accessing a tuple by tid (random order)
c_{sq}	accessing a tuple in sequential order
c_{sqf}	accessing the first tuple of a relation
c_{af}	"find first" operation on an alphanumeric index
c_{an}	"find next" operation on an alphanumeric index
c_{lsf}	"find nearest neighbor" operation on a location space index
c_{lsn}	"find next nearest neighbor" operation on a location space index
c_{fsf}	"find nearest neighbor" operation on a feature space index
c_{fsn}	"find next nearest neighbor" operation on a feature space index
c_{sc}	string comparison
c_{lsd}	distance computation in location space
c_{fsd}	weighted distance computation in feature space

Table 24.1: Costs of basic operations used in query processing.

In order to estimate the costs of each plan, we must make assumptions about the data distribution and the costs of the various operations. Table 24.1 contains a tabulation of the costs of basic operations used to process queries. The cost of many of these operations is a function of the relation on which they operate. $c_{x(y)}$ is the cost of performing operation x on relation or index y. `li` stands for `logical_images`. The cost of accessing the physical_images relation to retrieve the result image and the cost of the "display" operation are not included as it is always the same regardless of the selected execution plan. Let N_{pic} and N_{sv} be the number of tuples from class "picnic" and "scenic view", respectively. Let B_{pic} and B_{sv} be the number of disk blocks containing tuples from class "picnic" and "scenic view", respectively.

Equations 24.1, and 24.2 estimate the cost of responding to query 1 using the integrated and partitioned organizations, respectively.

$$C_{1_I} = c_{af(li\_cl)} + N_{sv} \times (c_{r(li)} + c_{an(li\_cl)}) \quad (24.1)$$

$$C_{1_P} = N_{sv} \times c_{sq(sv\_part)} \quad (24.2)$$

One difference between C_{1_I} and C_{1_P} is that in the integrated organization, there is an "alphanumeric find" operation on index `li_cl` that is not necessary in the partitioned organization. It is required in order to find the first scenic view tuple in this index. In addition, one more random access is required for each scenic view tuple in order to get the `img_id` from the `logical_images` relation. The other difference is that there are N_{sv} alphanumeric next operations in the integrated organization compared with N_{sv} sequential access operations in the partitioned organizations. The reason for this is that in the partitioned organization, the relation is scanned directly, whereas in the integrated organization, the index is scanned.

$$\begin{aligned} C_{2A_I} = \; & c_{af(li\_cl)} + N_{pic} \times (c_{r(li)} + c_{an(li\_cl)}) + \\ & B_{pic} \times [c_{af(li\_cl)} + N_{sv} \times (c_{r(li)} + c_{an(li\_cl)})] + \\ & N_{pic} \times N_{sv} \times c_{lsd} \end{aligned} \quad (24.3)$$

$$\begin{aligned} C_{2A_P} = \; & N_{pic} \times c_{sq(pi\_part)} + \\ & B_{pic} \times [c_{sqf(sv\_part)} + N_{sv} \times c_{sq(sv\_part)}] + \\ & N_{pic} \times N_{sv} \times c_{lsd} \end{aligned} \quad (24.4)$$

Equations 24.3 and 24.4 estimate the cost of responding to query 2 with plan A using the integrated and partitioned organizations, respectively. In both equations, the first line is the cost of reading all pic tuples, the second line is the cost of reading all sv tuples for each block, and the last line is the cost of checking the distance between each (pic,sv) pair. N_{InC_2} denotes the average number of tuples in the circular range specified in query 2 (C_2). $N_{sv\_InC_2}$ denotes the average number of scenic view tuples in C_2. Assuming a uniform distribution of symbols in space (i.e., there is an equal number of symbols in any given area), then $N_{InC_2} = \frac{area(C_2)}{A} \times N$, where N is the total number of tuples in the `logical_images` relation, A is the area covered by these tuples, and C_2 is the circular range specified in query 2. Assuming a uniform distribution of classifications among the symbols (i.e., there is an equal number of symbols from each classification in any group of symbols), then $N_{sv\_InC_2} = \frac{area(C_2)}{A} \times \frac{N}{CL}$, where CL is the number of different classifications in the database.

If these assumptions about the distribution of the classifications among symbols do not hold, then other methods are required to estimate the number of scenic view tuples in a given area. The portion of all tuples that belong to each classification can be recorded when populating the database by checking the `class` attribute and tallying the number for each classification. This data can then be used to estimate the distribution of the classifications among the symbols. Assuming that the distribution of classifications among any group of symbols is equal to the the total database distribution (i.e., the portion of tuples from each classification among any given group of symbols is equal to the portion of tuples from each classification in the entire database), then $N_{sv\_InC_2} = \frac{area(C_2)}{A} \times sv_p \times N$, where sv_p is the portion of the database tuples that belong to the "scenic view" class.

Plan P2A$_C$ performs a spatial join operation on the results of two selection operations on relation `logical_images`. The first select operation extracts all tuples of the relation that are of class "picnic", while the second select operation extracts all tuples of the relation that are of class "scenic view". The results of these two select operations are then joined according to a predicate based on the `loc` attribute. In our implementation of plan P2A$_C$, we perform the select and join operations simultaneously using a block nested loop join algorithm as follows. One of the classes is designated as the *inner class*, and the other is designated as the *outer class*. One block of tuples belonging into the outer class are read into a memory-resident buffer (using the index on attribute `class`). All tuples of the inner class are then read (one block at a time using the index on attribute `class`) and spatially joined with all tuples of the outer class that are in memory (by computing the predicate on the spatial attribute). This process is repeated with the next block of tuples of the outer class, until all tuples of the outer class have been read.

The main difference between C_{2A_I} and C_{2A_P} is that in the integrated organization the index is scanned sequentially, whereas in the partitioned organization the relation corresponding to the scenic view partition is scanned sequentially (as in the case of query 1). As a result, once again, there are considerably more "random access" operations in the integrated organization than in the partitioned organization.

Equations 24.5 and 24.6 estimate the cost of responding to query 2 with plan B using the integrated and partitioned organizations, respectively. Again, as in equations 24.3 and 24.4, the first line is the cost of reading all pic tuples, but the second line is the cost of finding sv tuples in the range (using index li_loc) for each pic.

$$\begin{aligned} C_{2B_I} &= c_{af(li\_cl)} + N_{pic} \times [c_{r(li)} + c_{an(li\_cl)}] + \\ &\quad N_{pic} \times [c_{lsf(li\_loc)} + N_{InC_2} \times (c_{r(li)} + c_{sc} + c_{lsn(li\_loc)})] \qquad (24.5) \\ C_{2B_P} &= N_{pic} \times c_{sq(pi\_part)} + \\ &\quad N_{pic} \times c_{lsf(sv\_loc)} + N_{sv\_InC_2} \times (c_{r(sv\_part)} + c_{lsn(sv\_loc)}) \qquad (24.6) \end{aligned}$$

The main difference between C_{2B_I} and C_{2B_P} is in the number of location-space "find next" operations and the number of random access operations.

In the integrated organization, all tuples `t` of any class in circle C_2 are retrieved from the spatial index. The `class` of `t` is then retrieved from the `logical_images` relation to see if it corresponds to a "scenic view". This requires a random access operation for each tuple in C_2. On the other hand, in the partitioned organization, only tuples of type "scenic view" are retrieved by the spatial index. Thus, there is no need for an additional random access to check the class of the tuple. In addition, since only a subset of the tuples in circle C_2 are "scenic view" tuples, the number of items retrieved by the spatial query in the integrated organization (i.e., N_{InC_2}) is larger than the number of items retrieved by the spatial query in the partitioned organization (i.e., $N_{sv\_InC_2}$).

Another significant difference between C_{2B_I} and C_{2B_P} is that the spatial index on which the search is performed is smaller in the partitioned organization since it only contains "scenic view" tuples (i.e., |`sv_loc`| < |`li_loc`|). As a result, $c_{lsf(sv\_loc)}$ and $c_{lsn(sv\_loc)}$ are less than $c_{lsf(li\_loc)}$ and $c_{lsn(li\_loc)}$, respectively. Therefore, the difference between the total cost of plan P2B in the partitioned organization and the total cost of plan P2B in the integrated organization is greater than in the case of plan P2A. The plan for the partitioned organization can be further improved by implementing a more sophisticated form of the *spatial join* operation between the two relations `scenic_part` and `pi_part` which correspond to "scenic view" and "picnic", respectively. The overall idea is that the join can be computed more efficiently by traversing both indices in parallel in such a way as to avoid comparing tuples which cannot satisfy the join condition. This operation has not been implemented in SAND yet. Once it is added, plan $P2B_P$ will be revised accordingly.

It is interesting to compare the costs of answering query 2 for one particular organization using plans P2A and P2B. For the integrated organization, we compare equations 24.3 and 24.5. In plan P2A$_I$, both relations are scanned sequentially via the alphanumeric index `li_cl`. For each picnic tuple, each scenic view tuple is checked to determine whether or not it is within the specified range. Thus, the total number of distance computations is $N_{pic} \times N_{sv}$. In addition, the same number of random access operations are also required in order to get the locations from the `logical_images` relations. In plan P2B$_I$, the spatial index is used and thus only tuples that are within the specified range need to be examined. The cost of this is the overhead involved in using the spatial index. In this case, this cost is N_{pic} location-space "find first" operations, and $N_{pic} \times N_{InC_2}$ location-space "find next" operations. These spatial operations involve distance computations as part of the incremental nearest neighbor operation. However, there is no need for any distance computations as part of the plan itself. Whether plan P2A$_I$ or plan P2B$_I$ is better depends on the size of the data set, the portion of these tuples that belong to each classification (termed the *contextual selectivity*), and on the portion of all tuples that fall in the range specified by the spatial component (termed the *spatial selectivity*). Assuming a high spatial selectivity (i.e., that the number of tuples in the spatial range is much smaller than the total number of tuples in the data set), plan $P2B_I$ should prove to be much more efficient than plan $P2A_I$. However, if the spatial selectivity is low, then plan $P2A_I$ may prove to be better. Similar observations can be made about the partitioned organization by comparing equations 24.4 and 24.6. Once a more efficient spatial join operator is implemented, as mentioned above, the difference will be even greater.

24.6 CONCLUDING REMARKS

Two different data organizations (integrated and partitioned) for storing logical images in relational tables were proposed. They differ in the way that the logical images are stored. Sample queries and execution plans to answer these queries were described for both organizations. Analytical cost analyses of these execution plans were given that indicated that the partitioned data organization is more efficient for queries that consist of both contextual and spatial specifications. On the other hand, the integrated organization is better for purely spatial specifications. Both organizations gave similar results for queries that consist of purely contextual specification.

Our definition of the class of images that we can handle is rather strict. Some of these restrictions can be relaxed. In particular, the requirement that there exists a function f which when given a symbol s and a class C returns a value between 0 and 1 indicating the certainty that s belongs to C can be omitted. In this case, we can store the feature vectors in the database rather than the classifications. For a comparison of using these two approaches, see [16]. Of course, more elaborate indexing methods are then required to respond to queries such as those presented in this paper.

24.7 ACKNOWLEDGMENTS

This work was supported in part by the National Science Foundation under Grants CDA-950-3994 and IRI-97-12715. We are grateful to Karttakeskus, Map Center, Helsinki, Finland for providing us the map data.

References

[1] W. G. Aref and H. Samet. Optimization strategies for spatial query processing. In *Proc. of the 17th Intl. Conf. on Very Large Data Bases*, pp. 81–90, Barcelona, Sept. 1991.

[2] S. K. Chang, E. Jungert, and Y. Li. The design of pictorial databases based upon the theory of symbolic projections. In *Design and Implementation of Large Spatial Databases — 1st Symp., SSD'89*, pp. 303–323, Santa Barbara, CA, July 1989. (Also Springer-Verlag Lecture Notes in Computer Science 409).

[3] C. Esperança and H. Samet. Spatial database programming using SAND. In *Proc. of the 7th Intl. Symp. on Spatial Data Handling*, vol. 2, pp. A29–A42, Delft, The Netherlands, Aug. 1996.

[4] C. Faloutsos. Access methods for text. *ACM Comp. Surveys*, 17(1):49–74, Mar. 1985.

[5] V. Gudivada and V. Raghavan. Design and evaluation of algorithms for image retrieval by spatial similarity. *ACM Trans. Info. Syst.*, 13(2):115–144, Apr. 1995.

[6] A. Gupta, T. Weymouth, and R. Jain. Semantic queries with pictures: the VIMSYS model. In *Proc. of the 17th Intl. Conf. on Very Large Databases*, pp. 69–79, Barcelona, Spain, Sept. 1991.

[7] G. R. Hjaltason and H. Samet. Ranking in spatial databases. In *Advances in Spatial Databases — 4th Intl. Symp., SSD'95*, pp. 83–95, Portland, ME, Aug. 1995. (Also Springer-Verlag Lecture Notes in Computer Science 951).

[8] R. Jain. NSF workshop on visual information management systems. *SIGMOD RECORD*, 22(3):57–75, Sept. 1993.

[9] R. Kasturi, R. Raman, and C. Chennubhotla. Document image analysis an overview of techniques for graphics recognition. In *Proc. of the IAPR Workshop on Syntactic and Structural Pat. Rec.*, pp. 192–230, Murray Hill, NJ, June 1990.

[10] R. C. Nelson and H. Samet. A consistent hierarchical representation for vector data. *Computer Graphics*, 20(4):197–206, Aug. 1986. (Also *Proc. of SIGGRAPH'86*, Dallas, Aug. 1986).

[11] W. Niblack, R. Barber, W. Equitz, M. Flickner, E. Glasman, D. Petkovic, and P. Yanker. The QBIC project: Querying images by content using color, texture, and shape. In *Proc. of the SPIE, Storage and Retrieval of Image and Video Databases*, vol. 1908, pp. 173–187, San Jose, CA, Feb. 1993.

[12] V. Oria, B. Xu, and M. T. Tamer. VisualMOQL: A visual query language for image databases. In *Proc. of the IFIP 2.6 4th Working Conf. on Visual Database Systems (VDB-4)*, pp. 186–191, L'Aquila, Italy, May 1998.

[13] A. Pentland, R. W. Picard, and S. Sclaroff. Photobook: Content-based manipulation of image databases. In *Proc. of the SPIE, Storage and Retrieval of Image and Video Databases II*, vol. 2185, pp. 34–47, San Jose, CA, Feb. 1994.

[14] D. Rotem. Spatial join indices. In *Proc. of the 7th Intl. Conf. on Data Eng.*, pp. 500–509, Kobe, Japan, April 1991. IEEE Computer Society Press.

[15] H. Samet and A. Soffer. MAGELLAN: Map acquisition of geographic labels by legend analysis. *Intl. Journal of Document Analysis and Recognition*, 1(2):89–101, June 1998.

[16] A. Soffer and H. Samet. Two approaches for integrating symbolic images into a multimedia database system: a comparative study. *VLDB Journal*, to appear.

[17] M. Swain. Interactive indexing into image databases. In *Proc. of the SPIE, Storage and Retrieval for Image and Video Databases*, vol. 1908, pp. 95–103, San Jose, CA, Feb. 1993.

[18] Virage. Virage web site. http://www.virage.com.

GPSR Compliance
The European Union's (EU) General Product Safety Regulation (GPSR) is a set of rules that requires consumer products to be safe and our obligations to ensure this.

If you have any concerns about our products, you can contact us on

ProductSafety@springernature.com

In case Publisher is established outside the EU, the EU authorized representative is:

Springer Nature Customer Service Center GmbH
Europaplatz 3
69115 Heidelberg, Germany

www.ingramcontent.com/pod-product-compliance
Ingram Content Group UK Ltd.
Pitfield, Milton Keynes, MK11 3LW, UK
UKHW012145240726
13966UKWH00001B/166

* 9 7 8 1 4 7 5 7 4 9 1 5 1 *